Economics and Biology

The International Library of Critical Writings in Economics

Series Editor: Mark Blaug

Professor Emeritus, University of London
Professor Emeritus, University of Buckingham
Visiting Professor, University of Exeter

This series is an essential reference source for students, researchers and lecturers in economics. It presents by theme an authoritative selection of the most important articles across the entire spectrum of economics. Each volume has been prepared by a leading specialist who has written an authoritative introduction to the literature included.

A full list of published and future titles in this series is printed at the end of this volume.

Economics and Biology

Edited by

Geoffrey M. Hodgson

Lecturer in Economics
The Judge Institute for Management Studies
University of Cambridge

THE INTERNATIONAL LIBRARY OF CRITICAL WRITINGS IN ECONOMICS

An Elgar Reference Collection

Published by
Edward Elgar Publishing Limited
Gower House
Croft Road
Aldershot
Hants GU11 3HR
England

Edward Elgar Publishing Company
Old Post Road
Brookfield
Vermont 05036
USA

British Library Cataloguing in Publication Data
Economics and Biology. – (International
Library of Critical Writings in Economics;
Vol. 50)
I. Hodgson, Geoffrey M. II. Series
330.01574

Library of Congress Cataloguing in Publication Data
Economics and biology / edited by Geoffrey M. Hodgson.
p. cm. — (International library of critical writings in economics; 50)
1. Economics—Methodology. 2. Biology-Methodology. 3. Sociobiology. 4. Biology, Economic. I. Hodgson, Geoffrey Martin, 1946– . II. Series.
HB131.E257 1995
330—dc20

94–47401
CIP

ISBN 1 85898 050 X

Printed in Great Britain by Galliard (Printers) Ltd, Great Yarmouth

Contents

Acknowledgements

The editor and publishers wish to thank the following who have kindly given permission for the use of copyright material.

American Association for the Advancement of Science for article: David J. Rapport and James E. Turner (1977), 'Economic Models in Ecology', *Science*, **195**, January–March, 367–73.

American Economic Association for articles: Edith Tilton Penrose (1952), 'Biological Analogies in the Theory of the Firm', *American Economic Review*, **XLII** (5), December, 804–19; Gregor Sebba (1953), 'The Development of the Concepts of Mechanism and Model in Physical Science and Economic Thought', *American Economic Review, Papers and Proceedings*, **XLIII** (1), May, 259–68; Gary S. Becker (1976), 'Altruism, Egoism, and Genetic Fitness: Economics and Sociobiology', *Journal of Economic Literature*, **XIV** (3), December, 817–26.

Annual Review Inc. for article: J. Maynard Smith (1978), 'Optimization Theory in Evolution', *Annual Review of Ecology and Systematics*, **9**, 31–56.

Association for Evolutionary Economics for article: Nicholas Georgescu-Roegen (1979), 'Methods in Economic Science', *Journal of Economic Issues*, **XIII** (2), June, 317–28.

Atlantic Economic Society for article: Gordon Tullock (1979), 'Sociobiology and Economics', *Atlantic Economic Journal*, September, 1–10.

Basil Blackwell Ltd for article: Joel Mokyr (1991), 'Evolutionary Biology, Technological Change and Economic History', *Bulletin of Economic Research*, **43** (2), April, 127–49.

Cornell University Press for excerpt: Morris A. Copeland (1958), 'On the Scope and Method of Economics', in Douglas F. Dowd (ed.), *Thorstein Veblen: A Critical Reappraisal*, Chapter 5, 57–75.

Economie appliquée for article: J.S. Metcalfe and M. Gibbons (1986), 'Technological Variety and the Process of Competition', *Economie appliquée*, **XXXIX** (3), 493–520.

Edward Arnold (Publishers) Ltd for article: Brinley Thomas (1991), 'Alfred Marshall on Economic Biology', *Review of Political Economy*, **3** (1), January, 1–14.

Elsevier Science Publishers BV for articles: Richard B. Norgaard (1987), 'Economics as Mechanics and the Demise of Biological Diversity', *Ecological Modelling*, **38**, September, 107–21; P.P. Saviotti (1988), 'Information, Variety and Entropy in Technoeconomic Development', *Research Policy*, **17**, 89–103; Mark E. Schaffer (1989), 'Are Profit-Maximisers the Best Survivors?: A Darwinian Model of Economic Natural Selection', *Journal of Economic Behavior and Organization*, **12** (1), March, 29–45; Ulrich Witt (1991), 'Economics, Sociobiology, and Behavioral Psychology on Preferences', *Journal of Economic Psychology*, **12**, 557–73.

Gordon and Breach Science Publishers for article: Geoffrey M. Hodgson (1993), 'Why the Problem of Reductionism in Biology Has Implications for Economics', *World Futures*, **37**, 69–90.

Helbing & Lichtenhahn Verlag AG for article: H. Thoben (1982), 'Mechanistic and Organistic Analogies in Economics Reconsidered', *Kyklos*, **35**, Fasc. 2, 292–305.

History of Economics Society for article: Neil B. Niman (1991), 'Biological Analogies in Marshall's Work', *Journal of the History of Economic Thought*, **13** (1), Spring, 19–36.

International Network for Economic Method for articles: Nicolai Juul Foss (1991), 'The Suppression of Evolutionary Approaches in Economics: The Case of Marshall and Monopolistic Competition', *Methodus*, **3** (2), December, 65–72; Elias L. Khalil (1992), 'Economics and Biology: Eight Areas of Research', *Methodus*, **4** (2), December, 29–45.

John Nightingale for his own article: (1993), 'Solving Marshall's Problem with the Biological Analogy: Jack Downie's Competitive Process', *History of Economics Review*, **20**, Summer, 75–94.

Kluwer Academic Publishers for articles: Sandra Herbert (1971), 'Darwin, Malthus, and Selection', *Journal of the History of Biology*, **4** (1), Spring, 209–17; W.S. Cooper (1989), 'How Evolutionary Biology Challenges the Classical Theory of Rational Choice', *Biology and Philosophy*, **4** (4), October, 457–81; Scott Gordon (1989), 'Darwin and Political Economy: The Connection Reconsidered', *Journal of the History of Biology*, **22** (3), Fall, 437–59.

Macmillan Press Ltd for excerpt: Elias L. Khalil (1993), 'Neo-classical Economics and Neo-Darwinism: Clearing the Way for Historical Thinking', in Ron Blackwell, Jaspal Chatha and Edward J. Nell (eds), *Economics as Worldly Philosophy: Essays In Political and Historical Economics in Honour of Robert L. Heilbroner*, 22–72.

MCB University Press for article: John M. Gowdy (1987), 'Bio-Economics: Social Economy Versus the Chicago School', *International Journal of Social Economics*, **14** (1), 32–42.

Past and Present Society, Banbury Road, Oxford for article: Robert M. Young (1969), 'Malthus and the Evolutionists: The Common Context of Biological and Social Theory', *Past and Present*, **43**, May, 109–41.

Philosophy of Science Association for excerpt: Elliott Sober (1981), 'Holism, Individualism, and the Units of Selection', in P.D. Asquith and R.N. Giere (eds), *Philosophy of Science Association 1980*, **2**, 93–121.

Southern Economic Journal for article: Lamar B. Jones (1989), 'Schumpeter verus Darwin: In re Malthus', *Southern Economic Journal*, **56** (2), October, 410–22.

University of Chicago Law School for article: J. Hirshleifer (1977), 'Economics from a Biological Viewpoint', *Journal of Law and Economics*, **XX** (1), April, 1–52.

Every effort has been made to trace all the copyright holders but if any have been inadvertently overlooked the publishers will be pleased to make the necessary arrangement at the first opportunity.

In addition the publishers wish to thank the Library of the London School of Economics and Political Science, and the Photographic Unit of the University of London Library for their assistance in obtaining these articles.

Introduction

Since the 1970s, a number of leading theorists have argued that economics is in a state of crisis. Indeed, since the publication of *The Crisis in Economic Theory* by Daniel Bell and Irving Kristol in 1981 the phrase in the title of the volume has become commonplace. Frequent complaints include the alleged lack of relevance of modern economic theory, the unrealism of its core assumptions, its failure to engage with real-world data, and its limited operational utility for policy.[1] However, the search for an alternative paradigm for economics has not yet been entirely successful. Not only do heterodox economists remain relatively few in number but after more than two decades they still fail to agree among themselves on the most viable alternative to orthodoxy.

Mechanical Analogies in Economics

Nevertheless, a number of important developments in the theory, history and philosophy of economics in the late 1980s and early 1990s give rise to the hope that the reconstruction of economic theory may be able to proceed henceforth with important results. These have to answer fundamental questions about the nature and conceptual basis of the subject.

It has been long recognized that modern economics is overly mechanistic in character, notably by Nicholas Georgescu-Roegen in his classic 1971 work *The Entropy Law and the Economic Process*. However, the publication in 1989 of Philip Mirowski's detailed, challenging and controversial thesis in his book *More Heat than Light* seemed to invest this observation with more substance and significance. Mirowski argued that the origins of neoclassical economics in the 1870s were intimately connected with developments in nineteenth-century physics, to the extent that pioneer theorists such as Léon Walras even adopted the mathematics of utility theory from analogous formulations in that science.

The use of physics in economics has an early precedent. Even at the formation of economic science, Adam Smith appealed specifically to Newtonian mechanics in his essay on 'The Principles which Lead and Direct Philosophical Enquiries: Illustrated by the History of Astronomy' (Smith, 1980). In broad terms there is no question that the founders of neoclassical economics simply regarded physics as a major inspiration. Several comentators have typified the kind of mechanistic ideas that permeate modern economics as essentially Newtonian, although Mirowski sees as crucial the additional influence of the energetics movement in physics in the latter half of the nineteenth century. Whatever the precise details of the account, the consensus is that economics is still heavily influenced by the kind of mechanistic thinking which dominated physics around the middle decades of the nineteenth century. In particular, the evidence for the substantial influence of physics on the architects of the 'marginal revolution' is substantial. Consider a number of selected examples.

Léon Walras (1834–1910), the originator of modern general equilibrium theory, wrote in 1874 that 'the pure theory of economics is a science which resembles the physico-mathematical sciences in every respect' (Walras, 1954, p. 71). Likewise, for his contemporary and co-thinker William Stanley Jevons (1835–82) the metaphor of physical science was all-pervasive:

> Utility only exists when there is on the one side the person wanting, and on the other the thing wanted ... Just as the gravitating force of a material depends not alone on the mass of that body, but upon the masses and relative positions and distances of the surrounding material bodies, so utility is an attraction between a wanting being and what is wanted. (Jevons, 1981, p. 80)

The allied economist Francis Edgeworth (1845–1926) was fond of similar analogies:

> As electro-magnetic force tends to a maximum energy, so also pleasure force tends toward a maximum energy. The energy generated by pleasure force is the physical concomitant and measure of the conscious feeling of delight. (Edgeworth, 1881, p. 25)

The innovative theorist Vilfredo Pareto (1848–1923) was also a consistent proponent of the mechanical metaphor. He saw 'the equations which determine equilibrium' as 'the equations of rational mechanics'. That is why 'pure economics is a sort of mechanics or akin to mechanics' (Pareto, 1953, p. 185).

With such evidence the prominent role of mechanical analogies in economics is clear, even if controversy is likely to persist over the details. Indeed, throughout much of the nineteenth and twentieth centuries, economists have assumed that the economy can be analysed as if it were a machine. Inspired by the manifest achievements of mechanics and engineering in the industrial revolution, pioneers of modern economic theory often made reference to the mechanical analogy. The metaphors of classical mechanics still pervade modern economic science. The question is then raised as to whether through this emulation economics has structured itself on the basis of an inappropriate theoretical metaphor.

Limitations of the Mechanistic Metaphor

It must be noted that by 'mechanics' we here refer to classical mechanics or physics before 1860. Hence any reference to statistical mechanics and other more recent developments in physics is excluded. It is the mechanistic metaphor of classical physics that is relevant and which remains influential for economics.

There are a number of problems involved in the use of the mechanistic metaphor in economics. For instance, movement is reversible in the 'conserved system' of Newtonian mechanics; there is no arrow of time. 'Classical mechanics only knows motion, whereas at the same time the processes of motion are completely reversible and in no way give rise to any qualitative changes' (Thoben, 1982, p. 293).

The derivation of the ideas of rationality and equilibria – the core concepts of modern mainstream economics – can be easily traced from the inheritance of mechanistic thought: 'Classical mechanics considers a system of material points upon which directional forces operate at a distance according to calculable laws of motion. The choice of paths is governed by the principle of least action, which may be termed the economic principle if we take the term in its widest sense as denoting a maximum–minimum principle' (Sebba, 1953, p. 269).

Hence economic agents optimize to the point of equilibrium as if they were particles subject to a combination of forces and obeying Newtonian mechanical laws.

Furthermore, information, learning and knowledge are difficult to incorporate in a mechanistic scheme. In classical mechanics there is no place for thoughts and ideas: all is mere matter, subject to Newtonian laws. As Norbert Weiner (1954, p. 29) remarked: 'In nineteenth-century physics it seemed to cost nothing to get information.'

It is not proposed here that the use of mechanistic thinking in economics has been entirely without value. Nevertheless, the limitations are severe: the mechanistic metaphor excludes knowledge, qualitative change and irreversibility through time. It entraps economics in equilibrium schema where there are no systematic errors and no cumulative development. Clearly much is missing with this way of modelling the economic world.

What are the Alternatives?

Can the 'crisis in economic theory' be rectified by ridding economics of the mechanical analogy, and replacing it by something else? Here an important division of opinion arises amongst the would-be reformers of economics. Some suggest that social sciences such as economics should eschew *all* metaphors from the physical and natural sciences. Instead, it is argued, economics should be founded on principles applicable exclusively to the socio-economic domain. Surprisingly, even some of the advocates of so-called 'evolutionary' economics take such a view. Notably, Joseph Schumpeter (1883–1950) wrote:

> it may be ... that certain aspects of the individual-enterprise system are correctly described as a struggle for existence, and that a concept of survival of the fittest in this struggle can be defined in a non-tautological manner. But if this be so, then these aspects would have to be analyzed with reference to economic facts alone and *no appeal to biology would be of the slightest use*. (Schumpeter, 1954, p. 789, emphasis added)

However, other 'evolutionary' economists make a very different stand. These include the 'old' institutional economists who follow the inspiration of Thorstein Veblen (1857–1929). Veblen (1919) argued that economics was not yet an 'evolutionary science' but it should take its inspiration from the biology of Charles Darwin (Hodgson, 1992; 1993c, ch. 9). Although they share the 'evolutionary' title with the Schumpeterians, it was Veblen rather than Schumpeter who embraced the metaphor taken from biology.

Just eight years before Veblen published 'Why Economics is Not an Evolutionary Science' (1898), Alfred Marshall (1842–1924) published the first edition of his *Principles*. Unlike his contemporaries such as Jevons and Walras, Marshall voiced an attachment to the biological analogy. In a later edition of the *Principles* he added the famous words: 'the Mecca of the economist lies in economic biology rather than in economic dynamics' (Marshall, 1961, p. xii). Nevertheless, it has been argued that Marshall's invocation of the biological analogy was partial and incomplete, and furthermore inspired in the main by Herbert Spencer rather than by Charles Darwin (Hodgson, 1993a; 1993c, ch. 7; Thomas, 1991). However, as elaborated by the contributions in Part IV of this volume, a part of the Marshallian tradition helps keep alive a version of 'economic biology' to this day.

Nevertheless, the elements inspired by biology in Marshall's thoughts were quickly diminished or even removed by his followers after his death (Foss, 1991). Biological analogies have no prominence in the post-war Marshallian textbooks. Even the Veblenian tradition made little further application of developments in biology after the 1920s. Partly as a reaction to 'Social Darwinism' and to the monstrous misapplication of the alleged results of biological science to the social and political under fascism, biological analogies became generally unpopular amongst liberal social scientists in the inter-war period.

The Post-war Re-emergence of Biological Analogies in Economics

An early post-war sign of the re-emergence of biological analogies in economics was in Armen Alchian's (1950) famous use of the 'natural selection' metaphor. This stimulated an important controversy over the application of evolutionary thinking to economics, including an important article by Edith Penrose (1952). After this controversy died down the exploration of the biological metaphor once more became the pursuit of a tiny minority, including Jack Downie (1955).[2]

In the late 1970s ideas from a distinct school of biological thought entered economics and took a specific form. Chicago School economists Gary Becker (1976), Jack Hirshleifer (1977) and Gordon Tullock (1979) seized the newly emergent discipline of 'sociobiology' (Wilson, 1975) and saw it as underpinning their individualistic assumptions and validating universal 'laws' spanning the biological and economic domains. Phenomena such as scarcity and individual competition were seen as common to both. Although the precedent was unacknowledged, this approach repeated many propositions fostered by the Social Darwinists of the late nineteenth century. As well as providing important targets of criticism (Gowdy, 1987), these episodes clearly demonstrate that biological analogies can be applied in quite different ways to the socio-economic sphere. There are very different intellectual traditions and kinds of biology to be drawn upon (Khalil, 1993).

The economics of Becker, Hirshleifer and Tullock was a perpetuation of the tradition of static, equilibrium theorizing. Accordingly, the dynamic and evolutionary aspects of biological thinking attracted them less. They were more concerned to attempt to base their allegedly universal assumptions concerning human behaviour on the bedrock of biological science.

An important but contrasting invocation of biology occurred in the early 1980s, with the publication of Richard Nelson and Sidney Winter's seminal book *An Evolutionary Theory of Economic Change*. As in the work of Alchian in the 1950s, here evolutionary thinking in biology was again foremost, with explicit analogies to the gene (routines in the firm), to mutation (the firm's search for new techniques) and to selection (profitable firms being favoured). Although the authors saw their work as being situated in the Schumpeterian tradition, such an explicit and extensive use of biological analogies would have discomforted Schumpeter. In fact, as an early reviewer pointed out (Eaton, 1984), Nelson and Winter had unknowingly resuscitated an important feature of the earlier Veblenian tradition of 'evolutionary economics'.

The result has been a steady exponential increase in the use of evolutionary analogies and models in economics. Indeed, if mainstream economics is characterized mainly by the assumption of rational choice and the context of static equilibrium, an evolutionary framework taken from biology offers the most consistent and fundamental challenge to these core ideas

(Cooper, 1989; Dosi and Egidi, 1991; Dosi *et al.*, 1988; Goldberg, 1975; Hodgson, 1993c, 1994; Schaffer, 1989) as well as providing an alternative theoretical nucleus.

Biology as an Alternative Metaphor in Economics: Some Problems

In part, the recourse to biology is based on the belief that real-world economic phenomena have much more in common with biological organisms and processes than with the mechanistic world of billiard balls and planets. After all, the economy involves living human beings, not merely particles, forces and energy. Nevertheless, there are risks involved in this switch of metaphors. We should again be reminded that biology has been grossly abused by social scientists in the past. As noted above, there has been the episode of 'Social Darwinism' and lamentable associations of biological thought with pro-aristocratic, racist, or sexist ideologies and political movements.

It is still wrongly assumed that evolutionary thinking involves the rejection of any kind of state subsidy or intervention on the basis of the supposed idea of the 'survival of the fittest'. However, it is wrong to assume that evolutionary theorizing always points to the optimality of competitive outcomes, or to laws of evolutionary 'progress', or to the sagacity of *laissez-faire*. According to modern theory, evolutionary processes do not necessarily lead to – by any reasonable definition – optimal consequences (Gould and Lewontin, 1979). Similar arguments apply in the economic as well as the biotic context. Evolutionary biology no longer sustains the dictum of Dr Pangloss in Voltaire's *Candide* that 'this is the best of all possible worlds' (Hodgson, 1991; 1993c, ch. 13).

Others would bar the biological analogy from social science with an emphasis on the alleged distinctiveness of the social and human domain, compared with the natural. This distinctiveness is supposedly established by the fact that humans are uniquely intentional or purposeful in the sense that they are more than programmed automata. Karl Marx expressed this well when he wrote in *Capital* that 'what distinguishes the worst architect from the best of bees is that the architect builds the cell in his mind before he constructs it in wax' (Marx, 1976, p. 284). However, it is ironic that such a view shares with much of modern mainstream biology the debatable assumption that fully purposeful action is not found among non-humans. More plausibly, the distinction between purposefulness and non-purposefulness is not an all-or-nothing affair; there are gradations of consciousness and intentionality found both within the human mind and in the minds of other species.

Another motivation for the rejection of the biological analogy in social science is the fear that the breakdown of the conceptual barriers between the two domains would imply that explanations of social phenomena would be wholly reduced to biological or genetic terms. In response, a Chinese Wall is thus built between the two sciences to keep out the genetic and other reductionist hordes. What is not recognized is that the very complexity of biological phenomena has created a strong anti-reductionist discourse inside that very discipline (Hodgson, 1993b). The potential allies on the other side of the wall are ignored. Furthermore, projects to unify the natural and physical sciences do not necessarily involve an overwhelmingly reductionist thrust, as several philosophers of science have argued (Bhaskar, 1979; Maull, 1977). The importation of biology is not necessarily a reckless effort to base all explanations of social phenomena on their alleged biological 'foundations'. Indeed, the breakdown of unsustainable conceptual barriers between the social and the natural worlds need not imply a search for ultimate analytical foundations at all.

However, it should be emphasized that the biological metaphor is not a panacea. Biology has internal disputes and problems of its own. Indeed, biological science is not itself free of mechanistic metaphor and reductionist methods. For instance, a significant number of biologists are committed to attempts to explain biological phenomena in physical or chemical terms. This reflects the widespread belief that science must proceed by breaking down phenomena into the smallest possible constituent units. Significantly, this 'reductionist' approach is associated with the fathers of classical mechanics: Galileo and Newton. But it is very doubtful that full reductionism can be achieved in more complex systems such as those found in biology. The systems are simply too complicated to yield to a full reductionist analysis. Analytical reduction is necessary to some limited extent, otherwise there would be no explanation in science, but it can never be complete. Despite this, the proclaimed aim of full reductionism is still common in many sciences today.

Notably, however, there are pronounced attempts to limit or transcend such strains of thought within biology itself. For example, a variety of forces and tensions point to an organicist ontology, a less rigid methodology and the transcendence of mechanistic thinking. Reductionism itself is queried and found wanting. Such features are found to some degree in the work of leading mainstream biologists such as Theodosius Dobzhansky and Ernst Mayr, as well as more heterodox scientists such as Niles Eldredge and Stephen Jay Gould, along with historians of biology such as Edward Manier (Dobzhansky, 1968; Eldredge, 1985; Gould, 1982; Manier, 1978; Mayr, 1985a).

All metaphors create difficulties as well as solutions. A problem with both the biological and the mechanical analogy is the conceptualization of the human agent. It has been argued by several critical economists that – despite the rhetoric – orthodox and mechanistic economics provides no room for real individual choice.[3] The same could be said for mainstream biology. Natural selection invokes genetic replication and random variation or mutation, but seemingly affords no role for intentionality, purposefulness or choice.

As with many 'hard core' metaphors, their transposition from one science to another may open up problems in their source as well as their destination. For instance, the problem of 'vitalism', involving choice, will and purpose, has been persistent within biology. Although 'vitalism' is now out of fashion, it raises real issues of importance, even if the notion is shunned by biologists who confine themselves to causal rather than intentional explanations. Dissenters to strict Darwinism, including Arthur Koestler (1967) have tried to instate concepts of will and purpose in the science, but with limited effect. Finally, there are novel reconstructions of the concept of causality in biology linking it to the phenomenon of organization (Campbell, 1985). This whole problem is not addressed in the present volume but it should not be ignored or underestimated. It is addressed at greater length elsewhere (Hodgson, 1993c, ch. 14).

The Exchange of Metaphor between Biology and Economics

The use of biological ideas in economics raises a number of philosophical questions. First, there is the inquiry into the extent to which existing mainstream economics has made use of metaphors from physics. Second, there is the issue of the possibility and desirability of replacing the mechanistic metaphors in economics by alternatives taken from biology. Third, there is the wider dispute over the possibility and desirability of using any metaphors taken from the natural and physical worlds in the social sciences. Fourth, there is the deeper question of the possibility or impossibility of avoiding the use of such metaphors in any science.

Clearly, these questions cannot be answered here. But it is important to emphasize that they strike at the fundamentals of any scientific project. Social and physical scientists often regard metaphors as mere literary ornaments, to be removed to reveal the essential theory below. Hence a motivation to use mathematics, from where it is assumed that literary frills and metaphors are excluded. However, modern philosophers of science take a very different view. Mary Hesse (1980, p. 111) complains that: 'It is still unfortunately necessary to argue that metaphor is more than a decorative literary device, and that it has cognitive implications whose nature is a proper subject of philosophic discussion.' Similarly, Max Black (1962, p. 237) concludes in a prominent study of metaphor and analogy in science: 'Metaphorical thought is a distinctive mode of achieving insight, not to be construed as an ornamental substitute for plain thought.'

Accordingly, several modern philosophers argue that metaphor is constitutive and indispensable for all science. Arguably, the constitutive transfers are at a deep and often unconscious level, affecting the ontology, epistemology and methodology of the subject. It may not even be a question of economics consciously aping physics as Mirowski (1989) suggests. With such 'deep level' transfers the contamination of economics by mechanistic thinking may be less deliberate but even more profound than Mirowski argues.

The argument that metaphorical transfer is at a deep as well as a more superficial level suggests that the removal of mechanistic thinking may be much more difficult than it appears at first sight. This is one reason given by some authors (Hodgson, 1993c; Khalil, 1992, 1993) – and in opposition to Mirowski – why it may be necessary to use one science to replace another, rather than to embark on a forlorn attempt to cleanse economics of natural and physical science. Such a strategy must give prominence to the organicist and non-reductionist strains in modern biology, rather than the atomistic and mechanistic alternatives found in the biology of Richard Dawkins (1976), George Williams (1966), Edward Wilson (1975) and others.

Much light is shed on these issues through an examination of an important episode in the history of ideas involving the transfer of ideas not from biology to economics – but in the opposite direction. This is the crucial and controversial question of the influence and metaphorical roles of 'political economy' in general, and the ideas of Adam Smith and Thomas Robert Malthus in particular, on the genesis of Charles Darwin's *Origin of Species*. This important case study is examined in the essays reproduced in Part III of this volume.[4]

Scott Gordon's (1989) essay is reproduced here, because it is an important case of a historian of social science arguing that political economy had no significant influence on the Darwinian revolution. A contrary view is argued in Hodgson (1993c, ch. 4). Note that to establish his controversial verdict, Gordon presents us with a narrow and sanitized version of classical political economy, free of metaphor, of ideology or of links with other sciences.

Gordon points out that Darwin did not read a great deal of political economy. He argues, further, that the 'perfect competition' of classical economics contrasts with competition in the natural world. In the former 'there is no rivalry at all' (Gordon, 1989, p. 455) since there is a multitude of firms all able to produce and sell at the current market price, whereas competition in nature involves rivalry and the 'struggle for existence'.

The latter point is easily dispensed with. Malthus's theory of population was different from the conception of competition in any kind of political economy – classical or otherwise – which stresses equilibrium outcomes. In contrast, Malthusian population theory did involve rivalry and a struggle for existence. Arguably, Gordon's account is defective for several other reasons. First, he neglects the general influence of Adam Smith on the contemporary intellectual climate, and particularly the individualistic mode of explanation championed by Smith. Second, he ignores the personal relationship between Charles Babbage and Darwin, and the influence of Babbage's ideas in political economy upon the biologist. Third, at the time at which Darwin was developing his theory, political economy enjoyed a high scientific status and was a widely popular subject for discussion (Berg, 1980, pp. 32 ff). Even if Darwin did not read all the major texts in political economy, as an intellectual moving in the scientific circles of Britain's capital city it is unlikely that he was not relatively knowledgeable of and significantly affected by such ideas at the time.

With the textual evidence available, it is possible to suggest that there was a transfer of ideas from political economy to Darwin's biology. Arguably, however, it was more to do with the spark of inspiration than the careful transfer of theorem and proof. Furthermore, although Darwin was clearly influenced by the political climate of his time (Desmond and Moore, 1991) it would be a mistake to caricature Darwin's theory simply as the import of bourgeois ideology into the natural world. This thesis is easily rejected:

> If it were true that ... the theory was the inevitable consequence of the Zeitgeist of early nineteenth-century Britain, of the industrial revolution, of Adam Smith and the various ideologies of the period, one would think that the theory of natural selection would have been embraced at once by almost everybody. Exactly the opposite is true: the theory was almost universally rejected. (Mayr, 1985b, p. 769)

It could thus be suggested that the 'deep level' transference of metaphor was of greater significance in this case than the real but more superficial contemporary ideological influences on Darwin's thought.

As noted above, the controversies surrounding the relationship between economics and biology in this period are of immense significance for the reform and development of modern economics. For instance, if biology was formed in part by economics then this suggests that the moulding of modern economics by modern biology may be a potentially fruitful enterprise. However, such a strategy involves taking heed of the tensions within and limitations of modern biology.

On this basis misgivings can be expressed over the importation into biology of models of optimizing behaviour taken from modern economics. For instance, David Rapport and James Turner's (1977) analyses of food selection, 'predator switching' and other biological phenomena involve indifference curves and other familiar analytical tools. Similarly Michael Ghiselin (1974) adopts the idea of 'methodological individualism' and the much older, pre-Darwinian metaphor of the biosystem as 'nature's economy'.[5] This modern instance of biology borrowing from economics not only reinforces the thesis of the historic relationship between the two disciplines but it also indicates that the potential or actual connection is not simply between unorthodox economics and the less reductionist versions of biology. Notably, the modelling of equilibria is found in mathematical biology as well as mainstream economics, despite the fact that Darwinian theory, as Veblen (1919, p. 37) clearly appreciated, offers unrelenting change and 'no final term'. As the Marshallian episode also indicates (Hodgson, 1993a), the biological metaphor does not provide a single or royal road to truth.

The Value of the Biological Metaphor in Economics

Despite all the problems and dangers, it is suggested here that modern biology provides a rich source of ideas and approaches from which a revitalized economics may draw. The application of an evolutionary approach to economics provides a number of advantages and improvements over the mechanistic paradigm. For instance, it enhances a concern with irreversible and ongoing processes in time (Dosi and Metcalfe, 1991), with long-run development rather than short-run marginal adjustments, with qualitative as well as quantitative change, with variation and diversity, with non-equilibrium as well as equilibrium situations, and with the possibility of persistent and systematic error-making and thereby non-optimizing behaviour.

In short, an evolutionary paradigm provides an alternative to the mainstream 'hard core' idea of mechanistic maximization under static constraints. The theory of rational choice at the core of mainstream economics relies on static assumptions, the notion of a stable or eventually constant decision environment, and the idea of global rationality, all of which are directly challenged by evolutionary theory.

Both economic and biotic systems are highly complex: that is another reason why ideas from biology are of relevance to economics. Biotic and economic systems both encompass tangled structures and causalities, involve continuous change and embrace huge variety. Partly for this reason, there is the difficult problem of the demarcation of levels of abstraction and choice of appropriate units of analysis. This issue has been faced up to and debated by a number of prominent biologists, but far less attention has been given to this by economists. The adoption of a biological metaphor may help to open up this vital methodological debate.

In biology there is an extended discourse concerning reductionism and the appropriate units of evolutionary selection. Furthermore, there is a debate over the viability of further theoretical reduction from genetics down to molecular biology, and even below to chemistry and physics (Sober, 1984). In contrast, confident in the Newtonian metaphor of the indivisible, 'individual' particle, mainstream economics traditionally proscribes discussion of the psychological or social foundations of individual purposes and preferences as being beyond the bounds of the subject.

In recent decades, and especially since the 1960s, there has been an increasing tendency for mainstream economists to attempt to explain all economic phenomena in terms of the utility-maximizing individuals which are supposed to make up the system. This 'methodological individualism' has acted to undermine Keynesian macroeconomics with its primary focus on aggregates at the systemic level. As argued elsewhere recognition of the shared problems of complexity in both biology and economics may lead economists to place less faith in methodological individualism and to recognize the legitimacy of levels and units of analysis above the individual (Sober, 1981; Hodgson, 1993b). This would involve the reinstatement of aggregative macroeconomics as an autonomous level of analysis.

Partly because of the acknowledged complexity of the phenomena which it attempts to analyse, biological science exhibits a theoretical pluralism. As David Hull (1973, pp. 3–36) points out, Darwin's methodology is not rigidly axiomatic. There is a rigorous deductive core, but it is deemed to prove little on its own and it is thus placed in the context of a mass of empirical material.

Hence in biology there are deductive arguments combined with contingent empirical premises and conclusions. Typically in biology a number of theories and explanations compete in their claims to identify the main, rather than the exclusive, cause in given real circumstances. Fortunately, biology does not present the near-monopoly of methods and approaches that appears to threaten to stifle economics today.

There is another reason why the turn to biology is of value and significance. As Fritjof Capra (1982) and others have argued, the Cartesian and Newtonian world-views have sanctioned habits of thought which involve an ultimately untenable conceptual division between humankind and the remainder of the natural world. Yet humans are living beings alongside others, and there are limits to the natural resources available and the tolerances of the ecosystems on the planet. The invocation of the biological metaphor surely helps remind us of these vital issues for the twenty-first century.

Conclusion

The mechanistic metaphor excludes knowledge, qualitative change, and irreversibility through time. It entraps economics in equilibrium schema where there are no systematic errors and no cumulative development. The value of an alternative metaphor from biology consists in part in its remedy to these deficiencies. In particular, the use of a biological metaphor suggests an alternative to methodological individualism and reductionism. Will economics emerge from its present crisis by taking this turn? The leading orthodox economist Frank Hahn (1991, p. 48) has predicted that in the next hundred years 'the subject will return to its Marshallian affinities to biology'. If this prediction is valid then a major reconstruction of economics will surely result.

Notes

1. For a selection of critical writings see Bell and Kristol (1981), Hahn (1991), Hodgson (1988), Friedman (1991), Leontief (1982), Mirowski (1986), Teece and Winter (1984), Ward (1972).
2. See Nightingale (1993). Downie's approach, emphasizing the necessary and dynamic role of variety in evolving economic systems, is developed by Metcalfe and Gibbons (1986).
3. See, for example, Loasby (1976), Shackle (1972).
4. The reader should also refer to an important essay – which for reasons of length it was impossible to reproduce here – by La Vergata (1985).
5. Additionally, sociobiologists make extensive use of constrained optimization techniques. A striking modern example of rebounding transference between the two disciplines is the use made by biologists of game theory by Maynard Smith (1982) and others. Maynard Smith added the concept of an evolutionary stable strategy to game theory and this idea was then transferred back to economics in the work of Sugden (1986).

Bibliography

Alchian, Armen A. (1950), 'Uncertainty, Evolution and Economic Theory', *Journal of Political Economy*, **58**, June, 211–22. Reprinted in Witt (1993).

Becker, Gary S. (1976), 'Altruism, Egoism, and Genetic Fitness: Economics and Sociobiology', *Journal of Economic Literature*, **14** (2), December, 817–26. Reprinted in this volume.

Bell, Daniel and Kristol, Irving (eds) (1981), *The Crisis in Economic Theory*, New York: Basic Books.

Berg, Maxine (1980), *The Machinery Question and the Making of Political Economy, 1815–1848*, Cambridge, Cambridge University Press.

Bhaskar, Roy (1979), *The Possibility of Naturalism: A Philosophic Critique of the Contemporary Human Sciences*, Brighton: Harvester.

Black, Max (1962), *Models and Metaphors: Studies in Language and Philosophy*, Ithaca, NY: Cornell University Press.

Campbell, John H. (1985), 'An Organizational Interpretation of Evolution', in David J. Depew and Bruce H. Weber (eds), *Evolution at the Crossroads: The New Biology and the New Philosophy of Science*, Cambridge, MA: MIT Press, pp. 133–67.

Capra, Fritjof (1982), *The Turning Point: Science, Society and the Rising Culture*, London: Wildwood House.

Cooper, W.S. (1989), 'How Evolutionary Biology Challenges the Classical Theory of Rational Choice', *Biology and Philosophy*, **4** (4), October, 457–81. Reprinted in this volume.

Dawkins, Richard (1976), *The Selfish Gene*, Oxford: Oxford University Press.

Desmond, Adrian and Moore, James R. (1991), *Darwin*, London: Michael Joseph.

Dobzhansky, Theodosius (1968), 'On Some Fundamental Concepts of Darwinian Biology', in Theodosius Dobzhansky, M.K. Hecht and W.C. Steere (eds) (1968), *Evolutionary Biology*, Amsterdam: North-Holland, pp. 1–34.

Dosi, Giovanni and Egidi, Massimo (1991), 'Substantive and Procedural Uncertainty', *Journal of Evolutionary Economics*, **1** (2), July, 145–68.

Dosi, Giovanni and Metcalfe, J. Stanley (1991), 'On Some Notions of Irreversibility in Economics', in Pier Paolo Saviotti and J. Stanley Metcalfe (eds) (1991), *Evolutionary Theories of Economic and Technological Change: Present Status and Future Prospects*, Reading: Harwood, pp. 133–59.

Dosi, Giovanni, Freeman, Christopher, Nelson, Richard, Silverberg, Gerald and Soete, Luc (eds) (1988), *Technical Change and Economic Theory*, London: Pinter.

Downie, Jack (1955), *The Competitive Process*, London: Duckworth.

Eaton, B. Curtis (1984), Review of *An Evolutionary Theory of Economic Change* by R.R. Nelson and S.G. Winter, *Canadian Journal of Economics*, **17** (4), November, 868–71.

Edgeworth, Francis Y. (1881), *Mathematical Psychics*, London: Kegan Paul.

Eldredge, Niles (1985), *Unfinished Synthesis: Biological Hierarchies and Modern Evolutionary Thought*, Oxford: Oxford University Press.

Foss, Nicolai J. (1991), 'The Suppression of Evolutionary Approaches in Economics: The Case of Marshall and Monopolistic Competition', *Methodus*, **3** (2), December, 65–72.

Friedman, Milton (1991), 'Old Wine in New Bottles', *Economic Jurnal*, **101** (1), January, 33–40.

Georgescu-Roegen, Nicholas (1971), *The Entropy Law and the Economic Process*, Cambridge, MA: Harvard University Press.

Ghiselin, Michael T. (1974), *The Economy of Nature and the Evolution of Sex*, Berkeley: University of California Press.

Goldberg, M.A. (1975), 'On the Inefficiency of Being Efficient', *Environment and Planning*, **7** (8), 921–39.

Gordon, Scott (1989), 'Darwin and Political Economy: The Connection Reconsidered', *Journal of the History of Biology*, **22** (3), Fall, 437–59. Reprinted in this volume.

Gould, Stephen Jay (1982), 'The Meaning of Punctuated Equilibrium and its Role in Validating a Hierarchical Approach to Macroevolution', in Roger Milkman (ed.) (1982), *Perspectives on Evolution*, Sunderland, MA: Sinauer Associates, pp. 83–104.

Gould, Stephen Jay and Lewontin, Richard C. (1979), 'The Spandrels of San Marco and the Panglossian Paradigm: A Critique of the Adaptationist Programme', *Proceedings of the Royal Society of London*, Series B, **205**, 581–98. Reprinted in Sober (1984).

Gowdy, John M. (1987), 'Bio-economics: Social Economy Versus the Chicago School', *International Journal of Social Economics*, **14** (1), 32–42. Reprinted in this volume.

Hahn, Frank H. (1991), 'The Next Hundred Years', *Economic Journal*, **101** (1), January, 47–50.

Hesse, Mary B. (1980), *Revolutions and Reconstructions in the Philosophy of Science*, Brighton: Harvester Press.

Hirshleifer, Jack (1977), 'Economics from a Biological Viewpoint', *Journal of Law and Economics*, **20** (1), April, 1–52. Reprinted in this volume.

Hodgson, Geoffrey M. (1988), *Economics and Institutions: A Manifesto for a Modern Institutional Economics*, Cambridge and Philadelphia: Polity Press and University of Pennsylvania Press.

Hodgson, Geoffrey M. (1991), 'Economic Evolution: Intervention Contra Pangloss', *Journal of Economic Issues*, June, **25** (2), 519–33.

Hodgson, Geoffrey M. (1992), 'Thorstein Veblen and Post-Darwinian Economics', *Cambridge Journal of Economics*, **16** (3), 285–301.

Hodgson, Geoffrey M. (1993a), 'The Mecca of Alfred Marshall', *Economic Journal*, **103** (2), March, 406–15.

Hodgson, Geoffrey M. (1993b), 'Why the Problem of Reductionism in Biology Has Implications for Economics', *World Futures*, **37**, 69–90. Reprinted in this volume.

Hodgson, Geoffrey M. (1993c), *Economics and Evolution: Bringing Life Back Into Economics*, Cambridge, UK and Ann Arbor, MI: Polity Press and University of Michigan Press.

Hodgson, Geoffrey M. (1994), 'Optimisation and Evolution: Winter's Critique of Friedman Revisited', *Cambridge Journal of Economics* (forthcoming 1994).

Hull, David L. (1973), *Darwin and His Critics: The Reception of Darwin's Theory of Evolution by the Scientific Community*, Cambridge, MA: Harvard University Press, pp. 3–36.

Jevons, William Stanley (1981), *The Papers and Correspondence of W.S. Jevons*, vol. 7, R. Black ed., London: Macmillan.

Khalil, Elias L. (1992), 'Economics and Biology: Eight Areas of Research', *Methodus*, **4** (2), December, 29–45. Reprinted in this volume.

Khalil, Elias L. (1993), 'Neo-classical Economics and Neo-Darwinism: Clearing the Way for Historical Thinking', in Ron Blackwell, Jaspal Chatha and Edward J. Nell (eds) (1993), *Economics as Worldly Philosophy: Essays in Political and Historical Economics in Honour of Robert L. Heilbroner*, London: Macmillan, pp. 22–72. Reprinted in this volume.

Koestler, Arthur (1967), *The Ghost in the Machine*, London: Hutchinson.

La Vergata, Antonello (1985), 'Images of Darwin: A Historiographic Overview', in David Kohn (ed.) (1985), *The Darwinian Heritage*, Princeton: Princeton University Press, pp. 901–72.

Leontief, Wassily (1982), Letter in *Science*, No. 217, 9 July, 104, 107.

Loasby, Brian J. (1976), *Choice, Complexity and Ignorance: An Enquiry into Economic Theory and the Practice of Decision Making*, Cambridge: Cambridge University Press.

Manier, Edward (1978), *The Young Darwin and his Cultural Circle: A Study of Influences which Helped Shape the Language and Logic of the First Drafts of the Theory of Natural Selection*, Dordrecht: Reidel.

Marshall, Alfred (1961), *The Principles of Economics*, 9th (variorum) edn, London: Macmillan.

Marx, Karl (1976), *Capital*, vol. 1, translated from the fourth German edition of 1890, Harmondsworth: Pelican.

Maull, Nancy (1977), 'Unifying Science Without Reduction', *Studies in the History and Philosophy of Science*, **9**, 143–62. Reprinted in Sober (1984).

Maynard Smith, John (1982), *Evolutionary Game Theory*, Cambridge: Cambridge University Press.

Mayr, Ernst (1985a), 'How Biology Differs from the Physical Sciences', in David J. Depew and Bruce H. Weber (eds) (1985), *Evolution at the Crossroads: The New Biology and the New Philosophy of Science*, Cambridge, MA: MIT Press, pp. 43–63.

Mayr, Ernst (1985b), 'Darwin's Five Theories of Evolution', in David Kohn (ed.) (1985), *The Darwinian Heritage*, Princeton: Princeton University Press, pp. 755–72.

Metcalfe, J. Stanley and Gibbons, Michael (1986), 'Technological Variety and the Process of Competition', *Economie appliquée*, **39** (3), 493–520. Reprinted in this volume.

Mirowski, Philip (ed.) (1986), *The Reconstruction of Economic Theory*, Boston: Kluwer-Nijhoff.

Mirowski, Philip (1989), *More Heat Than Light: Economics as Social Physics, Physics as Nature's Economics*, Cambridge: Cambridge University Press.

Nelson, Richard R. and Winter, Sidney G. (1982), *An Evolutionary Theory of Economic Change*, Cambridge, MA: Harvard University Press.

Nightingale, John (1993), 'Solving Marshall's Problem with the Biological Analogy: Jack Downie's Competitive Process', *History of Economics Review*, No. 20, Summer. Reprinted in this volume.

Pareto, Vilfredo (1953), 'On the Economic Phenomenon', *International Economic Papers*, No. 3.

Penrose, Edith T. (1952), 'Biological Analogies in the Theory of the Firm', *American Economic Review*, **XLII** (5), December, 804–19. Reprinted in this volume.

Rapport, David J. and Turner, James E. (1977), 'Economic Models in Ecology', *Science*, **195**, 367–73. Reprinted in this volume.

Schaffer, Mark E. (1989), 'Are Profit-Maximisers the Best Survivors?: A Darwinian Model of Economic Natural Selection', *Journal of Economic Behavior and Organization*, **12** (1), March, 29–45. Reprinted in this volume.

Schumpeter, Joseph A. (1954), *History of Economic Analysis*, New York: Oxford University Press.

Sebba, G. (1953), 'The Development of the Concepts of Mechanism and Model in Physical Science and Economic Thought', *American Economic Review (Papers and Proceedings)*, **43** (2), May, 259–68. Reprinted in this volume.

Shackle, George L.S. (1972), *Epistemics and Economics: A Critique of Economic Doctrines*, Cambridge: Cambridge University Press.

Smith, Adam (1980), 'The Principles Which Lead and Direct Philosophical Enquiries: Illustrated by the History of Astronomy', in W.P.D. Wightman (ed.), *Essays on Philosophical Subjects*, Oxford: Clarendon.

Sober, Elliott (1981), 'Holism, Individualism, and the Units of Selection', in P.D. Asquith, and R.N. Giere (eds) (1981), *Philosophy of Science Association 1980*, Vol 2, East Lansing, MI: Philosophy of Science Association, pp. 93–121. Reprinted in Sober (1984) and in this volume.

Sober, Elliott (ed.) (1984), *Conceptual Issues in Evolutionary Biology: An Anthology*, Cambridge, MA: MIT Press.

Sugden, Robert (1986), *The Economics of Rights, Co-operation and Welfare*, Oxford: Blackwell.

Teece, David J. and Winter, Sidney G. (1984), 'The Limits of Neoclassical Theory in Management Education', *American Economic Review (Papers and Proceedings)*, **74** (2), May, 116–21.

Thoben, H. (1982), 'Mechanistic and Organistic Analogies in Economics Reconsidered', *Kyklos*, **35**, Fasc. 2, 292–306. Reprinted in this volume.

Thomas Brinley (1991), 'Alfred Marshall on Economic Biology', *Review of Political Economy*, **3** (1), January, 1–14. Reprinted in this volume.

Tullock, Gordon (1979), 'Sociobiology and Economics', *Atlantic Economic Journal*, September, 1–10. Reprinted in this volume.

Veblen, Thorstein B. (1919), *The Place of Science in Modern Civilisation and Other Essays*, New York: Huebsch. Reprinted 1990 with a new introduction by W.J. Samuels, New Brunswick: Transaction.

Walras, Léon (1954), *Elements of Pure Economics, or The Theory of Social Wealth*, translated from the French edition of 1926 by W. Jaffé (1st edn 1874), New York: Augustus Kelley, p. 71.

Ward, Benjamin (1972), *What's Wrong With Economics*, London: Macmillan.

Weiner, Norbert (1954), *The Human Use of Human Beings*, 2nd edn, New York: Houghton Mifflin.

Williams, George C. (1966), *Adaptation and Natural Selection*, Princeton, NJ: Princeton University Press.

Wilson, Edward O. (1975), *Sociobiology*, Cambridge, MA: Harvard University Press.

Witt, Ulrich (ed.) (1993), *Evolutionary Economics*, Aldershot: Edward Elgar.

Part I
Biological and Mechanical Analogies

[1]

BIOLOGICAL ANALOGIES IN THE THEORY OF THE FIRM[1]

By Edith Tilton Penrose*

Economics has always drawn heavily on the natural sciences for analogies designed to help in the understanding of economic phenomena. Biological analogies in particular have been widely used in discussions of the firm. Probably the best known and most common of these analogies is that of the *life cycle,* in which the appearance, growth and disappearance of firms is likened to the processes of birth, growth, and death of biological organisms. Marshall's reference to the rise and fall of the trees in the forest is an oft-quoted example of this type of analogy. Recently, two additional biological analogies have been presented —a natural selection analogy, dubbed by one writer *viability analysis,* and the *homeostasis* analogy designed to explain some aspects of the behavior of firms. The former, like the life cycle analogy, is for use in long-run analysis only. The latter is exclusively for short-run analysis. Both are supposed to represent improvements on the existing theory of the firm at the core of which lies the chief target of attack—the assumption that firms attempt to maximize profits.

The purpose of this paper is to examine critically all three types of reasoning and to show that they lead in most cases to a serious neglect of important aspects of the problem that do not fit the particular type of analogical reasoning employed. The chief danger of carrying sweeping analogies very far is that the problems they are designed to illuminate become framed in such a special way that significant matters are frequently inadvertently obscured. Biological analogies contribute little either to the theory of price or to the theory of growth and development of firms and in general tend to confuse the nature of the important issues.

The "Life Cycle" Theory of the Firm

Implicit in the notion that firms have a "life cycle" analogous to that of living organisms is the idea that there are "laws" governing the de-

* The author is research associate and lecturer in political economy in The Johns Hopkins University.

[1] This paper is a by-product of my work on the theory of the growth of the firm in connection with a project on firm growth directed by G. H. Evans, Jr., and Fritz Machlup, and financed by the Merrill Foundation for the Advancement of Financial Knowledge. I am particularly indebted to Professor Machlup for his careful criticism of the manuscript and for many valuable suggestions, and to Professor Bentley Glass for safeguarding my ventures into biology.

velopment of firms akin to the laws of nature in accordance with which living organisms appear to grow, and that the different stages of development are a function of age. Were this implication not present, then the life cycle concept would amount to little more than a statement that if we look at the past we find that all firms had some sort of a beginning, a period of existence and, if now extinct, an end. Even if a careful collection of the relevant facts about groups of firms in like circumstances should establish a statistical pattern in which some affinity in origin, regularity in development and similarity in disappearance could be discerned, it might be interesting history and might enable one to deduce a variety of *ad hoc* theories but it would not be a theory of development without the further generalizations about the principles according to which the life cycle proceeds.

Whatever superficial plausibility such a theory may have had in the days of the "family firm,"[2] it lost even that when the publicly held corporation became the dominant type of firm. Even Marshall, who was an early exponent in economics of this theory of the growth of the firm, was doubtful about its applicability to the joint-stock company, and I would not spend much time on it now had it not been recently adopted and put forward with vigor by one of America's foremost economists. Kenneth Boulding has virtually called for a "life cycle" theory of the firm[3] and has categorically insisted that there is an "inexorable and irre-

[2] In a paper published on the sizes of businesses in the textile industries in parts of England from 1884 to 1911, S. J. Chapman and T. S. Ashton came out rather wholeheartedly in favor of a life cycle interpretation of the development of firms: "Indeed the growth of a business and the volume and form which it ultimately assumes are apparently determined in somewhat the same fashion as the development of an organism in the animal or vegetable world. As there is a normal size and form for a man, so but less markedly, are there normal sizes and forms for businesses." "The Sizes of Businesses, Mainly in the Textile Industries," *Jour. Royal Stat. Soc.*, Apr. 1914, LXXVII, 512. In this article the analogy between the firm and the biological organism is carried very far, but in a "belated appendix" Professor Ashton, in his characteristically cautious way, very much qualifies the analogy: "The picture of the growth of an industry outlined here recalls a well-known passage in which Dr. Marshall compared business undertakings with the trees of the forest; and other biological analogies spring so readily to mind that it may be more useful to point out the differences, rather than the similarities, between the life-history of businesses and that of plants, or animals, or men. Businesses are by no means always small at birth; many are born of complete or almost complete stature. In their growth they obey no one law. A few apparently undergo a steady expansion. . . . With others, increase in size takes place by a sudden leap. . . . " "The Growth of Textile Businesses in the Oldham District, 1884-1924," *Jour. Royal Stat. Soc.*, May 1926, LXXXIX, 572. Professor Ashton attributes some of the differences between the development of firms in the earlier (1884-1914) and later (1918-1924) periods to the development of the joint-stock company.

[3] ". . . we must go on further to discuss the problem of what determines the 'optimum' or equilibrium balance sheet itself, as this is also to some extent under the control of the firm. This should bring us directly into 'life-cycle' theory, and indeed one would have expected Marshall's famous analogy of the trees of the forest again to have led economists to a discussion of the forces which determine the birth, growth, decline, and death of a

versible movement towards the equilibrium of death. Individual, family, firm, nation, and civilization all follow the same grim law, and the history of any organism is strikingly reminiscent of the rise and fall of populations on the road to extinction. . . ."[4]

The purposes a life cycle theory of the firm would serve are obvious, yet the theory as a bare undeveloped hypothesis has existed for a long time and nothing has been done to construct from it a consistent theoretical system with sufficient content to enable it to be used for any purpose whatsoever.[5] The basic hypothesis is not one from which significant logical consequences can be deduced, such as can be deduced,[6] for example, from the proposition that firms attempt to maximize profits. Supplementary hypotheses about the kind of organism the firm is and the nature of its life cycle are required. Although we have a respectable collection of information about firms, it has not stimulated economists even to suggest the further hypotheses necessary to the development of a life cycle theory of the firm. This, I think, is primarily because the available evidence does not support the theory that firms have a life cycle characterized by a consistent transition through recognizable stages of development similar to those of living organisms. Indeed, just the opposite conclusion must be drawn: the development of firms does not proceed according to the same "grim" laws as does that of living organisms. In the face of the evidence one is led to wonder why the analogy persists and why there is still a demand for a life cycle theory of the firm.

The purpose of analogical reasoning in which we consciously and

firm. In fact the theory of the firm, and of the economic organism in general, has not developed along these lines . . . much of the static theory of the firm can be salvaged . . . nevertheless, even when this has been done we still do not have a life-cycle theory. . . ." Kenneth E. Boulding, *A Reconstruction of Economics* (New York: Wiley & Sons, 1950), p. 34.

[4] *Ibid.*, p. 38.

[5] The idea that a firm's vigor declines with age, which follows naturally from the notion that firms have life cycles, did, however, enable Marshall to maintain the possibility of competitive equilibrium even when firms operated under increasing returns to scale. Growth takes time, and Marshall argued that before a business man got big enough to obtain a monopolistic position, his "progress is likely to be arrested by the decay, if not of his faculties, yet of his liking for energetic work." And if conditions in an industry were such that new firms could quickly master the economies of scale, then it would be likely that the established firms would be "supplanted quickly by still younger firms with yet newer methods." See Alfred Marshall, *Principles of Economics* (London: Macmillan, 1920, 8th ed.) pp. 286-87; also p. 808, footnote 2. The importance of this decline in a firm's luck or skill for the Marshallian use of the concept of the representative firm is clearly brought out by G. F. Shove in the symposium on "Increasing Returns and the Representative Firm," *Econ. Jour.*, Mar. 1930, XL, especially 109.

[6] Theoretical models of competition between "populations" or of the conditions of population equilibria do not require the assumption that individuals *develop* in accordance with life cycle patterns but merely that there exist "birth" and "death" rates.

systematically apply the explanation of one series of events to another very different series of events is to help us better to understand the nature of the latter, which presumably is less well understood than the former. If the analogy has really helpful explanatory value, there must be some reason for believing that the two series of events have enough in common for the explanation of one, *mutatis mutandis,* to provide at least a partial explanation of the other. This type of analogy must be distinguished from the purely metaphorical analogy in which the resemblances between two phenomena are used to add a picturesque note to an otherwise dull analysis and to help a reader to see more clearly the outlines of a process being described by enabling him to draw on what he knows in order to imagine the unknown. Analogies of this sort are not only useful but almost indispensable to human thought.

The biological analogies of the firm are not of this metaphorical type or there would be no call to push them into service to help *explain* the development of firms. They are clearly related to the whole family of analogies between biological organisms and social institutions that flourished in profusion during the 19th century[7] but which are, for the most part, no longer popular among social scientists, although curiously enough they are apparently still popular among some biologists.[8] In the notion that a firm is an organism akin to biological organisms, there is an implication that, since all such organisms have something in common, we can use our knowledge of biological organisms to gain more insight into the firm. It is not an easy task even for the biologist to state unambiguously what is meant by an organism[9] or what distinguishes the biological organism from non-living matter. But in principle it is characteristic of biological organisms that they reproduce and have an identifiable pattern of development that can be explained by the genetic nature of their constitution.[10] Furthermore, the particular pattern of

[7] These analogies are, as a matter of fact, very old and are found in classical literature. It is not even clear whether their first use was to help in explaining the nature of biological organisms by analogy with social institutions or in explaining the nature of social institutions by analogy with biological organisms. See Oswei Temkin, "Metaphors of Human Biology," in *Science and Civilization,* Robert C. Stauffer, editor (Madison: University of Wisconsin Press, 1949).

[8] See, for example, a series of papers published under the general title "Levels of Integration in Biological and Social Systems," *Biological Symposia,* 1942, VIII, in the introduction to which the editor stated: "What these papers seem to be saying, in most general terms, is this: The organism and the society are not merely analogues; they are varieties of something more general . . ." (p. 5).

[9] See J. H. Woodger, "The 'Concept of the Organism' and the Relation between Embryology and Genetics," *Quart. Rev. Biol.,* May 1930, V, 6 ff. It should be noted that the concept of "organism" as used in philosophy, notably by Alfred Whitehead, has no biological connotation.

[10] Moreover, biological organisms have a form in a sense in which societies (and firms) do not. This was one of the objections to the use of the economic analogy to explain bio-

development that is supposed to characterize firms—birth, youth, maturity, old age, death—is characteristic only of biological organisms that reproduce sexually. Organisms whose reproductive processes are primarily asexual have in general a very different pattern of development in which *death* plays no part,[11] and certainly the development of firms shows no pattern similar even to that of organisms that reproduce asexually. Clearly the one thing a firm does not have in common with biological organisms is a genetic constitution, and yet this is the one factor that determines the life cycle of biological organisms.

The characteristic use of biological analogies in economics is to suggest explanations of events that do not depend upon the conscious willed decisions of human beings. This is not, of course, characteristic of biology as such, for some branches of biology are concerned with learning processes and decision making, with purposive motivation and conscious choice in men as well as animals. In this, biology overlaps sociology and psychology and, in a sense, even economics. Information drawn from these branches of biology can be useful in helping us to understand the behavior of men and consequently of the institutions men create and operate. In using such information, however, we are not dealing with analogies at all, but with essentially the same problems on a more complex scale. But, paradoxically, where explicit biological analogies crop up in economics they are drawn exclusively from that aspect of biology which deals with the non-motivated behavior of organisms or in which motivation does not make any difference.

So it is with the life cycle analogy. We have no reason whatsoever for thinking that the growth pattern of a biological organism is *willed* by the organism itself. On the other hand, we have every reason for thinking that the growth of a firm is willed by those who make the decisions of the firm and are themselves part of the firm, and the proof of this lies in the fact that no one can describe the development of any given firm or explain how it came to be the size it is except in terms of decisions taken by individual men. Such decisions, to be sure, are constrained by the environment and by the capacity of the men who make them, but we know of no *general* "laws" predetermining men's choices, nor have we as yet any established basis for suspecting the existence of such laws. By contrast no one would seriously attempt to explain the transition from infancy to manhood or the normal processes of aging in terms of

logical facts: "The economic metaphors . . . do not account for the biological phenomenon of form." O. Temkin, *op. cit.*, p. 184.

[11] And yet Boulding points out that the chief difference between biological and social organisms is the absence of sexual reproduction and argues that the "genetic processes in the social system are perhaps somewhat more akin to asexual reproduction . . .", *op. cit.*, p. 7.

such decisions, for we have every reason for thinking that these matters are predetermined by the nature of the living organism.

There can be no doubt, I think, that to liken a firm to an organism and then attempt to explain its growth by reference to the laws of growth of biological organisms is an ill-founded procedure. If it were no more than this, one could still question whether one should take the trouble of seriously analyzing the analogy. But, besides being ill-founded, this type of reasoning about the firm obscures, if it does not implicitly deny, the fact that firms are institutions created by men to serve the purposes of men. It can be admitted that to some extent firms operate automatically in accordance with the principles governing the mechanism constructed,[12] but to abandon their development to the laws of nature diverts attention from the importance of human decisions and motives, and from problems of ethics and public policy, and surrounds the whole question of the growth of the firm with an aura of "naturalness" and even inevitability.[13]

"Viability" Analysis

The second type of biological analogy I wish to discuss claims to have drawn on the principles of biological evolution and natural selection which were first put forth in a comprehensive form by Darwin. The discussion of the processes and progress of human society in terms of natural selection and evolution followed close on the introduction of these concepts into biology.[14] The analogy I am concerned with here avoids the crudities and attempts to avoid the value judgments that characterized the 19th century doctrines of Spencer and his followers in their application of these principles to society. It is very modern in its emphasis on uncertainty and statistical probabilities. Nevertheless, it

[12] See the discussion of homeostasis below. If analogies must be used, there is much to be said for comparing a firm to a machine that operates in accordance with the principles governing its physical organization, but the construction, evolution and uses of which are determined by a mechanic. However, neither type of analogical reasoning has much explanatory value.

[13] Not the least of the effects of this kind of reasoning is to bring "natural law" to the defense of the *status quo*. See the discussion in Richard Hofstadter, *Social Darwinism in American Thought* (Philadelphia: University of Pennsylvania Press, 1944) pp. 30 ff. and the quotation (p. 31) he gives from John D. Rockefeller: "The growth of a large business is merely a survival of the fittest. . . . The American Beauty rose can be produced in the splendor and fragrance which bring cheer to its beholder only by sacrificing the early buds which grow up around it. This is not an evil tendency in business. It is merely the working out of a law of nature and a law of God."

[14] This subject was widely debated throughout the Western world and the literature is far too extensive to cite. For a useful, though limited, bibliography, see Hofstadter, *op. cit.* The idea of the survival of the fittest, however, was first suggested to Darwin by a work in the social sciences—Malthus on population.

is open to the same basic objections that in my opinion adhere to all such biological analogies.

The purpose of the theory is to get around a logical difficulty alleged to be inherent in the assumption that firms attempt to maximize profits in a world characterized by uncertainty about the future. If uncertainty exists, firms cannot know in advance the results of their actions. There is always a variety of possible outcomes, each of which is more or less probable. Hence the expected outcome of any action by a firm can only be viewed as a distribution of possible outcomes, and it is argued that while a firm can select those courses of action that have an optimum distribution of outcomes from its point of view, it makes no sense to say that the firm *maximizes* anything, since it is impossible to maximize a distribution. Hence profit maximization as a criterion for action is regarded as meaningless. According to the "viability analysis," however, this is not a serious difficulty for the economist if he draws on the principle of natural selection and considers the adaptation required of firms by their environment.

The argument, originally set forth by Armen A. Alchian,[15] is as follows: To survive firms must make positive profits. Hence positive profits can be treated as the criterion of natural selection—the firms that make profits are selected or "adopted" by the environment, others are rejected and disappear. This holds whether firms consciously try to make profits or not; even if the actions of firms were completely random and determined only by chance, the firms surviving, *i.e.*, adopted by the environment, would be those that happened to act appropriately and thus made profits. Hence "individual motivation and foresight, while sufficient, are not necessary,"[16] since the economist with his knowledge of the conditions of survival can, like the biologist, predict "the effects of environmental changes on the surviving class of living organisms."[17]

Alchian argues that the introduction of the supplementary and realistic assumption of purposive behavior by firms merely "expands" the model and also makes it useful in explaining the nature of purposive behavior under conditions of uncertainty.[18] If firms do try to make profits even though (because of uncertainty) they don't know how to do so, then clearly they will have a motive for imitating what appears to be

[15] Armen A. Alchian, "Uncertainty, Evolution, and Economic Theory," *Jour. Pol. Econ.*, June, 1950, LVIII.

[16] *Ibid.*, p. 217.

[17] *Ibid.*, p. 220.

[18] "It is not argued that there is no purposive, foresighted behavior present in reality. In adding this realistic element—adaptation by individuals with foresight and purposive motivation—we are expanding the preceding extreme model." *Ibid.*, p. 217.

successful action by other firms. This explains conventional rules of behavior (traditional markups, etc.) which can be looked on as "codified imitations of observed success."[19] This is the evolutionary aspect of the theory: successful innovations—regarded by analogy as "mutations"—are transmitted by imitation to other firms. Venturesome innovation and trial and error adaptation are also purposive acts which, if successful, are "adopted" by the environment. Thus "most conventional economic tools and concepts are still useful, although in a vastly different analytical framework—one which is closely akin to the theory of biological evolution. The economic counterparts of genetic heredity, mutations, and natural selection are imitation, innovation, and positive profits."[20]

In accepting and enlarging upon Alchian's argument Stephen Enke has argued that, if competition were so intense that zero profits would result in the long run, economists could make "aggregate predictions" *as if* every firm knew how to secure maximum long-run profits. For with intense competition only firms that succeeded in maximizing profits would survive.[21] But under these circumstances, Enke notes, the economist can use the traditional marginal analysis and his predictions will be the same as they would be if he employed the "viability analysis." Which of the two he uses however is not "immaterial," since "the language of the former method seems pedagogically and scientifically inferior because it attributes a quite unreasonable degree of omniscience and prescience to entrepreneurs."[22]

There is much to be said about this revival of an old approach to human affairs and about its relation to the traditional marginalist approach in economics, in particular as to whether the two approaches really answer the same types of questions about the effect of "environmental" changes on price and output. In this paper I am not so much concerned to present an analytical critique of the theory as to discuss the applicability of the biological analogy and the implications involved in its use. Again we find that the characteristic of the analogy employed

[19] *Ibid.*, p. 218.

[20] *Ibid.*, p. 219. It should be noted that the treatment of imitation as analogous to genetic heredity is essential to give the principle of natural selection any evolutionary significance. Natural selection has two meanings: "In a broad sense it covers all cases of differential survival: but from the evolutionary point of view it covers only the differential transmission of inheritable variations." See Julian Huxley, *Evolution, the Modern Synthesis* (London: Allen & Unwin, 1942), p. 16.

[21] Stephen Enke, "On Maximizing Profits: A Distinction between Chamberlin and Robinson." *Am. Econ. Rev.*, Sept., 1951, XLI. The assumption of intense competition is essential for the results claimed by the authors of this approach, as we shall see below.

[22] *Ibid.*, p. 573.

is to provide an explanation of human affairs that does not depend on human motives. The alleged superiority of "viability" over marginal analysis lies in the claim that it is valid even if men do not know what they are doing. No matter what men's motives are, the outcome is determined not by the individual participants, but by an environment beyond their control. Natural selection is substituted for purposive profit-maximizing behavior just as in biology natural selection replaced the concept of special creation of species.

In biology the theory of natural selection requires the postulate that competition—a struggle for existence—prevails, but it is a postulate that rests firmly on observed facts. Darwin deduced the struggle for existence from two empirical propositions: all organisms tend to increase in a geometrical ratio, and the numbers of any species remain more or less constant.[23] From this it follows that a struggle for existence must take place. Translated into economic terminology, the explanation of competition in nature is found in the rate of entry. The "excessive entry" is due to the nature of biological reproduction. But how shall we explain competition in economic affairs where there is no biological reproduction? The psychological assumption of the traditional economic theory that businessmen like to make money and strive to make as much as is practicable performs a function in economic analysis similar to that of the physiological assumption in the biological theory of natural selection that the reproduction of organisms is of a geometric type—it provides the explanation of competition (and in economics, incidentally, also of monopoly). To be sure, the two assumptions rest on vastly different factual foundations and should not be treated as analogous. We can only say that there is some evidence that such a psychological motivation is widely prevalent and that we have found we can obtain useful results by assuming it. If we abandon this assumption, and particularly if we assume that men act randomly, we cannot explain competition, for there is nothing in the reproductive processes of firms that would ensure that more firms would constantly be created than can survive; and certainly from observations of the real world we can hardly assume that competition is so intense that zero profits will result in the long run or that only the best adapted firms can survive.

Although insisting it is not necessary, Alchian is prepared to assume that firms do strive for positive profits.[24] But I cannot see that even this is sufficient to explain the existence of competition sufficiently intense to enable the economist to assume that only the "appropriately adapted"

[23] See Julian Huxley, *op. cit.*, p. 14.

[24] "The pursuit of profits, and not some hypothetical undefinable perfect situation, is the relevant objective whose fulfilment is rewarded with survival. Unfortunately, even this proximate objective is too high." *Op. cit.*, p. 218.

firms will survive. Even with this modification firms would still be affected by environmental changes only when these changes cause losses. When changes in the environment opened up new opportunities without acting adversely on the old, then, on the assumptions of this analysis, firms would not respond at all to the new conditions since profits would already be positive and firms are assumed to be uninterested in increasing their profits.[25]

Once motivation is introduced the usefulness of the model becomes even more questionable. Great emphasis is laid on the predictive power of the viability theory. Therefore the essence of the theory cannot be that those firms best adapted to the economic environment will survive; this could easily become a circular argument. Rather it is that the economist can know what the conditions of survival are and therefore can know the characteristics of firms that will be required by these conditions of survival. Now, apart from the pardonable notion that economists have a special knowledge denied to firms[26]—which is quite appropriate if firms (but not economists) are treated as non-motivated organisms—this would seem reasonable provided either that environmental conditions are identifiable and are independent of the actions of the firm or, if they are dependent on the actions of firms, that the economist can know how firms will, by their actions, change the environment.

Once human will and human motivation are recognized as important constituents of the situation, there is no *a priori* justification for assuming that firms, in their struggle for profits, will not attempt as much consciously to adapt the environment to their own purposes as to adapt

[25] Once we admit that when opportunities for making money arise, some firms will prefer to take a chance on making more money rather than to rest content with less, we might just as well assume that firms act *as if* they were attempting to maximize profits, since, for the purpose of detecting the direction of change, we get more useful results from using this assumption than from any other that has yet been devised. It should be obvious that for this purpose marginal movements are the significant ones, yet the viability approach leaves us no way of predicting marginal movements except under special conditions and leaves us completely helpless if there is a pronounced lag between the introduction of a given environmental change and the effect of the change on the birth and death rates of firms, for "these long-run forces of adjustment operate in the main through the effect of altered conditions of survival and the births and deaths of firms." Enke, *op. cit.*, p. 572.

[26] For the life of me I can't see why it is reasonable (on grounds other than professional pride) to endow the economist with this "unreasonable degree of omniscience and prescience" and not entrepreneurs. Although this is incidental to our discussion, it seems to me that the logic of the argument runs somewhat as follows: It is impossible to know in advance what actions will yield maximum profits. Therefore firms cannot know in advance what they should do to maximize their profits. If there is intense competition, zero profits will be maximum profits and firms making negative profits will fail. Economists can know the conditions of survival. Therefore economists can know what type of firm will escape negative profits. Therefore economists can know what firms must do to make zero or positive profits. Therefore economists can know how maximum profits can be obtained. Therefore it is *not* impossible to know in advance what actions will yield maximum profits.

One can only suggest that firms should hire economists!

themselves to the environment. After all, one of the chief characteristics of man that distinguishes him from other creatures is the remarkable range of his ability to alter his environment or to become independent of it. Underlying the viability analysis is the assumption that, even if firms can and do make more or less intelligent choices, they can do nothing in unpredictable ways to "force" the environment to "adopt," and thus make successful, the results of their action.

The concept of the environment of firms on which the economist using "viability" analysis bases his predictions is by no means clear. There is little doubt that there are parts of the external environment of firms which are identifiable and which for all practical purposes we can safely assume will not be quickly or unpredictably altered by firms—geographical factors, the conditions of transportation, established government policies. There are other aspects of the environment that can be altered within fairly narrow limits and in more or less predictable ways—the amount of natural resources, the state of employment. There are still other aspects of the environment, equally important for survival, which we cannot assume are beyond the influence of firms and which can be unpredictably altered by them in a large number of ways—the state of technology, the tastes of consumers.

It is these unpredictable possibilities of altering the environment by man that create difficulties in comparing the economist to the biologist observing the processes of natural selection and studying the nature of adaptation. Animals, too, alter their environment, but in a rather unconscious fashion without much deliberation about different probable outcomes of their actions. The possibilities open to animals of affecting their environment in a given period of time are so much more restricted than those open to men that the biologist has a very much easier task, for the relative consistency of animal behavior and the relatively narrow limits within which animals can act give him a more secure basis for prediction.[27] If firms can deliberate, if they can weigh the relative profitability of assaulting the environment itself and if they can act in ways unknown to the economist, what are the "realized requisites of survival" that can give the economist confidence in his predictions? Alchian has treated innovations as analogous to biological mutations. But mutations are "alterations in the substance of the hereditary constitution" of an organism,[28] while innovations, though they may consist of changes in the constitution of firms, more often than not are direct attempts by

[27] As a matter of fact, it is doubtful if many biologists would agree that their powers of prediction are as sweeping as are implied here, particularly if man is included among the organisms with respect to whom the effects of environmental change are predicted.

[28] Huxley, *op. cit.*, p. 18.

firms to alter their environment. In other words, innovations are directly related to the environment of firms whereas the biologists tell us that genetic mutations are apparently completely unrelated either to the environment or to the agent inducing the mutation. The biologist cannot explain why mutations take the course they do while the economist, if he can assume with some justification that the activity of firms is induced by a desire for profits, has a plausible partial explanation of innovation.

It is not possible to go very far with this aspect of the matter because the authors of the viability approach have given us no hint of what they mean by the environment. It is vaguely referred to as an "adoptive mechanism"[29] but in view of the enormous complexity of the interrelationships in the economy, a prediction of the types of organisms that will survive a given change in the environment involves the prediction of a new general equilibrium and does not seem to me to be an "intellectually more modest and realistic approach"[30] than any other. After all, even the most ardent proponent of the marginal analysis never claimed that his tools enabled him to make such sweeping predictions as are implied here. By its very nature a prediction of the kinds of firms that will survive in the long run must take account of all the reactions and interactions that a given change in the environment will induce. With our present knowledge this is impossible, and the assertion that "the economist, using the present analytical tools developed in the analysis of the firm under certainty, can predict the more adoptable or viable types of economic interrelationships that will be induced by environmental change even if individuals themselves are unable to ascertain them"[31] places the wrong interpretation on the kind of thing the economist can do. If he can predict the consequences of environmental changes, it is not because certain types of interrelationships are more "viable" in a long-run sense, but because he has an idea of how people will behave. He knows little about long-run viability since he knows very little about all of the secondary and tertiary reactions that will in the end determine the "conditions of survival"—at least he has as yet given little convincing evidence of such knowledge.

Alchian's central objective of exploring the "precise role and nature of purposive behavior in the presence of uncertainty and incomplete

[29] "The suggested approach embodies the principles of biological evolution and natural selection by interpreting the economic system as an adoptive mechanism which chooses among exploratory actions generated by the adaptive pursuit of 'success' or 'profits.'" Alchian, *op. cit.*, p. 211.

[30] *Ibid.*, p. 221.

[31] *Ibid.*, p. 220.

information" is important[32] but the biological framework in which he has cast his model has led him to underestimate the significance of the very thing he claims to be exploring. After all, one of the more powerful effects of uncertainty is to stimulate firms to take steps to reduce it by operating directly on the environmental conditions that cause it and men have a greater power consciously to change their environment than has any other organism. A direct approach, stripped of biological trappings, to the problem of what happens when men try to reach an objective but don't know the "best" route, would not lead to underemphasis on the significance of purposive activity on the part of men. It is by no means "straightforward" to assume non-motivation,[33] for without motivation economic competition, leading to the elimination of all but the best adapted within a community, cannot be assumed. Hence, if the operation of natural selection through competition is made the guiding principle of the analytical technique, then an assumption equivalent to profit maximization must be made and the professed ***raison d'être*** of the viability approach disappears.

Homeostasis of the Firm

A third biological concept that has appeared in one form or another in economic literature is the concept of homeostasis.[34] Organisms are so constructed that there is a certain "equilibrium" internal condition which their bodies are organized to maintain. Any disturbance of the equilibrium sets forces in motion that will restore it. Kenneth Boulding considers that "The simplest theory of the firm is to assume that there is a 'homeostasis of the balance sheet'—that there is some desired quantity of all the various items in the balance sheet, and that any disturbance of this structure immediately sets in motion forces which will restore the status quo."[35]

Once again we find the characteristic of the biological analogy—action taking place in human affairs without the intervention of human decisions based on deliberation and choice. But here it is applied to describe a characteristic of organized activity and a possible method by which men may achieve certain objectives. The notion of homeo-

[32] *Ibid.*, p. 221.

[33] "It is straightforward, if not heuristic, to start with complete uncertainty and non-motivation and then to add elements of foresight and motivation in the process of building an analytical model. The opposite approach, which starts with certainty and unique motivation, must abandon its basic principles as soon as uncertainty and mixed motivations are recognized." *Ibid.*, p. 221.

[34] C. Reinold Noyes, for example, who believes that "economics is fundamentally a biological science" uses the physiological concept of the homeostasis of the body in his discussion of consumers' wants. See *Economic Man* (New York: Columbia University Press, 1948), pp. 29 ff.

[35] *Op. cit.*, p. 27.

stasis, treated simply as a principle of organization, does not obscure the importance of purposive behavior in human affairs but rather emphasizes its significance and illuminates its rôle in a complex social framework. This analogy is of the helpful descriptive sort: it is not claimed that the principles of physiology can explain the working of a firm.

Indeed, one could legitimately object to the appropriateness of including the "homeostasis theory" of the firm among the biological theories. Homeostasis is a word drawn from physiology, but it describes a characteristic of any activity that takes place within a framework so constructed that certain types of action are automatically induced without any interference from whatever agency is responsible for the construction. This notion can be extended from the physio-chemical reactions which take place within a living organism in order to maintain a constant internal environment, to include the operation of a thermostatically controlled heating or air conditioning system[36] and even the conduct of a game of tag according to predetermined rules.

Thus the managers of a firm may lay down rules for the operation of the firm which are determined with reference to some "ideal" interrelationship of the parts of the firm. The desired ratio of assets to liabilities, of inventories to sales, of liquid assets to fixed assets, etc., may be determined in advance and an organization so constructed that any disturbance of the desired ratio automatically sets in motion a process to restore it. There can be little doubt that the more complex an organization becomes, the more necessary it is to establish areas of quasi-automatic operation. The importance of routine as a means of taking care of some aspects of life in order that others may be given more attention has frequently been stressed.[37] The fact that many business decisions are not "genuine decisions," but are quasi-automatic and made routinely in response to accepted signals without a consideration of alternative choices has misled many into attacking the assumption that firms try to make as much money as they can—particularly where it can be shown that the rules governing the routine actions are not fully consistent with profit maximization.

This whole area of the behavior of the firm is still not adequately explained. Imitation of apparent success may, as Alchian suggests, account for some habitual and apparently irrational behavior. The persistence of routine action after the conditions for which it was appropriate have passed may also account for some of it; other partial

[36] See Kenneth Boulding, "Implications for General Economics of More Realistic Theories of the Firm," *Am. Econ. Rev.*, (Papers and Proceedings), May, 1952, XLII, 37 ff.

[37] For a well-balanced discussion of the rôle of habitual behavior and routine decisions in business activity see George Katona, *Psychological Analysis of Economic Behavior* (New York: McGraw-Hill, 1951), especially pp. 229 ff.

explanations have been suggested.[38] The theory of homeostasis provides a formal framework of explanation into which many routine responses can be fitted, but it throws no light at all—nor does it claim to—on why and how the "ideal" relationships between the relevant variables which the firm is now attempting to maintain were originally established or on the conditions under which decisions may be made to alter them.[39] Strictly speaking, the basic principle is not a biological one at all in spite of the name given it. It is a general principle of organization, examples of which may be found in biology, in mechanics and in social organization, and if one chooses to introduce into economics another mysterious word borrowed from another science—well, that is a matter of taste.

* * *

The desire to draw biological concepts into the explanation of social affairs is hard to understand since for the most part they add to rather than subtract from the difficulties of understanding social institutions. The observed regularities and the postulated explanations of nonmotivated biological behavior are related to chemical processes, thermal reactions and the like; they are unrelated to conscious deliberation by the organism itself. The appeal of such biological analogies to the social scientist plainly springs from a persistent yearning to discover "laws" that determine the outcome of human actions, probably because the discovery of such laws would rid the social sciences of the uncertainties and complexities that arise from the apparent "free will" of man and would endow them with that more reliable power of prediction which for some is the essence of "science." It should be noted that the distinction to be made is not that between human and non-human beings but between actions that are in some degree bound up with and determined by a reasoning and choosing process, no matter how rudimentary, and actions that are, as it were, "built into" the organism, or into the relationship between the organism and its environment, and cannot be altered by conscious decision of the organism itself.

Our knowledge of why men do what they do is very imperfect, but there is considerable evidence that consciously formulated human values do affect men's actions, that many decisions are reached after a conscious consideration of alternatives, and that men have a wide range of genuine choices. The information that we possess about the behavior of firms, small as it is, does furnish us with some plausible explanations

[38] *Ibid.*, p. 230.

[39] The homeostasis principle ". . . says nothing about what determines the equilibrium state itself. In biology this can generally be assumed to be given by the genetic constitution: in social organisms, the equilibrium position of the organism itself is to a considerable degree under the control of the organism's director," Boulding, *Reconstruction of Economics*, pp. 33-34.

of what firms are trying to do and why.[40] Biological explanations reduce, if they do not destroy, the value of this information and put nothing in its place.[41]

To treat the growth of the firm as the unfolding of its genetic nature is downright obscurantism.[42] To treat innovations as chance mutations not only obscures their significance but leaves them essentially unexplained, while to treat them directly as purposive attempts of men to *do* something makes them far more understandable. To draw an analogy between genetic heredity and the purposive imitation of success is to imply that in biology the characteristics acquired by one generation in adapting to its environment will be transmitted to future generations. This is precisely what does *not* happen in biological evolution. Even as a metaphor it is badly chosen although in principle metaphorical illustrations are legitimate and useful.[43] But in seeking the fundamental explanations of economic and social phenomena in human affairs the economist, and the social scientist in general, would be well advised to attack his problems directly and in their own terms rather than indirectly by imposing sweeping biological models upon them.

[40] As Jacob Marschak observed, "It would be a pity if we should not avail ourselves of that type of hypothesis provided by our insight—however imperfect or ambiguous—in the behavior of our fellow-men. This is our only advantage against those who study genes or electrons: they are not themselves genes or electrons." "A Discussion on Methods in Economics," *Jour. Pol. Econ.*, June 1942, XLIX, 445.

[41] If one attempts to apply the biological evolutionary principle to human activity, one must first show that human activity does not differ in kind from that of other organisms, and the argument of one noted biologist must be shown to be invalid: "Man differs from any previous dominant type in that he can consciously formulate values. And the realization of these in relation to the priority determined by whatever scale of values is adopted, must accordingly be added to the criteria of biological progress, once advance has reached the human level." Huxley, *op. cit.*, p. 575.

[42] Boulding, for example, finds "mysterious" the "problem of death and decay" of firms and asserts that "the question as to whether death is inherent in the structure of organization itself, or whether it is an accident is one that must remain unanswered, especially in regard to the social organization." "Implications for General Economics of More Realistic Theories of the Firm," p. 40.

It is surely unwarranted to confine the explanation of the disappearance of firms to some obscure thing, "inherent in the structure of organization itself" or to "accident," and it would not have been so confined if the very nature of the problem had not been prejudged and limited by the biological approach. I am not sure that there is any precise meaning at all in Boulding's statement and I suspect that this is the reason his question "must remain unanswered."

[43] But one should be discriminating in using them. The varieties of biological phenomena are so numerous that a parallel may be found somewhere for every conceivable type of social situation. There is even apparently a type of symbiotic growth among algae and fungi which combine to form characteristic lichens that can be compared to the growth of a firm by merger. Very curious "parallels" are sometimes drawn. For example, one biologist finds that "There is an interesting parallel in the need for salt by the organism and the epiorganism [*i.e.*, society]. The commodity is so important for the social group that it was one of the earliest and most prized objects traded . . ."! R. W. Gerard, *Biological Symposia, op. cit.*, pp. 77-78.

[2]

THE DEVELOPMENT OF THE CONCEPTS OF MECHANISM AND MODEL IN PHYSICAL SCIENCE AND ECONOMIC THOUGHT

By GREGOR SEBBA
University of Georgia

In the past two or three decades, pure economic theory has been mathematized to the extent that even the economist who knows his algebra and calculus is all but helpless when faced with the most recent advances. A determined effort is being made to construct economic theory as a rigorous, quantitatively predictive science. Although this effort is confined to a very small sector of what commonly goes under the title of economics, it happens to affect the heart of the theory. It is obviously not possible to foresee the future course of development in a field teeming with new ideas and approaches. But it is possible to spell out some of the implications of these ideas. Economic thought is rooted in the social order, and it has its effects upon the social order. What effects depends on what kind of thought and what kind of social order it is. Since the new thought tries to produce economic models analogous to physical world models, since its concept of predictiveness is that of the modern sciences of nature, it will be well to start out with an examination of the concepts of model and mechanism in both areas.

I

What is a model? We may say that it is a small machine representing a large machine. The catch lies in the word "representing." A small-scale but otherwise exact replica of the big mechanism is a model, but one that will interest only the hobbyist, the child, or the museum director. When a scientist builds a model he does not want to reproduce the whole mechanism. He wants to construct something that will do what the large mechanism does; and not all of it either, but only that which is of interest to him. It matters little how and why the model does it. The "Moniac" represents the flow of dollars by a flow of colored water. Colored water has nothing in common with dollars except that both are homogeneous, measurable quantities. That is enough for an analogue.

A thought model or theoretical model is a different thing. It is also a representation of an observable piece of reality, but the representation is made in the realm of thinking, not of reality itself. It took a very long time for the implications of this simple fact to be worked out.

Among the earliest physical world models are those of the Greek atomistic philosophers of nature who laid the foundation for the world view of modern science. To them the world of qualities as we experience it was not the ultimate, not the real world. There was no way of understanding it except by forming incomparable and often incompatible categories with which the mind cannot do very much. Therefore they conceived of an invisible "true" world behind the visible world—an intelligible, quantitative world of material particles whose mechanical arrangements and motions produce all the colorful and variegated phenomena we experience. Their world model was thus mechanistic, quantitative, non-normative, and non-teleological. It could not be mathematized, and its only link with the experienced world was through speculation about the ways in which the assumed real particles might produce the phenomena we observe.

In the sixteenth and seventeenth centuries another type of world model arises. The world model becomes visible, at least on principle. René Descartes explains his world model by the analogue of a large, closed barrel completely filled with small marbles. In the real universe the particles, originally set in motion by God, are moving as marbles would if they were infinitely small and divisible and if the barrel were astronomically large but still finite. Descartes did not try to mathematize this model, and he could not have done so had he tried. For there are no functional laws to be derived from it. But he did lay the ground for 250 years of modelmaking when he geometrized space as we intuitively experience it—as three-dimensional space outside time.

With Newton, physical models enter the realm of full mathematization and full predictiveness. His *Principia* of 1687 contains the greatest and most influential of all physical models; that of classical mechanics. Mechanistic economics, which arose almost a century later, is built in its image, as Professor Lowe has recently demonstrated. Classical mechanics considers a system of material points upon which directional forces operate at a distance according to calculable laws of motion. The choice of paths is governed by the principle of least action, which may be termed the economic principle if we take the term in its widest sense as denoting a maximum-minimum principle. Thus classical mechanics is an economic model, though it is not a model of the economy.

The laws of motion are true modern laws, establishing determinate functional relationships between measurable variables. As a model of the universe, classical physics is calculable in the sense that it renders it possible to find the world parameters by observation. The space of this universe is the timeless, three-dimensional space of Descartes. The mechanical processes in it are reversible.

It was thought for a long time that all physical models must be mechanical and that physical laws are "real" in some intuitive sense. But the process of physical inquiry led to a surprising fact. Physical laws and properties could be discovered not only by generalizing and formalizing quantitative observations. They could also be discovered by studying the mathematical structure of physical theory. If this examination revealed new unexpected mathematical properties, then it turned out to be safe to give them physical meaning. If verification failed, it was not because the physical interpretation of derived mathematical properties was illicit but because the original propositions were invalid. In other words, the convictions grew that mathematical and natural structures are isomorphic. The belief in this isomorphism is basic to modern physics.

This belief places physical models in a new light. Nature (defined as that reality which reaches us through our sense experiences) cannot be directly grasped. We can only rely on the isomorphism between two incommensurable realms: that of nature and that of thought. How do these two realms interconnect, or, stated differently, how are theoretical models geared to reality? The only link consists in the process of verifying theoretical prediction from the model by observation. This is necessary and sufficient. No complete part-by-part correspondence between model and reality is required or, strictly speaking, possible.

It is evident that thought models based on this conception can attain very great freedom from categories intuitively suggested by our sense experience. At the highest level, the mind builds autonomous mathematical structures called models, derives from them predictive statements about experience, and subjects these to the judgment of the senses through observation.

The models of modern field theory are no longer intuitively linked to reality. They transcend the limitations of mechanical explanation. In these pure thought constructs, timeless Euclidian space is replaced by a unified time-space concept deriving from a mathematics capable of dealing with "space" of any desired dimensions.

II

Classical economics made the tremendous discovery that the quantifiable features of a modern economy can be represented by a general mechanistic model capable of mathematization and presumably prediction. The emerging capitalistic system made economic processes increasingly rational and calculable while at the same time granting them a social ascendancy they had never before enjoyed. It swiftly transformed the old well-articulated society into something which, for a while at least, looked like a vast and rapidly increasing aggregate of more or less homogeneous human beings moving and acting under the impact of economic motivations imperiously overriding all others. It is not surprising that the quantifiable features of this new economy were thought to be all that mattered to economic theory. Everything else could be disposed of as random disturbances, trial and error, and friction—all thoroughly mechanical concepts. But the fact that the economy is imbedded in a social order unfolding in history asserted itself from the very beginnings of the science by repeated revolts against mechanistic theory. These nonmechanistic revolts so far failed to deal effectively with the quantitative features of the economy, nor have they produced satisfactory tools for analyzing the historical changes of social structures and the problems of social power which are just as much part of economic life as are the laws of the market.

The earliest mechanisms of economic theory need not detain us. It is with Adam Smith that the quantitative science of economics springs to life. His model is fundamentally a general mechanical equilibrium model—a complex servomechanism—but as yet incapable of mathematization. The model asserts that if the particles are left undisturbed in their movement along cost minimization paths, then the system as a whole will automatically attain equilibrium at maximal production and optimal distribution. This was at once a statement of theory and the expression of a guiding social myth.

Cournot provided one feature needed for the mathematization of the model when he introduced the schedule concept, together with the proper formalism of analytical geometry and calculus as the tools for analyzing time-reversible motion in Cartesian space along supposedly continuous curves and surfaces. This is still the dominant language of microeconomics.

The Lausanne school rose to the subsequent task of formalizing the general equilibrium system. Again a new formalism enters: the algebra of simultaneous linear equations. The solution was at once a triumph and a catastrophe. The proof that a sufficient number of equations is available to solve for all unknowns was mathematically decisive but in practice self-defeating.

R. G. B. Allen's *Mathematical Analysis for Economists,* published as late as 1938, illustrates the terminal stage of the classical approach. The word matrix is not mentioned in the book, and its chapter on determinants lists no economic applications. Yet the new theoretical movement had already been on its way for well over a decade when Allen's book was published.

This movement was not a sudden revolution. It started out harmlessly enough, trying to make classical theory rigorous and predictive. Yet its novelty becomes very clear when we compare the old distinction between "descriptive" and "theoretical" economics with the new concept of "econometrics" in which theory and observation are integrated on the theoretical plane itself. The new theory is driving towards full mathematization, not because of the advantages of mathematical over literary presentation, but because mathematization is the proper form of a purely quantitative theory. It is driving towards predictiveness, not because of the supposed usefulness of economic prediction, but because a non-predictive quantitative science is nonverifiable. It is driving towards rigor and abstractness, not because it wants to escape logical and historical fallacies, but because rigor and abstractness are the essence of mathematical structures and the source of their explanatory power. In short, the new theory is what it is because it understands the true nature of a quantitative science and accepts what inevitably follows.

It is from this point of view that we shall take a brief look at three outstanding types among the new economic models.

The first of these types is perhaps the best known and most easily accessible one: the dynamic macroeconomic model designed to explain and predict business cycles. This type of model introduces time and change into the timeless equilibrium system. It is strictly mechanistic, using such mechanical devices as shocks, lags, multipliers, accelerators, ceilings, etc. The structural parameters are derived from observation. The time of these models is still the reversible time of classical mechanics. Structural changes and growth factors are as yet treated as exogenous and reversible.

Another type of model is being developed by the new "theory of programming" or "allocation." The most easily accessible model of this type is the Leontief input-output model—a reconstruction of the equilibrium model designed to make it predictive and potentially dynamic. But the Leontief model is a wayside stop on the road from classical equilibrium mechanics to the new "normative" economics of allocation theory. This theory is of great generality, having already been applied to such diverse problems as the routing of wartime shipping, organizing the Berlin air lift, solving management problems, investigating theorems of welfare economics, and planning interindustry changes.

Here the distinction between "technical" and "economic" problems obviously no longer applies. In general allocation theory, economics is only a special case, just as economic systems are special cases of allocation systems. This represents one innovation. Another follows from the first. The concepts of price and market, consumers' preferences, etc., are no longer basic. They can be derived and defined in terms of the general allocation scheme. Hence theory is freed from the limitations of institutional setting. It can consider on equal terms the management of a firm, the workings of a market economy, and the decision-making of a central planning authority. Thirdly, it can be normative. Unlike classical theory, it is not confined to the question what the terminal state of the economic system will be, given its initial state and its laws of operation; normative economics can simultaneously consider the initial and the terminal state and select the minimum path from one to the other. The theory of allocations has the makings of a rigorous, predictive, general theory of planning.

Unlike the others, a third type of innovation—the theory of games—does not grow out of classical economics but goes down to foundations to build a new model of rational social behavior. Two brief remarks about it must suffice. First, the games model promises to explain power phenomena as the predictable consequences of rational social behavior. This would be a tremendous gain in realism over traditional theory, which treats power as irrational and exogenous if it treats it at all. Secondly, the model, if successful, would close the disturbing gap between micro- and macroeconomics, rigorously and without a formal break moving from one to the other.

We may summarize. Dynamic models try to predict macroeconomic developments by way of change mechanisms, econometrically linked to observation. Allocation theory reformulates the mechanical equilibrium model in a radically new way, leading towards a theory of planning. The theory of games replaces the classical mechanistic model by starting from the ground with a new model of rational social behavior itself.

III

To many economists, the new ventures must seem like an intellectual space opera: overzealous in their mathematicism, naïve in their simplification, and beautifully unrealistic in their flight towards unattainable predictive goals. But then, what is so realistic about the old science? How realistic can it be, considering that the economic reality it tries to explain is a graven image of its own making? As a rule, the economist studied economic theory before he began his regular, systematic observation of economic life. His picture of reality grows in him as uncounted casual and systematic observations are fused into a coherent whole under the organizing influence of his theoretical beliefs. Among these beliefs are some that represent a mythical survival of features of the Smithian model which have long since been abandoned. Theory therefore enters the economic image in its formative stage; hence, "verification" of theory by reference to the "generally accepted" image of reality is circular. Moreover, there is no guarantee that features of reality foreign to the prevailing model and myth will force themselves into their rightful place in this image.

Because of this hidden circularity and also because the economist tends to know the history of economic thought better than he knows the thinking of those who make economic history by operating a business, a curious attitude has developed towards patent discrepancies between observation and theory. In physics it is theory that becomes suspect when such discrepancies arise; in economics it is reality. A few excerpts from a round table discussion on *The Impact of the Union* (edited by David McCord Wright; Harcourt, Brace and Company, 1951) may illustrate this attitude. We quote (pages 117, 118-119, and 122; italics added):

BOULDING: *Why did we ever have a market?* It's rather baffling, because all the forces are arrayed against it. Everybody's individual interest is to be a monopolist.

KNIGHT: Always has been.

....

BOULDING: *The only thing wrong with capitalism is that nobody loves it* . . . this is something you have to take into the picture if this is going to be *social science and not just economics*. I mean all this ignorance. Why are people ignorant? Well, because as you say, we haven't succeeded in *putting truth into a myth*.

....

KNIGHT: I want to say one thing. Man is romantic. People hate trade. They hate profit . . . they hate truth. . . . *You can't get that out of the picture and talk about reality.*

CHAMBERLIN: Don't you think that another thing they hate is measuring things? *Part of their revolt against the market is due to the reduction of everything to quantitative measure.* . . .

KNIGHT: Some great author said the ability to do algebra is a form of low cunning. I have a great deal of sympathy with that. [Laughter.]

Now this is obviously not to be taken any too literally:

CHAMBERLIN: [What] is there ignorant about a monopolist . . . who thinks that by pursuing a monopolistic policy he can improve his own position?

FRIEDMAN: Nothing. He is absolutely right.

And out goes the "invisible hand." But the "myth" of the "invisible hand" stays to haunt the economist.

For one thing, he observes that the world is not as it ought to be, and since he has no proper tools in his kit to grip this eel-like fact, he is forced to call knowledge ignorance and to wonder why all these romantic people ever created the market.

What worries him still more is that he has failed to put what he continues to call "truth" into a "myth." He recognizes by now that the historical process that cast the economy into the mold of communicating markets has not cast the minds of men into the corresponding mold of underlying beliefs. But he still refuses to recognize that, faced with this fact, his concept of control is unrealistic and theoretically untenable. This concept of control consists in making it the theorist's task to tell the man who is about to jump from the bridge that he will drown if he does, and to leave it at that. If the man has common sense, he will stay on the bridge. If not, well, it's *his* funeral, isn't it? Control then consists of prediction offered as purely technical, neutral, powerless advice. The sons of Adam Smith fear control of man over man. And rightly so, for such control implies the dehumanization of the human realm. The ethos of classical economics revolts against this consequence. But its epistemology works towards it. So long as the theory is unpredictive, the conflict can remain unresolved and even undetected. But should the theory become predictive, it may yet turn against its origins and become instrumental in subverting economic freedom.

Moreover, the world this theory seeks to explain is no longer the world of Adam Smith. In the world of contemporary business the accent has shifted from the automatic workings of the market mechanism to technical control of predictible processes. The new approach to economics reflects this change of accent. Its concepts of prediction are those of a rigorous, fully mathematized science of nature. But the processes to which this concept is applied are social processes. That makes a difference.

IV

It has been argued that predictiveness is beyond the grasp of the new theory. But the arguments appear unconvincing. The practical obstacles have been called insuperable. They may be, but it is too early to say, what with so many analytical and computational power tools newly available. Again it is claimed that no model can possibly embody all the factors that do or may affect the phenomena studied. But the introduction of the strategically important factors alone would go a long way. Will structural changes make models obsolete as fast as they are constructed? If these changes are quantifiable, they can be built into a model. And if they are not quantifiable? Well, no pure economic theory proposes to predict them anyhow. How close to success are the modelmakers? That is a serious question, but not a fundamental one.

It is more profitable to think about the kind of prediction and control implied in the new ventures. Dynamic business cycle models may come to predict the quantitative effects of changes in the variables. This would make macroeconomic control through the control of strategic variables feasible. But if such models were to become predictive, their predictions would also have direct effects upon the economy. For men, unlike stars or particles, understand predictions and act upon them. To the extent that prediction alters the course of the predicted event, the publicizing of reliable predictions is therefore itself an act of control.

The theory of games, should it succeed, would provide a calculus of strategies for top-level policy making in large organizations. By making the behavior of "coalitions" understandable, it may also make it controllable.

Allocation theory has already been applied to organizing flow towards predetermined goals. But it also can attack the question what goals should be set. First, it can ask whether desired goals are attainable with given means. Secondly, it may measure different goals by some normative standard, and select the best one. Thirdly, it may give rise to the construction of goals different from, but equivalent to, those toward which the economy is freely moving. For example, it need not take consumers' preferences for granted. It may ask what other combination of preferences will produce equal satisfaction while being preferable on other grounds. This subjects the goals themselves to analysis and control. In fact, consumers' preferences are already under industry control in important fields. It is neither impossible nor fantastic to visualize that such control should be co-ordinated and centrally planned. Again, by considering prices, markets, etc., as structural factors of the system rather than as the results of the operation of economic laws, allocation theory brings a radically different kind of control into focus—control operating through structural changes in the economy rather than through legal restraints or manipulation of the market factors.

V

Is it legitimate to speculate so far ahead, having no more to go by than tentative theoretical beginnings of as yet small practical value? It is, unless we consider the making of theory and theoretical models a wholly arbitrary process. The theory maker must from the outset adopt a structural plan for his theory. To make the theory rigorous he must follow this plan as he goes on. To make it predictive he must constantly relate the model to observation. Once economic theory is conceived of as a mechanistic science dealing with quantitative phenomena, rigor and predictiveness must be accepted as its final form. Should all the present models fail, new models and new approaches would have to be tried until one of them succeeds or until it is discovered that none of them will, and why. Again, if predictiveness is achieved, then control must follow to the extent that economic phenomena are subject to planned human action.

To hope that men will for the sake of their freedom leave new means of control unused does not seem realistic. They will use the means of control and redefine freedom. They are doing it already.

They are also redefining control. They have to. They use control every day and are proud of it. When they look at their economic environment, they find the scene dominated by vast economic and political combines smoothly operating by a thoroughly rational system of internal controls. This is why programming theory is more realistic than the traditional theory of the firm and why the theory of games, if it can explain the behavior of "coalitions," will be more realistic than the traditional theory of market behavior. Control can no longer be identified with interference and with disturbing the natural harmony of the economy. The new models reflect the economy of our day as surely as Adam Smith's model reflected that of his time. But, of course, they may not succeed any better than his did.

At any rate, what happens in the present development of economic thought is worth watching. Economics is the pioneer among the social sciences; it is first in carrying the rigor and power of natural science into the social field with some initial theoretical success. This is not only a bold undertaking; it is also an inevitable and, above all, a grave undertaking. To obtain a just view of its implications it would be good to know what a rigorous, predictive theory of social processes can do, what it cannot do, and what it will do to society if it does what it can.

[3]

[MORRIS A. COPELAND]

On the Scope and Method of Economics

ONE of Thorstein Veblen's main, though not yet fully recognized, contributions to economics relates to the scope of the subject and the methods that should be employed in investigating it.

That this should be so is hardly surprising when we consider his special qualifications for such a contribution. Probably there was no contemporary economist who could match his familiarity with the then current developments in both biological and physical science and with the previous history of science. Moreover, along with his peculiarly wide background in science he had an extraordinary ability to understand sympathetically *Weltanschauungen* which differed widely from his own and from each other, e.g., those of Quesnay, Hume, and Marx.

The general nature of Veblen's contribution in the area of economic methodology is indicated by the title of his famous paper, "Why Is Not Economics an Evolutionary Science?" [1] He thought economics should be investigated in a manner that deserves the characterization, "modern scientific method," that it should be treated as a branch of natural science. He thought that, since the natural science approach to the study of the structure and functioning of living organisms had

[1] Reprinted in T. Veblen, *The Place of Science in Modern Civilisation* (New York, 1919), pp. 56–81.

Morris A. Copeland

come to be predominantly evolutionary or genetic and since economics is concerned with the functioning of one kind of living organism, man, scientific method in economics ought to mean an evolutionary or genetic approach. And as a result his conception of the scope of the subject was somewhat different from that of most of his contemporaries and indeed somewhat different from that of a good many economists today.

It will be convenient to consider what Veblen's proposal that economics should be an evolutionary science involves under the following headings: (1) his conception of evolution, (2) the historical relativity of economic truths, (3) the need for a sense of cultural perspective, (4) explanation, causation, and genetic process, (5) public policy, and (6) the scope of economics.

1. HIS CONCEPTION OF EVOLUTION

The conception of evolution Veblen had in mind when he proposed that economics ought to be approached as an evolutionary science was post-Darwinian rather than Hegelian or Bergsonian. This meant he had a post-Darwinian idea of the place of economics in the family tree of science, an idea of the place on which there is today widespread tacit agreement, even though this place carries implications that a good many economists would not accept. As I understand him, he thought of economics as a branch of that part of zoology concerned with man, a branch of functional anthropology. If one accepts the hypothesis that the *genus homo* like other *animal genera* is to be understood as having resulted from a process of natural evolution, this view of the scientific study of man seems an inescapable logical corollary. Of course it involves recognizing that in the case of the functional study of man three broad branches have become differentiated: physiology, which deals with the functioning of human bodily organs, tissues, and so on; psychology, which deals with the behavior of the individual human organism as a whole; and social science which deals with human group behavior.[2] If one takes a natural evolutionary

[2] The study of group behavior is indisputably a part of the job of the biologist in the case of other animals that have developed elaborate forms of group behavior, e.g., hymenoptera. I have discussed something of what it means to treat economics as a natural science in "Economic Theory and the Natural Science Point of View," *American Economic Review*, March 1931. Comparable questions for

Scope and Method of Economics

viewpoint and regards economics as a social science, he implicitly makes economics a subbranch of the branch of zoology concerned with the human animal.[3]

If economics is a branch of zoology, it seems reasonable that economists should look more to biologists than to physicists for methodological guidance. Certainly Veblen did. In much of his work he was concerned with the process of social evolution, and he conceived this process as very much like the process of evolution of species. Indeed he makes the analogy explicit when he speaks of "a post-Darwinian, causal theory of the origin and growth of species in institutions"[4] and of natural selection as applying to the process by which changes in conventions and habits of thought come about.[5]

Veblen's concept of social evolution surely merits high praise. And there are other aspects of this concept besides the analogy to the evolution of species to which it will be convenient to give attention at a later point. Also there are other applications of the methodology of biology to economics that it will be best to deal with later.

At the moment we may note that for Veblen looking more to biologists for methodological guidance meant looking less to physicists. For example, he seems to have had little or no use for the concept of equilibrium, which had been borrowed from mechanics. I concur in his strictures on the use of this concept in a normative sense and in his objection to the static implications that its usual sense entails. This does not rule the concept out of economics entirely, but it does rule out most of the use that has been made of it.[6]

---

psychology are dealt with in my paper, "Psychology and the Natural Science Point of View," *Psychological Review*, Nov. 1930.

Such a view of the anthropological studies seems a logically inescapable corollary of the hypothesis of natural evolution; but of course this corollary is not psychologically inescapable. Where the will to believe or disbelieve is strong, plausible rationalizations seem always to be forthcoming, and the idea that man is something more than a mere animal is a persistent one.

[3] Veblen does not seem to have said explicitly that he thought of economics in this way as a branch of natural science. I believe he took it to be a matter of course that such a view followed from the hypothesis of natural evolution. It happens that on the only occasion on which I met Veblen we discussed psychology and he made it clear that he thought the hypothesis of natural evolution required regarding psychology as a branch of natural science.

[4] *Place of Science*, p. 265.

[5] *Place of Science*, p. 149.

[6] See, for example, *Place of Science*, pp. 189 ff., for his comments on the concept of equilibrium. In one interpretation of Keynes's *General Theory* the con-

Morris A. Copeland

One other point suggested by the proposition that economics is a branch of zoology seems appropriate here, a comment on a curious out-of-place survival of an earlier conception of the family tree of knowledge. A century and more ago the division of academic labor was not between individual psychology and social science but between mental and moral philosophy. Mental philosophy was concerned with man as a passive, observing, and understanding being whose experiences were organized by association one with another; that is, it was concerned with the processes of perception, memory, and imagination. Moral philosophy was the study of man as a moral agent or active, decision-making being. Individual choice was then a part of the subject matter of moral philosophy, and the Benthamite school of moral philosophy provided a theory of individual choice that came to be widely accepted. But today individual choice is undeniably part of the subject matter of psychology. At the same time many economic texts written during the past decade, like their predecessors, offer as an "explanation" of consumer demand a purportedly general theory of individual choice that is obviously a refinement of Bentham's felicific calculus. It goes without saying that as a general theory it has no standing whatever among modern psychologists. Logically the economists who adhere to it should feel embarassed, but somehow they do not seem to.

2. THE HISTORICAL RELATIVITY OF ECONOMIC TRUTHS

Perhaps the most important and most far-reaching implication of the view that economics should be approached as an evolutionary science is the implication of the historical relativity of economic truths, the implication that the only economic propositions that can be said to be scientifically valid are historical truths. Every economic generalization that has scientific validity must be limited in its applicability to a specific historical period or to specific historical periods and to a specific culture or to specific cultures; i.e., it must refer to a particular society or societies.

---

cept of equilibrium there used is an illustration of a use that is neither normative nor static. Since many economists have insisted on a static interpretation of the *General Theory,* I may say I mean the interpretation Paul Samuelson gave it in his 1939 "Interactions" article. See *Readings in Business Cycle Theory* (Philadelphia, 1944), pp. 261 ff., where this article is reprinted.

Scope and Method of Economics

But this implication has a corollary relating to the nature of propositions that have scientific validity. Those who agree with Veblen in regard to the historical relativity of economics agree also that any scientifically valid descriptive economic generalization must be empirically definite. This means there should be facts relating to the communities or societies to which the generalization refers that support it and facts relating to other communities—possibly in some cases to nonhuman primate communities—that make the generalization inapplicable to them.

No doubt there are still a good many economists who are not prepared in such a thoroughgoing sense to give up the idea of economics as a deductive science conceived in the image of Euclid, and who would like to think of "the law of diminishing returns" or the proposition that the first derivative of an indifference curve is negative, the second positive, as a universal, timeless truth. But these economists will probably have to concede that neither the so-called law nor the indifference curve proposition is empirically definite in the sense just proposed. And it may be added that, when economics is conceived as a social science concerned with the group behavior of human beings, neither proposition is a proposition in economics. There are various senses for diminishing returns. In the sense in which universal validity can plausibly be claimed for this "law" it would appear to be a proposition in physical science. But I am not aware that any physical scientist has claimed it to be a physical law. As for the indifference map proposition I have just pointed out that it belongs to the field of psychology.

If the idea of the historical relativity of economic truths has not yet come to be generally accepted, I think it is reasonable to suppose that it is in process of becoming so.

3. THE NEED FOR A SENSE OF CULTURAL PERSPECTIVE

Another important implication of Veblen's contention that economics ought to be an evolutionary science is that an economist should have a sense of cultural perspective. This means that he should recognize that the scheme of values characterizing the cultural situation in which he happens to find himself has been preceded by other quite different and equally valid schemes of values and that there is reason to expect that it will be succeeded by still other equally valid schemes of values, and also that there are other equally valid schemes in other present-day cultures.

Veblen felt that many of his contemporaries lacked such a cultural perspective, that they treated economics not as an evolutionary science but as what he called "bourgeois homiletics." Thus he charged both J. B. Clark and G. Schmoller with a lack of perspective, because each of them naïvely accepted the righteousness or naturalness of the cultural situation prevailing at the time in his native land.

On the positive side the sense of cultural perspective would require adequate recognition of institutional facts in any explanation of the way an economy operates. For example, the distribution of income among factors of production cannot be adequately understood merely in terms of the hypostatized properties of a production function. "The productivity of labor, or of any conceivable factor in industry, is an imputed productivity—imputed on grounds of convention afforded by institutions that have grown up in the course of technological development." [7]

Again the sense of cultural perspective would rule out "the 'conjectural history' that plays so large a part in the classical treatment of economic institutions," e.g., the still prevalent account of the origin of trade that assumes it developed out of a putative barter stage anachronistically assumed to have the scheme of values characteristic of a society in which internal trade has already come to be a pervasive fact.[8] Veblen did not attempt a rounded scientific historical account of the origin of trade, but he did give us an indicative suggestion as to how trade might have arisen out of a prior cultural situation in which the scheme of values was definitely not of a bourgeois character. He suggested a predatory stage of culture in which the accumulation of booty was the basis of award of the highest popular esteem, and a process of evolution from this stage into one in which pecuniary employments became the means of entry into the leisure class.[9] My present concern is not to affirm the historical accuracy of

[7] T. Veblen, *The Instinct of Workmanship* (New York, 1914), p. 146.

[8] *Place of Science,* pp. 65–66. Another illustration of "conjectural history" that is still widely accepted is Adam Smith's account of the origin of money. Cf. the author's *A Study of Moneyflows in the United States* (New York, 1952), pp. 215–216.

[9] T. Veblen, *The Theory of the Leisure Class* (New York, 1899), chs. ii, ix.

this hypothesis—presumably a rounded scientific historical account would have to be a good deal more specific about places and about approximate dates than Veblen was. My present point is only that such an historical account of the genesis of the institution of trade would have to trace a process of evolution from a nontrade cultural scheme of values to the kind of scheme we have in cultures in which trade is a pervasive fact, and that Veblen's hypothesis involves a process of evolution of this sort.

4. EXPLANATION, CAUSATION, AND GENETIC PROCESS

In tracing the development of the higher learning Veblen identifies three ways in which men have sought to account for the facts of the world in which they lived. In the Middle Ages the scholastics, construing the facts on the assumption of a superpersonal, overruling authority conceived in the image of man, felt that to explain anything one must find a sufficient reason for it. On this view a law of nature is a divine decree and explaining it means adequately demonstrating the reason for it. But presently, under the cultural impact of the handicraft technology, men came to think not in terms of authoritative divine decrees, but in terms of the workmanship of Nature as a consummately skillful master craftsman.[10] Hence men came to seek an understanding of any fact of nature in terms of the efficient cause of it rather than the sufficient reason for it, in terms of an effect as a product and its cause as the event or action that produced it. More recently, under the influence of the machine technology, Veblen held that an "unteleological, mechanistic conception" of "a genetic process of cumulative change" had come to replace the more anthropomorphic concept of efficient cause.[11]

Veblen emphasized that the more archaic ways of thinking tended

[10] See, for example, *Instinct of Workmanship*, pp. 258 ff., 292, and *Place of Science*, pp. 11 ff.

[11] *Instinct of Workmanship*, pp. 326–327. But Veblen insisted that science still retained a definite amount of anthropomorphism. In particular he cited the bias against the idea of "action at a distance." See his famous comment that "Only the 'occult' and 'Christian' 'Sciences' . . . take recourse to 'absent treatment'" (*Place of Science*, p. 36). [For an extended discussion of this question, see Article 13 below by Philip Morrison.—EDITOR]

to survive longer in those branches of learning that were less closely involved with modern technology and in economics in particular. Thus the wide-spread insistence—then and even now—on explaining consumer demand and saving and labor supply in terms of the rational behavior of individuals, each maximizing his own utility, is an insistence that the only satisfactory way to account for human conduct is to find a sufficient reason for it.[12] Anyone who has much appreciation of the nature of present-day physical and biological science would want a much more modern approach. And among other things such an approach would surely concern itself with the cumulative process by which individuals' tastes have come to be what they are instead of merely taking these tastes as givens, as modern versions of the felicific calculus do.

Veblen made it clear that a scientific theory of consumer behavior would deal with tastes genetically. Indeed he offered a genetic hypothesis for the development of pecuniary canons of taste and for the irksomeness of humilific labor. Since our present concern is methodological, we need not attempt to pass on its empirical validity: we need only note its general nature. It is historical in that it traces an evolutionary process through time and within various geographical areas, even if the times and places are not very precisely specified. And the tracing runs in terms of a process of cumulative change and of a natural selection through the impacts of value standards and habits of thought on one another. Further, the genetic process it traces is a phylogenetic—not an ontogenetic—process; it is a process of change in the scheme of values prevalent in a community, not a change in the scheme of values of an individual human being. It is concerned with the kinds of choices consumers in a late Victorian community were making. It provides a theory or at least part of a theory of the market preference behavior of such a group (i.e., of the community). But this theory does not consist of an analysis of group demand into the demands of the individuals that compose it; it is a sociogenetic theory.

[12] *Place of Science,* pp. 235–237. His comment is on marginal utility theory, but of course it applies equally to indifference analysis. It may be added that this kind of explanation of individual choices lacks empirical definiteness in a sense slightly different from that proposed above. It is a theory that fits the way people have behaved after the fact, but it fits any hypothetical past behavior that did not actually take place equally well.

Scope and Method of Economics

In all these respects what Veblen proposes is surely an account of the kind economists ought to aim to give for the scheme of values in say the present-day United States that finds expression in household budget behavior; i.e., it is an account that conforms to the canons of modern science. But of course it is only a partial account, for instead of tracing the development of the standard of living it traces only the impacts of the institution of the leisure class on this standard.[13] Nonetheless, for our methodological purpose it is very instructive.

According to the neoclassical tradition consumer demand, saving, and labor supply are explained in terms of the rational, utility-maximizing behavior of individual consumers, savers, and laborers; business demands and supplies, in terms of the rational profit-maximizing behavior of individual entrepreneurs. Insisting on a profit-maximizing explanation, like insisting on a utility-maximizing explanation, means insisting on a sufficient reason approach. So also does writing a treatise on theory that says little or nothing about government demand and taxation (as several intermediate theory texts still do) because no comparable rationalization seems to fit the conduct of the affairs of government.

Veblen did not say explicitly that it becomes part of the job of economists, when they undertake to treat economics as an evolutionary science, to provide a genetic account of the development of government functions and expenditure requirements and of the tax structure. But certainly it is. As for business behavior, Veblen did not rule out profit-maximization.[14] But he did seek to provide a genetic account of the development of business enterprise as an institution, and he concerned himself with other aspects of business management beside profit-maximizing, e.g., with what he regarded as the increasingly remote contact of the businessman with the industrial and technological facts of his business.[15] But in addition to those aspects of business management he dealt with there are many that seem to call for a genetic approach rather than a rationalization in terms of

[13] Veblen did something also toward tracing the impacts of the machine technology on the standard of living. See T. Veblen, *The Theory of Business Enterprise* (New York, 1904), pp. 324 ff., 356 ff.; also *Instinct of Workmanship*, pp. 312 ff., where he points out that "Invention is the mother of necessity."

[14] "The business man's object is to get the largest aggregate gain from his business" (*Theory of Business Enterprise*, p. 93).

[15] *Instinct of Workmanship*, pp. 222 ff.

the maximizing of profits, e.g., the dividend policy of corporations (to which admittedly this type of rationalization does not apply). Also a genetic approach would seem to be needed to understand how the present mores of the accounting profession that define business profit and cost have come to be what they are.[16]

Veblen devoted a good deal of his attention to the evolution of the state of the industrial arts—a state which economists had not infrequently taken as given. In this connection he noted that, while currently most decisions to introduce technological changes are business decisions, this has by no means always been the case. Also he noted that, while currently there is a good deal of interest in inventing technological improvements, this was distinctly not so in what he termed savage cultures. But undoubtedly much the most significant feature of his account of the evolution of technology was his hypothesis of the merits of cultural borrowing.[17] Since this hypothesis is considered somewhat extensively elsewhere in this volume it may suffice here simply to mention it by way of underscoring the proposition that Veblen's accounts of sociogenetic processes are never mere historical narratives. He always endeavored to include an hypothesis or hypotheses in his account of such a process.

If one were to judge Veblen's account of the evolution of the leisure class or of technology in terms of the number of pages concerned with such matters one would doubtless be constrained to conclude that in both cases he leaned heavily on an hypothesis that involves differences in the hereditary complements of the psychological traits of different races and, in particular, differences in the vigor of such traits as the instincts of workmanship and of pugnacity. But this does not appear to be the case, and fortunately not, for interpretations of cultural evolution that run in these terms have not stood up well under the criticisms to which they have been subjected. Curiously, despite all that Veblen has to say about instincts and hereditary biases and propensities, his sociogenetic accounts do not seem to need them. In general they would apparently not suffer significantly if all refer-

[16] Veblen touches on this matter only incidentally, e.g., *Theory of Business Enterprise,* p. 155.

[17] See, for example, T. Veblen, *Imperial Germany and the Industrial Revolution* (New York, 1915), pp. 241 ff. [For extended discussions of this point see Articles 14, 15, and 16 below by Myron W. Watkins, Carter Goodrich, and Douglas F. Dowd.—EDITOR]

Scope and Method of Economics

ences to dolichocephalic blonds and brachycephalic brunettes were to be deleted. Essentially his sociogenetic accounts are stated in terms of a process of natural selection among institutions and other culture traits that results from the impacts of these culture traits on one another.

Veblen thought of the machine industry as undermining and requiring the rejection of the somewhat anthropomorphic concept of efficient cause, and of the concept of a genetic process of cumulative change as being the principal replacement for it. This view seems to have biased, indeed to have narrowed, the scope of his economic inquiries. A very large part of his work is concerned with such processes, with cultural evolution and with his theory of modern welfare which runs in these terms.[18] Also, as I understand him, he ruled out of his inquiries as not in accord with his conception of a scientific approach —i.e., not amenable to a genetic approach—much of the field now known as microeconomics.

For Veblen the prime example of a genetic process of cumulative change apparently was the evolution of the species of living organisms, although he doubtless had in mind other examples as well, particularly the ontogenies of various species of plants and animals and the genetic processes with which astrophysics is concerned. Now the obvious analogue of the phylogenetic process of the evolution of species in the field of social science is cultural evolution, and Veblen thought economists should be extensively concerned with this analogue. When it comes to dealing with things like the family system that change slowly, this means taking a very long-run view, a view that deals in eras that last for centuries. Hence a good deal of the time Veblen was concerned with periods such as the era of handicraft. It is true he did not confine himself to this very long-run view. But his genetic process concept meant a bias also in the type of shorter-run inquiries he undertook. The concept fits topics like the cultural incidence of the machine industry. He thought of the prevalence of mechanical processes as affecting everyone's ways of thinking and so leading to broad institutional changes. But he thought also that for some classes of the population the influence was particularly strong—for manual workers, engineers, and physical scientists. This extra-strong influence was a part of his hypothesis regarding the

[18] *Theory of Business Enterprise*, ch. vii.

development of trade unions,[19] also of his hypothesis regarding the growth of the kind of social unrest that includes agitation for revolutionary social reform.[20]

Again Veblen's concept of a genetic process of cumulative change fits the business cycle. Indeed one of his most ingenious contributions was conceiving the business cycle as just such a process, or rather as a concatenation of such processes, with prosperity tending to improve for a time but presently generating a crisis, a crisis resolving itself into depression, and depression tending to perpetuate itself until some outside influence converts it into prosperity.[21]

Veblen's analysis of the business cycle is about the only portion of his work that deals at all extensively with a topic economists in the neoclassical tradition would currently regard as a part of economic theory.

In general it is surely unfair to assume that any recent economist's notion of the scope of the subject is no broader than the parts of the field he has himself cultivated. And certainly Veblen never pretended to a balanced coverage of economics. Nonetheless, I think some significance attaches to the fact that he neglected so much of what is commonly regarded as the field of economic theory. I think his neglect helps to support the view that he would rule out most of microeconomics as unscientific. I believe time will prove him right in ruling out the search for sufficient reasons, though wrong in ruling out practically all the rest of microeconomics too, if this is what he meant.

But his view of the scope of economics must have been somewhat broader than the area covered by his own writings. It is significant that in discussing the cultural influence of the machine industry Veblen emphasized that, partly because of this influence, partly because of the influence of the price system, "modern science at large takes to the use of statistical methods."[22] It is true that he did not urge explicitly that economics should be a statistical as well as an evolutionary science. But he seems to have exerted a real push in this direction. Several of those who drew most heavily on Veblen for inspiration have certainly emphasized the statistical approach, notably Wesley Mitchell and Walter Stewart.

[19] *Theory of Business Enterprise*, pp. 327 ff. [20] *Idem*, pp. 336 ff.

[21] *Idem*, ch. vii. Veblen was something of a secular stagnationist.

[22] *Instinct of Workmanship*, p. 322.

Scope and Method of Economics

Perhaps it should be suggested at this point that if Veblen had given more explicit attention to the potential significance of statistics for economics he would almost certainly have had to broaden his concept of modern scientific method so as to include more than his genetic processes of cumulative change under the heading of scientific hypotheses.

5. PUBLIC POLICY

Veblen seems to have held, like many economists who were less disposed than he to deviate from the classical tradition, that policy judgments have no place in a scientific inquiry.[23] Like them, too, he was conspicuously unsuccessful in excluding such judgments from his economic inquiries.

One can gather the general outline of the kind of broad economic policy he was disposed to approve from *The Engineers and the Price System.*[24] This policy would entail avoiding "virtually all unemployment of serviceable equipment and manpower on the one hand, and all local and seasonal scarcity on the other." It would mean eliminating all sorts of wasteful and obstructive practices inherent "in the businesslike control of industry" (competitive sales effort is cited by way of illustration). And it would involve the abolition of absentee ownership, i.e., the abolition of intangible properties and of business proprietorship net worths as sources of individual income and as a basis for the "businesslike control of industry." But our present interest is not primarily in these particular policy propositions. Primarily it is that one does not have to probe far to find policy implications in Veblen's writings.

Public policy implications enter them at other points, too, and in ways that are quite significant parts of Veblen's methodological contribution. Much of his examination of the American economy of his day consists of analyses of various forms of business activities that are concerned with "making money" but that contribute somewhat un-

[23] *Place of Science*, pp. 19–20. But see my comment on the place of normative judgments in biological (including anthropological) science in the *American Economic Review*, March 1931, pp. 68–69.

[24] (New York, 1921). See ch. vi, "A Memorandum on a Practicable Soviet of Technicians," especially pp. 144, 152–154, 156–160.

Morris A. Copeland

certainly to "making goods," [25] and may even obstruct the processes of production. Several of these analyses are interesting anticipations of later developments.

One such analysis dealt with business price policy. He made it clear that he thought this is in general a kind of monopoly policy and that the usual situation is one "where the monopoly is less strict, where there are competitors." [26] His theory of monopolistic competition included an examination of selling cost as different from production cost and as largely competitive in nature.[27]

Several of Veblen's analyses that involve public policy implications had to do with what has come to be known as corporation finance.[28] In fact, they constitute one of the earliest attempts to deal analytically with this subject. Possibly his pioneering work in this area would have been more generally recognized had it not been for the fact that he emphasized financial operations and practices that involved making a good deal of money without contributing much to making goods, whereas the conventional treatment of corporation finance has tended to play down these aspects of the subject.

Although an analysis of a situation in which someone can make money without a significant positive contribution to production carries an inescapable public policy implication, Veblen seems to have thought that it was quite proper to include such analyses in an economic inquiry. Presumably he thought so because such analyses seem capable of being carried out on an objective basis. Possibly Veblen did not always succeed in maintaining his objectivity when he made them. But I think he was right about the possibility of making them objectively, and right in regarding them as an important part of the economist's job.

Another type of economic analysis involving policy implications in which Veblen was something of a pioneer has to do with the legal system and the contrast betwen the *de jure* freedom of the individual worker to contract for employment and the *de facto* coercion imposed by the limited alternatives open to him.[29] An interesting feature of

[25] The distinction between making goods and making money is Veblen's, but the language is Wesley Mitchell's.

[26] *Theory of Business Enterprise*, p. 54.

[27] *Idem*, pp. 55 ff.

[28] Especially *idem*, pp. 35 ff., 89 ff., and ch. v. [See Article 11 below by Joel Dirlam.—Editor]

[29] *Theory of Business Enterprise*, pp. 277 ff.

Scope and Method of Economics

Veblen's analysis of this contrast is the suggestion that the *de facto* situation had, up to the time of his writing, made more impression on juries than on the higher courts.

Still another way in which policy considerations entered into Veblen's investigations is illustrated by his *An Inquiry into the Nature of Peace and the Terms of Its Perpetuation.* In this inquiry he followed somewhat the procedure advocated by the elder Keynes.[30] That is, he started (despite his assumption of an instinct of pugnacity) with the policy premise that social conflicts—class conflicts as well as international conflicts—ought, if possible, to be avoided. Given this premise, the question of the prospects for peace and of the means of attaining it can be investigated objectively, or, as J. N. Keynes put it, as a part of political economy in the sense of a positive science. Much of Veblen's inquiry is concerned with the genetic processes leading to the development of great powers, both those powers that are "bent in effect on a disturbance of the peace" and those powers that "will fight on provocation"; most of the rest of the inquiry with speculation about possible and probable further developments on the basis of the then-current characteristics of these powers.

This method of separating "scientific" economic inquiry from ethical "nonscientific" inquiry involves a kind of dilemma. On the one hand, the separation may be effected through a genuine division of academic labor; i.e., the two inquiries may be conducted by different persons. In this case the economist becomes a kind of academic helot. On the other hand, the separation may be accomplished by a selection of the premise which defines the field of inquiry that is made by the economist himself. In this case, if he selects a policy premise to which many economists subscribe—say, avoiding wars or minimizing general unemployment—a significant enlargement of the policy inquiries that fall within the scope of economics may result, and the separation becomes mainly a matter of a clear labeling of the policy premise. Veblen took the second horn of this dilemma.

[30] T. Veblen, *An Inquiry into the Nature of Peace and the Terms of Its Perpetuation* (New York, 1917); J. N. Keynes, *Scope and Method of Political Economy* (London, 1890), ch. ii, secs. 4, 5, and Note B.

Morris A. Copeland

6. THE SCOPE OF ECONOMICS

Veblen did not say just what he thought the scope of economics should be. His concern with questions of the cultural incidence of economic institutions like the machine industry and the leisure class gave him a grand disregard of boundaries within the field of social science. Thus we find him discussing recent changes in a wide variety of our culture traits including religion, art, higher education, patriotism, gambling institutions, athletic events, styles in dress, the status of woman, and so on. No doubt the case for encouraging inquiries that cut across conventional subject-matter dividing lines in the way Veblen did is a strong one. And it may well be that we have developed a division of academic labor in the social sciences that is too minute. But some division of this field, even some division within the field of economics, clearly seems advisable.

It would, I take it, be quite consistent with Veblen's view to think of economics as marked off from the other social sciences that devote much of their attention to so-called industrialized societies on the basis of the institutions which are the economist's primary concern. Presumably he is primarily concerned with economic institutions such as technology, the division of labor, the price system, trade, money, the income and money circuit, the wage system, and property. Presumably, too, if the scope of economics is defined in this fashion, there will be primitive societies in which economic and other institutions are not clearly differentiated, societies that are mainly subjects of study for the general anthropologist and that the economist *as* economist will not deal with very extensively.

On Veblen's view, then, economists should concern themselves with economic institutions and closely related culture traits, probably with all important economic institutions and traits to be found anywhere in the world today apart from the relatively few remaining communities that have had little contact with modern industrialism. A major item in the task of economists should be to seek to understand each such institution or trait in terms of the genetic process of cumulative change by which it has come to be what it is. No doubt, too, economists should interest themselves in comparisons between similar institutions and similar institutional developments in different societies.

Scope and Method of Economics

Again on Veblen's view economists should engage in analyses involving various public policy questions—should concern themselves with the ways in which the pecuniary incentives in an economy encourage activities deemed not to be in the public interest, with the legal institutions which are supposed to provide just relations between individuals and the extent to which in fact they do so, with policy objectives on which there is something like a consensus and with the means by which they might be carried out as well as the prospects that these means may be forthcoming.

But there are other types of inquiry which economists should undertake, too. Some of these Veblen seems to have felt were merely descriptive and so not sufficiently theoretical to be called scientific: mere descriptions of things as they are, mere correlations between variables that seem to move together, mere narratives of the steps by which things have come to be what they are, mere statistical measurements of economic magnitudes, mere statistical economic time series. Other inquiries economists should engage in have to do with the way an economy operates or the way particular institutions or organizations in it operate. As I have noted, Veblen considered and made an important contribution to the theory of business cycles. But there are many other operational questions that should be investigated; presumably he would have included some, but not all, of these. It is not clear, for example, that he would have thought much attention should be paid to the way noncumulative changes in the supply and demand conditions in an industry influence the industry's prices and the income originating in it. Certainly studying such influences is an important part of the economist's job. Still other inquiries that are parts of that job relate to public policy questions. Thus one can study the genesis of public policies as well as of institutional structures. And while technically most of the other subjects economists should be concerned with that involve public policy questions could be considered as special cases of the types of inquiries noted above, there are a substantial number that these do not obviously suggest, e.g., public policy questions relating to taxation, to utility rates, to collective bargaining in the labor market, to international aid, to social security, to farm prices, to mergers.

If the push that Veblen gave to economics was not a particularly well-balanced push, it was nonetheless a signally important push forward. And there is good reason to think that, along with the recently widened knowledge of quite different present-day economic systems, we are getting a wider cultural perspective that will give a strong reinforcement to that push. It may well turn out that much the most important and most lasting of Veblen's contributions to economics is the proposition that economics ought to become an evolutionary science in fullest sense of what he intended by these words.

A POSTSCRIPT ON VEBLEN'S AUDIENCE

The primary corollary of the proposition that economics should be an evolutionary science is that the applicability of all economic theories should be restricted in respect to time and place. The applicability of Veblen's *Theory of the Leisure Class* is so restricted. One who reads it today is apt to think of changes in the forms of conspicuous leisure that have become prominent since he propounded it.

One of these is ideological. A person who is very securely a member of the leisure class and who in his pursuit of the higher learning has encountered heterodox socioeconomic philosophies may embrace leftist, even subversive ideas. It is not suggested that he is likely to do so with the intent of demonstrating the security of his leisure-class status, only that his doing so does have this effect. And since it does, embracing such ideas is clearly a form of conspicuous leisure. Apparently it is a form that has become prominent since 1899.

Most of Veblen's earlier articles appeared in the *Journal of Political Economy*, the *Quarterly Journal of Economics*, and the *American Journal of Sociology;* most of his later articles in the *New Republic*, the *Dial*, and the *Freeman*. There was a significant change between Veblen's earlier works and his works in the twenties in respect to the audience to which he addressed himself. His earlier works were addressed to his fellow professional economists and to other social scientists. His later works were of a more popular nature; some of them seem to have been written mainly for a group of members of the vicarious leisure class that had come to be among his most ardent admirers in the twenties, a group of lady lecture goers who had an amateur interest in social reform.

No doubt this group of admirers found Veblen's somewhat leftish social philosophy intriguing; embracing it was for them a form of conspicuous leisure. No doubt, too, they were attracted by his extensive vocabulary and the niceties of his diction; only one with sufficient leisure to be somewhat steeped in the higher learning could appreciate Veblenese.

But Veblen's theory of the cultural incidence of the machine industry assumed that radical social philosophies would appeal chiefly to manual workers, engineers, and physical scientists. No doubt he was right in thinking that the practice of a pecuniary employment inculcated a firm belief in the existing order. But there is no reason to think the inculcation extended to other members of the family; although not directly exposed to the machine industry, they might absorb some of its influence. Hence a wife or daughter—sometimes even a son—might find embracing pinkish ideas an enticing way to perform her—or his—vicarious leisure.

But the shift in the audience to which Veblen addressed himself surely indicates too that economists in the twenties were less interested in what he had to say than economists a quarter-century earlier had been. His earlier appeal was to colleagues many of whom had studied in Germany and had thereby gained something in the way of cultural perspective. The decline in interest in Veblen's ideas during the later years of his life is, I think, attributable at least in part to a temporary decline in cultural perspective due to the comparative lack of contacts of American economists outside the English-speaking world, a situation from which we have only recently begun to recover.

[4]

Jei JOURNAL OF ECONOMIC ISSUES
Vol. XIII No. 2 June 1979

Methods in Economic Science

Nicholas Georgescu-Roegen

According to the temper that has prevailed for some time now in the social sciences, but especially in economics, the contributions that deserve the highest praise are those using a heavy mathematical armamentarium; the heavier and the more esoteric, the more worthy of praise. Protests against this situation have not failed to be made sufficiently often to have deserved attention. What is more, protests of this kind were made not only by "verbal" economists, such as Thorstein Veblen and Frank H. Knight, but also by some who were well familiar with the mathematical tool, for example, Alfred Marshall, Knut Wicksell, and Lord Keynes.[1] Knight lamented that there are many members of the economic profession who are "mathematicians first and economists afterwards." The situation since Knight's time has become much worse. There are endeavors that now pass for the most desirable kind of economic contributions although they are just plain mathematical exercises, not only without any economic substance but also without mathematical value. Their authors are not something first and something else afterwards; they are neither mathematicians nor economists. How dangerous is the infatuation with pure mathematical symbolism is proved by the fact that voices from the circle of natural scientists have also often denounced it. Perhaps the strong-

---

The author is Distinguished Professor of Economics Emeritus, Vanderbilt University, Nashville, Tennessee, and was Visiting Professor at the Louis Pasteur University, Strasbourg, France, when this article was presented at the Annual Meeting of the Association for Evolutionary Economics, Chicago, Illinois, 29–30 August 1978. At that time he held an Earhart Foundation fellowship.

est example is that of Lord Kelvin, who did so in the preface to *Treatise on Natural Philosophy* (co-authored with P. G. Tait in 1883).[2]

T. C. Koopmans, perhaps the greatest defender of the use of the mathematical tool in economics, countered the criticism of the exaggeration of mathematical symbolism by claiming that critics have not come forward with specific complaints. The occasion was a symposium held in 1954 around a protest by David Novick.[3] But, by an irony of fate, some twenty years later one of the most incriminating *corpora delicti* of empty mathematization got into print with the direct help of none other than Koopmans. R. J. Aumann had already published in *Econometrica* an article dealing with the problem of a market in which there are as many traders as the real numbers, that is, as many as all the points on a continuous line.[4] In 1972, Koopmans presented to the National Academy of Sciences a paper by Donald Brown and Abraham Robinson for publication in its official periodical.[5] The authors assumed that there are more traders even than the elements of the continuum. Now, since the authors of both those papers and Koopmans are well versed in mathematics, they must have known the result proved long ago by George Cantor, namely, that even an infinite space can accommodate at most a denumerable infinity of three-dimensional objects (as the traders must necessarily be).[6]

But there are other examples that do not seem to constitute any flight of fancy and yet are just as much empty exercises with symbols. The only difficulty in seeing that they are just that is that the symbols are given names taken from the economic vocabulary: saving, investment, production capacity, and so forth. Such a case is the dynamic model of the most specific form, the model that has swept the economic profession off its feet, the Leontief dynamic model. That model is not an adequate analytical representation even of accretionary growth, let alone qualitative development.[7]

Another result of our concern with symbolism rather than with an adequate representation of facts is the completely faulty form by which standard economics represents a production process.[8] First, the standard production function does not distinguish between the agents of production—labor power, capital, and land—and the flow elements which form the object of the agents' activity, specifically, the transformation of some flows into others. As a result, mathematical economists have recently come out with a fantastic conjuring trick. We must not worry about the exhaustion of natural resources, since with the aid of the ubiquitous Cobb-Douglas production function it can be proved that capital equipment can be substituted without limit for those resources.[9] The proof pays no attention to the brute fact, namely, that increased capital implies increased use of resources to produce it and then to keep it up.

Second, the same traditional production function completely ignores the duration of the production process, say, the working day of a factory. The traditional form has no room for the elementary truth that doubling the working time doubles the output. The omission often leads to the confusion between the number of workers employed and the number of man-hours worked, a confusion particularly damaging in an analysis of unemployment.[10]

Mathematical formalism in the standard theory of production has reduced our analysis of this activity to one application of the Lagrangean multipliers after another, and little else. The graduate student who in an examination paper referred to Lagrange as "that great economist" was an insignificant casualty of the way we theorize about production.

Recent economic difficulties in many areas—unemployment, inflation, stagnation of undeveloped nations, and the energy crisis—have revealed the impotence of a professional knowledge consisting mainly of paper-and-pencil operations to prescribe some remedies, however imperfect. All this led Paul Samuelson, undoubtedly the sharpest analytical mind of all mathematical economists of this mid-century, to admit that "the malaise of which economists now suffer is not imaginary . . .: the respect that economists inspire among business circles is not what it used to be."[11] It is to be hoped that most of the errors introduced into our current mode of acting *as economists* by our infatuation with symbolism for symbolism's sake will be eliminated soon as a result of such developments and such authoritative admissions. Yet some bad habits of thought are likely to survive. By far the most crucial of these is the mechanistic epistemology. For as I shall now argue, most of the present faults and deviations have their origin in that *Weltbild*.

The Marquis Pierre Simon de Laplace, the man who had already made lasting analytical contributions to the science of mechanics and who had also written a famous treatise about *Mécanique Céleste,* in 1814 proclaimed with all his authority that absolutely everything in the universe is governed by the laws of mechanics and only by them.[12] He conceded, however, that the complete system of differential equations describing that mechanical system is so vast and the initial data so numerous that only a demiurgic intellect—to which we now refer as the Laplacean demon—could possibly collect all the data and find all the solutions. It is nothing but the imperfection of our minds that prevents us from using the laws of mechanics for knowing all the future (as well as all the past).

Thirty years after Laplace wrote this apotheosis of mechanics, something happened that tended to prove that mechanics has the power over existence as he described it. In 1846 a French astronomer, Urbain Leverrier, at the end of some calculations in which he confronted the astronomical observations of the known planets with the results of an appropriate mechanical system, was led to proclaim that there existed a still unknown planet, which, moreover, must be visible in a certain region of the sky. Direct observation of that region soon confirmed the existence of that planet, now called Neptune.

Neptune, therefore, was discovered not by scanning the firmament with a telescope, but "at the tip of a pencil." We can very well imagine the dream that this feat must have inspired in all social scientists, especially in economists. It is the dream of being able to predict the location of any share on the firmament of the Stock Exchange Market, whether tomorrow or one year from now, by solving certain equations that govern the motion of that market. Undoubtedly, the essence of that dream must still be nursed in the subconscious of many modern economists. The role of such a hope in the founding of the Cowles Commission is evidenced by several articles in the early volumes of *Econometrica*.

But Leverrier's success impressed everyone, scientist and philosopher as well. Mechanics reigned supreme as a science and as an epistemology. Wilhelm Wundt, by proclaiming in the 1880s that *"mechanics* is the beginning and the foundation for all explanatory natural science,"[13] was only describing the almost general scientific dogma of that time. And closer to our own time, a highly respected French mathematician argued completely along Laplacean lines: "Mechanics is the necessary foundation of all other sciences, insofar that they aim to be precise."[14]

It should be no wonder that in 1871 W. Stanley Jevons presented his plan for developing political economy as *"the mechanics of utility and self-interest."*[15] And years later, in 1906, Vilfredo Pareto upheld the idea.[16]

It was because of this orientation that the mathematical tool was introduced into political economy, a term so embarrassingly contradictory to what economists do nowadays that we have dropped it and replaced it by the neutral one, "economics." The methodological mutation by itself was a fortunate one, a point which I wish to emphasize again and again because I have continuously been read incorrectly on it. For mathematical models *are* useful in two situations.

The first is in engineering economics, which deals with circumscribed conditions, known prices and known coefficients of production, and seeks to find an optimizing solution. The best example I can cite is the *actual* application of linear programming to mixing gasoline or to shipping schedules—a highly fertile furrow opened by T. C. Koopmans.

The second is when a mathematical model is used to clarify an economic problem that exists as a problem prior to any modeling considerations.

Such problems are usually dialectical in nature (as I shall explain presently), and the models are only *similes* of our dialectical reasoning. They must not be interpreted as blueprints that tell us exactly what to do step by step. In economics, or any other social science, we cannot have tables such as those in use in engineering, or physics, or chemistry. The models may help us to probe into a dialectical reasoning, but they cannot show us the way. The important point is that we must first have such a reasoning.[17] It is precisely when we ignore this condition and introduce a model without any reference to a relevant problem that we indulge in idle mathematical "playotrics," the term used by Ragnar Frisch (in his unpublished opening address to the First World Congress of the Econometric Society) to stigmatize the present trend in econometrics.

But the fact that economics now breathes mechanics throughout is far more serious than playotrics. Almost all introductory manuals—those of the most respected authors included—describe the economic process by a circular diagram between "production" and "consumption." The explanation of the outcome of a market is identical with the principle of virtual displacements that is used in mechanics for determining the static equilibrium. Demand and supply schedules may move up and down, but the system always returns to any of the previous equilibria.[18] *Everything is reversible exactly as in mechanics,* where locomotion consists only of a change of place, not of quality.

The obvious truth, however, is that the economic system continuously changes *qualitatively*. To use a variant of one of Joseph Schumpeter's characteristic lessons, we do not keep producing one mail coach after another forever. We pass from traveling by coaches to traveling by trains, by automobiles, by planes, and, conceivably, by rockets.

The most important aspect of the economic process is precisely the continuous emergence of novelty. Now, novelty is unpredictable, but in a sense quite different from the way in which the result of a coin toss is unpredictable. In the latter case we can nevertheless predict an approximation of the frequency of, say, "tails," in a long sequence of *repeated* tossings. Each novelty, however, is unique in the sense that in chronological time it occurs only once.

Moreover, the novelty always represents a qualitative change. It is therefore understandable that no analytical model can deal with the emergence of novelty, for everything that can be derived from such a model can only concern quantitative variations. Besides, nothing can be derived from an analytical model that is not logically contained in its axiomatic basis. As has been argued by many famous mathematicians, any branch of mathematics is just a vast logical tautology. What is strictly novel in the historical development of mathematics is the *act of the discovery* of a "new" theorem, not the theorem itself. Novelty, on the other hand, is characterized by the fact that even after it has occurred it is as a rule impossible to explain it from the already known phenomenal laws. To wit, there are numberless *qualities* of chemical components that cannot be now logically deduced from the properties of their elements. Even some qualitative properties of such a common substance as water cannot be logically derived from the elementary properties of oxygen and hydrogen. But for an incontrovertible example let us consider a living creature, say, an elephant. The way an elephant behaves, that it is herbivorous, that it has a trunk, and so forth, cannot be explained by the properties of the chemical elements that constitute its body. If we know all these things it is because we have observed one elephant after another being born, maturing, and ultimately dying. Specifically, it is not the properties of elementary matter—carbon, oxygen, hydrogen, phosphorous, and so forth—that determine the behavior of the elephant, the mosquito, the human being, and so on down the line. On the contrary, all these behaviors reflect just as many properties of the chemical elements that are not manifest at the elementary level. Nature thus has an infinite number of properties.[10] It is because of this fact and because of the ever-present emerging novelty that the human mind cannot grasp actuality with the aid of analysis alone; it also must use dialectics.

Analysis and dialectics are the only methods by which we enter into mental contact with the phenomena around and even within us. But they are separated by an unbridgeable gap.

Analysis consists of a systematic description of actuality only with the aid of arithmomorphic concepts. The characteristic property of these concepts is that illustrated best by a number. To wit, the number "one," for example, stands completely isolated from all other numbers. There is no number that is at the same time "one" and not "one." For practical purposes a regular polygon with $10^{10^{10}}$ sides may be regarded as a circle, but the two concepts are as *discretely distinct* as the number "one" and that inaccessible number, $10^{10^{10}}$. Also, a number cannot change as time goes by. What "one" meant to the earliest minds that started to count is still valid today and will be so forever. The same is not true for most of our basic notions, as I shall explain presently.

Dialectical reasoning, on the other hand, employs dialectical concepts. These are concepts that are *distinct*, but not *discretely distinct*. Their characteristic feature is that they may overlap with their opposites; their meanings slide into their opposites. Whereas an arithmomorphic concept is separated from its opposite by a vacuous boundary (by a null set, as we say in mathematics), a dialectical concept is separated from its opposite by a *substantial* penumbra. It is within this penumbra that both A and non-A are true.

But one must note that this penumbra is not a perfectly defined arithmomorphic entity in the sense that we always know whether a given instance is within the penumbra or outside it. The dialectical penumbra does not divide the whole spectrum of the concept into three arithmomorphic domains: the domain of A, of non-A, and of both A and non-A.

The essence of dialectics viewed in this way is that the penumbra which separates a dialectical concept from its opposite is itself bordered by dialectical penumbras, which in turn are separated by dialectical penumbras, and so on in an infinite dialectical reduction.[20]

What the prevailing arithmomania ignores is that the most carefully constructed defense of positivism, of what its adepts like to call "no nonsense," cannot even get started without using dialectical concepts. Indeed, most of our fundamental concepts are dialectical: justice, democracy, good, evil, abstraction, workable competition, entrepreneur, farmer, occupation, belief, and so forth.

Any instance of an arithmomorphic concept will suffice as illustration. For example, a square ceases to be a square no matter how little we may change one of its angles. By contrast, any instance of a dialectical concept may be changed, sometimes even appreciably, without the concept being negated thereby. Think of it: Was the United States not a democracy when the minimum voting age was twenty-one? Or would the United States cease to be a democracy if the present age were lowered by one day? By one month? By one year? It certainly would no longer be a democracy if the age limit were set at seventy or at one.

A dialectical concept, therefore, while not discretely distinct, is nonetheless distinct. And if dialectical reasoning cannot be as precise in an engineering-like fashion as an arithmomorphic statement, dialectical reasoning can be perfectly *correct.* Here, just as in the art of painting, we should not blame colors for the horrible works some "painters" may produce with them. Open any good book on philosophical positivism and read almost any paragraph in order to see how splendidly correct dialectical reasoning can be. All our books would have to be thrown overboard if we insisted that dialectical "nonsense"—as dialectics is often disparaged—must never be used. "Not only are we aware of particular yellows, but if we have seen a sufficient number of yellows and have sufficient intelligence, we are aware of the universal *yellow;* this universal is the subject in such judgments as 'yellow differs from blue' or 'yellow resembles blue less than green does.' "[21]

The fundamental reason why we cannot do without dialectical concepts is that actuality, at least as seen by the human mind, continuously changes *qualitatively*. Recall the earlier illustration: Democracy is a dialectical concept because that condition is in constant flux, as we know from history as well as from the present variations from one place to another. The present democracy of the United States is not identical to that of Thomas Jefferson's time, nor is it identical to that found now in Switzerland, for example. Biological species is a dialectical concept precisely because it is the very seat of biological evolution. Attempts have been made to define "species" arithmomorphically. The unavoidable implication of these definitions is that all species were created once and for all, as completely immutable as, say, the proton. Human want also is a dialectical concept because it greatly varies with time and place. The human species would not have been able to have a durable biological existence had its wants been completely rigid, thus making adaptation impossible.

The most we can expect from an arithmomorphic model is to depict pure growth, or rather pure quantitative variations of qualitatively different but self-identical elements. A most telling case is offered by the recent developments in molecular biology. Before the discovery of the double helix, the main problem in biology was to explain pure growth, that is, how cells multiply by division so that the number of *identical* cells can grow, in principle, without limit. The difficulty was that for duplication one needs a template, a negative, as it were. The template, the recent findings explain, is within the nucleus itself: The chromosomal structure consists of two symmetrical patterns, each one capable by itself of producing its symmetrical image and thus of "recreating" the self-identical nucleus.

However, this arithmomorphic theory cannot explain at all the further process, that of development of a structural organism, let alone the relationship between the arithmomorphic structure of a gene and its manifestation through behavior.[22] Indeed, if the chromosomal structure is identical in all cells of an organism, because of its reproduction through the division of the helix, and if the chromosomal structure is the only code by which a cell operates, then the fertilized egg after its first division can produce only two other fertilized eggs identical to itself. And the same applies to the next division, to that after the next, and so on. How is it then possible to have development, that is, differentiation of cells according to their various qualitative functions—eye, stomach, brain, skin, and so forth?[23] It seems difficult to find a more striking illustration of Hegel's famous dictum: "Abstract self-identity has no life."[24]

Since evolutionary phenomena cannot be represented by an analytical model, all evolutionary domains confront the student with a difficulty of which we do not seem to be aware. To repeat, if we now know how an elephant lives, it is because and *only because* we have witnessed numberless lives of the elephant. Should we be suddenly confronted with a life-bearing structure from another world than ours, we could not possibly say what it feeds on, how long it may live on the average, or whether it is young or old. To know how long it may still live or whether or not it sheds its skin or some of its other organs we would have to observe it until its death. This is the dreadful predicament of any student of evolutionary phenomena, whether in biology, sociology, politics, art, or, to be sure, economics. We have not been and will not be able to witness another mankind emerging, developing, and finally bowing out of existence.

The upshot is that we cannot possibly have a bird's eye view of the future evolution of mankind. All we can have is a worm's eye view, that is, we can at most have some idea of what is likely to happen in the very near future. Certainly, this idea is based on the knowledge we may have derived from history and from the analytico-physiological study of the current trends. This method is that described by Karl Marx and Friedrich Engels in their dialectical principle, according to which out of the opposition between thesis and antithesis there emerges a new situation, the synthesis. But this principle should not be understood as an endless algorithm of the kind we find in analytical similes. A true algorithm can be used for as many steps as we may wish; this is why we can compute as many decimal digits of $\sqrt{2}$ as we please. But whereas at any given evolutionary juncture we may be able to determine the immediate synthesis, we cannot at the same time predict the thesis and the antithesis that will emerge from the new situation. They will emerge with time as novelties, not as predictions of our system of reasoning, whether dialectical or arithmomorphic.

The usefulness of the analytical models that represent similes of actual processes (divested, however, of any qualitative change) cannot be denied. But what matters most in the case of evolutionary structures is the emergence of novelties, of qualitative changes. For these aspects we have no other solution than that of a dialectical approach, involving in particular structural changes. This means to use *words,* instead of numbers, for truly qualitative changes cannot be represented by an arithmomorphic model. Qualities are not preordered, as numbers are, by their own special nature. The most relevant part of history is a story told in words, even when it is accompanied by some time series that mark the passage of time.

Unfortunately, the economics profession now concurs with W. J. Baumol's verdict that the works of Karl Marx and Joseph Schumpeter must not be imitated because they are "vague and impressionistic."[25] The consequence is seen in the fact that in our analysis of inflation or of unemployment we ignore structural effects completely. That our policy recommendations are thus wholly ineffective should not surprise us. Our science must orient itself toward a greater number of "vague and impressionistic" studies of the kind brought forward by Marx, Schumpeter, and several other less well-known economists (less well-known through no fault of their own). To this effect, I would like to close with an appropriate admonition by Schumpeter: "It is therefore misleading to reason on aggregative equilibrium [of the arithmomorphic models] as if it displayed the factors which initiate the change and as if disturbance in the economic system as a whole could arise only from those aggregates."[26]

Postscript

As a follow-up to the discussion prompted by this paper at the meeting, I should like to reproduce a poem by a famous engineer, one of the pioneers of thermodynamics and a colleague of Lord Kelvin at Glasgow University, William J. Macquorn Rankine, from his *Songs and Fables* (Glasgow: James Mackelhouse, 1870), p. 5.

"The Mathematician in Love"

Let *x* denote beauty, *y* manners well-bred,
z Fortune—this is essential—
Let *L* stand for love"—our philosopher said.
Then *L* is a function of *x, y* and *z*.
Of the kind known as potential.

Now integrate *L* with respect to *dt*
(*t*, standing for time and persuasion);
Then between proper limits, 'tis easy to see
The definite integral *Marriage* must be:
(A very concise demonstration).

Said he: "If the wandering course of the moon
By Algebra can be predicted,
The female affections must yield to it soon."
But the lady ran off with a dashing dragoon,
And left him amazed and afflicted.

Notes

1. See quotations in Nicholas Georgescu-Roegen, *The Entropy Law and the Economic Process* (Cambridge, Mass.: Harvard University Press, 1971), p. 341.
2. Lord Kelvin and P. G. Tait, *Treatise on Natural Philosophy*, reprinted as *Principles of Mechanics and Dynamics* (New York: Dover, 1962), Part I, p. viii. See also the very recent warning of a great scholar among British engineers, Reginald O. Kapp, quoted in Nicholas Georgescu-Roegen, *Energy and Economic Myths: Institutional and Analytical Economic Essays* (New York: Pergamon Press, 1976), p. 61.
3. Paul A. Samuelson et al., "Mathematics in Economics: Discussion of Mr. Novick's Article," *Review of Economics and Statistics* 36 (November 1954): 359–86. For Koopmans's statement, see p. 379.
4. R. J. Aumann, "Markets with a Continuum of Traders," *Econometrica* 32 (January 1964): 39–50.
5. Donald J. Brown and Abraham Robinson, "A Limit Theorem on the Cores of Large Standard Exchange Economies," *Proceedings of the National Academy of Science* 69 (May 1972): 1258–60.
6. Interestingly, Aumann admits that "the idea of a continuum of traders may seem outlandish to the reader" but argues that it is not more so than that of "a continuum of 'particles' in fluid mechanics." Mechanics thus seems to be the justification for any flight of fancy in economics.
7. Georgescu-Roegen, *Energy and Economic Myths*, chapter 9.
8. Ibid., chapters 2, 4, and 5.
9. See, for example, J. E. Stiglitz, "A Neoclassical Analysis of the Economics of Natural Resources," forthcoming in *Scarcity and Growth Reconsidered*, edited by V. Kerry Smith (Baltimore: Johns Hopkins Press, 1979).
10. See, for example, Edmond Malinvaud, *The Theory of Unemployment Reconsidered* (Oxford: Blackwell, 1977). See Jean-Paul Fitoussi and Nicholas Georgescu-Roegen, "Structure and Involuntary Unemployment," a paper presented at a conference of the International Association of Economics, Obernai, France (*Proceedings* forthcoming).
11. Paul A. Samuelson, "Les économistes ne sont plus ce qu'ils étaient," *Le Nouvel Economiste*, 31 October 1977 (my translation).
12. Pierre Simon de Laplace, *A Philosophical Essay on Probability* (New York: Wiley, 1902).
13. Wilhelm Wundt, *Logik*, 3d ed. (Stuttgart: F. Enke, 1906–1908), vol. 2, p. 274 (my translation).
14. Paul Painlevé, *Les axiomes de la mécanique: Examen critique* (Paris: Gauthier-Villars, 1922) (my translation).
15. W. Stanley Jevons, *The Theory of Political Economy*, 2d ed. (London: Macmillan, 1879), p. 21.
16. Vilfredo Pareto, *Manuale di economia politica* (Milan: Società Editrice Libraria, 1906), chapter 3, ¶ 4 (of which there exists now an English translation).
17. Nicholas Georgescu-Roegen, *Analytical Economics: Issues and Prob-*

lems (Cambridge, Mass.: Harvard University Press, 1966), pp. 116–24, and *Entropy Law*, chapter 11, section 4.

18. Georgescu-Roegen, *Energy and Economic Myths*, pp. 3–4, 236.
19. Georgescu-Roegen, *Analytical Economics*, pp. 61–64, and *Entropy Law*, chapter 5.
20. This dialectical thesis was first developed by the author in his *Analytical Economics*, pp. 22–46, and expanded in *Entropy Law*, chapters 2 and 3. On this thesis, see Phyllis Colvin, "Ontological and Epistemological Commitments and Social Relations in the Sciences: The Case of the Arithmomorphic System of Scientific Production," in *The Social Production of Scientific Knowledge*, edited by Everett Mendelsohn, Peter Weingart, and Richard Whitley (Dordrecht: Reidel, 1977), pp. 103–28; and Richard Mattessich, *Instrumental Reasoning and Systems Methodology* (Dordrecht: Reidel, 1978), pp. 301–304.

    There are claims that the recently set up mathematical concept of "fuzzy set" constitutes an analytical representation of our blurred and vague notions (which I call dialectical). It should be obvious that the dialectical penumbra cannot possibly be represented by any arithmomorphic boundary, anymore than the dialectical duration can be represented by the arithmetical continuum. Georgescu-Roegen, *Analytical Economics*, pp. 32–34, and *Entropy Law*, Appendix A.
21. Bertrand Russell, *Mysticism and Logic* (London: Allen and Unwin, 1932), p. 212.
22. I am speaking here of a definite *law* that would enable us to predict behavior in a general way. I am aware that some particular associations between one gene and some behavior have been established as a result of direct empirical registrations.
23. Georgescu-Roegen, *Entropy Law*, pp. 434–37.
24. G. W. F. Hegel, *Hegel's Science of Logic* (London: Allen and Unwin, 1951), vol. 2, p. 68.
25. W. J. Baumol, *Economic Dynamics*, 3d ed. (New York: Macmillan, 1970), p. 351.
26. Joseph A. Schumpeter, *Business Cycles* (New York: McGraw-Hill, 1939), vol. 1, p. 43.

[5]

KYKLOS, Vol. 35 – 1982 – Fasc. 2, 292–306

MECHANISTIC AND ORGANISTIC ANALOGIES IN ECONOMICS RECONSIDERED

H. THOBEN*

The sciences do not develop in complete isolation. On the contrary, there is interaction between the disciplines. By way of simply analogizing, the borrowing of jargon analytical tools and techniques or, in some cases by a mere transfer of metaphor. So far as economists are concerned, they have always had a sharp eye in looking for new tools they could borrow from other disciplines. 'They have taken their mathematics and their deductive techniques from physics, their statistics from genetics and agronomy, their systems of classification from taxonomy and chemistry, their model-construction techniques from astronomy and mechanics, and their methods of analysis of the consequences of actions from engineering' (SCHOEFFLER [1955, p. 40]). In this article we will try to go a bit deeper into the basic ideas that underly economic thinking, which can be identified as theoretical schemes that are borrowed from other sciences, by discussing two different conceptions of the economic system, the mechanistic and the organistic approach, that have been developed in analogy to classical mechanics and biology respectively.

I. THE MECHANISTIC ANALOGY

The mechanistic view on the economic system reflects Newtonian cosmology. It is analogous to the physical model NEWTON constructed in his *Principia* of 1687: that of classical mechanics. 'Classical mechanics considers a system of material points upon which

* University of Amsterdam, Netherlands.

directional forces operate at a distance according to calculable laws of motion. The choice of paths is governed by the principle of least action, which may be termed the economic principle if we take the term in its widest sense as denoting a maximum-minimum principle' (SEBBA [1953, p. 269]). Classical mechanics only knows motion, whereas at the same time the processes of motion are completely reversible and in no way give rise to any qualitative changes, or put in a more general way: 'the mechanistic view in a wider sense is held by everyone who believes himself to be an observer in an independent universe and who locates all events and objects uniquely in time and space' (MARGENAU [1950, p. 38–39]).

As LOWE [1951] demonstrated, mechanistic economics is modelled on classical mechanics. Starting from the basic hypothesis which underlies both classical mechanics and traditional economics and according to which the state of any 'whole' or 'aggregate' can be derived from the calculable behavior of its particles, LOWE derives three fundamental propositions on which any mechanistic theory is said to rest:

(a) 'All qualitative structures can be regarded as the aggregate of elementary, homogeneous quantities.
(b) These elementary quantities, far from behaving capriciously, conduct themselves as if they were exposed to well defined forces, notably the forces of push and pull.
(c) Hence the movements of the particles become calculable and can be formulated in general "laws" which permit us to determine the state of the aggregate' (LOWE [1951, p. 404]).

The great attraction of the mechanistic approach on the early economists may be related to the spectacular and successful attempts to rationalize observed regularities among phenomena in astronomy, biology, chemistry, mechanics, optics, thermodynamics and electrodynamics. The most convincing, however, was the fact that it became possible to make predictions that are fulfilled time after time.

No doubt, for the greater part it was its great success in the natural sciences that put the workers in the younger field of economics on the path of the mechanistic approach. It promised the possibility of mathematical formalization of the quantifiable aspects of the modern economy and the possibility of making reliable predictions.

Especially JEVONS and WALRAS give an explicit statement of their ambitions to construct a science of economics according to the basic pattern of mechanics. JEVONS writes about 'the *mechanics* of utility and selfinterest' and states that 'economics, if it is to be a science at all, must be a mathematical science' (JEVONS [1924, p. 3]). The same stand is taken by WALRAS. In his preface to the fourth edition of his *Elements* in 1900 he puts it as follows: 'It is already perfectly clear that economics, like astronomy and mechanics, is both an empirical and a rational science' (WALRAS [1977, p. 47]).

Later on in his book it becomes clear what his original intention has been, as he argues: 'If the pure theory of economics or the theory of exchange and value in exchange, that is, the theory of social wealth considered by itself, is a physico-mathematical science like *mechanics* or *hydrodynamics*, then economists should not be afraid to use the methods and language of mathematics' (WALRAS [1977, p. 71]).

The enthusiasm for the mechanistic approach is further illustrated by the pains FISHER [1925, p. 38f.] took to construct a very complicated model for the sole reason only to demonstrate the purely mechanical character of consumer behaviour. And then there is also F. KNIGHT, who considers mechanics 'as the sister science of economics' (KNIGHT [1935, p. 85]). The basic thought of this view is that the fundamental laws in economics are so general in character that they can be rightfully compared to the laws of the natural sciences. These last ones have 'their basis more or less obviously in the general principles of mechanics' (JEVONS [1924, p. XVII]). Economics is very closely related 'to the science of Statical Mechanics' (JEVONS [1924, p. VII]). A consequence of this conception of the economic system as a hypothetical mechanical system was the emphasis on quantitative magnitudes as prices and volumes. A concomitant effect was that the analysis of the economic system took place in isolation of other systems of social activity. In this way the search for causal laws could become the main theme of economic analysis. Phenomena that were irreconcilable with the supposed selfregulating operation of the system were considered as forces operating from outside the system, which the economist did not need to occupy himself with. The most far-reaching consequence of the mechanistic view is that it leads to the fiction of the '*homo economicus*', by which human behaviour is stripped from all its social-cultural facets and is reduced to the assumption that in economic life man acts in a purely mechanical way. In the conception of JEVONS and WALRAS the economic subject is essentially a rope-dancer. At the demand side it is assumed that every individual levels his marginal utilities and in this way balances his whole system of need satisfaction. Moreover, at the supply side of the economy every producer is constantly performing a balancing act by regulating the volume of production so as to equalize marginal costs and marginal revenues.

The mechanistic approach to economic analysis is not to be found in static general equilibrium theory only, however. Recent and less recent dynamic models, designed in order to explain and predict economic growth, the business cycle phenomenon or the interaction of both, have in general a strictly mechanistic character. It is all about mechanical concepts as impulse, multiplier, accelerator, ceiling, lags, etc. Changes in the structure of the economic system are considered as exogenous and unrelated to the outcome of the process of economic growth. In these models time is still the reversible time of classical mechanics. The mathematical form in which these models are formulated is that of difference or differential systems, which are highly characteristic of what might be called mechanical systems.

In the foregoing it is illustrated in what important way classical mechanics set an example for neoclassical economic theorizing. Part of its attraction can be explained by the success of mechanics in the natural sciences. However, according to SEBBA [1953, p. 261] also a number of historical factors contributed to the rise of the mechanistic approach in economics. In the developing capitalist system of the 19th century economic processes became increasingly rational and calculable while at the same time they were granted a social ascendancy they had never before enjoyed. There was a swift transformation of the old well structured society into what seemed to be in the beginning an aggregate of rather homogeneous human beings acting under a regime of overriding economic motivations. It is not surprising to SEBBA that the quantifiable features of this new economy were thought to be all that mattered to economic theory. In our opinion a third factor may be in question, one of a psychological nature. Scientists often have to start by constructing a mechanical analogy of a complex phenomenon in order to be able to understand the basic relations between the core variables. In this respect, the way by which FRISCH explains how he understood SCHUMPETER's theory on the relationship between innovations and business-cycles after constructing a mechanical analogy is quite illuminating. 'Suppose that we have a pendulum freely suspended to a pivot. Above the pendulum is fixed a receptacle where there is water. A small pipe descends all along the pendulum, and at the lower end of the pendulum the pipe opens with a value which has a peculiar way of functioning. The opening of the valve points towards the left and is larger when the pendulum moves towards the right than when it moves towards the left. Concretely one may, for example, assume that the valve is influenced by the air resistance or by some other factor that determines the opening of the valve as a function of the velocity of the pendulum. Finally we assume that the water in the receptable is fed from a constantly running stream which is given as a function of time' (FRISCH [1933, p. 203–204]).

The water that stores up in the receptacle above the pendulum represents SCHUMPETER's innovations. Those innovations descending down the pipe are the new ideas that are applicated in economic life and supply the energy to continue the business-cycles. The suggested psychological need for a mechanical analogy is confirmed by FRISCH himself, saying: 'Personally, I have found this illustration very useful. Indeed it is only after I had constructed this analogy that I really succeeded in understanding Schumpeter's idea' (FRISCH [1933, p. 203]).

Though it may be a useful vehicle for understanding economic problems, the mechanistic approach implies the fiction that human behaviour is essentially mechanical. This assumption remains highly problematical, or put in another way, 'in the case of celestial mechanics we can neglect the problem of whether the planets are moved by angels without causing any trouble at all for it is only the behavior of abstract time series of the positions of the planets that we are concerned with. In the case of economic and social systems, however, the "planets" that is, the commodities, prices and other statistical and abstract numbers with which we deal, are in fact moved by people who are not so well-behaved as angels, and we forget this fact at our peril' (BOULDING [1970, p. 74]).

MECHANISTIC AND ORGANISTIC ANALOGIES

II. THE ORGANISTIC ANALOGY

Though it was and still is the leading theoretical scheme, the mechanistic concept of the economic system is not the only scheme that is applied by economists. Biology too constituted a source of inspiration and was considered to have a certain heuristic value when formulating and analyzing economic problems. For example the German Historical School rejected the use of mechanical concepts in economic analysis. Its authors stressed the unity of social life, the interconnection of individual social processes and the organic as against the mechanistic, view of society (Roll [1973, p. 309]). Society, in its totality, had an organic existence apart from that of its members. Especially Roscher suggested that it was possible to discerne a 'physiology' of economic life. He conceives the economy as an organism functioning on the basis of a number of developmental laws, that are for him the laws of a lifecycle.

But a neoclassical economist like Marshall too, never was quite satisfied with studying the purely mechanical operation of abstract economic forces. 'The Mecca of the economist lies in economic biology rather than in economic dynamics' (Marshall [1924, p. XIV]), is a statement that cannot be misunderstood, although he adds that we have no other choice than to start with economic dynamics. Later on in his book he states that 'Economics is a branch of biology, broadly interpreted' [1924, p. 772]. A recent application of the biological or organical theoretical scheme can be found in Kornai's '*Anti-equilibrium*', a book which at the same time is meant to be a critique of (mechanistic) general equilibrium thinking in economics. In formulating the foundations for a theory of economic systems the above mentioned author bases his approach upon the idea that 'the economic system is a living organism, the functioning of which obeys certain laws' (Kornai [1971, p. 75]). More precisely, when the combined functioning and the interactions of the organizations within the economic system are analyzed, he refers to the difference made in biology between the so called autonomous or vegetative and the higher functions in the human organism. In general the autonomous functions concern the maintenance of the organism and operate almost completely beyond the will. The higher functions are regulated by the central nervous system, whereas at the same time the autonomous and higher functions interact to a certain degree. Then KORNAI continues by stating that 'a separation analogous to the one discussed above may be observed in the economic system. The "autonomous" and the "higher" functions, as well as the central processes of the two kinds of functions, are separated from each other to a certain extent both in individual organizations and in the economic system as a whole' (KORNAI [1971, p. 176]). Also in the chapter on adaptation and selection he refers to the biological analogies of social-economic processes. Adaptation concerns the way by which living organisms adapt to their environment and the changes that may occur in that environment. The individual will perish prematurely in case no minimum of adjustment takes place. And the species will become extinct when too few of the individuals adapt sufficiently. But DARWIN's natural selection operates in economic systems too. Organizations and even complete systems are born and die out. 'Different forms of behaviour and functional rules (mutations) arise; some of them become entrenched (because inherited): others prove to be unviable and disappear.' From this point of view natural selection projects the evolutionary perspective of an economic systems theory, in which the core of problems concerns structural change, factors of growth and innovation.

Another example comes from the work of BOULDING [1970, p. 8–9]: 'There are some striking parallels in the social system to the distribution which is so important in biological systems between the genotype and the phenotype, the genotype being the genetic code in the fertilized egg which organizes the growth and development of the phenotype – the living animal. In the social system what one has to look for are genotypical relationships which have the power of creating a process of development of social organization and role structure.' In short the approach mentioned above may be typified as an example of the organistic systems theory, whereas on a more abstract level the organistic systems theory in its turn forms a special field in general systems theory (MESAROVIC [1968]). The organistic approach was propagated in particular by VON BERTALANFFY [1950], a biologist and one of the founders (with BOULDING) of the Society for General Systems Research.

MECHANISTIC AND ORGANISTIC ANALOGIES

Some authors consider it a basic reorientation of scientific thinking in general. It is considered to be a retreat from the atomistic and mechanistic approach of the nineteenth century toward a holistic image of reality (SZTOMPKA [1974, p.56]). The basic characteristic of the systems approach is that the objects under study are considered as systems, *i.e.* as sets of interconnected elements representing a single whole. According to VON BERTALANFFY [1968, p.45] 'We may state as characteristic of modern science that the scheme of isolable units acting in one-way causality has proved to be insufficient. Hence the appearance in all fields of science of notions like wholeness, holistic, organismic, *Gestalt*, etc., which all signify that in the last resort we must think in terms of elements in mutual interaction'. SADOVSKY [1979, p.106] identifies the following informal signs of a system which characterise the more abstract systems approach.

1. First the system represents a certain wholeness from which follows, in particular, the fundamental irreducibility of its properties to the sum of the properties of the elements composing it, as well as non-deducibility of the properties of the whole from the latter.
2. Second, the system's nature is hierarchical: its every component can be regarded in its turn, as a system, while the system under study represents just a component of a broader system.
3. Third, in order to obtain sufficient knowledge about the system, the construction of a certain class of its descriptions is required, each of which being able to cover only certain aspects of the wholeness and hierarchy of a given system.

In BLAUBERG's [1979] opinion the development of the systems approach was in large measure necessitated by the methodological difficulties in conceiving and constructing complex integral objects, which were experienced in the second half of the 20th century by concrete scientific and technological knowledge. So in contrast to the mechanistic approach in economics the modern organistic (or cybernetic) approach, which is based on systems thinking, emphasizes the property of integrativity, *i.e.* the appearance as a result of interaction between parts of new qualities and properties at the level of the whole. The point is that these new qualities and properties are not inherent in the individual parts or their sum (BLAUBERG [1979, p. 69]).

Finally, contrary to the mechanistic approach one of the logical consequences of the systems approach is the idea that the observer and the observed influence one another mutually, whereby it is no longer possible to localize uniquely every event and every object in time and space. This is known as HEISENBERG's principle and as such it is part of modern quantumphysics. In what BOULDING [1970, p. 121] calls the 'generalized HEISENBERG principle' it is about the problem that 'when we try to obtain knowledge about a system by changing its inputs and outputs of information, the new inputs and outputs will change the system itself and under some circumstances change it radically'. Now, in the social sciences the generalized HEISENBERG principle is all-important: 'knowledge of the social sciences is an essential part of the social system itself; hence objectivity in the sense of investigating a world which is unchanged by the investigation of it is an absurdity.' Or put in another way, the moment that economic predictions and the policy recommendations derived from it are brought up for debate the interaction between observer and observed takes effect.

III. A CHOICE OF ANALOGIES: THE ENERGY LAWS

Apart from stating the fact that mechanistic as well as organistic analogies are used as a frame for thinking in economics, there still remains the problem on what rational arguments the choice between the two should be made. In the introduction of his '*Analytical Economics*' [1966] GEORGESCU-ROEGEN suggests that the strong relationship between the entropy law or second law of thermodynamics on the one hand and the economic process on the other, may provide us with a guide. So it is on the basis of the entropy law that he rejects the mechanistic approach and embraces an organistic point of view in economics [1971]. This standpoint has recently also been put forward again by ADAMS [1981] for the case of cultural anthropology. In this connection it is worth mentioning that the suggestion that in particular the second law of thermodynamics is of fundamental importance for the social sciences, was already made much earlier by WHITE [1943].

Put in a general way the entropy law states that there is a continuous and irrevocable degrading of energy taking place in the world, going from a state of low entropy to a state of high entropy or in the modern interpretation there is a continuous process of degrading from order into disorder. The material basis for every form of life is an entropic process and the idea is that the same goes for human social processes. In addition 'life' can be defined as the ability to evade the entropy law and to keep going a process of so called negative entropy, upgrading disorder into order. However a living being can only evade the degrading of its own structure. It cannot prevent the entropic degrading of the whole system, which includes its own environment too. On the contrary, at the present state of knowledge, the conclusion must even be that the presence of life accelerates the entropy of the total system.

This is exactly the point where biology comes in. As early as 1922 LOTKA conceived the entropy law as basic to natural selection, as he stated that 'In every instance considered, natural selection will so operate as to increase the total mass of the organic system, to increase the rate of circulation of matter through the system, and to increase the total energy flux through the system, so long as there is presented an unutilized residue of matter and available energy' [1922, pp. 151–154]. This evolutionary principle, also known as 'LOTKA's principle', explained the fundamental process whereby natural selection worked and evolution continuously searched for new forms of life, *i.e.* followed the direction of seeking disorder. It makes clear that life not only conforms to the entropy law but at the same time accelerates its operation. Then according to LOTKA's principle those life forms that give rise to a more extensive degrading of energy have a selective advantage over others and will outstrip their competitors.

Combining the second law of thermodynamics, LOTKA's principle and its clarification by 'PRIGOGINE's far-from-equilibrium theory' (PRIGOGINE/ROBERT and ALLEN [1977]) ADAMS applies these insights to anthropological theory. 'Culture provides human beings with the potentiality for extra-human extensions that allow them to capture energy and degrade it more rapidly and effectively. Thus, the societies that will be favored by natural selection are those that have cultures that so operate as to increase the total mass of the organic system, to increase the rate of circulation of matter through the system, and to increase the total energy flux through the system, so long as there is presented an unutilized residue of matter and available energy.' Following this line of thought ADAMS [1981] poses that human beings dedicate themselves to trying to 'survive', which means to continue to expend more energy for as long a time as is humanly possible. 'Complex social organizations have provided better and better ways of doing this, just as have the technological inventions that have provided the means by which energy could be at least consistently and, better, increasingly captured.'

However, as far as economics is concerned GEORGESCU-ROEGEN takes a more moderate position. First he establishes the fact that thermodynamics and biology have drawn continuously closer and that entropy now occupies a prominent place in the explanation of biological processes, especially the processes of change and evolution. Then he proceeds by stating that the economic process materially consists of a transformation of low entropy into high entropy, a process which is irrevocable. As a consequence in the longer run the economic process is inevitably dominated by a qualitative change which cannot be known in advance as in the case with the evolution of species in biology. So the economic process is an entropic process. As to the role of the entropy law itself he continues by putting that 'the important fact is that the discovery of the Entropy Law brought the downfall of the mechanistic dogma of classical physics which held that everything which happens in any phenomenal domain whatsoever consists of locomotion alone, and, hence, there is no irrevocable change in nature. It is precisely because this law proclaims the existence of such a change that before too long some students perceived its intimate connection with the phenomena peculiar to living structures. By now, no one would deny that the economy of biological processes is governed by the Entropy Law, not by the laws of mechanics' (GEORGESCU-ROEGEN [1971, p. XIII]). It is a law of elementary matter, the entropy law, that stresses the simple fact that from the purely physical viewpoint the economic process is not a mechanical analogue. Besides, the economic process is not automatic, but willed. In other words, the universal tendency to the downgrading of energy is the reason 'why the entropy reversal as seen in every line of production bears the indelible hallmark of purposive activity'.

However, this also means that the concept of *purpose*, of which many physicists admitted that it is a legitimate element of life activities where the final cause is in its proper right, is not only in its right place in the sciences of life but also constitutes an indispensable and useful tool of economic analysis.

It is the organistic analogy that can deal best with the purposive aspects of the economic process. Or as GEORGESCU-ROEGEN puts it, a biologist or a social scientist has to be a 'vitalist' and as a result has to be in the habit of looking for a purpose. 'It is all right for an economist to rest satisfied with the explanation of a catastrophic crop by some efficient causes triggered by random events. However, the science served by him is ordinarily interested in problems, involving human actions. And so he will not arrive at a penetrating understanding if he refuses to look for the purposes that move men' [1971, p. 195].

IV. CONCLUSION

The main results of this reexamination of the mechanistic and organistic analogy may now be summarized. First of all it is a well known fact that the main theoretical currents of scientific economics have to this day retained the characteristics of a 'mechanistic' system. On the other hand history provides us with periodic attacks against this application of the principles of classical mechanics in economics. However, the older principal critics, like the Historical, Romanticist, and Institutional schools, have confined themselves in the main to pointing out weaknesses in the classical and neoclassical approach, without offering any workable alternative in its place (LOWE [1951]). This does not in itself prove, of course, that the dominant approach is valid.

With the downfall of the mechanistic dogma of classical physics in physics itself, triggered by the entropy law, there is no longer a solid base for arguing that scientific economics should develop in analogy to classical physics and astronomy. At the same time one has to admit that the economic process is an entropic process, which implies that from a physical point of view the economic process cannot be captured in a mechanical analogue. This job is done better by an organical analogue, especially where it leaves room for the analysis of qualitative change and takes into account the purposiveness of human behaviour.

Besides, scientific developments in the last three decades in the new fields of general systems theory and cybernetics, may provide the organistic approach with the analytical tools so as to make it a workable alternative instead of the traditional method. So the final verdict must be in favour of the organical analogy. Once the choice is made in favour of the organistic approach the economist may proceed by borrowing from the conceptual apparatus of cybernetics and of a general systems theory, which may possibly help him to improve and broaden his understanding of the economic process.

REFERENCES

ADAMS, R.N.: 'Natural selection, Energetics and "Cultural Materialism"', *Current Anthropology*, Vol. 21 (1981), December.

VON BERTALANFFY, L.: 'An outline of general systems theory', *British Journal for Philosophy of Science*, Vol. 1 (1950), pp. 134–165.

VON BERTALANFFY, L.: *General System Theory*, New York 1968.

BLAUBERG, I.: 'System and Wholeness Concepts', *Social Sciences*, Vol. 10 (1979), pp. 65–79.

BOULDING, K.: *Economics as a Science*, New York 1970.

FISHER, I.: *Mathematical Investigations in the Theory of Value and Prices*, New Haven 1925 (First edition 1892).

FRISCH, R.: 'Propagation problems and impulse, problems in dynamic economics', in: *Economic Essays in honour of Gustav Cassel*, London 1933.

GEORGESCU-ROEGEN, N.: *Analytical Economics: Issues and Problems*, Cambridge: Harvard 1966.

GEORGESCU-ROEGEN, N.: *The Entropy Law and the Economic Process*, Cambridge: Harvard 1971.

JEVONS, W.S.: *The Theory of Political Economy*, London 1924.

KNIGHT, F.H.: *The Ethics of Competition*, New York 1935.

KORNAI, J.: *Anti-equilibrium, On economic systems theory and the tasks of research*, Amsterdam 1971.

LOTKA, A.: 'Contribution to the energetics of evolution', *Proceedings of the National Academy of Sciences*, Vol. 8 (1922), pp. 151–154.

LOWE, A.: 'On the Mechanistic Approach in Economics', *Social Research*, Vol. 18 (1951), pp. 403–434.

MARGENAU, H.: *The nature of Physical Reality*, New York 1950.

MECHANISTIC AND ORGANISTIC ANALOGIES

Marshall, A.: *Principles of Economics* (8th ed.), New York 1924.

Mesarovic, M. D. (Ed.): *Systems theory and biology*, Berlin 1968.

Prigogine, I.; Robert, H. and Allen, P.: 'Long-term trends and the evolution of complexity', in: *Goals in a global community*, Edited by E. Laszlo and J. Bierman, New York 1977.

Roll, E.: *A History of Economic Thought*, London 1973.

Sadovsky, V.: 'The Methodology of Science and Systems Approach', *Social Sciences*, Vol. 10 (1979), pp. 93–110.

Schoeffler, S.: *The failures of economics: a diagnostic study*, Cambridge, Mass. 1955.

Sebba, G.: 'The Development of the Concepts of Mechanism and Model in Physical Science and Economic Thought', *American Economic Review, Papers and Proceedings*, Vol. 43 (1953), pp. 259–268.

Sztompka, P.: *System and function, Toward a Theory of Society*, New York 1974.

Walras, L.: *Elements of pure economics*, translated by W. Jaffé, Fairfield 1977 (first edition 1874).

White, L.: 'Energy and the evolution of culture', *American Anthropologist*, Vol. 45 (1943), pp. 335–356.

SUMMARY

This article is about the analogies that underly economic thinking. Two conceptions of the economic system are discussed. First the traditional approach, which views the economic system as a hypothetical mechanical system, in which the state of the whole can be derived from the calculable behavior of its parts. Second, the organistic approach which uses the analogy to a living organism, in which the whole has qualities and properties that are not inherent in the parts or their sum. It is argued that economics should drop the mechanistic analogy to classical physics and astronomy and develop along the lines of organistic systems theory and cybernetics.

Part II
Economics and Sociobiology

[6]

Altruism, Egoism, and Genetic Fitness: Economics and Sociobiology

By GARY S. BECKER

The University of Chicago

I am indebted to Jack Hirshleifer, Guity Nashat, George J. Stigler, and Edward O. Wilson for very helpful comments.

I. *Introduction*

ECONOMISTS generally take tastes as "given" and work out the consequences of changes in prices, incomes, and other variables under the assumption that tastes do not change. When pressed, either they engage in *ad hoc* theorizing or they explicitly delegate the discussion of tastes to the sociologist, psychologist, or anthropologist. Unfortunately, these disciplines have not developed much in the way of systematic usable knowledge about tastes.

Although economists have been reluctant to discuss systematically changes in the structure of tastes, they have long relied on assumptions about the basic and enduring properties of tastes. Self-interest is assumed to dominate all other motives,[1] with a prominent place also assigned to benevolence toward children[2] (and occasionally others), and with self-interest partly dependent on distinction and other aspects of one's position in society.[3] The dominance of self-interest and the persistence of some benevolence have usually been explained by "human nature," or an equivalent evasion of the problem.

The development of modern biology since the mid-nineteenth century and of population genetics in the twentieth century made clear that "human nature" is only the beginning, not the end of the answer. The enduring traits of human (and animal) nature presumably were genetically selected under very different physical environments and social arrangements as life on earth evolved during millions of years. It is not difficult to understand why self-interest has high survival value under very different circumstances,[4] but why should altruistic behavior, sometimes observed among animals as well as human beings, also survive?

This kind of question has been asked by some geneticists and other biologists especially during the last two decades. Their work has recently been christened "soci-

[1] For example, Adam Smith said, "We are not ready to suspect any person of being defective in selfishness" [9, 1969, p. 446], and "it is not from the benevolence of the butcher, the brewer, or the baker, that we expect our dinner, but from their regard to their own interest" [10, 1937, p. 14].

[2] According to Alfred Marshall, ". . . men labor and save chiefly for the sake of their families and not for themselves" [6, 1920, p. 228].

[3] Nassau Senior said, "the desire for distinction . . . may be pronounced to be the most powerful of human passions" [8, 1938, p. 12].

[4] Ronald Coase argues convincingly that Adam Smith, especially in his *Moral Sentiments*, was groping toward an explanation of the importance of self-interest in terms of its contribution to viable social and economic arrangements (see Coase [5, 1976]).

obiology" by Edward Wilson in an important book that organizes and develops further what has been done. According to Wilson, "the central theoretical problem of sociobiology [is]: how can altruism, which by definition reduces personal fitness, possibly evolve by natural selection?" [12, 1975, p. 3].

Sociobiologists have tried to solve their central problem by building models with "group selection"; these models can be illustrated with the particular variant called "kin selection." Suppose that a person is altruistic toward his brother and is willing to lower his own genetic fitness[5] in order to increase his brother's fitness. If he lowers his own fitness by b units as a result of his altruistic behavior, he increases his brother's fitness by say c units. Since they have about one half of their genes in common, his altruism would increase the expected fitness of his own genes if $c > 2b$. In particular, it would then increase the expected fitness of the genes that contribute to his altruism. Therefore, altruism toward siblings, children, grandchildren, or anyone else with common genes could have high survival value, which would explain why altruism toward kin is one of the enduring traits of human and animal "nature."

The approach of sociobiologists is highly congenial to economists, since they rely on competition, the allocation of limited resources—of say food and energy—efficient adaptation to the environment, and other concepts also used by economists. Yet sociobiologists have stopped short of developing models having rational actors who maximize utility functions subject to limited resources. Instead they have relied solely on the "rationality" related to genetic selection: the physical and social environment discourages ill-suited behavior and encourages better-suited behavior. Economists, on the other hand, have relied solely on individual rationality and have not incorporated the effects of genetic selection.[6]

I believe that a more powerful analysis can be developed by joining the individual rationality of the economist to the group rationality of the sociobiologist. To illustrate the potential, the central problem of sociobiology, the biological selection of altruistic behavior, is analyzed using recent work by economists on social interactions (see Becker [2, 1974] and Becker and Tomes [3, 1976]). I will show that models of group selection are unnecessary, since altruistic behavior can be selected as a consequence of individual rationality.

II. *An Economic Model of Altruism*

Consider first the effect of altruism on consumption and wealth, the usual focus of economists. Essentially by definition, an altruist is willing to reduce his own consumption in order to increase the consumption of others. Two considerations suggest that the own consumption of egoistic persons (or animals) would exceed that of equally able altruistic persons (or animals[7]). The own consumption of egoists would be greater if the wealth of egoists and altruists were equal because altruists give away some of their wealth to be con-

[5] Genetic selection is defined as "the change in relative frequency in genotypes due to differences in the ability of their phenotypes to obtain representation in the next generation" [12, Wilson, 1975, p. 67]. Genetic fitness is the relative contribution of one genotype to the next generation's distribution of genotypes, where a genotype is "the genetic constitution of an organism," and a phenotype is "the observable properties of an organism" [12, Wilson, 1975, p. 585, 591].

[6] Of course, economic analysis has sometimes been related to biological evolution: Alfred Marshall believed that economic systems evolve in the same way as biological systems do, and maximizing behavior has been said to be prevalent essentially because of the selection and survival of maximizers (see Armen A. Alchian [1, 1950]). However, biological selection has not been integrated into and combined with the main body of economic analysis: it has been an occasional appendage rather than an integral part.

[7] Although the following discussion might be as applicable to animals as to persons, I simplify the presentation by referring only to persons.

sumed by others. Moreover, the wealth of egoists apparently also would tend to be greater because egoists are willing to undertake all acts that raised their wealth, regardless of the effects on others, whereas altruists voluntarily forgo some acts that raise their wealth because of adverse effects on others.

These forces are potent, but they are not the whole story, and a fuller analysis shows that the consumption and wealth of altrusitic persons could exceed that of egoistic persons, even without bringing in social controls on the behavior of egoistic persons. Let us consider systematically the behavior of h who is altruistic toward an egoist i. By definition of altruism, h is willing to give some of his wealth to i, but how much is he willing to give? That surely depends on his degree of altruism, his and i's wealth, the "cost" of giving, and other considerations.

The economic approach assumes that all behavior results from maximizing utility functions that depend on different commodities. If, to simplify, the allocation and transfer of time is neglected, and both h and i consume a single aggregate of market goods and services, the utility function of an altruist h can be written as

$$U^h = U^h(X_h, X_i),^8 \qquad (1)$$

where X_h and X_i are the own consumptions of h and i respectively. The budget constraint of h can be written as

$$pX_h + h_i = I_h, \qquad (2)$$

where h_i is the dollar amount transferred to i, and I_h is h's own income. If h transfers to i without any monetary loss or gain—"dollar for dollar"—the amount received by i equals the amount transferred by h, and i's budget constraint would be

$$pX_i = I_i + h_i, \qquad (3)$$

where I_i is i's own income. By substitution of (3) into (2), the basic budget constraint for h is derived:

$$pX_h + pX_i = I_h + I_i = S_h, \qquad (4)$$

where S is called h's "social income."[9]

The equilibrium condition for maximizing the utility function given by equation (1) subject to the social income constraint given by (4) is

$$\frac{\partial U^h/\partial X_h}{\partial U^h/\partial X_i} = \frac{MU_h}{MU_i} = \frac{P}{P} = 1. \qquad (5)$$

Then h would transfer just enough resources to i so that h would receive the same utility from increments to his own or to i's consumption. Put differently, h would suffer the same loss in utility from a small change in his own or i's consumption.

Clearly, h's altruism is relevant not only to transfers of income, but also to the production of income. He would pursue all actions that raised his (real) social income and refrain from all that lowered it because his utility would be increased by all increases in his social income. Since the latter is the sum of his own and i's own income, he would, in particular, refrain from actions that raised his own income at the expense of a greater reduction in i's own income. This was referred to earlier when it was said that altruists have lower personal income (or wealth) than egoists because altruists do not take advantage of all opportunities to raise their own income.

[8] With many market goods and services, his utility function can be written as

$$U^h = U^h[X_{h_1}, \ldots, X_{h_m}, g(X_{i_1}, \ldots, X_{i_m})],$$

where X_{h_j} and X_{i_j} are the consumptions of the jth good by h and i respectively, and g is a function that would have the same indifference curves as i's utility function if h's welfare partly depended on i's welfare.

[9] See Becker [2, 1974]. The essentials of the economic analysis of altruism in the present section are taken from that paper.

Note, however, that some actions of altruistic *h* could increase his utility and own consumption while reducing his own income, a combination that is impossible for an egoist. Suppose that *h* could increase his social income by actions that lowered his own income and raised *i*'s even more. Since *h*'s utility would increase, he would increase both his own and *i*'s consumption, as long as neither were an inferior good. He could increase his own consumption only by reducing his transfers to *i* because his own income declined; this is consistent with an increase in *i*'s consumption because *i*'s own income increased. Therefore, *h*'s own consumption would increase even though his own income declined, and *i*'s own consumption would increase even though transfers from *h* declined. Consequently, if an egoist and altruist began with the same consumption—the own income of the altruist necessarily being greater—events could raise the consumption of the altruist above that of the egoist at the same time that they lowered the difference in their incomes.

The most important consideration benefitting altruists, however, and one that seems puzzling and paradoxical at first, is that egoistic *i* has an incentive to act "as if" he too were altruistic—toward *h*—in the sense that it would be to *i*'s advantage to raise the combined incomes of *i* and *h*. In particular, *i* would refrain from actions that lowered *h*'s own income unless *i*'s was raised even more, and *i* would lower his own income if *h*'s were raised even more.

Why should egoist *i* act as if he were altruistic? Consider the consequences to him (all that he cares about) of doing the contrary; for example, let *i* raise his own income at the expense of lowering *h*'s even more. Since *h*'s social income and utility decline because the sum of his own and *i*'s income declines, *h* would want to reduce his own and *i*'s own consumption. Then *h* would have to reduce his transfers to *i* by more than the increase in *i*'s income. Therefore, as long as *h*'s transfers remained positive, *i*'s own consumption and welfare would be reduced by *h*'s response. If *i* anticipated correctly *h*'s reaction, *i* would refrain from these actions. A similar argument shows that *i* would benefit from his own actions even if they lowered his income as long as they raised *h*'s income even more: for *h* would increase his transfers to *i* by more than the reduction in *i*'s income.

In other words, by linking *i*'s consumption with his own, the altruistic *h* discourages egoistic *i* from actions that lower *h*'s consumption because then *i*'s consumption would also be lower. Moreover, *i* would not refrain from harming other egoistic persons not linked to *h*. Therefore, the intuitively appealing conclusion that the own consumption of egoistic persons exceeds that of equally able altruistic persons is seriously qualified when interaction with others is incorporated. Even though an altruist gives away part of his income and refrains from some actions that raise his own income, his own consumption might not be less than that of an egoist because the beneficiaries of his altruism would consider the effect of their behavior on his consumption. These beneficial indirect effects on the behavior of others may dominate the direct "disadvantages" of being altruistic. Moreover, these indirect effects need not be minor and could greatly exceed the amount transferred to *i*. For example, assume that *h* transfers $1000 and that *i* could increase his own income by $800 at the cost of harming *h* by $5000. Since *i* would not take these actions, *h*'s altruism has increased his income by $5000, or by five times the amount transferred to *i*.

The analysis is easily extended to incorporate altruism by *h* toward egoistic persons *j*, *k*, . . . , as well as *i*. Then *h* would transfer resources to *j*, *k*, . . . , as well as *i*, and maximize a utility function of all these consumptions subject to a social income constraint equal to the sum of all these own incomes. Following the previous analysis, it can be shown that *h* would refrain from actions that raised his own income if the combined incomes of *i, j, k,* . . . were lowered even more. Moreover, he would lower his own income if their combined incomes were raised even more.

Furthermore, not only *i* but each of the others would lower his own income if *h*'s were raised more and would refrain from raising his own income if *h*'s were lowered still more. Therefore, *h* may give away more of his income, and refrain from more actions that raise his own income, yet he would benefit more too because more people would consider the effects of their behavior on him. Consequently, although the direct effects reducing his own consumption are stronger for an altruist toward many persons than toward a single person, the indirect effects are also stronger. The own consumption of an altruist toward many persons also need not be less than that of an equally able egoist.

The most important new consequence of multi-person altruism relates to the behavior of recipients toward each other. Although *i, j, k,* . . . are all egoistical and do not give or receive transfers from each other, each has an incentive to consider the effects of his behavior on the others. For example, *j* would not raise his own income if the sum of the incomes of *i, k,* . . . were reduced still more, and *j* would lower his own income if their incomes were raised still more. Elsewhere I have called this the "rotten-kid" theorem (see Becker [2, 1974]), although its applicability is not restricted to interaction among siblings.

To prove this theorem, assume the contrary; for example, let *j* raise his income and lower *k*'s still more. Then *h*'s social income (and utility) would be reduced because it is the sum of *j*'s, *k*'s, and the others' own incomes. Consequently, *h* would reduce the consumption of both *j* and *k*, assuming that these consumptions are superior goods to him, and would reduce his transfers to *j* by more than *j*'s increase in income and raise his transfers to *k* by less than *k*'s decrease in income. In the end, *j* as well as *k* (and everyone else) would be worse off; if *j* could anticipate *h*'s reaction, he would refrain from raising his income at greater expense to *k*.

Even though *i, j, k,* . . . are completely egoistical, they are linked together through *h*'s altruism. Their own interest, not altruism, motivates them to maximize the sum of their own and *h*'s incomes—that is, to maximize *h*'s social income. This provides another reason why an altruist's own consumption may not be less than an egoist's consumption: beneficiaries of his altruism consider all indirect as well as direct effects of their behavior on his own consumption. They do not consider the effect of their behavior on the consumption of other persons not linked to this altruist.

Note that a sufficiently large redistribution of income away from *h* and toward *i, j, k,* . . . would make *h* unwilling to transfer resources to some of these persons, say to *k*. Then *k* and *h* would continue to be interested in maximizing the same social income only if the income redistribution induced *k* to transfer resources to *h* (or induced someone else, like *j*, to transfer to *k*). That is, *k*'s (or someone else's) altruism—*h*'s altruism toward *k* and *k*'s toward *h* is an example of "reciprocal altruism"[10] —would increase the robustness of the conclusions with respect to large redistri-

[10] The term "reciprocal altruism" is used in a different and misleading way in sociobiology. It refers not to true altruism, but to one type of simulated altruism: a person helps others in the expectation or hope that he will be helped by them in the future (see Wilson [12, 1975, pp. 120–21]). This is more appropriately called "social exchange" by sociologists (see Peter M. Blau [4, 1968]).

butions of income within the group initially related through h's altruism.

Each person in the group linked by an altruist's transfers has an incentive to maximize the group's total income, even if most are egoistical. The group's income could be maximized in the absence of altruism if the "government" imposed appropriate taxes and subsidies, or if members bargained with each other only to take actions that benefitted the group as a whole. However, appropriate voluntary agreements and government action often are not achieved, especially when governments are primitive or subject to many pressure groups, contract law is not well developed, or other private transactions costs are sizable. Therefore, whereas the private behavior induced by the rotten-kid theorem in an altruistic situation *automatically* maximizes group income, government responses or the Coase theorem (on private bargaining)[11] do not.

Recipients of h's transfers are encouraged to act "as if" they are altruistic to each other and to h by the adverse reaction from h when they act egoistical. Therefore, the rotten-kid theorem is essentially a theorem about the incentive that egoists have to *simulate* altruism when they benefit from someone else's altruism. More generally, an egoist has an incentive to try to simulate altruism whenever altruistic behavior increases his own consumption through its effect on the behavior of others. For example, egoist n may have an incentive to act as if he were altruistic toward j, in the sense that he would voluntarily transfer resources to j, maximize their combined own incomes, reduce his transfers when their combined own income fell, *etc.*, if this discourages j from actions that harm n.

If egoists can always perfectly simulate altruism whenever altruistic behavior raises their own consumption, then, of course, the own consumption of true altruists would not exceed that of true egoists; they would be equal when egoists perfectly simulated altruism. We could still conclude, however, that "apparent" altruistic behavior—either true or simulated altruism—could increase own consumption, and that is important. Moreover, if altruism could be perfectly simulated, transactions and negotiation costs must be sufficiently small so that the Coase theorem could prevail. Conversely, if the Coase theorem broke down, say because of sizable bluffing and other bargaining costs, altruism could not be perfectly simulated, for otherwise the Coase theorem would prevail. When altruism cannot be perfectly simulated, the own consumption of altruists could exceed, perhaps by a good deal, the consumption of equally able egoists.

III. *Genetic Fitness and the Economic Model of Altruism*

Since sociobiologists are more concerned with selection and genetic fitness than with consumption and wealth *per se*, I can bring out sharply the relationship between this economic analysis of altruism and the central problem of sociobiology by reformulating the utility function to depend only on genetic fitness. Then altruistic h would have the function

$$U^h = U^h(f_h, f_i), \tag{6}$$

where f_h and f_i measure the fitness of h and i respectively, and the utility function of egoist i would depend only on his own fitness. Since genetic fitness depends directly on birth and death rates of offspring and on own life expectancy only to the extent that it influences the number of offspring, even an egoist must be somewhat concerned about the well-being of mates and children.

In the language of the household production approach to consumer behavior,[12]

[11] The rotten-kid theorem, therefore, is a powerful substitute for the Coase theorem when there is altruism.

[12] An exposition can be found in Michael and Becker [7, 1973].

genetic fitness is a commodity produced by households using their own time and goods, their skills, experience and abilities, and the physical and social environment. For example, the fitness of h would be produced according to

$$f_h = f_h(X_h, t_h; S_h, E_h), \quad (7)$$

where t_h is the time he directly[13] uses to produce fitness—as in the care and protection of children—S_h is his stock of skills and other human capital, and E_h is the environment.

If t, S, and E were exogenous, fitness could be changed only by changing the input of goods. With the exception of a small part of the human population during the last 100 years or so, access to food and perhaps some other goods has been the main determinant of fitness throughout the biological world. The close relation between fitness and goods can be made transparent by writing the production function for fitness as

$$f = aX, \quad (8)$$

where a depends on the biological species, and the parameters t, S, and E.[14] Fitness does not have a market price, since it is not directly purchased, but does have a "shadow" price, defined as the value of the goods used in changing fitness by one unit:

$$\pi = \frac{\partial(pX)}{\partial f} = \frac{p}{a}, \quad (9)$$

[13] A brief but suggestive discussion of the allocation of time (and energy) in the biological world can be found in Wilson [12, 1975, p. 143].

[14] A more appropriate formulation might be

$$f = \alpha X,$$

where α depends on the species, and X is produced by the function

$$X = \psi(t, S, E).$$

For present purposes, however, this formulation and the one in the text are essentially equivalent.

where p is the (constant) price or cost of X.

Altruistic h is willing to transfer some of his goods to i because he is willing to reduce his own fitness in order to improve i's fitness. This is precisely the definition of altruism in sociobiology: "When a person (or animal) increases the fitness of another at the expense of his own fitness, he can be said to have performed an act of *altruism*" [12, Wilson, 1975, p. 117].

The budget constraint for h can be derived by substituting equation (8) into equation (4):

$$\frac{pf_h}{a_h} + \frac{pf_i}{a_i} = I_h + I_i = S_h,$$

or by equation (9),

$$\pi_h f_h + \pi_i f_i = S_h. \quad (10)$$

h's social income is partly spent on his own and partly on i's fitness: the sum of the shadow values placed on their fitnesses equals his social income.

The equilibrium condition for maximizing h's utility function (6) subject to his budget constraint (10) is, with positive transfers,

$$\frac{\partial U_h}{\partial f_h} \bigg/ \frac{\partial U_h}{\partial f_i} = \frac{\pi_h}{\pi_i} = \frac{a_i}{a_h}. \quad (11)$$

If h and i were equally efficient producers of fitness, $a_h = a_i$, and h would transfer goods to i until he was indifferent between equal increments to his own and to i's fitness. If h were a more efficient producer of fitness, $a_h > a_i$, and he would be discouraged from promoting i's fitness: he would receive more utility from an increment to i's fitness than from an equal increment to his own fitness because his own fitness is cheaper to produce.

The important point is that all the earlier results on the consumption of goods apply equally to this analysis of fitness. Both the altruist h and the egoistical recipient i maximize the *sum* of their real incomes and would raise one of them only when the other were not reduced even more. In terms of fitness, they maximize the sum of the values placed on fitness and would increase the fitness of one only if the shadow value of its increase was not less than the shadow value of the decrease in the other's fitness:

$$\pi_h df_h + \pi_i df_i \geq 0. \qquad (12)$$

For example, if $\pi_i > \pi_h$ because h is more efficient at producing fitness, any increase in h's fitness would have to be at least π_i/π_h times as large as the decrease in i's fitness.

I concluded earlier that although an altruist forgoes some own consumption to raise the consumption of others and forgoes some opportunities to raise his own income to avoid lowering the income of others, his own consumption may exceed that of an equally able egoist because the beneficiaries of his altruism are discouraged from harming him. Reasoning along the same lines, the same conclusion can be reached for altruism with regard to genetic fitness: although an altruist forgoes some own fitness to raise the fitness of others, and so forth, his own fitness may exceed that of an equally able egoist because the beneficiaries of his altruism are discouraged from harming him.

Therefore, two apparently equivalent statements about altruism by Wilson are in fact quite different. He says ". . . altruism . . . *by definition* reduces personal fitness . . ." [12, 1975, p. 3, my italics], yet simply defines an act of altruism "[w]hen a person (or animal) increase the fitness of another at the expense of his own fitness . . ." [12, 1975, p. 117]. Using the latter definition, I have shown that altruism may actually increase personal fitness because of its effect on the behavior of others. Consequently, altruism does not by (Wilson's or my) definition necessarily reduce personal fitness.

This conclusion is highly relevant in answering the central question of sociobiology: "how can altruism . . . evolve by natural selection?" [12, Wilson, 1975, p. 3]. If altruism, on balance, raises own genetic fitness, then natural selection would operate in its favor. A central focus of sociobiology would be to identify when biological and social conditions have a sufficient effect on the behavior of the beneficiaries of altruism so that own fitness is increased by altruism.

Note that the extensive evidence among animals of what appears to be altruistic behavior[15]—for example, baboons expose themselves to danger to protect relatives—is not inconsistent with altruism increasing personal fitness because the effects of altruism on the behavior of beneficiaries have not been considered. Note, moreover, the incentive to try to simulate altruism whenever true altruism raises personal fitness, and sociobiologists have found it difficult to distinguish simulated altruism from true altruism.[16]

Even if altruism lowers fitness, and the sociobiologist's group selection must be used to explain how altruism evolves by selection, the actual trade-off between an altruist's and a beneficiary's fitness may be much more favorable to selection of altruism than the apparent trade-off. For example, if h were altruistic toward a brother i with about half his genes in common, kin selection would favor h's altruistic (and other) genes only if he could increase i's fitness by at least two units for every unit reduction in his own fitness. Since according to equation (12) he would be willing to exchange a unit of his own fitness for at least π_h/π_i units of i's, apparently his altruistic genes can be selected only if $\pi_h > 2\pi_i$, or only if his brother is more than twice as efficient in producing fitness as he is.

[15] See Wilson [12, 1975, pp. 121–28].

[16] The literature on altruism among animals reveals how difficult it is to distinguish true from simulated and other apparent altruism (see Wilson [12, 1975, pp. 123–25]).

Yet when all the effects of his altruism on i are considered, his genes may be strongly selected even when i is much less than twice as efficient as he is. Assume, for example, that the total loss in h's fitness from his altruism would be 5 units if he and i were equally efficient producers of fitness. Assume further that the total gain to his brother would be 15 units—the gain to his brother *must* be at least as large as his own loss since his altruism cannot decrease their combined fitness (by equation (12) when $\pi_h = \pi_i$). Instead of the apparent rate of exchange of one unit of his brother's fitness for one unit of his own, or the 2 to 1 minimum rate required to select his altruistic genes, he adds three units to his brother's fitness for each unit of his own loss.

The utility function (6) and the analysis can again be generalized to include altruism by h toward $j, k, \ldots$ as well as i. He would try to maximize the sum of his own and their real incomes, and would affect different fitnesses only if the sum of the shadow values of the changes were non-negative:

$$\pi_h df_h + \pi_i df_i + \pi_j df_j + \pi_k df_k + \ldots \geq 0. \tag{13}$$

Each beneficiary of h's altruism also maximizes the group's total real income and is constrained in his behavior by equation (13); in particular, each would reduce the fitness of another member of the group only if the value of the reduction were less than the value of the increase in his own fitness.

The sociobiological literature contends that a major conflict arises between parents and children because the altruism of parents toward children exceeds the altruism of children toward each other: ". . . there is likely to evolve a conflict between parents and offspring in the attitudes toward siblings: the parents will encourage more altruism than the youngster is prepared to give" [12, Wilson, 1975, p. 343], or "Conflict during socialization need not be viewed solely as conflict between the culture of the parent and the biology of the child; it can also be viewed as conflict between the biology of the parent and the biology of the child" (quoted in Wilson [12, 1975, p. 343] from Robert L. Trivers [11, 1974]). My analysis denies that such a conflict exists when parents are altruistic because children have an incentive to act as altruistically toward each other as their parents want them to, even if children are really egoistical. This application of the more general result on the simulation of altruism by beneficiaries led to the name "the rotten-kid" theorem.

Of course, the substitution between the fitness of parents and children that is due to the parent's altruism might not maximize the selection of his altruistic genes. However, the actual substitution may be much more favorable to the selection of his genes than substitution given by the shadow prices of fitness. For example, if these prices were equal, a parent would be willing to give up a unit of his fitness to increase the fitness of each child by a unit; yet his altruism might be strongly selected: both his and his children's fitness might actually exceed what they would be if he were not altruistic or the reduction in his fitness might be much less than the increase in their's.[17]

IV. *Conclusion*

Sociobiologists have explained the strong survival throughout most of the biological world of altruism toward children and other kin by group selection operating through the common genes of kin. Using an economic model of altruism, I have

[17] If $\pi_h = \pi_i = \pi_j = \pi_k, \ldots$, then necessarily by equation (13)

$$G_c + L_h \geq 0,$$

where L_h is the total change in the parent's (h) fitness that results from his altruism, and G_c is the total change in his children's fitness. It could also be that

$$G_c > -2L_h,$$

or even that L_h as well as $G_c > 0$.

explained its survival by the advantages of altruism when there is physical and social interaction: kin have had much interaction with each other because they have usually lived with or near each other. Since the economic model requires interaction, not common genes, it can also explain the survival of some altruism toward unrelated neighbors or co-workers, and these are not explained by the kin selection models of sociobiologists (but perhaps can be explained by their other models of group selection).

I have argued that both economics and sociobiology would gain from combining the analytical techniques of economists with the techniques in population genetics, entomology, and other biological foundations of sociobiology. The preferences taken as given by economists and vaguely attributed to "human nature" or something similar—the emphasis on self-interest, altruism toward kin, social distinction, and other enduring aspects of preferences—may be largely explained by the selection over time of traits having greater genetic fitness and survival value.[18] However, survival value is in turn partly a result of utility maximization in different social and physical environments. To demonstrate this I have shown how the central problem of sociobiology, the natural selection of altruism, can be resolved by considering the interaction between the utility maximizing behavior of altruists and egoists.

REFERENCES

1. ALCHIAN, ARMEN A. "Uncertainty, Evolution, and Economic Theory," *J. Polit. Econ.*, June 1950, *58*, pp. 211–21.
2. BECKER, GARY S. "A Theory of Social Interactions," *J. Polit. Econ.*, Nov./Dec. 1974, *82*(6), pp. 1063–93.
3. ——— AND TOMES, NIGEL. "Child Endowments and the Quantity and Quality of Children," *J. Polit. Econ.*, August 1976.
4. BLAU, PETER M. "Interaction: Social Exchange," in *International encyclopedia of the social sciences.* Volume 7. Edited by D. E. SILLS. New York: Macmillan, Free Press, 1968, pp. 452–58.
5. COASE, RONALD H. "Adam Smith's View of Man," *J. Law Econ.*, Oct. 1976, Forthcoming.
6. MARSHALL, ALFRED. *Principles of economics.* Eighth edition. London: Macmillan, 1920.
7. MICHAEL, ROBERT T. AND BECKER, GARY S. "On the New Theory of Consumer Behavior," *Swedish J. Econ.*, Dec. 1973, *75*(4), pp. 378–96.
8. SENIOR, NASSAU. *An outline of the science of political economy.* Library of Economics edition. New York: Farrar & Rinehart, [1836] 1938.
9. SMITH, ADAM. *The theory of moral sentiments.* Reprint of 1853 edition. Introduction to 1969 edition by E. G. WEST. New Rochelle, N.Y.: Arlington House, [1759] 1969.
10. ———. *The wealth of nations.* Modern Library edition of 1904 edition, "copied" from original fifth edition and edited by EDWIN CANNAN. New York: Random House, [1789] 1937.
11. TRIVERS, ROBERT L. "Parent-Offspring Conflict," *American Zoologist,* Winter 1974, *14*(1), pp. 249–64.
12. WILSON, EDWARD O. *Sociobiology.* Cambridge, Mass.: Harvard University Press, 1975.

[18] A few years ago Robert T. Michael and I already suggested that "if genetical natural selection and rational behavior reinforce each other in producing speedier and more efficient responses to changes in the environment, perhaps that common preference function has evolved over time by natural selection and rational choice as that preference function best adopted to human society" [7, 1973, p. 392, fn. 2].

[7]

ECONOMICS FROM A BIOLOGICAL VIEWPOINT*

J. HIRSHLEIFER
University of California, Los Angeles

I. Economics and Biology

THE field variously called population biology, sociobiology, or ecology is concerned to explain the observed interrelations among the various forms of life—organisms, species, and broader groupings and communities—and between forms of life and their external environments. The subject includes both material aspects of these interrelations (the geographical distributions of species in relation to one another, their respective numbers, physical properties like size differences between the sexes) and behavioral aspects (why some species are territorial while others flock, why some are monogamous and others polygamous, why some are aggressive and others shy).

From one point of view, the various social sciences devoted to the study of mankind, taken together, constitute but a subdivision of the all-encompassing field of sociobiology.[1] The ultimately biological subject matter of economics in particular has been recognized by some of our leading thinkers.[2] There is however a special link between economics and sociobiology over and above the mere fact that economics studies a subset of the social behavior of one of the higher mammals. *The fundamental organizing con-*

* Thanks for comments and suggestions, far too numerous and important to be fully responded to here, are due to: Armen Alchian, Shmuel Amir, Edward C. Banfield, Gary Becker, Eric L. Charnov, Ronald Cohen, Harold Demsetz, Michael Ghiselin, Joel Guttman, Bruce Herrick,, Gertrude Himmelfarb, David Levine, John G. Riley, Vernon L. Smith, Robert Trivers, and James Weinrich.

[1] See chapter 27 of E. O. Wilson's authoritative text Sociobiology (1975) [hereinafter cited as Sociobiology], and also *id.*, Biology and the Social Sciences, Daedalus (forthcoming).

[2] "But economics has no near kinship with any physical science. It is a branch of biology broadly interpreted." Alfred Marshall, Principles of Economics 772 (9th Variorum ed. 1920). See also Kenneth E. Boulding, A Reconstruction of Economics ch. 1 (1950). Also relevant, of course, are the famous passages in The Wealth of Nations where Adam Smith attributed the emergence of the division of labor among mankind, and its failure to develop among animal species, to a supposedly innate human "propensity to truck, barter, and exchange." Adam Smith, An Inquiry into the Nature and Causes of the Wealth of Nations 15-18 (Edwin Cannan ed. 1937).

cepts of the dominant analytical structures employed in economics and in sociobiology are strikingly parallel.[3] What biologists study can be regarded as "Nature's economy."[4] Oswald Spengler perceived (and regarded it as a serious criticism) that Darwin's contribution represented "the application of economics to biology."[5] Fundamental concepts like scarcity, competition, equilibrium, and specialization play similar roles in both spheres of inquiry. And terminological pairs such as species/industry, mutation/innovation, evolution/progress, mutualism/exchange have more or less analogous denotations.

Regarded more systematically, the isomorphism between economics and sociobiology involves the intertwining of two levels of analysis. On the first level, acting units or entities choose strategies or develop techniques that promote success in the struggle or *competition* for advantage in given environments. The economist usually calls this process "optimizing," the biologist, "adapting." The formalizations involved are equations of constrained maximization. The second, higher level of analysis examines the social or aggregate resultant of the interaction of the striving units or agents. The formalizations here take the form of equations of equilibrium. (In more general versions, the static solutions may be embedded in "dynamic" equations showing the time paths of approach to solution states.) The solutions on the two levels are of course interdependent. The pursuit of advantage on the part of acting units takes place subject to opportunities and constraints that emerge from the social context, while the resulting social configuration (constituting at least part of the environment for each separate agent) depends in turn upon the strategies employed by the advantage-seeking entities.

Among the methodological issues that might arise at this point are two with somewhat opposed thrusts: (1) Given the validity of a sociobiological outlook on human behavior, are we not claiming too much for economics? What role is there left for the other social sciences if economics can be regarded as essentially coextensive with the sociobiology of human behavior? (2) But alternatively, are we not claiming too little for economics (and a fortiori for the other social sciences) in adopting the reductive interpretation of human behavior implicit in the sociobiological approach? May it not be the case that the cultural evolution of the human species has carried it into a realm where biological laws are determinative of only a minor fraction of behavioral phenomena? (Or perhaps economics is the discipline that regards

[3] A somewhat similar argument is made in the very recent paper by David J. Rapport & James E. Turner, Economic Models in Ecology, 195 Science 367 (1977).

[4] Michael T. Ghiselin, The Economy of Nature and the Evolution of Sex (1974).

[5] Gertrude Himmelfarb, Darwin and the Darwinian Revolution 396 (1959).

mankind as merely sociobiological in nature, while the other social sciences treat of the higher aspects of human culture?)

Consideration of the second group of questions will be reserved for the concluding sections of this paper. With regard to the first—a seeming claim that the domain of economics is coextensive with the total sphere of all the social sciences together—a unified social-science viewpoint is adopted here, in which economics and other social studies are regarded as interpenetrating rather than compartmentalized. The traditional core area of compartmentalized economics is characterized by models that: (a) postulate rational self-interested behavior on the part of individuals with given preferences for material goods and services, and (b) attempt to explain those interactions among such individuals that take the form of market exchanges, under a fixed legal system of property and free contract. That only a very limited portion of human behavioral association could be adequately represented under such self-imposed analytical constraints has often been pointed out to economists by other social scientists. In recent years economics has begun to break through these self-imposed barriers, to take as subject matter all human activity that can be interpreted as goal-directed behavior constrained by and yet, in the aggregate, determinative of resultant social configurations. Significant innovative instances of the application of techniques of economic analysis to broader social issues include Schelling and Boulding's works on conflict and warfare, Downs and Buchanan and Tullock on political choice, and Becker on crime and marriage.[6] And each of these efforts has been followed by a growing literature, in which both economists and other social scientists have participated.[7] The upshot is that (at least in their properly scientific aspect) the social sciences generally can be regarded as in the process of coalescing. As economics "imperialistically" employs its tools of analysis over a wider range of social issues, it will *become* sociology and anthropology and political science. But correspondingly, as these other disciplines grow increasingly rigorous, they will not merely resemble but will *be*

[6] Thomas C. Schelling, The Strategy of Conflict (1960); Kenneth E. Boulding, Conflict and Defense (1962); Anthony Downs, An Economic Theory of Democracy (1957); James M. Buchanan & Gordon Tullock, The Calculus of Consent (1962); Gary S. Becker, Crime and Punishment: An Economic Approach, 76 J. Pol. Econ. 169 (1968); *id.*, A Theory of Marriage: Part I, 81 J. Pol. Econ. 813 (1973).

[7] In the earlier "classical" era the compartmentalization of economics within such narrow boundaries had not yet taken place. Adam Smith in particular discussed law, government, psychology, and the biological instincts promoting and hindering social cooperation—as well as economics in the narrow sense—throughout his works. See R. H. Coase, Adam Smith's View of Man, 19 J. Law & Econ. 529 (1976); Leonard Billet, The Just Economy: The Moral Basis of the Wealth of Nations, 34 Rev. Soc. Econ. 295 (1976). In a sense, then, economics is in the process of returning to the classical view of the whole man.

economics. It is in this sense that "economics" is taken here as broadly synonymous with "social science."[8]

One of the obvious divergences between economics and sociobiology, it might appear, is that men can consciously optimize—or so we often like to think—whereas, for all but a few higher animals, the concepts of "choice" or "strategy" are only metaphorical. What happens in the biological realm is that, given a sufficiently long run, *natural selection* allows survival only of entities that have developed successful strategies in their respective environments. So the result is sometimes (though not always, as we shall see) *as if* conscious optimization were taking place. The idea that selective pressure of the environment can do the work of conscious optimizing (thus freeing us of any need to postulate a "rational" economic agent) has also received some controversial discussion in the economics literature. This topic will be reviewed in Section III.

After these preliminaries, the central portions of the paper will survey some of the main parallels and divergences in economic and sociobiological reasoning. Since this is written by an economist with only an amateur interest in the biological sciences, attention will be devoted to "what message sociobiology has for economics" rather than to "how we can set the biologists straight."

II. Some Mutual Influences

The most famous example of the influence of an economist upon biological thought is of course the impact of Malthus upon Darwin and Wallace. The codiscoverers of evolution each reported that Malthus' picture of the unremitting pressure of human population upon subsistence provided the key element leading to the idea of evolution by natural selection in the struggle for life.[9] Malthusian ideas of compounded growth also play a role in modern

[8] Marx's "economic interpretation of history" can be regarded as an earlier instance of intellectual imperialism of economics, but its connection with this modern development is limited. Marx's economic interpretation was a *materialistic* one. He contended that the essentially autonomous progress of the methods and organization of material production was decisive for shaping the entirety of social relationships in every era. True or false, this is a *substantive* proposition essentially independent of the *methodological* stance of modern economic imperialists. The latter analyze marriage, fertility, crime, law, revolution, etc., with the tools of economic analysis without necessarily asserting that these patterns of social interaction are determined by "materialistic" considerations (such as the ownership of the means of production) as contended by Marx.

[9] Oddly enough, this example is not really a valid one, for the borrowing was already from biology to economics in Malthus' own thought! Malthus drew his ideas about human populations from a biological generalization attributed to Benjamin Franklin on the first page of the Essay on the Principles of Population: "It is observed by Dr. Franklin that there is no bound to

biological theory. The "Malthusian parameter," as defined by biologists, represents the exponential rate at which a population will grow as limited by its genetic capabilities and constrained by the environment.[10]

In the very recent period a number of biologists have come to make significant use of tools and approaches of economics. Michael T. Ghiselin[11] has urged fellow biologists to adopt the "methodological individualism" of economics in preference to the open or disguised "teleologism" of assuming optimizing behavior on the part of higher-level groupings and species. A few instances of recent biological optimization studies that seem to be consciously modelled upon economic analytical techniques can be cited: (1) Rapport[12] showed that the extent of "predator switching" from one prey species to another in response to changes in relative abundance could be expressed in terms of shapes of the predator's indifference curves and opportunity frontier; (2) Gadgil and Bossert[13] interpreted various characteristics of organisms' life histories—such as the timing and scale of reproductive effort and the determination of survival probabilities at various ages—as the resultant of a balance between "profit" (that is, gain) and "cost" (that is, foregone gain or opportunity cost) in choosing strategies to maximize the Malthusian parameter of population growth. (3) Trivers[14] demonstrated that several aspects of parental behavior, in particular the differing extent in various species of male versus female "investment" in care of offspring, could be explained in terms of differences in the selectional return on investment to the male and female parents (that is, in terms of the comparative propagation of their respective genetic endowments); (4) Cody[15] examined the conditions determining the relative competitive advantages of "generalist" versus "specialist" strategies in the exploitation of a mixed-resource environment. (5) E. O. Wilson[16] employed linear programming models to

the prolific nature of plants or animals but what is made by their crowding and interfering with each other's means of subsistence." See Gertrude Himmelfarb, *supra* note 5, at ch. 7.

[10] The classical definition by R. A. Fisher, The Genetic Theory of Natural Selection, ch. 2 (2nd rev. ed. 1958) as applied by him to a population of mixed ages, corresponds to what the economist would call the *internal rate of return* on investment (the growth rate of invested capital). Fisher, in fact, uses the metaphor of a business loan to explain the concept.

[11] Michael T. Ghiselin, *supra* note 4. See also the review by Harold Demsetz, On Thinking Like an Economist, 1 Paleobiology 216 (1975).

[12] David J. Rapport, An Optimization Model of Food Selection, 105 Am. Naturalist 575 (1971).

[13] Madhav Gadgil & William H. Bossert, Life-Historical Consequences of Natural Selection, 104 Am. Naturalist 1 (1970).

[14] Robert L. Trivers, Parental Investment and Sexual Selection, in Sexual Selection and the Descent of Man, 1871-1971, at 136 (B. Campbell ed. 1972).

[15] Martin L. Cody, Optimization in Ecology, 183 Science 1156 (1974).

[16] Sociobiology, *supra* note 1, at ch. 16.

determine the optimal number and proportion of castes in the division of labor among social insects. (6) Charnov[17] develops an optimality theorem for foraging animals, in which the forager terminates exploitation of a given food patch when the marginal energy intake falls to equality with the average return from the habitat.

But the more significant intellectual influence has been in the other direction, from biology to social science. The success of theories of evolution and natural selection in the biological realm led quickly to the body of thought called "Social Darwinism"—the most characteristic figures being the philosopher Herbert Spencer in England and the economist William Graham Sumner in America. On the scientific level Social Darwinism represented an attempt to explain patterns of social stratification as the consequence of the selection of superior human types and forms of organization through social competition. To a considerable extent, its exponents went on to draw the inference that such existing stratification was therefore ethically *justified*. The political unpalatability of this conclusion has led to an exceptionally bad press for Social Darwinism—at the hands of other social scientists, jurists, and philosophers, as economists after Sumner have scarcely discussed the question. The Social Darwinists, or some of them at least, did confuse descriptive with moral categories so as to attribute excessive beneficence to natural selection on the human level. In the real world, we know, success *may* sometimes be the reward of socially functional behavior, but also sometimes of valueless or disruptive activities like monopolization, crime, or most of what is carried on under the heading of politics.

It would be incorrect to assume that Darwinism is necessarily conservative in its social implications. The implications would seem to be radical or conservative according as emphasis is placed upon the necessity and importance of mutability and change (*evolution*) or upon final states of harmonious adaptation as a result of selection (*equilibrium*).[18] Similarly, racist and imperialist theories, on the one hand, and pacifist and universalist theories, on the other hand, could both be founded on Darwinian ideas.[19] The first would emphasize the role of ongoing struggle, and the latter the role of social instinct and mutual aid, in promoting selection of human types. And even among those for whom the key lesson of Darwinism is the competitive struggle for survival, there are a variety of interpretations, ranging from individualistic versions of Spencer and Sumner to a number of collectivist

[17] Eric L. Charnov, Optimal Foraging: The Marginal Value Theorem, 9 Theoret. Pop. Biology 129 (1976).

[18] On this see R. C. Lewontin, 5 Int'l Encycl. Soc. Sci., Evolution: The Concept of Evolution 202 (1968).

[19] See Richard Hofstadter, Social Darwinism in American Thought ch. 9 (rev. ed. 1955) and, especially, Gertrude Himmelfarb, *supra* note 5, at ch. 19.

versions: the idea of superior or fitter social classes (Karl Marx), or systems of law and government (Bagehot),[20] or of course racial groups.[21]

In the spectrum of opinion that went under the name of social Darwinism almost every variety of belief was included. In Germany, it was represented chiefly by democrats and socialists; in England by conservatives. It was appealed to by nationalists as an argument for a strong state, and by the proponents of laissez-faire as an argument for a weak state. It was condemned by some as an aristocratic doctrine designed to glorify power and greatness, and by others, like Nietzsche, as a middle-class doctrine appealing to the mediocre and submissive. Some socialists saw in it the scientific validation of their doctrine; others the negation of their moral and spiritual hopes. Militarists found in it the sanction of war and conquest, while pacifists saw the power of physical force transmuted into the power of intellectual and moral persuasion.[22]

But the too-total rejection of Social Darwinism has meant a lack of appreciation of its valid core of scientific insights: (1) that individuals, groups, races, and even social arrangements (democracy versus dictatorship, capitalism versus socialism, small states versus large) are in never-ending competition with one another, and while the results of this competition have no necessary correlation with moral desert, the competition itself is a fact with explanatory power for social phenomena; (2) that the behavior of mankind is strongly influenced by the biological heritage of the species, and that the forces tending toward either cooperation or conflict among men are in large part identical with phenomena observable in the biological realm.

The sweeping rejection of biological categories for the explanation of human phenomena, on the part of social scientists, is strikingly evidenced by the concluding paragraph of Hofstadter's influential and penetrating study:

Whatever the course of social philosophy in the future, however, a few conclusions are now accepted by most humanists: that such biological ideas as the "survival of the fittest," whatever their doubtful value in natural science, are utterly useless in attempting to understand society; that the life of man in society, while it is incidentally a biological fact, has characteristics that are not reducible to biology and must be explained in the distinctive terms of a cultural analysis; that the physical well-being of men is a result of their social organization and not vice versa; that social improvement is a product of advances in technology and social organization, not of breeding or selective elimination; that judgements as to the value of competition between men or enterprises or nations must be based upon social and not allegedly biological consequences; and, finally, that there is nothing in nature or a naturalistic philosophy

[20] Walter Bagehot, Physics and Politics (1st Borzoi ed. 1948) (1st ed. 1875).

[21] Gertrude Himmelfarb, *supra* note 5, at 407. The subtitle of the Origin of Species is "The Preservation of Favoured Races in the Struggle for Life," and there is no doubt that Darwin himself applied this conception to the competition among races of mankind.

[22] *Id.* at 407.

of life to make impossible the acceptance of moral sanctions that can be employed for the common good.[23]

This statement is on solid ground in rejecting attempts to draw moral claims from biological premises. But it promotes confusion in confounding these claims with—and therefore rejecting out of hand—the entirely scientific contention that man's biological endowment has significant implications for his social behavior.

Following Nicholson,[24] Darwinian evolution involves four main factors: the occurrence of *variations*, some mechanism of *inheritance* to preserve variations, the Malthusian tendency to *multiplication* (leading sooner or later to *competition* among organisms), and finally environmental *selection*. From this broad point of view it is clear that there may be cultural evolution even apart from any biological change. Hofstadter seems to regard the forms of human association and the patterns of human social and cultural change as almost entirely free of biological determinants—apart, presumably, from permanent human characteristics like degree of intelligence which determine and constrain the *possibilities* of cultural advance. In contrast, the sociobiological point of view is that cultural and biological change cannot be so totally dichotomized; cultural tracking of environmental change is a group-behavioral form of adaptation, which interacts in a variety of ways with genetic and populational responses.[25] There is cultural evolution even in the nonhuman sphere, as animals discover successful patterns of behavior which then spread by learning and imitation. Apart from the direct implications for population composition (those individuals who succeed in learning more efficient behavior survive in greater numbers), there may be genetic consequences in that the behavioral changes may modify the conditions of selection among genetic mutations and recombinations.[26]

Along this line, the anthropologist Alland[27] emphasizes that culture itself should be regarded as a kind of biological adaptation. And there is a long tradition among biologists which encourages attention to the implications of human biological origins for social behavior and institutions. Among the important recent instances are J. Huxley, Fisher, Dobzhansky, Lorenz, Tiger and Fox, and of course E. O. Wilson.[28] On the more popular level are

[23] Richard Hofstadter, *supra* note 19, at 204.

[24] A. J. Nicholson, The Role of Population Dynamics in Natural Selection, in 1 Evolution After Darwin: The Evolution of Life 477 (S. Tax & C. Calender eds. 1960).

[25] See Sociobiology, *supra* note 1, at 145.

[26] Ernst Mayr, The Emergence of Evolutionary Novelties, in 1 Evolution After Darwin, *supra* note 24, at 349, 371.

[27] Alexander Alland, Jr., Evolution and Human Behavior ch. 9 (1967).

[28] Julian S. Huxley, The Living Thoughts of Darwin (rev. ed. 1958); R. A. Fisher, *supra* note 10; Theodosius Dobzhansky, Mankind Evolving (1962); Konrad Lorenz, On Aggression (Mar-

such works as Ardrey (1961 and 1970) and Morris.[29] But these ideas have won relatively little acceptance among social scientists.

Turning now to economics, the relevance of quasi-biological (selectional) models has been the topic of controversial discussion since Alchian's paper in 1950.[30] Alchian argued that environmental selection ("adoption") could replace the traditional analysis premised upon rational profit-maximizing behavior ("adaptation") as a source of verifiable predictions about visible characteristics of business firms. This discussion, which has interesting parallels within biology proper, will be reviewed next.

III. Biological Models of the Firm: Optimization Versus Selection

Alchian contended that optimization on the part of the business firm (profit maximization in the traditional formulation) was an unnecessary and even unhelpful idea for purposes of scientific explanation and prediction. While profit is undoubtedly the firm's goal, the substantive content of profit *maximization* as a guiding rule erodes away when it is realized that any actual choice situation always involves profit as a probability distribution rather than as a deterministic variable.[31] And even if firms never attempted to *maximize profit* but behaved purely randomly, the environment would nevertheless select ("adopt") relatively correct decisions in the sense of meeting the *positive realized profit* condition of survival.[32] Without assuming profit maximization, therefore, the economist can nevertheless predict that relatively correct (viable) adaptations or decisions will tend to be the ones observed—for example, the employment of low-skilled workers becomes less viable a practice after imposition of a minimum-wage law.

Enke[33] expanded on Alchian's discussion, with a significant shift in point of view. He suggested that, *given sufficient intensity of competition*, all policies save the optimum would in time fail the survival test. As firms pursuing successful policies expand and multiply, absorbing a larger fraction of the market, a higher and higher standard of behavior becomes the mini-

---

jorie Wilson trans. 1966); Lionel Tiger & Robin Fox, The Imperial Animal (1971); Sociobiology, *supra* note 1.

[29] Robert Ardrey, African Genesis (1961); *id.*, The Social Contract (1970); Desmond Morris, The Naked Ape (1967).

[30] Armen A. Alchian, Uncertainty, Evolution, and Economic Theory, 58 J. Pol. Econ. 211 (1950), reprinted in Armen A. Alchian, Economic Forces at Work 15 (1977).

[31] *Id.* at 212.

[32] *Id.* at 217.

[33] Stephen Enke, On Maximizing Profits: A Distinction Between Chamberlin and Robinson, 41 Am. Econ. Rev. 566, 571 (1951).

mum criterion for competitive survival. ***In the long run, viability dictates optimality.*** Consequently, for long-run predictive purposes (under conditions of intense competition), the analyst is entitled to assume that firms behave "as if" optimizing.

"As if" optimization is of course what the biologist ordinarily has in mind in postulating that organisms (or, sometimes, genes or populations) "choose" strategies leading to evolutionary success. Two levels of the optimization metaphor in biology may be distinguished. First, there are axes along which the organism can be regarded as having a degree of actual choice (what size of territory to defend, how much effort to devote to the struggle for a mate, what intensity of parental care to confer upon offspring). Here we speak only of "as if" optimizing because we do not credit the animal with the intelligence necessary for true (nonmetaphorical) optimization. Secondly, there are axes along which the organism cannot exercise choice in any meaningful sense at all (whether or not to be an unpalatable insect, whether or not to be a male or a female). Nevertheless, such is the power of selection that the optimization metaphor often seems workable for "choice" of biological characters even on this second level.

There is, however, a serious problem here not yet adequately treated in either economics or biology. If, as applies in almost all interesting cases, the strategic choice is *among probability distributions,* what is the "optimum"? According to what criterion does natural selection select when strategies have uncertain outcomes?

In evolutionary theory, the "as if" criterion of success (the maximand) is generally postulated to be *fitness*: the ratio of offspring numbers to parent numbers at corresponding points in the generational life cycle.[34] In a deterministic situation, no doubt it is better adaptive strategy to choose higher fitness over lower. (Or, translating from metaphorical to literal language, in the long run the environment will be filled by those types of organisms who have developed and passed on to descendants traits permitting higher multiplication ratios.) But what if the situation is not deterministic, so that some or all of the strategies available generate probability distributions rather than definite deterministic numbers for the fitness ratio? In such circumstances the strategy that is optimal in terms of *mean* fitness—that yields the highest mathematical expectation of offspring per parent—might be quite different from the strategy that rates highest in terms of viability (that minimizes the probability of extinction). Where such a conflict arises, some biologists have suggested that viability considerations dominate over mean fitness.[35]

[34] See R. A. Fisher, *supra* note 10, at 37; Edward O. Wilson & William H. Bossert, A Primer of Population Biology 51, 73-76 (1971).

[35] See, for example, George C. Williams, Adaptation and Natural Selection 106 (1966).

No solution to this general problem in evolution theory will be offered here.[36] The point to be underlined is that Enke envisaged a situation where the outcome of each alternative policy option for the firm is *objectively* deterministic, although *subjectively* uncertain from the point of view of the firm's decision-maker (acting under limited information). Under these conditions there really does exist an objectively optimum course of action leading to maximum profit, which intense competition (even in the absence of knowledge) ultimately enforces—in Enke's view—upon all surviving firms. Alchian sometimes seems to have the same idea.[37] In saying that *maximum* realized profits is meaningful while *maximizing* profit is not, he means that one cannot "maximize" a probability distribution representing subjective uncertainty about profit, but there is nevertheless a deterministic or objective "maximum" of profit that could be attained if the knowledge were available. Usually, however, Alchian seems to have in mind the quite different case in which the outcomes are intrinsically or *objectively* probabilistic, rather than merely subjectively uncertain because of imperfect knowledge. Here there does not exist any unequivocal optimum, and Enke's argument does not apply. For Alchian, it is in such an environment that viability (positive realized profit) becomes the relevant success criterion.

Independent of Alchian's introduction of the viability argument, but parallel in its implications, was Herbert A. Simon's contention[38] that firms are better regarded as "satisficing" than as optimizing. Starting from a psychological rather than evolutionary orientation, Simon contended that decision-makers are conservative about modifying established routines yielding satisfactory results—unless forced to do so by exogenous changes that threaten unacceptable outcomes. The reason given was informational: the

[36] A number of the complex issues involved may be briefly alluded to. In balancing extinction probability against multiplication ratio, a long-term (multi-generational) point of view must be taken. In any such long-term comparison there will be some prospect of changes in the external environment and even in the genetic constitution of the organism's descendants over time. Even if a high-mean-fitness strategy pays off, the extinction risk being avoided, eventually diminishing-returns constraints (what the biologists call "density-dependent effects") are likely to be encountered—so that the one-generation high-multiplication ratio cannot be indefinitely maintained. On both these grounds the probability distribution for "fitness" measured in terms of a *single* generation's multiplication ratio may give misleading results. A high extinction probability is more acceptable if descendants will spread into a number of different environments or otherwise diversify so that the extinction risks have a degree of independence of one another. In this case, while many lines of descent may be extinguished, others are likely to survive and multiply. Finally, flexibility is an important consideration; a very advantageous strategy might include a capacity to mutate between high-mean-fitness and low-extinction-probability characters over time.

[37] Armen A. Alchian, *supra* note 30, at 212.

[38] Herbert A. Simon, A Behavioral Model of Rational Choice, 69 Q. J. Econ. 99 (1955); *id.*, Theories of Decision-Making in Economics and Behavioral Science, 49 Am. Econ. Rev. 253 (1959).

decision-maker who recognizes the inadequacy of his knowledge, or the costs of performing the computations necessary for determining optimality even if he had all the relevant data, does not find that it pays even to attempt to optimize.[39] Simon did allow for a long-run approach toward optimization under stationary conditions in the form of a gradual shift of the decision-maker's "aspiration level" toward the best outcome attainable. But, he emphasized, business decisions take place in a context of ever-recurring change; the process of gradual approximation of optimality can never progress very far before being confounded by events. Thus, for Simon as for Alchian, the environment primarily plays a selective role in rewarding choice of *viable* strategies. Simon, in contrast with Alchian, chooses to emphasize how this process has in effect been internalized into the psychology of decision-makers.

A closely related aspect of the optimizing-selection process is the question of "perfection." It is possible in evolutionary models alternatively to emphasize the *achieved state of adaptation*, or the *process of adaptive change* toward that state. In the biological realm a high state of perfection on the organismic level has been attained: ". . . organisms in general are, in fact, marvellously and intricately adapted, both in their internal mechanisms, and in their relations to external nature."[40] The high degree of perfection is evidenced by the fact that the vast majority of mutations, which follow a random law, are harmful to the organism rather than beneficial. An important and less obvious consequence of the high degree of perfection is that the environment, as it changes under a variety of random influences, is always (from the organism's viewpoint) tending to deteriorate. So even relatively well-adapted organisms, or particularly such organisms, require the ability to track environmental changes. In the economic sphere, in contrast, we do not—though perhaps we should—think in terms of a very high degree of perfection in the adaptations of individuals or firms.[41] The argument in terms of perfection has been at the heart of much of the critical discussion of the biological model in economics.

[39] Of course, behavior might be optimized *subject to these informational constraints*. While it seems possible to adopt such an interpretation, there may be operational or even logical difficulties in calculating "the optimal amount of departure from optimality" See Sidney G. Winter, Optimization and Evolution in the Theory of the Firm, in Adaptive Economic Models 73, 81-85 (Richard H. Day & Theodore Graves eds. 1975).

[40] R. A. Fisher, *supra* note 10, at 44.

[41] But note that a high degree of such "selfish" adaptation, on the part of private economic agents, need not imply optimality of the Invisible-Hand variety on the *social* level. Similarly in the biological domain, perfection on the level of the organism does not imply that the entire biota, or even smaller aggregates like single species, have been optimally adapted to the environment. See Gordon Tullock, Biological Externalities, 33 J. Theoret. Biology 565 (1971); Michael T. Ghiselin, *supra* note 4. This point will be discussed further below.

Penrose[42] criticized Alchian by contending, in effect, that the achieved state of economic adaptation is generally *too perfect* to be accounted for by merely random behavior on the part of businessmen. Although high states of adaptation are indeed attained in the biological sphere even without rational optimizing, that is due, she argued, to the extreme intensity of competition forced by organisms' innate urge to multiply—the Malthusian principle. This urge being lacking in the economic sphere, and competition therefore less intense, the businessman's purposive drive to make money is required to supply the analogous driving force.[43]

Of course, the *desire* to make money is not enough. The key point of the Penrose criticism is that this desire must, for the most part, be realized. Businessmen must expect to be successful if they are to enter the competitive arena. And any such expectation would be too regularly refuted to persist if actual outcomes realized were no better than would ensue from random action. So the Penrose image is one of a changing environment (else there would not be much in the way of profit opportunities) very effectively tracked by rationally optimizing businessmen.

The selectional processes of Nature, driven by random variation and Malthusian competition, are profligately wasteful of life and energy.[44] An implication of the Penrose thesis is that the wastage cost of economic selection should be considerably less than that of biological selection.[45] Quantitative estimates of the selectional wastage cost (bankruptcies, abandonments, etc.) would be of interest, therefore, in providing some measure of the prevalence and success of rational optimization.[46]

While Penrose argued that the observed degree of adaptation in the econ-

[42] Edith Tilton Penrose, Biological Analogies in the Theory of the Firm, 42 Am. Econ. Rev. 804, 812 (1952); *id.*, Biological Analogies in the Theory of the Firm: Rejoinder, 43 Am. Econ. Rev. 603 (1953).

[43] Edith Tilton Penrose, Biological Analogies in the Theory of the Firm (1952), *supra* note 42, at 812.

[44] See J. B. S. Haldane, The Cost of Natural Selection, 55 J. Genetics 511 (1957); William Feller, On Fitness and the Cost of Natural Selection, 9 Genetical Research 1 (1967).

[45] Not all biological adaptive mechanisms are random in their working, however. Mutations and genetic combinations are completely random, but patterns of activity (for example, feeding, mating) often are not. Even lower animals display simple purposive behavior, such as escape maneuvers when threatened. And there is a great deal of adaptive *learning* on the nonhuman level.

[46] To some extent, market experiments—while failing to capture the full richness and variety of economic environments—do provide insights as to the rapidity of convergence to optimal solutions. Vernon L. Smith, Experimental Economics: Induced Value Theory, 66 Am. Econ. Rev., pt. 2, at 274 (Papers & Proceedings, May 1976), in surveying such experiments is generally quite impressed by the ability of experimental subjects to approximate optimal (rather than merely viable) behavior. Experiments on economic choices even on the part of animals provide evidence of a considerable degree of "rationality". John H. Kagel, Howard Rachlin, Leonard Green, Raymond C. Battalio, Robert L. Basmann & W. R. Klenn, Experimental Studies of Consumer Demand Behavior Using Laboratory Animals, 13 Econ. Inquiry 22 (1975).

omy is *too perfect* to be accounted for by blind environmental selection, Winter's critique[47] is based on the opposite contention—that the state of adaptation is *too imperfect* to be accounted for by a process that leads to the same outcomes "as if" firms actually optimized. His argument is therefore directed against Enke's extension of the selectional model, against the idea that in the long run viability requires optimality, rather than against Alchian's original version. The main evidence of imperfection cited by Winter is the prevalence in business practice of conventional rules of thumb (for example, a pricing policy of fixed percentage markups) even where seemingly in conflict with profit-maximizing behavior.[48]

Winter contributed interesting suggestions about the nature of *inheritance* and *variation* in economic selectional models. For Alchian, the inherited aspect of the firm was described as "fixed internal conditions"[49]—in effect, simple inertia due to the fact that the firm is more or less the same from one day to the next. Variation was attributed to imitation of successful firms,[50] or simply to trial-and-error exploration. For Winter the inherited element, analogous to the biological genotype, is represented by certain more permanent aspects of the firm (its "decision rule"). This is to be distinguished from the specific decision made in a given context, which is analogous to the biological phenotype. What the environment selects is the correct action, even though it be the chance result of a rather inferior decision rule. In natural selection as well, well-adapted and less well-adapted genotypes might be represented at a given moment by the same phenotype. But, over a number of generations, natural selection working together with the Mendelian laws of inheritance will tend to fix the superior genotype in the population.[51] The economic mechanism of repeated trials is somewhat different, as no genetic recombination is involved. But surely we can expect that, as a variety of selectional tests are imposed over time, those firms providing a merely lucky action-response to a particular environmental configuration will tend to be selected against as compared with those following a more correct decision rule.[52]

[47] Sidney G. Winter, Jr., Economic "Natural Selection" and the Theory of the Firm, 4 Yale Econ. Essays 225 (1964); *id.*, Satisficing, Selection, and the Innovating Remnant, 85 Q. J. Econ. 237 (1971); *id.*, *supra* note 39.

[48] Sidney G. Winter, Jr., Satisficing, *supra* note 46, at 241.

[49] Armen A. Alchian, *supra* note 30, at 216.

[50] And "innovation" to imperfect imitation that happens to be successful!

[51] Suppose a dominant allele A at a certain gene locus is the superior type, and the recessive allele a is inferior. Then the heterozygote Aa will be represented by the same phenotype (and so be subjected in the current generation to the same selection) as the homozygote AA. But in the next and succeeding generations, the descendants of AA will on the average do better than those of Aa—ultimately extinguishing the inferior allele.

[52] Winter appears to doubt this. Sidney G. Winter, *supra* note 39, at 97; *id.*, Economic "Natural Selection", *supra* note 46, at 257-58.

In his first article Winter employed the term "organization form" for what his later papers call "decision rule" or "rule of action." While the intended referent is the same, and is indeed better described by the words "decision rule" or "rule of action," the initial term had interesting implications that might well have been pursued. "Organization form" would ordinarily be understood to mean something like corporation or partnership, large firm or small, etc. This is a more visible and operational concept than "decision rule." Since even the best decision rule (in the usual sense of that term) might not make possible survival of a firm with an ill-adapted organization form, we should really think of three levels of selection—action, decision rule, and organization form.[53]

The broadly similar views of Alchian and Winter represent, it might be noted, a Lamarckian evolutionary model. Lamarck believed (as did Darwin) that acquired characters can be inherited, and also that variations tend to appear when needed. Failure-stimulated search for new rules of action (Winter), taking in particular the form of imitation of observed success (Alchian), is—if the results are assumed to be heritable—certainly in the spirit of Lamarck. The Lamarckian model is inapplicable to inheritance and variation (whether somatic or behavioral) mediated by the *genetic* mechanism, but it seems to be broadly descriptive of *cultural* evolution in general, and of economic responses in particular.[54]

Perhaps Winter's most important contribution in this area is his actual modelling of possible *selectional equilibrium* situations. Space does not permit adequate exposition or review of these formulations here, but the following summary may be suggestive:

> Those organization forms which have the lowest zero growth price are viable, others are not. Or, to put the matter another way, price will tend to the lowest value at which some firm's organization form still yields non-negative growth. Firms whose organization forms result in decline at that price will approach zero scale as time goes on, leaving the firms which have the minimum zero growth price to share the market.[55]

This language suggests the "long run zero-profit equilibrium" of the competitive industry, reinterpreted in terms of the biologists' population equilibrium condition of zero growth. But Winter is at pains to show that even a

[53] George J. Stigler, The Economies of Scale, 1 J. Law & Econ. 54 (1958) employed, though without placing any emphasis upon biological analogies, a selectional model called *the survivor principle* to draw inferences about efficient plant and firm sizes in a variety of industries. The same method could evidently be applied to other firm characteristics that could be described as "organizational forms."

[54] Since behavioral changes, by modifying the conditions of selection, may *lead* to changes in genetic compositions of populations, to a degree Lamarckism plays a role even in the modern theory of genetic evolution. See C. H. Waddington, The Nature of Life ch. 4 (1961).

[55] Sidney G. Winter, Economic "Natural Selection", *supra* note 46, at 253.

firm with the lowest possible zero-growth price (lowest minimum of Average Total Cost curves) might—as a result of using an inappropriate decision rule—not actually be a survivor in selectional equilibrium. So the traditional competitive equilibrium might not be generated, or, once generated, might not respond in the standard way to changes in exogenous determinants.[56] One reason for this divergence from the traditional result, however, is that Winter's model is limited to the single adjustment mechanism of *firm growth*. Among the factors not considered, *entry pressure* on the part of new firms and (a more surprising omission in view of the previous emphasis) *failure-stimulated search* on the part of unsuccessful existing firms would tend to force a progressively higher state of adaptation upon survivors.

In his 1971 article Winter indicates that in order to achieve the optimality properties of the standard competitive model an "innovating remnant" is needed. This category consists of firms that are, for unexplained reasons, inveterate searchers who will ultimately hit upon any as-yet-undiscovered superior decision rules.[57] But new entrants, upon whom standard theory relies to discipline firms already in the industry, can also serve this exploratory role. A fruitful approach, consistent with biological observation, would be to recognize that one of the many possible survival strategies adopted by organisms (firms) is a tendency to search—and at any moment of time there will be a balance between organisms searching for new niches and organisms adapting to existing ones. (This point will come up again when competitive strategies are discussed below.)

It is a rather odd accident that biological models entered into economic thought in connection with the theory of the *business firm*—a highly specialized and consciously contrived "cultural" grouping. To some extent, as just seen, evolution theory is applicable to firms: inheritance, variation, competition, selection, adaptation—all play roles in explaining the observed patterns of survivorship and activity. Still, if biological models were being explored afresh for possible relevance to economic behavior, one's first target for consideration would naturally be the *individual* together with the *family*—entities of direct biological significance. Without any preconceived limitation of attention to the business firm, several aspects of economic theorizing will now be examined from a biological orientation: the nature and provenance of preferences; the evolution of patterns of competition, cooperation, and conflict; and resulting tendencies toward equilibrium, cycles, and progressive change.

[56] In a more recent work, Richard R. Nelson & Sidney G. Winter, Neoclassical vs. Evolutionary Theories of Economic Growth: Critique and Prospectus, 84 Econ. J. 886 (1974) have developed simulation models of growth in which firms and industries evolve over time by a selectional process, one not describable as a path of moving equilibrium.

[57] Sidney G. Winter, Satisficing, *supra* note 46, at 247.

IV. Elements of Economic Theorizing: A Biological Interpretation

The contention here is that the social processes studied by economics, or rather by the social sciences collectively, are not mere analogs but are rather *instances* of sociobiological mechanisms—in the same sense in which chemical reactions have been shown to be a special class of processes following the laws of physics.[58] For this to be in any way a useful idea, it remains to be shown that a more general sociobiological outlook can in fact provide social scientists with a deeper and more satisfactory explanation of already-known results, or better still can generate new ones.[59]

A. *Utility, Fitness, and the Provenance of Preferences—Especially, Altruism*

Modern neoclassical economics has forsworn any attempt to study the source and content of preferences, that is, the goals that motivate men's actions. It has regarded itself as the logic of choice under conditions of "given tastes." But many of the great and small social changes in history have stemmed from *shifts* in people's goals for living. The very terminology used by the economist—preferences, wants, tastes—tends not only to trivialize these fundamental aims and values, but implies that they are arbitrary or inexplicable (*de gustibus non est disputandum*). Nor have the other social sciences, to whom the economists have unilaterally delegated the task of studying preferences, made much progress in that regard. The healthy aggrandizing tendency of modern economics requires us, therefore, to overstep this boundary like so many others.

No doubt there is a large arbitrary element in the determination of wants. Individuals are idiosyncratic, and even socially influenced preferences may reflect chance accidents in the histories of particular societies. But it is equally clear that not all preferences for commodities represent "mere taste." When we learn that Alabamans like cooling drinks more than Alaskans do, it is not hard to decipher the underlying physiological explanation for such differences in "tastes." Unfortunately, the refusal of modern economics to examine the biological functions of preferences[60] has meant that the bridge

[58] Compare Alexander Alland, Jr., *supra* note 27, at 194-97 and Edward O. Wilson, Biology and the Social Sciences, *supra* note 1.

[59] And, of course, it is possible that the more general science of sociobiology might benefit from results independently achieved in the special fields of the human sciences.

[60] Recent reformulations of consumer theory by Kelvin J. Lancaster, A New Approach to Consumer Theory, 74 J. Pol. Econ. 132 (1966) and Gary S. Becker, A Theory of the Allocation of Time, 75 Econ. J. 493 (1965) treat commodities as packages of more fundamental characteris-

between human physiology and social expressions of desires has been studied by no one (except, perhaps, by practitioners of empirical "human engineering").

On a very abstract level, the concept of *homeostasis* has been put forward as the foundation of wants: the individual is postulated as acting to maintain vital internal variables within certain limits necessary for optimum functioning, or at least for survival.[61] But homeostasis is too limited a goal to describe more than very short-run human adaptations. And in any case, the internal "production function" connecting these internal variables with external social behavior has somehow fallen outside the domain of any established field of research.

Of more critical importance to social science than tastes for ordinary commodities are preferences taking the form of attitudes toward other humans. Anger and envy are evidently antisocial sentiments, while benevolence and group identification promote socialization. Socially relevant attitudes differ from culture to culture: in some societies hierarchical dominance is a prime motive for action, in others not; in some, marital partners value fidelity highly, in others promiscuity is regarded as normal; in some cultures people cluster closely together, in others they avoid personal contact. The programmatic contention here is that such preference patterns, despite seemingly arbitrary elements, have survived because they are mainly adaptive to environmental conditions. (No strong emphasis will be placed upon the issue of whether such adaptations are cultural or genetic in origin, in line with the argument above that the ability to evolve cultural traits is itself a kind of genetic adaptation.) This contention will surely not be always found to hold; in the biology of plants and animals as well, it is often unclear whether a particular morphological or behavioral trait is truly adaptive or merely an accidental variation. Nature is unceasingly fertile in producing random modifications. But if a trait has survived, as a working hypothesis the biologist looks for an adaptive function.[62]

As a nice example, in a famous passage in *The Descent of Man* Darwin asserted that for hive bees the instinct of maternal hatred rather than maternal love serves an adaptive function. He went on to generalize that, for animals in general (and not excluding mankind), "sentiments" or social attitudes are but a mechanism of adaptation.[63] The anthropologist Ronald

---

tics which constitute the true desired entities. But without a biological interpretation, this reformulation merely pushes the arbitrariness of tastes one step farther back.

[61] Richard H. Day, Adaptive Processes and Economic Theory, in Adaptive Economic Models, *supra* note 39, at 1.

[62] Though whether the function is adaptive to the individual only, or alternatively to some larger social group to which he belongs, may remain subject to controversy.

[63] Michael T. Ghiselin, *supra* note 4, at 218-19. Adam Smith, it might be noted, argued that

Cohen[64] has similarly pointed to variations among cultures in degrees of "affect" (that is, of interpersonal emotional attachment) as adaptive responses to environmental circumstances.

The biological approach to preferences, to what economists call the utility function, postulates that all such motives or drives or tastes represent proximate aspects of a single underlying goal—fitness. Preferences are governed by the all-encompassing *drive for reproductive survival*. This might seem at first absurd. That all humans do not solely and totally regard themselves as children-making machines seems evidenced by phenomena such as birth control, abortion, and homosexuality. Or, if these be considered aberrations, by the large fractions of income and effort devoted to human aims that compete with child-rearing—among them entertainment, health care beyond the childbearing age, personal intellectual advancement, etc. Yet, all these phenomena might still be indirectly instrumental to fitness. Birth control may be a device leading *on net balance* to more descendants rather than fewer; health care beyond the childbearing age may more effectively promote the survival and vigor of children or grandchildren. And, as we shall see shortly, even a childlessness strategy *may* be explicable in fitness terms!

In any attempt to broaden the application of economic reasoning, to make it a general social science, a key issue is the problem of altruism (the "taste" for helping others): its extent, provenance, and determinants. Old-fashioned, narrow economics was often criticized for employing the model of economic man—a selfish, calculating, and essentially nonsocial being.[65] Of course, it was impossible to postulate such a man in dealing with that essential social grouping, *the family*. Neoclassical economics avoided the difficulty by abandoning attempts to explain intrafamily interactions! Some economists formalized this evasion by taking the household rather than the individual as the fundamental *unit* of economic activity; in effect, they postulated total altruism within and total selfishness outside the family.

Modern economic "imperialists" have been dissatisfied both with the excessively restrictive postulate of individual selfishness and with the exclusion of intrafamily behavior from the realm of economic analysis. The modern view postulates a generalized preference or utility function in which selfishness is only the midpoint of a spectrum ranging from benevolence at one extreme to malevolence at the other.[66] But, standing alone, this is really

the desires (or passions, appetites, or sentiments) driving men have been implanted (as by a wise Providence) to promote the survival of the species. See R. H. Coase, *supra* note 7.

[64] Ronald Cohen, Altruism: Human, Cultural or What?, 2 J. Soc. Issues, No. 3, at 39, 46-51 (1972).

[65] A criticism quite inapplicable, as already observed, to Adam Smith's view of man. See note 7, *supra*.

[66] See, for example, Gary S. Becker, A Theory of Social Interactions, 82 J. Pol. Econ. 1063 (1974).

an empty generalization. Where any individual happens to lie on the benevolence-malevolence scale with regard to other individuals still remains a merely arbitrary "taste." And yet we all know that patterns of altruism are not merely arbitrary. That a parent is more benevolent to his own child than to a stranger's is surely capable of explanation.

From the evolutionary point of view the great analytical problem of altruism is that, in order to survive the selectional process, altruistic behavior must be profitable in fitness terms. It must somehow be the case that being generous (at least sometimes, to some beneficiaries) is selectively more advantageous than being selfish!

A possible semantic confusion arises here. If altruism were defined simply as accepting injury to self in order to help others, without countervailing benefit of any kind, then indeed natural selection would quickly eliminate altruist behavior. When biologists speak of altruism they do not mean to rule out offsetting or redeeming mechanisms making unselfish behavior profitable in some sense; indeed, their analysis requires that such exist.[67]

The redeeming mechanisms identified by biologists seem to fall into two main categories. In the first, altruistic behavior survives because, despite initial appearances, a fuller analysis shows that *the preponderance of benefit or advantage is really conferred on the self.* We may, though paradoxically, call such behavior "selfish altruism"; being ultimately selfish, such altruism does not require compensation or reciprocity to be viable. In the second class of redeeming mechanism compensation does take place; Trivers[68] has termed such behavior "reciprocal altruism." Reciprocal altruism, apart from motivation, approaches what economists would of course call *exchange*. It will be discussed, in connection with that topic, in Section B following.

The clearest cases of selfish altruism, of behavior only seemingly unselfish, stem from the fact that *in the biological realm there are two levels of self.* On one level is the morphological and physiological constitution of the organism (the phenotype); on the other level the organism's genetic endowment (the genotype). The genetic constitution may contain recessive genes that are not expressed in the phenotype; perhaps even more important, the phenotype is subjected to and modified by environmental influences that leave the genotype unaffected. "Unselfish" action defined as behavior that injures the organism's phenotypical well-being may yet tend to propagate the organism's genotype. Indeed, since all living beings eventually die, ultimately

[67] Still another semantic difficulty is suggested by a remark like the following: "If an individual's utility function has the well-being of another party as argument, there need be no conflict between (selfishly) maximizing utility and (unselfishly) helping the other." Here maximizing utility is taken as the *definition* of selfish behavior, a verbal device that only evades the real substantive issue: to explain *how* it is that aiding others can viably enter an individual's utility function.

[68] Robert L. Trivers, The Evolution of Reciprocal Altruism, 46 Q. Rev. Biology 35 (1971).

the only way to achieve a payoff in fitness terms is to help certain other organisms—most notably, of course, one's offspring—carry one's genetic endowment beyond the death barrier.

The mechanism rewarding this type of altruist behavior is called *kin selection.*[69] Maximization of fitness from the point of view of the genotype often dictates a degree of altruism from the point of view of the phenotype—not only to offspring, but more generally to close relatives. Setting aside a number of qualifications, we might say that any individual should be willing to give his life to save two of his brothers (since full sibs have at least half their genes in common), or four half-brothers, or eight cousins, etc. Put another way, the "as if" maximand governing choice of evolutionary strategy is not the organism's *own* fitness but its *inclusive* fitness—the reproductive survival, with appropriate discounting for distance of relationship, of all those organisms sharing its genetic endowment.

Before proceeding to draw out some of the implications of altruism motivated by kin selection, a word of caution: actual behavior always represents the *interaction* of two determining factors—on the one side preferences, on the other side opportunities (constraints). We cannot directly infer altruistic preferences from cooperative behavior; in some environments the limited opportunities available may dictate that even enemies cooperate in the interests of selfish survival. Nor can we directly infer malevolence from hostile behavior; in some environments even brothers may be impelled to fight one another for survival.

Compare parent-to-offspring altruism with sib-to-sib altruism. Parental altruism is behaviorally much the more evident, and yet the degree of kinship (proportion of shared genes) in the two cases is exactly the same! The reason for the difference is that brothers and sisters are ordinarily in much closer *competition* with one another than parents are with children.[70] Why then the famed maternal hatred and sisterly altruism among ants? The explanation is remarkable. Due to the unusual method of sex determination called haplodiploidy, sisters in ant colonies (the queen and worker castes) are more closely related to one another than they are to their own offspring (or would be, if they had offspring)![71] The notoriously lazy male drones, on the other hand, have only the ordinary degree of kinship with other colony members.

Yet it must not be assumed that parents and offspring never compete.

[69] W. D. Hamilton, The Genetical Evolution of Social Behavior I, 7 J. Theoret. Biology 1 (1964).

[70] For many species, the struggle for food or shelter among members of a litter is a matter of life or death.

[71] Robert L. Triver & Hope Hare, Haplodiploidy and the Evolution of the Social Insects, 191 Science 249 (1976).

Each offspring's selfish interest lies in having its parents' full devotion. But the parent aiming at reproductive survival strives for an optimal allocation of care and protection over *all* his or her offspring—past, present, and future. One nice implication is described by Trivers.[72] Intergenerational conflict occurs during the period when additional parental care, still desirable from the offspring's point of view, is no longer optimal for the parent (who must consider his opportunity cost in the form of the potential fitness gain in caring for a new batch of offspring). But the *intensity* of such "weaning conflict" is a function of the offspring's expected degree of relationship with his sibs of the later batch. If an offspring in a promiscuous species foregoes maternal care, his sacrifice will probably operate to the benefit of mere half-sibs; in permanently mating species, to the benefit of full sibs. Hence the prediction, which is in fact confirmed, that offspring will be somewhat less "selfish" (weaning conflict will be less intense) in species following the stable-family pattern.[73]

Another point of interest: why are parents generally more altruistic to offspring than offspring to parents—since the degree of relationship is the same? The reason turns on their disparate *opportunities* for helping one another. The offspring may initially require care simply in order to survive, while the parents usually have energy available over their own immediate survival needs. As the offspring develop self-sustaining capacity over time, parental devotion diminishes. Still another factor is the asymmetry in time. In terms of fitness comparisons, offspring generally have greater "reproductive value," that is, offspring are more efficient at producing future descendants for parents than parents are in producing future relatives (sibs and their descendants) for offspring.[74] This is of course clearest when parents have entirely completed their reproductive activity. And, as seen above, the sibs are likely anyway to be pretty close competitors. Yet, in appropriate biological environments, offspring sometimes do curtail personal reproduction to help parents rear sibs.[75]

What of altruism *within* the parental pair? From the biological viewpoint, alas, the parental partner is just a means to the end of selfish reproductive survival. He or she is undoubtedly to be valued, but only as a kind of specialized livestock! Trivers[76] has explored in detail the mixed cooperative-competitive incentives for parents. Each requires the other to achieve reproductive survival, yet each is motivated to load on to the other

[72] Robert L. Trivers, Parent-Offspring Conflict, 14 Am. Zoologist 249 (1974).

[73] In human polygamous families, full sibs reputedly display greater mutual altruism than half-sibs. But I am unaware of any hard evidence on this point.

[74] R. A. Fisher, *supra* note 10, at 27-30.

[75] Sociobiology, *supra* note 1, at 125.

[76] Robert L. Trivers, *supra* note 14.

a disproportionate share of the burden. The relatively smaller male investment in germ cells (sperm vs. egg) tends to lead to desertion, promiscuity, or to polygyny as ways for males to maximize numbers of descendants. The female, having already made a substantial somatic commitment in each reproductive episode, is less well placed than her mate to refuse additional parental commitment. (Females sometimes have means of cheating through cuckoldry, however.) The actual expression of one or more of these nonaltruistic tendencies depends upon the specific opportunities provided by the environmental situations of each species. There are situations in which parental pairs are models of mutual devotion, most notably in difficult environments where the survival of offspring requires full concentrated teamwork on the part of both parents.[77]

Let us now go beyond the kin-selection mechanism favoring altruism directed at close relatives. Wynne-Edwards[78] propounded the broader view that altruistic behavior may be favorably selected because it promotes the good of the species as a whole even though adverse to individual fitness—an example being voluntary restriction of number of offspring in times of food scarcity. Or, more generally, it has been argued that in environments where within-group altruism strongly promotes group success (as will often be the case), altruism tends to evolve through a process of *group selection*. For example, ant colonies that cooperate more efficiently will thrive and multiply, in comparison with colonies whose altruism is not so fully developed.

But biologists recognize a serious difficulty here, equivalent to what economists call a "free-rider problem." To wit, the bearer of a gene dictating altruistic behavior tends to be negatively selected *within* his group as against fellow group members who are nonaltruists. Thus, *individual* selection opposes *group* selection; the altruistic groups may thrive, but always tend to become less and less altruistic while doing so. Even if the altruist groups drive all others to extinction, they themselves tend to end up nonaltruistic.

One important consideration might make it appear, at first sight, that the argument for selection of *kin-directed* altruism (that it is really selfish behavior, genotypically speaking) extends with almost equal force to broader within-group altruism—and indeed, even to cooperation on the level of the species as a whole. There is a strong degree of relationship (in the sense of correlation of genetic endowments) even among "unrelated" members of the same species. At many, or even the great majority of loci, genes are *fixed* in any given species;[79] everyone has both genes in common at any such locus. So even individuals chosen at random in a species may well share 70 or 80 per cent of their genetic endowments.

[77] Sociobiology, *supra* note 1, at 330.

[78] V. C. Wynne-Edwards, Animal Dispersion in Relation to Social Behavior (1962).

[79] R. A. Fisher, *supra* note 10, at 137.

This fact would seem to imply a very heavy "selfish" payoff, genotypically speaking, for altruistic behavior toward any conspecifics whatsoever. (And, of course, the correlation will tend to be closer, and so the payoff greater, within localized social groupings having any degree of inbreeding.) The flaw in this argument is that group selection for altruistic behavior is not governed by *overall* correlations of genetic endowments, but by the presence or absence of the *specific* gene or genes determining altruist behavior. The "free-rider problem" operates equally effectively to favor noncarriers of the altruist gene, whether or not the individuals concerned otherwise have high or low correlations of genetic endowments. The altruist gene, metamorphically speaking, only "wants" to help *its* close relatives—organisms likely to be bearing the same specific gene. Given that the altruist gene is initially rare, it is highly unlikely that both parents carry it. Thus there is only a 50 per cent chance that one's full brother is a fellow carrier, and essentially no chance that a random conspecific is.

Still, it remains true that, from the point of view of the organism's overall genotype, altruism has a higher value for promoting fitness the higher the genetic correlation with the beneficiary. The mechanism governing the spread of the specific altruist gene might be thought of as the "supply" factor, with the overall genotypical benefit as the "demand" factor, in the process. The idea is that the free-rider problem is more likely to be overcome the greater the benefit from doing so.[80]

Two different types of process for overcoming the free-rider problem seem to have been identified by biologists: genetic drift, and group dispersal-reassortment. Genetic drift refers to variation of gene frequencies due simply to random fluctuations in the process of genetic recombination associated with mating. It may so happen that, despite the free-rider factor acting systematically to reduce within-group frequency of the altruist gene, by sheer random fluctuation the gene may nevertheless become fixed in the group.[81] Once every member of the mating group possesses *only* altruist genes, there can be no within-group selection against altruists (unless the nonaltruist gene is reintroduced by mutation or by entry of outsiders.) Such a development is highly improbable, unless the group is very small. And yet, Nature's experiments over time have been so unimaginably numerous that the improbable does happen from time to time. The improbability is sharply reduced for colonial species that "bud off" mating pairs to found new colonies.[82] Here the altruist gene need only become fixed from time to time in a minimally-sized group—a mating pair. Such a pair may then found a colony

[80] I am indebted to Joel Guttman for this point.

[81] J. Maynard Smith, Group Selection and Kin Selection, 201 Nature 1145 (1964).

[82] R. C. Lewontin, The Units of Selection, 1 Ann. Rev. Ecology & Systematics 1, 13-14 (1970).

which will be favorably group-selected in competition with other colonies. With successive "buddings off" from such a thriving colony, the altruist genes may spread and eventually preponderate.

The second process, often mixed with the first, involves regular dispersal and reassortment of groups having larger and smaller proportions of altruist genes.[83] *Within* each of the two classes of groups, prevalence of the altruist gene is progressively reduced by individual selection. Yet, if the collective advantage of altruist behavior is sufficiently large, it may be that groups with larger altruist representation increase in numbers so much relative to the others that the *overall* representation of the altruist gene increases in the population at large. If the groups regularly disperse and reassort themselves at some stage in the life cycle, this process can continue. (Failing dispersal and reassortment, on the other hand, individual selection will ultimately tend to drive out the altruist genes.)

A quite different sort of altruistic behavior, not necessarily involving close kin or even fellow carriers of the altruist gene, still falls into the selfish category. An instance appears in the development of alarm calls in birds.[84] A caller who alerts the flock to a predator, it is hypothesized, is thereby subjected to a higher risk (by attracting attention to itself). This behavior can be viable in fitness terms in certain circumstances, provided that it is only *comparatively* (not absolutely) disadvantageous to the caller. Thus, the altruism is merely *incidental* to selfish behavior. (The alarm may discourage the predator entirely or at least reduce his efficiency, so that the caller benefits on balance.) Still, under such "incidental altruism" even the *comparative* disadvantage tends to lead to elimination of the altruistic caller types by natural selection in favor of other group members (free riders). The saving feature here is that flocks are fluid, ever-changing aggregations. The caller gets only a small benefit, but gets it every time; the noncaller occasionally gets a big benefit from a free ride, but otherwise loses by refraining from calling. This tends to lead to an interior solution with a mixed population of callers and noncallers, for as the callers increase in numbers, the marginal advantage of being a noncaller (receiving more free rides) increases.[85]

Incidental altruism of the alarm-call type is an instance of what economists would term the *private provision of a public good.* Olson[86] argues that

[83] David Sloan Wilson, A Theory of Group Selection, 72 Proc. Nat'l Acad. Sci. USA 143 (1975).

[84] Robert L. Trivers, *supra* note 67, at 43-44.

[85] Eric L. Charnov & John R. Krebs, The Evolution of Alarm Calls: Altruism or Manipulation, 109 Am. Naturalist 107 (1975) [letter to the ed.].

[86] Mancur Olson, Jr., The Logic of Collective Action ch. 1 (Harv. Econ. Stud., vol. 124, 1965).

such a provision is more likely to be found in small groups, and particularly so where there are size or taste disparities within the group. (The larger members, or of course the more desirous ones, are the most motivated to provide the public good; the smaller, or the less desirous, are more likely to be the free riders.) Buchanan[87] has a somewhat different analysis, showing that substantial amounts of the public good might be provided even without such disparities. For Buchanan the main factor is the wealth enhancement that each group member derives from the purchase of the public good by others. On the one hand such purchases by others impel him to cut back his own purchases (the free-rider effect), but on the other hand the wealth enhancement stops him from cutting back all the way to zero (income effect).

Summing up, we have seen how altruistic behavior may prove to be viable in selectional terms even in the absence of any reciprocation. Over the course of human and pre-human evolutionary development, drives or instincts promoting such behavior have evolved and ultimately taken the form that the economist so inadequately calls preferences. And what is true for the specific "taste for altruism" holds in considerable degree for preferences in general—that these are not arbitrary or accidental, but rather the resultants of systematic evolutionary processes. This does not mean that such attitudes are now immutable. On the contrary, the inbuilt drives themselves contain the capability of expressing themselves in diverse ways depending upon environmental circumstances, which will in turn be modified by cultural evolution. The main lesson to be drawn, therefore, is not that preferences are biologically determined in any complete way—but rather, that they are scientifically analyzable and even in principle predictable in terms of the inheritance of past genetic and cultural adaptations together with the new adjustments called for by current environmental circumstances.

B. *Exchange and Other Competitive Strategies*

Exchange, the sole form of social interaction traditionally studied by economists, is a particular competitive strategy in the great game of life—one involving a mutually beneficial relation among two or more organisms. It fits into the more general category called "mutualism" by biologists, of which there are both interspecific and intraspecific examples. Among the former are the symbiosis of alga and fungus that constitutes a lichen, the pollination-nectar exchange between bees and flowers, the presence of nitrogen-fixing bacteria on the roots of leguminous plants, and the resident protozoa in the gut of the termite that facilitate digestion of cellulose. Particularly interesting are the complementary associations among somewhat higher animals, which can be regarded as involving a degree of conscious-

[87] James M. Buchanan, The Demand and Supply of Public Goods (1968).

ness and discretionary choice. Here mutualism approaches the economic concept of exchange.

In the absence of legal enforcement of compensation for acts conferring advantages on others, such patterns of mutual aid in the biological realm may represent instances of altruism on the part of one or more of the participants.[88] A nice example of what Trivers[89] called reciprocal altruism is the interaction wherein certain fish species feed by grooming other, larger species—who in return refrain from eating their cleaners.

The key question for the selectional advantage of such reciprocal aid (in economic terms, for the viability of a pattern of exchange or "market") is control of cheating. As Trivers points out, this is a Prisoner's Dilemma—a special case of the more general public-good situation. However great the advantage jointly to the trading pair of establishing a reciprocal relationship, it pays each member to cheat if he can. The big fish, once having been properly groomed, would seem to be in a position to profit by snapping up his helper. (The little cleaner fish often does his work actually within the mouth of his client.) On the other side of the transaction, mimics have evolved that imitate the characteristic markings of the true cleaners. Upon being permitted to approach the big fish, the mimic takes a quick bite and then escapes!

The problem here is essentially the same as the cheating, sale of "lemons," or "moral hazard" that arises in a number of market contexts.[90] While these phenomena threaten market viability, given the mutual advantage of trade the market can tolerate *some* slippage through cheating, provided it is kept within bounds.[91] A number of devices have evolved, in both market and biological contexts, to limit the degree of slippage. The market cheater may be punished by law, the mimic cleaner fish by being (with some probability) caught and eaten. Noncheaters in markets establish personal reputa-

[88] But even in human interactions, exchange very often takes place without legally enforceable contracts. This is true not only for trading among primitive peoples, but for highly sophisticated transactions under the most modern conditions. Stewart Macaulay, Non-contractual Relations in Business: A Preliminary Study, 28 Am. Sociol. Rev. 55 (1963). And in the sphere of "social exchange" among humans (George C. Homans, Social Behavior as Exchange, 63 Am. J. Sociol. 597 (1958)) legal enforcement is ordinarily out of the question.

[89] Robert L. Trivers, *supra* note 67. Trivers also classes alarm calls in birds under reciprocal altruism. But, as argued above (and in line with his detailed analysis), the benefit to the calling bird in no way depends upon reciprocation in the form of self-sacrificing behavior on the part of other birds. Alarm calls appear to represent incidental altruism, under the more general heading called "selfish altruism" in the previous section.

[90] See George A. Akerlof, The Market for "Lemons": Qualitative Uncertainty and the Market Mechanism, 84 Q. J. Econ. 488 (1970); Michael R. Darby & Edi Karni, Free Competition and the Optimal Amount of Fraud, 16 J. Law & Econ. 67 (1973).

[91] Richard Zeckhauser, Risk Spreading and Distribution (Aug. 1972) (Discussion paper No. 10 Kennedy Sch. Harv. U.).

tions and brand names, while cleaner fish develop (so it is claimed) a regular clientele of satisfied customers.

Mutually advantageous exchange is facilitated by altruistic motivations; the emotions of affection and sympathy have evolved, Trivers contends, because they provide a better guarantee of reciprocity than any mere calculated advantage of doing so. Put another way, altruism economizes on costs of policing and enforcing agreements.[92]

Becker[93] has contended that sympathetic motivation may be required *only on one side* of reciprocal-altruism interactions. The other party can be quite selfish in his aims, yet may still find cooperative behavior advantageous. Consider a selfish beneficiary of a parent's benevolence: a "rotten kid." The key proposition is that the rotten kid may still act benevolently toward the parent, simply in order to maximize the latter's capacity to bestow benefits upon him. And, in these circumstances, the mutual advantage of cooperative behavior may be such that even the "unselfish" parent ends up *selfishly* better off than he would if he were not altruistic! Consequently, in biological terms, no loss of fitness on either side is involved. This altruistic "contagiousness"—unselfish motivation on one side breeding cooperative behavior on the other side—would seem to promote the evolution of mutual aid patterns. Let one party be so motivated, for whatever reason (for example, altruism on the part of the parent could evolve simply from kin selection), and we will tend to observe reciprocity and mutual aid.[94]

More generally, Trivers argues that human evolution has developed a balance between the abilities to engage in and to detect and suppress subtle cheating while participating in reciprocal interactions. The sense of justice, what Trivers calls "moralistic aggression," is an emotion that involves third parties as additional enforcers to punish cheaters. Finally, the selectional advantage of these emotions has led to evolution of the ability to simulate or mimic them—to hypocrisy. Note once again how these emotional qualities, absent from the makeup of "economic man," turn out to have an important place in the biological economy of human relationships. Economics can, as the economic imperialists allege, deal with the whole human being, and indeed *must* do so even to explain the phenomena in its traditional domain of market behavior.

[92] See also Mordecai Kurz, Altruistic Equilibrium (Stan. U. Inst. for Math. Stud. in Soc. Sci., Econ. Ser., Rep. No. 156, 1975).

[93] Gary S. Becker, Altruism, Egoism, and Genetic Fitness: Economics and Sociobiology, 14 J. Econ. Lit. 817 (1976).

[94] There is one important limitation, however. The benevolent party must be in a position to have the last word, the last move in the interaction. If "rotten kid" has the last free choice of action, he may ruthlessly destroy his parent (Shakespeare's Regan and Goneril in relation to King Lear), so that the interaction would not be viable in selectional terms. See J. Hirshleifer, Shakespeare vs. Becker on Altruism: The Importance of Having the Last Word, 15 J. Econ. Lit. 5 (1977).

The chief biological example of *intraspecific* exchange is of course mating interaction. Here vying for trading partners, sexual competition, not only has market parallels but is of course an important economic phenomenon in its own right. In some human societies marriage partners are explicitly sold, but more generally the marriage relationship constitutes a form of "social exchange."[95] The competition for mates in the biological realm displays many familiar and some unexpected parallels with market phenomena.

Health and vigor in sexual partners are obviously desirable qualities, correlated with the probability of generating and rearing viable offspring. As a means of demonstrating these qualities (that is, of advertising), sexual displays, combats, and rituals have developed.[96] There is a nice analogy here with recent economic theories of "competitive signalling."[97] Some characteristics may be acquired by economic agents not because they *confer* competitive superiority, but only because they *demonstrate* a preexisting superiority (in potential for mutually advantageous exchange). Just as success in display or combat, even in cases where biologically useless in itself, may signal sexual vigor—so educational attainment, even where of itself useless in contributing to productivity, may yet be a signal of useful qualities like intelligence.

Another desirable quality in a mate is possession of territory, generally by the male.[98] This is advertised in birds by the call. Presumably it is not the artistic excellence of the male's call that attracts the female, but the mere announcement effect—since the quality of the product (of the territory) is evident on inspection.[99] But for goods whose quality can be determined only by experience, the main message conveyed by advertising is simply that the product is worth the effort of advertising![100] Sexual displays seem to fall in this category.

Sexual competition also provides parallels with what is sometimes called

[95] An economic analysis quantifying some of the determinants of polygynous marriages appears in Amyra Grossbard, Economic Analysis of Polygyny: The Case of Maiduguri, 17 Cur. Anthrop. 701 (1976).

[96] "Advertising" is also observed in some interspecific exchanges, for example, showy flowers and fragrances designed to attract the attention of pollinating insects.

[97] See Michael Spence, Competitive and Optimal Responses to Signals: An Analysis of Efficiency and Distribution, 7 J. Econ. Theory 296 (1974); Joseph E. Stiglitz, The Theory of "Screening": Education and the Distribution of Income, 65 Am. Econ. Rev. 283 (1975); John G. Riley, Information, Screening and Human Capital, 66 Am. Econ. Rev., pt. 2, at 254 (Papers & Proceedings, May 1976).

[98] While the most obvious illustrations of sexual competition involve male competition for females, females compete for males as well. This is reasonably evident in the human species.

[99] It seems, however, that there may be some selection for excellence in the call. The reason appears to be that well-developed calls are correlated with age which is a good indicator of ability in birds. (Personal communication from M. Cody.)

[100] On this see Phillip Nelson, Information and Consumer Behavior, 78 J. Pol. Econ. 311 (1970), and especially *id.*, Advertising as Information, 82 J. Pol. Econ. 729 (1974).

"excessive" or "destructive" competition for trade. Cheating is once again a factor, as it pays males to mimic vigor by convincing displays even if they do not actually possess it. (The "coyness" of the female is said to have evolved to prevent premature commitment of her limited reproductive capacity to males with only a superficially attractive line.)[101] Sexual combats may go beyond mere demonstration and actually harm the vanquished party, or sometimes the victor as well. Biologists have devoted considerable attention to cases like the peacock, where the extreme development of sexual ornaments appears to be disfunctional to the species or even to the individual. The explanation seems to be that positive *sexual selection* can to a degree overcome a disadvantage in terms of *natural selection*—the peacock with a splendid tail does not survive so well or so long but is more likely to find a mate. Such a development requires that male ornamentation and female preference evolve in parallel, which when carried to an extreme degree may represent a rather unstable equilibrium.[102]

In economic exchange, another mechanism of competition is *entry and exit*—variation of numbers to equalize on the margin the net advantages of the various types of activity. This also operates in sexual competition; the sex ratio varies to equalize the advantage of being a male or a female! Other things equal the equilibrium male/female sex ratio is 1/1. Taking any offspring generation, exactly half its genetic endowment is provided by male parents and half by female parents. Hence, if one sex were scarcer than the other in the parent generation at mating age, its *per capita* representation in the offspring generation's genes (genetic fitness) would be greater. If the disproportion persisted, it would pay in fitness terms to have offspring of the scarcer sex, and an adaptive response in this direction would correct the disparity. Even such practices as disproportionate infanticide of females will not affect the equilibrium 1/1 ratio. (This outcome displays the power of individual as opposed to group selection, since a 1/1 ratio is not the most "efficient" from the point of view of species growth. In terms of group selection it would generally be much more desirable to have a larger proportion of females.)

One factor that does distort the equilibrium sex ratio has been described by Trivers and Willard.[103] It is nearly universal among mammals that male parents have a higher *variance* in number of offspring than female parents. (A single male can father hundreds or even thousands of offspring, but the female's reproductive capacity is much more severely limited.) Also, healthy, vigorous parents tend to have healthy, vigorous offspring and physically

[101] See Sociobiology, *supra* note 1, at 320.

[102] R. A. Fisher, *supra* note 10, at 152.

[103] Robert L. Trivers & Dan E. Willard, Natural Selection of Parental Ability to Vary the Sex Ratio of Offspring, 179 Science 90 (1973).

weak parents, weak offspring. Taken together, these two considerations imply that it pays stronger parents to have *male* offspring; strong male children will tend to engender a relatively larger number of descendants. Conversely, it pays weaker parents to have *female* offspring, to minimize exposure to this variance. Thus an explanation is provided for the otherwise mysterious tendency of the human male/female sex ratio to rise with socio-economic status[104] (since status tends to be correlated with health and vigor). More generally, the normally higher early male mortality is explained. Prenatal and postnatal mechanisms discriminating against males permit stronger parents (who will suffer relatively less early mortality among their offspring) to end up with relatively more male children and weaker parents with relatively more female children.

Even *interest,* Trivers[105] suggests, ultimately has a biological origin. *Reproductive value* (the average number of offspring an organism will engender in the future) declines with age in the childbearing life phase. A loan today involves a cost to the lender in fitness terms; since his reproductive value upon repayment will be less, the repayment would have to be proportionately greater to make up the difference.

So exchange in a variety of forms, and with many familiar implications, exists in the biological realm. But what does seem to be a specifically human invention is the *organized* market, a form of exchange involving "middlemen" specialized to trading activity. This must have been what Adam Smith really had in mind in his otherwise too-sweeping assertion that "the propensity to truck, barter, and exchange" is specifically associated with the human species.[106] Sexual competition and cleaning symbioses provide sufficient evidence to the contrary. And associations such as pack membership also undoubtedly involve "social exchange."

But competition for trading partners remains only one very special type of biological competition. The more general concept used by biologists is illustrated in Figure I.[107] Let N_G and N_H signify numbers of two populations G and H. Then if $\dot{N}_G$, the time-derivative of N_G, is a negative function of N_H, and N_H of N_G, the two populations are called competitors. In the diagram we

[104] Sam Shapiro, Edward R. Schlesinger & Robert L. Nesbitt, Jr., Infant, Perinatal, Maternal, and Childhood Mortality in the United States (1968).

[105] Robert L. Trivers, *supra* note 67.

[106] "It is common to all men, and to be found in no other race of animals, which seem to know neither this nor any other species of contracts." Adam Smith, *supra* note 2, at 15-18. Simmel, who adopted a broad view of exchange as equivalent to *compromise,* also regarded the process as a human invention. Georg Simmel, Conflict 115 (Kurt H. Wolff trans. 1955). But compromise surely occurs in nonhuman interactions.

[107] These curves have already been expounded and analyzed in the economic literature by Kenneth E. Boulding, A Reconstruction of Economics, *supra* note 2; *id.*, Conflict and Defense, *supra* note 6.

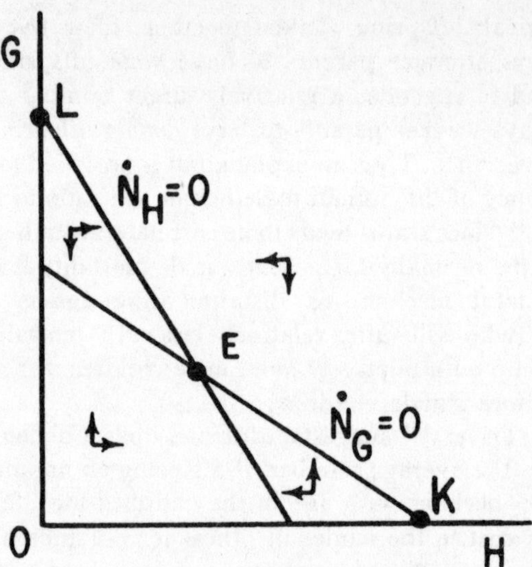

FIGURE I
Two Competitive Populations, Stable Coexistence Equilibrium

can draw for population G what the economist would call a "reaction curve" showing the population levels for which $\dot{N}_G = 0$, and similarly for population H. Since the populations are competitors, the reaction curves have negative slope. Their intersection will be a state of equilibrium. (Whether the equilibrium is stable or unstable depends upon the relative slopes at the point of intersection—as will be explored further in the next section.) If the reaction curves are *positively* sloped as in Figure II, the two populations are complementary rather than competitive. (Again, depending upon the relative slopes, the intersection point may be stable or unstable.) Finally, there is a mixed case, typified by predator-prey interactions, where the reaction curve of the predator has $\dot{N}_G$ as an increasing function of the prey population N_H, while $\dot{N}_H$ is a falling function of N_G. (Again the equilibrium at the intersection may or may not be stable.)

Competition in the general sense exists because some resource of relevance for two or more organisms is in scarce supply. The consequent *universality of competition* (the "struggle for existence") was of course the main message Darwin drew from Malthus. The ecologists speak of an organism's "fundamental niche" as the volume of abstract resource space in which it can exist—and of the "realized niche" as the volume which it actually occupies. Where niches overlap, there is competition. These considerations have one very essential implication: *that competition is generally more severe the more similar the organisms*. The more similar the organisms, the greater the niche

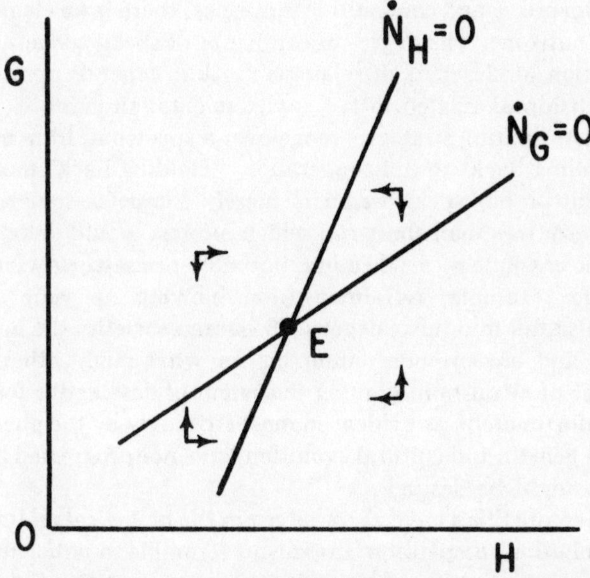

FIGURE II
Two Complementary Populations, Stable Coexistence Equilibrium

overlap. In particular, *intra*species competition tends to be more intense than *inter*species competition.[108] For example, territorial birds exclude conspecifics but to a greater or lesser extent tolerate birds of other species. And, we have seen, competition tends to be particularly severe within families and especially among litter-mates; the high correlation of genetic endowments and of positions in the generational life cycle, plus physical proximity, make for near identity of resource requirements (niches).

There are two opposing forces which together constitute what might be called the "dilemma of sociality." On the one hand, altruistic preferences or motivations stem mainly from degree of relationship (from correlation of genetic endowments), not only among close kin but extending to more distant relatives. And even, perhaps, to a degree over the entire species. (Other things equal, a man's genes would tell him to favor his fellowman fighting with a bear.) This is the main socializing force. On the other hand, competition, which opposes socialization, tends to be most intense precisely where degree of relationship is closest. (The other man will often be a closer competitor than the bear.) In consequence, as organisms strike some balance

[108] Charles Darwin, The Origin of Species ch. 3 (Mentor ed. 1958) (1st ed. 1859). In exceptional cases, however, as when population density is held down by other forces such as predation, intraspecies competition may not be very severe.

between cooperative and competitive strategies, there is an element of instability in the outcome. The degree of conflict or of social cooperation is not a simple function of closeness of relationship, but depends upon the specific details of kinship as related to the environmental situation.

Competition-limiting strategies range over a spectrum, from minimal patterns of "holding back" to full cooperation. "Holding back" means that the economic unit or biological organism merely competes somewhat less intensely for resources than short-run selfish interest would dictate. An obvious economic example is cartelization, but more praiseworthy forms of holding back—for example, refraining from blowing up your competitor's premises—also fall into this category. In human societies the institutions of government and law provide reinforcers for what might otherwise be the too-frail force of altruism in limiting the extent of destructive forms of competition. Unfortunately, as evidenced most strikingly by the phenomenon of war, human genetic and cultural evolution have not progressed as far in this direction as might be desired.

Limits on competition have also evolved in the biological realm. In what is called "exploitation competition" organisms scramble to utilize resources but ignore competitors, whereas, in "interference competition," they gain resources precisely by hampering competitors.[109] Interference may take the milder form, as in territoriality, of fighting only as necessary to deny a limited zone of resource access to others. But more aggressive versions also exist, of direct attack upon conspecifics—even of cannibalism, where the competitor himself is converted into a resource. This is relatively rare, however. Presumably, extreme forms of interference strategies have mainly proved disfunctional to the groups or species evolving them, and have therefore been selected against. (*Group* selection need not be involved here, as there is a fitness loss to the individual to the extent that his own descendants are inclined to eat one another up.) Biologists have observed that interference competition is more likely to evolve when resource limitations are particularly severe. In economic affairs as well, "cut-throat competition" is a product of hard times. When organisms are occupying unfilled environments, on the other hand, or firms are interacting in a growing market, competition takes place mainly through the externality of resource depletion (in economic terms, bidding up prices of inputs or driving down prices of products).

Another important means of limiting competition is *specialization*. It is useful to distinguish the specialization that results from competitive pressure, on the one hand, from the kind of cooperative specialization more

[109] S. J. McNaughton & Larry L. Woolf, General Ecology ch. 11 (1973); Sociobiology, *supra* note 1, at chs. 11, 12.

properly called *the division of labor.* Unfortunately, there has been some confusion on this score. The valuable pioneering study on biology and economics by Houthakker[110] confounds the two categories. The very important analysis by the biologist Ghiselin,[111] on the other hand, distinguishes what he calls the *competitive* division of labor (represented by the subdivision of ecological niches in the biological sphere, corresponding to product or locational differentiation in the economy) from the *cooperative* division of labor. In the former case (which, preferably, ought to be termed simply competitive specialization) there is no mutual dependence or complementarity among the entities. Each would be better off if the others were to vanish. The latter type of differentiation, the division of labor proper, is associated with true alliance—to achieve a common end, or at least for mutual benefit where a degree of complementarity exists.

In competitive specialization in the biological realm, each of the contending species is forced away from the zone of resource overlap—not only in locational terms, but in the form of divergent evolution of characters. This process of character displacement, resulting in an equilibrium *separation distance* between the species,[112] is completely parallel to the economic mechanisms described in our textbooks under the heading of product-differentiation competition and locational competition ("monopolistic competition"). But on the other hand, the biologists emphasize, such specialization is constrained by the possibility that a generalist of intermediate character might outcompete the set of specialist types.[113] Relative abundance and certainty of resources favor specialists; relative scarcity and unpredictability favor generalists.

Biologists, having developed a more subtle and elaborate approach to this question of specialization/generalization strategies than economists, recognize a variety of different dimensions of "generalist" competition against specialists. Individuals of a species might tend to a common intermediate character, able to make tolerably good use of a range of resources. Or the *individuals* might be specialized, yet the *species* show enough inter-individual variety to generalize its command over resources. Still another form of generalization is *plasticity,* whereby the species is enabled to change its character in response to environmental shifts.[114] Such plasticity might be genetically determined if the population maintains a reserve of variety in the

[110] Hendrik S. Houthakker, Economics and Biology: Specialization and Speciation, 9 Kyklos 181 (1956).

[111] Michael T. Ghiselin, *supra* note 4, at 233-40.

[112] S. J. McNaughton & Larry L. Woolf, *supra* note 108, at 312-24.

[113] Martin L. Cody, *supra* note 15.

[114] See the discussion of "adaptability" in George J. Stigler, The Theory of Price 129-30 (3rd ed. 1966).

form of a largely heterozygotic genetic composition. Or failing this, it may have evolved a high mutation rate as a way of tracking the environment. Finally, even with a fixed genetic constitution the capability for learning and *behavioral* adaptation may exist to a greater or lesser extent. The human species, of course, has concentrated upon becoming a generalist of this last type.

Turning now to cooperation in the true sense, we arrive at what is properly called the division of labor. Since competition is most intense when organisms are all attempting to do the *same* thing (to occupy the same niche, to use the same resources), one way out is for individuals or groups to cooperate by doing *different* things. For the group, or rather for each member thereof, command over resources is thereby extended.

The division of labor in Nature penetrates profoundly into the deepest aspects of the differentiation of living matter. In multicelled organisms the parts unselfishly cooperate to serve the whole, which is of course warranted by the fact that all the cells of an individual organism are genetically identical (save the germ cells, of course). Sexual differentiation also represents an evident instance of the cooperative division of labor in the interests of reproductive survival. Here altruism is less perfect, in that each member of the parental team is altruistic toward the other only to the extent necessary for promoting the reproductive survival of his or her own genetic endowment.[115] Nevertheless, the mechanism works well enough to have won out, for the most part, over asexual reproduction. Going beyond this most elemental social unit—the male-female pair—the *family* involves a related type of role differentiation: that associated with the generational life cycle. This provides a temporal division of labor; each generation plays its role, in due course, in promoting the reproductive survival of the parent-offspring chain. While altruism between generations is by no means unlimited, as seen above, the differentiation of tasks ties together the interests of the family group.

For larger cooperative associations, necessarily among more remotely related organisms, specialization through the division of labor with its concomitant of social exchange must, to be viable, become compensatingly productive as the force of altruism is diluted. Traditional economics, epitomized by Adam Smith, demonstrated the economic advantage of the division of labor even for a group of entirely selfish individuals. The sociologist Durkheim,[116] in contrast, claimed that the division of labor generates a kind of superorganismic "solidarity." He argued that the economic

[115] Robert L. Trivers, *supra* note 14.

[116] Emile Durkheim, On the Division of Labor in Society 39-229 (George Simpson trans. 1933).

benefits of the division of labor are picayune compared to this solidarity, a union not only of interests but of sentiments (as in the case of friends or mates). As so often occurs in social analysis, however, Durkheim fails to distinguish properly between desires (preferences) and opportunities. If there is any superorganismic tie among individuals, it can only be (according to the hypothesis accepted here) their sharing of genetic endowments. Yet in many important instances of the division of labor (for example, bees and flowers) there is no genetic association at all. The cooperative division of labor in such cases is no more than an alliance for mutual benefit. With genetic sharing it is no doubt easier for cooperation to evolve, but superorganismic ties are not sufficient causes and certainly not necessary consequences of the division of labor.

The human species, of course, has carried the division of labor to extraordinary lengths. The extent to which this represents genetic versus cultural evolution is not a simple matter to resolve. The regulation of cheating, necessary to make exchange and therefore the division of labor possible, has, as we have seen, been achieved in Nature to some degree. Even emotional supports for exchange, like the sense of justice ("moralistic aggression") may represent genetically evolved characters. On the other hand, human culture has evolved institutional supports for exchange and the division of labor—property, law, and government.

Analysis on the part of economists of the determinants of the division of labor has gone little beyond Smith's famous proposition: ". . . That the division of labour is limited by the extent of the market."[117] Houthakker,[118] taking the standpoint of the individual, views him as the potential beneficiary of a number of activities some or all of which may however be disharmonious if undertaken together. The choice to be made is for individuals either to act as nonspecialists and incur costs of internal coordination, or else to separate and distribute the activities via a division of labor that entails costs of external coordination. Here Smith's "extent of the market" is taken as the inverse of inter-individual transaction costs, the absence of which would facilitate specialization with external coordination. Stigler's analysis[119] is fundamentally similar, though concentrating on firms as decision units rather than individuals. Again there are a number of activities, all desirable or even essential in the production of output, but diverging mainly in offering economies or diseconomies of *scale*. The firms would do better to divest themselves of at least the increasing-returns activities, if a specialized external supplier were available. As the *industry* expands, such specialized

[117] Adam Smith, *supra* note 2, at 17-21.

[118] Hendrik S. Houthakker, *supra* note 109.

[119] George J. Stigler, The Division of Labor is Limited by the Extent of the Market, 59 J. Pol. Econ. 185 (1951).

suppliers become economically viable entities. Thus, for Stigler, "extent of the market" signifies *aggregate* scale of output.

The discussion by the biologist Ghiselin[120] provides many apt illustrations: for example, that an insect colony must reach a certain size before it pays to have a specialized soldier caste. But Ghiselin is inclined to stress that there are important advantages of nonspecialization, such as the existence of complementarities among certain activities (for example, teaching and research). In addition, there may be sequential rather than individual specialization, as when members of an ant colony all progress through a common series of different productive roles in the course of the life cycle.

Following up a suggestion by Ghiselin, it might really be better to think in terms of "combination of labor" rather than "division of labor." Division is the first step; it is the combination (external coordination) that produces the result. Apart from the division of labor as a form of *complementary combination* of individuals undertaking different specialized tasks, there is also the possibility of *supplementary combination* whereby individuals reinforce one another in performing the *same* task. A simple example would be men tugging on a rope to move a load; such "threshold phenomena" are quite important and widespread. Wherever scale economies for a given activity dictate a minimum efficient size greater than the full output of a single individual, we would expect to see a mixture of complementation and supplementation, of specialization and multiplication of numbers, in the general process of cooperation through the combination of labor.

A number of other dimensions of choice have been explored by biologists. One such is between "K-strategies" and "r-strategies." K symbolizes the carrying capacity of the environment, that is, the species number N^* at which the time-rate of change $\dot{N} = 0$. The symbol r signifies the maximum rate of Malthusian growth, which obtains under conditions where the environment is not constraining. The r-strategists are opportunist species, who pioneer and settle new unfilled environments. The K-strategists are solider citizens, who compete by superior effectiveness in utilizing the resources of relatively saturated environments. The r-strategists thus make their living from the recurrence of disequilibrium situations (entrepreneurial types, we would say). But their success can only be transient; ultimately they will be displaced by the more efficient K-strategist species. The r-strategists tend to be characterized by high early mortality, as they must continually disperse and take long chances of finding new unsaturated habitats. A high birth rate is therefore a necessity. Among other tendencies are rapid maturity, small body size, early reproduction, and short life. K-strategists, in contrast, tend to develop more slowly, have larger body size, and longer life.[121] Their

[120] Michael T. Ghiselin, *supra* note 4, at 233-47.

[121] Sociobiology, *supra* note 1, at 101.

inclination is to produce a smaller number of more carefully optimized offspring.[122]

Analogs in the world of business exist for a number of these strategies. In the high-fashion industry we observe high birth rates and death rates of firms, in public utilities the reverse. In general, pioneering strategies tend to be more suitable for small firms—which survive better in highly changeable environments.

But as applied to *firms*, as emphasized previously, biological reasoning is only a metaphor. In particular, firms do not follow the reproductive laws of biology: small firms do not give birth to other small firms, and firms of one "species" (industry) may transfer to another. By way of contrast, human individuals, families, races, etc. *are* biological entities which may be regarded as choosing competitive strategies. Martial races may concentrate on success through politics, conflict, or violence ("interference strategy"); others may have proliferated and extended their sway through high birth rates; others through lower birth rates but superior efficiency in utilizing resources ("exploitation strategy"). The *r*-strategist pioneering human type was presumably selected for in the early period of American history—a period long enough for genetic evolution, though cultural adaptation may have been more important. This type was not entirely antisocial; altruist "pioneer" virtues such as mutual defense and sharing in adversity can emerge under *r*-selection. In the present more crowded conditions the preferred forms of altruism represent "urban" virtues of a negative rather than positive sort: tolerance, nonaggressiveness, and reproductive restraint.[123] Even today it seems likely that a suitable comparison of populations in environments like Alaska on the one hand and New York City on the other would reveal differential genetic (over and beyond merely cultural) adaptations.[124]

C. *The Results of Social Interaction—Equilibrium Versus Change*

Equilibrium in biology has one striking feature with no close counterpart in economics: a dualism between processes taking place simultaneously on the level of *organisms* and on the level of *genes*.

In dealing with the interactions of *organisms* the biologist generally uses a partial-equilibrium model, taking genetic compositions as fixed. He then

[122] Compare the discussion of "high-quality" and "lower quality" children in Gary S. Becker, An Economic Analysis of Fertility, in Demographic and Economic Change in Developed Countries ([Univ.] Nat'l Bur. Econ. Res., 1960); Marc Nerlove, Household and Economy: Toward a New Theory of Population and Economic Growth, 82 J. Pol. Econ. 200 (1974).

[123] Sociobiology, *supra* note 1, at 107-08.

[124] Many such associations of human genetic types with historical and geographical determinants are elaborated in Ellsworth Huntington, Mainsprings of Civilization (1945). While his work remains highly controversial, and not all of his instances are convincing, that some racial characters are indeed adaptive (for example, the dark skin of Africans, the body shape of Eskimos) is evident.

asks such questions as: (1) For a given species G, what will be the limiting population number in a particular environment (the "carrying capacity" of the environment for that species)? (2) Or, with two or more interacting populations, G and H, what will be their respective equilibrium numbers N_G and N_H. And, in particular, will one drive the other to extinction, or might they even *both* become extinct? (The last possibility may seem surprising. Yet a predator might conceivably be so efficient as ultimately to wipe out its prey, in which case its own extinction may follow.) (3) Where new species may enter an environment by migration, thus offsetting loss of species from extinction, what is the equilibrium number of distinct species, and how do the species partition the total biomass?

To take up the second of these three questions, it was remarked above that the intersection of the two reaction curves of Figure I (two competitive populations) might be a stable or an unstable equilibrium point. It will be evident, by consideration of the nature of the interaction (as illustrated by the arrows showing the directions of change of the two populations from any N_G, N_H point in the positive quadrant), that the intersection equilibrium as shown is stable. Thus, we have here a coexistence solution at point E. If the labels on the reaction curves were reversed, however, it may be verified (by making appropriate changes in the arrows showing the directions of change) that the coexistence equilibrium would be unstable. Depending upon the initial situation, population H would drive G to extinction at point K, or population G would drive H to extinction at point L.

A similar analysis of the complementary populations in Figure II will show that the coexistence equilibrium at point E is again stable. But if the labels on the reaction curves were reversed, the populations would jointly (depending upon the starting point) either decay toward zero or explode toward infinity. (Of course, in the latter case another branch of at least one of the reaction curves would eventually be encountered, beyond which the rate of change of population would again become negative.)

The arrows of directional change in the predator-prey diagram of Figure III show that a kind of spiral or cobweb exists around the intersection point E. Depending upon the slopes of the curves, the cobweb could: (a) repeat itself indefinitely, (b) converge to the coexistence equilibrium at E, or (c) oscillate explosively. In the latter case the result may be extinction of the predator (if the spiral first hits the prey axis, since the prey can continue to survive without the predator), or the extinction of both (if the spiral first hits the predator axis, in the case where the predator cannot continue to survive without prey). The theoretical tendency of predator-prey interactions toward cycles in population numbers has in fact been confirmed in empirical observations.[125]

[125] S. J. McNaughton & Larry L. Wolf, *supra* note 108, at ch. 10.

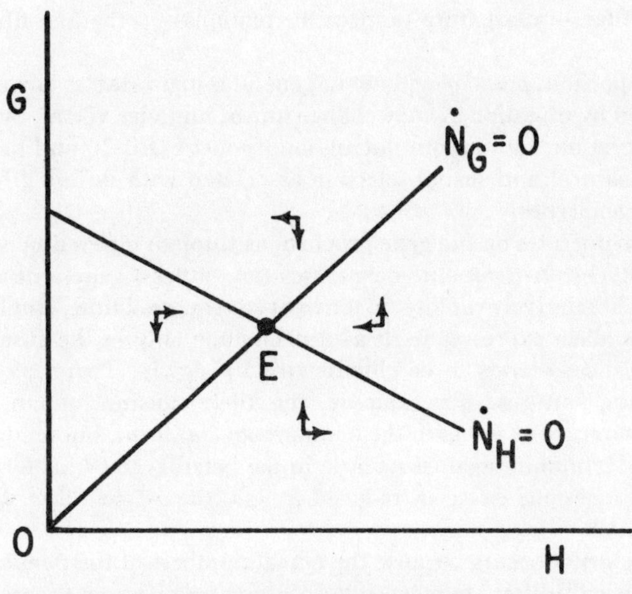

FIGURE III
Predator-Prey Interaction

These models have rather direct analogies with a number of processes in the realm of the human sciences. The reaction-curve format closely parallels Lewis F. Richardson's models of arms races[126] and Lanchester's equations of combat.[127] Economists will of course recognize the duopoly solutions associated with Cournot.[128]

Biological models of equilibrium on the *genetic* level are again of a partial-equilibrium nature, since they typically involve only processes within a single population. The simplest version of such models is known as the Hardy-Weinberg Law. If at a particular gene locus two alleles A and a exist, under sexual reproduction there are three possible genotypes: AA, Aa, and aa. With random mating, if selective and other pressures determine the proportions p and q (where $p + q = 1$) for the prevalence of alleles A and a respectively, then the equilibrium proportions for the genotypes will be p^2 for AA, $2pq$ for Aa, and q^2 for aa. This equilibrium is reached extremely

[126] Lewis F. Richardson, Variation of the Frequency of Fatal Quarrels with Magnitude, 43 J. Am. Stat. A. 523 (1948). See, on this, Anatol Rapoport, Fights, Games, and Debates ch. 1 (1960). Some extensions are provided in Kenneth E. Boulding, Conflict, *supra* note 6, at chs. 2, 4, 6. Kenneth E. Boulding, Reconstruction, *supra* note 2, proposed that these models serve as the core of an "ecological" reorientation of economics.

[127] See F. W. Lanchester, Aircraft in Warfare (1916); Philip M. Morse & George E. Kimball, Methods of Operation Research (1951).

[128] See R. G. D. Allen, Mathematical Analysis for Economists 200-04 (1938).

rapidly, in fact—apart from random fluctuations—in the first filial generation.[129]

The proportions p and q will not in general remain stable, however. They are affected by mutation (A may change into a, and vice versa), by gene flow due to migration, by random fluctuation ("genetic drift"), and most importantly by natural and sexual selection associated with differing fitnesses of the three genotypes.

Selection operates on the gene proportions through differential survival of the phenotypes. A *dominant* deleterious (low-fitness) gene will tend to be extinguished relatively rapidly, in terms of generational time. But a *recessive* deleterious allele expresses itself as a phenotype only in the case of the *aa* genotype, and so tends to be eliminated only slowly. There may be other complicating features. For example, the allele causing human sickle-cell anemia is a recessive lethal in the homozygote (*aa*) form, but tends to confer a degree of immunity against malaria in the heterozygote (*Aa*) form. Where malaria is a serious cause of reduced fitness, the a-type allele will not be eliminated.[130]

"Genetic drift" occurs because the actual numbers of the phenotypes *AA*, *Aa*, and *aa* will differ stochastically to a greater or lesser degree from the respective mean values p^2, $2pq$, and q^2. The most important consequence is a tendency toward the loss of heterozygosity, that is, genetic drift tends ultimately to fix a single allele in the population. Genetic drift operates more powerfully upon smaller populations, of course, and elimination obviously is much more likely to occur for an allele that is already rare. Note that even a superior-fitness allele, if sufficiently rare, might well be eliminated by stochastic fluctuations. (It was genetic drift that was called on above to explain the occasional fixing of low-individual-fitness "altruist" genes in some populations.)

Somewhat tenuous analogies exist between genes and ideas, between mutation and invention, etc.[131] A human population might increase fitness by "mutations" like a new form of social organization or the invention of a new tool or weapon. And ideas, like genes, are subject to the selectional test of competition. But the laws of the generation and propagation of ideas are so different from those of genes that the comparison does not really seem fruitful.

Some broader parallels might still be of interest, however. Sexual reproduction may be interpreted as a device that (among other things) provides populations with a *reserve of variability of characters*. Heterozygosity makes

[129] 1 William Feller, An Introduction to Probability Theory and its Applications 94-95 (1950).

[130] Edward O. Wilson & William H. Bossert, *supra* note 34, at 68-70.

[131] See Kenneth E. Boulding, *supra* note 2, at 7.

a range of different phenotypes available for selection in each generation, thus permitting the tracking of environmental shifts while delaying the loss of potential characters that might turn out to be useful in the future. Asexual organisms, lacking this reserve of variability, are more vulnerable to environmental shifts. In effect, sexual reproduction provides species with "memory," though at the cost of some loss of efficiency. In each generation, as was seen above, each of the combinations *AA*, *Aa*, and *aa* will generally be "recalled" and tried again—so long as $0 < p < 1$. And in actuality, more than two alleles are often "stored" at a given locus, and in addition there may exist other, more complex forms of genetic recombination or recall. The widened opportunities provided by sexual reproduction are related to the issue of satisficing versus optimizing discussed at several points previously. In the absence of "memory" of alternative possibilities, a biological entity could not successfully stray very far from any current combination that leads to even minimally satisfactory outcomes—since it cannot remember anything old, it can scarcely afford to learn something new. The mental development of the human species, culminating in speech and writing, has permitted the vast development of *cultural* memory independent of genetic storage of variability, thus widening the ability to explore alternatives and approach closer to true optimization.

Another feature that operates to store variety in the economic system is *the law of diminishing returns*, in its various forms. Rising marginal cost tends to lead to interior or coexistence solutions; entities or forms of organization that are favored by environmental changes tend to increase in prevalence, but not ordinarily so totally as to drive out all others. Thus, a capacity for rapid response to change tends to be preserved.[132] The concept corresponding to diminishing returns in biology is called "density dependence," though biologists tend to call upon this mainly to explain why single populations do not increase without limit.[133] With respect to competing populations the biologists have a proposition that seems to run counter to diminishing returns in economics—Gause's Exclusion Principle. The idea is that no two species that fill the same ecological niche can permanently coexist.[134] Here, at least, it would seem that the biologists can learn from us. Because of diminishing returns to any form of expansion (density-dependent effects), coexistence equilibria in the same niche should be perfectly possible. Ultimately, the same forces preventing a single *organism* from monopolizing a

[132] On the other hand, the less stringent inheritance process in economics—the ability of a "mutation" to spread by mere imitation—means that storage of alternative productive techniques or forms of organization is not so vital.

[133] Edward O. Wilson & William H. Bossert, *supra* note 34, at 106-09.

[134] *Id.* at 156-58.

niche against conspecifics also tends to control the expansion of the species as a whole against its competitors.[135]

Biologists, as compared with economists, seem to devote relatively more effort to the description of processes of ongoing *change* as opposed to processes leading to *equilibrium* in the sense of stationary states. This is historically understandable, in that modern biology was faced at the outset with the great polemical problem of winning public acceptability for the fact of evolutionary change. In consequence, perhaps, biologists do not seem to have developed (or at any rate do not pay much attention to) concepts of *general* equilibrium. They do not seem, to cite one example, to have felt the need for integrating the two partial-equilibrium developments described above—one on the level of population numbers, the second on the level of genetic composition. On the other hand, they have developed models showing the working of a rich variety of mechanisms of change—mutation and recombination, selection and migration, learning, genetic drift, etc.—as well as useful generalizations concerning the extent and prevalence of certain patterned responses to change such as mimicry, convergence, character release, speciation, and the like.

Related to the intellectual problem of the relative importance of equilibrium versus change is an issue that has concerned both disciplines—the question that biologists call teleology. In Panglossian terms, is this the best of all possible worlds? Or, if not the best just yet, does our world at least progress toward such a desirable goal?

In biology, the teleological theme seems to underlie the concluding sentence of *The Origin of Species*:

> Thus, from the war of nature, from famine and death, the most exalted object which we are capable of conceiving, namely, the production of the higher animals, directly follows. There is grandeur in this view of life, with its several powers having been originally breathed by the Creator into a few forms or into one; and that, whilst this planet has gone cycling on according to the fixed law of gravity, from so simple a beginning endless forms most beautiful and most wonderful have been, and are being evolved.[136]

Darwin's language suggests, though it does not quite say, that evolution is directed by some higher force and that its results represent in some sense progress. Herbert Spencer and others went further to develop an evolutionist ethics—moral conduct is *defined* as that which contributes to better adaptation and progress toward higher forms. T. H. Huxley, Darwin's great sup-

[135] While the law of diminishing returns makes coexistence equilibrium *possible*, corner solutions are not necessarily ruled out.

[136] Charles Darwin, *supra* note 107.

porter, declared: "The absolute justice of the system of things is as clear to me as any scientific fact."[137]

The alternative mechanistic view, that evolution is an entirely undirected process, is almost universally and emphatically postulated by modern biologists.[138] Ghiselin[139] contends further that hidden teleology lurks wherever adaptation is explained in such terms as "the good of the species" or "the good of the community." But this accusation does not seem warranted. The scientific question is simply whether the mechanistic processes of evolution can lead to the emergence of characters benefiting larger groups although harming the individual bearer. That this is at least possible, as in the devotion of parents to offspring, can scarcely be denied. More generally, the genetic-relationship argument for altruism (kin selection) shades gradually in diluted form to groups up to the level of the species, and possibly beyond. Since Nature does select simultaneously on both the organism and the gene level—and on higher population and community levels as well—and since groups of genes or groups of individuals may become coadapted in a variety of ways and so coselected, it would seem that some of Nature's productions could validly be interpreted as responding to "the good of the group" rather than solely of the organism (or the gene).

Yet, it is evident, the argument of "perfection" does not hold with any force above the organism level. The many forms of destructive competition in Nature—from sexual combats within species to predation between species—preclude any inference of a universal harmonious adaptation to the nonliving environment.[140] Still, it seems that there may be at least some slow long-run pressure in this direction.[141]

A related question is the degree to which *cultural* evolution, which necessarily concerns group rather than individual traits, is adaptive. Again, one can hardly make any strong arguments for perfection of cultural adaptation. And yet, selection processes are certainly at work which tend to destroy societies that have somehow evolved seriously maladapted cultures.[142]

[137] Quoted in Gertrude Himmelfarb, *supra* note 5, at 382. Huxley was later to totally reverse his position, going on to argue that ethical progress required *combating* the natural tendency of the cosmic processes. *Id.* at 385.

[138] Mechanism is not, any more than its opposite (the postulate of design or purposiveness) a scientifically provable proposition. It is a working hypothesis.

[139] Michael T. Ghiselin, *supra* note 4.

[140] See Gordon Tullock, *supra* note 41.

[141] H. E. Frech, III, Biological Externalities and Evolution: A Comment, 39 J. Theoret. Biology 669 (1973). One possible instance is the tendency of disease parasites to evolve in the direction of reduced virulence (Sociobiology, *supra* note 1, at 116). It is sometimes contended that the beneficial bacteria living within our bodies have evolved from harmful ones.

[142] See Alexander Alland, Jr., *supra* note 27, at 171; Sociobiology, *supra* note 1, at 560;

The main classical tradition in economics has similarly been subjected to criticism on grounds of teleology. Adam Smith's view,[143] that under laissez-faire an "invisible hand" leads to a kind of *harmony* of private interests, has been attacked as apologetics for the capitalist system—as a tendentious attempt to prove that what exists is indeed the best of all possible worlds. Setting questions of motivation aside, it is indeed true that much of the intellectual effort of modern theorizing has gone into proving social optimality—in the very special sense of *Pareto-optimality*—of idealized versions of the laissez-faire capitalist economy. (Or, in some cases, of the welfare-state or even the socialist economy!) More specifically, what has been shown is that the equilibrium outcome under an unregulated economy with fully defined property rights is a social optimum in the sense that it would not be possible to improve the situation of any individual (in his own eyes) without harming one or several individuals (in their own eyes).

However, these results might equally well be interpreted as anti-apologetics. For, the idealized conditions necessary to make them valid evidently do not fully apply to any actual capitalist (or welfare-state or socialist) economy. And in fact, economists have devoted major energy to examination of forces leading to failures of Pareto-optimality—natural monopoly, oligopoly, externalities, and public goods being leading examples.

The lack of the institution of *property*—founded, in turn, upon the larger institutions of *law* and *government*—in the economy of Nature is an important element explaining the "imperfection" of social adaptations in the biological realm. Some observers have regarded animal *territoriality* as closely analogous to property, but this is incorrect. Territory in Nature is held only so long as it is continuously and effectively defended by the force of its possessor. Property does sometimes need to be defended by force, but what makes it property is the availability of impersonal enforcement through the law of the community.[144] To the extent that the property system is effective, a degree of progressive cultural adaptation tends to take place over time. Individuals need not expend energy in combat or other contests for possession, but are instead motivated to search out mutually advantageous ways of employing property so as to achieve a more complete division of

---

Ronald Cohen, *supra* note 63; William H. Durham, Resource Competition and Human Aggression, Part I: A Review of Primitive War, 51 Q. Rev. Biology 385 (1976).

[143] "By pursuing his own interest he frequently promotes that of the society more effectually than when he really intends to promote it." Adam Smith, *supra* note 2, at 423.

[144] Melvin C. Fredlund, Wolves, Chimps and Demsetz, 14 Econ. Inquiry 279 (1976) claims to have found that property in this sense does exist, at least in primitive form, in some animal communities.

labor. In particular, they are motivated to find ways around the failures of Pareto-optimality mentioned above.[145]

Yet, lest this seem too unguardedly hopeful, it must be pointed out that the institutions of law and government are powerful mechanisms that may be employed to achieve many private or group ends quite apart from Pareto-optimality. Law and government may destroy some individuals for the benefit of others, may penalize rather than promote the division of labor, may undermine rather than support the institution of property. Nor can we say on scientific grounds that law and government "ought not" do so. But to the extent that they do not, the progress of adaptation to the environment will be hampered or even reversed.

V. Points of Comparison—A Tabular View

Tables 1 and 2 have been designed as a way of pulling together, without undue repetition, the strands of the preceding discussions. The first table is an attempt to systematize, in a comparative way, the entities or units of action as viewed by biologists and by economists. The second table is intended to display, again in a comparative way, the *processes* of action and interaction involving these entities.

For the economist the fundamental acting unit or agent is of course the *individual.* Individuals organize into many types of composite units for purposes of joint action—these are the "Cooperative Groups" in Table 1. A useful though somewhat rough distinction can be made between "unselfish" groupings, whose dominant feature is the existence of altruistic preference functions connecting the goals of the members, and "selfish" aggregations where cooperative action is motivated only by mutual anticipation of selfish gain.

The family is of course the standard example of a supposedly "unselfish" grouping. As explained at length above, some or all participating family members may actually be motivated to a greater or lesser degree by considerations of personal advantage rather than by other-regarding love and concern. But for the most part, family associations respond to supra-individual goals (kin selection). A variety of other communal associations ("brotherhoods")—social, religious, and the like—also exist, at least purportedly, to unite the members thereof in unselfish fellowship.

Economics, in contrast with other social sciences, has concentrated attention upon the "selfish" associations in the next line of the Table. These include *alliances* of all sorts: the firm in the realm of economics, the gang for criminal activity, political parties and other associations for achieving or

[145] R. H. Coase, The Problem of Social Cost, 3 J. Law & Econ. 1 (1960).

TABLE 1
ACTING ENTITIES, UNITS, AND GROUPS

	ECONOMIC SYSTEM	BIOLOGICAL SYSTEM A	BIOLOGICAL SYSTEM B
AGENTS	Individuals	Organisms	Genes
COOPERATIVE GROUPS			
"Unselfish"	Families, "brotherhoods"	Reproductive associations	(None)
"Selfish"	Firms, parties and other political associations, gangs, exchange associations	Packs, mutualists	Organisms, chromosomes and other gene linkages
COMPETITIVE CLUSTERS	Industries, crafts and professions, other contending sets (of gangs, parties, nations, etc.)	Sexes, species, set of niche competitors	Set of alleles, of genotypes
UNIVERSAL GROUP	Society	Biota	Gene pool

exercising power. "Exchange associations" are links in the division of labor. Just as the "unselfish" associations are in fact not completely so, similarly the "selfish" combinations typically have and may indeed require a certain social cement in the form of feelings of fraternity and community (altruism). This cement is perhaps least binding in the case of exchange associations, but even there at least a simulation of uncalculated fellowship between the parties may be essential for good business. While the state or polity falls into the "selfish" grouping, its survival in the face of military competition probably requires a high degree of unselfish patriotic sentiment.

The next major heading represents "Competitive Clusters." The term, for lack of a better, is intended to represent aggregations of units that are mainly *striving against* rather than *cooperating with* one another. Here there may be no sense of actual association on the part of the participants, the cluster being merely a discrete *classification* as viewed by an observer. Such an aggregate of closely competing firms we call an industry, of competing workers a craft or profession, etc. We lack accepted single words for clusters of competing gangs, of competing parties and political associations, of competing nations, etc. (Sometimes we refer to them as the players in the political game, the diplomatic game, and so forth.) The members of cooperating groups may do *different* things, so as to complement one another; or they do the same thing, where scale economies make supplementation a more advantageous cooperation technique than complementation. But members of competitive clusters are trying to do the same thing in a rivalrous sense, in a context where the success of one entity to some extent precludes that of others.

Here again, the distinction is not always so sharp. Contending groups or individuals generally have some mutual interest in limiting at least the degree of competition. They are better able to find this opportunity for mutual gain if an element of "brotherhood" is thought to exist among the competitors. Trade unions (often actually called "brotherhoods") call on class sentiment to limit the competition among workers.

Finally, at the bottom line we have the "Universal Group"—society itself. Society as an entirety is a complex structure of cooperating and competing elements.

In the biological realm, as was indicated earlier, there are two interwoven *systems* of thinking—here simple denoted *A* and *B*. In *A* the organism is the fundamental unit, in *B* it is the gene. In system *A* the egg serves to reproduce the chicken, in system *B* the chicken is the means of reproducing the egg (that is, the gene). Genes are chemical units that have somehow evolved ways of reproducing themselves. (Not that they "want" to do so, of course, but rather that once self-reproduction somehow came about it tended to be selected by Nature for survival.) In system *A* there are "unselfish" (kin-selected) cooperative groupings like the family, here more abstractly called reproductive associations. But in system *B* there are no "unselfish" genes!

Now consider the "selfish" cooperative groupings of individual organisms in system *A*—packs or other alliances (within or between species) whose members gain by mutual association in feeding or defense or reproduction. The leading analog in system *B* is the *organism* itself. That is, the individual organism represents a kind of alliance of the various genes making up its genetic endowment! As a rather less important point, study of the details of the process of genetic reproduction reveals that the genes are themselves not isolated but are organized into chromosomes and other linkages whose prospects for reproduction are connected in various ways.

The most obvious instance of the "Competitive Cluster" category in system *A* is the species itself—regarded as the aggregate of its competing individual members. While competition is severest within a species, interspecific competition also occurs where the potential niches of different species overlap. Each *sex* also represents a competitive cluster (that is, all males compete against one another, as do all females) within a sexually reproducing species. In system *B* the set of competing alleles at a given locus, and the set of alternative genotypes, are instances of competitive clusters. Finally, the "Universal Group" is the entire biota in system *A*. In system *B* the gene pool represents the universe in which various forms of cooperation and competition may take place.

In Table 2 the chief point of interpretation to be emphasized is that the

TABLE 2
PROCESSES AND RELATIONSHIPS

	ECONOMIC SYSTEM	BIOLOGICAL SYSTEM
OBJECTIVE FUNCTION	Subjective preferences ("tastes")	Reproductive survival ("fitness")
PRINCIPLE OF ACTION	Optimization [alternatively, "satisficing"]	"As if" optimization
OPPORTUNITIES	Production Exchange via market Crime, war Family formation	Exploitation of resources Mutualism Predation, war Reproduction
PRINCIPLE OF COMPETITIVE SELECTION	Economic efficiency	Superior "fitness"
PRINCIPLES OF EQUILIBRIUM		
a) Short-run	Markets cleared	?
b) Long-run	Zero-profit	Reproductive ratio = 1
c) Very long-run	Stationary state	Saturated environment
"PROGRESS"	Accumulation, technological advance	Evolution: improved adaptation via mutation, recombination, migration, drift, and behavioral adjustment
SOCIAL OPTIMALITY CONCEPTS	Pareto-optimality	None (?)

biological processes and mechanisms represent more general classes into which the economic ones fall as particular instances. Where standard economics takes the satisfaction of preferences as the primitive objective or "utility function" of the acting individuals, biological theory suggests that what seems like mere preference or taste evolves out of the objective dictates of reproductive survival. As to the principle of action or behavior, the process of calculated optimization postulated in standard economics can be regarded as a special instance of the uncalculated "as if" optimization dictated by the selective forces of Nature. The thrust of the "satisficing" controversy in descriptive economics is that, even in the economic sphere, explicit optimization cannot always serve as the principle of action.

The *opportunities* available to organisms in the biological realm can be categorized in ways that seem familiar to the economist. Exploitation of resources is akin to production; mutualism corresponds to exchange; predation and war have obvious analogs in human society. Biology's emphasis on reproduction corresponds to the range of choices involved in family formation in the social context.

In terms of selective processes at work, the biological environment chooses for superior fitness, the analog being superior economic efficiency in the processes studied by standard economics. However, since economic efficiency is not propagated by mechanisms closely analogous to inheritance in biology, the processes of competition in the two areas are not closely comparable.

Economics distinguishes three levels of equilibrium: (1) short-run exchange equilibrium (market-clearing); (2) long-run entry/exit equilibrium, in which there is no longer any net advantage from redirection of resources (zero-profit condition); and (3) a hypothetical very long-run stationary state where there is no longer any advantage to the formation of new resources (by accumulation). There seems to be no close analog in biology to the short-run concept. The equivalent of the long-run equilibrium condition of economics can be taken to be the biological situation where each type of population (on the organism level) or each type of allele (on the genetic level) has a reproductive ratio ("fitness") equal to unity. And one can also imagine a hypothetical very-long-run equilibrium condition in which the environment is so totally saturated as to leave no niche for the formation of new life entities.

"Progress" takes place in the economy in two main ways: accumulation of resources by saving and technological advance. In biology the analogous process is of course *evolution*, the improvement of adaptation to environment by a variety of processes.

Finally, we have the question of social optimality. In biology, the standard mechanistic view seems to leave no room for such a concept. In economics we have the one rather debatable, and in any case highly limited, criterion of Pareto-optimality. While Pareto-optimality is usually regarded as a normative concept, it does have positive content in one respect—that there is at least a weak tendency in the competitive economy to move toward Pareto-optimal outcomes. Despite the "teleological" ring of the argument, it is conceivable that a similar tendency, toward solving the Prisoners' Dilemma by arriving at cooperative rather than conflictual outcomes, may be operating, however weakly, in the biological realm.

VI. Economy, Biology, and Society

I have tried here to trace some of the implications of Alfred Marshall's view that economics is a branch of biology. Or, in more sweeping terms, of the contention that the social sciences generally can fruitfully be regarded as the sociobiology of the human species.[146] Yet, at the same time, it was suggested, we might well claim that certain laws of the economizing

[146] Compare Sociobiology, *supra* note 1, at ch. 27, and E. O. Wilson, Biology, *supra* note 1.

process—optimization on the individual level, and equilibrium on the societal level—apply to biology as well.[147] Viewed this way, economics can be regarded as the general field, whose two great subdivisions consist of the natural economy studied by the biologists and the political economy studied by economists proper.[148] Considerable light has been shed, I believe, upon many of the questions and results of the social sciences. These involve broad issues like the provenance of tastes (including, what is particularly essential for social processes, individuals' "taste" for *altruism*), the balance between optimization and selection in governing social outcomes, the forces favoring cooperation versus conflict as competitive strategies in social interaction, and the determinants of specialization in human productive activities. And some specific phenomena as well: the correlation of the male/female sex ratio with socioeconomic status, the recent tendency to have smaller numbers of "higher-quality" children, the predominance of small firms in transient economic environments, positive interest or time-preference, and minimum separation distances in locational or product-differentiation situations.

It was not very debatable, perhaps, that the sociobiological approach does have *some* utility for social science purposes. But how much? The central question is whether or not the human species has entered a new domain of experience where general biological laws will have only negligible relevance or have even been abolished by the unique developmental advances achieved by mankind. Among such might be included: (1) the transcending importance of cultural as opposed to genetic change; (2) the degree of intelligence and awareness, suggesting that man can henceforth regulate and control the evolutionary process by deliberate cultural and even genetic modifications of the human material itself—quite apart from operations on the environment; (3) the invention of weapons of intraspecies competition that threaten the survival of all mankind; and (4) what might hopefully be a countervailing factor, man's possession of moral, spiritual, and ethical values.

At this point it is possible only to pose the question, not to answer it. In terms of the proximate goal of research strategy, perhaps it is sufficient to say that the sociobiological approach holds out great hope for breaking down not only the "vertical" discontinuity between the sciences of human behavior and more fundamental studies of life but also the "horizontal" barriers among the various social studies themselves.

[147] See Martin L. Cody, *supra* note 15; David J. Rapport & James E. Turner, *supra* note 3.

[148] Michael T. Ghiselin, *supra* note 4.

[8]

Sociobiology and Economics

GORDON TULLOCK*

It is a striking fact that the world's first professor of economics in a way founded modern biology. Both Darwin and Wallace, the two co-inventors of the evolutionary hypothesis specifically acknowledged their debt to Malthus.

In spite of this close connection at the beginnings of modern biology, however, the two disciplines had very little contact with each other until about 1960 and in fact still have far less contact than I think is desirable. It is true that colleges of agriculture normally had departments of agricultural economics as well as various applied biology specialties and individuals from two disciplines sometimes worked together on the same project. The projects were, however, highly applied and there is no sign of the kind of interdisciplinary fertilization which would have led the biologist to use economic methods or vice versa.

The lack of cross fertilization between two disciplines which had been so close together at the beginning is only superficially surprising. They were indeed very greatly different in structure until very recently. Economics from the beginning has been structurally rather similar to physics in being based on complex theoretical propositions and empirical research to validate them. Before the computer revolution the empirical work was comparatively crude and theory was heavily emphasized. Since the advent of the computers and the new statistical tools which have been developed to make the best use of them empirical work in economics has come into its own. It has now become as important as theoretical work.

Biology, however, although it had the vast overarching theory of natural selection was essentially a non-theoretical or basically empirical science at the operating level. With the exception of genetics which became a very highly developed mathematical science early in the twentieth century, most biological work was essentially observational or experimental and had little direct connection to the theory of evolution. Indeed it had little direct connection with any very sophisticated theory at all.

The situation began to change in the thirties with the work of such men as Fisher but basically the revolutionary impact of the new theoretical ideas was a development of the 1960's and 1970's.

Essentially the change was the result of a major theoretical insight. It was realized that the theory of evolution was not only a grand overarching theory but that it had things to say in detail about individual specie. It was possible to make theoretical deductions from the theory of evolution and then to test them by examining the detailed data.

The general form of this new work can perhaps be seen from an article in the current journal of The American Naturalist.[1] Needless to say in both economics and biology not all articles follow the pattern of theory development followed by empirical testing. As in physics in both biology and economics there are many articles which are only theoretical and other articles which simply test empirically propositions developed theoretically elsewhere.

The similarity between the two disciplines is not limited, however, to the fact that they are

*Virginia Polytechnic Institute & State University.

[1] Diane W. Davidson, "Size variability in the worker caste of a social insect (Veromessor pergandei Mayr) as a function of the competitive environment." *The American Naturalist*. Vol. 112, No. 985, pp. 523-32.

now following what we might call the Popper-pattern of hypothesis and test with the hypothesis deduced from a central overarching set of theories. There is also a very close resemblance in the general structure of the theory. In both cases the theory involves maximization against constraints.

To begin with biology one of the consequences of evolution would be that most species now existent should be at least reasonably efficient. With some knowledge of the environmental conditions faced by the specie it is possible to deduce efficient patterns of behavior or physical design and then test to determine whether this deduction is correct. Most of the theoretical biology articles do indeed follow that pattern. The close similarity between this and economics is obvious. The individual economic entities are seen as maximizing utilities subject to constraints and a deduction as to the behavior is drawn from knowledge of the constraints. This is then tested.

The two procedures are also subject to rather similar limitations. Firstly, the assumption that the individual specie is efficient or the individual is maximizing utility is rarely directly tested. In fact, of course, the experiment of necessity is an indirect test of it but most biologists and economists are sufficiently convinced of these foundation stones of their work so that they use them without much skepticism. To a considerable extent, of course, this conviction is based on earlier work.

Secondly, in both cases the deductions are a little dubious. In economics we are never really clear in our minds as to exactly what will maximize utility for some given individual. We therefore use proxys and fortunately there is a fairly simple widely used set of proxy which appears to have enough agreement with the real world so that there is no great difficulty. In biology the problem is we do not really know the entire environment of any species in perfect detail and we do not know the mechanical limitations on the design of species in similar perfect detail. Thus, the hypothesis that it is efficient is not perfectly fitted to the real world. This once again makes the situation rather similar to that in economics.

It can be noted from the above that I am claiming what amounts to a mapping of biology in economics. I do not claim that they can be deduced from each other but only that the particular technical apparatus now dominant in the two disciplines happens to be almost identical with the result that individuals can easily shift from one to the other. I myself have been writing articles, notes, comments, etc. in biology for nearly 10 years now.[2] Their quantity is not great but after all I am not a professional biologist. It is hard for an outsider to judge quality, particularly with his own work, but there is at least one objective test available from the citation index. My articles, notes, etc. have received considerably more than the average number of footnote references.

The reason for pointing out my own success in putting articles in biology is not entirely vanity although I will not claim that is not partly involved. The real point is to indicate the two disciplines are close enough together so that it is fairly easy to switch from one to the other. Indeed, it could be argued that I have never left economics, that all of my "biological" articles are simply economics articles in which I have rather unusual sets of entities maximizing a rather unusual utility function.

[2] For example see "Biological Externalities," *Journal of Theoretical Biology*, 33, December 1971, pp. 379-92; "Altruism, Malice, and Public Goods," *Journal of Social and Biological Structures*, I, January 1978, pp. 3-9; "Switching in General Predators: A Comment," *Bulletin of the Ecological Society of America*, 51, September 1970, pp. 21-4; "The Coal Tit as a Careful Shopper," *The American Naturalist*, 105, January-February 1971, pp. 77-80; "Altruism, Malice, and Public Goods: A Reply to Frech," *Journal of Social and Biological Structures*, 1978, 1, pp. 187-9; "On the Adaptive Significance of Territoriality: A Comment," *The American Naturalist*, Vol. 113, No. 5, pp. 772-5; and "Economics and Sociobiology: A Comment," *Journal of Economic Literature*, September 1976, pp. 502-6.

TULLOCK: SOCIOBIOLOGY AND ECONOMICS

So far I have said nothing about sociobiology. This discussion of a relationship between economics and biology in general, however, is a necessary preliminary to the discussion of the relationship between economics and sociobiology.

One might call the new theoretical biology "micro" deductions about plants and animals in terms of efficiency. Natural selection is assumed to guaranty that the genes provide for efficiency in the individual animal and we can thus make deductions. This is not true only of the physical design of the animal. Insofar as behavioral patterns are inherited they also would be selected for efficiency in the same way and hence the same kind of deduction can be made. There is now quite an extensive biological literature dealing with this particular topic.

Among the many behavioral patterns which might be inherited would be those which lead to social behavior. These also are subject to the same analysis and there is here again a considerable modern literature. This field is called sociobiology.

Since the techniques of economics map a more general biological example it follows that they would also map the sociobiology reasoning. It is thus fairly easy for economists to make contributions in the sociobiology area. I should say that in my opinion it would be equally easy for a biologist to make the reverse transition into economics and indeed one of them, Garrett Hardin, has done so. I have thus come to what I think is the intersection between economics and sociobiology. As we have noticed I think it is of less total significance than the intersection between economics and modern biology in general but it still doubtedly exists.

Further, from the standpoint of an economist sociobiology is undeniably more interesting than the rest of biology simply because it is closer to what he normally studies. Further, it is clear that study of non-human societies will broaden the approach that an economist has in his studies of human societies. Nevertheless, I believe for reasons which will be given shortly that there is little more direct aid which any student of human society can get from sociobiology. I should like to qualify the above statement, however, by saying that I do not feel confident this will remain true in the future.

There are two problems, one of which is human society is clearly very drastically different from most animal societies and, the second is that we do not understand most animal societies very well anyway. But let me elaborate. I would like to begin with a very brief statement with respect to the first point that is that human societies are not very similar to animal societies and turn to a fairly lengthy discussion of the second that we don't understand animal societies very well and then return to a discussion of the differences between the evolutionary experience of humans and of animals.

Beginning then with the differences in human societies and animal societies the first thing that must be noted is that it is large. The importance of this observation, however, is reduced when we realize how immense the differences are among animal societies.[3] Consider the difference between a hyena pack and a slime mold. To put it mildly it is not obvious that the difference between human society and a hyena pack is greater than the difference between the hyena pack and the slime mold. Ectroprocts, sponges, and jelly fish are all societies which are radically different from the social insects. We observe great differences between human society and those animal societies, mainly the social insects and mammals, which we understand best. This does not prove that the differences between societies of the social insect and mammals on the one hand and sponges on the other are not even greater.

---

[3] As far as I can tell there are also social plants. A cluster of blackberry bushes for example or an elm grove would probably be called societies if it were not that we restict the term in ordinary usage to animals only.

The existence of this wide range of societies raises the perfectly genuine possibility, emphasized by Wilson, that we may be able to develop a general theory of society for which all of the known social groupings would be seen as special instances. We could in this theory move from one type of social structure to another by just changing some of the parameters. Although this is a hope for the future we are definitely not there now. A great deal of study of such little known societies as the social spiders, the sponges and the ectoprocts is needed before we can tell whether this possibility is a real one.

The difficulty of lack of knowledge in this area can be illustrated by the fact that Wilson mentions sponges only three times in his massive sociobiology and apparently doesn't understand them. I make this point not to criticize Wilson. Certainly all of us have gaps in our knowledge but simply to point out that even such an extremely well informed man as he is ignorant of one of the major categories of animal society.

Let me now turn to a more detailed discussion of the gaps in our knowledge of animal societies. I should like to begin with a criticism of what I call the haploidy theory of society in the general category of ants, bees and wasps. That these animals like their non-social relatives have an unusual method of reproduction is obvious and it seems quite possible this unusual method of reproduction had something to do with the development of social life in this family. There is, however, a difference between the origins of a society and how that society itself works.

The hypothesized close relationship between the sisters of a queen and her offspring depends on the assumption that the queen has not mated with more than one male. Further, in about half of all ant specie there is more than one queen in the nest. Indeed the aggressive and rapidly expanding argentine ants are a multi-queen specie. If they achieve world dominance, which seems possible, we will have a theory of ant society which doesn't fit the most prominent single example of such society.

It must be admitted, of course, the haploidy does provide a particularly simple explanation of how social life might have originated. In fact it has, however, originated in widely different areas including, of course, the termites, whose societies so closely resemble the ants. This seems to indicate that the haploidy is at best a facilitating factor in the development of social organization and not a necessity.

There is another older theory of functioning of the social organization of such species as the ant and termite which in fact works a little bit better than the haploidy theory since it does include the termites but also has its defects. This theory simply points out that a reproduction is confined to the queen in the ant and the royal pair in the termite. Hence the workers do not pass on their own genes. The genes which control the workers, therefore, are not designed to promote survival of the workers but promote survival of the reproductives. This means the survival of the whole nest which is necessary for the survival of the reproductives.

This theory is I think somewhat wider in its potential application than the haploidy theory since it does apply to the termites. It suffers, however, once again from the fact that a number of ants nests have more than one queen and some termites nests have more than one royal pair.

This theory, further, like the haploidy theory, falls completely apart when applied out of social insect areas. Indeed it doesn't even fit one particular group of social insects, the social spiders.

Explaining animal society, however, is easier with the social insects than with those much more ancient societies, the slime molds and the sponges. In both of these cases apparently undifferentiated amoeba like single cell animals[4]

[4] Those which wander around freely in the environment in the case of the slime molds but in the case of the sponge confine their activities to moving through the jelly like interior of the sponge itself.

at one stage in their life cycle get together and form a reproductive body in which as far as we can see thousands of these cells are given an opportunity to contribute their genes to the next generation but many many more such cells are not. All of our theories of transmission of a social habit from one generation to another fail in these cases. If we are to have a general theory of sociobiology we must at the very least explain these societies.

Thus, although we may in the long run develop a general theory of society from study of all existent social animals[5] we are a long way from it. This does not, of course, prove that we should not attempt generalizations from our present rather inadequate data base. It does, however, indicate that we should put little reliance on these generalizations until we have been able to test them with further research.

In having called for more research with respect to, in essence, the hereditary basis of social behavior among non-humans I should now like to criticize the current theory of animal societies. Apparently this behavior is explained to a very considerable extent by references to the term "altruism." In another place I have argued that at least one potential mechanism for what biologists call "altruism" kin selection will not bear the weight put upon it.[6]

Leaving that issue aside I should like to here argue that altruism is neither necessary nor the likely explanation of social behavior in animals except in those particular cases where the society consists of a single reproductive (or single pair of reproductives) and the remaining members of the society cannot directly reproduce. In this latter case the relationship between the let us say individual bee and the hive is, from the standpoint of evolution, very similar to the relationship between a skin cell and its body. In both cases there cannot be any direct reproduction and all genetic messages must be carried by the reproductive specialists. That the non-reproductives whether bees or skin cells are programmed to sacrifice for the whole nest or organism is not surprising. Even here, however, the word "altruism" has to be given a rather unusual meaning to make it apply.[7]

Since the bulk of animal societies do not meet the above test I would like to turn here to another possible organization principle which may explain them. I do not claim, of course, to have complete explanations for them, all that will be presented here is a very brief outline of how I think we should think about them and the approach which I think might be fruitful.

I said before that altruism was not necessary or terribly useful in explaining society. Let me begin by proving that it is not necessary. The proof is ridiculously simple. The very large volume of economic research which is used to explain human society characteristically does not make any use of altruism whatsoever.[8] Outside the family (and economics have mainly dealt with relations outside the family), individuals are normally assumed to be engaged in simple straight forward selfish maximization with no regard for others. Economists are aware, of

[5] And once again I would suggest looking into the problem of social plants.

[6] For example see "Altruism, Malice, and Public Goods," *Journal of Social and Biological Structures*, I, January 1978, pp. 3-9; H. E. Frech, III, "Altruism, Malice, and Public Goods: Does Altruism Pay?" *Journal of Social and Biological Structures*, I, April 1978, pp. 181-5; "Altruism, Malice, and Public Goods: A Reply to Frech," *Journal of Social and Biological Structures*, I, April 1978, pp. 187-9; and a general symposium on the subject is scheduled for an early issue of the *Journal of Social and Biological Structures*.

[7] Some years ago I wrote a book, *Coordination without Command: The Organization of Insect Societies*, which explains how I think these societies work. Unfortunately I was unable to find a publisher but anyone curious can obtain a copy for the cost of xeroxing.

[8] In earlier days human society was also explained by altruism or to be more precise benevolence. See the Earl of Shaftsbury, "Characteristics of Men, Manners, Opinions," *Times*, 3 Vol , 3rd Edition (N.P. 1723) and Francis Hutchinson, "A Short Introduction to Moral Philosophy." (N. P. 1747)

course, that this is not a 100 percent realistic assumption. Human beings are undeniably altruistic although when we say that human beings are altruistic we are using the word in a different and more conventional sense than the biologist's use of the same word. Economists indeed have investigated human altruism and for that matter intra-family relations. The bulk of economic theory, however, is based on straight forward non-altruistic assumption.

This theory without any altruism is undeniably the best available theoretical explanation of any society, probably because we are more interested in human society than in others. Further, it is by now very thoroughly validated by empirical research. Most of this research is statistical investigation of real world behavior but there is a fair although not overwhelming vol ume of straight forward experimental research.

The fact that the theory is empirically validated although it tends in most applications to ignore human altruism which is a real phenomena may surprise the reader, but apparently human altruism outside the family is a fairly small matter. The average person is apparently willing to give something between 1 and 3 percent of his income to help others. The deviance between the real world with this minor degree of altruism and the non-altruistic theory is small enough so that it does not interfere with the empirical tests. Of course, as I have said several times economists do on occasion directly investigate altruism or incorporate altruism into their investigation of other subjects if it appears that in this particular case it will be of greater significance than normal.

Since this is an example of an elaborate theoretical justification of the most complex society we know[9] it is obvious that theoretical explanations of societies do not necessarily depend on altruism. This, of course, does not prove that animal societies do not depend on altruism merely that it is not a necessary foundation. In this connection it is notable that towards the end of *Sociobiology* Wilson extends his altruism idea to human society and says that humans have worked out a form of reciprocal altruism called contract. Perhaps he is correct and that is why we carry out contracts but it is certainly not the explanation normally given by other students of human society.

The conventional explanation is that human society is based not on altruism but on a social arrangement which in many cases (but unfortunately not in all) change the selfish advantage of the individual so that he helps others because it is in his own self interest even though he is uninterested in their well-being. Of course, in fact he is not completely uninterested in their well-being but the degree to which he is altruistic is relatively small compared to his drive to aid himself. Society would collapse if it depended on the rather modest bit of extra familia altruism which we do observe among human beings for its basic functioning.

These special social arrangements, however, are not found in animal societies so far as I know.[10] This social contrivance I would like to call "government" although the use of the term will be very broad and will include those very primitive societies in which there is no formal government but in which anyone who wishes to remain active and prosperous had better be well thought of by the other members of the little tribe or community.

Basically "government" in my meaning involves some kind of apparatus which will "enforce" certain rules. The details vary immensely from society to society and the rules which are "enforced" are equally varying but basically in all cases the violating individual or group is faced

[9] Notably the theory seems to work very well with simple societies too. See *Penny Capitalism: A Guatemalan Indian Economy*, sol tax Washington: U.S. Government Printing Office, 1953.

[10] The closest animal parallel that I know of occurred in some of the mammals who operate in packs. In these packs the dominant animal may "keep order" by attacking any of his inferiors who fight among themselves.

not only by the people whom he is directly harming but with outsiders who have overwhelming force and who will coerce him if he puts them to the test.

An example of this would be hierarchical control in which the lower official who refuses to obey orders from his duly constituted superiors faced not the possibility of a fight with that superior but coercion by a much larger body. Another example, human property is different from animal territoriality in that the trespasser does not have to be ejected by the owner himself, he can call in third parties.

This institution permits humans to engage in a great deal more cooperative activity than do animals although in those particular cases in which all members in the given animal society are decended from the same reproductives and only these reproductives can found new societies, another principle of cooperation which is even stronger is available.

This, however, is an indication that our society is not like that of most other animal societies. How then do they work? To answer this question let us talk very briefly about the problem of agreement and cheating. Consider two entities. If they interact there may be some gain from an agreement between them which patterns their behavior so that the total output is larger than it would be if they were acting independently. Note, that although usually there is some such "agreed improvement" possible it does not follow that it is present in all cases and in most cases it will involve only part of the activity of the two entities.

Once the agreement has been made it may well be the advantage of one or the other or indeed both of the parties to cheat on the agreement. Putting it in human terms they don't keep their promises. One of the functions of human government, of course, is to see to it that they do keep voluntary agreements and to compell them to carry out "social agreements" such as laws, constitutions, etc. This kind of thing is unfortunately absent in all animal societies of which I know. Bees do not keep order in their nests by having special police bees patrol the comb. But this does not mean that cooperation is totally impossible in animal society, merely that it cannot be carried to its optimal degree.

In many cases there is an agreement optimum and an independent adjustment optimum. The independent adjustment equilibrium may involve favorable interaction or at least the avoidance of unfavorable interaction between the two entities. To see the point consider Figure I. Here we have a standard prisoner's dilemma with the social optimum in the upper left hand corner and the usual prediction that without an enforced agreement the outcome would be the lower right hand corner. Both students of human society and students of biology would predict the lower right hand corner as the result of independent adjustment.

FIG. I

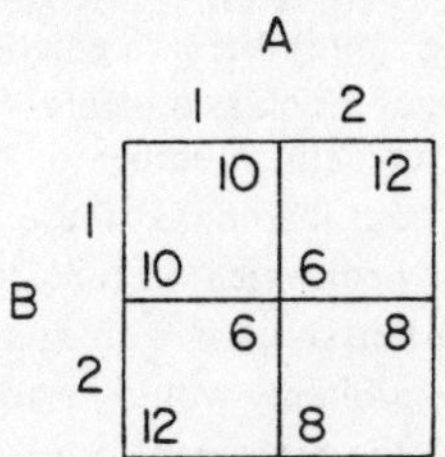

Now consider Figure II which is identical to Figure I except that a third strategy has been

FIG. II

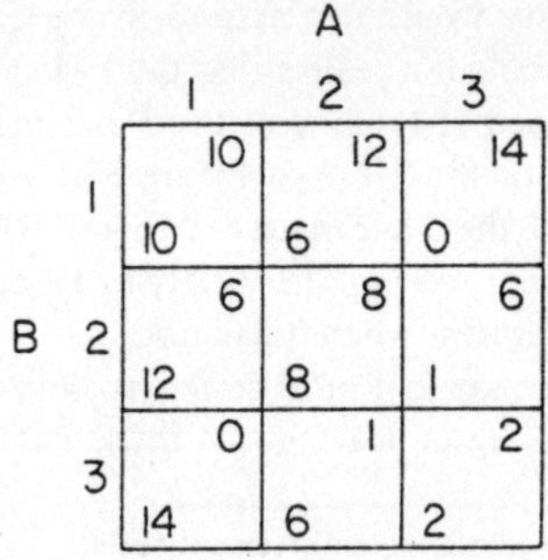

added for each of the two players. This has a saddle point at the middle or 2 - 2 square which, of course, was the solution also to Figure I. The parties do not play strategy three and thus end up worse off individually than they would with strategy two because the independent adjustment equilibrium of this particular game is the playing of strategy two by each party. Note, however, that this is the independent adjustment equilibrium and not the agreement equilibrium. A society which could enforce an agreement would achieve the 1 - 1 square[11] instead of the 2 - 2 square.

It is clear that an individual entity interacting with another will not select that strategy which injures the other entity most unless there is something in it for himself. Hence, the actual strategy chosen will of necessity not be the worst conceivable strategy from the standpoint of the two interaction entities. Thus, one can always allege there is something in the way of cooperation in the sense simply the two entities do not injure each other as much as possible.

Granted the immense number of species it seems not at all improbable that there would be some in which the equivalent of our 2 - 2 square would involve a fair amount with apparent cooperation. There probably would be none which actually reached the agreement equilibrium in the upper left hand corner but this might be far from obvious to the observer. The observer might see only a functioning society of some sort, i.e., 2 - 2 and notice that it could fall to the 3 - 3 square. The prospects for further cooperative activity would not necessarily be visible and hence would not realize that the 1 - 1 square existed. Instead of looking at the 3 x 3 matrix of Figure II or the 2 x 2 of Figure I he would be looking at the 2 x 2 matrix of Figure III. He might, therefore, feel that the society had reached optimal adjustment when it had not.

It seems to me that most animal societies we observe once again leaving out those cases in

FIG. III

B \ A	2	3
2	8 (B), 8 (A)	1 (B), 6 (A)
3	6 (B), 1 (A)	2 (B), 2 (A)

which there is specialization of reproduction would be in this independent adjustment equilibrium. Hence they would never be fully efficient but the efficiency losses might not be very visible from the outside standpoint. We should, however, in each case seek out the reason why from a standpoint of each individual entity it is sensible to be in the society and not "free ride."

Let me now turn to my final subject which is why I do not believe we can learn much about human society from animal society although once again I am not sure this is so. Humans have had a dramatically different evolutionary experience over the last million years perhaps over the last two million years than any other specie. Firstly, it would appear that at least as far as two million years ago humans exercised dominance over most other specie in their immediate environment. Presumably in this very early day they were rarely attacking elephants and they may well have avoided lions and tigers but certainly they were also regarded as dangerous by these powerful animals. The bones found associated with human artifacts in periods which are recent enough so that the bones survived indicated that very early human beings were eating even the largest and most powerful of their competing specie.

A specie like humans or like the present day lion[12] who is top of the preditor chain faces quite different evolutionary conditions than other species. Lions like human beings are not subject to predation by other species. Their main causes of death are attacks by con-specifics i.e. murder by another lion, disease and starvation.

[11] Disregarding, of course, enforcement costs.

[12] Assuming he is not in competition with human beings.

Protection against disease is largely non-behavioral, i.e. such mechanism as the white corpuscles. Defense against starvation in both the lion and the human species or at least the human specie until quite recently does involve behavioral modification.

One of the more important behavioral defenses against over-exploitation of resources leading to starvation, however, leads us to the third cause of death, aggression by con-specifics. Either a lion pride or a human tribe that finds its resource base a little weak always has the alternative of turning on neighboring prides or tribes and driving them back in order to increase its own resource space. That this type of behavior is common in human history is clear. Presumably it was also common in prehistory and indeed it may have been more common since the alternative ways of dealing with the same problem were probably much less developed than they were in the historic period. Lions certainly engage in this kind of activity although I have yet to read an account of a boarder war between two lion prides similar to that described by Kruuk[13] for hyenas.

It is in general a principle of biology that the competitors for any given entity who are most to be feared are other members of its own specie. In the case of a dominant or top of the food chain animal this takes a particularly obvious form in that the animal must fear murderous attacks from its con-specifics and indeed if it is to maintain control of a suitable resource base for its survival it must be prepared to win in such battles. Putting it differently, the evolution would select very very strongly for efficiency in combat with con-specifics.

Note, that I am not alleging that evolution would develop aggression or a tendency to fight when there is nothing to be gained by it. If some particular lion is aggressive in the sense that it seeks out fights with other lions when there is nothing to be gained thereby one can predict that its genes will be eliminated because obviously the more fights the more likely it is to be badly injured. The same would be true with human beings. Evolution led to combat efficiency but not necessarily to any particular desire to engage in combat.

In general, however, it would appear that human beings have been for a very long time now, certainly at least 500.000 years, subject to a good deal less competitive pressure than most species. We have a fairly slow reproduction rate. In addition our social and for that matter eating habits are such as to make us particularly suitable for propagation of germ diseases. Under the circumstances our effective reproduction rate even if there were no competition for resources would have been fairly slow until the development of modern medicine. This does not mean that we were not subject to selection but the selective pressure was relatively weak.

Further, the principle direction of evolutionary advance in human beings was the development of a larger brain i.e. a large apparently non-programmed computer which could be used to solve all sorts of problems. It developed in the old stone age but seems to be quite suitable for quantum mechanics, writing novels, and participating in national politics. Really it can't have very much hardwiring and must be mainly designed for self-programming.

These facts led to a situation in which although human beings did not, of course, escape from evolutionary selection, the selection ceased to have the tight restrictive characteristics it has on most specie. The situation in which human beings found themselves did not provide a single unique behavior pattern which was most efficient. It seems fairly certain that very early in the human race, individuals began to specialize in such things as making weapons or hunting. Further, technological development although slow does seem to have been characteristic of

[13] Hans Kruuk, *The Spotted Hyena*, A Study of Predation and Social Behavior, ed. George B. Schaller, Chicago and London: The University of Chicago Press, 1972, p. 335.

the human race for at least the last 500.000 years. Now consider the rule of thumb that it takes at least a hun'dred generations to fix a gene. In the human case that would be 2000 years. Any behavior control gene to be selected would have to pass the test of being efficient even over a period of 2000 years during which time the technology both of fighting and of making a living by whatever means was used by that particular tribe would certainly have changed at least some. Further, the gene going through one hundred generations would probably pass through people who had different behavioral specialities in the tribe. The witch doctor, the maker of stone axes and the common hunter would all have to be benefitted by that gene if it were to be selected. It does not seem likely that this would lead to tight genetic control of behavior, and, of course, in the last 50.000 years technological changes have been fast enough so that selection in general would be against any specific behavioral patterns.

As a result of this unique evolutionary background, human beings do a great many things which are contrary to the survival of their genes. The obvious single example is our tendency to put large resources into decorations of various sorts. We also spend a great deal of time in activities which have only entertainment value and which clearly do not increase the likelyhood that our genes will be transmitted. We also have a rather mysterious trait, altruism, which leads us to help people who are in no way related to us. This obviously has negative survival value in any tightly evolving specie. Under the loose restraints with which human beings are faced, however, it was possible for it to develop. Putting it all together human beings have a number of traits which would not have developed had we been subject to severe selective pressure. These traits are not likely to be found in species whose evolutionary background is different from ours. This raises great doubts as to whether our societies will closely resemble non-human societies. Note, however, it only raises great doubts, it does not prove that there is not some general science of society which covers both human society and the slime mold.

The general theme of this paper has been that we are unlikely to learn very much about human society by studying animal societies. They are fascinating subjects in and of themselves and clearly are suitable subjects for scientific investigation. In particular a large number of them are practically unknown and could repay intensive study. I would not anticipate, however, that the result of such study would be knowledge of our own society.

32

Bio-Economics: Social Economy Versus the Chicago School

by John M. Gowdy
Rensselaer Polytechnic Institute, Troy, New York

Introduction

The description "bio-economics" is currently being claimed by two opposing schools of thought. For one group of economists, led by Kenneth Boulding, Herman Daly and Nicholas Georgescu-Roegen, the term is chosen to emphasise the biological foundations of our economic activity. They remind us that the human species, as members of the animal kingdom, live as other species do, by taking low entropy from the natural environment and discharging it back into that environment as high-entropy waste. The economic system is thus viewed as a sub-set of larger processes taking place in the natural world. This school questions the reductionism typical of modern science and seeks to build an alternative approach based on a holistic view of nature and society.

For Chicago School economists the "imperialism" goes the other way, from economics to the rest of the world. Tullock [42, p. 3] describes the new theoretical biology as " 'micro' deductions about plants and animals in terms of efficiency". Becker[4] extends the economist's concept of individual rationality to group rationality as postulated by socio-biology. Hirshleifer[28] would extend the domain of economics even further. According to him, what biologists study is "nature's economy". Adaptation in the biological world can be described by the tools of neo-classical economics; organisms "optimise" so as to maximise "fitness". In Hirshleifer's view economics can be regarded as *the* field of inquiry, whose two great sub-divisions are the natural economy studied by biology and political economy studied by economists[28, p. 52]. From this point of view then, scientific analysis of the entire natural world may be brought under the domain of the economic way of thinking.

The Chicago School and the New Ecology

To the Chicago School bio-economics means extending the axioms and methodology of economics to the biological world. Microeconomic concepts are used to examine bits and pieces of natural phenomena. For example, Becker and Tomes[5] present a "bioeconomic" model of the family which attempts to extend the assumption of individual utility maximisation to the biological family. Among other things they assume that all members of the family, present and future, have identical utility functions and the children are produced asexually. As Daly[9] points out, the article is particularly interesting as an example of the absurd lengths to which some economists will go to force the natural world into the assumptions of classical theory. Other Chicago School economists view the adaptation of organisms to their environment as being analogous to "optimising" by the firm or the consumer. Adaptation is thereby reduced to a constrained maximisation problem, where "fitness", defined by Hirshleifer as "the ratio of offspring numbers to parent numbers at corresponding points in the generational life cycle"[28, p. 10], is the single-valued function to be maximised.

This view of nature is found in early ideas of ecology first formulated by biologists at the turn of the century. In 1910 Hermann Reinheimer described organisms as "traders" or "economic persons"[48, p. 291]. Reinheimer wrote:

> ...every day, from sunrise until sunset, myriads of (plant) laboratories, factories, workshops and industries all the world over, on land and in the sea, in the earth and on the surface soil, are incessantly occupied, adding each its little contribution to the general fund of organic wealth[48, p. 291].

From that time on the new science of ecology increasingly reflected the dominant ideology of the market economy. In the 1930s H.G. Wells and Julian Huxley[44, p. 961] described ecology as "the extension of economics to the whole world of life". Important figures in the "New Ecology" school were Charles Elton, August Thienemann, and Joseph Grinnell. Elton[14] suggested the principle of the "food chain" in which certain economic roles are performed. Plants are all "producers" and animals are either first- or second-order "consumers"[48, pp. 259-97].[1] Thienemann moved ecology even closer to economics by using the terms "producer", "consumer", "reducer" and "decomposer" to describe more complex ecological relationships. Grinnell coined the term "niche", to which he defined as the "status" or "occupation" of an organism in the community[48, p. 298]. In his view population pressure causes an intense competition for food that results in the emergence of only one species for each niche. Any existing species, then, has won its place by being efficient.

Perhaps the most important step in the new ecology movement was A.G. Tansley's[41] formulation of the concept of the ecosystem. As in Georgescu-Roegen's work in economics, Tansley's starting point was the Second Law of Thermodynamics or the Entropy Law. For Tansley, however, the Second Law became a means to reduce the study of ecology to rigid physical laws. All of nature could be reduced to a system of equations describing energy flows among organisms. Thus, the goal of the new science of ecology became the construction of a series of accounts which would describe nature's economy in terms of an energy theory of value. More recent biologists who have called for the adoption of the "methodological individualism" of economics include Ghiselin[20], Rapport[36] and Cody[8].[2]

So the new ecology, far from being a "subversive science"[38], cast the natural world in terms of the highly stylised, quantitative world of the corporate economy. Ecology today is statistical rather than teleological, reductionist rather than holistic. It is this tradition in ecology that the Chicago School bio-economists draw upon. The ideas have flowed from economics to biology and back again. In the 1970s Becker and Hirshleifer suddenly "discovered" that one of the dominant paradigms in ecology had much in common with economic theory. What they failed to see was that this commonality was the result of a common ideological milieu and was not due to common characteristics of the respective subject matter, as perceived by the Chicago School.

Brief mention should be made here of the Chicago School's adoption of socio-biology[46] to examine questions of economic policy[32, 7]. Both Becker and Hirshliefer use socio-biology to justify reactionary political views. Becker uses Wynne-Edwards' theory of altruism to argue that assistance to the poor does no good, since its effects will be diffused through intra-family redistributions[3,7]. Not to be outdone, Hirshleifer asserts:

> Sociobiology means that individuals cannot be molded to fit into socialist societies such as the Soviet Union without a tremendous loss of efficiency[49].

The ideological implications of Chicago School socio-biology are clearly expressed in an article appearing in *Business Week*:

> Bio-economics says that government programs that force individuals to be less competitive and selfish than they are genetically programmed to be are preordained to fail[49, p. 100].

When microeconomic concepts are applied to biology the original focus of ecology on interdependence and co-operation within an ecosystem all but disappears. There are several problems with the new ecology point of view, in terms of economics as well as biology. Among these are (1) the extension of the "ordinalist fallacy" to the realm of biology, and (2) the lack of any notion of duration or adaptation through time, which leads to an emphasis on competition to the exclusion of co-operation and interdependence. Among standard economists there is also an implicit denial that humans are bound by the rules that govern the rest of the universe.

The ordinalist fallacy[1, 16] is the representation of utility by a single-valued function; the notion that what consumers seek to maximise can be reduced to a single number no matter how diverse the components of the utility bundle[27]. When one extends this reasoning to the realm of evolutionary biology the difficulties are compounded. What is it that organisms maximise? In the natural world many goals are readily observable. Individual organisms apparently seek to maximise their lifespans, the number of surviving offspring, the number of their species, the long-term duration of their species, or any number of other, frequently conflicting, goals.

A second problem with Chicago School bio-economics is that it contains no sense of history. In Hirshleifer's view the "purpose" of an organism is the growth in species numbers; not balance, survival, or duration, but growth in numbers. Evidence against this idea may be seen in the biological world as well as in the economic world, where agents try to occupy niches where they will not be subject to competition. Once a niche is successfully occupied they do not, in general, try to displace other entities from "better" niches. Various species of sharks, for example, have remained unchanged for millions of years both in morphology and in absolute numbers. Biological organisms, like firms, "satisfice" rather than maximise. Again, the Chicago School describes the natural world in terms of the ideology of free market competition. Nature "red in tooth and claw" becomes a metaphor for the dominant social mythology of perfection through cut-throat competition. In fact, many biologists, including Darwin himself, have been struck by co-operation and interdependence as major themes in nature. This interdependence, the "web of life", tempers not only the idea of conflicts within nature but also the inevitability of the conflict between man and nature. Darwin writes:

> If we choose to let conjecture run wild, the animals, our fellow brethren in pain, diseases, death, suffering and famine — our slaves in most laborious works, our companions in our amusements — they may partake[of] our origin in one common ancestor — we may be all netted together (*Notebooks on Transmutation*, quoted in [48, p. 180]).

An important implicit, if not explicit, view in political economy is that humans are somehow outside the natural world. For Adam Smith it was the "propensity to truck, barter, and exchange one thing for another" that sets humans apart from other animal species. This characteristic "is common to all men, and to be found in no other race of animals"[39, p. 12]. This division between humans and the rest of the world sometimes became, in later writings in political economy, a conflict between good and evil. It became the job of humans to "amend the course of nature" to bring the natural world under human control so as to bring nature "more nearly into conformity with a higher standard of justice and goodness"[35, p. 44]. John Stuart Mill wrote:

> All praise of civilization, or art or contrivance is so much dispraise of nature, an admission of imperfection which it is man's business and merit to be always endeavouring to correct or mitigate[35, p. 15].

Malthus, too, saw nature as something apart from humans, as a force which severely limited mankind's desires and aspirations. Parson that he was, however, Malthus thought that the suffering imposed by nature was ultimately a good thing:

> The Supreme Being has ordained that the earth shall not produce good in great quantities till much preparatory labour and ingenuity has been exercised upon its surface[33, p. 204].

Among contemporary economists, nature's "imperfection" is justification both for the wholesale destruction of nature and for the belief that the human economy is somehow immune to the laws governing the rest of the natural world. In the field of biology Darwin's theory of evolution was most vehemently opposed on the grounds that humans had "souls" and therefore could not possibly be subject to the same natural laws governing other members of the animal kingdom. Among many contemporary economists the "free market" has replaced the soul as the factor which makes us immune from the forces that limit the success of other species. Hirshleifer[3] writes:

> The lack of the institution of *property* — founded, in turn, upon the larger institution of *law* and *government* — in the economy of Nature is an important element explaining the 'imperfection' of social adaptations in the biological realm.

In this view, the free market and the institution of private property enable humans to make a system more "perfect" than the natural one. In the human economy scarcity need not be a problem because humans can "truck, barter, and exchange". The problem is that scarcity in this view is strictly a one-dimensional problem of allocating a given amount of goods among consumers or inputs among firms. Given an array of goods and an initial distribution of these goods among consumers, the free market will ensure a Pareto-optimal distribution. The notion of Pareto optimality says nothing about constraints on the absolute amount of production, that is, nothing about the absolute standard of living or its duration. Pareto optimality is a static concept, dependent on a given point on the production possibilities frontier (relative scarcity), which says nothing about constraints on this frontier through time (absolute scarcity).

The legitimate offspring of the Chicago School, supply-side economics, has taken this view to its logical absurdity and declared the economy to be totally independent of any laws of nature. George Gilder[21] writes: "Because economies are governed by thought, they reflect not the laws of matter but the laws of mind". In the same vein, Julian Simon would have us believe that "in the end, copper and oil come out of our minds"[12]. The upshot of these arguments is that resources are not meaningfully finite. Human imagination, prodded by the forces of a free economy, will overcome any potential scarcity imposed by nature. These ideas are not new and are not confined to those defending a *laissez-faire* economy. The sociologist, Lester Ward, writing at the turn of the century, also drew a distinction between "the economy of nature" and "the economy of the mind". He argued that nature was competitive, anarchistic and inherently wasteful, while the human economy could be planned for the utmost efficiency. The "collective brain of society", human reason, could correct nature's shortcomings[43]. Central to all these views is the idea that human institutions are superior to those found in nature, and that they will overcome nature's limits. The economy is seen as a circular, self-contained system independent of the natural world.

Ecological Bio-Economics

To another group of economists, tied to the social economy school, "bio-economics" means viewing the economy as a sub-system of the natural world. To distinguish this group from the Chicago School we will use the cumbersome term ecological bio-economics. The best known members of this group are Boulding, Daly, Miernyk, and Georgescu-Roegen. Their views are in sharp contrast to the "economic imperialism" discussed above, as well as to an "ecological reductionism" that sees economic prices as reflecting embodied energy. Like the new ecology school in biology the ecological bio-economists take the Entropy Law as the starting point for much of their work. Humans, like other living things, survive by extracting low entropy from their environment. In contrast to other species, however, modern humans are able to live the way they do, not by living off the flow of solar energy, but by drawing down the stocks of sunlight stored in fossil fuels. The "mineralogical bonanza" that mankind has reaped has made possible the tremendous advances in technology over the past 200 years and has accommodated the vast increases in population through the application of energy and petrochemicals in agricultural production. Members of the ecology school of economics point out that, contrary to the picture painted in standard textbooks, the economy is not a circular-flow system. It is maintained by low-entropy resources flowing from the environment to the economy and it necessarily pumps high-entropy waste back into the environment.

The ecological school can also claim a long intellectual heritage. The English Romantic poets, Wordsworth, Coleridge, and Blake, saw harmony in nature and wanted humans to be part of that harmony. In the "Rime of the Ancient Mariner" the sailor thoughtlessly kills an albatross, one of God's creatures. His soul is lost in torment until he sees the beauty of nature's harmony:

He prayeth best, who loveth best
All things both great and small;
For the dear God who loveth us,
He made and loveth all.

Bio-Economics 37

The Romantic poets were in the forefront of a battle against the reductionism that was sweeping across scientific disciplines in the nineteenth century. John Stuart Mill, quoted earlier as seeing humans in a struggle against nature, was influenced by the Romantic poets at least at some periods in his life[13], and can also be quoted by steady-state supporters:

> It must always have been seen, more or less distinctly, by political economists, that the increase in wealth is not boundless: that at the end of what they term the progressive state lies the stationary state. . . [which] I am inclined to believe would be, on the whole, a very considerable improvement on our present condition[10].

Alfred Marshall[31], in support of a biological model of the economy rather than a mechanical one, wrote:

> In the later stages of economics, when we are approaching nearly to the conditions of life, biological analogies are to be preferred to mechanical.

The Anglo-American philosopher Alfred North Whitehead, one of the forerunners of the modern ecology movement, presented a systematic critique of the mechanistic viewpoint of scientific thought of the eighteenth century. That century's view of nature was based on the mechanistic outlook of Galileo, Descartes and Newton. To Whitehead this was "one-eyed reason, deficient in its vision and depth"[48, p. 316]. What was missing from the mechanical, reductionist view was an appreciation of relatedness. To Whitehead:

> Nature is a structure of evolving processes. The reality is the process. It is nonsense to ask if the colour red is real. The colour red is an ingredient in the process of realisation. The realities of nature are the pretension in nature, that is to say, the events in nature[46, p. 74].

Whitehead's criticism is that the reductionist nature of Western science does not allow us to see the whole. His insistence that nature should be seen as a whole rather than as an unrelated series of discrete parts was a major influence on members of the ecological school of economics, including Nicholas Georgescu-Roegen.

For Georgescu-Roegen the term bio-economics,

> . . .is intended to make us bear in mind continuously the biological origin of the economic process and to spotlight the problem of mankind's existence with a limited store of accessible resources, unevenly located and unequally appropriated[18].

He draws on the work of Erwin Schrodinger[37] who points out that life exists by drawing low entropy from the surrounding environment. Life is able to concentrate low entropy in part of the system although the overall level of entropy in the whole system increases. Another influence on Georgescu-Roegen was the biologist, Alfred Lotka[30]. Lotka saw that all species, including humans, go about their business of living by using the physical organs with which they were biologically endowed at birth. Lotka called these *endosomatic* organs. For most animals these endosomatic organs dictate how they live, where they live, even the "social structure" of their communities. Humans, however, are the only species to make extensive use of *exosomatic* organs, organs outside the body. These may be considered as "detachable limbs" such as spears, clubs, knives, cars, planes, etc, and all the things that are the physical manifestation of human culture. Exosomatic evolution is the reason why humans have been so successful in colonising the world, in creating the high material standard of living for most of the world's population.

Exosomatic evolution, however, has confronted humans with two major predicaments. The first of these is mankind's addiction to the comfort provided by these exosomatic organs. The production of the various gadgets and implements that extend our bodies draws down the finite stock of available energy and matter stored in the earth, and causes increasing deterioration of the earth's biosphere. The second predicament is the social conflict generated by exosomatic evolution. Georgescu-Roegen[18] argues that exosomatic organs become the object of social conflict. Endosomatic organs, being the property of the individual, cannot be the object of class conflicts. When production becomes a social activity, however, it becomes difficult to determine who produces what and it is no longer clear how the fruits of production should be distributed. Exosomatic organs, being the end result of hundreds of thousands of years of cultural evolution, are not the natural product of any individual, yet certain individuals are able to expropriate them precisely because it is not clear who created them.

The message of ecological bio-economics is that the economic system is an extension of human biological evolution. Like other biological entities the economy survives by extracting low entropy from a limited environment. The main points of this approach are these:

(1) an appreciation of man's economic activity as a part of nature, not as a self-renewing, circular flow independent of the environment;

(2) the realisation that the stocks of non-renewable energy and matter are finite, as is the assimilative capacity of the environment;

(3) from (1) and (2) a knowledge that economic growth cannot continue indefinitely. There is compelling evidence that we are nearing the limits of the earth's capacity both in terms of available fossil fuels and in terms of the biosphere's ability to accept further pollution without severe damage to its life support systems.

How do these points relate to social economy and what are the implications of the bio-economic viewpoint to economic theory and policy?

New Directions for Social Economy — The Implications of Bio-Economics

It is commonly argued that neo-classical theory remains dominant because there is no other body of theory to take its place. In fact, this is not the case. In recent years economic events have rocked the economics profession to a degree not seen since the Great Depression. These challenges have resulted both in a growth in "ultra-orthodoxy" typified by the supply-side and rational expectations groups, and in renewed interest in challenges to orthodox thought. Within the latter, several schools of competing thought have gained adherents. Among those schools are post-Keynesians, Marxians, institutionalists, and social economists. Ecological bio-economics has been most closely identified with social economics, although one would have to say that it still remains outside any of the major dominant alternative schools of thought.

Within the framework of the bio-economic viewpoint, Georgescu-Roegen has proposed a comprehensive alternative to neo-classical general equilibrium theory.

His theory of production takes into account the unidirectional nature of economic change and sees resource exhaustion and environmental pollution as an integral part of the economic process. His view of the economic process was first presented in 1971, in *The Entropy Law and the Economic Process*, and has been refined and extended since then[17]. Unfortunately his work in production theory has been largely ignored, both by mainstream economists and by those who are more sympathetic to his views.

In terms of economic theory, ecological bio-economics has two major implications. First, the fact that the economic system is continually undergoing evolutionary change implies that a general equilibrium approach is untenable. Second, again drawing upon analogies with biology, co-operation and interdependence are more important concepts in describing economic reality than is competition.

General equilibrium theory, based on the mechanical model of the universe, presents a strictly deterministic model. Given the assumptions of the neo-classical model, the firm, if it is to survive, cannot in any meaningful sense dictate its own actions. With a near-infinite number of firms and perfect knowledge on the part of all agents in the economy, the best a firm can do is fill an available ready-made niche. If it acts within certain externally determined parameters it will make a normal profit and survive; if it does not meet these predetermined conditions it will fail[25].

A current controversy within the field of evolutionary biology has great relevance for general equilibrium theory in economics. This is the notion of "punctuated equilibria". In this view evolution proceeds unevenly. Long periods of statics are broken by periods of rapid change. Gould writes:

> For millions of years species remain unchanged in the fossil record and then abruptly disappear, to be replaced by something that is substantially different but closely related[29, p. 885].

The same sort of pattern of relatively uneventful periods punctuated by rapid change can be seen in economic history. If economic change is characterised by periods of relative calm, broken by sudden disruptions, a problem arises for the adaptationist or "survival of the fittest" view of economic evolution. Catastrophic events, such as wars or depressions, must be seen as more than simple magnifications of the natural process of weeding out the less fit firms. If periodicity exists in economic history it places the emphasis on external rather than on internal (efficiency) phenomena in economic change. Firms, like the dinosaurs 160 million years ago, may be well adapted to a particular environment only to be swept aside as external conditions suddenly change. The marginal approach of neo-classical general equilibrium theory may be appropriate to the interstitial periods but it is inadequate to explain the periodic sweeping changes that characterise economic history. And, of course, it is these periods of sweeping change that are critical for economic evolution and economic policy. By this view then, marginal analysis is flawed not because it is wrong but because it yields precise answers only to comparatively unimportant parts of the economic problem.

A second major theoretical implication of ecological bio-economics is that co-operation and interdependence are more important in describing economic reality than is competition. Spencer's phrase "survival of the fittest" describes the Chicago School view of the economy. The most efficient firms survive, the others perish and the result is a steady progression towards a better world. As Boulding[4, p. 18] and others have pointed out, however, this is really a tautology:

> If we ask 'fit for what?' the answer is 'to survive', so that all we have is a survival of surviving, which we knew anyway, and unless fitness — that is, survival value — can be specified in some way, the principle is quite empty.

In Boulding's view, a much better phrase would be "the survival of the fitting". Economic systems, like ecosystems, have myriad niches within which survival is possible. When one looks objectively at the biological or economic environment, the striking feature is interdependence and "mutual aid" to use Kropotkin's term.

The above theoretical considerations have important policy implications. The neo-classical theory of general equilibrium means that the only legitimate policy action of government is to keep the market "free". Obviously, once a perfect system has been established any change will make that system worse than before. Some neo-classical economists grudgingly admit that some instances of market failure are present and that some action is necessary to correct externalities or to provide public goods. In general, however, the Chicago School argues that while market failure may be present, government action is so imperfect it will invariably make the situation worse.

On the other hand, ecological bio-economics suggests that what exists may be largely a matter of chance. There is no divine justification for whichever particular economic arrangement exists at a particular time. The existence of pure uncertainty and periods of random disruptive change may offer a rationale for government guidance and intervention.

Perhaps the most important policy implication of ecological bio-economics is that we must act now to conserve the earth's dwindling mineralogical and biological resources. The economy is not a circular self-contained system, but is dependent for its survival on inputs from a non-renewable stock of natural resources and outputs to a finite environment.

The policy implications of this view are summarised by William Miernyk[34]:

> Bio-economists urge policies that will force conservation of the world's dwindling endowment of energy and natural resources. They place more emphasis on an equitable distribution of goods and services than do conventional economists. They also recognize the need for steady progress on the technological front, perhaps even more so than their conventional brethren. The 'winding down' phase of the world economy can be stretched only by using our scarce resources more efficiently in the future than we have in the past.

Although there are many uncertainties involved in the policy implications of bio-economics, one thing is clear. The growth-oriented economic policies of the past are no longer adequate to address the problems of the present. Acid rain, the destruction of tropical forests, the alarming rate of species extinction, and the greenhouse effect all point to the fact that man's economic activity has reached the point where it is causing irreparable damage to its environmental base. There is now a fundamental conflict between economic growth and the preservation of the environment. The key policy problems emerging at the end of the growth-oriented economy revolve around the issues of population, conservation and redistribution.

A bio-economic viewpoint implies not only zero population growth but ultimately a reduction in population as the world's agricultural system shifts from fossil fuel-based production to organic agriculture. At the least this means policies promoting family planning and the elimination of government subsidies for large families. Conservation means reducing the throughput of energy and matter in the economy. Policies here include fuel-efficiency standards, pollution taxes, the development of public transportation, and numerous other policies that have been widely discussed in the environmental economics literature.

The final implication of bio-economics is the one most difficult to deal with. This is the problem of redistribution in a non-growing or even shrinking economy. As the economic pie ceases to grow, policy makers will be forced to come to grips with long-neglected questions of unequal income distribution. No economic growth in the context of politics as usual means an increasingly unequal distribution of income and economic opportunity, a pattern we have seen since the 1970s. The Western world seems to be moving towards what has been referred to as a "two-thirds society", a society where the top two-thirds enjoy selfish prosperity while the bottom third continues to become a permanent underclass. In order to develop viable alternatives, therefore, bio-economics must formulate policies to address problems within the economic system itself as well as policies dealing with the interface between the economic system and the ecosystem.

Notes

1. Later in life Elton worried that "in giving priority to economic productivity, especially in regard to the production of large cash crops from the land, the human environment itself may gradually become dull, unvaried, charmless, and treated like a factory rather than a place to live"[13, 48,p. 300].

2. The economic ecologists are discussed by Hirshleifer[28].

3. This idea was expressed in the thirteenth century by Thomas Aquinas who postulated such an impassable chasm between humans and other animals when he contended that when God created the world he gave animals instinct and man the free intelligence of angels[45, p. 42].

References

1. Armstrong, W.E., "Utility and the 'Ordinalist Fallacy' ", *Review of Economic Studies*, June 1958, pp. 172-181.
2. Artin, T., *Earth Talk*,, New York, Grossman Publishers, 1973.
3. Becker, G.S., "Altruism, Egoism and Genetic Fitness: Economics and Socio-biology", *Journal of Economic Literature*, September 1976, pp. 817-26.
4. Becker, G.S., "A Theory of Social Interactions", *Journal of Political Economy*, Vol. 82, November/December 1974, pp. 1063-1093.
5. Becker, G.S. and Tomes, N., "An Equilibrium Theory of the Distribution of Income and Intergenerational Mobility", *Journal of Political Economy*, December 1979, pp. 1153-1189.
6. Boulding, K.E., *Evolutionary Economics*, Beverly Hills, Sage Publications, 1981.
7. Cherry, R., "Biology and Sociology and Economics — An Historical Analysis", *Review of Social Economy*, October 1980, pp. 141-154.
8. Cody, M.L., "Optimization in Ecology", *Science*, Vol. 183, 22 March, 1974, pp. 1156-64.
9. Daly, H.E., "Chicago School Individualism versus Sexual Reproduction: A Critique of Becker and Tomes", *Journal of Economic Issues*, March 1982, pp. 307-12.
10. Daley, H.E., *Steady State Economics*, San Francisco, W.H. Freeman, 1977.
11. Daley, H.E., "The Circular Flow of Exchange Value and the Linear Throughput of Matter-Energy: A Case of Misplaced Concreteness", *Review of Social Economy*, December 1985, pp. 279-97.
12. Daley, H.E., "Ultimate Confusion: The Economics of Julian Simon", *Futures*, October 1985, pp. 446-50.

13. Davis, E.G., "Mill, Socialism and the English Romantics: an Interpretation", *Economica*, August 1985, pp. 345-58.
14. Elton, C., *Animal Ecology*, 1927, Revised edition, New York, 1966.
15. Elton, C., *The Pattern of Animal Communities*, London, 1966.
16. Georgescu-Roegen, N., "Choice, Expectations and Measurability", *Quarterly Journal of Economics*, November 1954, pp. 503-34.
17. Georgescu-Roegen, N., "Feasible Recipes and Viable Technologies", *Atlantic Economic Journal*, March 1984, pp. 21-31.
18. Georgescu-Roegen, N., Inequality, Limits and Growth from a Bioeconomic Viewpoint", *Review of Social Economy*, December 1977, pp. 361-75.
19. Georgescu-Roegen, N., *The Entropy Law and the Economic Process*, Cambridge, Massachusetts, Harvard University Press, 1966.
20. Ghiselin, M.T., "The Economy of the Body", *American Economic Review*, May 1978, pp. 233-7.
21. Gilder, G., *Wealth and Poverty*, New York, Basic Books, 1981.
22. Gowdy, J.M., "Biological Analogies in Economics: A Comment", *Journal of Post-Keynesian Economics*, Summer 1983, pp. 676-8.
23. Gowdy, J.M., "Evolutionary Theory and Economic Theory: Some Methodological Issues", *Review of Social Economy*, December 1985, pp. 316-24.
24. Gowdy, J.M., "Marx and Resource Scarcity: An Institutionalist Approach", *Journal of Economic Issues*, June 1984, pp. 393-400.
25. Gowdy, J.M., "Non-Darwinian Evolutionary Economic Change", under review.
26. Gowdy, J.M., "Radical Economics and Resource Scarcity", *Review of Social Economy*, October 1981, pp. 165-180.
27. Gowdy, J.M., "Utility Theory and Agrarian Societies", *International Journal of Social Economics*, 1985, pp. 104-117.
28. Hirshleifer, J., "Economics From a Biological Viewpoint", *The Journal of Law and Economics*, 1977, pp. 1-52.
29. Lewin, R., "Evolutionary Theory Under Fire", *Science*, Vol. 210, 21 November 1980.
30. Lotka, A., *Elements of Mathematical Biology*, (1924), New York, Dover Books, 1956.
31. Marshall, A., *Principles of Economics*, eighth edition, London, Macmillan, 1920.
32. McCain, R., "Critical Reflections on Sociobiology", *Review of Social Economy*, October 1980, pp. 123-140.
33. Malthus, T., *An Essay on the Principle of Population*, (1798), New York, Penguin Books, 1970.
34. Miernyk, W., *The Illusions of Conventional Economics*, Morgantown, West Virginia, West Virginia University Press, 1982.
35. Mill, J.S., *'Nature' and 'Utility of Religion'*, New York, Bobbs-Merrill, 1958.
36. Rapport, D.J. and Turner, J.E., "Economic Models in Ecology", *Science*, Vol. 195, 28 January 1977, pp. 367-73.
37. Schrondinger, E., *What is Life?*, (1944), Cambridge, Cambridge University Press, 1967.
38. Shepard, P. and McKinley, D., *The Subversive Science*, Boston, Houghton Mifflin, 1969.
39. Smith, A., *The Wealth of Nations*, New Rochelle, Arlington House, no date.
40. Snyder, G., *Turtle Island*, New York, New Directions Books, 1974.
41. Tansley, A., *Practical Plant Ecology*, London, Allen and Unwin, 1923.
42. Tullock, G., "Sociobiology and Economics", *Atlantic Economic Journal*, September 1979, pp. 1-10.
43. Ward, L., *Dynamic Sociology*, (1897), New York, D. Appleton, 1924.
44. Wells, H.G. and Huxley, J., *The Science of Life*, Garden City, Doubleday, Doran & Co, 1938.
45. Wheeler, W.M., *Essays in Philosophical Biology*, Cambridge, Massachusetts, Harvard University Press, 1939.
46. Whitehead, A.N., *Science and the Modern World*, (1925), New York, Mentor Books, 1948.
47. Wilson, E.O., *Sociobiology*, Cambridge, Harvard University Press, 1977.
48. Worster, D., *Nature's Economy*, Cambridge, Cambridge University Press, 1977.
49. "A Genetic Defense of the Free Market", *Business Week*, 1978.

[10]

Journal of Economic Psychology 12 (1991) 557–573
North-Holland

Economics, sociobiology, and behavioral psychology on preferences

Ulrich Witt *

University of Freiburg, Freiburg, Germany

Received May 28, 1990; accepted July 16, 1991

Economists have become increasingly interested in hypotheses from sociobiology as a source of inspiration for filling gaps in the economic model of behavior. To avoid borrowing eclectically and arbitrarily from neighboring disciplines, this paper attempts to outline in a systematic way the similarities and differences between the approaches taken in economics and sociobiology. In doing so, special attention is given to an empirical theory of preferences that is lacking in economics. Here, inspiration from sociobiology would seem to be particularly useful. The considerations in the paper suggest that sociobiological arguments may indeed be helpful, albeit at a very elementary level only. A more comprehensive theory cannot ignore the influences of innate learning mechanisms in higher living beings. An elaborated theory of preferences in economics will have to acknowledge and incorporate insights from behavioral psychology.

1. Introduction

In recent years an increasing number of economists have been interested in discussing whether or not hypotheses from sociobiology might have a role to play in economics (Becker 1976; Hirshleifer 1977a; Tullock 1977; Hayek 1979; Margolis 1982; Tietzel 1983; Sugden 1986; Ursprung 1988; Güth and Yaari 1992). At first sight, economics and sociobiology do seem to have some things in common. In economics, scarcity and competition figure prominently as basic facts around

* I would like to thank R.J. Herrnstein, J. Irving-Lessmann S.A. Kauffman, and the participants of the European Sociobiological Society meeting in Brussels for helpful discussions related to earlier drafts of the paper. Thanks also to three anonymous referees of the present journal and W. Fred van Raaij for their detailed comments and recommendations. The usual disclaimer of course applies.

Author's address: U. Witt, Faculty of Economics, University of Freiburg, Europaplatz 1, 7800 Freiburg, Germany.

which theory has been built. In sociobiology, as in biology in general, competition and scarcity of natural resources also play a role, for instance, where habitat space (Milinski 1984) or reproduction opportunities, which are usually competitive, are scarce (on mating opportunities, see Waage 1979; Harcourt et al. 1981; on rearing offspring, see Trivers 1972). Here too, theoretical attempts to explain observable behavior reflect these basic conditions (see, e.g., Wilson 1975: ch. 3 and 6), though at a less prominent level.

Apart from that, however, the basic interpretation of behavior is markedly different in the two disciplines. Sociobiology, with its roots in the Darwinian theory of natural selection, is concerned with behavioral traits as represented in whole populations and produced by the principles of variation, selection and replication. In contrast, economics, at least the microeconomic theory discussed here, is deeply committed to the idea of individual autonomy. It has traditionally tried to explain behavior on the basis of a calculus of 'rational' decision making. Many components of the rational choice model are, of course, left unspecified, or are only specified in a purely ad hoc manner. A striking example are the hypotheses on individual preferences and on human information processing.

Thus, the economic model of behavior is actually incomplete and needs to be complemented with additional empirical hypotheses. Such an extension cannot only be expected to improve the explanatory power of microeconomic theory, but may also offer some new insights into particular features of evolution in the socioeconomic realm. In order to extend the boundaries of economic theory, an interdisciplinary dialogue seems necessary in which sociobiology may indeed play a role. However, a more elaborate theory will have to consider, in addition, the influences of innate learning mechanisms in higher living beings. This leads, in a natural way, to research topics traditionally investigated in psychology.

The paper proceeds as follows: section 2 discusses in more detail both the similarities and the differences between economics and sociobiology. Section 3 presents the basic structure of the economic theory of behavior and explains what is lacking. Special concern will be given to the hypotheses on individual preferences, i.e. on what people like/dislike and why. Section 4 considers how sociobiology might be helpful here from an economist's point of view. It will be shown that important insights can be gained, but that additional hypotheses are needed to deal with the kind of behavior which economists usually consider. These hypotheses, to be taken from the domain of the behavioral sciences and psychology, are briefly outlined in section 5 together with some implications. Section 6 contains some concluding remarks.

2. Scarcity and competition in economics and biology

It has often been argued that there are significant similarities between economics and biology and, sometimes, even modest forms of mutual inspiration in particular with regard to the theory of natural selection (Marshall 1938 passim; Hirshleifer 1977b, 1982; Fao 1982; Ghishelin 1978; Schweber 1977; Bowler 1989: 164–175). Since Malthus (1797), relative scarcity of resources, a key feature in the realm of economics, has been related to variations in generative behavior. Darwin's theory of genetic fitness is intimately related to competition and scarcity of resources, as reproductive success of the phenotype is a relative measure which depends on competitive advantage of particular traits in situations where increasing population density entails decreasing chances for survival and for raising offspring. Where these traits are behavioral ones, the proper domain of sociobiology (cf. Wilson (1975) and Krebs and Davies (1984) for introductions) is entered.

Both sociobiology and economics are interested in explaining observable behavior in terms of the obvious or, in case of genetic fitness, latent competition induced by scarcity. The former discipline relates the outcome primarily to the organisms' innate physical and behavioral traits which may or may not enable them to exceed the reproduction rates of rival individuals or rival species. In the socioeconomic sphere, the outcome depends to a usually much more significant extent on an elaborate framework of social behavioral regularities (institutions) as, for instance, rules of conduct, entitlement rights, and law. These are often presupposed implicitly when, for example, competition in the market place is discussed.

Even on an intra-individual level, the allocation of an organism's own scarce resources, time and energy, to alternative options available to the organism/individual may be identified as a competition phenomenon. This internal competition is not independent of external scarcity conditions since the latter may affect both the prospects for success and the relative costs of competing options (Wilson 1975: ch. 6). In the Darwinian theory of natural selection, the problem is treated as one of genetic adaptation, and specialization of both, the organism and its parts, is explained by this. Similarly, (micro-) economic theory suggests that observable human behavior can be explained as a response to the prevailing conditions of external scarcity, but the internal choice of one course of action over another is usually interpreted as a matter of deliberate (rational) decision making.

In pursuing such analogies, obvious differences between the two disciplines with respect to the role of competition and scarcity should not be overlooked. First, while in economics the notions of scarcity and competition are themselves at the center stage of theorizing, they have a role to play in biology only to the extent to which they can help to explain differences in genetic fitness. Second, in biology, scarcity, if it is relevant, is measured in terms of 'objective' criteria such as supply of energy, water, and calories per member of a population in a given habitat. In economics no such objective, easily verified, criteria are used. Since the overthrow of objectivist concepts such as the labor theory of value by the 'subjectivist revolution' of the 1870's, scarcity has been defined in terms of subjective evaluations and desires of the individuals involved or, in economic terminology, relative to their individual preferences (Kauder 1965). As a consequence, intra-individual discrimination between competing options is, in the perspective of economics, a highly subjective matter, and this certainly entails an individualistic bias for the whole theory.

3. The economic model of behavior

The simple explanatory scheme which underlies the economic theory of behavior consists of three hypotheses: (1) people are supposed to perceive a set of alternative courses of action and outcomes, but know that only a subset is actually feasible because resources commanded by the individual are scarce; (2) people are supposed to evaluate the alternatives according to their subjective desirability, i.e. according to individual preferences; (3) it is suggested that the alternative most preferred by the individual can be inferred from choices actually observed. This basic construction has also been applied quite successfully by other social scientists as, for instance, in the theory of social exchange in social psychology (Thibaut and Kelley 1959) and sociology (Homans 1961), or in a more sophisticated form in the 'expectancy × value'-approach in psychology (Atkinson 1982).

The three hypotheses taken together provide the basis on which, even with only a very limited knowledge of the particular subjective preferences, attempts are made to predict the effect of *changing* conditions of scarcity on individual behavior. Consider a simple example of an individual's choice of nutrition. Suppose, for convenience, that the individual can only allocate a fixed amount of her/his time to collecting or producing some form of nutrition A and/or some form B at a constant level of physical effort where A and B strongly differ in taste.[1] With respect to the individual preference it is usually assumed that: (i) the individual evaluates A and B positively and is able to consistently assess alternative bundles of A and B (completeness and transitivity assumption); (ii) for any given amount of A and B obtaining more of at least one of them is a preferred situation (no satiation occurs within the relevant domain); (iii) the desire for A (for B) declines relative to that for B (for A) the more of A relative to B (of B relative to A) the individual disposes of (convexity assumption).

If the time constraint is binding, it represents the scarcity condition and prevents the individual from increasing consumption in total. In order to get more of A some amount of B has to be sacrificed and vice versa. In this situation the individual is bound to choose the mix which (s)he prefers most among the combinations which are feasible given the time constraint. Once a choice is made, this means, of course, that the opportunity of choosing any other consumption mix has been foregone. In general, any kind of chosen behavior thus entails 'opportunity costs' in the form of the next best alternative that, though feasible, has not been chosen. Now imagine that due to some event in the natural or social environment scarcity conditions change so that more time is needed to obtain a unit of A while the time needed to obtain a unit of B is unchanged. This means that the opportunity costs of consuming A have been increased as the amount of B that can be obtained in place of each unit of A is now greater than before. Given that assumptions (i)–(iii) hold, the economic model predicts that individual behavior is

[1] The advantage of this simple choice problem is that it can easily be reproduced in animal experiments where A and B are different food pellets or liquids for which animals have to work by pressing different food/liquid dispenser levers (cf. e.g. Silberberg et al. 1987; Hursh et al. 1989).

likely to respond by consuming relatively more of the relatively less scarce form of nutrition B. [2]

To put it in more general terms, the theory suggests that individual behavior adjusts to changing conditions of scarcity, if these affect the subjectively perceived opportunity costs, with a tendency to economize on resources which become relatively scarcer and vice versa. This basic hypothesis was originally developed as a description of the outcome of conscious, or 'rational', decision making, which was believed be characteristic for solving economic problems. In fact, the theory has often been presented with normative connotations and its formal basis, the apparatus of constrained maximization, has been used to develop the foundations of economic decision-making skills, e.g. in operations research. However, recent years have witnessed a growing belief among economists and also experimental psychologists that the approach has general explanatory power and can successfully be applied to investigating all sorts of human behavior (see McKenzie and Tullock (1978), Hirshleifer (1985) and Radnitzky and Bernholz (1986) for surveys of different applications) and non-human behavior (see Kagel et al. (1980) and Hursh (1984) for surveys).

The problem with at least some of the attempts to apply to the economic model is that they come very close to being pseudo-explanatory in the following sense. If the postulated preferences and/or constraints may be specified ad hoc, any kind of choice behavior can be made rational, i.e. can be derived from the economic model (Rosenberg 1979; Rachlin 1980; Boland 1981). Such ad hoc specifications are not unusual (see, e.g., Hamermesh and Soss (1974), Blinder (1974), Azzi and Ehrenberg (1975) for particularly obvious cases). They originate from the fact that economics has failed to develop a body of general, empirically meaningful, hypotheses about what people have preferences for as well as about how they perceive actions, outcomes, and constraints. Instead, perfect perceptual skills (perfect information) and

[2] There is one exception. If the costs of acquiring A increase, this diminishes the feasible overall amount of nutrition in all bundles in which A is included. If A and B do not only taste different but A, unlike B, also covers elementary nutritional needs, e.g. for caloric intake, the overall reduction in feasible nutrition may induce the individual to consume even more of A as there may be no other way of satisfying the minimal caloric needs. This exceptional case is known in economics as the 'Giffen paradox'. Although there are only rare empirical examples in the economic literature (see Koenker 1977), several of the animal experiments mentioned in fn. 1 have been designed to produce, and claim to have found empirical evidence for, the Giffen effect.

formal properties of preference orders (completeness, transitivity, convexity and others) have simply been assumed without much empirical investigation.

With respect to the notion of constraints, the perfect information assumption tacitly presupposes, however, that a change in scarcity conditions is always subjectively realized, by the individual decision maker, in exactly the same way as the outside observer sees it. Furthermore, it is implicitly assumed that the recognition of the choice set is otherwise invariable or, if there is a variation, it is irrelevant. With respect to preferences, the formal properties discussed cannot substitute for empirical hypotheses about what people prefer since these are necessary for any empirical explanation. The only pertinent statement which can be deduced is that individual preferences do not change (explicitly asserted by Stigler and Becker 1977). In terms of the original, static, method in which the economic model of behavior was developed the shortcomings may have been overlooked. In such a framework, individual behavior, which actually emerges from an ongoing learning and decision-making process, appears as simple a-temporal one-shot decision making for which information and tastes can safely be assumed to be invariably given.

A systematic discussion of the theoretical background of preferences and perceived constraints, largely drawing on results from psychology, has only recently begun. Models of bounded perception and memory capacity (Simon 1976, 1982), of perception biases and decision heuristics (Kahneman et al. 1982; Machina 1987; Frey 1988), and of non-maximizing behavior (Vaughan and Herrnstein 1987) have been developed. It has also been recognized that perception of choices involves an imaginative element which cannot be conceptualized within a wholly adaptive framework (Shackle 1983; Witt 1989). Obviously, these psychological insights have considerably improved the theoretical foundations of a behavioral model of decision making. What is still necessary is a debate on individual preferences. As will be argued in the next section, such a debate might profit, though possibly only indirectly, from insights taken over from sociobiology.

4. What sociobiology might have to say on preferences

The lack of an empirical theory about the content of individual preferences in economics is unsatisfactory, given the prominent role assigned to preferences in its individualistic approach. The lack may in part result from the fact that neither preferences nor the way in which they emerge in the human mind are directly observable by the economist. Only with respect to a very limited number of alternatives, a 'snap-shot' of individual preferences may, at best, be indirectly identified from the alternatives a person says (s)he prefers or actually chooses (cf. Wong (1978) on the theory underlying such preference revelation experiments).

Can sociobiology help to provide the missing hypotheses? From the point of view of sociobiology, it may seem straightforward to assume that preferences are genetically determined. In line with the population oriented perspective, the preferences of human individuals could then be treated in a way which is fundamentally no different from the one in which other inherited personal traits or even morphological features are analyzed with regard to their survival value. Indeed, it can easily be imagined how the theory of natural selection could be applied here. Natural selection should favor preferences which, under the prevailing environmental conditions, increase the probability of having surviving offspring. Thus, innate preferences should have evolved so that the choice behavior they induce comes close to maximizing the genetic fitness of the respective phenotype.

On the basis of this conjecture, it seems possible to arrive at quite definite predictions about some items humans should have (innate) preferences for: air, water or other drinkable liquid, sleep, any measure that helps maintain body temperature, nutrition, sexual activity, maternal care, and so on. Such preferences can be expected to enhance genetic fitness when they induce the choice of those items rather than others in a certain mix per period of time. Even some more formal properties of preference orders might be assessable on the basis of the genetic fitness criterion. In fact, this could be so for the entire rational choice model (see Ursprung 1988).

As the very notion of preferences is not directly related to something observable, and as the level at which individual preferences are defined is, thus, a matter of pragmatic decision, it could be asked, of course, why a preference for own genetic fitness should not be stipulated immediately. For such a unique preference the items just mentioned would be assigned only an instrumental value. (If genes had preferences they would certainly choose that way.) An assumption like this seems straightforward in particular with regard to the problem of reciprocal altruism. Sociobiology has indeed discussed it in this connection, but the idea was not ultimately upheld.

In a seminal work on the apparent paradox of reciprocal altruism, Trivers (1971) had originally cast the problem theoretically in the form of an ordinary prisoner's dilemma game in which the payoff to each individual player is defined in terms of a genetic fitness measure. As is well known, the 'rational choice' game theory, to which Trivers thus referred, presumes that the payoffs correspond to the players' preferences in the form of a monotonic transformation, and that players deliberately choose among strategies according to some decision criterion (dominant strategy, maximin, etc.) which is but a special application of the standard economic theory of behavior set out in the hypotheses (1)–(3) above. In the further discussions, however, sociobiology turned away from such an interpretation and, instead, developed an 'evolutionary' game theory (Maynard Smith 1982; Selten 1983). According to this, the cooperative or the non-cooperative strategy in the game (or a mixture of both) is adopted by the individual as a matter of genetic disposition. This amounts to a 'hard-wired' committal which conflicts with the very notion of deliberate or, if you like, opportunistic choice on the basis of individual preferences. [3]

What sociobiology might have to say about preferences is therefore best summarized by rather concrete specifications of items like those mentioned above. Unfortunately, it is not clear how insights like these could be helpful for an economist faced with the problem of explaining ordinary economic choice behavior in a modern economy. What do the insights contribute to understanding why some people spend a fortune in motor sports rather than donating their money to charitable organizations that help save the lives of road casualties? Why some invest in or consume education while others start to earn money as unskilled workers as soon as possible? Why some people prefer to have two or three houses rather than two or three children? Can any of these

[3] It is worth mentioning that, in the evolutionary interpretation, quite general conditions under which altruistic behavior can survive and propagate in a population can be given (Boorman and Levitt 1973; Axelrod and Hamilton 1981), while in the rationalist interpretation, the proof for the existence of a cooperative solution (assuming no information on the players' past record) still depends on rather specific assumptions (Kurz 1977; Kreps et al. 1982; Neyman 1985; Rubinstein 1986). A convergence of the two interpretations can be imagined. It would require showing that a pre-commitment to always being cooperative is a dominant strategy in a repeated (rational choice) game in which players hold preferences for own genetic fitness; for a first attempt in that direction cf. Güth and Yaari (1992).

economic decisions be explained as the result of a corresponding innate preference which, in turn, helps to increase genetic fitness?

The answer is by no means obvious. However, the last question raises the more fundamental issue of the degree to which the behavior of homo sapiens is still controlled by selection pressure. The recent debate about microevolution versus macroevolution and the state of Darwinian theory in biology has emphasized, among other things, that a large latent genetic variability is always present (Gould 1982; Stebbins and Ayala 1985). In a stationary environment, such variability does not find much phenotypic representation if selection pressure is tight. In an environment where genetic reproduction is assured for largely varying forms of economic behavior – an environment that mankind, as a species, seems to have been able to create – this may, however, be different.

Are individual preferences other than those that enhance genetic fitness immediately then just a matter of genetic variance? Is the huge number of different ordinary, but not arbitrary, choices which everybody makes in economic life perhaps determined by genetically fixed preferences and their natural – now no longer latent – inter-individual variance? A definite answer to these questions is hardly possible. What occurs as a result of sheer genetic variance in such an 'affluent' environment is, in the sense of the – functional – theory of natural selection, non-functional and is therefore not explicable within such a theory. A different explanation is thus clearly needed. In the next section such an explanation will be offered. It is based on the hypothesis of an innate learning mechanism in human behavior which explains much of the variety of individual preferences as being acquired.

5. Innate learning mechanisms and socioeconomic evolution

In the previous section, it was mentioned that preferences are not directly observable properties ascribed to the individual by an outside observer. Certain properties may, however, be inferred indirectly by appropriately designed revelation procedures. It is interesting now that, in developing a theory of revealed preferences, economists have tried to solve basically the same problem encountered in behavioral psychology when an attempt is made to determine 'reinforcers' empirically, that is those items which have the power to reinforce operant behavior of an organism (Lea 1978, 1983). In fact, in a suitable preference revelation experiment with mammals some basic items can be expected to be found as objects of the individual preferences which have been identified in laboratory experimentation with mammals (Millenson 1967) as 'primary' reinforcers: air, water, sleep, warmth, nutrition, sexual activity, maternal care, love and affection, physical activity, and novelty. Quite plausibly, these items have already been mentioned in the previous section as candidates for innate preferences.

Besides these innate, primary reinforcers, behavioral psychology suggests the existence of so-called 'secondary' or conditioned reinforcers. They are acquired in a conditioning or learning process which builds on the innate learning capacity shared by all vertebrates and man (Skinner 1966; Pulliam and Dunford 1980: 11–44). According to this theory, learning of secondary reinforcers takes place by simple association with primary reinforcing events. If an originally neutral stimulus is systematically paired with a primary reinforcing stimulus, an association is established in such a way that the learned stimulus can eventually act as a substitute, at least for a limited time. A stimulus associated with conditioned reinforcers can also acquire reinforcing power in this way. It can easily be imagined how, given man's large associative capacity, a most developed hierarchy of learned reinforcers emerges from the very simple innate learning mechanism.

In the light of this theory, some instructive conclusions can be drawn with regard to individual preferences. Their variety can obviously be explained as the result of a permanent learning process, a slow process of preference formation and change. In an individual lifetime history of conditioning, a more or less long chain of learned associations leads from the few innate preferences to those actually revealed in current everyday life. In this process, the current environmental conditions have a crucial impact. They determine the extent to which individually chosen actions are rewarding or non-rewarding and thus affect the ongoing conditioning process. Environment means here largely other individuals' actions and reactions or, ultimately, preferences. Thus, much of the 'socialization' process which human individuals go through with decreasing intensity during their lifetime is simply an attempt by the individual's social environment (parents, teachers, peers, superiors) to form or change the individual's preferences.

The mutual dependence of the individual preference formation processes within a group or even society has two important implications with respect to societal evolution. First, at each point in time, the state of preferences collectively reached imposes constraints on the individual changes. The result is a path-dependency of all individual processes of preference change. This means that, at any moment of time, the present state of a person's preferences crucially hinges upon the previous history of the individual's preference formation (for an interesting attempt in this direction cf. Kapteyn et al. 1980). Second, the collective features of the preference formation process are likely to be subject to frequency-dependency effects. The presence of such effects means that individual changes depend on whether, and with which relative frequency, the same changes have already occurred with others. This can give rise to typical features of non-linear dynamics – abrupt change and hysteresis (Witt 1991).

In the broader perspective of societal evolution, the theory of collective preference formation processes proposed here supports the theory of cultural evolution as outlined by Hayek (1979). It suggests a distinct source of change besides, and largely independent of, phylogenetic change on the one side and cultural change, as far as it is intellectually created, on the other. Sociobiology is particularly concerned with the impact of phylogenetic evolution and may thus indeed be able to explain satisfactorily primitive forms of preference differentiation and social behavior as a result of genetic adaptation to the selection environment faced by early man. As inherited attributes, they are still present in many instinctive reactions and evaluations of modern man. As opposed to this, human intelligence and imagination – the creation, registering, and proliferation of human knowledge – are often viewed as the only other source of evolution, in particular of the evolution of human culture. In fact, it has recently been speculated that intellectual evolution functions as a new and independent mechanism based on the same principles of the variation, selection, and replication, but acting substantially faster (Dawkins 1976: ch. 11; Popper 1984).

The notion developed above suggests a different view. Collective preference formation processes can be seen as underlying the spontaneous emergence of civilized interactions in the more recent history of mankind. In this perspective, culture rests, at least in part, on behavioral regularities exhibited by the individuals involved which are neither genetically fixed nor necessarily a result of deliberate human creation. The process of collectively learning of preferences is adaptive in that it depends on whether individually rewarding or non-rewarding experiences are produced. It works independently of deliberate, intellectual activities. Reward is not necessarily the result of deliberate choice or design, nor must the individual be able to grasp why (s)he becomes positively or negatively conditioned; in fact, the latter may be difficult given the complicated interactive process.

From this brief sketch of the interactions between preferences and socioeconomic evolution it is already apparent that the present view is different, yet partially compatible with the theory of co-evolutionary processes and of cultural transmission that have been advanced in the sociobiological tradition in recent years (Durham 1978; Lumsden and Wilson 3981; Gavalli-Sforza and Feldman 1981; Boyd and Richerson 1985). In distinguishing a driving force and a mechanism of cultural evolution 'between instinct and reason' (Hayek 1979), the view suggested here is obviously more remote from the genetic than from the co-evolutionary view. Accordingly, the process of learning and change is not limited to transmission between generations. If it is not in a phase of self-stabilizing stasis, the process may therefore produce substantially more rapid transformations within only one or two generations as has been evident in the last two hundred years. Indeed, for the research interests of sociobiology, in contrast to those of economics, a time horizon as short as this is perhaps of no significance. However, the dynamic features of the potentially rapid intra-generational transitions still need serious interdisciplinary exploration.

6. Conclusions

In their respective domains economics and sociobiology face some problems which are quite similar. Yet, the ways in which these problems are approached in the two disciplines differ significantly. A comparison of the two approaches is therefore instructive. This is true also for what economics and sociobiology have to say on preferences. The individualistic economic theory of behavior claims that human beings choose those actions which they prefer most from a constrained set of feasible actions. However, what is lacking is an empirical theory of what it is that individuals have preferences for – a theory about the content of preference orders – which is necessary to avoid a pseudo-explanatory attitude of rationalizing all behavior by suitably specifying the underlying preferences. The question has thus been raised here as to whether sociobiology might contribute to developing such a theory.

In discussing this question it has been argued that the population-oriented rather than individualistic perspective of sociobiology can provide some insights albeit on a very elementary level only. A more elaborate theory must also explain higher, culturally formed, behavior. Such a theory may be obtained by recognizing the influences of innate learning mechanisms in higher living beings. According to such a theory, which refers to the conditioning model developed in behavioral psychology, the formation of, and change in, individual preferences appear as processes of a life-long interactive learning that starts from basic and rather uniform genetic dispositions and develops into highly differentiated, idiosyncratic forms. As a consequence, preferences have to be assessed as partly genetically determined and partly acquired from the specific cultural influences of the respective social environment.

References

Atkinson, J.W., 1982. 'Old and new conceptions of how expected consequences influence action'. In: N.T. Feather (ed.), Expectations and actions: Expectancy–value models in psychology. Hillsdale, NJ: Erlbaum. pp. 17–52.

Axelrod, R. and D. Hamilton, 1981. The evolution of cooperation. Science 212, 1390–1396.

Azzi, C. and R. Ehrenberg, 1975. Household allocation of time and church attendance. Journal of Political Economy 83, 27–56.

Becker, G.S., 1976. Altruism, egoism, and genetic fitness: Economics and sociobiology. Journal of Economic Literature 14, 817–826.

Blinder, A.S., 1974. The economics of brushing teeth. Journal of Political Economy 82, 887–891.

Boland, L.A., 1981. On the futility of criticizing the neoclassical maximization hypothesis. American Economic Review 71, 1031–1036.

Boorman, S.A. and P.A. Levitt, 1973. A frequency-dependent natural selection model for the evolution of social cooperation networks. Proceedings of the National Academy of Sciences (USA) 70, 187–189.

Bowler, P.J., 1989. Evolution – The history of an idea (rev. ed.). Berkeley, CA: University of California Press.

Boyd, R. and P.J. Richerson, 1985. Culture and the evolutionary process. Chicago, IL: University of Chicago Press.

Cavalli-Sforza, L.L. and M.W. Feldman, 1981. Cultural transmission and evolution: A quantitative approach. Princeton, NJ: Princeton University Press.

Dawkins, R., 1976. The selfish gene. Oxford: Oxford University Press.

Durham, W.H., 1978. 'Toward a coevolutionary theory of human biology and culture'. In: A.L. Caplan (ed.), The sociobiology debate. New York: Harper & Row. pp. 428–448.

Fao, B., 1982. Marshall revisited in the age of DNA. Journal of Post Keynesian Economics 5, 3–16.

Frey, B.S., 1988. Ein ipsatives Modell menschlichen Verhaltens. Analyse und Kritik 10, 181–205.

Gishelin, M.T., 1978. The economy of the body. American Economic Review 68, Papers and Proceedings, 233–237.

Gould, S.J., 1982. 'The meaning of punctuated equilibrium and its role in validating a hierarchal approach to macroevolution'. In: R. Milkman (ed.), Perspectives on evolution. Cambridge: Sinauer Association. pp. 83–105.

Güth, W. and M. Yaari, 1992. 'An evolutionary approach to explain reciprocal behavior in a simple strategic game'. In: U. Witt (ed.), Explaining process and change: Approaches to evolutionary economics. Ann Arbor, MI: Michigan University Press. pp. 23–24.

Hamermesh, D.S. and N.M. Soss, 1974. An economic theory of suicide. Journal of Political Economy 82, 83–92.

Harcourt, A.H. et at., 1981. Testis weight, body weight and breeding system in primates. Nature 293, 55–57.

Hayek, F.A. , 1979. 'The three sources of human values'. In: F.A. Hayek, Law, legislation, and liberty. London: Routledge.

Hirshleifer, J., 1977a. Shakespeare vs. Becker on altruism: The importance of having the last word. Journal of Economic Literature 15, 500–502.

Hirshleifer, J., 1977b. Economics from a biological viewpoint. Journal of Law and Economics 20, 1–52.

Hirshleifer, J., 1982. Evolutionary models in economics and law. Research in Law and Economics 4, 1–60.

Hirshleifer, J., 1985. The expanding domain of economics. American Economic Review 75(6), 53–68.

Homans, G.C., 1961. Social behavior. New York: Harcourt Brace.

Hursh, S.R., 1984. Behavioral economics. Journal of Experimental Analysis of Behavior 42, 435–452.

Hursh, S.R., T.G. Raslear, R. Bauman and H. Black, 1989. 'The qualitative analysis of economic behavior with laboratory animals'. In: K.G. Grunert and F. Ölander (eds.), Understanding economic behavior. Dodrecht: Reidel. pp. 393–407.

Kagel, J.H., R.C. Battalio, L. Green and H. Rachlin, 1980. 'Consumer demand theory applied to choice behavior of rats'. In: J.E.R. Staddon (ed.), Limits to action. New York: Academic Press. pp. 237–267.

Kahneman, D., P. Slovic and A. Tversky (eds.), 1982. Judgement under uncertainty: Heuristics and biases. Cambridge: Cambridge University Press.

Kapteyn, A., T. Wandsbeek and J. Buyze, 1980. The dynamics of preference formation. Journal of Economic Behavior and Organization 1, 123–157.

Kauder, E., 1965. A history of marginal utility theory. Princeton, NJ: Princeton University Press.

Koenker, R., 1977. Was bread giffen? The demand for food in England circa 1790. Review of Economics and Statistics 59, 225–229.

Krebs, J.R. and N.B. Davies (eds.), 1984. Behavioral ecology (2nd. ed.). Oxford: Blackwell.

Kreps, M.D., P. Milgrom, J. Roberts and R. Wilson, 1982. Rational cooperation in the finitely repeated prisoner's dilemma. Journal of Economic Theory 27, 245–252.

Kurz, M., 1977. 'Altruistic equilibrium'. In: B. Balassa, R. Nelson (eds.), Economic progress, private values, and public policy. Amsterdam: North-Holland. pp. 177–200.

Lea, S.E.G., 1978. The psychology and economics of demand. Psychological Bulletin 85, 441–446.

Lea, S.E.G., 1983. 'The analysis of need'. In: R.L. Mellgren (ed.), Animal cognition and behavior. Amsterdam: North-Holland. pp. 31–63.

Lumsden, C.J. and E.O. Wilson, 1981. Genes, mind, and culture – The coevolutionary process. Cambridge, MA: Harvard University Press.

Machina, M.J., 1987. Choice under uncertainty: Problems solved and unsolved. Economic Perspectives 1, 121–154.

Malthus, J.R., 1797. An essay on the principle of population. 2 vols. Cited according to the 7th ed. of 1914. Reprinted London: Everyman.

Margolis, H., 1982. Selfishness, altruism, and rationality. Cambridge: Cambridge University Press.

Marshall, A., 1938. Principles of economics (8th ed.). London: Macmillan.

Maynard Smith, J., 1982. Evolution and the theory of games. Cambridge: Cambridge University Press.

McKenzie R.B. and G. Tullock, 1978. The new world of economics – Exploration into the human experience (2nd ed.). Homewood, IL: Irwin.

Milinski, M., 1984. Competitive resource sharing: an experimental test of a learning rule for ESSs. Animal Behavior 32, 233–242.

Millenson, J.R., 1967. Principles of behavioral analysis. New York: Macmillan.

Neyman, A., 1985. Bounded complexity justifies cooperation in the finitely repeated prisoner's dilemma. Economic Letters 19, 227–229.

Popper, K.R., 1984. 'Evolutionary epistemology'. In: J.W. Pollard (ed.), Evolutionary theory: Paths into the future. Chichester: Wiley. pp. 239–255.

Pulliam, H.R. and C. Dunford, 1980. Programmed to learn: An essay on the evolution of culture. New York: Columbia University Press.

Rachlin, H., 1980. 'Economics and behavioral psychology'. In: J.E.R. Staddon (ed.), Limits to action – The allocation of individual behavior. New York: Academic Press. pp. 205–236.

Radnitzky, G. and P. Bernholz, (eds.), 1986. Economic imperialism: The economic approach applied outside the traditional areas of economics. New York: Paragon House.

Rosenberg, V., 1979. Can economic theory explain everything? Philosophy of Social Sciences, 509–529.

Rubinstein, A., 1986. Finite automata play – The repeated prisoner's dilemma. Journal of Economic Theory 39, 83–96.

Schweber, S.S., 1977. The origin of the *origin* revisited. Journal of History of Biology 10, 229–316.

Selten, R., 1983. Evolutionary stability in extensive two-person games. Mathematical Social Sciences 5, 269–363.

Shackle, G.L.S., 1983. 'The bounds of unknowledge'. In: J. Wiseman (ed.), Beyond positive economics. London: Macmillan. pp. 28–37.

Silberberg, A., F.R. Warren-Boulton and T. Asano, 1987. Inferior-good and Giffen-good effects in monkey choice behavior. Journal of Experimental Psychology 13, 292–301.

Simon, H.A., 1976. 'From substantive to procedural rationality'. In: S.J. Latsis (ed.), Method and appraisal in economics. Cambridge: Cambridge University Press. pp. 129–148.

Simon, H.A., 1982. Models of bounded rationality. Vol. 2, Behavioral economics and business organization. Cambridge, MA: MIT Press.

Skinner, B.F., 1966. 'Operant behavior'. In: W.K. Honig (ed.), Operant behavior – Areas of research and application. New York: Meredith Corp. pp. 12–32.

Stebbins, G.L. and F.J. Ayala, 1985. The evolution of Darwinism. Scientific American 253, 54–64.

Stigler, G.J. and G.S. Becker, 1977. De gustibus non est disputandum. American Economic Review 67, 76–90.

Sugden, R., 1986. The economics of rights, cooperation and welfare. New York: Basil Blackwell.

Thibaut, J.W. and H.H. Kelley, 1959. The social psychology of groups. New York: Wiley.

Tietzel, M., 1983. Ökonomie und Soziobiologie – oder: Wer kann was von wem lernen? Zeitschrift für Wirtschafts- und Sozialwissenschaften 103, 107–127.

Trivers, R.L., 1971. The evolution of reciprocal altruism. Quarterly Review of Biology 46, 281–299.

Trivers, R.L., 1972. 'Parental investment and sexual selection'. In: B. Campbell (ed.), Sexual selection and the descent of man. Chicago, IL: Aldine. pp. 139–179.

Tullock, G., 1977. Economics and sociobiology: A comment. Journal of Economic Literature 15, 502–506.

Ursprung, H.W., 1988. Evolution and the economic approach to human behavior. Journal of Social and Biological Structure 11, 257–279.

Vaughan, W., Jr. and R.J. Herrnstein, 1987. 'Stability, melioration, and natural selection'. In: L. Green and J.H. Kagel (eds.), Advances in behavioral economics, Vol. 1. Norwood, NJ: Ablex. pp. 185–215.

Waage, J.K., 1979. Dual function of the damselfly penis: Sperm removal and transfer. Science 203, 916–918.

Wilson, E.O., 1975. Sociobiology – The new synthesis. Cambridge, MA: Belknap Press.

Witt, U., 1989. 'Subjectivism in economics – A suggested reorientation'. In: K.G. Grunert and F. Ölander (eds.), Understanding economic behavior. Dodrecht: Reidel. pp. 409–431.

Witt, U., 1991. 'Reflections on the present state of evolutionary economic theory'. In: G. Hodgson and E. Screpanti (eds.), Rethinking economics: Markets, technology, and economic evolution. Aldershot: Edward Elgar. In press.

Wong, S., 1978. The foundations of Paul Samuelson's revealed preference theory. London: Routledge & Kegan Paul.

Part III
Classical Economics and the Darwinian Revolution

[11]

MALTHUS AND THE EVOLUTIONISTS:

THE COMMON CONTEXT OF BIOLOGICAL AND SOCIAL THEORY[1]

I

AMONG SOME HISTORIANS OF SCIENCE A NEW AWARENESS IS DEVELOPING, and its sense is that our work is much less unlike that of other historians than we have hitherto supposed. Both historians of science and other sorts of historians are coming to see that their interests cannot be compartmentalized, that — to put it crudely — science happened in history and has influenced historical events increasingly. That there was a need for these changes in attitude implies that both historians of science and other sorts of historians have tended to make two related assumptions: first, that scientific ideas and findings can be dealt with as relatively unequivocal units with fairly sharply defined boundaries and clear-cut linear influences; and second, that "non-scientific" factors played relatively little part in shaping the development of scientific ideas. There have been reactions against these assumptions, which have, however, led to a rather polarized situation with "internalists" and "externalists" conducting relatively unconnected studies.[2] What has not been evident is an approach which considers that varied influences and varying interpretations coming from inside and outside the "scientific" community as traditionally defined, are the rule and not the exception. Rather than having internalists *versus* externalists in the history of science, with both of these groups relatively separated from other sorts of historians, an approach might be developed which routinely considers social and political factors in scientific research and scientific factors in social, economic and political history. What have been seen as

[1] An earlier version of this paper was presented to the Stubbs Society, Oxford on 2 February 1968. I should like to thank the following people for their generous help in revising it: John Burrow, John Dunn, Jeremy Mulford, P. M. Rattansi, Margot Waddell, Charles Webster, and Sheila Young.

[2] For an excellent discussion of current problems in the historiography of science, see Thomas S. Kuhn, "History of Science", in David L. Sills (ed.), *International Encyclopedia of the Social Sciences* (New York, 1968), xiv, pp. 74-83.

peripheral or specialist interests for both historians of science and other historians might come to be seen as constitutive of the studies of both.

This paper is a case study which attempts to break down barriers, in one small area, between the history of science and other branches of history. For Malthus was undoubtedly important in the history of political, economic and welfare theory and was at the same time a crucial and acknowledged influence in the evolutionary debate. In considering his influence I also want to show just how available his theory was for interpretation in very different senses both by various evolutionists and by others whose views were markedly different. In a sense I want to marry history of socio-economic theory and history of biology or — to alter the metaphor — to show that Malthus, Paley, Chalmers, Darwin, Charles Lyell, Herbert Spencer, A. R. Wallace and others were part of a single debate. Indeed, even some aspects of Marxist apologetics and Soviet biological theory can be included in this common context. In doing this I hope to counter at least two sorts of analysis which have attempted either to absorb Darwin into social theory or to diminish Malthus's rôle in the development of evolutionary theory.[3] Instead

[3] For examples, see Thomas Cowles, "Malthus, Darwin, and Bagehot: a Study in the Transference of a Concept", *Isis*, xxvi (1936), pp. 341-8, esp. p. 341; Leo J. Henkin, *Darwinism in the English Novel* (New York, 1940), p. 47; Conway Zirkle, "Natural Selection before the 'Origin of Species' ", *Proc. Amer. Philos. Soc.*, lxxxiv (1941), pp. 71-123, esp. pp. 99-104; Alexander Sandow, "Social Factors in the Origin of Darwinism", *Quart. Rev. Biology*, xiii (1938), pp. 315-26, esp. pp. 322-4; Kenneth E. Bock, "Darwin and Social Theory", *Philosophy of Science*, xxii (1955), pp. 123-34 and "Theories of Progress and Evolution", in Werner J. Cahnman and Alvin Boskoff (eds.), *Sociology and History: Theory and Research* (Glencoe, Illinois, 1964), pp. 21-41; Douglas Bush, "Evolution and the Victorian Poets", in *Science and English Poetry: a Historical Sketch, 1590-1950* (New York, 1950), ch. v, esp. pp. 113-14; Charles C. Gillispie, *Genesis and Geology: the Impact of Scientific Discoveries upon Religious Beliefs in the Decades before Darwin* (Cambridge, Mass., 1951; repr. New York, 1959), pp. 38, 212, 215-16, 227; Loren Eiseley, *Darwin's Century: Evolution and the Men who Discovered It* (London, 1959; repr. New York, 1961), pp. 53, 101-2, 179-82, 331-2; Gertrude Himmelfarb, *Darwin and the Darwinian Revolution* (London, 1959), pp. 132-9 and "The Specter of Malthus", in *Victorian Minds* (New York, 1968), pp. 82-110; H. J. Habakkuk, "Thomas Robert Malthus, F.R.S. (1766-1834)", *Notes & Records of the Royal Society*, xiv (1959), pp. 99-108; Samuel M. Levin, "Malthus and the Idea of Progress", *Jl. Hist. Ideas*, xxvii (1966), pp. 92-108, esp. p. 102; Sydney Smith, "The Origin of 'The Origin' as Discerned from Charles Darwin's Notebooks and his Annotations in the Books he read between 1837 and 1842", *Advancement of Science*, no. 64 (1960), pp. 391-401. The connection between Malthus and evolutionary theory is surprisingly not mentioned in Walter Bagehot, "Malthus", in Mrs. Russell Barrington (ed.), *Works and Life of Walter Bagehot* (London, 1915), vii, pp. 212-26, or in Kenneth Smith, *The Malthusian Controversy* (London, 1951).

of seeing Malthus as an influence outside of biology, I should like to indicate the ways in which his theory and its assumptions about nature were at once pervasive in the biological literature of the first decades of the century and a part of an ongoing debate within natural theology which was at least as important to Darwin and Wallace as the question of the mechanism of evolution.[4] Finally, I want to suggest that the distinction between social and biological issues — which was, in turn, based on the distinction between man and animals which evolutionary theory was supposed to break down from 1859 onwards — was broken down in principle well before the turn of the century.[5]

II

When one looks back at Malthus from a post-Darwinian vantage point, his principle of population — the Malthusian law that population, when unchecked, increases geometrically while at most the food supply can increase arithmetically[6] — can be seen as a natural law about man. It is an important step in the series of developments which overcame the belief that man and his environment were in harmony, and it resulted in man's being seen as an animal — a part of nature in mind and body. From this point of view then, Malthus was a biologist, a human ecologist. Indeed, it was Evolutionism which brought the distinction between mind and body into question: if man is considered a person for social purposes, he remains an organism from a biological point of view. Looking back once again, one sees Malthus as the source of the view of nature which led to Social

[4] It is a contentious claim that the evolutionary debate occurred almost wholly *within* the context of natural theology rather than as a conflict between science and theology. For evidence to support this claim see, Walter F. Cannon, "The Problem of Miracles in the 1830's", *Victorian Studies,* iv (1960), pp. 5-32; "The Basis of Darwin's Achievement; a Revaluation", *ibid.,* v (1961), pp. 109-34; Robert M. Young, "The Impact of Darwin on Conventional Thought", in Anthony Symondson (ed.), *The Victorian Crisis of Faith* (in press).

[5] This paper has a subsidiary historiographic aim. The method of textual exegesis used in sections III-VIII is intended to provide some reassurance that influence studies need not find themselves in quite the parlous conceptual limbo which some recent criticisms imply. See Quentin R. D. Skinner, "The Limits of Historical Explanation", *Philosophy,* xli (1966), pp. 199-215, and John M. Dunn, "The Identity of the History of Ideas", *ibid.,* xliii (1968), pp. 85-104, whose position is closer to my own.

[6] For expositions and criticisms of Malthus's theory see Smith, *The Malthusian Controversy,* p. 275; cf. bks. 3 and 4; Antony Flew, "The Structure of Malthus' Population Theory", *Australasian Jl. Philos.,* xxxv (1957), pp. 2-20.

Darwinism — the social struggle for existence, the survival of the fittest.[7]

In the writings of Condorcet and Godwin, Utopian speculation had reached a stage which contemplated indefinite progress toward the complete absence of struggle among men: no illness, no sexual urge, no cares. William Godwin's place in the history of economics, social theory and literature has been assessed. In the history of evolutionary theory, however, his rôle has, as far as I know, received no attention. It was essentially a negative one, but it was significant nonetheless. His views on the indefinite perfectibility of man beyond all the constraints of the earth, animal nature and social conflict provided the limiting case of eighteenth-century optimism. In the early editions of his *Political Justice*, Godwin argued that man could transcend both inorganic and organic nature as well as his own passions. Reason was supreme, birth and death could conceivably cease to occur, and society could approach perfect harmony. The significance of this view for the history of evolutionary theory is that it so affronted Malthus's sense of reality that it occasioned his *Essay*.[8] Even though Malthus softened his doctrine in later editions, it altered the image of nature from benign harmony to an inexorable imbalance between nature's supply of sustenance and man's need for both food and sex. It was this doctrine which served as an important catalyst for the development of evolutionary theory. Godwin had gone too far in removing man from nature. Malthus's reaction

[7] There can be no doubt of the contemporary significance of Malthus's theory. For example in his essay on Malthus in *The Spirit of the Age* (1825) William Hazlitt implied that it was an open question whether or not Malthus had "endeavoured to spread a gloom over the hopes and more sanguine speculations of man, and to cast a slur upon the face of nature . . .": William Hazlitt, "Mr. Malthus", in *The Spirit of the Age, or Contemporary Portraits* (1825; repr. London, 1904), p. 159; among twentieth-century historians, Basil Willey claimed that ". . . Malthus had raised a spectre which haunted half the century; Nature was niggardly rather than profuse, and, without stern measures, population would soon outrun means of subsistence": Basil Willey, "Origins and Development of the Idea of Progress", in *Ideas and Beliefs of the Victorians* (London, 1949; repr. New York, 1966), p. 43; Humphrey House refers to Malthus's principle of population as "the theory which overshadowed and darkened all English life for seventy years" and "one of the greatest causes of pessimism" of the period: Humphrey House, "The Mood of Doubt", in *ibid.*, p. 74.

[8] [Thomas Robert Malthus], *An Essay on the Principle of Population, as it Affects the Future Improvement of Society, with Remarks on the Speculations of Mr. Godwin, M. Condorcet, and Other Writers* (London, 1798), pp. i, 10-15; William Godwin, *Enquiry Concerning Political Justice, and its Influence on Morals and Happiness* (London, 1793; 2nd ed., 1796). I am not here concerned with the development of Godwin's views or with the debate between Godwin and Malthus in the early decades of the nineteenth century. See Ford K. Brown, *The Life of William Godwin* (London, 1926).

provided the essential change of perspective for putting man into nature once and for all. As William Hazlitt put it, Malthus's *Essay* "made Mr. Godwin and the other advocates of Modern Philosophy look about them".[9]

The second major occasion of Malthus's reaction was another version of belief in inevitable progress, that of Condorcet, whose *Esquisse des progrès de l'esprit humain* was composed while revolutionary Paris was at the height of the Terror and its author was under sentence of death and in hiding.[10] These circumstances help to highlight the incongruity between man's hopes as described in his optimistic essay and the actual environment in which he found himself. Condorcet believed that reason and science would lead to indefinite perfectibility.[11] Free inquiry, liberty and justice would increasingly triumph over tyranny, superstition and prejudice, and science provided the model for man's enlightenment.[12] Human life would be prolonged indefinitely, and both the physical and mental constitution of man would undergo limitless improvement. Slavery and war would cease, and the acquired perfections of an individual might be transmitted to the next generation by inheritance. Improvements in domesticated animals lent credence to this hope.[13] There was a possibility that the population might exceed the means of subsistence, but this day was far away and posed no threat to the indefinite perfectibility of the human race.[14]

Malthus observes, in the additions made to the *Essay* in 1817, that

> It is probable, that having found the bow bent too much one way, I was induced to bend it too much the other, in order to make it straight. But I shall always be quite ready to blot out any part of the work which is considered by a competent tribunal as having a tendency to prevent the bow from becoming finally straight, and to impede the progress of truth.[15]

Malthus concentrates first on the *impediments* to progress, and the perspective on man's place in nature was radically changed.[16]

[9] Hazlitt, *The Spirit of the Age*, p. 161.

[10] Marie-Jean-Antoine-Nicolas Caritat, Marquis de Condorcet, *Esquisse d'un tableau historique des progrès de l'esprit humain, Ouvrage posthume de Condorcet* (Paris, 1795), trans. June Barraclough (London, 1955); Malthus, *Essay*, 1st edn. (1798), ch. 9; James G. Frazer, "Condorcet on Human Progress", in *The Gorgon's Head and Other Literary Pieces* (London, 1927), pp. 369-83; Alexandre Koyré, "Condorcet", *Jl. Hist. Ideas*, ix (1948), pp. 131-52.

[11] Condorcet, *Sketch* (1955 edn.), pp. 142, 193-202.

[12] *Ibid.*, pp. 149 sqq., 186-96.

[13] *Ibid.*, pp. 200-1.

[14] *Ibid.*, pp. 180, 188-9.

[15] [William Empson], "Life, Writings, and Character of Mr Malthus", *Quarterly Rev.*, lxiv (1836), p. 494.

[16] Malthus, *Essay*, 6th edn. (1826), i, p. 1.

III

Malthusianism played a central rôle in a debate in which social and biological ideas were part of a common intellectual context. Smith points out that nearly every issue of the *Quarterly* and *Edinburgh Reviews* contains an article on or reference to the Malthusian debate.[17] Malthus's biographer says that it rained refutations of Malthus for thirty years:[18] the resulting controversy sprouted everywhere. Malthus's ideas were as commonplace in the first half of the nineteenth century as Freud's were in the twentieth. One partial bibliography of the controversy (1793-1880) is thirty pages long.[19] In 1825, Hazlitt reported that Godwin was something of a living ghost, while Malthus was one of those rare men who "has not left opinion where he found it".[20]

Robert Wallace, Godwin, Condorcet and even Paley, among many others, had acknowledged some version of potential disproportion between population and food supply, but the *perspective* within which they viewed it prevented them from taking it seriously as a genuine prospect for mankind. The problem was absorbed in the general aura of optimism, and lingering doubts were put to sleep with the promise of progress overcoming the obstacle should it arise.[21]

William Paley considered the issue more directly. That is, he accepted the fact of the conflict, but he placed it in a perspective which was still fundamentally optimistic. He reacted in a way which was to become characteristic of sophisticated theologians' responses to scientific findings: not to deny the fact but to absorb it in a generalization which was once again comforting. The ways of God were reconciled to man. The earlier generation had not felt the need for reconciliation so acutely. Paley addressed himself to Malthus's theory in his *Natural Theology* (1802). The last chapters are concerned with the personality, natural attributes, unity and goodness of

[17] Smith, *The Malthusian Controversy*, p. 49.

[18] James Bonar, *Malthus and His Work* (1885), 2nd edn. (London, 1924), p. 2.

[19] J. A. Banks and D. V. Glass, "A List of Books, Pamphlets, and Articles on the Population Question, published in Britain in the period 1793 to 1880", in D. V. Glass (ed.), *Introduction to Malthus* (London, 1953), pp 79-112

[20] Hazlitt, *The Spirit of the Age*, pp. 19, 160.

[21] Malthus, *Essay*, 1st edn. (1798), pp. iii-iv, 7; 6th edn. (1826), i, p. iii (preface to 2nd edn.). For a discussion of a number of Malthus's precursors, see Smith, *The Malthusian Controversy*, ch. i. Cf. Erasmus Darwin, *Zoonomia* (London, 1794-6), p. 570 and *Phytologia* (London, 1799), p. 556; Stillman Drake, "A Seventeenth-Century Malthusian", *Isis*, lviii (1967), pp. 401-2; James Bonar, *Theories of Population from Raleigh to Arthur Young* (London, 1931; repr. 1966).

the Deity.[22] He begins this part of his argument by rejecting the gradual origin of species by natural means.[23] It is when he turns to the Goodness of the Deity that he defends design: "Nor is design abortive. It is a happy world after all". "But pain, no doubt, and privation exist, . . .". "Evil, no doubt, exists; but it is never, that we can perceive, the *object* of contrivance".[24] Animals devouring one another is, however, a worrying case. Can this be deemed evil? No, since immortality would otherwise be out of the question; pursuing prey affords pleasure to the pursuer; and a quick death is preferable to a slow one.[25] Nature is very fecund; indeed it displays "*superfecundity*". Think of gnats and plagues of mice. This excess is easy to regulate, much easier than it would be to replenish a scarcity. Even so, nature cannot receive and support all her progeny. Superabundance requires destruction, otherwise any animal could overrun the world. "It is necessary, therefore, that the effects of such prolific faculties be curtailed. In conjunction with other checks and limits, all subservient to the same purpose, are the *thinnings* which take place among animals, by their action upon one another". Species keep one another within bounds. "Though there may be the appearance of failure in some of the details of Nature's works, in her great purposes there never are". Paley concludes quite comforably: "We have dwelt the longer on these considerations, because the subject to which they apply, namely, that of animals *devouring* one another, forms the chief, if not the only instance, in the works of the Deity, of an economy, stamped by marks of design, in which the character of utility can be called in question".[26] But, of course, the contrivances are beneficial if only we take a broad view. He provides benevolent justifications for private property, bodily pain (noting the comfort that derives from the cessation of the latter), disease, mortal disease ("The horror of death proves the value of life".), and death ("All must be changed".)[27]. When Paley arrives at an explicit statement of the Malthusian doctrine, it is expressed in the same — perhaps even more — reassuring terms, under the heading of the evils of civil life. Paley says that these

> are much more easily disposed of than physical evils: because they are, in truth, of much less magnitude, and also because they result from a kind of

[22] William Paley, *Natural Theology: or, Evidences of the Existence and Attributes of the Deity. Collected from the Appearances of Nature* (London, 1802), new edn. (London, 1816), chaps. 23-7.

[23] *Ibid.*, pp. 360-79.

[24] *Ibid.*, pp. 392, 399, 401.

[25] *Ibid.*, pp. 402-8.

[26] *Ibid.*, pp. 408-13

[27] *Ibid* , pp. 421-32; cf. pp. 421-2.

> necessity, not only from the constitution of our nature, but from a part of that constitution which no one would wish to see altered. The case is this: Mankind will in every country *breed up* to a certain point of distress. . . . The order of generation proceeds by something like a geometrical progression. The increase of provision, under circumstances even the most advantageous, can only assume the form of an arithmetic series. Whence it follows, that the population will always overtake the provision, will pass beyond the line of plenty, and will continue to increase till checked by the difficulty of procuring subsistence. ([fn.] See a statement of this subject, in a late treatise upon population.) Such difficulty therefore, along with its attendant circumstances, *must* be found in every old country: and these circumstances constitute what we call poverty, which necessarily imposes labour, servitude, restraint.[28]

He argues that this process may hurt some but increases the *mean* happiness of all, and he goes on to extol the benefits of good government, religion, clean living, and "the possession of well-directed tastes and desires, compared with the dominion of tormenting, pernicious, contradictory, unsatisfied, and unsatisfiable passion". The chapter concludes with gentle defences of distinctions in civil life, distribution of money, station and property. He says, for example, "The distinctions of civil life are apt enough to be regarded as evils, by those who sit under them; but, in my opinion, with very little reason".[29] Nature's harmony and man's moral agency are the universal reassurances for Paley.

A contemporary said of Malthus: "We have repeatedly heard him say that the two converts of whom he was most proud were Dr. Paley and Mr. Pitt".[30] Pitt *did* drop his bill for extending poor relief to large families. He grasped Malthus's point: God would not provide food for all the mouths but more than enough mouths for all the food. Paley was a less clear-headed convert. Although he accepted the words of Malthus's theory, he saw it in a context which was very different from the one which was generated as a result of Malthus's influence on others. In Paley's hands and in those of many scientists who tried to include Malthus within a complacent natural theology, the Malthusian principle was a means for periodically re-establishing the harmony of nature. Far from being a mechanism for change, it was a defence of the *status quo* both in nature and in society. The Malthusian law led to suffering and death, and even to extinction of species, but not to a change in the constitution of nature. I am not suggesting that Malthus felt that his *Essay* could not be reconciled with natural theology. In fact, the first edition (which Paley read) contained two concluding chapters which were explicitly concerned with the relationship between his view and "our ideas of the power, goodness and foreknowledge of the Deity" — Malthus's attempt, as

[28] *Ibid.*, pp. 432-3. [29] *Ibid.*, pp. 434, 435-9, 444-7.
[30] [Empson], *Edin. Rev.*, xliv, p. 483.

he put it, to "Vindicate the ways of God to man".[31] His intention is to look the *actual* phenomena of nature full in the face. If this view gives, as he says "a melancholy hue" to human life[32] then this view must be explained and justified. It is explained in terms of the necessity for evil in order to produce exertion, exertion to produce mind, and mind to produce progress.[33] "Necessity has with great truth been called the mother of invention".[34] Man is sinful, inert, sluggish, and averse to labour, unless compelled by necessity. "Had population and food increased in the same ratio, it is probable that man might never have emerged from the savage state".[35] Once man reached the civilized state, the Malthusian law became a check upon further progress. Paley almost exclusively stressed harmony and benevolence at the expense of the unpalatable facts. Harmony, not struggle, was the keynote. The disharmony between man and nature which Malthus had made the basis of his antidote to optimism was not prominent in Paley. He did not go to the extremes of Condorcet and Godwin in arguing that men were indefinitely perfectible and could live indefinitely long, but he did emphasize that pain and death and extinction were adjustments in order to re-establish harmony.

Lest these views be considered the ultimate in sanguine approaches to pain and suffering, it is worth noting that they represent a considerable modification of Paley's earlier ideas on population. Seventeen years earlier, in his *Principles of Moral and Political Philosophy*, he had argued that the quantity of happiness in a given district depends on the number of people and that "... the collective happiness will be nearly in the exact proportion of the numbers, that is, twice the number of inhabitants will produce double the quantity of happiness; ..." "... consequently, the decay of population is the greatest evil that a state can suffer; and the improvement of it [is] the object which ought, in all countries, to be aimed at in preference to every other political purpose whatsoever". He noted that food supply was an "insuperable bar" but that the bar never operates, since there is so much fertile land, and man is such an industrious cultivator.[36]

[31] Malthus, *Essay*, 1st edn. (1798), p. 349, quoting Alexander Pope's *Essay on Man*.

[32] *Ibid.*, p. iv. [33] *Ibid.*, pp. 360-1. [34] *Ibid.*, p. 358. [35] *Ibid.*, pp. 361-4.

[36] William Paley, *The Principles of Moral and Political Philosophy* (London, 1785; *Works*, London, 1825), iv, pp. 478-81. In an unpublished MS., "The Crisis, a View of the Present Interesting State of Great Britain, by a Friend of the Constitution", Malthus wrote in 1796: "I cannot agree with Archdeacon Paley, who says, that the quantity of happiness in any country is best measured by the number of people. Increasing population is the most certain possible sign of the happiness and prosperity of a state; but the actual population may be only a sign of the happiness that is past": quoted in [Empson], *Edinburgh Rev.*, xliv, p. 482; cf. p. 479.

Increase of population was an unqualified good, and his argument is devoted to means of furthering this end. In the light of Paley's earlier views, the statements in his *Natural Theology* are most temperate.

Since Darwin was strongly influenced by both Malthus and Paley, this is the appropriate place to make the point that their respective rôles in the development of his evolutionary theory were strikingly different. Although Paley accepts Malthus's theory, he does so in a way which was unlikely to draw Darwin's attention to the significance of conflict in nature. Darwin read Paley's *Natural Theology* while an undergraduate at Cambridge (indeed, everyone did: it remained a set book for all undergraduates until 1921). He tells us in his autobiography that the logic of Paley's *Evidences* and his *Natural Theology*

> gave me as much delight as did Euclid. The careful study of these works, without attempting to learn any part by rote, was the only part of the Academical Course which, as I then felt and as I still believe, was of the least use to me in the education of my mind. I did not at that time trouble myself about Paley's premises; and taking these on trust I was charmed and convinced by the long line of argumentation.[37]

Although a strong case can be made for the influence of Paley on Darwin's view of adaptation, it would be extremely difficult to maintain that Paley's version of Malthus could have influenced or did influence Darwin when he was casting about for a mechanism for evolutionary change seven years later. It was when he read Malthus in 1838 that he was struck by an interpretation of nature which reinforced that gained from Lyell (who also uses Malthus to explain problems of ecology and extinction) and from the study of domesticated animals. Thus, Paley and Malthus influenced Darwin in very different ways. Paley stresses perfect adaptation; Malthus stresses conflict. These were, at one level, antithetical. Darwin synthesizes them. Struggle both *explains and produces* adaptation.[38]

[37] *The Autobiography of Charles Darwin 1809-1882 with original omissions restored*, ed. Nora Barlow (London, 1958), p. 59.

[38] Many of Darwin's examples in *On the Origin of Species* are the same as Paley's. Where Paley had considered each adaptation to be a separate proof of God's wisdom, power, and goodness, Darwin considered it a problem requiring a natural explanation. Nevertheless, Darwin retained the requirement that each adaptation must be beneficial: "Natural selection will never produce in a being anything injurious to itself, for natural selection acts solely by and for the good of each. No organ will be formed, as Paley has remarked, for the purpose of causing pain or for doing an injury to its possessor": Charles Darwin, *On the Origin of Species by Means of Natural Selection or the Preservation of Favoured Races in the Struggle for Life* (London, 1859), p. 201.

IV

Malthus dropped the chapters on natural theology from the second edition of his *Essay*, although it is still possible to see his original theodicy at work.[39] He also acknowledged his authorship, increased its bulk many times, and changed the subtitle. The first subtitle had referred to the principle of population "as it affects the future improvement of society, with remarks on the speculations of Mr. Godwin, M. Condorcet, and other writers". The second edition (1803) referred to "a view of its past and present effects on human happiness; with an inquiry into our prospects respecting the future removal or mitigation of the evils which it occasions". Malthus turns his attention from speculations on the perfectibility of man and society to amassing data on the effects of the principle and to a new check on population which does not come under the head of either vice or misery. He softens some of the harshest conclusions of the first essay by including this factor of "moral restraint" from marriage.[40] As with the exclusion of natural theology, the distinction between editions is not complete. The doctrine of moral or prudential restraint from marriage until one could support a wife and family was not absent from the first edition, but it was not stressed.[41] Even so, Malthus was right to distinguish the second edition as "a new work".[42] Another important change in the second and later editions was that the *Essay* became less of a personal polemical tract. The criticisms of Godwin and Condorcet remained, but the attack on the poor laws, which was secondary in the *Essay* of 1798, usurped the position of the attack on perfectibility. The doctrine of "moral restraint" and the criticism of public charity provided the source for a very different interpretation of Malthus which replaced Paley's harmonious view of nature based on a deist's view of God with a Calvinist interpretation of the Deity as an implacable Old Testament Judge.

Paley's *Natural Theology* provided the inspiration for a series of remarkable works which — in eleven volumes — bored the public with a dropsical version of the thesis that all of nature shows design and that the argument is cumulative, case by case. The earl of Bridgewater left £8,000 for a work

> On the Power, Wisdom, and Goodness of God, as manifested in the Creation; illustrating such work by all reasonable arguments, as for instance the variety

[39] For example, see Malthus, *Essay*, 6th edn. (1826), i, p. 92; ii, pp. 5, 42-3, 84-5.

[40] *Ibid.*, i, pp. vii-viii (preface to 2nd edn., 1803), 15, 15n-17n.

[41] Malthus, *Essay*, 1st edn. (1798), ch. iv.

[42] Malthus, *Essay*, 6th edn. (1826), i, pp. v-vi (preface to 2nd edn., 1803).

and formation of God's creatures in the animal, vegetable, and mineral kingdoms; the effect of digestion, and thereby of conversion; the construction of the hand of man, and an infinite variety of other arguments; as also by discoveries ancient and modern, in arts, sciences, and the whole extent of literature.

The intentions of the will were carried out by the President of the Royal Society, the archbishop of Canterbury, and the bishop of London, who, in turn, chose the Rev. Thomas Chalmers, Professor of Divinity in the University of Edinburgh, to write the first of the eight works, entitled *On the Power, Wisdom and Goodness of God as Manifested in the Adaptation of External Nature to the Moral and Intellectual Constitution of Man,* which appeared in two volumes in 1833, and went through six editions.[43] The *Bridgewater Treatises* are of interest, because they constituted an encyclopedia of pre-evolutionary natural history. They were commissioned and appeared while Darwin was on the 40,000 mile voyage of the Beagle around the world, during which he studied the distribution of fossils, of live animals and of South American species. These were the facts which led him to believe that species might be mutable. Chalmers's treatise is particularly interesting for two reasons. First, it was one of *two* on man (N.B. nature was adapted to man, not the other way around): a separate one was commissioned on man's body;[44] and, second, because Chalmers was besotted with the Malthusian Law, which he interpreted very differently from Paley. Sin and moral restraint were the most important concepts in Chalmers's natural theology. Where Malthus had stressed a dismal law of nature alleviated by moral restraint, Chalmers focused on moral restraint itself.

Chalmers saw his life's work as the unification of religious doctrine and *laissez faire* economic theory. His writings embraced natural theology, political economy, and geology (a not unusual combination in the period). In his *Political Economy* (1832) he argued that "the right economic condition of the masses is dependent on their right moral conditions, that character is the parent of comfort, not vice

[43] *The Bridgewater Treatises on the Power Wisdom and Goodness of God as Manifested in the Creation.* Treatise I: Thomas Chalmers, *The Adaptation of External Nature to the Moral and Intellectual Constitution of Man* (London, 1833), i, pp. ix-xi; W. H. Brock, "The Selection of the Authors of the Bridgewater Treatises", *Notes and Records of the Royal Society,* xxi (1966), pp. 162-79.

[44] John Kidd, *On the Adaptation of External Nature to the Physical Condition of Man* (London, 1834).

versa".[45] Since at least 1808 he had been arguing in particular against state charity on Malthusian grounds. He claims that more state charity means an end to individual industry. If there is more charity, the demand will rise to exhaust it. He says that Malthus's theory would have convinced him even without examples. "But it seldom happens that a speculation so apparently paradoxical is so well supported by the most triumphant exemplifications".[46]

> It is quite vain to think that positive relief will ever do away the wretchedness of poverty. Carry the relief beyond a certain limit, and you foster the diseased principle which gives birth to poverty. . . . The remedy against the extension of pauperism does not lie in the liberalities of the rich; it lies in the hearts and habits of the poor. Plant in their bosoms a principle of independence — give a high tune of delicacy to their characters — teach them to recoil from pauperism as a degradation.[47]

The panacea was that men should reform their habits by means of the influence of the Scriptures. Only ten per cent of pauperism could be attributed to genuine misfortune: the rest was moral sloth. "The shame of descending [into pauperism] is the powerful stimulus which urges them to a manly contest with the difficulties of their situation, and which bears them through in all the pride of honest independence".[48]

Chalmers's *Political Economy,* published a year before his *Bridgewater Treatise,* repeated this point *ad nauseam.* Its subtitle conveys the context: *On Political Economy, in Connection with the Moral*

[45] William Hanna and Dugald Macfadyen, "Thomas Chalmers", in *The Encyclopedia Britannica,* 11th edn. (New York, 1910), v, p. 810; cf. William Hanna, "Thomas Chalmers", in *ibid.,* 8th edn. (Edinburgh, 1854), vi, pp. 403-7; Thomas Chalmers, *On Political Economy, in Connection with the Moral State and Moral Prospects of Society* (Glasgow, 1832), pp. 126, 134, 457; Leslie Stephen, *The English Utilitarians* (London, 1900), ii, pp. 242-50; Hugh Watt, *Thomas Chalmers and the Disruption* (London, 1943).

[46] Letter dated 7 February 1811, quoted in William Hanna, *Memoirs of the Life and Writings of Thomas Chalmers, D.D., LL.D.* (Edinburgh, 1862), i, pp. 381-2.

[47] *Ibid.,* p. 384. "It is in the power of charity to corrupt its object; it may tempt him to indolence — it may lead him to renounce all dependence on himself — it may nourish the meanness and depravity of his character — it may lead him to hate exertion, and resign without a sigh the dignity of independence. It could easily be proved, that if charity were carried to its utmost extent, it would unhinge the constitution of society. It would expel from the land the blessings of industry. Every man would repose on the beneficence of another; every incitement to diligence would be destroyed. The evils of poverty would multiply to such an extent as to be beyond the power of the most unbounded charity to redress them; and instead of an elysium of love and plenty, the country would present the nauseating spectacle of sloth and beggary and corruption" (*ibid.,* p. 381).

[48] *Ibid.,* p. 385; cf. [Thomas Chalmers], "Causes and Cure of Pauperism", *Edinburgh Rev.,* xxviii (1817), pp. 1-31; xxix (1818), pp. 261-302.

State and Moral Prospects of Society. Chalmers's litany is represented by the following passage:

> It is not by means of economic enlargements, but of moral principles and restraints, that the problem of our difficulties is at length to be fully and satisfactorily resolved. No possible enlargement from without will ever suffice for the increasing wants of a recklessly increasing population. We look for our coming deliverance in a moral change, and not in any, or in all, of those economic changes put together, which form the great panacea of so many of our statesmen. Without the prudence, and the virtue, and the intelligence of our common people, we shall only have a bulkier, but withal as wretched and distempered a community as ever; and we repeat, that a thorough education, in both the common and Christian sense of the term, forms the only solid basis, on which either the political or economic wellbeing of the nation can be laid.[49]

The criticisms of a contemporary reviewer help to illuminate this use of the moral theory in Malthus in an extreme form (in contrast with Paleyian harmony on the one hand and with Darwinian naturalism on the other). G. Poulett Scrope, who had distinguished careers in both political economy and geology, begins his review of Chalmers's *Political Economy* in the *Quarterly* by praising Chalmers as a pastor but adds that

> we cannot pretend to rate him so highly as a political arithmetician. ... We shall not be suspected of undervaluing the efficacy of a Christian education, when we hesitate to believe that this is the only desideratum in our civic and national economy, or the only remedy for the existing evils of our social conditions capable of affording us the least glimpse of hope.[50]

(Where some feared education lest the poor read Tom Paine, Malthus advocated the study of political economy, and Chalmers the Bible). Scrope points out Chalmers's well-known inveterate hostility to any public provision for the poor — his adherence to the Malthusian theory of population, and the Malthusian remedy for its apparent excess, "the prudential check".

> The one main principle to which every argument on every subject is there referred, and by which every question is decided, is the Malthusian axiom, ... From this axiom the obvious deduction is, that all enlargements of the means of subsistence do more harm than good ..., that all improvements in agriculture are curses and that we should not increase subsistence but check the increase of the persons to be subsisted![51]

[49] Chalmers, *Political Economy*, p. 240; cf. pp. 31-2, 58, 70-1, 134, 297-8, 305, 328, 357, 386-7, ch. xiv, pp. 421, 433-4, 438-9, 446-7, 522, 554, etc. Although Chalmers's place in Joseph A. Schumpeter's *History of Economic Analysis* (London, 1954) is confined to "Some of Those Who Also Ran", his work was influential in Scotland, and his *Political Economy* was considered by Schumpeter to be "a book of considerable importance" (pp. 486-7).

[50] [G. P. Scrope], "Dr. Chalmers *On Political Economy*", *Quart. Rev.*, xlviii (1832), p. 39.

[51] *Ibid.*, p. 40.

Economic remedies for improving the condition of the lower classes only generate further misery "for the very reason that they are immediately beneficial"! — thereby encouraging breeding.[52]

> It is, indeed, [Scrope continues] an extraordinary *monomania* which affects these gentlemen. The idea of an ultimate limit to the globe's possible productiveness tyrannizes over their imaginations, and gives rise to the strangest opinions and rules of conduct. Dr. Chalmers overtops them all: his whole soul is absorbed by the frightful prospect of the time when every rood of soil on the face of the earth shall maintain its full complement of human beings . . . .[53]

Scrope feels that "to persuade us to have recourse to it [the Malthusian specific] NOW, is indeed right midsummer madness — the *ne plus ultra* of moonstruck, Lauptan philosophy".[54] In the concluding passages he says, "We submit, therefore, that the true policy deducible from the Malthusian premises, is, that we should not merely abolish the poor laws, but go on to dispatch the surplus population as it appears". Recovering himself, Scrope grants that Chalmers, having himself exhausted all other palliatives as self-defeating,

> brings us in triumph to the "*argal*" at which he has been all along straining, viz. that since nothing can make food keep pace with population, all our efforts should be turned to make population keep pace with food; and the only specific for this is "prudential restraint upon marriage", self-imposed by each individual, and inculcated by a Christian education.[55]

This has the effect, he concludes, of freeing the government "from all responsibility for the sufferings of the mass of the community, by throwing the blame entirely on *Nature* and the improvidence of the poor themselves, and declaring the evil to admit of no remedy from any possible exertions of the legislature".[56]

Chalmers's natural theology removes Malthus's theory from the status of something to be explained away *à la* Paley and places it at the centre of a different interpretation of nature. Indeed, to turn now to his *Bridgewater Treatise,* Chalmers explicitly takes Paley to task for stressing God's natural attributes at the expense of his moral ones.[57] Academic natural theologians like Paley, he continues, are

[52] *Ibid.*, p. 44. There was a clear warrant for this conclusion in Malthus's *Essay,* 6th edn. (1826): "The most general rule that can be laid down on this subject is, perhaps, that any *direct* encouragements to marriage must be accompanied by an increased mortality": i, p. 329; cf. p. 462 and ii, pp. 81-2.

[53] [Scrope], *Quart. Rev.*, xlviii, p. 45.

[54] *Ibid.*, p. 62.

[55] *Ibid.*, p. 67.

[56] *Ibid.*, pp. 68-9. It was on just this point (which was echoed by J. S. Mill) that Marx, Engels, Henry George and A. R. Wallace parted company with Malthus. See sections VI and VIII below.

[57] Chalmers, *Bridgewater Treatise,* ii, pp. 98-9.

apt to stress God's benign virtues and "to overlook the virtues of the Lawgiver and Judge".

> When we take this fuller view of God's moral nature — when we make account of the righteousness as well as the benevolence — when we yield to the suggestion of our own hearts, that to Him belongs the sovereign state, and, if needful, the severity of the lawgiver, as well as the fond affection of the parent — when we assign to Him the character, which, instead of but one virtue, is comprehensive of them all — we are then on firmer vantage-ground for the establishment of a Natural Theology, in harmony, both with the lessons of conscience, and with the phenomena of the natural world.

When we consider only the infinite benevolence of the Deity, we produce a natural theology which cannot explain "the numerous ills, wherewith the world is infested". It remains a complete mystery why "there should be any suffering at all".[58] Chalmers has no such problem: ". . . it will be found," he says, "that the vast amount of human wretchedness, can be directly referred to the waywardness and morbid state of the human will — to the character of man, and not to the condition which he occupies".[59] Thus, the Malthusian law becomes the centre of both political economy and natural theology.[60]

There is a perfectly good basis in Malthus's *Essay* for Chalmers reading: "Hard as it may appear in individual instances, dependent poverty ought to be held disgraceful. Such a stimulus seems to be absolutely necessary to promote the happiness of the great mass of mankind; and every general attempt to weaken this stimulus, however benevolent its intention, will always defeat its own purpose".[61] His specific proposals reflected no hesitation over applying strong sanctions: "To this end, I should propose a regulation to be made, declaring, that no child born from any marriage, taking place after the expiration of a year from the date of the law, and no illegitimate child born two years from the same date, should ever be entitled to parish assistance".[62] The Dickensian workhouse was, in part, a consequence of the views which Malthus and Chalmers shared.

Chalmers does not shrink from the existence of evil, suffering, and struggle, but all are absorbed into a moral context. This is what is most remarkable about his treatise. The choice of author and his treatment of the subject in terms of a stern, Old Testament, judicial and vengeful God, instead of the psychological and even the ethical

[58] *Ibid.*, pp. 100-3.
[59] *Ibid.*, p. 112.
[60] There are two long passages from Chalmers's *Bridgewater Treatise* which draw out the consequences of his position: see Appendix below.
[61] Malthus, *Essay*, 6th edn. (1826), ii, pp. 82-3; cf. pp. 84, 86, 108-9.
[62] *Ibid.*, pp. 337-8; cf. bk. iv, ch. viii, *passim*, and i, pp. 256, 399.

discussions of the day, is significant. Indeed, the failure to discuss the data of man's relationship to nature is also significant. In spite of the title of the treatise, man is considered neither naturalistically nor psychologically. (Aspects of the psychological theories of Thomas Brown are discussed but only those which are concerned with the conscience.)

In complaining about the redundancy of the *Bridgewater Treatises*, another reviewer of Chalmers says that

> Dr. Chalmers is in fact the only writer amongst the eight who occupies a territory which he may call his own. But the manner in which he came into the possession of it will not, perhaps, be deemed perfectly legitimate. That able divine was requested to point out the adaptation of external nature to man's intellectual and moral constitution. This certainly must be admitted to be a task of extreme difficulty in the execution. We all perceive the relation of external nature, composed of the fertile earth, its varied produce, the sea, the atmosphere, the sun, and especially our own satellite, to our physical necessities; but their adaptation to the intellect, which seeks higher objects of contemplation, is not so obvious. Dr. Chalmers was, therefore, reduced to the necessity of considering men in general as "external nature", in relation to an individual of the species; by this contrivance he has been enabled to shape his theme to his own studies, and to furnish us with two volumes on metaphysics and ethics! The books will doubtless have their admirers, but we apprehend that they are not of the class of literature which the Earl of Bridgewater had in his view when he made his will.

He goes on to say that Chalmers's work in the pulpit, the professorial chair, and the closet of the political economist are admirable and worthy of respect for his genius. Nevertheless, these volumes are disappointing. Ordinary ideas are complicated by endless mazes of language and neologisms.[63] In sum, an unworthy work. However, in the context of a study of the uses to which Malthus's theory was put, Chalmers's view represents the extreme of an anti-naturalist interpretation in a sense which was different from his contemporaries. The most relevant contrast is with the eighteenth-century optimists. Where Godwin and Condorcet predicted indefinite progress by means of reason and the effort of thought, Chalmers held out the same hope if men would only obey their consciences and engage in the requisite moral struggle: if they failed to do so they would suffer the penalties of a Stern Judge.

V

Paley emphasized nature's harmony, and Chalmers concentrated on the wars of nature and society in an entirely moral context. Darwin took Paley's answers and converted them into questions. Adaptations needed explaining: they were not each evidence of

[63] [Anon.], "The Bridgewater Treatises. The Universe and Its Author", *Quarterly Rev.*, l (1833), pp. 4-5.

piecemeal designs; they came to be. How? It is here that he removed "moral restraint" from the Malthusian doctrine, which he then applied in the first instance to animals, not to man, and used as an answer to the question of how Paley's beautiful adaptations came to be. The Malthusian doctrine is then, secondarily, reapplied to man. In the crucial passage in Darwin's *Autobiography,* written thirty years after the event, he gives the proper emphasis to his reading of Malthus:

> In October 1838, that is, fifteen months after I had begun my systematic inquiry, I happened to read for amusement Malthus on *Population,* and being well prepared to appreciate the struggle for existence which everywhere goes on from long-continued observation of the habits of animals and plants, it at once struck me that under these circumstances favourable variations would tend to be preserved, and unfavourable ones to be destroyed. The result of this would be the formation of a new species. Here, then, I had at last got a theory by which to work; but I was so anxious to avoid prejudice, that I determined not for some time to write even the briefest sketch of it.[64]

In order to demonstrate this influence, it is worth exploring Darwin's remarks on Malthus, moving backwards from his mature work to his earliest evolutionary notebooks. In *The Variation of Animals and Plants under Domestication* (1868), he recalls the genesis of his theory. As he pondered the evidence gathered in his travels in South America, he was left with an

> inexplicable problem [of] how the necessary degree of modification could have been effected [for evolution to have occurred], and it would have thus remained forever, had I not studied domestic productions, and thus acquired a just idea of the power of Selection. As soon as I had fully realized this idea, I saw, on reading Malthus on *Population,* that Natural Selection was the inevitable result of the rapid increase of all organic beings; for I was prepared to appreciate the struggle for existence by having long studied the habits of animals.[65]

In the first edition of *On the Origin of Species* (1859) Darwin introduces his argument by reviewing the order of presentation. His first chapters are devoted to the subjects of variation under domestication and under nature. The summary continues, "In the next chapter the Struggle for Existence among all organic beings throughout the world, which inevitably follows from their high geometrical powers of increase, will be treated of. This is the doctrine of Malthus, applied to the whole animal and vegetable kingdoms". More are born than can survive. This leads to struggle for existence; any slight favourable variation will lead to a better

[64] Darwin, *Autobiography,* p. 120.

[65] Charles Darwin, *The Variation of Animals and Plants under Domestication* (London, 1868), i, p. 10; cf. Darwin, *The Descent of Man and Selection in Relation to Sex,* 2nd edn. (London, 1874), pp. 44-6.

chance of survival and be naturally selected, and this new form will be propagated to future generations.[66] In 1859 he wrote to A. R. Wallace, as follows:

> You are right, that I came to the conclusion that selection was the principle of change from the study of domesticated productions; and then, reading Malthus, I saw at once how to apply this principle. Geographical distribution and geological relations of extinct to recent inhabitants of South America first led me to the subject: especially the case of the Galapagos Islands.[67]

In the passage in his autobiography in which he mentions the effect of reading Malthus, he continues, "In June 1842 I first allowed myself the satisfaction of writing a very brief abstract of my theory in pencil in 35 pages; and this was enlarged during the summer of 1844 into one of 230 pages, which I had fairly copied out and still possess".[68] In the 1844 *Essay*, he writes:

> It is the doctrine of Malthus applied in most cases with ten-fold force. As in every climate there are seasons for each of its inhabitants of greater and less abundance, so all annually breed; and the moral restraint, which in some small degree checks the increase of mankind, is entirely lost. Even slow-breeding mankind has doubled in twenty-five years, and if he could increase his food with greater ease, he would double in less time. But for animals, without artificial means, *on an average* the amount of food for each species must be constant; whereas the increase for all organisms tends to be geometrical, and in a vast majority of cases at an enormous ratio.[69]

In the pencil sketch of 1842, written as cryptic notes, Darwin again stresses the importance of removing moral restraint from Malthus's doctrine in order to arrive at his own theory:

> But considering the enormous geometrical power of increase in every organism and as every country, in ordinary cases, must be stocked to full extent, reflection will show that this is the case. Malthus on man — in animals no moral [check] restraint — they breed in time of year when provision most abundant, or season most favourable, every country has its season — calculate robins — oscillating from years of destruction. ... the pressure is always ready ... a thousand wedges are being forced into the economy of nature. This requires much reflection; study Malthus and calculate rates of increase and remember the resistance — only periodical. ... In the course of a thousand generations infinitesimally small differences must inevitably tell; ...[70]

If one looks closely at Darwin's working notebooks, which he began in 1837 as a place to put all his notes and reflections on the "species question", there is unequivocal evidence for Malthus's rôle in the actual formation of Darwin's idea. Sometime between

[66] Darwin, *Origin of Species*, pp. 4-5.
[67] *More Letters of Darwin*, ed. Francis Darwin (London, 1903), i, pp. 118-19.
[68] Darwin, *Autobiography*, p. 120.
[69] Charles Darwin, "Essay of 1844", in Charles Darwin and Alfred Russel Wallace, *Evolution by Natural Selection* (Cambridge, 1958), pp. 116-17.
[70] Charles Darwin, "Sketch of 1842", in *ibid.*, pp. 46-7.

28 September and 12 October 1838, he read Malthus. One can often go directly to Darwin's marginal notes in assessing the rôle of some of the influences on him, but in this case he was in London and almost undoubtedly read his brother's copy. In his notebook "D" he wrote (at a later date), "Towards close I first thought of selection owing to struggle".[71] Among the pages excised by Darwin for use in writing his great, never-published, work entitled *Natural Selection,* one finds the following passage:

> [Sept] 28th. We ought to be far from wondering of changes in numbers of species, from small changes in nature of locality. Even the energetic language of Decandolle does not convey the warring of the species as inference from Malthus — increase of brutes must be prevented solely by positive checks, excepting that famine may stop desire. — in nature production does not increase, whilst no check prevail, but the positive check of famine & consequently death. I do not doubt every one till he thinks deeply has assumed that increase of animals exactly proportionate to the number that can live. — . . .
>
> Population is increase at geometrical ratio in FAR SHORTER time than 25 years — yet until the one sentence[72] of Malthus no one clearly perceived the great check amongst men. — there is spring, like food used for other purposes as wheat for making brandy — Even a *few* years plenty, makes population in man increase & an *ordinary* crop causes a dearth. take Europe on an average every species must have some number killed year with year by hawks by cold &c. — even one species of hawk decreasing in number must affect instantaneously all the rest. — The final cause of all this wedging, must be to sort out proper structure, and adapt it to changes. — to do that for form, which Malthus shows is the final effect (by means however of volition) of this populousness on the energy of man. One may say there is a force like a hundred thousand wedges trying [to] force every kind of adapted structure into the gaps in the oeconomy of nature. or rather forming gaps by thrusting out weaker ones. —[73]

In notebook "E", begun in October 1838, Darwin writes, "Epidemics seem intimately related to famine, yet very inexplicable". (This refers to the chapters on epidemics in Malthus's essay). Darwin goes on quoting Malthus and adds his own italics and exclamations:

> "It accords with the most *liberal!* spirit of philosophy to believe that no stone can fall, or plant rise, without the immediate agency of the deity [Malthus wrote 'divine power']. But we know from *experience!* that these operations

[71] "Darwin's Notebooks on Transmutation of Species, Part III", ed. Sir Gavin de Beer, *Bull. British Museum* (*Natural History*), *Historical Series,* ii, no. 4 (1960), p. 128. Dr. Sydney Smith has been most generous in guiding me through the labyrinth of dates and excised passages of Darwin's notebooks.

[72] Footnote by Sir Gavin de Beer: "This note, written on 28 September 1838, makes it possible to identify the sentence in T. R. Malthus's *Essay on the Principle of Population* which enabled Darwin to see how the pressure of natural selection is inevitably brought to bear. It was in the 6th edition, London 1826, vol. i, p. 6: 'It may safely be pronounced, therefore, that the population, when unchecked, goes on doubling itself every twenty five years, or increases in a geometrical ratio.' "

[73] "Part VI, Pages Excised by Darwin", *ibid.,* iii, no. 5 (1967), pp. 162-3.

of what we call nature, have been conducted *almost!* invariably according to fixed laws: and since the work began, the causes of population & depopulation have been probably as constant as any of the laws of nature with which we are acquainted." — This applies to one species — I would apply it not only to population & depopulation, but extermination and production of new forms — this number and correlations.[74]

On the next page Darwin first mentions "my theory" and the small changes involved in the slow process; subsequent pages mention "the theory" and "my theory".

It appears, then, that it was the removal of Malthus's idea of "moral restraint", and an emphasis on the concept of "population pressure" which left a natural law about plants and animals, that characterized Darwin's interpretation. He was, in effect, reverting to the purity of the inescapable dilemma of Malthus's first edition. It is "the strong law of necessity" which Malthus emphasizes repeatedly in both editions, even though in the second it lies side by side with the partial palliative of "moral restraint". References with this deterministic basis appear in tens of places in both editions and might themselves have influenced Darwin's application of the principle to man: for example, "Elevated as man is above all other animals by his intellectual faculties, it is not to be supposed that the physical laws to which he is subjected should be essentially different from those which are observed to prevail in other parts of animated nature",[75] One could go on to cite Malthus's analogies of population studies with the laws of mechanics and ballistics and the invocation of Newton, as well as his opposition to miraculous explanations, but there are sources enough for these elements of Darwin's view. In particular, Charles Lyell's *Principles of Geology,* which was the work which most influenced Darwin (as it did Wallace and Spencer), contains many references of this kind, including innumerable passages on struggle: for example, "In the universal struggle for existence, the right of the strongest eventually prevails; and the strength and durability of a race depends mainly on its prolificness, in which hybrids are acknowledged to be deficient". Without working systematically I have seen fifteen other references to struggle in volume two alone.[76] Indeed, Lyell used the concept of struggle to

[74] "Part IV", *ibid.,* ii, no. 5 (1960), p. 160; cf. *ibid.,* iii, no. 5 (1967), p. 166 (Darwin's pp. 6, 9). The quotation is from Malthus, *Essay,* 6th edn. (1826), i, p. 529.

[75] Malthus, *A Summary View of the Principle of Population* (London, 1830), reprinted in *Introduction to Malthus,* pp. 121-2. This nicely summarizes statements which are scattered throughout the 1826 edition of Malthus's *Essay,* the one which Darwin read.

[76] Charles Lyell, *Principles of Geology, being an Attempt to Explain the Former Changes of the Earth's Surface by Reference to Causes Now in Operation,* 2nd edn. (London, 1833), ii, p. 58; cf. pp. 125, 136-7, 147, 148, 153, 160, 163, 165, 172, 173, 175, 179, 180-8.

explain many of the facts of geographical distribution and of extinction but refrained from applying it to the problem of the origin of new species. It seems that Malthus legitimized the idea of a law of struggle, impressed Darwin with the intensity of struggle, and provided a convenient natural mechanism for the changes which Darwin was studying in the selection of domesticated varieties. It gave Darwin the analogy he needed to move from artificial to natural selection, and this was the essential step in his reasoning: indefinite variation and natural selection could produce new species.

VI

Whereas Darwin had returned from six years of fieldwork with the question of evolution in his mind, Alfred Russel Wallace had gone to the field convinced that evolution occurs and attempted to find out how. He had been led to this conclusion by Robert Chambers's *Vestiges of the Natural History of Creation* and George Combe's phrenological doctrines, along with Lyell's *Principles*, and Darwin's *Journal of Researches*.[77] The fact that he came to these questions about ten years after Darwin and as a result of reading Chambers and Combe, gave a different emphasis to his enquiries. It was man's place in nature which interested him most. Darwin wrote more on plants than on animals and more on animals than on man. His work on *The Descent of Man* was, as he said, unoriginal. With Wallace it was different. The ubiquitous Malthusian principle operates as a benevolent dispensation to keep man in touch with the laws of nature in the influential works of Chambers and Combe.[78] But, in the same period 1844-5, Wallace read Malthus's *Essay* itself. Speaking of this period Wallace says in his autobiography:

> But perhaps the most important book I read was Malthus's "Principles of Population", which I greatly admired for its masterly summary of the facts and logical induction to conclusions. It was the first work I had yet read treating of any of the problems of philosophical biology, and its main principles remained with me as a permanent possession, and twenty years later gave me the long-sought clue to the effective agent in the evolution of organic species.[79]

[77] It should be recalled that between 1838 and 1858 Darwin kept the existence of his theory of evolution by natural selection a closely guarded secret, known only to a few close friends. His *Journal of Researches* helped to raise the question of evolution in Wallace's mind but gave no hint of Darwin's solution to the problem of the mechanism by which evolution might occur.

[78] [Robert Chambers], *Vestiges of the Natural History of Creation* (1844), 12th edn. (London, 1884), pp. 227, 405 ff.; George Combe, *The Constitution of Man Considered in Relation to External Objects*, 5th edn. (Boston, 1835), pp. 191, 220-1.

[79] A. R. Wallace, *My Life. A Record of Events and Opinions* (London, 1905), i, pp. 232, 234-5, 254-5; cf. Wallace, *The Wonderful Century. Its Successes and Failures*, 4th edn. (London, 1901), chaps. xiii and xvi.

Wallace was then in his early twenties. A few pages later he refers to the reading of Malthus as one of the two events which formed the turning point in his life, "without which work I should probably not have hit upon the theory of natural selection and obtained full credit for its independent discovery".[80] Indeed, Wallace first uses the concept of struggle as applied to man in a Malthusian context. In 1853, he wrote, "It is the responsibility and self-dependence of manhood that calls forth the highest powers and energies of our race. It is the struggle for existence, the 'battle of life', which exercises the moral faculties and calls forth the latent spark of genius".[81] Similarly, in his 1855 paper in which Wallace advocates evolution without supplying a mechanism, he quotes a passage from Lyell describing the struggle for existence.[82] But his theory still lacked the essential ingredient, the concept that only the fittest survive the struggle for existence. When Wallace did hit upon the idea of survival of the fittest, it was in the context of ethnological investigations into the origin of human races in the Malay Archipelago. We have four accounts of this from Wallace, and they all exhibit the feature of beginning with Malthus's theory applied to the human species and then extended to other species.

> ... while again considering the problem of the origin of species, something led me to think of Malthus' Essay on Population (which I had read about ten years before), and the "positive checks" — war, disease, famine, accidents, etc. — which he adduced as keeping all savage populations nearly stationary. It then occurred to me that these checks must also act upon animals, and keep down their numbers; and as they increase so much faster than man does, ... it was clear to me that these checks in their case must be far more powerful, ... While vaguely thinking how this would affect any species, there suddenly flashed upon me the idea of *the survival of the fittest* — ...[83]

The second one, written in 1903, also contrasts animals and man in degree of effect.[84] The *locus classicus* for Wallace's version of the theory (and indeed, one of the most dramatic descriptions of a scientific discovery) occurs in his autobiography and shows clearly that recalling Malthus's theory was the crucial experience in the formulation of his own hypothesis.[85]

Three years later (and sixty-four years after the event) Wallace

[80] Wallace, *My Life*, i, p. 240.

[81] A. R. Wallace, *A Narrative of Travels on the Amazon and Rio Negro* (London, 1853), p. 129. My interpretation of Wallace owes much to an excellent article by H. Lewis McKinney, "Alfred Russel Wallace and the Discovery of Natural Selection", *Jour. Hist. Med. and Allied Sciences*, xxi (1966), pp. 333-57.

[82] See McKinney, *op. cit.*, p. 346.

[83] Wallace, *The Wonderful Century*, p. 139.

[84] See McKinney, *op. cit.*, p. 354.

[85] For the full text of Wallace's account, see Appendix below.

took the trouble to re-read the sixth edition of Malthus's essay and to supply the Linnean Society with his recollection of the chapters which had, as he recalled, impressed him most. It was not the passages on natural law or the strictures on improvability and the hope from the exercise of "moral restraint" of the second volume but the cumulative effect of chapters three to twelve, especially three to eight, of volume one. These contain 150 pages of excruciatingly detailed travellers' accounts and histories of the checks on the population of primitive societies, parts of the world outside Europe and Scandinavia, and ancient Greece and Rome. It is a catalogue of details of bestial life, sickness, weakness, poor food, lack of ability to care for young, scant resources, famine, infanticide, war, massacre, plunder, slavery, cold, hunger, disease, epidemics, plague, and abortion. Wallace goes on to list passages which particularly struck him and concludes:

> I then saw that war, plunder and massacres among men were represented by the attacks of carnivora on herbivora, and of the stronger upon the weaker among animals. Famine, droughts, floods and winter's storms would have an even greater effect on animals than on men; while as the former possessed powers of increase from twice to a thousand-fold greater than the latter, the ever-present annual destruction must also be many times greater . . . Then there flashed upon me . . .

and so on, including a ringing debt of gratitude to Lyell's "Immortal Principles of Geology" which impressed him even more deeply.[86] Wallace had been working as a naturalist and pondering the problem of the origin of species for thirteen years; he had published a paper on the theory *sans* mechanism three years earlier. As a naturalist he needed no more facts. He needed a new perspective, and an ethnology steeped in struggle provided it to his fitful mind.[87]

Wallace's later views can also serve to introduce the negative side of Malthus's influence in biological and social theory. While his interest in man and the origin of races had led to his co-discovery of the mechanism of natural selection, Wallace's belief in the perfectability of man led him to turn away from the all-sufficiency of the survival of the fittest. He came to make exceptions about man's

[86] A. R. Wallace, "Selections from Malthus's Essay on Population which suggested the Idea of Natural Selection", in *The Darwin-Wallace Celebration held on Thursday, 1st July, 1908, by the Linnean Society of London* (London, 1908), pp. 111-8.

[87] While the influence of Malthus on the actual formation of Darwin's theory is unequivocal, it should be noticed that all of Wallace's accounts were written well after the event and are liable to the reservations mentioned by Skinner, *Philosophy*, xli, pp. 206-10. I find Wallace's retrospective account completely convincing (see Appendix below) and feel that in each of the cases discussed in this article it is possible to gain a precise idea of the aspects of Malthus's ideas which were influential. Even so, Skinner's reservations do seem to have some conceptual force in the case of Wallace.

brain, and his aesthetic and moral faculties and to turn increasingly to the anticipation of human needs by some force transcending nature.[88] Having rejected the principle of utility as an adequate explanation of human evolution, it is not surprising that he went further and rejected its Malthusian source. He wrote to Darwin in 1881 that Henry George's *Progress and Poverty* had convinced him that Malthus's law did not apply at all to human evolution. George argued that nature could not be blamed for man's failure to distribute her bounty fairly.[89] Voluntarist co-operation and reform replaced struggle as the mechanism for social change.[90] Wallace came to agree with George that Malthus's theory has no bearing "whatever on the vast social and political questions which have been supported by reference to it". He saw *Progress and Poverty* as "making an advance in political and social science equal to that made by Adam Smith a century ago".[91] George has been called "arguably the most potent socialist influence in his generation".[92] By the time he wrote *The Wonderful Century* in 1898, Wallace's socialist hopes for the future of society led him to reject social struggle completely, and to

[88] The development of Wallace's divergence from Darwin on the question of the adequacy of natural selection to explain human evolution can be traced in the following articles by Wallace: "The Development of Human Races under the Law of Natural Selection" (1864) repr. in *Natural Selection and Tropical Nature* (London, 1891), ch. viii; "Sir Charles Lyell on Geological Development and the Origin of Species", *Quart. Rev.*, cxxvi (1869), pp. 379-94; "The Limits of Natural Selection as Applied to Man" (1870) repr. in *Natural Selection and Tropical Nature,* ch. ix; *Darwinism. An Exposition of the Theory of Natural Selection with Some of Its applications* (London, 1889), ch. xv. Darwin was very troubled by Wallace's views. He wrote to Wallace in 1869, "I hope you have not murdered too completely your own and my child". At p. 391 of Wallace's article on Lyell, Darwin has written in his copy "No", followed by a shower of exclamation marks. In the same year he wrote to Wallace, "If you had not told me, I should have thought that [your remarks on Man] had been added by someone else. As you expected, I differ grievously from you, and I am very sorry for it": *More Letters of Darwin,* ii, pp. 39-40; cf. pp. 31-7, 93. For discussions of this controversy, see George J. Romanes, *Darwin, and After Darwin* (Chicago, 1895), ii, ch. i; Loren Eiseley, *Darwin's Century* (London, 1959), ch. xi.

[89] Henry George, *Progress and Poverty. An Inquiry into the Casue of Industrial Depression and Increase of Want with Increase of Wealth . . . The Remedy* (New York, 1879; repr. New York, 1962), pp. 98, 130-41, 485-504, 525, 549-50, 558-9.

[90] A. R. Wallace, "Human Progress, Past and Future" (1892), repr. in *Studies, Scientific and Social* (London, 1900), ii, ch. xxvii; *Alfred Russel Wallace. Letters and Reminiscences,* ed. James Marchant (London, 1916), ii, pp. 139-65.

[91] *Letters and Reminiscences,* i, pp. 317-19; cf. i, pp. 15-16.

[92] I am indebted to A. R. K. Watkinson of Pembroke College, Cambridge for drawing my attention to George's influence; cf. Peter d'A. Jones, *The Christian Socialist Revival, 1877-1914* (Princeton, 1968), pp. 48-57.

embrace a belief in inevitable progress with no mechanism specified.[93] When, near the end of his life, Wallace reconsidered the question "Is Nature cruel?" and discussed the purpose and limitations of pain, he provided a neat way of reconciling Malthusian struggle in the animal world with a non-Malthusian view of human progress. His solution was almost Cartesian in its simplicity. Animals felt much less pain than men — almost none at all. Indeed, uncivilized races felt less than civilized ones.[94]

VII

Before venturing further into the relations between Malthus, evolution and socialism, I want to turn to the last of the three most eminent evolutionists. While Wallace drew away from Malthus and the all-sufficiency of the mechanism for human evolution suggested by "the survival of the fittest" (as his interest in social issues developed), Herbert Spencer provides the penultimate case which I wish to consider. His main interest was always man and society. According to John Burrow's excellent work *Evolution and Society, a Study of Victorian Social Theory,* Spencer, like Darwin and Wallace, drew his mechanism of evolution from Malthus's population theory.[95] Burrow is mistaken but in an interesting way. In 1851 Spencer published his first book, a defence of *laissez faire* social theory in opposition to the manipulations of the Benthamites. *Social Statics* contained views (derived in part from phrenology) which served as the basis of his later evolutionary thinking.[96] In 1852 he wrote an essay entitled "The Development Hypothesis" in which he advocated evolution but provided no detailed discussion of the mechanism by which evolution occurred. The main thesis of his brief argument was that "continual modifications due to change of circumstances"

[93] Wallace, *The Wonderful Century,* "Appendix — The Remedy for Want in the Midst of Wealth". I have discussed the issues involved in the views of Darwin, Wallace, George, and Spencer in " 'Non-Scientific' Factors in the Darwinian Debate", *Actes du XIIe Congrès International d'Histoire des Sciences, 1968* (in press).

[94] A. R. Wallace, *The World of Life. A Manifestation of Creative Power, Directive Mind and Ultimate Purpose* (London, 1911), ch. xix.

[95] John Burrow, *Evolution and Society. A Study in Victorian Social Theory* (Cambridge, 1966), p. 183.

[96] Herbert Spencer, *Social Statics: or The Conditions Essential to Human Happiness Specified, and the First of Them Developed* (London, 1851); cf. 2nd edn. (London, 1892), pp. 120 n, 266 n; R. M. Young, "The Development of Herbert Spencer's Concept of Evolution", *Actes du XIe Congrès International d'Histoire des Sciences* (Warsaw, 1967), ii, pp. 273-8.

was much more plausible than special creation.[97] In the same year he published an essay entitled "A Theory of Population, Deduced from the General Law of Animal Fertility". The natural inference is that belief in evolution combined with the population theory and applied to animal fertility, produced the same result as it had in the theories of Darwin and Wallace. On the contrary, there was no such synthesis in Spencer's theory. The Malthusian law is not mentioned until a few pages before the end, where pressure on population is called the proximate cause of progress. The principle of natural selection is also mentioned but not developed or extended beyond human society.[98]

After pointing out these passages in retrospect, Spencer remarks in his autobiography:

> It seems strange that, having long entertained a belief in the development of species through the operation of natural causes, I should have failed to see that the truth indicated in the above-quoted passages, must hold, not of mankind only, but of all animals; and must everywhere be working changes among them. ... Yet I completely overlooked this obvious corollary — was blind that here was a universally-operative factor in the development of species.

The reasons which he gives for this oversight are ignorance of the phenomena of variation and his belief in the inheritance of acquired characteristics.[99] Lyell had attempted to refute Lamarck's theory (which included "use inheritance") in the *Principles of Geology,* and this refutation was almost universally accepted. With characteristic perversity, Spencer rejected Lyell's refutation and became a convinced Lamarckian. The main feature of Spencer's explanation was not population pressure but Progress itself. Spencer agreed with Lamarck that nature had an inherent progressive tendency. He garbled the Lamarckian theory and considered the mechanism of this progress to be the inheritance of learned modifications. Indeed, his next work, begun almost immediately, was on psychology. Inspired by G. H. Lewes's *Biographical History of Philosophy* and informed by a copy of J. S. Mill's *Logic* which George Eliot gave him, Spencer abandoned the psychological theory of phrenology and became an associationist. Spencer's *Principles of Psychology,* published in 1855, contained a consistent evolutionary interpretation of all learning and an extension of associationism from the *tabula*

[97] Herbert Spencer, "The Development Hypothesis", repr. in *Essays: Scientific, Political, & Speculative* (London, 1901), i, pp. 1-7.

[98] Herbert Spencer, "A Theory of Population, Deduced from the General Law of Animal Fertility", *Westminster Rev.,* i (1852), pp. 498-501.

[99] Herbert Spencer, *An Autobiography* (London, 1904), i, pp. 389-90.

rasa of the individual to that of the race. Habits are inherited as built-in dispositions in the nervous system.[100]

In the introduction, in his collected *Essays,* to an essay written two years later and entitled "Progress: Its Law and Cause" Spencer says, "Though the idea and illustrations contained in this essay were eventually incorporated in *First Principles,* yet I think it well here to reproduce it as exhibiting the form under which the General Doctrine of Evolution made its first appearance".[101] The works under review in the original essay in the *Westminster Review* were von Humbold's *Cosmos,* the ninth edition of Lyell's *Principles of Geology,* and the fourth edition of William Carpenter's *Principles of Comparative Physiology.* Thus, Spencer's topics are: the universe, the earth, and life — typical Spencerian subject matter. He does not ignore struggle, but he certainly subordinates it to his own explanatory factors: Lamarckian inheritance of acquired characteristics, the concept of physiological division of labour, and that mysterious process which seems to be the key to all change — the transformation "from homogeneity to heterogeneity". Within this framework the idea of struggle is mentioned with no special emphasis. For example, he says, "The authority of the strongest makes itself felt among a body of savages as in a herd of animals, or a posse of schoolboys".[102] He had made similar statements in *Social Statics*[103]. This is not related to Malthusianism or described as a force for change in its own right but is an example of the transformation from homogeneity to heterogeneity, resulting in division of labour in society. He says at an earlier stage that the law of organic progress is the law of all progress — in the development of the earth, life, society, government, manufacture, commerce, language, literature, science, art. "From the earliest traceable cosmical changes down to the latest results of civilization, we shall find that the transformation of the homogeneous into the heterogeneous, is that in which Progress essentially consists".[104] "Progress is not an accident, not a thing within human control, but a beneficient necessity".[105]

[100] Herbert Spencer, *Principles of Psychology* (London, 1855), esp. parts iii-iv; *An Autobiography,* i, ch. xxxi; David Duncan, *The Life and Letters of Herbert Spencer* (London, 1908), ch. vii, and Appendix B, "The Filiation of Ideas". The development of Spencer's psychological theory is discussed in detail in my forthcoming book, *Mind, Brain, and Adaptation in the Nineteenth Century* (Oxford, in press), chs. v-vi.

[101] Spencer, *Essays,* i, p. 8. The version of this essay in Spencer's *Essays* is considerably altered from the original one in the *Westminster Review,* xi (1857), pp. 445-85, from which the following quotations are taken.

[102] *Ibid.,* p. 453.

[103] Spencer, *Social Statics,* pp. 322, 378-81, 388, 399; cf. *An Autobiography,* i, p. 363.

[104] Spencer, *Westminster Rev.,* xi, p. 447.

[105] *Ibid.,* p. 484.

In 1886 Spencer pointed out that although he had been heavily criticized for continuing to believe in the inheritance of acquired characteristics, Wallace had abandoned the survival of the fittest as a mechanism for human evolution, and in his later writings Darwin was allowing an increasingly greater rôle for mechanisms other than natural selection in the evolution of animals.[106] Indeed, the closer he got to mind and society, the more Darwin employed use-inheritance. Spencer says in the preface to a separately published edition of 1887 that the reason he had clung so tenaciously to the inheritance of acquired characteristics in biological theory was because it had such important implications for psychology, ethics and sociology.[107] These implications led him to write the essay, which was entitled "The Factors of Organic Evolution". He granted that the Malthusian factor might operate in mental phenomena of simpler kinds, but "use and disuse" was the chief factor in the development of man and society. Unless this were so, he pointed out, we could not be assured that society would progress *en masse* as quickly as it is seen to be doing. Progress on the Malthusian model was too indirect and too slow.[108] Far from being an application of Malthus, the sanguine belief in inexorable evolutionary progress which was characteristic of Spencer was more reminiscent of the doctrines which prompted Malthus to write the polemical first edition of his *Essay on the Principle of Population*. Spencer's *laissez faire* optimism is far closer to Rousseau, Condorcet and Godwin than to Malthus. True, Spencer had a place for struggle, but it basked in the light of Progress. This must be the real source of nature's energy. Thus, Spencer's evolutionary theory provides a negative case: it was fundamentally anti-Malthusian. Although he considered the Malthusian mechanism in the same period when he was working out his evolutionary theory, he passed it by, for it did not provide a sufficient guarantee of social progress, and he had turned to biology in search of that certainty.

VIII

There are a number of ways one could develop this progression involving the uses to which Malthus was put, the most obvious being to attempt a British version of Hofstadter's *Social Darwinism in American Thought*. Malthus, Darwin and Spencer provided the

[106] See above, note 88; Peter Vorzimmer, "Charles Darwin and Blending Inheritance", *Isis*, lv (1963), pp. 371-90.

[107] Herbert Spencer, *The Factors of Organic Evolution* (London, 1887), pp. iii-iv: this preface does not appear in the collected *Essays*.

[108] *Ibid.*, pp. 70-5, cf. pp. 9, 19-22, 29-33, 36-7, 41, 45-6.

rationalization for British imperialism as well as for the American robber barons.[109] But a tidier solution is to recall the Marxist view of Malthus and of the mechanism of evolution. When Marx first read Darwin's *Origin of Species* in 1860, he wrote to Engels that "although it is developed in the crude English style, this is the book which contains the basis in natural history for our view".[110] In fact, he wrote to Darwin in 1880 asking permission to dedicate the English edition of *Das Kapital* to him. Darwin politely refused, since he did not want his views to be associated with attacks on Christianity and Theism.[111]

For all their enthusiasm over Darwin's naturalistic interpretation of man, Marx and Engels found themselves embarrassed by Darwin's avowed debt to Malthus's population theory, since they had denounced the latter as a libel against the human race and Malthus as a plagiarist, a bought advocate, a shameless sycophant of the ruling classes who had well-earned the hatred of the English working classes.[112] In the *Dialectics of Nature,* Engels wrote that "Darwin did not know what a bitter satire he wrote on mankind and especially on his countrymen, when he showed that free competition, the struggle for existence, which the economists celebrate as the highest historical achievement, is the normal state of the *animal kingdom*".[113]

Marx and Engels were attempting to prize Darwin and Malthus apart. This has remained the Marxist line on Malthus, as Ronald Meek's edition of *Marx and Engels on Malthus* shows. An article in the *Modern Quarterly* illustrates the position: Fyfe argues that Marx exposed Malthus as a bourgeois fraud and that Malthusian theories "serve to disguise the fact that human suffering is due to the defects of a political system, by seeking to explain it as due to the operation of natural phenomena".[114] The value of neo-Malthusian theories

[109] Richard Hofstadter, *Social Darwinism in American Thought* (rev. edn., Boston, 1955); *Social Darwinism: Selected Essays of William Graham Sumner,* ed. Stow Persons (Englewood Cliffs, New Jersey, 1963); Walter Bagehot, *Physics and Politics, or Thoughts on the Application of the Principles of 'Natural Selection' and 'Inheritance' to Political Economy* (London, 1869); Benjamin Kidd, *Social Evolution* (London, 1894); *The Science of Power* (London, 1918).

[110] Quoted in *Marx and Engels on Malthus,* ed. Ronald L. Meek (New York, 1954), p. 171. Darwin wrote in 1879, "What a foolish idea seems to prevail in Germany on the connection between Socialism and Evolution through Natural Selection": *The Life and Letters of Charles Darwin,* ed. Francis Darwin (London, 1887), iii, p. 237.

[111] Sir Gavin de Beer, *Charles Darwin* (London, 1963), p. 266; cf. Gertrude Himmelfarb, *Darwin and the Darwinian Revolution* (London, 1959), p. 316 and ch. xix.

[112] *Marx and Engels on Malthus,* pp. 22-3.

[113] *Ibid.,* pp. 185-6; cf. pp. 173-88.

[114] James Fyfe, "Malthus and Malthusianism", *Modern Quart.,* vi (1951), p. 202.

to the capitalist and imperialist is "to deflect attention from the real causes of desperately low living standards by setting up pseudo-scientific 'laws' ".[115] Why do Marxists oppose Malthus's theory? For the same reason that earlier meliorists had done: it limits man's self-improvement and stresses struggle as an almost inescapable *impediment* to progress rather than as a mechanism for inevitable progressive change. Fyfe argues that in the U.S.S.R. "within our lifetimes the unlimited possibilities of man's control over his environment, once an assertion of a reasoned belief, a prediction, are being realized in actuality".[116]

Twentieth-century expressions of the intimate fusion of social and evolutionary theory which characterized the nineteenth-century debate were not confined to the pages of the *Modern Quarterly*. Indeed there was a smooth transition to very recent debates on the laws of biological inheritance. (It would be misleading to suggest that there are many such examples which support my general thesis as aptly as the following). G. H. Lewes and Herbert Spencer were the inspiration of Pavlov's classical research on conditioned reflexes,[117] and it is only very recently that the Darwinian version of evolution, including the Watson-Crick solution of the genetic code, could be taught, and the relevant scientific subjects could be studied, in the Soviet Union. The belief in changing animal (and human) nature by the "Lamarckian" inheritance of acquired characteristics was an orthodoxy. A statement by the Praesidium of the U.S.S.R. Academy of Sciences claimed in 1948 that the Russian version of "Lamarckianism" — the Lysenko-Michurin theory of inheritance — was the only acceptable one, "because it is based on dialectical materialism and on the revolutionary principle of changing nature for the benefit of the people".[118] Ten years later, as Soviet geneticists began an orderly retreat from this position, a reviewer of the waning orthodoxy pointed out that the proponents of Michurinism "assert that [the] gene theory of heredity opposed to it is a pseudoscientific, idealistic

[115] *Ibid.*, p. 207.

[116] *Ibid.*, p. 210. The arguments used by Marxists are reminiscent of those used by Henry George: Malthus was an apologist for the *status quo*, and by blaming nature for poverty he relieved men of the inclination to improve their lot by social change. See *ibid.*, pp. 23-5 and above notes 56, 75, 89-93.

[117] Sir Geoffrey Jefferson, *Selected Papers* (London, 1960), p. 40; Mary A. B. Brazier, "Russian Contributions to an Understanding of the Central Nervous System and Behavior", in *The Central Nervous System and Behavior*, ed. M. A. B. Brazier (New York, 1959), pp. 102-3; Horace W. Magoun, "Evolutionary Concepts of Brain Function Following Darwin and Spencer", in *Evolution After Darwin*, ed. Sol Tax (Chicago, 1960), ii, pp. 188, 193-5, 204.

[118] Quoted in A. E. E. McKenzie, *The Major Achievements of Science* (Cambridge, 1960), ii, p. 146.

conception of development associated with the reactionary ideology of the imperialistic bourgeoisie". The disagreement between Lysenko-Michurinist believers in inheritance of acquired characteristics and the neo-Darwinian geneticists was "not the conflict of two points of view in a single system; it is a class struggle between two systems, two ideologies". The ideology "of bourgeois scientists makes it utterly impossible for them to discover objective laws of nature, and they are, so to speak, forced consciously or unconsciously to distort these laws in accordance with the class interests of the bourgeoisie, to create a 'pseudoscientific reactionary' genetics — the gene theory of heredity".[119] This is a blatant example of the dominance of political ideology over well-attested scientific findings in the twentieth century, but it was also an international scandal. When it became clear that Watson and Crick were likely to win a Nobel Prize for their pseudo-scientific reactionary findings, modern genetics was finally allowed to begin developing in the Soviet Union. Nevertheless, it is not unlikely that a future historian will find that the neat division between biological and social science which most current scientists believe to have been established, is less absolute than it now appears.

IX

I have tried to show how five aspects of Malthus's *Essay on the Principle of Population* were developed by different figures in the debate on man's place in nature in the nineteenth century. First, his theodicy was muted by Paley, who (as the eighth edition of the *Britannica* put it) absorbed struggle in a "higher illumination than Reason alone affords us".[120] Second, the palliative of "moral restraint" which was added to the second edition of Malthus's *Essay*

[119] N. V. Turbin, "Philosophical Problems in Contemporary Genetics", *Problems of Philosophy,* no. 2 (1958), pp. 112-27. Lest it be thought that this example has been chosen for simple political reasons, it should perhaps be added that the United States Government took the trouble to translate a series of articles written in this vein and to join with the Josia Macy Jr. Foundation and the National Science Foundation in distributing them without charge to scientists: *The Central Nervous System and Behaviour. Translations from the Russian Medical Literature* (Bethesda, Maryland, 1960), p. 946. The following articles are also of particular interest for my historical purposes: I. T. Frolov, "Determinism and Teleology", pp. 186-205; N. I. Nuzhdin, "Methodological Problems in Contemporary Genetics", pp. 736-63; N. N. Zhukov-Verezhnikov and A. P. Pekhov, "Genetics of Microorganisms and Present-Day Views on Heredity", pp. 1023-42.

[120] Henry Rogers, "William Paley", in *The Encyclopedia Britannica,* 8th edn. (Edinburgh, 1859), xvii, p. 205.

became a scourge for the punishment of the sinful in the hands of Thomas Chalmers. Both Paley and Chalmers had interests in the established order of society and of nature. Third, Darwin seized on the image of nature as at war and used Malthus's view of natural law as applied to man as his authority for extending the principle of selection from the breeders' wishes to nature, that is, from artificial to natural selection. Once "moral restraint" was discounted, the law of struggle became the source of the marvellous adaptions of the natural theologians. Fourth, Wallace was impressed by the actual phenomena of human suffering in the environment, and having grasped this with respect to man, he applied it analogously to all of nature. Wallace also serves as a transitional figure for the fifth reading of Malthus. Progress became a watchword for his later writings on man and society. As this occurred, Malthus was progressively abandoned. Spencer's preoccupations with social progress were such that Malthus never found a place in his evolutionary theory, since Malthus had stressed the impediments to Godwin's and Condorcet's belief in indefinite progress. These impediments were also anathema to the social philosophy of Marx and Engels, who wanted to embrace Darwin while rejecting Malthus. Similarly, and perfectly appropriately, their Russian interpreters embraced the theory of learning and its extension to the race which was furthest from the Malthusian doctrine. They, like Spencer, wanted evolution only as a scientific guarantee for indefinite social progress.

It is hoped that this case study may have provided some evidence for the theses that influences in the history of science can be exploited as variously as in political and social history and that claims for progressive separation of "objective" natural science and woolly social science can find no support in the history of evolutionary theory. The integration of the history of science with other aspects of history is now established in seventeenth-century studies. It would appear that historians of the nineteenth century could well apply this approach to their period with similar interesting results.

King's College, Cambridge *Robert M. Young*

[12]

RESEARCH NOTE

Darwin, Malthus, and Selection

SANDRA HERBERT
Museum of History and Technology
Smithsonian Institution
Washington, D. C.

Occasionally in history a matter of interpretation comes to be settled by the addition of new evidence. This is what is happening in the debate over Darwin's reading of Malthus—the time at which Darwin first read him and the extent to which he was influenced by him. Previously lost pages from Darwin's "Notebooks on Transmutation of Species" were published in 1967. These pages establish the dates on which Darwin was reading Malthus and record Darwin's immediate response to the importance of what he was reading for his own ideas on the origin of species. A passage dated September 28, 1838, taken from "D." the third notebook on species, reads as follows:

> 28th. We ought to be far from wondering of changes in numbers of species, from small changes in nature of locality. Even the energetic language of Decandolle does not convey the warring of the species as inference from Malthus.—increase of brutes must be prevented solely by positive checks, excepting that famine may stop desire.—in nature production does not increase, whilst no check prevail, but the positive check of famine & consequently death. I do not doubt every one till he thinks deeply has assumed that increase of animals exactly proportionate to the number that can live— . . .
>
> Population is increase[d] at geometrical ratio in *far shorter* time than 25 years—yet until the one sentence of Malthus no one clearly perceived the great check amongst men.—[there is spring, like food used for other purposes as wheat for making brandy.—Even a *few* years plenty, makes population in man

Journal of the History of Biology, vol. 4, no. 1 (Spring 1971), pp. 209–217.

> increase & an *ordinary* crop causes a dearth.] Take Europe on an average every species must have same number killed year with year by hawks, by cold &c.—even one species of hawk decreasing in number must affect instantaneously all the rest.—The final cause of all this wedging, must be to sort out proper structure, & adapt it to changes.—to do that for form, which Malthus shows is the final effect (by means however of volition) of this populousness on the energy of man. One may say there is a force like a hundred thousand wedges trying force every kind of adapted structure into the gaps in the oeconomy of nature, or rather forming gaps by thrusting out weaker ones.—[1]

Interpretations of the importance of Malthus to Darwin made before this passage was discovered erred in several directions. The most obvious and correctable error was misjudging the time when Darwin read Malthus. For example, Gavin de Beer, editor of the Darwin notebooks, estimated the reading to have taken place after the third notebook was filled. Thus de Beer could cite the following passage from the third notebook, now known to have been written after Malthus, as evidence that Darwin had no need of Malthus in coming to the notion of natural selection: "(All this agrees well with my views of those forms slightly favoured getting the upper hand & forming species.)[2] Believing

1. *"Darwin's Notebooks on Transmutation of Species,"* Parts I–IV, Edited, with Introduction and Notes by Sir Gavin de Beer; Addenda and Corrigenda, edited by Sir Gavin de Beer and M. J. Rowlands; Part VI (excised pages) edited by Sir Gavin de Beer, M. J. Rowlands, and B. M. Skramovsky, *Bulletin of the British Museum (Natural History) Historical Series,* vol. 2, nos. 2–6, and 3 no. 5 (London, 1960–1967); Part VI, pp. 134–135, excised from the third notebook. Darwin's pagination is used throughout in citations from the notebooks; De Beer's Parts I, II, III, and IV correspond to Darwin's "B", "C", "D", and "E". Other notebooks in the series kept during 1837–39 include "A" on geological topics and "M" and "N" on the human aspect of transmutation with regard to views of philosophers and moralists and to the reinterpretation of human behaviour that would be required by transmutationist theory.

In the passage quoted those sentences in brackets appear in between the lines of the text in smaller and darker script. Fortunately for the dating of the passage we have Darwin's own word. Otherwise the date would be difficult to set as there are succeeding entries in the notebook with earlier dates. Darwin apparently decided on September 11 to begin a separate section on "Generation" towards the back of the book on page 152. There are thus two separate runs of dates in the notebooks which did not, of course, prevent the paper-saving Darwin from using free space in the notebooks without respect to chronological order of entry. Nevertheless, the Malthus entry seems to have been made in order since the entry begun on page 134 continues at the top of page 135 and since the entry on the bottom of page 136 dated September 29th continues without interruption for three pages.

2. *Ibid.*, pt. III, p. 175. Since this sentence is taken from the section of

that Darwin wrote this sentence without benefit of Malthus, de Beer then assessed the importance of Malthus to Darwin to be the "mathematical demonstration of the insufficiency of food supplies if numbers increased too fast and the consequent inevitableness of the penalties."[3]

Other interpreters, while not assigning a date to Darwin's reading of Malthus, yet concurred with de Beer's general conclusion that Darwin was indebted to Malthus for the notion of the tendency toward the geometrical expansion of population rather than for any help in the definition of the notion of selection. Gertrude Himmelfarb, for example, suggested that "In general, what Malthus was concerned with was not how the struggle for existence affected the quality of the population but simply how it limited its numbers."[4] Loren Eiseley, also puzzled by Darwin's expressed indebtedness to Malthus, concluded: "It may well be that Darwin really received only an increased growth of confidence in his previously perceived idea through reading the Malthusian essay. The geometrical growth of life as expressed by Malthus greatly impressed him and may have turned his thoughts more intensively upon the struggle for existence."[5] Giving a slightly different emphasis, Stephen Toulmin and June Goodfield have agreed that "Darwin did not learn anything new from Malthus," but have traced what Malthusian seed there was in Darwin's discovery to a new focus on the "struggle for the means of subsistence".[6]

Now that the date for Darwin's critical reading of Malthus is secure, however, the puzzle over why Darwin himself credited so much to this event still exists if the above interpretations are not altered. Gavin de Beer, for one, has remained faithful to his prior conclusion that Darwin already had accepted selection as a mechanism for evolution before reading Malthus. De Beer's reconstruction of the discovery of natural selection has it that Darwin was actively looking for a natural corollary to artificial selection when he read Malthus. In substantiating his claim, de

---

the notebook on "Generation" [footnote 1], its date may still be questioned. This last dated page in this section is page 163, dated September 25. What probably happened was that Darwin inserted this parenthetical remark concerning his new insight into a longer speculation, left unquoted, on the variation caused by change in physical circumstance.

3. *Ibid.* Introduction by Sir Gavin de Beer, p. 29.

4. Gertrude Himmelfarb, *Darwin and the Darwinian Revolution* (New York: Doubleday, 1959), p. 159.

5. Loren Eiseley, *Darwin's Century* (New York: Doubleday Anchor Books, 1961), pp. 181–182.

6. Stephen Toulmin and June Goodfield, *The Discovery of Time* (New York: Harper & Row, 1965), p. 203.

Beer cites Darwin's own words in a letter to Alfred Russel Wallace: "I came to the conclusion that selection was the principle of change from the study of domesticated productions; and then, reading Malthus, I saw at once how to apply this principle." [7]

Unfortunately, as clear as this citation is, the notebooks that Darwin kept at the time do not substantiate such a straightforward account of the discovery of natural selection. The most that can be substantiated by the notebooks on the point of the selective survival of the most fit is that Darwin considered the possibility that, somehow, only the well-adapted might survive and breed. In the first notebook, for example, there is speculation on this topic, though the distinction between individuals and species is not yet clear: "The father being climatized, climatizes the child. Whether every animal produces in course of ages ten thousand varieties (influenced itself perhaps by circumstance) and those alone preserved which are well adapted." [8] Darwin, however, could see no signs that only the "well-adapted" were preserved, and, not having the Malthusian fund of excess individuals to work with, he did not develop that line of thought. In regard to "artificial selection"— the phrase was not used—the record before Malthus is equally ambiguous. Darwin could refer to the existence of "two grand classes of varieties; one where offspring picked, one where not" [9]; but he could also remark, "It certainly appears in domesticated animals that the amount of variation is soon reached—as in pigeons no new races.—" [10]

Surveying all the comments in the notebooks made before Malthus, it does not seem that Darwin held a sufficiently unambiguous notion of artificial selection to have enabled him to anticipate finding, as a mechanism for evolution, a similar process at work in untended nature. Rather, it would seem, the

7. Gavin de Beer, *Charles Darwin* (New York: Doubleday Anchor Books, 1965), pp. 100–101. Quoted from *More Letters of Charles Darwin*, ed. Francis Darwin, 2 vols. (New York: D. Appleton & Co., 1903), dated from Down, April 6, 1859, to Alfred Russel Wallace, vol. 1, p. 118. For some reason de Beer lists the date as being 1858. Domestic species maintained no balanced relationship against each other; thus there was no world or system of domestic species to analogize with the species of the undomesticated world of nature. Domestic species were of value to Darwin before Malthus not as a miniature of the larger world of species but for their presentation of the facts of variation and the opportunity they afforded for study of the laws of inheritance.

8. "Darwin's Notebooks," pt. I, p. 90.

9. *Ibid.*, Addenda and Corrigenda, p. 106, from the second notebook.

10. *Ibid.* Addenda and Corrigenda, p. 104, from the third notebook.

discovery of natural selection made the domestic analogy much more clear to Darwin than it had been before.

It is clear from the evidence of the third notebook prior to the entry concerning Malthus that Darwin was developing two lines of thought in his search for rules governing transmutation. First, he was looking for the causes of variation among what he designated as external agencies (as, for example, climate) and as internal agencies (the "laws of organization"— growth, reproduction, and the connection between mental and physical discussed under the title of "habit"). Second, he was trying to discover the rules of inheritance. The third notebook abounds in cases recorded to prove or disprove what seemed most likely to him from a transmutationist point of view that the least variable structures in a species were the oldest. Although Darwin never abandoned his early interest in either of these two questions, they were no longer crucial to him once he had natural selection to rely on. Thus, for example, one can contrast the keen-eyed attention he was paying to habit six months before reading Malthus with the comparative detachment attending discussions of habit later. The following passage is from the second notebook: "According to my views, habits give structure, therefore habits precede structure, therefore habitual instincts precede structure."[11] Indeed, two weeks before reading Malthus Darwin could declare the structure of a species formed over a long time by habit to be superior to a "mere monstrosity propagated by art".[12] The following passage, written eight months after Malthus, puzzles again over external and internal agencies only to conclude:

> All that we can say in such cases is that the plumage has not been so injurious to bird as to allow any other kind of animal to usurp its place—& therefore the degree to injuriousness must have been exceedingly small.—This is a far more probable way of explaining, much structure, than attempting anything about habits.[13]

It was not that Darwin no longer suspected habit of having some role in the occurrence of new variations in structure but that, after Malthus, with selection as the primary mechanism for species change, he could afford to put off "attempting anything about habit."

If the role of Malthus in Darwin's development of the idea of

11. *Ibid.*, pt. II, p. 199.
12. *Ibid.* pt. III, p. 107.
13. *Ibid.* pt. IV, p. 147.

natural selection was more complicated than pictured by traditional interpretation, then what precisely was that role? Of the three elements comprising the theory of natural selection—individual variability, the tendency toward overpopulation, and the selective factors at work in nature—Darwin certainly owed little to Malthus concerning variability, for Darwin had already spent much energy documenting the differences and similarities of individuals belonging to the same or related species. The recurrent difficulty Darwin experienced in future years with individual variation related to its causes, not to its fact.

The tendency toward overpopulation is another matter. As all his students have agreed, Darwin on his own entertained little notion of such a tendency as universal, nor was he, at the time of reading Malthus in late September 1838, engaged in speculations relating to such an idea. Nevertheless, Darwin's great forerunner, Charles Lyell, had at least raised the issue of fertility. First, though not very seriously, Lyell had quoted the Italian geologist Giovanni Brocchi to say that species might "degenerate" and, like old men, lose their capacity to reproduce as fruitfully as in their prime. Second, and again from Lyell, domestic species could be said to be less fertile than their uncultivated cousins. At the place where this suggestion appeared in the sixth edition of the *Principles of Geology*, Darwin penciled a firm "no" but also inserted some heavy question marks.[14] Slightly closer to the population issue as raised by Malthus was the credit Lyell gave overpopulation as a stimulant to species migration, though there are no marks alongside this passage in Darwin's copies of the *Principles*.[15]

All in all, the closest Darwin came to the notion of population held by Malthus was in the awareness of a typical constancy in numbers of individuals belonging to a given species in a given area. Yet the manner in which this notion was raised was so far from any consideration of the potential productive powers of a species, or of any two parents, that is prevented Darwin from arriving at natural selection on his own. For Lyell and Darwin assumed that most species tend to produce as many young as may be necessary to maintain their population at its present level. The reasoning of parents who have three children in order

14. Marginalia in Darwin's copy, now at the University Library, Cambridge, of Charles Lyell, *Principles of Geology*, 3 vols., (London: John Murray, 1840), III, 42.

15. Lyell, *Principles*, 6th ed. (1840), III, 119. This passage occurs in the fifth edition (1837) as well, where it went unmarked by Darwin, but does not appear in the previous (first) edition which Darwin owned. Reading Malthus apparently sensitized Darwin to the issue of birth rates.

to assure that two will survive to adulthood is not unlike Lyell and Darwin's picture of the reproductive activity of most species.[16] This assumption was linked to the belief that the amount of life which could be maintained in a given area was constant. Such a view is represented by this passage from the first edition of the *Principles:*

> In the first place it is clear, that when any region is stocked with as great a variety of animals and plants as the productive powers of that region will enable it to support, the addition of any new species, or the *permanent* numerical decrease of one previously established, must always be attended either by the local extermination or the numerical decrease of some other species.[17]

That Darwin supported this view is evidenced by this entry from the second notebook:

> The *quantity of life* on planet at different periods depends on relations of desert, open ocean, etc. This probably on long average equal quantity, 2° on relation of heat and cold, therefore probably fewer now than formerly. The *number of forms depends* on the external relations (a fixed quantity) and on subdivision of stations and diversity, this perhaps on long average equal.[18]

16. Even after integrating Malthusian over reproduction into his theory, Darwin remained sensitive to the checks within a species against maximum reproduction. In his own copy of Malthus' *An Essay on the Principles of Population* [Lond., 6th ed. 1826, I, 29; inside front cover, "C. Darwin April 1841"; Cambridge U. Lib.], Darwin reminds himself in the margin that even in the savagest life not every man marries for wives must generally be bought.

All in all, before reading Malthus for himself, Darwin was not excited by the issue of rate of reproduction *per se*, especially compared to someone who was such as Alexander von Humboldt. In Darwin's copies of Humboldt's *Political Essay on the Kingdom of New Spain* (trans. J. Black, New York, 1811, 2 vol.; inscribed "C. Darwin, Buenos Aires 1832;" Camb. U. Lib.) and his *Personal Narrative of Travels to the Equinoctial Regions of the New Continent*, 1799–1809 (trans. Williams, 6 vols., Lond., 1819–1829; "J. S. Henslow to his friend C. Darwin on his departure from England upon a voyage round the world"; Cambridge U. Lib.) Darwin did not choose to mark Humboldt's tallying of birth and death rates among various peoples or his citations from Malthus even though his markings show he gave attention to other portions of the works.

17. Lyell, *Principles*, 1st ed., II, 142.

18. "Darwin's Notebooks," pt. VI, p. 147, excised from the second notebook. For a similar statement from Darwin as of 1860 see *Sir Charles Lyell's Scientific Journals on the Species Question*, ed. Leonard Wilson (New Haven and London: Yale University, 1970), pp. 344–346.

Obviously, this attitude toward population does not touch on the Malthusian point of the tendency toward overpopulation, except that both views assumed the amount of life the earth could support to be fairly constant.

Yet, for Darwin, the manner in which Lyell treated numbers and species blurred the distinction between reproduction as a separate problem from competition. What was peculiar to the Lyellian point of view, particularly as it is represented in the quotation above, was the similar treatment accorded individuals and species. Indeed, it can be said that Lyell tended to treat individuals and species in the same breath. Where Lyell's conflation of species and individuals misled Darwin in his search for a mechanism for species change was in Lyell's very persuasive and forceful presentation of the struggle for existence in nature. Here is a typically Lyellian passage on selection which sounds so much like the *Origin of Species* that it is difficult to see at first glance what Darwin, or Malthus, could add to the concept:

> If we consider the vegetable kingdom generally, it must be recollected, that even of the seeds which are well ripened, a great part are either eaten by insects, birds, and other animals, or decay for want of room and opportunity to germinate. Unhealthy plants are the first which are cut off by causes prejudicial to the species, being usually stifled by more vigorous individuals of their own kinds. If, therefore, the relative fecundity or hardiness of hybrids be in the least degree inferior, they cannot maintain their footing for many generations, even if they were ever produced beyond one generation in a wild state. In the universal struggle for existence, the right of the strongest eventually prevails; and the strength and durability of a race depends mainly on its prolificness, in which hybrids are acknowledged to be deficient.[19]

On closer reading, however, we see that Lyell is not really speaking of competition between individuals of the same group to represent that group in nature. All that he is saying with respect to intraspecific competition is that the "unhealthy" or the obviously abnormal will die. The "more vigorous individuals of their own kinds" is not enlarged on, for Lyell tended to see the division between "vigorous individuals" and "unhealthy" ones as sharp—no doubt because he spent relatively little time examining the differences between individuals regarded as belonging to the same species and made his distinctions between the two

19. Lyell, *Principles*, 4th ed., II, 391.

groups for the purposes of argument. Rather, the kind of selection always uppermost in his mind was that resulting in the extinction of some species—that is, in the competition between various species and races, to maintain their place on an earth with limited amount of life space. Thus we see in his ringing sentence on the "universal struggle for existence" where the "right of the strongest eventually prevails" that he is referring primarily to the competition between groups, for the sentence concludes: "and the strength and durability of a *race* depends mainly on its prolificness, in which hybrids are acknowledged to be deficient." [20] Aware that the distinction I am making is one of degree of emphasis, I believe that is is correct to say that Lyell's vision and depiction of the struggle for existence focused on the struggle between species—that is, its concentration was interspecific rather than intraspecific.

Once this distinction is made, it becomes easier to understand why Darwin, who accepted Lyell's presentation of competition without protest, did not come to natural selection sooner than he did or, more interestingly, was not thinking in that direction at the time he read Malthus. For to see selection as a mechanism for evolution it was necessary to concentrate on the competitive edges to nature—predation, famine, natural disaster—as they played upon the individual differences of members of the same group. Since, save for the work of breeders and horticulturists, this was largely an act of imagination, Lyell's concentration on competition at the species level could well have numbed—and I believe did—Darwin to the evolutionary potential of the "struggle for existence" at the individual level. Malthus, by showing what terrible pruning was exercised on the individuals of one species, impelled Darwin to apply what he knew about the struggle at the species level to the individual level, seeing that survival at the species level was the record of evolution, and survival at the individual level its propulsion. For that reason it is just that Thomas Malthus be ranked as contributor rather than catalyst to Darwin's new understanding, after September 28, 1838, of the explanatory possibilities of the idea of struggle in nature.[21]

20. *Ibid.* (italics added).

21. Since this article was accepted for publication, several articles have appeared on the subject: Frank N. Egerton, "Humboldt, Darwin, and Population," *J. Hist. Biology*, 3 (Fall 1970), 325–360; Peter Vorzimmer, "Darwin, Malthus, and the Theory of Natural Selection," *J. Hist. Ideas*, 30 (October 1969), 527–542, and Robert M. Young, "Malthus and the Evolutionists: the Common Context of Biological and Social Theory," *Past & Present*, 43 (May 1969), 109–145.

[13]

Schumpeter versus Darwin: In re Malthus*

LAMAR B. JONES
Louisiana State University
Baton Rouge, Louisiana

> It was Lena who had introduced me to the valuable idea that modes of seeing were matters of destiny, that what is sent forth by the seer affects what is seen. She liked to give the example of Whistler the painter when he was taken to task by a woman who said, "I never see trees like that." He told her, "No ma'am, but don't you wish you could?"
>
> Saul Bellow, *More Die of Heartbreak*

I. Introduction

This paper seeks to explore the impact of Thomas Robert Malthus upon the research conducted by Charles Robert Darwin. The justification for the undertaking stems from the perceived void in the pages of histories of economic analysis concerning the Malthus-Darwin linkage. For example, in the recently published four volume critical assessments of *Thomas Robert Malthus* [44] not one of the one hundred articles contains anything meaningful about the relationship of Malthus's work to Darwin's creation of evolutionary biology. Yet, among present-day historians of science, and among scientists concerned with Darwin's work, "The relationship between Darwin and Malthus is perhaps the issue in Darwin studies on which there has been most discussion and disagreement [27, 953]."

Economists have, of course, long accorded to Malthus an influence on Darwin. However, the direction and degree of that influence has not, in the literature of economics, been well developed. Instead, a kind of folklore has been built up, bearing only a tangential relationship to reality, and when an economist with prestige repeats or embellishes the folklore the legends exude an aura of credibility. All too often folklore and legend remain an operative but inaccurate or imprecise interpretation of the history of the discipline of economics. Consequently, the inter-generational transmission of the history of the discipline in shaping events—in the matter at hand, evolutionary biology—is either misunderstood or substantially lost, making economics and economists the poorer for it. To illustrate the problem and to create a starting point for what follows, J. A. Schumpeter's treatment of the Malthus-Darwin linkage in the pages of his widely read *History of Economic Analysis* will serve as *locus classicus*.

Schumpeter clearly admired Darwin, ranking *The Origin of Species* as the greatest scientific book of all times. In typically Schumpeterian exuberance he wrote that ". . . the *Origin of Species* and the *Descent of Man* . . . have secular importance for mankind's cosmic conceptions . . .

*For his thorough reading of a draft of this paper I am indebted to Professor Robert F. Hébert of Auburn University. As always, his comments were trenchant.

comparable with that of the heliocentric system [36, 188, 445]." No small praises, these, but when it came to accepting Darwin's own observations about Malthus, Schumpeter's admiration cooled considerably. In what ought to be especially intriguing words for economists to read, Darwin wrote, in his *Autobiography*, the famous tribute: "In October 1838, that is, fifteen months after I had begun my systematic enquiry, I happened to read for amusement Malthus on *Population*, ... Here, then, I had at last got a theory by which to work [10, 120]." Schumpeter's reaction was hardly accepting:

> It seems very hazardous, to be sure, to dissent from a man's statements about his own mental processes. But quite insignificant events or suggestions may release a given current of thought; Darwin himself did not include Malthus' work in the Historical Sketch . . . [Here the reference is to the "Historical Sketch" added by Darwin in 1866 to the third and later editions of the *Origin of Species*.], though he did refer to it in his introduction; and the mere statement that "more individuals are born than can possibly survive" (which, moreover is doubtful Malthusianism) is, in itself not more than a platitude. I am afraid, therefore, that service rendered by economics to the evolution of the Darwinian doctrine bears some analogy to the service rendered to Rome by the celebrated geese [36, 445–6].[1]

What a tangle! Schumpeter, one of the foremost proponents of econometrics, a man who wanted economics to move closer to the physical sciences, casts doubt about the reliance a renowed scientist, Darwin, said he placed upon the writings of a competent mathematician and political economist, Malthus. Is Schumpeter correct in his observation? The analysis which follows attempts to detail both the "true" extent of the Malthus-Darwin linkage, and thereby respond to Schumpeter. The provocative question is this: What did Darwin find useful in Malthus's writings? The way to approach an answer is to first examine what Darwin actually wrote that pertained to Malthus. The results are, arguably, not favorable to the Schumpeterian view.

II. Darwin's References to Malthus: The Written Record

Darwin's research notebooks[2] record that in contrast to his statement in his *Autobiography* he opened Malthus's 6th edition of the *Essay On Population* on September 28, 1838. And, of course, he was reading earnestly, not for "amusement." As Gruber has observed, Darwin was searching for something that would tie his thoughts together in a more holistic way; for a vehicle that would carry him to explanatory structure [20, 118–9]. Did Malthus provide the coherence? The crucial entry which supports contention that Malthus provided the link Darwin needed is found in the "D" notebook, Darwin's third notebook on "Transmutation of Species," written from July 15 –

1. The role of the geese of Rome are detailed in *Livy*, published by The Heritage Press, 1972, pp. 485–6. As for Schumpeter's comment about Darwin's inclusion of a historical sketch, one should know that *On the Origin of Species* was changed substantially through the five revisions. These changes may be followed in Morse Peckham's *The Origin of Species By Charles Darwin A Variorum Text*. Philadelphia: University of Pennsylvania Press, 1959. References to Malthus were never altered in any of the five revisions.

2. The matter of Darwin's notebooks is a bit involved. The "Notebooks On Transmutation Of Species," the so-called "B, C, D, and E Notebooks," first appeared in print in 1960, in celebration of the 100th anniversary of publication of Darwin's *Origin*. The series edited by Gavin de Beer are in the *Bulletin of The British Museum (Natural History) Historical Series*, 2:2, 2:3, 2:4, 2:5, 2:6, London, 1960. In 1967, pages that Darwin had excised from the Transmutation Notebooks were found and published. These pages are in the aforementioned *Bulletin*, 3:5, 1967. The "Notebooks on Man, Mind and Materialism," "Old and Useless Notes," and "The Essay On Theology and Natural Selection," are in total transcribed and annotated by Barrett in Gruber, and Barrett [20, 259–424]. The same work contains extracted passages from the Transmutation notebooks.

October 2, 1838. Kohn has reproduced the entry, which is in two separable layers of writing. The roman print identifies the initial entry. The italicized passages are Darwin's interlined comments located near their original position in the "D" notebook.[3] Kohn believes that the passage marks the moment when,". . . as an immediate result of reading Malthus, Darwin first formulated his theory of natural selection [26, 140]." For Gruber the entry marks the point of Darwin's "Malthusian insight," that moment when he". . . recognized the force of the idea of evolution through natural selection [20, 7]." The entry reads as follows:

> *I do not doubt, every one till he thinks deeply has assumed that increase of animals exactly proportiona[l] to the number that can live.—*
> [September[28th.[1838] We ought to be far from wondering of changes in number of species, from small changes in nature of locality. Even the energetic language of ['Malthus' *del*] Decandoelle does not convey the warring of the species as inference from Malthus.—
> *increase of brutes, must be prevented solely by positive checks, excepting that famine may stop desire.—*
> in nature production does not increase, whilst no check prevail, but the positive check of famine & consequently death . . . population is increase at geometrical ratio in *FAR SHORTER* time than 25 years—
> *there is spring, like food used for other purposes as wheat for making brandy.—*
> yet until the one sentence of Malthus no one clearly perceived the great check amongst men.—
> *Even a few years plenty, makes population in man increase & an* ordinary *crop causes a dearth.*
> take Europe on an average every species must have same number killed, year with year, by hawks, by cold & c—even one species of hawk decreasing in number must affect instantaneously all the rest.—
> *The final cause of all this wedging, must be to sort out proper structure. & adapt it to change.—to do that, for form, which Malthus shows, is the final effect, (by means however of volition) of this populousness, on the energy of man*
> one may say there is a force like a hundred thousand wedges trying [to] force every kind of adapted structure into the gaps in the oeconomy of nature, or rather forming gaps by thrusting out weaker ones.—[26, 140–1; 15 (1967), 162–3].

In notebook "E," Darwin's fourth notebook on Transmutation of Species," kept from October 1838 to July 10, 1839, he wrote, after several statements about epidemics—he was, Young writes, reading Malthus's passages on epidemics—this quotation from page 529 of Malthus's 6th edition [p. 529], adding his own italics and exclamations:

> It accords with the most *liberal!* spirit of philosophy to believe that no stone can fall, or plant rise, without the immediate agency of the deity [Young interjects that Malthus wrote "divine power"]. But we know from *experience!* that these operations of what we call nature, have conducted *almost!* invariably according to fixed laws: and since the work began, the causes of population & depopulation have been probably as constant as any of the laws of nature with which we are acquainted.—This applies to one species—I would apply it not only to population & depopulation, but extermination and production of new forms—this number and correlations [45, 128–9; 15, 160].

A few pages below this entry is the following: "It/may/be said, that wild animals will vary, according to my Malthusian views, within certain limits, but beyond them not,— . . . [15, 175]."

But Darwin's interest in Malthus extended beyond the direct natural selection insight. In his

3. The entry referred to emerged in the discovery of excised pages that Darwin had removed from the "E" notebook. It is this reference to Malthus that enabled the date of Darwin's reading of Malthus's *Essay* to be moved back from October 4, 1838 to September 28, 1838. See *Bulletin of The British Museum (Natural History) Historical Series*, 3:5, 1967, p. 1.

research notebooks "M and N," Darwin focused on links between man and animals, including evolution of intelligence, emotions, sanity and insanity, as well as other psychological topics. In the "Essay on Theology and Natural Selection" and in a set of papers labeled as "Old and Useless Notes" Darwin probed a variety of issues, such as free will, effects of atheism on morality, the moral sense and metaphysics. In brief, he was interested in potentially relevant questions and problem areas which might pertain to his overall research thrust. Malthus's name appears in these works.

In the "N" notebook, dealing with, "Man, Mind and Materialism" there is an October 4, 1838 entry pertaining to Malthus: "Malthus on Pop. p. 32 origin of Chastity in women,—rationally explained—on the wish to support a wife a ruling motive—Book IV, Chapt. I on passions of mankind, as being really useful to them: This must/be studied before my view of origin of evil passions [12, 332]." In miscellaneous notes, the "Old and Useless Notes," a notebook entry for October 2, 1838, dealing with emotions in man, reads: "No check were necessary to the vice of intemperance, circumstances made the check—the licentiousness jealousy & everyone being [Gruber and Barrett have suggested the next word is 'named,' but Darwin's entry is not readable] to keep up population, with the existences of so many positive checks.—(This is encroaching on views in second volume of Malthus) [13, 390]." And in a set of notes for his "Essay on Theology and Natural Selection" there is an entry, written in 1838, arguing against the Bridgewater Treatises: "inconvenience! *extinction*, utter *extinction!* let him study Malthus & Decandoelle." The very next entry reads: "The final cause of innumerable eggs is explained by Malthus [14, 416, 419]."

What is important about these various entries is that in them Darwin demonstrates that his involvement with Malthus's intellect was not only deep, in the specific aspect of struggle and natural selection, but also broad in scope and subject. Malthus was more important than a superficial glimpse would reveal.

From the notebooks Darwin's writings move toward more comprehensive structure for the key account of his theory of evolutionary biology. In 1842 to, in his words, ". . . allow myself the satisfaction of writing a very brief abstract of my theory in pencil" he produced a 35 page essay [10, 120]. In 1844, this abstract was expanded to 250 pages, and it was extracts from this "work on Species," as Darwin titled it, that were read, along with A. R. Wallace's competing paper, by Lyell and Hooker before the Linnean Society of London on July 1, 1858. The late Sir Gavin de Beer, in the 1958 commemorative reprinting of both the 1842 and 1844 Darwin papers, and Wallace's essay, wrote in the introduction that the eighteen pages of abstracted material presented to the Linnean Society in 1858 "were among the most pregnant ever printed, and deserve to rank with those of Isaac Newton, since they provided for the realm of living things the first general principle capable of universal application [17, 1]." Malthus is prominent in both Darwin's 1842 and 1844 works. In the 1842 essay there is this important development; a powerful presence of Malthusian influence.

> *Natural selection*. DeCandolle's war of nature—seeing contented face of nature—may be well at first doubted; we see it on borders of perpetual cold. But considering the enormous geometrical power of increase in every organism and as every country, in ordinary cases, must be stocked to full extent, reflection will show that this is the case. Malthus on man—in animals no moral restraint—they breed in time of year when provision most abundant, or season most favourable, every country has its season—calculate robins—oscillating from years of destruction. If proof were wanted let any singular change of climate occur here, how astoundingly some tribes increase, also introduced animals, the pressure is always ready—capacity of alpine plants to endure

> other climates—think of endless seeds scattered abroad—forests regaining their percentage—a thousand wedges being forced into the economy of nature. This requires much reflection; study Malthus and calculate rates of increase and remember the resistance—only periodical [7, 46–7].

In the 1844 essay there is a smoothing of text, and part of the 1842 passage concerning Malthus becomes this, which served as the opening paragraph in the extracted version read to the Linnean Society.

> NATURAL MEANS OF SELECTION
>
> De Candolle, in an eloquent passage, has declared that all nature is at war, one organism with another, or with eternal nature. Seeing the contented face of nature, this may at first be well doubted; but reflection will inevitably prove it is too true. The war, however, is not constant, but only recurrent in a slight degree at short periods; and hence its effects are easily over looked. It is the doctrine of Malthus applied in most cases with ten-fold force [9, 259].

The remainder of the 1842 portion concerning Malthus was included in the 1844 Essay, in slightly revised form, as follows:

> Lighten any check in the least degree, and the geometrical powers of increase in every organism will almost instantly increase the average number of favoured species. Nature may be compared to a surface on which rest ten thousand sharp wedges touching each other and driven inward by incessant blows. Fully to realize these views much reflection is requisite. Malthus on man should be studied;
>
> . . . .
>
> Reflect on the enormous multiplying power *inherent and annually in action* in all animals; reflect on the countless seeds scattered by a hundred ingenious contrivances, year after year, over the whole face of the land; and yet we have every reason to suppose that the average percentage of each of the inhabitants of a country usually remains constant [8, 118].

In the *Origin of Species*, which Darwin rushed to publication in 1859, there are two explicit references to Malthus, neither of which changed in five revisions of the text. In the Introduction there is this: "In the chapter the Struggle For Existence amongst all organic beings throughout the world, which inevitably follows from their high geometrical power of increase, will be treated of. This is the doctrine of Malthus, applied to the whole animal and vegetable kingdoms [11, 5]." And in Chapter III there is an expanded version of the Malthus passage in the Introduction: "It is the doctrine of Malthus applied with manifold force to the whole animal and vegetable kingdoms; for in their case there can be no artificial increase in food, and no prudential restraint from marriage [11, 63].

The *Origin* was an abstract of Darwin's "big book" his work which he identified as "Natural Selection" but which he never completed. An edited from manuscript version has recently been published. In it there are several references to Malthus, the most important of which reads:

> Nevertheless the doctrine that all nature is at war is most true. The struggle very often falls on the egg & seed, or on the seedling, larva & young; but fall it must sometime in the life of each individual, or more commonly at intervals on successive generations & then with extreme severity. This struggle & destruction follows inevitably in accordance with the law of increase so philosophically enunciated by Malthus . . . .
>
> . . . .
>
> Yet all living beings, if not destroyed, even the slowest breeders, tend to increase in geometrical proportion & often at enormous ratio [41, 175–6].

And, there is in Darwin's *The Variation of Animals and Plants Under Domestication*, 1868, this: ". . . I saw, on reading Malthus on Population, that Natural Selection was the inevitable result of the rapid increase of all organic beings; for I was prepared to appreciate the struggle for existence by having long studied the habits of animals [5, 10]."

In *Descent of Man*, 1871, Darwin uses Malthus's name twice. In the first instance: "There is reason to suspect, as Malthus has observed, that the reproductive power is actually less in barbarous, than in civilized races." And, in the second instance, pertaining to discussion of population checks in primitive societies: "Malthus has discussed these several checks, but he does not lay stress enough on what is probably the most important of all, namely infanticide . . . and abortion [6, 44, 46]."

The need for Malthus was not paramount in *Descent of Man*, the case had been made, in Darwin's mind, for natural selection was surely, for him, a founded theory. But Darwin had not abandoned Malthus after publication of the *Origin*. As passages from the following letters convey, he never was less than open about Malthus's importance to his research. In a letter to A. R. Wallace, on April 6, 1859, Darwin wrote: "You are right that I came to the conclusion that selection was the principle of change from the study of domesticated productions; and then, reading Malthus, I saw at once how to apply this principle." To Asa Gray, June 8, 1860, commenting on a review of the *Origin* in the *Dublin Natural History Review*: "The article is a curiosity of unfairness and arrogance; but as he [the author was Samuel Haughton] sneers at Malthus, I am content, for it is clear he cannot reason." And, to A. R. Wallace, July 5, 1866, commenting on the term "Natural Selection." "I doubt whether the use of any term would have made the subject intelligible to some minds, clear as it is to others; for do we not see even to the present day Malthus on Population absurdly misunderstood? This reflection about Malthus has often comforted me when I have been vexed at this misstatement of my views [16, 118, 153–4, 270–1]."

III. The Literature: A Survey[4]

"Malthus misunderstood?" Why? Did Darwin see more than did Schumpeter? If so what did he see? How does one, at this juncture, take the grand gauge of position and sort out the "true" linkage between Malthus and Darwin? Among scientists and historians of science there is clear agreement that Malthus was at least a contributor, whether a necessary element or not is not agreed upon. Some argue for more than a mere contribution, preferring instead to view Malthus as absolutely critical to Darwin's theoretical discovery, in short, a positive catalyst. The debate is continuous present-day discourse, not a proverbial dead horse to be flogged, but a vital part of modern perspective on the development of science, as well as an active part of science in the making. To pursue the matter is to broaden perspective.

Appropriately, therefore, the question to pose is: What could Malthus have provided for Darwin that he did not already have? At the low end of the gauge is de Beer's 1958 observation that almost nothing was offered: "I can hardly doubt that with his [Darwin's] knowledge of organisms and the tyranny of conditions, his experience would have crystallized out into 'a theory by which to work' even without the aid of Malthus [17, 27]." At the high end of the gauge is Herbert's 1977 observation: ". . . because of the enormous impact of Malthus on Darwin's work biology remains permanently indebted to the field of political economy [23, 216]."

4. Part III brings to mind the story of Professor M. M. Knight, an economic historian on the faculty of the University of California at Berkeley and brother of Frank H. Knight, who was once heard shouting at a doctoral student who had submitted a draft of his dissertation for reading: "God-damnit! You don't have to use all of your notes!" I have *not* used all of my notes in Part III.

Along the contours of the gauge from de Beer to Herbert are numerous possibilities. The reasons for the diversities of perspective are located in the fragmentation of Darwin's work, for his theory is not a monolithic structure, but rather a composite of several theories: speciation, common descent, gradual evolution, and natural selection, for example. Accordingly, the various perspectives concerning the linkages between Malthus and Darwin do not neatly fit under one heading. Arbitrarily they are grouped under three broad categories: mathematical, struggle for existence and balance of nature, and contextual derivations. But argumentative overlaps exist. What is said under one heading might well fit under another.

Mathematical Influences

For Gillispie, [19], the *Origin* was quantitative in method and matter of thought—"it was crucial for Darwin's success that he began with the Malthusian ratio," . . . Indeed, it was of far more significance for his success than was the question of its validity." The ratio let Darwin make clear to the scientific community that his reasoning ". . . was concerned with quantity and circumstance," and therefore he was, accordingly, liberating biology from its old heritage of typology. Through Malthus, Gillispie argues, Darwin found in good part the basis for atomism, the method he needed to link biology to Newtonian physics, and thereby treating biological order as no different than contemporary atomic physics, an order of chance to be understood through techniques of mathematical probability [19, 339, 340–1].

Mayr, supports this proposition, arguing that Darwin had brought to biology "population thinking," which of course was Malthusian derived, and because the populationist stresses the uniqueness of everything in the world populationism is directly opposed to typology. In short, atomism, chance, and probability mathematics are inherent in the approach Darwin took; "natural selection is inconceivable except through population thinking [30, xix–xx]."

For Schweber, Darwin got from Malthus's statement of population growth all he needed to crystallize his theory: "The requirements that the theory be quantitative, predictive, and deterministic," had, "been fulfilled [37, 304]." Additionally, "The transition from the specific Malthusian statement—that populations; if unchecked, increase geometrically on a fixed time scale—to a formulation in terms 'of the strongest possible tendency to increase' marks an important shift in Darwin." Why? Because, "the specific Malthusian statement allowed one to look at the initial and the final configurations and then try to interpolate between these in terms of a most probable history [38, 230–31]."

For Pancaldi, it was the transfer into biology of human demography that had such profound effects on Darwin's theory. This transfer was made easier, however, ". . . because of the prestige Malthusian views and political economy enjoyed in Britain for ideological and political reasons [34, 262]." And, of course, in terms of biological data the human numbers were the only numbers, hence Darwin's interest in Malthus's tables in the *Essay on Population*.

Struggle for Existence and Balance of Nature

For Young, ". . . Malthus legitimized the idea of a law of struggle, impressed Darwin with the intensity of struggle, and provided a convenient natural mechanism for the changes which Darwin was studying in the selection of domesticated varieties . . . ." From Malthus Darwin got the analogy he needed to move from artificial to natural selection, ". . . this was the essential step in his reasoning: indefinite variation and natural selection could provide new species." Moreover, Young argues that Malthus's influence was inside of biology, not outside. His theory and its assumption concerning nature were prevalent in the biological literature in the first few decades of the nineteenth century. Also useful to Darwin was Malthus's participation in the debate within natural theology [45, 130, 110–1].

For Vorzimmer, the "great watershed" in the development of Darwin's theory came with the reading of Malthus. Why? Because Darwin had reached the point where he understood that adaptation was the end, selection the means, and changing conditions were the initiating force, but the motive force was missing—a natural source was needed. The answer: "Malthusian struggle precipitated by changing conditions produces permanent modification or extinction of species." Additionally, Malthus impressed upon Darwin ". . . the great pressures bearing upon each *individual* being and the resultant struggle among offspring of the same parents" [42, 539].

For Herbert, Darwin would not reach natural selection as a mechanism until he traversed population, and he was blocked in this by his reading of Lyell who concentrated on competition at the species level. Darwin was numbed to the evolutionary potential of struggle for existence at the individual level, but after Malthus Darwin understood ". . . the terrible pruning exercised on *individuals* of one species." Malthus made Darwin see that ". . . survival at the species level was the record of evolution, and survival at the individual level its propulsion [22, 214–217]."

Bowler supports the essence of Herbert's argument, but does so by arguing that the idea of struggle was used quite differently by Malthus and by Darwin, with the concept used by Darwin occupying only a subsidiary position for Malthus. Specifically, Malthus by calling Darwin's attention to intra-species competition, which only was a minor part of Malthus's emphasis, led Darwin to the real core of the idea of a struggle for existence. Malthus had argued for inter-species struggle, man against his environment, and only in his mention of primitive tribal warfare did he at all deal with intra-species competition. By raising intra-species struggle to the status of a major driving force in nature, Bowler argues that Darwin added a new dimension ". . . which cannot be seen as a continuous development from earlier social debates [2, 648]."

Burkhardt finds the reading of Malthus changing for Darwin his understanding of the process by which organic change takes place. Malthus's ability to make Darwin see intra-species struggle and the importance of individual differences in this struggle is the major contribution Malthus made [4, 339]. This view is fully supported by Mayr, [32], and by Sober, [40], both of whom viewed the contribution Malthus made to Darwin to be the turning toward intra-species competition and away from the good of the species to the good of the individual organisms.

Contextual Derivatives

For Vorzimmer, Darwin found Malthus's influence to be both direct, in the sense of providing a principal element of the selective process, and indirect, in the sense of providing an all encompassing context through which Darwin could tie together a number of previously disconnected thoughts [42, 539, 541–2]."

Ospovat argues that "The theodicy of the *Origin* is essentially the theodicy of Malthus: to wit: "Thus, from the war of nature, from famine and death, the most exalted object which we are capable of conceiving, namely, the production of the higher animals, follows." But, for Ospovat, "Malthus and natural selection did not at once succeed in altering the natural theological structure of Darwin's earliest theories," for, "from the opening pages of his first transmutation notebook, across the Malthusian divide, to beyond the 'Essay of 1844' Darwin did not really abandon his belief in perfect adaptation [33, 220, 221–23]." Malthus's influence was therefore one of gradualism, forcing Darwin to ultimately, by 1859 and the *Origin*, opt for struggle and natural selection through competition; for differential adaptation.

For Kohn, it was not until he read Malthus, in 1838, that Darwin could move forward to accomplish ". . . the personal revolution of his own perception of adaptation," and when "he truly abandoned perfect adaptation for the concept of differential adaptation." To Kohn's mind the issue about Malthus is settled: he was the precipitator of Darwin's first formulation of the theory of natural selection by evolution. Moreover, "without Malthus's contribution . . . the emotional tone of the event remains controversial [26, 140, 142]."

Schweber sees ". . . the dynamical explanations that Darwin advanced in the *Origin* as the amalgamation of two great insights, the first of which was the Malthusian mechanism which carried Darwin to the high point of his theorizing. The second, not directly applicable here, was the use of Scottish thought about individualism to explain the principle of divergence [39, 35–6].

Gruber believes it was out of Malthus's context of social theory in which complex interrelationships such as intertwining population growth, social class differences, and human sexuality were matters of intense controversy, that "Darwin abstracted one key idea out of context and turned it upside down—from the scourage of humanity to the motor of evolution [21, 31]."

Hodge and Kohn argue against a sudden insightful theoretical breakthrough from the Malthus reading, arguing instead that Darwin's theorizing underwent complex developments both before and after his "meeting" with Malthus [24, 185].

IV. Conclusion

Is Darwinism the product of Malthusianism? Or is it more prudent to view Malthus's contribution as a very specific one, the proportional arithmetic and nothing else? Was Malthus's role, as Mayr ultimately concluded, merely ". . . that of a crystal tossed into a saturated fluid [31, 492]?"

No doubt the debate about the Malthus-Darwin linkage will continue, and remain controversial. The question, at this point, to ask is what, if anything, has been resolved? It seems certain that Schumpeter understated the importance of Malthus to Darwin, but in all fairness Schumpeter did not have available the various and important notebooks, though he did have access to everything else Darwin had written, from 1842 on. Why did he not take Darwin at his word, for certainly the references to Malthus were strong, continuous, and never out of Darwin's frame of reference about his own work? Is it as Schweber suggests, that we put our own proclivities into the issues and simply attribute to Malthus what best suits us? Schumpeter may have done just that, for his references to Malthus are quite caustic, in both the *History of Economic Analysis* [36, 446, 578, 581–2] and in *Capitalism, Socialism, and Democracy* [35, 115].

However, do those who interject Malthus into Darwin beyond Darwin's own references do what Gillian de Beer suggests: ". . . privilege Darwin's reading of Malthus . . . since it released and disturbed him creatively?" Or should we not entertain the possibility that is all too true, that "Books read do not stay inside their covers. Once in the head they mingle." Darwin was reading much more than just Malthus in 1838, as his reading notebooks point out [43].

Is Manier not believable in the view that "Darwin's distinctive task was to take both evidence and conceptual machinery from a number of diverse fields, and persuasively and coherently to represent his own novel integration of that material [29, 187]?"

Is not the *Origin* written in a fashion that is the language "really spoken by men [1, 561]?" Is it not the language of Malthus that one finds? And why not? How else could Darwin have penetrated so provocatively the intellects of his contemporaries. And surely the Malthusian ratios fit well, for as Browne comments, "More than any other contemporary topic, arguments over population brought simple arithmetic into the lives and homes of the people [3, 55]." Darwin's use of Malthus's ratios injected into biological science arithmetical procedures that were part of the general push toward numbers throughout society. Moreover, the ratios helped popularize his theory. And why should Malthus not be an effective vehicle for Darwin? John Herschel, an opinion leader in scientific circles, and a man for whom Darwin had great respect, described Malthus, in 1831, " 'as one of the most profound but at the same time popular writers of our time [34, 262].' "

But it is imprudent to ascribe too much to Malthus concerning theological, literary, and ideological input to Darwin. What needs to be made clear is that there is a clear case for Malthus being part of the ongoing scientific debate toward which Darwin was headed when he first read the *Essay on Population*. It is today Malthusian instability, in the minds of some scientists, that propels evolutionary biology. As Depew and Weber, 1988, have so recently observed:

> Darwin's task, as . . . the structure of the *Origin of Species* shows, was to refute the standing presumption, associated with Paley, that no natural law could account for functional organic traits. By envisioning the *environment* as a *closed* Malthusian space defined by intense competition, Darwin provoked the 'pressures' and 'forces' that could cause this effect, with no need to invoke any extrasystematic cause, least of all a divine one. In this way, Darwin's theory was understood as delivering up the biological world to the same Newtonian framework that had already captured the physical and chemical worlds [18, 332].

For F. A. Hopf, "By basing his theory of evolution on the Malthusian instability, Darwin . . . offers an enticing possibility of unifying physics and biology [25, 267]."

If reputable, active scientists see things as do Depew, Weber, and Hopf, then clearly there is considerable substance to the Darwin view that Malthus was important to him. And while there are different perspectives about the vitalness of this linkage is that not the result, to parody something Hopf wrote, of giving one historian of science ice, the other water, telling them it is the same substance, then giving them imprecise thermometers? Some confusion has to result. So is it with perspectives on the Malthus-Darwin linkage. The measuring devices concerning the relationship are too multi-dimensional to achieve unity of opinion. Nevertheless, it seems quite fair to make several concluding observations about the matter. First, Darwin's explicit references to Malthus should be accepted at face value. Had Schumpeter thought about matters a bit more, surely he would have recognized that Malthus's emphasis upon competitive struggle for survival among humans did play a significant role in the development of Darwin's thought, as did the population arithmetic, and population thinking, which pointed toward statistical analysis and probability theory. Also a reading of Darwin's views about Malthus suggest other avenues, theology for example, that Malthus opened for him.

But what appears as explicit links to Malthus may not be the major role Malthus played in Darwin's life. Darwin's letters, which were available to Schumpeter, hint toward a deeper less obvious influence. Perhaps Darwin saw in Malthus what Whistler saw in the trees he painted, something no one could see, or would see. For reasons only Darwin knew he seems to have found some character trait in Malthus that he admired, some ineffable quality. Perhaps it was courage.[5]

5. Malthus wrote in Chapter XIX of the *Essay On Population* these words: "The Supreme Being would appear to us in a very different view if we were to consider him as pursuing the creatures that had offended him with eternal hate and torture . . ." [28, 284]. As Antoney Flew points out this is a remarkably advanced passage—Malthus, an ordained clergyman of the Church of England is unequivocably rejecting the doctrine of Hell as a punishment of ever-lasting torment. In Darwin's *Autobiography* [10, 87] it was this "damnable doctrine" which reconciled Darwin to his loss of religious faith: "I can indeed hardly see how anyone ought to wish Christianity to be true . . . ."

Interestingly, Darwin was until after the Beagle's voyage destined for the same religious orders as Malthus held. Schumpeter's first marriage was to the daughter of an official of the Church of England.

Darwin's long and dangerous voyage in a small ship may have sharpened his awareness of the characteristics that make some men more worthwhile than others. Malthus seems to have been for Darwin a good man, a reliable shipmate, in a sense, who had earlier entered and survived the stormy waters of intense controversy aroused by his views. Darwin's experiences with controversy were to be more intense and bitter than were Malthus's, but he weathered them with the same degree of restraint and dignity that Malthus exhibited.

For economists what value is there in deeper exposure of the Malthus-Darwin linkage? Mayr offers the intriguing thought that it is not at all far-fetched to consider evolutionary biology as a bridging concept between the physical sciences on the one hand and the social sciences and humanities on the other [31, 77]. The fact that Alfred Marshall and Charles Darwin shared the same motto—*Natura non facit saltum*—has for years caused a certain puzzlement for many economists. In all probability Marshall, who was in time not at all far from Darwin, recognized that there were limits to the development of economic science if it attempted to pursue the physical sciences as the relevant model. Most certainly his great *Principles of Economics* contains several important references to biology. The recent attempts to advance the concepts of sociobiology have, for example, in spite of rather harsh ideological attacks upon them, opened perspectives about economics as ultimately a biological science. Economics and biology have much in common, including the truth that almost all "laws" in each have exceptions and controversy is not unknown among the practitioners of each craft. Modern biology seems to rely less and less upon the language and conceptual framework of the physical sciences, and as it does so it finds probabilistic generalizations more useful than universal laws [31, 846–7]. The fact that Darwin found in the writings of Malthus much that was useful suggests that economists might find today much that is useful in modern Darwinian biology. For most surely Darwin is more relevant now than at any time. It would seem a great pity if economics moved inward toward minaturization, toward quantum purposelessness and ignored the relevancy of biology. For, as Mayr suggests, the integration of all three: social science, biology, and physical science may ultimately produce a comprehensive science. To ignore the possibility for integration, to ignore the intertwined outlooks of Malthus and Darwin, and what they portend, is, for economists, a way to miss the broader currents of their discipline. For, in a very real way, pursuit of the Malthus-Darwin interaction provides a respite, a moment to reflect on the direction and course of economics. Moreover, reflection on Malthus's contribution to biology should do nothing to lessen one's pride in being an economist.

References

1. Beer, Gillian. "Darwin's Reading and the Fictions of Development," in *The Darwinian Heritage*, edited by David Kohn. Princeton: Princeton University Press, 1985, pp. 519–42.

2. Bowler, Peter J., "Malthus, Darwin, and The Concept of Struggle." *Journal of the History of Ideas*, 37, 1976, 631–50.

3. Browne, Janet, "Darwin's Botantical Arithmetic and the 'Principle of Divergence,' 1854–1858." *Journal of the History of Biology*, Spring 1980, 53–89.

4. Burkhardt, Richard W., Jr., "Darwin on Animal Behavior and Evolution," in *The Darwinian Heritage*, edited by David Kohn. Princeton: Princeton University Press, 1985, pp. 327–66.

5. Darwin, Charles. *The Variation of Animals and Plants Under Domestication*. London: John Murray, 1868.

6. ———. *Descent of Man*, 2nd ed. New York: D. Appleton and Company, 1915.

7. ———. "Sketch of 1842," in Darwin, Charles and Wallace, Alfred Russel, *Evolution By Natural Selection*. Cambridge: International Congress of Zoology and The Linnean Society of London, 1958, pp. 41–90.

8. ———. "Essay of 1844," in Darwin, Charles and Wallace, Alfred Russel, *Evolution By Natural Selection*. Cambridge: International Congress of Zoology and The Linnean Society of London, 1958, pp. 91–258.

9. ———. "On The Variation of Organic Beings In A State Of Nature," the extracted version of his "Essay of 1844,: as presented to the Linnean Society of London in 1858, in Darwin, Charles and Wallace, Alfred Russel, *Evolution By Natural Selection*. Cambridge: International Congress of Zoology and The Linnean Society of London, 1958, pp. 259–63.

10. ———. *The Autobiography of Charles Darwin*, edited by Nora Barlow. London: Collins, 1958.

11. ———. *On The Origin of Species*, a Facsimile of the First Edition. Cambridge: Harvard University Press, 1964.

12. ———. "The Notebooks on Man, Mind and Materialism," in *Darwin On Man*, edited by Howard E. Gruber and Paul H. Barrett. New York: Dutton, 1974, pp. 263–381.

13. ———. "Old and Useless Notes," in *Darwin On Man*, edited by Howard E. Gruber and Paul H. Barrett. New York: Dutton, 1974, pp. 382–413.

14. ———. "Essays on Theology and Natural Selection," in *Darwin On Man*, edited by Howard E. Gruber and Paul H. Barrett. New York: Dutton, 1974, pp. 414–22.

15. ———. "Transmutation of Species Notebooks," in *Bulletin of the British Museum (Natural History) Historical Series*, 2:2, 2:3, 2:4, 2:5, 2:6, 1960, pp. 27–200; and 3:5, 1967, pp. 129–176.

16. Darwin, Francis, editor. *More Letters Of Charles Darwin*, Vol. I. New York: D. Appleton and Company, 1903.

17. de Beer, Gavin, "Foreword," in Darwin, Charles and Wallace, Alfred Russel. *Evolution By Natural Selection*. Cambridge: International Congress of Zoology and The Linnean Society of London, 1958, pp. 1–22.

18. Depew, David J. and Bruce H. Weber, "Consequences of Nonequilibrium Thermodynamics for the Darwinian Tradition," in *Entropy, Information, and Evolution*, edited by Bruce H. Weber, David J. Depew, and James D. Smith. Cambridge: The MIT Press, 1988, pp. 317–54.

19. Gillispie, Charles Coulston. *The Edge of Objectivity*. Princeton: Princeton University Press, 1960.

20. Gruber, Howard E. and Paul H. Barrett, *Darwin On Man*. Dutton: New York, 1974.

21. ———, "Going the Limit: Toward the Construction of Darwin's Theory (1832–1839)," in *The Darwinian Heritage*, edited by David Kohn. Princeton: Princeton University Press, 1985, pp. 9–34.

22. Herbert, Sandra, "Darwin, Malthus, and Selection," *Journal of the History of Biology*, Spring 1971, pp. 209–17.

23. ———. "The Place of Man in the Development of Darwin's Theory of Transmutation." *Journal of the History of Biology*, Fall 1977, pp. 155–227.

24. Hodge, M. J. S. and David Kohn, "The Immediate Origins of Natural Selection," in *The Darwinian Heritage*, edited by David Kohn. Princeton: Princeton University Press, 1985, pp. 185–206.

25. Hopf, F. A., "Entropy and Evolution: Sorting Through The Confusion," in *Entropy, Information, and Evolution*, edited by Bruce H. Weber, David J. Depew, and James D. Smith. Cambridge: The MIT Press, 1988, pp. 263–74.

26. Kohn, David, "Theories to Work By: Rejected Theories, Reproduction, and Darwin's Path to Natural Selection." *Studies in History of Biology*, 4, 1980, 67–170.

27. La Vergata, Antonello, "Images of Darwin: A Historiographic Overview," in *The Darwinian Heritage*, edited by David Kohn. Princeton: Princeton University Press, 1985, pp. 901–72.

28. Malthus, Thomas Robert. *An Essay On The Principle Of Population*. Edited by Antoney Flew. New York: Penguin Books, 1970, p. 284.

29. Manier, Edward. *The Young Darwin and His Cultural Circle*. Boston: R. Reidel Publishing Company, 1978.

30. Mayr, Ernst, "Introduction," in Darwin, Charles, *On The Origin of Species*, Facsimile of the First Edition. Cambridge: Harvard University Press, 1964, pp. vii–xxvii.

31. ———. *The Growth of Biological Thought*. Cambridge: The Belknap Press of Harvard University Press, 1982.

32. ———. "Darwin's Five Theories of Evolution," in *The Darwinian Heritage*, edited by David Kohn, 1985, pp. 755–72.

33. Ospovat, Dov, "Darwin After Malthus," *Journal of the History of Biology*, Fall 1979, pp. 211–30.

34. Pancaldi, Guiliano, "Darwin's Intellectual Development (Commentary)," in *The Darwinian Heritage*, edited by David Kohn. Princeton: Princeton University Press, 1985, pp. 259–64.

35. Schumpeter, Joseph A. *Capitalism, Socialism, and Democracy*. New York: Harper and Brothers, Publishers, 1942.

36. ———. *History of Economic Analysis*, edited from manuscript by Elizabeth Boody Schumpeter. New York: Oxford University Press, 1954.

37. Schweber, Silvan S., "The Origin of the *Origin* Revisited." *Journal of the History of Biology*, Fall 1977, pp. 229–309.

38. ———, "Darwin and the Political Economists: Divergence of Character," *Journal of the History of Biology*, Fall 1980, pp. 195–289.

39. ———. "The Wider British Context in Darwin's Theorizing," in *The Darwinian Heritage*, edited by David Kohn. Princeton: Princeton University Press, 1985, pp. 35–70.

40. Sober, Elliott, "Darwin on Natural Selection: A Philosophical Perspective," in *The Darwinian Heritage*, edited by David Kohn. Princeton: Princeton University Press, 1985, pp. 867–900.

41. Stauffer, R. C., editor. *Charles Darwin's Natural Selection*. Cambridge: Cambridge University Press, 1975.

42. Vorzimmer, Peter, "Darwin, Malthus, And The Theory of Natural Selection." *Journal of the History of Ideas*, 30, 1969, 572–42.

43. ———, "The Darwin Reading Notebooks (1838–1860)." *Journal of the History of Biology*, Spring 1977, 107–53.

44. Wood, John Cunningham, editor. *Thomas Robert Malthus*. London: Croom Helm, 1986.

45. Young, Robert M., "Malthus And The Evolutionists: The Common Context of Biological And Social Theory." *Past and Present*, May 1969, pp. 109–45.

[14]

Darwin and Political Economy: The Connection Reconsidered

SCOTT GORDON

Department of the History and Philosophy of Science
Indiana University
Bloomington, Indiana 47405

Department of Economics
Queen's University
Kingston, Ontario K7L 3N6

INTRODUCTION

Addressing a joint session of the American Association for the Advancement of Science and the History of Science Society in 1934, Thomas Cowles asserted that the idea of evolution is a "classic example" of "the transference of a concept from one field of investigation to another." However, he went on to say, "it is not generally recognized . . . that the idea of evolution originated in the social sciences, even though Darwin crystallized it in the field of biology, whence it has been taken over into the whole range of current thought" (Cowles 1936–37:341). In speaking of the "social sciences" as the source of the idea of evolution Cowles was not referring to the interest of economists and other social scientists in the general phenomenon of social development but, much more specifically, to the statement by Charles Darwin, and also by Alfred Russel Wallace, that each was indebted to Thomas Robert Malthus's *Essay on Population* for a key element in their independently formulated theories of natural selection. In the half-century that has elapsed since Cowles's paper, a substantial literature has been generated on this topic, utilizing newly available Darwin documents. Nevertheless, it cannot be said that a consensus has been reached. Some accept Darwin's and Wallace's avowals that Malthus furnished a crucial notion that enabled them to develop the theory of natural selection.[1] Others take the view that Darwin and Wallace exaggerated their indebtedness to Malthus, and that he served only as the fortuitous immediate

1. For example, Michael T. Ghiselin argues that Malthus's *Essay* shifted Darwin's attention from competition among species to competition among the individuals of the same species, thus supplying the populational focus that is essential to Darwin's theory of natural selection (Ghiselin 1969:59; see also Vorzimmer 1969, and Herbert 1971).

Journal of the History of Biology, vol. 22, no. 3 (Fall 1989), pp. 437–459.

supplier of a catalyst for ideas that, at least in Darwin's case, were ready to fall together in a "prepared mind."[2] Other historians see a distinct connection between Darwin's thinking about the species problem and the general conception of "competition" in the contemporary literature of economic theory.[3] Still others adopt an even wider angle of observation, seeing the theory of evolution by natural selection as reflecting the economic and social environment of Darwin's time.

In this paper I shall first discuss the role of the "Malthusian theory of population" in the development of Darwin's thought. I use quotation marks here because the remarks by Malthus that impressed Darwin did not capture the essentials of the *theory* of population growth that Malthus actually advanced and that was accepted by the economists of the period. In the second section I shall examine the contention that Darwin was conversant with the economic literature of the period and was indebted to it for a great deal more than the principle of organic superfecundity. In the final section I shall comment on the apparent parallelism between Darwinian theory and classical economics in the role they ascribed to "competition."

MALTHUS AND DARWIN

According to his reading notebooks, Darwin read Malthus's *Essay* twice, in the fall of 1838 and the spring of 1847 (Vorzimmer 1977). It was the first of these readings, fifteen months after he had begun systematic work on transmutation, that Darwin referred to in his autobiography thirty-eight years later as having given him "a theory by which to work" (Darwin 1958:120). Darwin read the sixth edition of the *Essay*,[4] but it will be useful if

2. Ernst Mayr writes: "[T]he role of Malthus was very much that of a crystal tossed into a saturated fluid. If Darwin at this moment had read Franklin's pamphlet or some of the natural-history literature stressing super-fecundity and its consequences, it is quite likely that it would have electrified him just as much as did the sentence in Malthus [on the geometric rate of population growth]. It was a clear case of the 'prepared mind' seeing something that he had not seen when he was not prepared" (Mayr 1982:493).

3. For example, Stephen Jay Gould says: "Darwin's theory of natural selection . . . was essentially Adam Smith's economics read into nature. Without Adam Smith and the whole school of Scottish economics, I doubt that Darwin would ever have thought of it" (Gould 1982:62; see also Gould 1987:103).

4. There are two copies of the sixth edition of the *Essay* in the Darwin archives in Cambridge. According to Howard E. Gruber, one of these (the one that Darwin read in 1838) belonged to Charles's brother Erasmus. The second, which has many markings in Darwin's hand, was apparently purchased in 1841

we pay some attention to the first edition, and to the circumstances that led Malthus to write it.

When Robert Malthus[5] sat down, in 1798, to write what he correctly described as an "essay" on population, he was not an economist. He had graduated as Ninth Wrangler in the mathematics tripos at Cambridge in 1788 at age twenty-two, was ordained shortly thereafter, and spent the next ten years living quietly as a curate in a country parish — so quietly, in fact, that his modern biographer refers to this period as a "fallow decade" (James 1979:40). Little is known of what he did during this decade; there is no evidence that he had much interest in the literature that was becoming identified as "Political Economy"[6] or, indeed, in political and social questions more generally. Robert's father, Daniel Malthus, was greatly interested in such matters, however, and especially in the proposals for the comprehensive restructuring of society that flooded from the presses in the era of the French Revolution (see Manuel and Manuel 1979). It was, apparently, Robert's conversations with his father that led him to compose an essay to confute the contentions of utopianist social philosophers that a perfect social order could be constructed. There was, he felt, a fatal flaw in all such schemes: the people of any utopia will outbreed their capacity to produce the things needed for their "subsistence." This is unmistakably the central thesis of the first edition of the *Essay*.[7] By 1798 the bloom

and was the one he read in 1847. The pages of the second volume of this copy are uncut (see Gruber 1974:7).

5. The author of the *Essay on Population* is very frequently referred to in the modern literature as "Thomas Malthus," but within his family he was always called "Robert" or "Bob" (James 1979:1).

6. The term "Political Economy" did not become firmly established as designating a branch of "Moral Philosophy" until the second decade of the nineteenth century. It was adopted by writers on economic questions partly because the Greek word *oikonomia* — a compound of *oikos* (household) and *nomos* (law) — which Aristotle had used to describe the science of estate management (compare the modern "Home Economics"), was insufficient to capture the national, and international, focus of their interests; and partly in order to differentiate these writers from the French disciples of François Quesnay, who were called *les économistes*. Historians of economics now use the term "classical economics" to refer to the mainstream theoretical literature of the century from Adam Smith's *Wealth of Nations* to the emergence of "neoclassical economics" in the 1870s.

7. Its full title was *An Essay on the Principle of Population, as it affects the Future Improvement of Society, with Remarks on the Speculations of Mr. Godwin, M. Condorcet, and other Writers*. Some idea of the variety of contemporary utopian thought may be obtained by noting that Godwin was an ultraanarchist, contending that the destruction of all government, indeed all social

of enthusiasm for the opportunities offered by the overthrow of the *ancien régime* in France was fading fast under the presssure of events (Napoleon declared himself "First Consul" the following year); Malthus set out to deliver the *coup de grace* to the idyllic notions of any "perfectibilists" who, like his father, had not yet been fully disillusioned.

In the first (anonymous) edition of the *Essay*, after a few pages of introductory matter on "the advocates of the perfectibility of man and of society," Malthus gets down to work:

> I think I may fairly make two postulata.
>
> First, That food is necessary to the existence of man.
>
> Secondly, That the passion between the sexes is necessary, and will remain nearly in its present state.
>
> . . .
>
> Assuming then, my postulata as granted, I say, that the power of population is indefinitely greater than the power in the earth to produce subsistence for man.
>
> Population, when unchecked, increases in a geometrical ratio. Subsistence increases only in an arithmetical ratio. A slight acquaintance with numbers will show the immensity of the first power in comparison with the second.
>
> By that law of our nature that makes food necessary to the life of man, the effects of these two unequal powers must be kept equal.

---

institutions, would allow a beneficent natural harmony to emerge; while Condorcet echoed Plato's prescription of a highly organized and rigidly controlled social order, but one in which, as Francis Bacon had urged a century earlier, scientists rather than philosophers would play the role of society's governors. Malthus intended to reveal an irremediable defect, not only in these, but in all varieties of "perfectibilism."

John Langdon Brooks says that the immediate cause of Malthus's decision to write the *Essay* was a controversy over legislation to change the Poor Law (Brooks 1984:3). He gives no evidence to support this. Malthus devotes 27 pages (out of 396) in the first edition to a criticism of the Poor Law, but he introduces the book with 10 pages on the utopian philosophy and, after giving his population argument, devotes 122 pages to Godwin and Condorcet.

Dov Ospovat is even further off the track in saying that Malthus, "like most of the political economists of his school, supposed that society runs according to divinely appointed laws, which laws must, therefore be on the whole good" (Ospovat 1979:218). Historians of economics have pointed out that none of the prominent classical economists, not even Adam Smith, held such a view (see, e.g., Robbins 1952; Gordon 1968; Coats 1971). Moreover Malthus, when he became an economist, adopted quite the opposite stance on some of the important issues of contemporary debate, such as unemployment. One of the main objectives of Malthus's original *Essay* was to attack proponents of the natural harmony thesis such as William Godwin.

> This implies a strong and constantly operating check on population from the difficulty of subsistence. That difficulty must fall somewhere; and must necessarily be severely felt by a large portion of mankind. (Malthus 1926:11—14)

Malthus did not regard his "principle of population" as novel. He acknowledged that it had been stated previously by David Hume, Adam Smith, and "probably by many writers that I have never met with" (Malthus 1926:8).[8] His originality was, in his opinion, the use of the principle to refute the claims of the perfectibilists. But, to his surprise, it was the population principle itself, rather than his antiutopian use of it, that caught public attention. He lost no time in capitalizing on his unexpected success: a second edition was published (no longer anonymously) in 1803, greatly enlarged by the addition of large amounts of statistical data on human populations, but no longer focusing on the flaw that Malthus originally viewed himself as having found in utopian social philosophy.[9] Four more editions appeared during his lifetime, steadily expanding the empirical material but not changing the form or essential content of the second edition. In 1805 Malthus was appointed "Professor of General History, Politics, Commerce, and Finance" at the newly founded training college for the East India Company's officials at Haileybury, began to write on subjects other than population, and became one of the leading members of the emerging group of "political economists" — but his public reputation continued to be that of a writer on population and the originator of what the great essayist William Hazlitt described as the "revolting ratios." By the time that Darwin read the *Essay*, "Malthusianism" was a well-established eponym for the problem of overpopulation.

8. Malthus's modesty in this regard was not excessive. Many others had previously noted the exponential growth characteristics of population, and in the second edition he expanded his list of precursors considerably. Robert Wallace is particularly noteworthy because he made detailed calculations of the number that would result from an initial pair after different lengths of time on various assumptions as to procreation rates, life span, etc. (see Hartwick 1988).

9. The second edition was entitled *An Essay on the Principle of Population: or, a View of its Past and Present Effects on Human Happiness, with an Inquiry into our Prospects Respecting the Future Removal or Mitigation of the Evils which it Occasions.* This title was retained in the subsequent editions. In the preface to the second edition, Malthus said that his object in writing the *Essay* originally was "to account for much of the poverty and misery observable among the lower classes of people in every nation, and for those reiterated failures in the efforts of the higher classes to relieve them." This serves as an accurate statement of the main focus of the second (and later) editions, but as a declaration of his intent in 1798 it was disingenuous.

The *Essay on Population* that Darwin picked up on September 28, 1838, to read, as he says in his autobiography, "for amusement," differs from the first edition in more respects than the elimination of the discussion of utopian social philosophy and the addition of empirical data. Even in the first edition, Malthus had weakened his case against the perfectibilists by admitting that the "passion between the sexes" could be satisfied, without procreation ensuing, by "vice" (contraception, prostitution, and other "irregular" sexual practices),[10] but in the second edition he undermined it altogether by adding "moral restraint" (abstinence, prudential postponement of marriage) as a controlling factor — thus, in effect, making procreation a matter of voluntary choice rather than a biological imperative.[11] Equally important was a subtle change that took place in Malthus's presentation of the "ratios" that had captured so much attention. The ratios are there — up front, so to say — in the opening pages of the volume that Darwin held in his hands, and Malthus even spells out with illustrative numbers (presumably for the mathematically innocent) the difference between a geometric and an arithmetic growth rate, but they are presented as generalizations founded on empirical experience rather than as *a priori* postulates.[12] The most significant change is in the treatment of the arithmetic growth rate of "subsistence": this now appears as a maximum rate of growth of agricultural production, which is constrained irremediably by the limitation of "room" — that is, the amount of arable land. Malthus does not use the term, but the reasoning clearly involves the "law of diminishing returns."

In the literature that has developed in recent years on the Malthus-Darwin connection, the juxtaposition of the two ratios is commonly treated as capturing the essence of Malthus's theory of

10. Discussing procreation among "savages" in the *Descent of Man*, Darwin criticized Malthus's discussion of the "checks" to population growth for failing to "lay stress enough on what is probably the most important of all, namely infanticide, especially of female infants, and the habit of procuring abortion" (Darwin 1874:44—5).

11. Patricia James emphasizes this difference between the first and second editions: "Malthus' quarto [the second edition] represented what would now be called a break-through. His book is a landmark because he affirmed that population — procreation — was something which man not only could, but should, as a duty, attempt to control. . . . Malthus initiated a new era when he maintained that population growth should be limited by prudence, rather than dramatically checked by disease and famine" (James 1979:109).

12. Malthus's assertion, repeated by Darwin, that a human population, in an unconstraining environment, doubles in twenty-five years, was derived from Benjamin Franklin's (1755) pamphlet on the population of the British colonies in America. See Zirkle (1957) for an interesting discussion of this.

population.[13] But here we have a mystery that requires some unraveling: the ratios play no role in classical economics, despite the fact that population theory is an essential element in it. David Ricardo, whose work established the basic methodology and much of the substantive content of classical economics, paid generous tribute to Malthus for his theory of population, but he did not mention the ratios at all in his *Principles of Political Economy and Taxation* (1817). John Stuart Mill, whose *Principles of Political Economy with Some of Their Applications to Social Philosophy* (1848) became the standard work on economics that was not replaced for half a century, was a strong "Malthusian" who seized every opportunity that offered itself to point out that no permanent improvement in man's condition is possible unless population growth is constrained. He mentioned Malthus's ratios, but only to describe them as an "unlucky attempt to give numerical precision to things that do not admit of it," and added that they are, moreover, "wholly superfluous to his [Malthus's] argument" (Mill 1965:353). Malthus himself must have held a similar view on the latter point, since the ratios are totally absent from the discussion of population in his own *Principles of Political Economy Considered with a View to Their Practical Application* (1820). He also omitted the ratios from an article on population that he prepared for the *Encyclopedia Brittanica* and reprinted as *A Summary View of the Principle of Population* (1830).

If the ratios did not constitute Malthus's real population theory, what did? In the first edition, if we get beyond the ratios and do not permit them to control our understanding of what we read, a straightforward argument emerges: While the *potential* rate of population growth is very large, the *actual* rate is normally much

13. See, for example, Cowles (1936—37), Flew (1957), Young (1969), Moore (1979:312), Gruber (1985), and Ruse (1975; 1986:158). The same presentation of Malthus is sometimes contained in introductory textbooks in biology. I have examined seven widely used textbooks and find that, of the five that refer to Malthus, two express his argument as the comparison of geometrical and arithmetical ratios.

If this were Malthus's real theory, it would be even more remarkable that the *Essay* should have become, as Ashley Montagu (a severe critic of Malthus) describes it, "the most important book on population ever published" (Montagu 1952:130). Malthus recognized that the law of geometric growth applies to all species. But the food of one organism (except for those possessing the capacity of photosynthesis) consists of other organisms, so how can one say, of all species, that food supply increases at a slower rate than the eaters? Moreover, so far as man is concerned, the reproductive capacity of the organisms he feeds upon is much greater than his own. This flaw in the ratios version of Malthusian theory was pointed out by various critics in Malthus's own lifetime.

smaller. The actual growth rate at any moment of time reflects the operation of two factors: the quantity of food available (H), and the quantity of food that is required to meet the "subsistence" requirements of the existing population (S). Whenever H exceeds S the population will increase; whenever H is less than S it will decline; when H equals S it will remain constant. This is the essential line of argument that Malthus maintains in subsequent editions of the *Essay* and in his other writings. It is what Ricardo, Mill, and the other classical economists adopted as the "Malthusian theory of population."

As advanced in the first edition of Malthus's *Essay*, this argument is incomplete, at least so far as most human populations are concerned. All but the most primitive of human societies engage in agriculture; that is to say, they do not merely exploit existing food supplies, they produce additional quantities. The relations, therefore, between H and S are more complex. If food were produced "arithmetically" in the sense that every additional unit of productive effort yielded the same incremental harvest as before, there could never be any overpopulation since every additional person could raise an undiminished increment of food.[14] As one critic of Malthus asked: "Does not God send two hands with every stomach?" The answer of course is that food is not raised by labor alone; arable land is also needed, and God fails to send additional acres of it. Obviously, population growth cannot be unlimited. In a finite world, as Malthus pointed out, the surface of the earth will inevitably be covered by humans (or any other species) if procreation is not constrained.[15] But Malthus did not see clearly how to complete his theory in 1798; the missing piece of the puzzle was supplied, in 1815, by the discovery of the law of diminishing returns.[16]

14. This is not the "arithmetic ratio" that Malthus expresses in the first edition as a time function — i.e., the pattern of food-supply growth over time. What economists call a "production function" — i.e., output produced as a function of the quantity of human effort and other production factors used — is a quite different notion.

15. This is true of *any* growth rate. Malthus and Darwin were both fond of globe-covering calculations, which they presented, erroneously, as if globe-covering would result specifically from *geometric* growth.

16. This was one of those numerous occasions in the history of science when more than one person hit on the same idea, independently, at about the same time — one of Robert Merton's "multiples" (Merton 1973). The notion of diminishing returns in agriculture can be found in the eighteenth-century literature, but not until 1815, when no less than four persons (Malthus, Ricardo, Edward West, and Robert Torrens) expressed it clearly in print, did it became part of the corpus of economic theory. J. S. Mill called the law "the most

The classical economists did not make use of analytical diagrams, as modern ones do, but the precise nature of the law of diminishing returns and its relation to the Malthusian argument can be most easily understood by such a device. In the accompanying diagram (see Fig. 1) the sigmoid curve describes the harvest of food (H) as a function of the quantity of labor (L) applied to a plot of land of given size and fertility. This is the "production function" of food for a specific agricultural technology. Beyond the inflection point at X the total harvest continues to increase as more labor effort is applied, but the incremental yield, or, as economists say, the "marginal product," steadily diminishes. In mathematical terms, the second partial derivative of the H function is negative for quantities of L greater than X. This characteristic of such a production function is what is meant by the "law of diminishing returns."[17] Because of this, the yield per

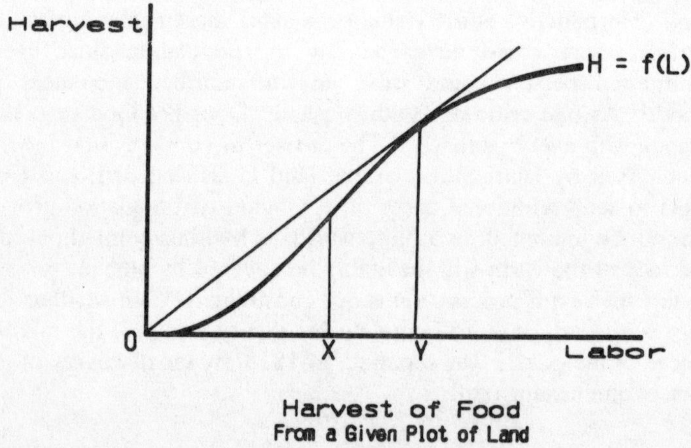

Fig. 1. Harvest of food from a given plot of land.

---

important proposition in political economy" (Mill 1965:174). With a long stretch the law can be read into certain passages in the first edition of Malthus's *Essay*, but no stretching is needed to see it in the sixth.

17. It may be worth noting that though the sigmoidal form of the H function resembles the famous Pearl-Reed curve, the two are not the same. The H function is a hypothetical curve of food production, while the Pearl-Reed curve is generated by an equation fitted to the time-series data of U.S. population and projected into the future. The H function purports to delineate, in purely theoretical terms, a causal relation; the Pearl-Reed curve is an empirical description. The negative second derivative of the Pearl-Reed curve, however, is not derived from the data — it is an inherent characteristic of the type of mathe-

unit of labor applied (*H/L*) will also commence to fall at some point to the right of *X* (more precisely, where a ray drawn from the origin becomes tangential to the *H* function — at *L* equal to *Y*). If we now assume that the available supply of agricultural labor is proportional to the population, it follows that, on account of the law of diminishing returns, an increasing population will eventually result in a decline in the amount of food per capita.[18] When this falls to the level of "subsistence," population growth will cease. This is what Malthus and the other classical economists meant by population being constrained by "the difficulty of obtaining subsistence."[19]

---

matical equation that Pearl and Reed choose to apply to the time-series data. They select a logarithmic parabola because it has properties that they consider essential: when projected it approaches an asymptote, and therefore displays, after a point, a negative second derivative. Interestingly, they refer to Malthus as having been the first to point out "the *a priori* grounds" for depicting population growth by a curve with such properties (Pearl and Reed 1920).

18. Populations have increased greatly since Malthus's time, but in many countries the production of food per capita has also increased, even with a reduced proportion of the labor force devoted to agriculture. This does not invalidate the law of diminishing returns; it calls attention to the fact that it is a "static" law, holding only for a given state of production technology. Agricultural technology was improving in the early nineteenth century, but the classical economists persistently believed that such improvements were fast approaching a limit.

19. Malthus frequently speaks of "subsistence" as food, which conveys the impression that he has a notion of minimum physiological requirements in mind. But a careful reading reveals that he construes subsistence as primarily a sociological datum, reflecting the conventional view, in a particular society, of a minimum "standard of living." Ricardo defines subsistence as "the quantity of food, necessaries and conveniences become essential . . . from habit" (1951:93). Since conventional norms may change, this means that population growth can be constrained by a rise in the subsistence norm as well as by a reduction in food and other consumption goods. Most of the classical economists regarded this as the best way of solving the population problem. For example, Ricardo: "The friends of humanity cannot but wish that in all countries the labouring classes should have a taste for comforts and enjoyments, and that they should be stimulated by all legal means in their exertions to procure them. There cannot be a better security against a superabundant population" (1951:100). Mill persistently argues in his *Principles*, and other writings, that the way to control population growth is to raise the standard of living of the lower classes, and to educate them in the need for, and the means of, contraception. As a young man he had been arrested for distributing birth control literature in Hyde Park. He could not agree with Malthus that contraception only substitutes "vice" for "misery," but he gave him full credit for the notion that the specter of overpopulation can be exorcised: "The doctrine that . . . the progress of society must 'end in shallows and miseries,' far from being, as many people still believe, a wicked invention of Mr. Malthus . . . can only be successfully combatted on his principles. . . . The publication of Mr. Malthus' Essay is the era from which better views of this subject must be dated" (Mill 1965:753).

This kind of argument makes no appearance in Darwin's published or unpublished writings, and it is difficult to see how he could have made any use of it in developing his theory of evolution. In saying that Malthus provided him with "a theory by which to work" Darwin does not mean Malthus's real theory of population, nor indeed the juxtaposition of the two ratios. He never referred to the arithmetical rate of food growth,[20] only to the revelation (conveyed by the geometrical ratio) that plants and animals in the wild state procreate at such a fast rate that a large proportion of the progeny cannot survive. As many historians have pointed out, all that Darwin derived from Malthus was the notion of superfecundity. From it, the notion of a "struggle for existence" (a phrase Malthus used) follows.

Did Darwin not know, before reading Malthus, that the procreation of most animals is greatly in excess of that which would reproduce the existing population? Surprising as it may seem to us today, Darwin's view (which apparently was the common opinion of biologists at the time) was that species in the wild produce only as many progeny as can survive. Writing in his notebook the day he began reading Malthus's *Essay*, Darwin says:

> I do not doubt that every one till he thinks deeply has assumed that increase of animals exactly proportional to the number that can live. . . . Population is increased at geometric ratio . . . yet until the one sentence of Malthus no one clearly perceived the great check . . . [that] is a force like a hundred thousand wedges trying to force every kind of adapted structure into the gaps in the oeconomy of nature or rather forming gaps by thrusting out weaker ones.[21]

Even if we grant the proposition that it was the notion of

20. In the excerpt from Darwin's unpublished manuscript that Lyell and Hooker read to the Linnean Society on July 1, 1858, the following appears: "The amount of food for each species must, *on an average*, be constant whereas the increase of all organisms tends to be geometrical" (George 1964:61, Darwin's emphasis). If Darwin meant by this that, except for short-term variations, the food supply available to a population is constant, then he regarded it not as increasing arithmetically, but as not increasing at all. If he meant by "average" that the food available *per member of the population* was constant, then there could never be any shortage of food no matter how rapidly the population were to increase.

21. Quoted by Vorzimmer (1969). Sandra Herbert says that before reading the *Essay*, "the closest Darwin came to the notion of population held by Malthus was in the awareness of a typical constancy in numbers of individuals belonging to a given species in a given area. . . . Lyell and Darwin assumed that most species tend to produce as many young as may be necessary to maintain their population at its present level" (Herbert 1971:214).

superfecundity that put his mind on the trail of natural selection, it may seem strange that Darwin was so struck by reading Malthus, since, as historians have pointed out, he must have encountered the notion many times before in books and papers that he is known to have read (Gruber 1974:162—163; Schweber 1980). Some historians have suggested that it was the specifically mathematical or quantitative form of Malthus's ratios that impressed Darwin (Vorzimmer 1969; Ruse 1975) — but his earlier reading included items that contain similarly precise expressions of the idea of superfecundity. Perhaps Ernst Mayr is right in saying that if Darwin had read any one of many other disquisitions on population in the fall of 1838 "it would have electrified him just as much as did the sentence in Malthus" (Mayr 1982:493). But it needs to be recalled that, in 1838, Malthus was not just one of many writers on population: he was known far and wide as the inventor of the ratios and the promulgator of the doctrine that social progress is threatened by man's tendency to excessive procreation. Even if Darwin had been "electrified" by some other writer, it is highly likely that he would have promptly gone to Malthus's *Essay*, to consult the author who was commonly referred to as the originator of these ideas.[22]

In 1858, when A. R. Wallace hit on the principle of natural selection, Malthus's name and the doctrine of overpopulation were still indelibly coupled. Wallace had read the *Essay* (like Darwin, the sixth edition) in 1844 or 1845 (McKinney 1966; Young 1969) — that is, before he had developed an interest in biology. It was some fourteen years later that he had the insight that led him to write his famous paper "On the Tendency of Varieties to Depart Indefinitely from the Original Type," and more than sixty years after reading the *Essay* that he cited it as having been the source of his inspiration. In preparing a contribution for the semicentennial celebration of the Darwin-Wallace submission to the Linnean

22. "[E]ven a cursory look at the Victorian periodicals of the 1830s makes it clear that the laws governing the growth of population were central to many of the political and economic issues being debated at the time and that it would have been difficult for anyone reading the *Edinburgh Review* or the *Quarterly Review*, as Darwin did, not to be familiar with Malthus' thesis" (Schweber 1980:195—196).

If nothing else, the great debate over the Poor Law Amendment Act of 1834 would have fixed Malthus's name in the public mind as the prime exemplar of the overpopulation thesis. The act was widely characterized (especially by the *Times* and other opponents) as inspired by "Malthusian" doctrine. Ironically, Nassau W. Senior, who played the leading role in devising and promoting the act, was one of the few prominent economists of the period who did not agree with Malthus on the subject of population.

Society that was to take place in 1908, Wallace reexamined the *Essay* in order to identify what it was that had impressed itself so firmly on his mind when he had first read it, but he could not fix upon anything specific and concluded that it was the "cumulative effect" of Malthus's description of the forces that "keep down the populations of savage and barbarous nations" (Brooks 1984:184). But perhaps Wallace was searching in the wrong place. In 1858, every educated Englishman would have associated the idea of overpopulation with Malthus. When Wallace perceived the evolutionary significance of superfecundity, it is highly likely that he would have identified it as a "Malthusian" notion even if he had never read the *Essay*. On matters of this sort there can be no hard evidence, since mental processes leave no records, but one may hazard the hypothesis that it was the public image of Malthus in Victorian England rather than the *Essay* that induced Wallace to credit him with the seminal idea.

So far, in examining the Malthus-Darwin connection, I have focused upon the notion of superfecundity. On this point the role of Malthus would appear to be even less than that of "a crystal tossed into a saturated fluid" (Mayr 1982:493). But Malthus's significance for the history of evolution theory would have to be reevaluated upward rather than downward if Michael Ghiselin (1969:49, 59) and others are correct in maintaining that the *Essay* induced Darwin to focus on *populations* and to think of the "struggle for existence" as a contest among the members of the same species in a habitat. Charles Lyell had construed the struggle for existence as competition between species or, more generally, the struggle of a species to survive in its organic and physical environment. Peter Vorzimmer (1969) contends that Malthus's focus on *one* species, man, enabled Darwin to recognize the significance of competition among the individual members of a species (see also Herbert 1971). The move to intraspecific competition was, without question, a crucial step in the development of a theory of evolutionary change by natural selection that construes the individual as the unit of selection. The contention that Darwin was indebted to Malthus for it cannot be dismissed, but this ought not to be regarded as more than a speculation. No documentary evidence has been offered in support of this thesis, and one must keep in mind that it is not what Darwin himself, in his notebooks and reminiscences, attributed to Malthus.[23]

23. In the introduction to the *Origin* Darwin speaks of "the doctrine of Malthus" as "the Struggle for Existence amongst all organic beings throughout the world." In chap. 3 he refers to "the doctrine of Malthus" as "a struggle for

For Ghiselin, the attraction of this thesis seems to be bound up with a philosophical stance: the epistemological and ethical merits of individualism, as opposed to a holistic or essentialist focus upon groups, such as species or classes (Ghiselin 1969:59–61). If we pursue this line of inquiry as part of the history of evolution theory, we are, as Ghiselin recognizes, drawn immediately into the question of the influence upon Darwin of, not only Malthus's *Essay on Population*, but the scientific methodology and social philosophy of the classical economists. Ricardo, Mill, and the other leading figures of the classical school adopted a strong individualist stance, in their positive analysis of economic processes and in their normative evaluation of public policy. All economic phenomena, in their view, must be explained in terms of the behavior of self-interested individuals; and all public policies must be judged in terms of their effect upon the welfare, not of the abstract general community, but of the sensate persons who compose it. In the Victorian era, no line of thought adopted the individualist stance of Benthamite utilitarianism to a greater degree than Political Economy.[24]

DARWIN AND POLITICAL ECONOMY

All educated Englishmen of Darwin's era knew something about Political Economy — or, at least, about what its leading practitioners said (or were supposed to have said) regarding the great public issues of the day such as the Poor Law, the Factory Acts, and the Corn Laws. Darwin did not have much interest in

existence, either one individual with another of the same species, or with individuals of distinct species, or with the physical conditions of life." Such passages do not contradict Ghiselin's thesis, but they do not provide it with much support since Malthus's name is not identified specifically in such passages with intraspecific struggle.

24. Schweber suggests that Darwin's focus on the individual organism derived from an earlier source: "I believe that it was by reading the writings of Adam Smith and the other Scottish Common Sense philosophers that Darwin initially got his emphasis on individuals as the units for his theory of natural selection" (Schweber 1977:277). He gives no reference to anything Darwin wrote that would support this. In the same paper Schweber refers to Darwin as adopting "the Scottish view of trying to understand the whole in terms of the individual parts and their interactions." This is a questionable interpretation of the Scottish moral philosophers, since one of the striking characteristics of their thought is their insistence upon the view that man is, by nature as well as nurture, a *social* animal, and their emphasis upon the need to study the various social institutions through which human actions are organized into a coordinated collective enterprise (see, e.g., Bryson 1968).

contemporary public affairs,[25] and we cannot ascertain the influence of Political Economy upon him by examining his views on such matters. Silvan S. Schweber (1980), however, maintains that Darwin had more immediate knowledge about Political Economy through direct acquaintance with its professional literature, and that this played a significant role in the development of his ideas. In evaluating this contention, the first thing we must do is examine the documentary materials that enable us to ascertain the extent to which he was familiar with this literature.

Darwin's reading notebooks covering the period from 1838 to 1860 (Vorzimmer 1977) contain only two citations of books on economics, aside from Malthus's *Essay on Population* and William Godwin's response to it: J. R. McCulloch, *Principles of Political Economy* (read in the spring of 1840), and J. C. L. Simonde de Sismondi, *New Principles of Political Economy* (September 1847). McCulloch's book was a popular rendition of David Ricardo's difficult-to-read *Principles*, the foundation book of classical Political Economy; Darwin made no notebook entry giving his view of it, as he frequently did concerning the things he read. Sismondi's book was a frontal attack on the methodology and content of Ricardian economics; its author (then deceased) had been the husband of an aunt of Darwin's wife. Next to Darwin's record of it in the notebook is the single word "poor."[26] There are a number of other items peripheral to Political Economy, such as Adam Smith's *Theory of Moral Sentiments* (May 1842: ". . . skimmed parts; ought to be studied for comparison of man & animals. . . .") and J. S. Mill's *On Liberty* (March 1859: "very good") — but these, and other items on social questions, have no relevance to the present subject because Darwin could not have obtained any information from them about Political Economy as a delimited domain of investigation.

More significant, in my view, are certain items that are missing from the list. Adam Smith's *Wealth of Nations* does not appear;[27]

25. "Charles Darwin was not what you would call politically *engagé*. He did participate in public affairs from time to time and to a limited extent. But he chose to live the major part of his adult life in a quiet place, and he protected himself from becoming publicly embroiled in matters that would distract him from his vast scientific undertakings" (Gruber 1974:69).

26. The Darwin libraries at Down House and Cambridge University do not contain copies of McCulloch's and Sismondi's books, so we do not know whether he made any marginal or end notes in them. (I am indebted to Marsha Richmond for searching for these books in the Darwin archives.)

27. Schweber says, "We can legitimately infer that Darwin read Smith's

nor does Ricardo's *Principles* or J. S. Mill's *Principles*. The absence of Mill's book from Darwin's reading (and the lack of any reference to it in his writings) is especially noteworthy. Mill enjoyed a wide reputation as one of the stellar intellectuals of the age. His *System of Logic* (1843) alone was sufficient to place him in the front rank of contemporary philosophers, and to qualify him as a thinker of special importance in the philosophy of science. His *Principles of Political Economy* was, from the time of its publication in 1848, generally regarded as the authoritative statement of classical economics, and was studied carefully by anyone seriously interested in the subject.[28]

We might also note, in this connection, Darwin's reading of Harriet Martineau's publications. Martineau became well known in the early 1830s as the author of a series of twenty-four didactic novelettes published under the general title *Illustrations of Political Economy*. In these she essayed to instruct the general public in the mysteries of the subject and to show that it had provided scientific proof of the principle of laissez-faire (Gordon 1971). She followed up with similar writings on the Poor Law, and taxation, and then turned to other subjects such as the methodology of science, mesmerism, how to keep cows, Auguste Comte's philosophy, and the government of India. Several of her publications are recorded in Darwin's reading notebooks, but none of these entries refers to any of her works on economics. Presumably, he had no desire to be instructed by her on that subject.

Wealth of Nations at some stage of his studies at Edinburgh, though there is no record of it" (1980:265). If it had been as important to the development of Darwin's ideas on species divergence as Schweber claims, surely he would have consulted it again.

Darwin's C notebook in 1839 contains, in a list of items "To Be Read," the entry "Du Stewart works, & lives of Reid, Smith, & giving abstract of their views" (Barrett et al. 1987:325). A similar reminder is contained in the M notebook (ibid., p. 559). Schweber infers from this that Darwin read Dugald Stewart's biography of Smith ("Account of the Life and Writings of Adam Smith, LL.D.," first published in the *Transactions* of the Royal Society of Edinburgh, 1794, and frequently reprinted thereafter). But there is no hard evidence to substantiate this; the only notes on Stewart contained in Darwin's notebooks refer to Stewart's own views on certain topics, not Smith's (ibid., pp. 604—606).

28. Schweber's (1980) account of Political Economy fails to note that Ricardo and Mill were its leading spokesmen. He refers to Richard Jones, Malthus's successor at the East India College, as "probably the most respected political economist in England" and discusses him at length. Jones was, in fact, a minor figure, not highly regarded by the economists of the era. Historians of economics typically award him little more than a footnote reference, on account of his exhortation that economists should do historical studies rather than follow the abstract theoretical methodology of Ricardo.

If we turn from the record of Darwin's reading to his own writings for evidence of an interest in Political Economy, we draw a complete blank. So far as I have been able to ascertain, none of the prominent economists of the era was so much as mentioned by him, and there is no indication that he was at all interested in the subjects they investigated. The central questions of Political Economy — such as the explanation of economic value, the determinants of the distribution of income, and the controlling factors of economic growth — make no appearance, even obliquely, in Darwin's writings. Schweber (1980, 1985) contends that Darwin was indebted to the classical economists for the notion of division of labor, which, he claims, was what led him to the idea of species divergence. This is difficult to credit. The division of labor, as the classical economists employed it, explains the *functional* specialization of persons and geographic regions; it has little, or nothing, to do with the *morphological* differentiation that characterizes species divergence. Moreover, if it were true, nevertheless, that the notion of division of labor was the seed of species divergence in Darwin's mind, he did not need to have any knowledge of Political Economy in to order to apprehend it since the idea was common in the general literature of the time and, especially in the writings of Henri Milne-Edwards, was even prominent in professional biology.[29]

Finally, we should note that Darwin, on one occasion at least, explicitly stated his views on the subject of Political Economy. In July 1881 he received a letter from A. R. Wallace, saying that he had just read a book that impressed him immensely and that he wished to call to Darwin's attention: namely, Henry George's *Progress and Poverty* (first published in the United States in 1879). "It is," said Wallace, "the most startling novel and original book of the last twenty years, and if I mistake not will in the future rank as making an advance in political and social science equal to that made by Adam Smith a century ago." In his reply, Darwin said: "I will certainly order "Progress and Poverty," for the subject is a most interesting one. But I read many years ago some books on political economy, and they produced a disastrous effect on my mind, viz. utterly to distrust my own judgment on the subject and to doubt much everyone else's judgment!" (Marchant 1916, 1:317—318). One might reasonably infer that Darwin was

29. Herbert Spencer, second in importance only to Darwin in the spread of evolutionism as a general intellectual outlook, elevated the progressive development of differentiation into a "law" of evolutionary development, but he derived the notion from the biologists Milne-Edwards and Karl von Baer rather than Adam Smith or the classical economists.

alluding to his reading of McCulloch and Sismondi, for there is no evidence that he read any other "books on political economy." Historians of science have good reason to be skeptical concerning the accuracy of a scientist's account of his intellectual development, especially when recollected many years later, but in this case, all the evidence we have supports the conclusion that Darwin was speaking the unvarnished truth.

THE CONCEPT OF "COMPETITION"

In December 1860, Karl Marx wrote to his close friend and collaborator Friedrich Engels that he had been reading Darwin's *Origin of Species*. "Even though it is developed in the clumsy English fashion," he said, "this is the book which contains the historico-natural basis for our views [on capitalism]."[30] Since then, many writers, not all Marxists, have pointed to parallels — and, indeed, a causal connection — between the Darwinian theory of evolution and the competitive capitalism of the Victorian era and its intellectual ambience.[31] That Darwin, like other great men, was a "child of his time" is a proposition that cannot be denied, but neither can it be supplied with much in the way of hard evidence by the historian who is in search of the origin of a scientific idea.[32] This paper is concerned, not with the relation of Darwin to the socioeconomic and general intellectual environment of Victorian England, but with a more restricted relationship — namely, that between his theory of evolution and classical Political Economy. One more issue remains to be addressed: Can Darwin's theory of natural selection be traced to the concept of *competition* that the

30. For this, and for other comments by Marx and by Engels on Darwin, see Ureña (1977). In 1931 the Marx-Engels Institute in Moscow made note of a letter supposedly written by Darwin to Marx in 1880, in which Darwin declines the writer's request for permission to dedicate a forthcoming book to him. This has often been noted by scholars as a testament to Marx's high opinion of Darwin — but it is now known that Darwin's correspondent was not Marx but his son-in-law, Edward Aveling (Ureña 1981).

31. See, for example, Sandow (1938), Lewontin (1968), Young (1969, 1971), and Gale (1972). R. C. Lewontin is among the most insistent in advancing this thesis. In his view, the initial emergence of evolution, as a general concept, "was deeply embedded in the economic and social conditions of the industrial West." Darwin's specific theory was, like all of "bourgeois science," a product of the "bourgeois revolution" that accompanied the rise of industrialism. Lewontin notes also that Darwin came from a family of prominent industrialists, which he pointedly calls, in relation to evolution theory, "no accident."

32. Concerning the historiography on Darwin, La Vergata says that "nowhere is the tendency to resort to easy formulas more evident than in the frequency with which Darwin's view is linked to the British competitive ideology" (1985:913).

classical economists used in constructing their analysis of a capitalistic market economy?[33]

Without question, competition is a vital component of both Darwinian theory and the Ricardian economic model. But the concept is quite different in the two contexts. In Darwinian theory it refers to a "struggle for existence" that only some can win; all others lose, and suffer the supreme penalty. In the context of classical economics, competition is not a mortal contest with such a categorical distinction between winners and losers; in fact, the classical model depicts a world where, as in Alice's Wonderland, "everyone wins and all must have prizes." This is difficult to credit unless one is aware of the fact that the early economists, instead of naming technical concepts by using Greek or Latin roots as biologists do, frequently used familiar English words in ways that did not match their connotation in common speech; sometimes, as their technical use was extended, such terms departed greatly from the common meaning. "Competition" was one of these: as used by the classical (and modern) economists, it denotes a state of affairs that the ordinary person might well describe as one where "competition," as ordinarily understood, is *absent*.

When one refers in common speech to competition between producers, what springs to mind is the rivalry of large firms as sellers (or as buyers) in commercial markets where there are only a small number of such firms. This is, indeed, a situation characterized by "struggle," and it may be a veritable "struggle for existence" in which bankruptcy is the commercial counterpart of death in Darwin's theory of natural selection. But according to economists, this is a state of affairs in which competition is "imperfect." The classical model of the market economy hypothesizes a state in which there are so many producers (and consumers) of each (homogeneous) commodity that no one of them can have any influence upon its price or other conditions of sale. In this world of "perfect competition" there is no rivalry at all, since every producer (or consumer) can sell (or buy) as much as he wishes at the going market price. In the market for corn, for example, there are construed to be so many farmers (and eaters)

33. I do not undertake here to consider whether Darwin may have been influenced by the concept of competition that was attributed to the classical economists by popular writers. He must have read some of the many criticisms of Political Economy that pictured it as seeking to justify an economic system based upon incessant conflict and combat. Whether his notion of the "struggle for existence" derived from such sources is a question I cannot answer. The focus of my inquiry here is whether the leading economists advanced a concept of competition that is similar to Darwin's.

that nothing any one of them may do can appreciably affect the conditions facing the others. (The corn farmers of the United States do not consider themselves to be competing with one another; but the economist regards them as engaged in "perfect competition.") Few such "perfect" markets exist in today's world or, for that matter, in the world of the classical economists, but this was adopted as the paradigmatic market for the purposes of analysis.[34]

The Darwinian model might be described as a "zero-sum game": the supply of food and the other necessities of existence for a population of organisms is a given quantity; if one member of the population obtains more, there is, necessarily, less for others. But humans do not simply forage a given stock of food or occupy a given niche in the "economy of nature": they *produce* food and modify the niche. The model of the classical (and modern) economists is a "positive-sum game," and "competition" appears in it as part of the mechanism by which that sum is made as large as possible in a production economy that operates in a regime of private enterprise. The less-efficient producers in such a model are not necessarily eliminated; they may survive, and indeed flourish, by specializing in the performance of those functions in which their deficiencies are minimized.[35] Even if Darwin had been fully cognizant of the way in which the concept of competition was used in Political Economy, he could not have made any use of it in developing his theory of natural selection.

CONCLUSION

It seems to me that no substantial support can be provided for the thesis that the Darwinian theory of evolution drew significantly

34. I cannot go into the technical reasons why the classical economists adopted this concept of competition. Suffice it to say that until the differential calculus was applied to economics, there was no way of dealing with rivalrous relations among economic entities. It may be worth noting that Karl Marx, though he was convinced that production was being "concentrated in fewer and fewer hands," used the concept of perfect competition as a heuristic device in developing his model of a capitalistic economy.

35. This is Ricardo's celebrated theory of "comparative advantage," which he developed in the context of international trade. Ricardo showed, by means of a numerical illustration for two countries and two commodities, that even if one country is more efficient than the other in the production of both commodities, total production is larger if each concentrates upon one of them than if they do not specialize. The theorem applies, not only to geographic specialization, but to specialization among all entities, including individual persons. This remains today the only significant contribution that has been made to the economic analysis of the division of labor since Adam Smith.

upon ideas in contemporary Political Economy. What Darwin may have derived from Malthus was not an integral part of the theory of population that the classical economists, including Malthus, put forward. He did not know the literature of Political Economy; and if he had been acquainted with it, he would not have been able to derive anything from it that was important for the theory of natural selection. The judgment that "with Darwin's theory there was a real transfer of knowledge from political economy to biology" (Pancaldi 1985:262) cannot be sustained.

Acknowledgments

For reading and commenting upon an earlier draft of this paper I wish to thank Roy Gardner, John Hartwick, Jack Hirschleifer, and a referee of this journal.

REFERENCES

Barrett, Paul H.; Gautrey, Peter J.; Herbert, Sandra; Kohn, David; and Smith, Sydney, eds. 1987. *Charles Darwin's Notebooks, 1836–1844*. Ithaca: Cornell University Press.

Bowler, Peter J. 1985. "Scientific Attitudes to Darwinism in Britain and America." In Kohn (1985), pp. 641–681.

Brooks, John Langdon. 1984. *Just before the Origin: Alfred Russel Wallace's Theory of Evolution*. New York: Columbia University Press.

Bryson, Gladys. 1968. *Man and Society: The Scottish Inquiry of the Eighteenth Century*. New York: Kelley.

Coats, A. W., ed. 1971. *The Classical Economists and Economic Policy*. London: Methuen.

Cowles, Thomas. 1936–37. "Malthus, Darwin, and Bagehot: A Study in the Transference of a Concept." *Isis, 26*:341–348.

Darwin, Charles. 1874. *The Descent of Man, and Selection in Relation to Sex*. Revised ed. New York and London: Merrill and Baker.

—— 1958. *The Autobiography of Charles Darwin*. Ed. Nora Barlow. London: Collins.

—— 1968. *The Origin of Species*. Ed. J. W. Burrow. Harmondsworth: Penguin.

Flew, Anthony. 1957. "The Structure of Malthus' Population Theory." *Australasian J. Phil., 35*:1–20.

Franklin, Benjamin. 1755. *Observations Concerning the Increase of Mankind and the Peopling of Countries*. Boston.

Gale, Barry G. 1972. "Darwin and the Concept of a Struggle for Existence: A Study in the Extrascientific Origins of Scientific Ideas." *Isis, 63*:321–344.

George, Wilma. 1964. *Biologist Philosopher: A Study of the Life and Writings of Alfred Russel Wallace*. New York: Abelard-Schuman.

Ghiselin, M. T. 1969. *The Triumph of the Darwinian Method*. Berkeley: University of California Press.

Gordon, Scott. 1968. "Laissez-Faire." In *International Encyclopedia of the Social Sciences, 8*: 546–549. New York: Macmillan.

—— 1971. "The Ideology of Laissez-Faire." In Coats (1971), pp. 181–205.

Gould, Stephen Jay. 1982. Interview. *U.S. News and World Report*, March 1.

—— 1987. *An Urchin in the Storm*. New York: Norton.

Gruber, Howard E. 1974. *Darwin on Man: A Psychological Study of Scientific Creativity*. New York: Dutton.

—— 1985. "Going the Limit: Toward the Construction of Darwin's Theory (1832–1839)." In Kohn (1985), pp. 9–33.

Hartwick, John M. 1988. "Robert Wallace and Malthus and the Ratios." *Hist. Polit. Econ., 20*:357–379.

Herbert, Sandra. 1971. "Darwin, Malthus, and Selection." *J. Hist. Biol., 4*:209–217.

James, Patricia. 1979. *Population Malthus: His Life and Times*. London: Routledge and Kegan Paul.

Kohn, David. 1985. *The Darwinian Heritage*. Princeton: Princeton University Press.

La Vergata, Antonello. 1985. "Images of Darwin: A Historiographic Overview." In Kohn (1985), pp. 901–972.

Lewontin, R. C. 1968. "The Concept of Evolution." In *International Encyclopedia of the Social Sciences, 5*:202–209. New York: Macmillan.

Malthus, Thomas Robert. 1926. *First Essay on Population*. London: Macmillan. This is a facsimile reprint of the first edition of 1798.

—— 1951. *Principles of Political Economy Considered with a View to Their Practical Application*. New York: Augustus M. Kelley. This is a reprint of the second edition, 1836; the first edition was published in 1820.

—— 1953 [1830]. *A Summary View of the Principle of Population*. London: John Murray. Reprinted in D. V. Glass, ed., *Introduction to Malthus*. London: Watts.

Manuel, Frank E., and Manuel, Fritzie P. 1979. *Utopian Thought in the Western World*. Cambridge, Mass.: Harvard University Press.

Marchant, James. 1916. *Alfred Russel Wallace: Letters and Reminiscences*. New York: Cassell.

Mayr, Ernst. 1982. *The Growth of Biological Thought: Diversity, Evolution, and Inheritance*. Cambridge, Mass.: Harvard University Press.

McKinney, H. Lewis. 1966. "Alfred Russel Wallace and the Discovery of Natural Selection." *J. Hist Med., 21*:333–357.

Merton, Robert K. 1973. *The Sociology of Science: Theoretical and Empirical Investigations*. Chicago: University of Chicago Press.

Mill, John Stuart. 1965. *Principles of Political Economy, with Some of their Applications to Social Philosophy*. Toronto: University of Toronto Press.

Montagu, Ashley. 1952. *Darwin: Competition and Cooperation*. New York: Schuman.

Moore, James R. 1979. *The Post-Darwinian Controversies: A Study of the Protestant Struggle to Come to Terms with Darwin in Great Britain and America*. Cambridge: Cambridge University Press.

Ospovat, Dov. 1979. "Darwin after Malthus." *J. Hist. Biol., 12*:211–230.

Pancaldi, Giuliano. 1985. "Darwin's Intellectual Development (Commentary)." In Kohn (1985), pp. 259–263.

Pearl, Raymond, and Reed, Lowell J. 1920. "On the Rate of Growth of the Population of the United States since 1790 and Its Mathematical Representation." *Proc. Nat. Acad. Sci., 6*:275–288.

Ricardo, David. 1951. *On the Principles of Political Economy and Taxation*. Cambridge: Cambridge University Press. First edition 1817.

Robbins, L. C. 1952. *The Theory of Economic Policy in English Classical Political Economy*. London: Macmillan.

Ruse, Michael. 1975. "Darwin's Debt to Philosophy: An Examination of the Influence of the Philosophical Ideas of John F. W. Herschel and William Whewell on the Development of Charles Darwin's Theory of Evolution." *Stud. Hist. Phil. Sci.*, *6*:159–181.

—— 1986. *Taking Darwin Seriously: A Naturalistic Approach to Philosophy.* Oxford: Basil Blackwell.

Sandow, Alexander. 1938. "Social Factors in the Origin of Darwinism." *Quart. Rev. Biol.*, *19*:315–326.

Schweber, Silvan S. 1977. "The Origin of the *Origin* Revisited." *J. Hist. Biol.*, *10*:229–316.

—— 1980. "Darwin and the Political Economists: Divergence of Character." *J. Hist. Biol.*, *13*:195–289.

—— 1985. "The Wider British Context in Darwin's Theorizing." In Kohn (1985), pp. 35–69.

Ureña, Enrique M. 1977. "Marx and Darwin." *Hist. Polit. Econ.*, *9*:548–559.

—— 1981. "A Note on 'Marx and Darwin.'" *Hist. Polit. Econ.*, *13*:772–773.

Vorzimmer, Peter. 1969. "Darwin, Malthus, and the Theory of Natural Selection." *J. Hist. Ideas*, *30*:527–542.

—— 1977. "The Darwin Reading Notebooks (1838–1860)." *J. Hist. Biol.*, *10*:107–153.

Young, Robert M. 1969. "Malthus and the Evolutionists: The Common Context of Biological and Social Theory." *Past and Present*, *43*:109–145.

—— 1971. "Evolutionary Biology and Ideology: Then and Now." *Sci. Stud.*, *1*:177–206.

Zirkle, Conway. 1957. "Benjamin Franklin, Thomas Malthus, and the United States Census." *Isis*, *48*:58–62.

Part IV
Alfred Marshall and Economic Biology

[15]

Review of Political Economy, 3.1 (1991), pp. 1–14

Alfred Marshall on economic biology

Brinley Thomas *University of California, Berkeley*

This article examines the sequence of ideas which led Marshall to conclude that economic growth is organic in nature and that its analysis must be based on a biological not a mechanical analogue. At the outset of his career in the early 1870s, when he was attempting to reconcile increasing returns with atomic competition, Marshall came up against the problem of irreversibility; he had to discard his long-period curves because they were interdependent and irreversible. Volume I of the *Principles* (1890), particularly Book V, was an analysis of mechanical equilibrium, and it was to be followed by Volume II on dynamics. When Marshall replied to a critic of the *Principles* in the *Economic Journal* in 1898, he gave an illuminating account of his methodology and declared that 'the Mecca of the economist is economic biology rather than economic dynamics'. He failed to produce Volume II of his *Principles* because by the end of the 1890s he had changed his mind on important theoretical matters. He would have had to write a treatise on economic biology, and he must have felt that this was a task for his successors, not for him.

Two outstanding critics of standard economics, Kenneth Boulding and Nicholas Georgescu-Roegen, have argued powerfully that the mechanical analogue should be replaced by an evolutionary approach (Boulding, 1981; Georgescu-Roegen, 1971). In recent years the challenge has evoked a growing response; a significant number of economists are exploring economic biology and there are signs that cliometricians are beginning to question the dominant influence of mechanical models on their work.[1] The patron saint of this movement is Alfred Marshall, whose famous declaration provides a motto: 'The Mecca of the economist is economic biology rather than economic dynamics' (1898: 43). As we celebrate the centenary of the first edition of Marshall's *Principles* (1890), it is fitting to explore Marshall's case for economic biology and to assess the contribution which he made to advance the cause.

[1] Sigüenza (1982: 1560) gives a list of contemporary economists in the English-speaking world interested in the biological method. For economic biology and economic history see Mokyr (1989).

2 *Alfred Marshall on economic biology*

I The Darwinian legacy

By about 1875 Marshall had completed his ideas on the theory of value, but he did not publish his work at that time, partly because he was grappling with the problems raised by time and increasing returns. During this fertile period he stood at the confluence of two great intellectual traditions – the classical or Newtonian (Adam Smith, Ricardo, John Stuart Mill), and the Darwinian (Paley, Malthus, Darwin). The Darwinian tradition can be traced to William Paley who, in the words of Keynes (1933: 108), '. . . was for a generation or more an intellectual influence on Cambridge only second to Newton. Perhaps in a sense *he* was the *first* of the Cambridge economists'. In 1785 Malthus, in his first year as an undergraduate in Cambridge, was tutored by William Frend, a pupil of Paley's, and it is significant that in that year Paley's *Principles of moral and Political philosophy* was published. This book left a deep mark on the mind of the young Malthus and had a strong influence on the *Essay on population* (1798).

Paley's *Principles* also helped to mould the thinking of the young Charles Darwin. The central idea was that:

> . . . the functions and structures of an organism are to be explained in terms of its own good – not in terms of the desires or needs of any other species, man not excepted . . . An Augustinian, confronted with a remarkable natural phenomenon, must seek its utility for man; if he cannot find it he is in a bad way . . . A Paleyan, in contrast, asking *what is the function of this structure or ability in the life of the organism possessing it?* necessarily becomes a close and attentive student of nature. Paley made naturalists: Darwin was one of them (Hardin, 1960: 57–58).

In his autobiography Darwin (1958: 59) recalled that, when he was an undergraduate in Cambridge, Paley's books:

> . . . gave me as much delight as did Euclid. The careful study of these works, without attempting to learn any part by rote, was the only part of the Academical Course which, as I then felt and as I still believe, was of the least use to me in the education of my mind. I did not at that time trouble myself about Paley's premises; and taking these on trust I was charmed and convinced by the long line of argumentation.

Malthus's *Essay* had a dramatic influence on the process of thought leading to the theory of evolution. Darwin related how in October 1838 he happened to be reading the *Essay* when it suddenly struck him that in the struggle for existence favourable variations would tend to be preserved and unfavourable ones destroyed and this would lead to the formation of new species. He concluded triumphantly (1958: 120): 'Here then I had at last got a theory by which to work'. Malthus's theory was also responsible for a crucial change in Darwin's approach – the substitution of *individuals* for *species* as the unit of population analysis. The intellectual contributions of the two great pioneers were dissimilar: 'Paley stresses adaptation; Malthus stresses conflict. These were at one level antithetical. Darwin synthesizes them.

Struggle both *explains and produces* adaptation' (Young, 19 : 118). The young generation of intellectuals was swept off its feet by the Darwinian revolution. For Marshall the writings of Herbert Spencer were even more significant than those of Darwin; he remembered how '... a saying of Spencer sent the blood rushing through the veins of those who a generation ago looked eagerly for each volume of his as it issued from the press' (1975: Volume 1, 109).

II Irreversibility and evolution

At the outset of his career Marshall had come up against the problem of reconciling increasing returns with competitive conditions. Sometime in the early 1870s it became clear to him that, given increasing returns, the long-period supply curve is irreversible. The first account of this is to be found in *The pure theory of foreign trade and domestic values*, written around 1873 and privately printed in 1879.[2] The following quotation indicates the nature of the problem:

> In economics every event causes permanent alterations in the conditions under which future events can occur ... When any casual disturbance has caused a great increase in the production of any commodity, and has thereby led to the introduction of extensive economies, these economies are not readily lost. Developments of mechanical appliances, of division of labour and of means of transport, and of improved organisation of all kinds, when they have been once obtained are not readily abandoned (1975: Volume 2, 201–202).

Because of irreversibilities such as learning by doing and economies of scale, there can be no swing back along the long-period curve. In his diagram Marshall inserted a dotted line below the original curve to demonstrate the point (1975: Volume 2, 203). However, this device is misleading since the problem cannot be resolved within the static ambit of Marshall's diagram. There was not much conviction in his hope that '... the unsatisfactory character of these results ... may conceivably be much diminished in a later age by the gradual improvement of our scientific machinery' (1961: Volume 1, 809). He drew on his creative imagination to try to shore up the edifice; three of his well-known concepts – the representative firm, external economies and market imperfection – were brought into play to serve the purpose. In the end, however, it was all in vain, as one can see from a significant change made in Book IV, Chapter XIII of the sixth edition of the *Principles*. In the earlier editions beginning with the second, the 'trees of the forest' passage reads as follows:

> 'As with the growth of trees so it is with the growth of businesses. As each kind of tree has its normal life, in which it attains its normal height, so the

[2] Reprinted by the London School of Economics and Political Science in 1930 in its Series of Reprints of Scarce Tracts in Economic and Political Science.

4 *Alfred Marshall on economic biology*

> length of life during which a business of any kind is likely to retain full vigour is limited by the laws of nature combined with the circumstances of place and time, and the character and stage of development of the particular trade in which it lies' (1961: Volume 2, 343–44).

In the sixth edition (1910) this was replaced by the following sentences:

> 'And as with the growth of trees, so *was* it with the growth of businesses as a general rule before the great recent development of vast joint-stock companies, which often stagnate but do not readily die. Now that rule is far from universal, but it still holds in many industries and trades' (1961: Volume 1, 316 – my italics).

As G. F. Shove pointed out (1942: 729), '. . . this inconspicuous change of wording really knocks away – so far as a large and growing section of industry is concerned – the main prop on which the reconciliation between atomic competition and increasing returns had rested'. Marshall spent a great deal of time exploring the facts of industrial change in Britain and the USA, and by the first decade of this century he had seen ample evidence of the decline of competition and the emergence of large-scale corporations wielding monopolistic power. These significant empirical discoveries ran counter to his benign 'trees of the forest' story. When firms are reaping substantial internal as well as external economies, the competitive process tends to result in an increase in monopoly. In these circumstances, particularly when division of labour among industries is a major element in economic growth, the concept of the 'representative firm' loses all meaning. When Marshall produced the sixth edition of his *Principles* in 1910, he was compelled to face the implications of these fundamental developments.

The irreversibility problem has far-reaching consequences. Evolution may be defined as the history of a system undergoing irreversible changes (Lotka, 1956: 24). The long-period supply and demand curves are interdependent; in Marshall's words, '. . . every movement of the exchange index entails some alteration in the shapes of the curves and therefore in the forces which determine its succeeding movements' (1975: Volume 2, 164). Therefore, the theory of economic growth cannot be based on the mechanical analogue: it must be a theory of organic growth on biological lines. In models of organic growth, time (T) is historical time – a continuous series of 'moments' entailing qualitative change – whereas in mechanical models time is 'the measure of an interval (T^{i}, T^{ii}) by a mechanical clock' (Georgescu-Roegen, 1971: 135). Mechanical laws are invariable with respect to historical time; in the mechanical world each 'moment' is exactly like any other.

Marshall did not concern himself with the wide implications of irreversibility, the theory of organic growth, when he was writing his *Principles*. The proof of this may be seen by examining the papers which he wrote on economic progress in the 1870s and 1880s. His major contributions in this area were the following:

1) 1875: Lectures on 'Some features of American industry'.
2) 1877: 'Foreign trade in its bearing on industrial and social progress' (Chapters 4 and 5 of the abortive book on the theory of foreign trade).
3) 1879: A lecture course on 'Economic progress' given in Bristol.
4) 1880–82: Notes on the theory of economic growth – a neoclassical growth model.
5) 1883: Lectures on Henry George's *Progress and poverty*.

The most telling item in this list is the mathematical model (written some time between 1880 and 1882) which was found among the manuscripts in the Marshall Library (Marshall, 1975: Volume 2, 305–16). In the words of John K. Whitaker, '. . . for the first time we have really clear and explicit evidence of a neoclassical author actually working in terms of what has come to be known as "the neoclassical aggregate growth model" ' (Marshall, 1975: Volume 2, 305). 'It goes in some ways beyond anything appearing in the modern growth-theory literature, even though its sophistication falls short in other ways' (Whitaker, 1974: 15). This was magnificent but it was not *organic* growth. It was inspired by Book 4 of John Stuart Mill's *Principles* which Marshall regarded as 'the most advanced and modern part' of Mill's work (1975: Volume 2, 306). In the manuscript notes for the first lecture on 'Economic progress' delivered at Bristol in 1879, Marshall said that he planned '. . . to endeavour to show that all or almost all the piles of statistics which state how some things have fallen and others have risen in value may be reduced under a few simple laws' (1975: Volume 2, 306). These were the laws of neoclassical growth in the tradition of mechanical reasoning. The model failed to throw any light on the main object of the exercise, an analysis of the forces governing the long-run movement of the rate of interest. Marshall saw no future in it. His arguments against Henry George's *Progress and poverty* were firmly rooted in the marginal productivity theory of distribution set out in the *Economics of industry*. None of the pre-1885 essays on economic growth showed any evidence of the use of biological ideas. After 1881 Marshall seems to have turned away from problems relating to economic growth (Whitaker, 1974: 15).

III The treatment of 'time' in the *Principles*

Principles of economics, Volume 1, was essentially a treatise on economic statics to be followed by Volume 2 on dynamics. In the second edition in 1891 the former Books 5 and 6 were merged to make the new Book 5 on '. . . demand and supply as crude forces pressing against one another and tending to a mechanical equilibrium, (Pigou, 1925: 318). In the preface to this edition Marshall wrote: 'To myself personally the chief interest of the volume centres in Book V: it contains more of my life's work than any other part: and it is there, more than anywhere else, that I have tried to deal with unsettled questions of the science' (1961: Volume 2, 40). Books 4 and 6, contain biological language relating, for example, to the principles of continuity and substitution. The purpose of those sections, as Marshall explained in the preface to the fourth edition (1898), was '. . . to lay stress on the essentially organic character of the larger and broader problems towards which we are working our way' (1961: Volume 2, 44). Presumably he was here thinking of the biological analysis which would appear in Volume 2.

According to Marshall's plans in 1887 the second volume would cover 'Foreign Trade, Money and Banking. Trade Fluctuations, Taxation, Collectivism, Aims for the Future' (1975: Volume 1, 36). This volume was never completed. Part of the type for it set up in 1904 remained unused until 1919 when it was incorporated in *Industry and trade* (1921: vi); Marshall was told that this lag was something of a record! The main ideas on foreign trade which had been thought out in the 1870s did not appear in print under Marshall's own name until the publication of *Money, credit and commerce* in 1923, shortly before his death. At the end of his life, Marshall was struggling to put together material for yet another book to be called 'Progress: its economic conditions'.

Writing to the Dutch economist, N.G. Pierson, in 1891, Marshall described the objective of the *Principles* as follows:

> The book was written to express one idea, and one only. That idea is that whereas Ricardo & Co. maintain that value is determined by Cost of production, and Malthus, MacLeod, Jevons and (in a measure) the Austrians that it is determined by utility, each was right in what he affirmed but wrong in what he denied. They none of them paid, I think, sufficient attention to the element of *Time*. That I believe holds the key of all the paradoxes which this long controversy has raised. When Ricardo spoke of Cost of production as determining value he had in mind periods as to which cost of production is the dominant force; when Jevons emphasized utility, he had in mind shorter periods. The attempt to work all existing knowledge on the subject of value into one continuous and harmonious whole, by means of a complex study of the element of Time permeates every book, almost every page of my volume. It is the backbone of all that, from a scientific point of view, I care to say (1975: Volume I, 97–98).

Marshall's achievement was based on his central concern with the fact that the nature and causes of equilibrium depend on the length of time over which the market extends. The great problem was broken up into parts with the aid of *ceteris paribus*, culminating in the full static equilibrium of the industry. On the surface it would seem that Marshall thought of Time in the ordinary nontechnical sense; his term 'normal' refers to 'long periods of several years', and 'secular' denotes a period covering one generation to another. However, this is taking matters too literally. As the late Sir John Hicks (1965: 50) pointed out, the 'short' and 'long' periods have no relation to the kind of 'period' used in dynamic economics. They are 'technical terms of Marshallian economics'. 'Time' in Book 5 is neither the ordinal variable which applies to strictly mechanical systems nor the cardinal variable which applies to genuinely biological systems: it is a hybrid. Further light can be thrown on this by considering how biological is the analysis in the *Principles*.

Marshall's deep interest in the element of *time*, the source of the greatest difficulties in economics, helped to determine his attitude to the mathematical method:

> For many important considerations, especially those connected with the manifold influences of the element of time, do not lend themselves easily to mathematical expression: they must either be omitted altogether, or clipped and pruned till they resemble the conventional birds and animals of decorative art. And hence arises a tendency towards assigning wrong proportions to economic forces; those elements being most emphasized which lend themselves most easily to analytical methods (1961: Volume 1, 850).

IV Economic biology: substance or promise?

In the first edition of the *Principles* the opening paragraph of Book 5 was confined to stating that the book would be devoted to the balancing of the forces of demand and supply. In the fourth edition in 1898 that paragraph was replaced by a new one which stated that the mechanical equilibrium analysis of Book 5 ('corresponding to the mechanical equilibrium of a stone hanging by an elastic string or of a number of balls resting against one another in a basin') was a preliminary to an advanced study which would be biological in character – the balancing of the forces of life and decay (1961: Volume 1, 323 and Volume 2, 350). Marshall regarded Book 6 as an analysis of demand and supply more and more from a biological point of view, and he thought this was particularly true of the chapter on the 'Influence of progress on value' (1898: 50).

One cannot help feeling that in 1898, when Marshall was on the defensive against critics of the *Principles*, he tended to exaggerate the biological element in his previous work. A striking example is that in 1898 he defined his concept of the 'representative firm' as biological rather than mechanical, and declared, *ex post*, that 'its application to the theory of value is one mark of the gradual transition from the mechanical view of the composition of forces ... to the biological notion of composite organic development' (1898: 50). There was no mention of biological meaning when the notion of the representative firm was introduced in the first edition of the *Principles* (1961: Volume 2, 346). If the 'representative firm' is a biological concept, is it not strange that two-thirds of the references to it in the *Principles* are in Book 5 which is devoted to mechanical equilibrium analysis?

How much economic biology is there is the *Principles*? In the preface to the first edition Marshall emphasized the notion of continuity with regard to development and stated that writings such as those of Herbert Spencer and Hegel's *Philosophy of History* had '... affected more than any other the substance of the views expressed in the present book' (1961: Volume 1, ix). He regarded the law of substitution as '... nothing more than a special and limited application of the law of survival of the fittest ...' (1961: Volume 1, 597). If continuity and substitution are biological concepts, it has been suggested that Marshall really had in mind the notion of an economy in a biosystem (Levine, 1983: 276–93).

One must distinguish between biological analogies and biological analysis. There are sound reasons for concluding that Marshall was for the most part indulging in analogies or figures of speech. First, we have already shown that in the decade and a half leading up to the *Principles* Marshall's thinking on economic development was based on neoclassical, mechanical models. His publications on economic progress in that period contained no biological analysis. He was a marginal-productivity theorist who in the 1880s worked out his own formulation in terms of production functions and their partial derivatives, but these were not displayed in the *Principles* (1975: Volume 1, 96). His handling of development problems was also influenced by his macroeconomic growth modelling. The famous chapter on the 'Influence of progress on value', far from being a contribution to economic biology, was an elegant essay on economic history scantily dressed up in biological finery.

Secondly, the significance attached to the principle of continuity with regard to development simply echoes the motto of the *Principles* – *natura non facit saltum*. It was Marshall's general philosophy of history that nature does not make jumps, and when the Mendelians came along with their big jumps he was careful to neglect that kind of biology. The important fact for him was '... the accumulated effects of forces which, though weak at first, get greater strength from the growth of their own effects; and the universal form, of which every such fact is a special embodiment, is Taylor's Theorem' (1961: Volume 1, 844). In the seventh edition (1916) he added the following statements:

> This conclusion will remain valid even if further investigation confirms the suggestion, made by some Mendelians, that gradual changes in the race are originated by large divergences of individuals from the prevailing type. For economics is a study of mankind, of particular nations, of particular social strata; and it is only indirectly concerned with the lives of men of exceptional genius or exceptional wickedness and violence (1961: Volume 1, 844).

The Hegelian influence was strong and always present; it helped to shape the peculiar features of his time analysis. He did not use the concept of 'time' which is appropriate to mechanical models; nor did he follow through his pioneering work on irreversibility to develop the concept of 'time' required for the analysis of organic growth.

The nearest Marshall gets to economic biology is in Book 4 on 'Industrial organization'. He starts with '... the many profound analogies which have been discovered between social and especially industrial organization on the one side and the physical organization of the higher animals on the other' (p. 240–41). Then he moves on to suggest in effect that biology takes over part of economics, since there is '. . . a fundamental unity of action between the laws of nature in the physical and in the moral world' (p. 241). This was explained as follows:

> This central unity is set forth in the general rule, to which there are not many exceptions, that the development of the organism, whether social or physical, involves an increasing subdivision of functions between its separate parts on the one hand, and on the other a more intimate connection between them. Each part gets to be less self-sufficient, to depend for its wellbeing more and more on other parts, so that any disorder in any part of a highly-developed organism will affect other parts also (p. 241).

In developing his thesis Marshall goes beyond analogy. In a few pages he summarizes the 'bearings in economics of the law that the struggle for existence causes those organisms to multiply which are best fitted to derive benefit from their environment' (p. 241). Book 4, Chapter 8 of the *Principles*, the wording of which, with a few minor changes, dates from the first edition, reads like an early blueprint of a book on economic biology. If Marshall had got around to it, this chapter would have been the nucleus of a large section of his Volume 2.

One of the puzzles about Marshall is why in the 20 years after 1890 he did not fulfil his ambition to write Volume 2 of his *Principles*. His own explanation, in the preface to *Industry and trade* (1919), was that, '. . . my progress has been delayed, not only by weak health and constitutional unfitness for rapid work; but also by heavy professional duties till 1908; by preparing evidence and memoranda for various Royal Commissions on currency and other matters; and by service on the Royal Commission on Labour, 1891–5, during which I received from working men and other witnesses, and from members of the Commission, the most valuable education of my life' (1921: vi–vii). Mrs Marshall described how, '. . . he wasted a great deal of time because he changed his method of treatment so often. In 1894 he began a historical treatment, which he called later on a White Elephant, because it was on such a large scale that it would have taken many volumes to complete. Later on he used fragments of the White Elephant in the descriptive parts of *Industry and Trade*' (Pigou, 1925: 58). Is it not probable that, in giving so much time to those Royal Commissions, the revising of his *Principles* and various professional activities, Marshall was really creating for himself a series of alibis? In December 1902 he informed his publishers that '. . . I am giving myself up to my Second Volume with ever increasing resoluteness so far as I am free. But I have not much freedom, and my progress is not fast' (Whitaker, 1990: 201). Could it have been that there were over-riding intellectual reasons why he could not accomplish the big task?

10 *Alfred Marshall on economic biology*

In a letter to J.B. Clark in November 1902 when he was 60 years of age, Marshall said that he had changed much since the years before 1870 when he worked out his theory of value. He added this revealing sentence:

> I then believed it was possible to have a coherent though abstract doctrine of economics in which competition was the only dominant force; and I then defined 'normal' as that which the undisturbed play of competition would bring about: and now I regard that position as untenable from an abstract as well as from a practical point of view (1961: Volume 2, 97).

This was a striking admission for him to make. During the 1890s the old doubts generated by the irreversibility problem must have come back with renewed force. Was he satisfied with his handling of the element of time which he had described in the preface to the first edition as 'the centre of the chief difficulty of almost every economic problem'? Had he changed his mind about what he had achieved in the *Principles*. He had never taken much notice of critics. However, an attack on the *Principles* in the *Economic Journal* in 1897 by an US economist, Arthur T. Hadley (1897: 477–85), drew from Marshall a spirited reply in an article. 'Distribution and exchange', in the *Journal* in 1898. It is an important statement of his views on methodology. It was in this article that he first declared that 'the Mecca of the economist is economic biology rather than economic dynamics' (see Marshall, 1898: 43).

Hadley's criticism was summarized as follows:

> The problem of distribution is essentially a kinetic one . . . Marshall in general uses static methods for static problems and gets correct solutions. When he attempts to make connections with the kinetic problem the result is less satisfactory. The unsatisfactory character of these results is recognised by Marshall in his discussion of the deficiencies of the statical method in economics; but he fails to see that those deficiencies make themselves chiefly felt when that method is applied to problems which are not statical at all (Hadley, 1897: 485).

In his reply Marshall apologised for the delay in bringing out his second volume and gave a careful account of what he meant by 'static' and 'dynamic'. In the static stage the analogy of physics is appropriate; the variables do not change their character as they move through time; the forces of demand and supply tend towards a mechanical equilibrium, and much use is made of partial equilibrium analysis. 'The purpose of the statical method is to fix our attention on some centre, which for the time we regard as either at rest or in steady movement; to consider the tendencies of various elements to mutually adjust themselves relatively to that centre, or perhaps to change the position of that centre' (1961: Volume 2, 67). In the dynamic stage there is no analogy with the physical sciences; variables change their character as they move through time; the analysis is biological and the balance or equilibrium is between the organic forces of life and decay. Marshall went out of his way to insist that though the treatment in Book

5 is static it does not lack 'living force and movement'. There is a good deal of dynamics in the *Principles* '. . . if the terms are interpreted as in physical science' (Volume 2, 48). This is not the sort of dynamics required for the analysis of organic growth.

Written eight years after the appearance of the *Principles*, the 1898 article shows how far Marshall's position had moved since 1870. In *The pure theory of foreign trade and domestic values* he had stressed that movements in the economic sphere alter '. . . the magnitude if not the character of the forces that govern succeeding movements' (1975: Volume 2, 163). In the 1898 statement the emphasis is on changes in the *character* of the forces, as the following paragraph shows:

> The catastrophes of mechanics are caused by changes in the quantity and not in the character of the forces at work; whereas in life their character changes also. 'Progress' or 'evolution', industrial and social, is not mere increase or decrease. It is organic growth, chastened and confined and occasionally reversed by the decay of innumerable factors, each of which influences and is influenced by those around it; and every such mutual influence varies with the stages which the respective factors have already reached in their growth. In this vital respect all sciences of life are akin to one another, and are unlike physical sciences. And therefore in the later stages of economics, when we are approaching nearly to the conditions of life, biological analogies are to be preferred to mechanical, other things being equal. (Marshall, 1898: 47–48).

Marshall repeated his famous sentence about 'the Mecca of the economist' in every preface to the *Principles* from the fifth edition (1907) on, and he left it at that. Economic biology remained promise rather than substance.

V Conclusion

Looking back in 1919 Marshall referred to weak health as one of the causes of his delays. However, a decline in vitality is difficult to believe in view of all that he achieved between 1890 and 1910. He could have chosen to produce Volume 2 of his *Principles* containing a substantial contribution to economic biology: instead he brought out seven editions of Volume 1, each of which according to his own estimate entailed a full year's work (Guillebaud, 1942: 349). If he seemed to have lost control over his material it was probably because the ideas he had up to 1887 about the contents of Volume 2 had changed by the end of the 1890s. He had come to realize more and more that the study of organic growth necessitated a break with his neoclassical system as definite as the break which he had made with the Ricardo-Mill system. His great achievement in the first half of his career had been that, in the words of Keynes (1933: 177–78), '. . . he had worked out within him the foundations of little less than a new science, of great consequence to mankind.' By about 1900 he must have become convinced that, if Volume 2 was to be true to his high standards, he would have to work out within him the foundations of yet another science – economic biology. If that was so, one could hardly blame him for regarding this as a task for his successors not for him.

Marshall's basic insight was that the study of economic growth must mean the abandonment of mechanical equilibrium models based on the reversibility of time. This message was not heeded by his successors. The revival of growth theory which came after the Keynesian revolution was dominated by neoclassical model building, and its influence was widespread. Aggregate growth models became the ruling fashion and were applied to all countries irrespective of culture or history. Robert E. Lucas Jr, outstanding among today's neoclassical theorists, has explained what he does in these words: 'This is what I mean by the "mechanics" of economic development – the construction of a mechanical, artificial world, populated by the interacting robots that economics typically studies, that is capable of exhibiting behavior the gross features of which resemble those of the actual world that I have just described' (Lucas, 1988: 5). The late Sir John Hicks, in a penetrating review of modern growth theory, reached the following conclusions:

> Growth theory, say since Harrod and Domar (or perhaps since von Neumann) has been the scene of a tremendous come-back of equilibrism. Trying to push on beyond Keynes it has slipped back behind him . . . So long as attention was fixed on ratios (and the growth rate itself is a ratio) the Steady State could be absorbed into full-blown equilibrium economics, in which one point of time is just like another. It was just as much 'out of time' as the Stationary State itself . . . It is my own opinion that [Steady State economics] has been rather a curse. It has encouraged economists to waste their time upon constructions that are often of great intellectual complexity but which are so much out of time, and out of history, as to be practically futile and indeed misleading (Hicks, 1976: 142–43).

Subsequent developments of dynamic equilibrium theories suffer from similar disabilities: 'Though these are not Steady State theories, they are nevertheless equilibrium theories. One point of time is not like another, even in the ratio sense; yet the whole of the plan is looked at together. The plan is mutually determined; there is no movement from past to future, except in the sense that there is also a movement from future to past. There is no room for the unexpected' (p. 114). This trenchant verdict, with its emphasis on the irreversibility of time, would have been applauded by Marshall.

The sequence of ideas described in this paper contains an element of the paradoxical. The relevant methodological issues were thoroughly explored almost a century ago. When Marshall recognized the full implications of irreversibility he rejected his mechanical model of growth and called for a biological approach. Yet, strangely enough, when the study of economic growth became a major preoccupation in the 1950s and 1960s Marshall's conclusions were ignored, and mechanical models similar to the one which he discarded became a prominent element in economics curricula everywhere. The prevalence of mechanical equilibrium and steady-state modelling had the effect which Marshall had warned against – 'a tendency towards assigning wrong proportions to economic forces, those elements being most emphasized which lend themselves most easily to analytical methods' (1961: Volume 1, 850). This is particularly the case when such models are applied to less developed countries with cultures very different from those of developed countries. Two major problems to be explained are the large differences in growth rates between countries and between periods; and yet, in a comprehensive review of growth theory, F.H. Hahn and R.C.O. Matthews (1964: 889 – 90) concluded that '. . . it would be difficult to claim that any of the models we have discussed goes far towards explaining these differences or predicting what will happen to them in the future'. The solution of empirically important problems such as these will be facilitated by the current shift towards economic biology and the development of theories of growth which will be 'in time' not 'out of time'.

VI References

Boulding, K. 1981: *Evolutionary economics*. Beverley Hills: Sage Publications.

Darwin, C. 1958: *The autobiography of Charles Darwin, 1809–82*, edited by N. Barlow. London: Collins.

Georgescu-Roegen, N. 1971: *The entropy of law and the economic process*. Cambridge, MA: Harvard University Press.

Guillebaud, C.W. 1942: The evolution of Marshall's *Principles of economics*. *Economic Journal* 52, 330–49.

Hadley, A.T. 1897: Some fallacies in the theory of distribution. *Economic Journal* 7, 477–86.

Hahn, F.H. and **Matthews, R.C.O.** 1964: The theory of economic growth: a survey. *Economic Journal*, 74, 779–902.

Hardin, G. 1960: *Nature and man's fate*. London: Jonathan Cape.

Hicks, J.R. 1965: *Capital and growth*. London: Oxford University Press.

——— 1976: Some questions of time in economics. In Tang, A.M., Westfield, F.M. and Worley, J.S., editors, *Evolution, welfare and time in economics: essays in honor of Nicholas Georgescu-Roegen*, Lexington, MA: Lexington Books, 135–51.

Keynes, J.M. 1933: *Essays in biography*. London: Macmillan.

Levine, A.L. 1983: Marshall's *Principles* and the 'biological viewpoint': a reconsideration. *Manchester School*, 51, 276–93.

Lotka, A.J. 1956: *Elements of mathematical biology*. New York: Dover Publications.

Lucas, R.E., Jr 1988: On the mechanics of economic development. *Journal of Monetary Economics* 22, 3–42.

Marshall, A. 1898: Distribution and exchange. *Economic Journal* 8, 37–59.

14 *Alfred Marshall on economic biology*

——— 1921: *Industry and trade*. London: Macmillan.

——— 1961: *Principles of economics*, ninth (variorum) edition with annotations by C.W. Guillebaud. London: Macmillan.

——— 1975: *The early economic writings of Alfred Marshall, 1867–1890*, edited by J.K. Whitaker. London: Macmillan.

Mokyr, J. 1989: Evolutionary biology, technological change, and economic history. Mimeograph.

Pigou, A.C., editor, 1925: *Memorials of Alfred Marshall*. London: Macmillan.

Shove, G.F. 1942: The place of Marshall's *Principles* in the development of economic theory. *Economic Journal* 52, 294–329.

Sigüenza, M. 1982: Review of Boulding's *Evolutionary economics. Journal of Economic Literature* 20, 1558–61.

Whitaker, J.K. 1974: The Marshallian system in 1881: distribution and growth. *Economic Journal* 84, 1–17.

——— 1990: What happened to the second volume of the principles? The thorny path to Marshall's last books. In Whittaker, J.K., editor, *Centenary essays on Alfred Marshall*, Cambridge: Cambridge University Press.

Young, R.M. 1969: Malthus and the evolutionists: the common context of biological and social theory. *Past and Present* 43, 109–45.

[16]

BIOLOGICAL ANALOGIES IN MARSHALL'S WORK

BY

NEIL B. NIMAN

I. INTRODUCTION

Alfred Marshall, who once proclaimed that "the Mecca of the economist lies in Economic Biology," is remembered more for the mechanical analogies contained in the appendices of his *Principles of Economics*. Subsequent revisions of Marshall based on the mechanical principles he incorporated into the theory of the firm (Robbins 1928; Pigou 1928), the theory of competition (Robinson 1933; Chamberlin 1933), and the theory of value (Hicks and Allen 1934), succeeded in completely removing the corpus of economic theory from the domain of biology. The unimportance attached to biological analogies forms the basis for the position advocated by Philip Mirowski (Mirowski 1984a, 1984b, 1989) that the true fascination of the neoclassical economist is with physics and not biology.

Mirowski has identified the rise of neoclassical economics with the adoption of the physics metaphor and includes Marshall on his list of neoclassical economists despite "his defence of Ricardo vis-à-vis Jevons; his soft-pedalling of the mathematical method; his insistence of the basic continuity of economics from Adam Smith to his time; his persistent praise of organic metaphors." The reason for that classification is, according to Mirowski, that "all these activities are attempts to incorporate energetics into economics while controlling or perhaps altering some of its more objectional aspects" (Mirowski 1984a, p. 375). What Mirowski fails to identify is Marshall's belief that while "the mechanical analogy is apt to be the more definite and vivid...as the science reaches to its highest work..., the tone becomes more and more that of a biological science" (Marshall 1898, p. 317-18). Thus if neoclassical economics is nothing more than physics, then it becomes a subject for debate as to whether economics has reached its "highest work," but what is not subject for debate is the conclusion that must be drawn that Marshall was not a neoclassical economist in the sense that

University of New Hampshire. I would like to thank Philip Mirowski, who encouraged me to write this paper, and the members of the Kress Society for their helpful comments. An earlier version of this paper was presented at the Kress Society Seminar held at Harvard University in April 1990.

Journal of the History of Economic Thought, 13, Spring 1991.

Mirowski uses the term. While "physics envy" may have swept many of the early proponents of neoclassical economic theory, the purpose of this paper is to demonstrate that Marshall was not a member of that group, and that the biological metaphor had an important and significant role to play in the construction of his economic theory.

II. RECENT INTERPRETATIONS OF MARSHALL

Over the last hundred years, many articles have appeared focusing on various broad themes found in Marshall's *Principles*. These themes include Marshall's appeals to the natural sciences; his "moralising imp"; his relegation of mathematics to an appendix; his careful attention to history and real-world events; his use of inductive as well as deductive reasoning; and his painstaking attempts to maintain continuity between his innovative ideas and the major ideas of the classical economists. Explanations for the existence of these individual themes have been traced to Marshall's desire to 1) professionalize economics; 2) provide ethical foundations for economic behavior; 3) provide an engine for policy analysis; or 4) denigrate W. S. Jevons's view that the principles underlying marginal utility represent a radical break with the classical tradition. Instead of there existing a myriad of explanations for why these various themes can be found in the *Principles*, they are rather variations on one central theme: that theme being one of economic biology.

Professionalization through scientific foundations. A. W. Coats has characterized the position of economics in the later part of the nineteenth century as "profoundly discouraging" because "its public reputation had fallen owing to the combined effects of a sharp public reaction against classical economics, an increased concern about current economic and social problems, and the disruptive methodological wrangles among the leading economic writers" (Coats 1967, p. 707). John Maloney (1985) offers the view that Marshall set out to professionalize economics to rectify this situation. Professionalization would establish not only an identity for the economists, but would create a vaunted place for economics within the context of social discourse, and therefore save economics from the indifference of the general public.

In his inaugural address as Professor of Political Economy at Cambridge, Marshall notes that the biological sciences have been ascending throughout the nineteenth century, and economics (along with the moral and historical sciences), has changed as the result of the development of "clearer ideas about the nature of organic growth" (Marshall 1885, p. 154). By sharing in biology's "rising tide," economics was able to keep pace with changes in the academic and professional communities,[1] and to benefit from being associated with a natural science that had attracted widespread support and interest.[2] Perhaps more important, Marshall felt that developments in biological sciences had a strong influence on the development of economic reasoning, and as a result, "the human as distinguished from the mechanical element is taking a more and more prominent place" (Marshall 1920, p. 765). Therefore Marshall views economic reasoning as

> passing onward from that early stage in the development of scientific method, in which the operations of Nature are represented as conventionally simplified for the purpose of enabling them to be described in short and easy sentences, to that higher stage in which they are studied more carefully, and represented more nearly as they are, even at the expense of some loss of simplicity and definiteness, and even apparent lucidity. And in consequence general reasoning in economics has made more rapid progress, and established a firmer position in this generation in which it is subject to hostile criticisms at every step, than when it was at the height of its popularity and its authority was seldom challenged (ibid., p. 766).

Scientific foundations for an ethical position. The widespread interest in biology in the nineteenth century can be attributed to the work of Charles Darwin and the subsequent broad acceptance of evolution as a theoretical construct. However, according to Peter Bowler, "Darwin's theory should be seen not as the central theme in nineteenth-century evolutionism but as a catalyst that helped bring about the transition to an evolutionary viewpoint within an essentially non-Darwinian conceptual framework" (Bowler 1988, p. 5). For while the process of natural selection is non-teleological and does not connote any type of progress, the majority of those who jumped on the Darwinian bandwagon viewed evolution as an orderly, progressive, and goal-directed process. Thus a man like Alfred Marshall, prone to making "pious asides and prim moralisings" (Shove 1942, p. 316), would certainly find comfort in constructing analogies that were consistent with the domi-

1. Mirowski (1989, p. 265) recounts an attempt in 1877 to oust political economy from the British Association for the Advancement of Science on the grounds that research had not been conducted and reported in a scientific manner. In 1878, J. K. Ingram constructed a defense through the assertion that political economy resembled biology in many important respects. This enables Mirowski to draw the conclusion that "Marshall's recourse to biological analogies can be understood as a continuation of that strategy, as part of his larger project of building a stable professional identity for economics."

2. Bowler (1988, p. 47) refers to a study by Hull, Tessner and Diamond confirming "that approximately three-quarters of the British scientific community accepted evolution during the years 1859-1870," and to a survey by Elegard of the periodical press that "revealed a widespread popular conversion in the same period."

nant theory of evolution that prevailed at the end of the nineteenth century.[3] The progressive interpretations of evolution would provide a desirable backdrop for Marshall and his *Principles*, which is "infused throughout with an effluvium of moral maxims, ethical prescriptions, and public-policy insistences" (Levitt 1976, p. 427).

Marshall wanted to promote a view of economic progress where economic and moral advancement are inextricably linked. His theory of progress contains three propositions: 1) "Every increase in the physical, mental and moral vigour of a people makes them more likely, other things being equal, to rear to adult age a large number of vigorous children"; 2) "every increase of wealth tends in many ways to make a greater increase easier than before"; leading to the conclusion that 3) "every increase of wealth and every increase in the numbers and intelligence of the people increased the facilities for a highly developed industrial organization, which in its turn adds much to the collective efficiency of capital and labour" (Marshall 1920, p. 314).[4]

The adoption of biological foundations enabled Marshall to legitimate his ethical prescriptions and pronouncements about economic and social progress in part because "the rules of scientific explanation which were developed in the seventeenth century banished purposes, intentions, and anthropomorphic expressions from scientific explanations. Biologists, however, had never been very good at confining their explanations to matter, motion, and number" (Young 1985, p. 93). Thus as Maloney has observed "to make ethical judgments and yet persuade oneself science had not been left behind, the manufacture of biological and evolutionary metaphors was needed" (ibid., p. 199). The treatment of ethical issues incorporated in a theory of social and economic progress was therefore consistent with the dominant view of evolution, and places Marshall within the intellectual mainstream.

History vs. theory. Darwin's theory of evolution is based on the principle that variation between members of a given population provides the basis for selection, and selection is a process that chooses those characteristics best suited to survive in a particular environment. While a generalized principle (the theory of natural selection) can explain how change will occur, the actual changes themselves are dependent on the composition of existing populations. Thus a "biological economics" that is consistent with Darwin-

3. The desire to moralize can be traced to Marshall's Anglican background, his interest in Utilitarianism, membership in the Grote Club, and the influence of Sidgwick and Spencer.

4. It is important to note that, for Marshall, economic progress is limited by the biological progress of the human organism. "In fact our new command over nature, while opening the door to much larger schemes for industrial organization than were physically possible even a short time ago, places greater responsibilities on those who would advocate new developments of social and industrial structure. For though, institutions may be changed rapidly; yet if they are to endure they must be appropriate to man: they cannot retain their stability if they change very much faster than he does" (Marshall 1920, p. 249).

ian principles will attempt to construct generalized principles in concert with observations of the actual environment where activity takes place. Because of the importance of variation, Marshall comments that "Darwin's development of the laws of struggle and survival gave perhaps a greater impetus to the careful and exact study of particular facts than any other event that has occurred" (Marshall 1897, p. 298).

By drawing connections between the theory of evolution and economic theory, Marshall is able to justify the liberal use of inductive as well as deductive reasoning, and to justify his assertion of the need to direct careful attention toward historical fact. For Marshall, a biological approach is important because "the matter with which the chemist deals is the same always: but economics, like biology, deals with a matter, of which the inner nature and constitution, as well as the outer form, are constantly changing" (Marshall 1920, p. 772). Adoption of a biological approach requires the careful study of actual events because the evolutionary process depends on the composition of existing populations. This leads Marshall to the position that "the study of theory must go hand in hand with that of facts: and for dealing with most modern problems it is modern facts that are of the greatest use" (ibid., p. 39). "It is obvious that there is not room in economics for long trains of deductive reasoning; no economist, not even Ricardo, attempted them" (ibid., p. 781).

Continuity with classical theory. Marshall viewed his *Principles* not as representing a radical break from the classical tradition, but rather as advancing and generalizing the classical position. Thus while he is critical of the classical economists because they "attributed to the forces of supply and demand a much more mechanical and regular action than is to be found in real life: and they laid down laws with regard to profits and wages that did not really hold even for England in their own time" (ibid., pp. 762-63), he is careful to stress that "some of the best work of the present generation has indeed appeared at first sight to be antagonistic to that of earlier writers; but when it has had time to settle down into its proper place, and its rough edges have been worn away, it has been found to involve no real breach of continuity in the development of the science" (ibid., p. v).

One potential explanation for why Marshall emphasized continuity in the development of economic thought has been offered by A. W. Coats, who utilizes Marshall's professional sense of etiquette (where claims to originality are not allowed) to provide an explanation why Marshall "disapproved of Jevons' claims, why there are no "labels of salesmanship" in the *Principles,* and why his "references to the question of priority are extremely reserved" (Coats 1967, p. 710).[5] A different explanation, however, can be

5. Thus it was left to Keynes (1924) and Shove (1942) to make the case that Marshall's ideas flow from Ricardo and are not a "'compromise' or 'synthesis' between Ricardian doctrines and those of other schools" (Shove 1942, p. 295). Whether Marshall's ideas predated the work of Jevons, Walras, and Menger is extensively discussed by Whitaker (1975, pp. 37-52).

tied to Marshall's use of biological analogies. Marshall states in his inaugural lecture as Professor at Cambridge: "if the subject-matter of a science passes through different stages of development..., the laws of the science must have a development corresponding to that of the things of which they treat" (Marshall 1885, p. 154). Thus given that the subject matter of the science is biological in nature, and that Marshall viewed the biological process of evolution as being gradual (Moss 1982), changes in economic science, he thought, must also be gradual and therefore maintain continuity with the past.

III. THE IMPORTANCE OF BIOLOGY IN MARSHALL'S THOUGHT

Marshall's interest in biology stems from his belief that economists have "owed much to the many profound analogies which have been discovered between social and especially industrial organization on the one side and the physical organization of the higher animals on the other" (Marshall 1920, p. 240). The commonality between economics and biology is found in the division of labor. While modern economics finds its roots in the division of labor, the relationship between the division of labor and the theory of evolution is perhaps less well known. In cataloging the relationship between Darwin's ideas about evolution and those of the classical economists, S. Schweber points to three important influences: 1) as an undergraduate at Cambridge, Darwin was acquainted with various utilitarian tracts on moral and political philosophy and read works by W. Paley, J. R. McCulloch, and J.-C. Sismondi; 2) Darwin became familiar with the work of T. R. Malthus in 1838; and 3) Darwin was heavily influenced by Henri Milne-Edwards, a French zoologist whose writings were, in turn, heavily influenced by Smithian themes with respect to the division of labor. The influence of Milne-Edwards is ascribed particular influence by Schweber because it provided Darwin with the license to "use the metaphor of the industrial economy and its driving force–competition and division of labor--in a biological context.... It allowed him to ascribe the principles of the physiological division of labor to an eminent zoologist and philosopher of biology, rather than to the political economists" (Schweber 1980, p. 256).

While political economy may have formed a basis for Darwin's theory of evolution, changes in the biological sciences enabled Marshall to develop biological foundations that invited an investigation of the motives underlying economic behavior and of the appropriate actions taken in response to these motives. Rather than focusing on the broad category of wealth, biology has led the movement toward paying "a greater attention to the pliability of human nature, and to the way in which the character of man affects and is affected by the prevalent methods of the production, distribution and consumption of wealth" (Marshall 1920, p. 764). The creation of biological foundations enabled the focus to shift from the wealth of the nation to "human beings who are impelled, for good and evil, to change and progress" (ibid., p. xv), thus leading Marshall to conclude: "The growth of mankind in numbers, in health and strength, in knowledge, ability, and in richness of character is the end of all our studies" (ibid., p. 139). A shift in focus away from a study of wealth in the broader sense lends itself to the development of new techniques that may be of value in discussing the individual consumer or firm. Marginal analysis supported the movement towards a disaggregated approach by providing a framework that was capable of identifying and quantifying meaningful relationships on the level of the individual. Marginal analysis is however only a tool, and does not necessitate a fundamental restructuring of the classical science of wealth.

For Marshall, the error of the classical economists was not that they had a preoccupation with deductive reasoning at the expense of history and statistics, but that they did not have the opportunity for sharing in the benefits ascribed to the advances in biological science. The classical economists "regarded man as, so to speak, a constant quantity, and gave themselves little trouble to study his variations" (Marshall 1885 pp. 154-55). Yet it was these "variations" that were of interest at the end of the nineteenth century, because without variation the mechanism of natural selection becomes inoperable, and without natural selection, there is no dynamic for evolutionary change. Thus an evolutionary approach to economic analysis must first begin by acknowledging the existence of differences between individual economic agents. The adoption of biological foundations enabled Marshall to create a broader view of economic phenomena. What can be explained is not only how the expansion of wealth is related to the division of labor, but why labor can be divided, and how the process of division produces economic relationships that ultimately determine the creation of wealth. Thus human behavior becomes a noteworthy topic in terms of the wants created by individuals, and the organizing principles that are adopted in order to best satisfy those wants.

Human wants that originate from biological necessity become more "subtle and various" as "man rises in civilization, as his mind becomes developed, and even his animal passions begin to associate themselves with mental activities" (Marshall 1920, p. 86). The ability to satisfy wants depends not only on the characteristics of the individuals within a population, but also on the organization of activities designed to satisfy those wants. For Marshall, "Knowledge is the most powerful engine of production" and "Organization aids knowledge." Thus "it seems best sometimes to reckon Organization apart as a distinct agent of production" (ibid., pp. 138-39). Within the context of Marshall's firm, competitive market forces drive entrepreneurs to combine capital and labor in order to produce a definite quantity of a particular good. Production activity depends not only on a technical set of blueprints, but on the ability of the entrepreneur to create an organization that can effectively identify and utilize the resources required to carry out production, and can respond well to the competitive pressures emanating from the market (Niman 1991). As the firm evolves, it discovers new opportunities that enable the firm to grow and develop. Later, the businessman in charge of it experiences a "decay, if not of his faculties, yet of his liking for energetic work" (Marshall 1920, p. 286) and the firm is ultimately left behind by stronger competitors.

Because firms are created by individuals in order to satisfy wants as determined by the individuals within the population, the means for producing goods and the types of goods chosen to be produced are also determined by biological principles. Thus just as the principle of substitution guides individual decision-making in order to maximize utility, "the law of substitution–which is nothing more than a special and limited application of the law of survival of the fittest–tends to make one method of industrial organization supplant another when it offers a direct and immediate service at a lower price" (ibid., p. 597).

While human beings are organisms governed by biological laws, and economic institutions are created by individuals in order to facilitate the satisfaction of human wants and therefore are subject to the same biological laws, how organizations interact with themselves and human beings is characterized by Marshall not as a biological process, but as a mechanical process. Interaction between individuals and firms within a given population takes place within the confines of the market. Market activity occurs within the context of a given set of wants and a fixed ability to satisfy those wants. The biological factors that lead to the establishment of a particular market position fall to the background as the workings of the market emerge to center stage. The process of exchange and the functioning of the market are not determined by biological principles but rather by physical laws.

IV. SIMPLE AND COMPOUND EVOLUTION

The biological economics of Alfred Marshall does not exclude physical laws from economic activity, it merely acknowledges that the basis for mechanical relationships is located in biological properties of the underlying individuals and organizations. Physical laws coexist with biological properties in a manner consistent with the belief widely held in the nineteenth century of a basic uniformity of nature (Young 1985, p. 123). Marshall's acceptance of this continuity is perhaps best illustrated by the phrase "Natura non facit Saltum." On that view, evolution is a gradual process as conceived by Darwin and before him by Charles Lyell in his uniformitarian geology which rejected the notion of catastrophic earth movements in favor of gradual change (Bowler 1988, p. 23).

Marshall's acceptance of a basic unity found in nature and his subsequent mixing of metaphors is not the result of a desire to mimic the physicist, but rather can be attributed to the influence of Herbert Spencer. Marshall acknowledges the influence of Herbert Spencer in the preface to the first edition of his *Principles*, and Keynes (1924, p. 13) quotes Mary Marshall's account of how her husband would read Spencer during rest stops while hiking in the Alps. Spencer shared the dominant nineteenth century belief in the basic unity of science and offered a theory of evolution that could explain changes in organic and inorganic matter. For Spencer, evolution and dissolution are the dynamic principles that explain the continuous redistribution of matter and motion. Evolution is associated with the integration of matter and concomitant dissipation of motion, while dissolution is the absorption of motion and concomitant disintegration of matter (Spencer 1966, p. 228). In describing the process of evolution, Spencer draws a distinction between simple and compound evolution. Simple evolution prevails when the movement towards integration results in a single redistribution of matter into a coherent whole. Compound evolution occurs when the initial redistribution of matter leads to secondary redistributions. In other words, if evolution proceeds gradually through various stages, at each stage additional forces may come to bear and effect the outcome of the evolutionary process. Whether secondary redistributions occur depends on the quantity of contained motion and the speed by which motion dissipates during the course of evolution.

For Spencer, organic matter tends to unite larger quantities of contained motion with a greater degree of cohesion, and therefore the integration of matter and corresponding loss of motion is better characterized by compound rather than by simple evolution (Spencer 1896, p. 89). During the course of compound evolution, "matter passes from a relatively indefinite, incoherent homogeneity to a relatively definite, coherent heterogeneity; during which process the retained motion undergoes a parallel transformation" (Spencer 1966, p. 321). The distinction between simple and compound evolution reflects Spencer's view that "science concerns itself with the co-existences and sequences among phenomena: grouping these at first into generalizations of a simple or low order, and rising gradually to higher and more extended generalizations" (ibid., p. 103).

A similar pattern can be observed in Marshall's use of biological and mechanical analogies where "there is a fairly close analogy between the earlier stages of economic reasoning and the devices of physical statics," but "in the later stages of economics better analogies are to be got from biology than physics." Consequently, "economic reasoning should start on methods analogous to those of physical statics, and should gradually become more biological in tone" (Marshall 1898, p. 314). As a result, mechanical analogies are found to be suitable by Marshall when articulating the underlying "Foundations" described in a manner characteristic of simple evolution, and biological analogies are reserved for describing higher order generalizations characterized by compound evolution.

Exchange is portrayed by Marshall as an activity where firms having produced a given stock of goods, and consumers with a particular set of preferences, come to a centralized location to trade. Competition acts as a force which directs price movements until an equilibrium is achieved that represents a balance between supply and demand. This activity can be described in terms of simple evolution because the integration of matter (construction of an equilibrium set of prices), and the corresponding dissipation of motion (the exchange of goods), is completed with the creation of a unique set of equilibrium prices. In order to describe the market in terms of simple evolution, Marshall relies on the use of mechanical analogies where the balancing forces correspond "to the mechanical equilibrium of a stone hanging by an elastic string, or of a number of balls resting against one another in a basin" (Marshall 1920, p. 323).

In contrast, Marshall's treatment of the firm utilizes biological analogies to describe a growth and development process that parallels Spencer's description of compound evolution. Firms move from a less coherent to a more coherent form by increasing knowledge in order to improve organization and the efficiency of production. As knowledge increases, the entrepreneur is able to take advantage of internal and external economies that reduce costs and increase profitability. As firms become more successful at exploiting various economies, they become increasingly heterogeneous because no two firms have the same opportunities and therefore do not have equal ability to realize fully all economies.[6] Thus firms, just as the "trees in the forest," vary in terms of their relative success, and industries become populated by a distribution of firms that are successful to varying degrees.[7]

Marshall therefore constructed a theory where economic agents are characterized by biological analogies representing the process of com-

6. Heterogeneity exists for Marshall because "every locality has incidents of its own which affect in various ways the methods of arrangement of every class of business that is carried on in it: and even in the same place and the same trade no two persons pursuing the same aims will adopt exactly the same routes.... Each man's actions are influenced by his special opportunities and resources, as well as by his temperament and his associations" (Marshall 1920, p. 355).

7. For Marshall, the trees in the forest represent an accurate description of the growth of business. As the young trees "struggle upwards through the benumbing shade of their older rivals..., few only survive...; one tree will last longer in full vigor and attain a greater size than another; but sooner or later age tells on them all. Though the taller ones have a better access to light and air than their rivals, they gradually lose vitality; and one after another they give place to others, which, though of less material strength, have on their side the vigour of youth" (Marshall 1920, pp. 315-16).

pound evolution, but engage in exchange activity within the confines of the market and in that respect are characterized by mechanical analogies representing the process of simple evolution. Marshall mixes his metaphors because of a belief that "two things may resemble one another in their initial stages; and a comparison of the two may then by helpful: but after awhile they diverge; and then the comparison begins to confuse and warp the judgment" (Marshall 1898, p. 314). Thus, "in the earlier stages of economics, we think of demand and supply as crude forces pressing against another, and tending towards a mechanical equilibrium; but in the later stages, the balance or equilibrium is conceived not as between crude mechanical forces, but as between the organic forces of life and decay" (ibid., p. 318). The mixing of metaphors where biological agents interact with mechanical markets however creates a serious problem for Marshall. The problem is how to describe the workings of the market in terms of simple evolution when the participants are not themselves simple.

V. MECHANICAL LAWS AND BIOLOGICAL PRINCIPLES

While belief in the uniformity of nature was widely accepted in the nineteenth century, the attempt to integrate physical and biological phenomena proved to be no simple task. In discussing the relationship between Darwin and Isaac Newton, S. Schweber notes that scientists in the nineteenth century attempted to construct universal laws by looking at the dynamical response of the organism (system) in terms of the dynamics of the parts (elements):

> But Darwin recognized that the analogy with gravity broke down at the next level of biological organization. One could not describe the dynamics of a community of organisms simply from the pairwise interaction of the organisms and from interaction of the organisms with the environment. Living systems were infinitely more complicated than Newton's planetary system. Biological "elements" had characteristics that were changing in time: they had history. All of the interactions of organisms whether with one another or with the environment were non-additive, non-instantaneous and exhibited memory. It was the ahistorical nature of the objects with which physics dealt that give the Newtonian scheme the possibility of a simple, mathematical description. It was precisely the *historical* character of living objects which gave biological phenomena their unique and complex features (Schweber 1985, p. 49).

The difficulty characterized by Schweber is not one of integrating statics (physics) and dynamics (biology), but rather how to reconcile two dynamic processes when the elements do not share identical characteristics.

This same fundamental difference between biological and physical elements was recognized by Marshall, and forms the basis for distinctions between mechanical and biological analogies as seen in the following passage:

> But the catastrophes of mechanics are caused by changes in the quantity and not in the character of the forces at work: whereas in life their character changes also. "Progress" or "evolution," industrial and social, is not mere increase and decrease. It is organic growth, chastened and confined and occasionally reversed by the decay of innumerable factors, each of which influences and is influenced by those around it; and every such mutual influence varies with the stages which the respective factors have already reached in their growth. In this vital respect all sciences of life are akin to one another, and are unlike physical sciences (Marshall 1898, p. 317).

Within the context of Marshall's *Principles*, the difficulties encountered in terms of reconciling mechanical laws and biological principles are most pronounced when attempting to construct an industry supply curve. By utilizing the biological metaphor with respect to the firm, Marshall is highlighting the heterogeneous nature of firms resulting from the process of compound evolution. However, this heterogeneity makes it difficult to identify the normal costs of production in an industry, and therefore creates serious difficulties for constructing an industry supply curve (Sraffa, 1926). Without a supply curve, Marshall would be unable to describe how competitive forces lead to an equilibrium between quantity supplied and quantity demanded within the context of simple evolution.

The difficulty Marshall experiences results from his belief that while "the Mecca of the economist lies in economic biology...a volume on Foundations must...give a relatively large place to mechanical analogies" (Marshall 1920, p. xiv). Or perhaps another way to express this is that a volume on foundations should attempt to concentrate as much as possible on the process of simple evolution where matter undergoes only one redistribution, in order to avoid confusing the reader and run the risk of obscuring important underlying principles. However, Marshall's other motives involving professionalization, historicism, moralization, and continuity lead him to stray and attempt to integrate compound evolution in the form of biological principles as much as possible. To resolve the difficulties created by having a "mechanical" market along with a "biological" firm, Marshall must either present a unified theory that incorporates a biological market, or a mechanical firm. A complex conception of the market based on the more advanced notion of compound evolution would have eliminated the problem of inconsistency, but one can only speculate with Laurence Moss (1990) that Marshall's failure to do so was either because Marshall was not capable of developing such a conception of the market, or because he intended to develop such an approach later on, perhaps in his projected volume 2 of his *Principles*.

Rather than following the route requiring a change in how market processes are conceptualized, Marshall chose instead to alter his working concept of the firm. When attempting to apply his theory of the firm in order to construct an industry supply schedule, Marshall realizes that "we cannot then regard the conditions of supply by an individual producer as typical of those which govern the general supply in a market.... [T]hus the history of the individual firm cannot be made into the history of an industry" (Marshall 1920, p. 459). To remedy this problem, Marshall utilizes the representative firm in constructing a supply schedule. A representative firm is an "average firm," one which has had "a fairly long life, and fair success, which is managed with normal ability, and which has normal access to the economies, external and internal, which belong to that aggregate volume of production" (ibid, p. 317). By creating a representative firm, Marshall was able to hold biological factors constant in order to then study how activity is structured within the context of a market governed by physical laws.

VI. THE DISAPPEARANCE OF BIOLOGICAL ECONOMICS

The use of a representative firm in order to more clearly articulate the mechanical processes underlying the creation and distribution of value creates two difficulties. The first arises in defining the concept of equilibrium. In a population where no two firms are the same, it becomes difficult to identify the relevant quantities associated with supply. Uniformity between cost conditions must be identified before a mechanical equilibrium can be established. Marshall avoids this problem by creating a representative firm in order to construct an equilibrium not between actual participants but between representative firms. However, while a representative firm may be in equilibrium, since no firm is the representative firm, actual firms in an industry may not be in equilibrium (Pigou 1928). Thus while the industry may be in equilibrium, individual firms in that industry will only be in equilibrium if they all share the same basic characteristics as the representative firm. The second difficulty exists because, as a population evolves, new characteristics will become prevalent and alter the profile of the representative member of the population. Thus any analysis based on a representative firm must be historically specific and cannot be generalized to all situations at all points in time. Therefore while exchange activity (governed by physical laws) may remain invariant between historical periods, the population will change with respect to preferences, behavior, and actions between periods.

The difficulties created by the use of a representative firm are inherent in a biological approach that is based on the acknowledgement that variation exists within a given population. Rather than preserving the "biological" elements of Marshall's theory, however, the subsequent development of economic theory in the twentieth century rejected the biological metaphor. One possible explanation of why economics rejected biology can be attributed to the state of the biological sciences at the beginning of the twentieth century. Just when the difficulties inherent in Marshall's evolutionary approach to economic theory were being exposed, the genetic revolution that occurred at the turn of the century was thoroughly discrediting the nineteenth century conception of developmental evolution (Bowler 1988, p. 105). Thus Marshallian economics was left without underlying ideological and scientific foundations just at the time when it was itself coming under attack from within the economics profession. With evolutionary theory falling out of favor in the scientific community, a reconstruction of economic theory would have to look toward the other sciences for support in solving the problems confronting Marshallian economics in the 1920s and 1930s. Appealing to biology (a science in turmoil and disrepute) would have limited appeal and a negative impact on maintaining the position of economics in the new scientific order, while an amended framework without the complications of biological factors could be nicely inserted into the physics metaphor. Thus Gerald Shove offers the observation that the movement away from the biological to the mechanical approach can be explained in part as resulting from an "itch for precise results," and "the fact that among the natural sciences physics has once more taken over the lead from biological studies" (Shove 1942, p. 323).

The completion of the Darwinian revolution (the synthesis of genetics and selection) in the 1930s passed by virtually unnoticed by economists, as the development of economic theory focused almost exclusively on the construction of a statical framework based on physical laws. Thus while Marshall made comparisons between the chemist and biologist, Pigou (1922) was interested in comparing mathematicians and physicists. Rather than continuing on the path of attempting to integrate biology into economics, various ideas found in Marshall were modified in order to accommodate mechanics as the 'Mecca' for the economist. Theoretical devices such as the representative firm became equilibrium firms (Pigou 1928), and equilibrium concepts were developed that are no longer consistent with nonhomogeneous economic agents (Moss 1984).

VII. BIOLOGY AND MARSHALL'S ECONOMICS

Marshall acknowledged that biological organisms live within the context of certain physical laws, and attempted to integrate both biological and mechanical analogies into a coherent framework. The approach he adopted acknowledges that while physical laws determine how individuals within the context of the market interact, the individuals themselves are the product of biological principles. Human beings adapt to the physical environment and, as part of the adaptation process, attempt to exert control over the environment through the construction of economic institutions. While these institutions themselves may operate within the context of physical laws, they are defined in terms of the biological organisms that have created them.

Marshall attempted to build an economic theory based on natural science foundations, and it is established here that he relied on both mechanical and biological analogies to express economic principles. The remaining question is whether Marshall felt that the physics and biology metaphors were interchangeable, or whether there existed some other underlying agenda that could explain why one metaphor was utilized to explain certain aspects of Marshall's theoretical framework, and why the other metaphor was employed to explain the remainder. The answer to this question can be discovered by looking at the influence of Herbert Spencer and Marshall's twin goals of, on the one hand, providing a simple framework for presenting the foundations underlying economic theory, and on the other hand, of promoting economics as a distinct course of study that could make meaningful statements about the real world.

Marshall's development of theoretical foundations was constructed within the context of what Spencer would describe as simple evolution. Goods are brought to market, relative prices are established, and an equilibrium is obtained. For expressing the general principles underlying the theory of value, mechanical analogies provided the clearest and simplest expression. A complete discussion of the theory of value for Marshall, however, included a description of the creation of wants and the means for satisfying these wants. The discussion of consumers and firms is carried out not within the framework of simple evolution but rather in terms of compound evolution. Compound evolution is utilized because of the relative complexity found in the description of human wants and productive activities. Insofar as the source of wants and want satisfaction is found in human behavior, it is perhaps understandable why biological rather than mechanical analogies would be appropriate for this context.

Are we therefore able to conclusively determine whether Marshall was a closet physicist, or a self-styled biologist? Marshall can be accused of being a physicist insofar as he attempted to integrate biological economic agents into a mechanistic market framework. However, if Marshall was nothing more than a physicist, then he would not have left the confines of simple evolution when describing economic phenomena. If neoclassical economics represents the appropriation of physics, then Marshall would not have found it necessary to introduce a discussion of want-creation and satisfaction based on the concept of compound evolution. The development of neoclassical economics in the twentieth century has demonstrated that a theory of value can be constructed within the context of a representative firm with a given set of production opportunities and a representative consumer with a given set of preferences. Thus it would not have been necessary for Marshall to enter into an extended discussion of how wants are created and satisfied if his goal was merely to create foundations for economics based on physics.

Marshall's extensive use of the biological metaphor went far beyond the goal of establishing a simple and basic foundation for economic analysis. The biological metaphor assumed importance because it could be used to illustrate

the dynamics underlying the process of compound evolution, a process that closely approximates real economic phenomena. If Marshall is to be found at fault, it is for his failure to conceptualize market processes in terms of compound rather than simple evolution. Marshall failed as a biologist by adopting a conception of markets that necessitated the elimination of biological agents from the framework. If Marshall had rectified this problem by creating a compound conception of market evolution, then biology might have won the day, and the subsequent development of economic analysis might have taken a different turn.

REFERENCES

Bowler, P. 1988. *The Non-Darwinian Revolution*, Johns Hopkins University Press, Baltimore.

Chamberlin, E. 1933. *The Theory of Monopolistic Competition*, Harvard University Press, Cambridge.

Coats, A. W. 1967. "Sociological Aspects of British Economic Thought (CA. 1880-1930)," *Journal of Political Economy*, 75, 706-29.

Dosi, G., C. Freeman, R. Nelson, G. Silverberg, and L. Soete, eds. 1988. *Technical Change and Economic Theory*, Pinter Publishers, London.

Hicks, J. R. and R. G. D. Allen. 1934. "A Reconsideration of the Theory of Value," *Economica*, 1, 52-76, 196-219.

Jones, L. 1989. "Schumpeter versus Darwin: In re Malthus," *Southern Economic Journal*, 56, 410-22.

Keynes, J. M. 1924. "Alfred Marshall," *Economic Journal*, 34, 311-72, reprinted in Pigou 1966.

Kohn, D., ed. 1985. *The Darwinian Heritage*, Princeton University Press, Princeton.

Levine, A. L. 1983. "Marshall's Principles and the 'Biological Viewpoint': A Reconsideration," *The Manchester School*, 3, 276-93.

Levitt, T. 1976. "Alfred Marshall: Victorian Relevance for Modern Economics," *Quarterly Journal of Economics*, 90, 425-44.

Maloney, J. 1985. *Marshall, Orthodoxy and the Professionalisation of Economics*, Cambridge University Press, Cambridge.

Marshall, A. 1885. "The Present Position of Economics," reprinted in Pigou 1966.

______. 1897. "The Old Generation of Economists and the New," reprinted in Pigou 1966.

______. 1898. "Mechanical and Biological Analogies in Economics," reprinted in Pigou 1966.

______. 1920. *Principles of Economics, Eighth Edition*, Macmillan, London.

Mirowski, P. 1984a. "Physics and the 'Marginalist Revolution,'" *Cambridge Journal of Economics*, 8, 361-79.

______. 1984b. "The Role of Conservation Principles in 20th Century Economic Theory," *Philosophy of the Social Sciences*, 14, 461-73.

______. 1989. *More Heat Than Light*, Cambridge University Press, Cambridge.

Moss, L. 1982. "Biological Theory and Technological Entrepreneurship in Marshall's Writings," *Eastern Economic Journal*, 8, 3-13.

______. 1990. "Evolutionary Change and Marshall's Abandoned Second Volume," presented at the Kress Society Seminar.

Moss, S. 1984. "The History of the Theory of the Firm from Marshall to Robinson and Chamberlin: The Source of Positivism in Economics," *Economica*, 51, 307-18.

Nelson, R. and S. Winter. 1982. *An Evolutionary Theory of Economic Change*, Harvard University Press, Cambridge.

Niman, N. 1991. "The Entrepreneurial Function in the Theory of the Firm," *Scottish Journal of Political Economy*, forthcoming.

Pigou, A. C. 1922. "Empty Economic Boxes: A Reply," *Economic Journal*, 32, 458-65.

______. 1928. "An Analysis of Supply," *Economic Journal*, 38, 238-57.

______. 1966. *Memorials of Alfred Marshall*, A. M. Kelly, New York.

Robbins, L. 1928. "The Representative Firm," *Economic Journal*, 38, 387-404.

Robinson, J. 1933. *The Economics of Imperfect Competition*, Cambridge University Press, Cambridge.

Schweber, S. 1980. "Darwin and the Political Economists: Divergence of Character," *Journal of the History of Biology*, 13, 189-195.

______. 1985. "The Wider British Context in Darwin's Theorizing," in D. Kohn, ed. 1985. *The Darwinian Heritage*, Princeton University Press, Princeton.

Shove, H. 1942. "The Place of Marshall's Principles in the Development of Economic Theory," *Economic Journal*, 52, 294-329.

Spencer, H. 1896. *The Principles of Biology*, D. Appleton and Company, New York.

______. 1966. *First Principles. Fourth Edition.* Otto Zeller, Osnabruk.

Sraffa, P. 1926. "The Laws of Returns Under Competitive Conditions," *Economic Journal*, 36, 535-50.

Whitaker, J. 1975. *The Early Economic Writings of Alfred Marshall*, 1867-1890, The Free Press, New York.

Young, R. 1985. *Darwin's Metaphor*, Cambridge University Press, Cambridge.

Methodus December 1991

The Suppression of Evolutionary Approaches in Economics : The Case of Marshall and Monopolistic Competition

Nicolai Juul Foss
(Copenhagen Business School)

> "A discipline, a region of the world of thought should seek *to know itself*. Like the individual human being, it has received from its origins a stamp of character, a native mode of response to the situations confronting it. Right responses, "responsability" will require of the profession as of the individual an insight into the powers and the defects of the tool which history has bequeathed to it" (Shackle 1972, p.24).

Introduction : Evolutionary Approaches in Economics

The inspiration that Charles Darwin is said to have received from Thomas Malthus's work on population questions, as well as from the broadly evolutionary social theorizing of the Scottish Enlightenment, when groping towards the theory of natural selection, is well-known (Jones 1980). He thus continued a tradition of cross-fertilization between the sciences of the biological and the sciences of society that can be said to have started with Bernard Mandeville taking the bee-hive as model of society. And Darwin in his turn was to provide tremendous inspiration for a school of social scientists and moralists, later to be dubbed "social Darwinists". Today this cross-fertilization is alive and well, biologists adopting the social scientists' game-theoretic tools for the analysis of animal conflict, and social scientists turning increasingly towards theories of cultural evolution and showing increasing interest in the provocative works of sociobiologists.

Given the fact that economists were among the early sources of inspiration for the emerging theory of natural selection, and given the fact that competiti in the marketplace has always been something of a paradigmatic example of "struggle for existence", one should perhaps have expected economists to be among the social scientists most enthusiastically adopting results from evolutionary biology and endorsing evolutionary modes of thought. Sifting through the pages of an advanced modern *formal* economic text-book will quickly dispel such expectations, however. One seeks in vain for anything that can properly be said to constitute an evolutionary *model*.

The role reserved for evolutionary reasoning in economics is *methodological*: To provide a justification of the Friedmanite "assumptions-don't-matter"-thesis (Friedman 1953) in a specific context. More precisely, to undergird the notion that in the long run behavioral forms will converge towards maximizing, those forms that failed to do so having been selected out in the process. And aside from methodology, evolutionary reasoning enters economists' explanations almost exclusively in the form of what Nelson/Winter (1982) call "appreciative theory" (as distinct from "formal theory"): The unformalized story-telling that accompany the economist's explanation to the outsider. The sort of explanation, in short, that is the domain of the bread-and-butter-economist, *or* the defender of Friedmanite instrumentalism.

Going back approximately one hundred years in the history of economic doctrines will confirm that such a subordinate role was not always the one allotted to evolutionary reasoning. In a famous article, Thorstein Veblen (1898) castigated contemporary marginalist economics for its supposedly Newtonian slant, calling for an evolutionary economics. As has often been pointed out, he chose the wrong target for his aggressive verbal gymnastics, namely the Austrians, who were certainly the most processual in their theorizing among contemporary marginalists, those who, in other words, could most appropriately be said to have presented rudiments of evolutionary reasoning. What is, furthermore, interesting about the context of Veblen's article is that a work that could in many respects be said to have honored Veblen's call for an evolutionary economics *had* in fact appeared eight years earlier: Alfred Marshall's *Principles of Economics*.

Economic folklore has it, however, that Marshall constructed what has been passed down as price - theory -at least of the "intermediate"specie- virtually from scratch. It is to Marshall that we owe the graphic instrumentarium of basic price theory, with its temporal distinctions, cost curves, etc. In addition to such heuristics, we owe the concept of perfect competition and pure monopoly and their graphic representations to Marshall. And this folklore is often accompanied by the belief that Marshall supplied the explication of cost- and supply-curves to the larger neoclassical edifice, Jevons , Menger and Walras having on the whole neglected the supply side. Over the last two decades, the original marginalists have, however, been "de-homogenized" (Jaffé 1976): It has become increasingly clear that their respective doctrines were different in many dimensions . This paper can be said to extend this de-homogenization somewhat, with particular reference to Alfred Marshall. Our de -homogenization exercise will not contrast Marshall with other contemporary marginalist, however, but rather with later generations' interpretation of Marshall's economics. Focusing on the role of the representative firm in Marshall's theorizing we will obtain an indication of the extent to which evolutionary reasoning can be said to be present in Marshall's work ("*Marshall and the Representative Firm*"). The original Marshallian meaning of the representative firm was to be twisted and transformed in theoretical developments on the British price-theoretical scene in the 1920's and 1930's. And it is precisely in the fate that Marshall's representative firm suffered that we will be able to diagnose one dominant reason why evolutionary reasoning lost the grip it once had in the economics profession.

Recent work on the theory of path-dependency has shown how small early historically events may lock-in a social development course on a potentially suboptimal path, from which it cannot escape except without very high social costs (Arthur 1988 ; David 1985). On the intellectual level, it was precisely small events in the history of economic doctrines - particularly the theory of monopolistic competition - that were responsible for the lock-in of economics (or rather : the theory of the firm)on an intellectual trajectory in which evolutionary reasoning had no role to play ("*Post-Marshallian Developments*"). This lock-in, furthermore, had the effect that important potential explananda for economics - particularly the process of technological change - were for a very long time excluded from the menu of explananda that could legitimately be addressed with economic tools. Or, at least, these explananda could only be addressed with strong affronts to realism. With respect to problem-solving capacity, then, the intellectual standard that was locked-in in the early 'thirties was definitely suboptimal.

Marshall and the Representative Firm

Although Marshall's Victorian admiration for results from the evolutionary biology of his day is a generally acknowledged fact (Jones 1980) -as well as easily confirmed by a cursory reading of *Principles*- the exact status and role of evolutionary reasoning in Marshall's thought is somewhat more controversial. At one extremum of the interpretive spectrum we find Loasby's (1989) claim that Marshall's theorizing was indeed genuinely evolutionary in nature. And at the other end, we confront A.L. Levine's (1980) open irritation over Marshall's "biological folklore", "fantasia" and "near-mystique", all of which finds its "..crescendo in that biological folk-tale which is the lifecycle of the firm " (p.269). Here is one of Marshall's discussions of "that biological folktale" in operation :

> "..the very conditions of an industry which enables a new firm to attain quickly command over new economies of production, render that firm liable to be supplanted quickly by still younger firms with yet newer methods. Especially where the powerful economies of production, on a large scale are associated with the use of new appliances and new methods, a firm which has lost the exceptional energy which enabled it to arise, is likely ere long quickly to decay; and the full life of a firm seldom lasts very long " (Marshall 1925, p.287).

And a little later, we confront the more explicitly "biological" "trees in the forest"-analogy:

> ".. we may read a lesson from the young trees in the forest as they struggle upwards through the benumbing shade of their older rivals. Many succumb on the way, and a few only survive; those few become stronger with every yea, they get a larger share of light and air with every increase of their height, and at last in their turn they tower above their neighbours... One tree will last longer in full vigour and attain a greater size than another; but sooner or later age tells on them all..And as with the growth of trees, so was it with the growth of business as a general rule before the great recent development of vast joint-stock companies, which often stagnate, but do not readily die" (ibid., p.316-316).

Although this imagery has often been ridiculed (e.g. Penrose 1952), a standard interpretation of the theoretical role of Marshall's life-cycle theory of the firm has arisen over the last decades, stemming in essence from Gerald Shove's (1942) centenary article. The background for this interpretation was the "Empty Economic Boxes" - debates on the analytical meaning and empirical significance of Marshall's discussion of returns of scale, sparked off by Clapham (1922), culminating in Sraffa (1926), and continued in the famous "increasing returns-symposium" in *The Economic Journal* 1930. Sraffa pointed out, of course, that competitive equilibrium is totally incompatible with increasing returns. The problem with this - in an exegetical sense - was that Marshall had not postulated horizontal average-revenue-curves, but had nevertheless insisted on analyzing "competition".

Marshall himself had been very well aware of the problem that Sraffa highlighted; 'there is more than one discussion in *Principles* of a firm enjoying increasing returns of scale (e.g. 1925,p.459n). *The* problem for Marshall, however, was to combine increasing returns with some notion of "competition". The rational reconstruction of this "reconciliation exercise" (Levine 1980) usually proceeds in terms of a) external economics, b) Chamberlianian product-differentiation, and c) the life cycle -theory of the firm (Shove 1942).

The point about external economies is easily summarized: By placing the burden of increasing returns on the systemic interaction of groups of firms in networks - generating positive technological externalities - it was possible to maintain that individual firms were characterized by only constant returns to scale (Marshall 1925, p. 284,615), thus preserving "competition". Pigou (1928) gave a rigorous geometrical explication of this aspect of "the reconciliation exercise".

The concept of competition that was adequate to Marshall's intentions was not, in Shove's (1942) interpretation, a "numbers" concept per se. Rather, Marshallian competition is a matter of product differentiation, and Marshallian equilibrium a Chamberlinian "group equilibrium", where the outputs of individual firms are "adapted to special tastes", and therefore "produced on a small scale" (Marshall 1925, p. 357-358), but where ".. the force of advertising keeps many rivals in the field for a long time" (ibid., p. 392).

And then, finally, we have the life cycle-theory of the firm, an idea that in lieu of an economic theory of economic organization - supplying a rationale for the organizational lethargy so essential to Marshall's argument - to later generations of formal economists could only be interpreted as a typical manifestation of that typical Marshallian methodological malady : The ad hoc-elevation of quasi-empirical generalizations to the status of theoretical propositions of significance and depth.

It is clear from the foregoing that what is necessary and analytically permissible within the boundaries marked off by the neoclassical theory of the firm-for a "reconciliation" of increasing returns and "competition" is strictly speaking Chamberlinian product-differentiation only. But this is precisely the conclusion that the theorists of monopolistic competition drew from Sraffa's "abandon the path of free competition and turn in the opposite direction, namely towards monopoly" (1926, p.187). What, then, is new and interesting in the conventional rational reconstruction of Marshall's "reconcialiation" of increasing returns and "competition" ?

A perhaps better understanding of Marshall's intentions may be obtained by interpreting him as a genuinely evolutionary theorist. Here we should remind ourselves of the basic mechanisms of evolutionary change. These are the principle of variation, that members of a population differ with respect to at least one characteristic with selective significance; the principle of heredity, that there exist copying mechanisms to ensure continuity over time in the form of the species under investigation; and the principle of selection, that some forms are better fitted to environmental pressures and thus increase in relative significance.

The illegitimacy of transferring these concepts uncritically to the social domain is well-recognized among economists, who have usually (though not always) guarded their analogues to variation / mutation (innovation), heredity (the firm as a repository of knowledge, imitation of successful behavioral rules), and selection (competitive market selection) (Downie 1958; Winter 1975; Nelson/Winter1982) with strong reservations. Without entering into a detailed discussion of the precise equivalents in Marshall's (or other economists') work to the above mentioned basic evolutionary concepts, we may note that Marshall has at least one clear analogue, namely an analogue to the principle of variation; a concept that underlay his " trees in the forest"- story (which is, of course, a rudimentary selection-story).

Marshall's analogy, then, is his analytical starting point in a concept of the industry that allows variation among firms with respect to the allocation of entrepeneurial competence, cost structure and innovative performance. It is basically the inclusion of this variety that motives that Marshall's concept of industry equilibrium has no room for an equilibrium *firm*; long run industry equilibrium is a matter of equality between aggregate market demand and supply only. There is simply no pretension that individual firms are in equilibrium.

Analytically, this may be represented by a conventional statistical instrumentarium, defining the population of firms in terms of a probability distribution and its characteristic moments (Downie 1958). Marshall's long run-equilibrium is not, however, stationary in terms of the individual firms composing it; organizational birth, sclerosis and death is an integral part of this equilibrium. Marshall's problem was then to reason analytically under such circumstances.

Enter the representative firm. The representative firm was the analytical device that Marshall employed to handle complexity. And to a very large extent it is under the impact of attempts to understand the analytical meaning and significance of this concept - and very much so in the process of transformation that this concept underwent-that the embryonic evolutionary theorizing in Marshall's work was suppressed. Briefly, it was "the new establishment in value theory" (Shackle 1967)-best represented by the theorists of monopolistic competition - which in the course of attempts to give clear meaning to the concept of the representative firm thoroughly twisted this and transformed it into the concept of the uniform equilibrium firm. Furthermore, the industry came to be defined as a collection of totally identical equilibrium firms. And this analytical innovation was totally inconsistent with any meaning that can plausibly be ascribed to an evolutionary conceptualization of market activity. But not only came a change in analytical approach. This change arose in tandem with changes in the explananda that could be addressed with price- theoretical tools. There was a substantial Kuhnian "loss of content": Such Marshallian themes as entrepeneurship, growth of firms, internal organization, etc., became relegated for decades from the universe of discourse of formal economic theory, Strange story, isn't it? Let's see how it happened.

Post-Marshallian Developments : The Elimination of Evolutionary Approaches

The most analytically problematic of the concepts making up the total Marshallian edifice was the supply-curve (Sraffa 1926; Robinson 1933). The difficulties stemming from this concept were basically a manifestation of Marshall's attempt to handle fundamental *variety* among firms, in terms of their products, age, internal organization, innovative capabilities, etc. Since every firm in a given industry at a given point of time was at a particular stage of its life cycle, having acquired "a special market" for its products etc, one could not in general ".. regard the conditions of supply by an individual producer as typical of those which govern the general supply in a market" (Marshall 1925, p.459).

It is this element of variety among firms that motivated the introduction of the representative firm, that firm which has cost of production equal to the industry average in long run equilibrium, is of average size, and earns "normal" profit. The representative firm is a heuristic fiction, not to be found in any given industry, but what exactly is its analytical significance? Is it merely a statistical summary measure? Or does it have analytical significance, as e.g. a device for comparative static analysis, knowledge of the cost structure of the representative firm allowing qualitative predictions about the average industry response when changing e.g. industry demand? This is, as Lionel Robbins (1928) pointed out, unclear.

What *can* be said about the representative firm, however, is that it served as a conceptual bridge between Marshall's dynamic conception of firms and his static industry concept. The total population of firms may be static, individual firms, however, constantly change: "..firms rise and fall, but .. the representative firm remains always of the same size" (Marshall 1925, p. 367).

Marshall's conception of the representative firm became virtually eliminated by two articles published in the same year, Robbins (1928) and Pigou (1928). Robbins pointed out, as mentioned, the unclear analytical status of the representative firm. But more fundamentally, he made clear that (general) equilibrium was not inconsistent with variety among firms. The obvious implication - which Robbins did not, however, made - was that Marshall's long run-equilibrium was an equilibrium composed of equilibrium firms.

Pigou (1928) came closer to this. He made clear that for the purposes of comparative static analysis, Marshall's analytical starting point in a population of heterogenous disequilibrium firms - a "state of things the direct study of which would be highly complicated" (ibid., p.239) - was strictly speaking totally unnecessary. In order to understand this "state of things" it was necessary to make references to individual firms preceding histories of innovation, their preceding strategic interaction, the allocation of entrepreneurial competence in the population of managers etc. Pigou insisted on the possibility - and desirability - of eliminating this analytical complexity. For there is "a way round" ;In long run- equilibrium, the contraction and expansion of firms will "net out" on the aggregate level - this, after all, is one obvious interpretation of the representative firm. And application of Occam's razor dictates that for the purpose of constructing a industry supply-curve, variation in the population of firms is *irrelevant*. This

> ".. gives warrant for the conception of what I shall call the *equilibrium firm*. It implies that there *can* exist some firm, which, whenever the industry as a whole is in equilibrium... will itself also individually be in equilibrium" (ibid., p.240).

The specific significance of "the equilibrium firm", the firm which sets price equal to marginal cost, was that this construction allowed Pigou to graphically explicate marginal - and average cost-curves - derived, in today's language , from the expansion path of the production function for given factor prices and with technology stationary - in the illustration of "internal" and "external" economies and their relative weight. And this allowed Pigou to formulate a partial response to Sraffa's attack on Marshall: By maintaining that the equilibrium firm produced on its minimum efficient scale, all "economies" had to be "external".

But Pigou's contribution was to acquire a much wider significance than being limited to merely a contribution to internal Marshallian discussions. First, Pigou gave economics the conceptualization of the firm as *a production function*; Pigou (1928) is the first contribution to economic theory in which the firm is identified with a U- formed average cost-curve and the derived marginal cost-curve (Moss 1984, p.312). And on the basis of this, Pigou was able to take an important step forward in the axiomization of market theory: Never before had long run-equilibrium been defined as equality between price, marginal and average cost.

Second, with his introduction of the equilibrium firm, Pigou took an important step towards the definitive distortion of Marshall's concept of the representative firm : The identification of the representative firm with an arbitrary firm selected from a population of uniform firms postulated in the work of Robinson (1933) and Chamberlin (1933). The " historical" aspect of Marshall's representative firm - a miniature portrait of the dynamic developments in an industry - began to be lost with the introduction of the equilibrium firm . The significance of firms, organizational and technical trajectories for the understanding of their contemporary activities became increasingly neglected; the ahistorical firm began to become a reality.

Third, Pigou's contribution introduced an explanatory innovation that was wholly complementary to the above-mentioned ones : Pigou was the first to subsume *the theory of the firm* under the methodical approach that Spiro Latsis has dubbed "*single exit situational determinism*". Latsis (1976b) presented a general characteristic of this approach to social-scientific explanation:

> "Some behavior may be said to be predominantly artificial ..in the following sense : it can be understood in terms of an organism seeking a conventional goal and adapting to a largely "man-made" environment. The burden of explanation is in such cases born by the description of the artificial environment and there is almost no reference to the structure and properties of the behaving organism . The point about single-exit situations is that we need to know little if anything about the behaving organism's inner structure and organisation" (p.58).

Pigou's derivation of cost curves from the expansion path of the production function may be regarded as a manifestation of "single exit situational determinism": Holding technology and relative prices fixed, it is industry levels (and changes) of demand that determine cost minimizing factor utilization and demand. And changes in the positioning of cost curves are not the result of the firm's own action; rather, they derive from "external economies", contrasting strongly with Marshall's emphasis on the firm's cost-reducing incremental process-innovations, carried through by energetic entrepreneur/managers.

It is, however, the theory of monopolistic competition which ultimately instituted the equilibrium firm with its accompanying assumptions in economic theory; Pigou never went so far as to operate with a population of identical firms. *And it is not until the advent of the theory of monopolistic competition that we can meaningfully talk about a neoclassical theory of firm behavior*. It is decidedly not the case - as Spiro Latsis (1976a) implicitly assumes in his methodological discussion of the significance of the theory of monopolistic competition-that the theory of perfect competition was well-developed before the theory of monopolistic competition. On the very contrary, these two theories were to a large extent a simultaneous analytical innovation. In my interpretation of the development of the neoclassical theory of the firm, Pigou's and others' preceding contributions are best thought of as contributions "hardening" (cf . Weintraub 1984 on the "hardening"of general equilibrium theory) the neoclassical program in the context of the theory of the firm, Robinson and Chamberlin being the ones who finally succeeded in establishing a full-blown neoclassical theory of the firm. How did this come about?

First of all, Chamberlin and Robinson gave the representative firm a very strange twist. A Robinsonian firm, for instance,

> ".. is always in equilibrium.. [and].. firms are alike in respect of their costs and the conditions of demand for their individual outputs. Since we have assumed that all firms are alike, each must be supposed to act

in the same way, so that a single price always rules throughout the whole market" (Robinson 1932, p544-546).

This made possible a new interpretation of the industry, one that turned Marshall completely on his head: Instead of defining an industry relative to products produced, an industry came to mean a collection of firms with identical technology and cost-structures. And of course, with every firm confronted with a falling demand curve, and the names of firms entering into the utility - functions of households, there simply was nothing except costs left to define an industry (Shackle 1967, p.49)

The problem-situation from which Robinson's work emerged is briefly summed up by herself: "..the chief aim of this book is to carry out [Sraffa's] pregnant suggestion that the whole theory of value should be treated in terms of monopoly analysis" (1933,p.XIII). Retrospectively, Robinson saw the Depression as an important external stimulus for her following Sraffa's "pregnant suggestion":

"The notion that every firm is facing a falling demand curve for its own product and that profits are maximized at the output for which marginal revenue is equal to marginal cost, provided an explanation for a situation in which firms could work their plants at less than full capacity and still earn a profit" (1933[1969],p.VI).

This "situation", in contrast , was a Kuhnian anomaly for what Robinson took to be the theory of perfect competition. It is not surprising, then, that "The Economics of Imperfect Competition" excels in polemics against the descriptive realism of perfect competition. What is astonishing, however, is that this polemic is *anonymous*; perfect competition is attributed "older text-books" (Robinsin 1933, p.3) without any references.

Which may these "older textbooks" be? This is a puzzle, since the perfect competition model as we know it (which is almost identical to Robinson's conception) is simply not to be found in any textbook before Robinson (1933) (consult for corrobating overviews. Dennis 1977 and Stigler 1957). Robinson's introduction to the second edition of Robinson (1933) gives us a clue, however; for here it is Pigou who is attributed perfect competition's "neat, logical system (p. V)". And it was Pigou, as we have seen, who took some very important steps toward the conception of the neoclassical firm. We seem thus to led toward the following observation : It was the theorists of monopolistic competition who supplied the neoclassical theory of the firm with its Kuhnian exemplar, the theory of firm behavior under perfect competition. In the process of polemizing against perfect competition, Chamberlin and Robinson constructed their own target, bringing together hitherto dispersed elements - e.g. full mobility (J.M.Clark , Knight), perfect information (Knight) the equilibrium firm (Pigou) firms as price-takers (Pigou), etc. - under a rigorous geometrical treatment. A comparative survey over the situational constraints that firms confront in this theory may argue my case a bit more comprehensively:

1. *Independence of actions* (parametric rationality, price-taking): "*Perfect competition* prevails when the demand for the output of each producer is perfectly elastic" (Robinson 1933, p.18). This is *not* in Marshall.
2. *Complete relevant knowledge*: "..each firm is always in equilibrium" (Robinson 1932, p.544). This is *not* in Marshall.
3. *Free entry/exit*: Totally free entry/exit is *not* in Marshall. Robinson's (1933, p. 93-94) discussion clearly implies the necessity of this assumption for her results.
4 .*Homogenous products* : "An *industry* is any group of firms producing a single commodity" (ibid., p.17). Totally homogenous commodities are *not* in Marshall, who reserved the specific industry-definition for the relevant problem-situation of the analyst.
5. Large number of producers: ".. the number of sellers is large so that the output of any one seller is a negligibly small proportion of the total output" (ibid.). This *is* in Marshall, although Marshall does not seem to have associated this with price-taking.

And these situational constraints were of course wedded to the fundamental behavioral assumption of neoclassical economics in the context of the firm, the notion of profit maximization.Thus arose the neoclassical program in the context of the theory of the firm. This is what motivates Shackle's(1967, p.11) somewhat surprising attribution to Robinson of "a new invention, the theory of the firm". Surely, it would be much more correct to say that Robinson was instrumental in demolishing what existed of a theory of the firm proper in English economic thought. Her contribution (and Chamberlin's) was an important step toward the axiomization of the theory of *markets*, not firms.

It is now easy to see how , why and when the embryonic evolutionary conceptualization of firms and markets that was present in Marshall's thought was swept in the dustbin. With the introduction and subsequent institutionalization of the *ahistorical, fully adapted, uniform equilibrium* firm in economic theory, there could be absolutely *no* scope for appeal to evolutionary reasoning within the theory of the firm. There could be no variety (no trees in the forest), no "heredity" (in the Marshallian sense of the firm as a repository of changing knowledge), and no competitive market selection (no trees/firms "succumbing on the way"). The Marshallian evolutionary insights were completely lost, and Marshall was subsequently attributed models, he would have regarded as "scientific toy[s] rather than engines for practical work" (Marshall 1925, p.460). Only equilibrium states and perfect adaptation remained.

Following Sraffa's "pregnant suggestion", Robinson had set up the wrong problem for herself: The choice was not between partial versus general equilibrium per se, but between partial and general *equilibrium* analysis on the one hand, and firm growth, disequilibrium, competitive struggle etc. on the other.

Concluding Reflections

The episode described in the preceding pages is of course only one manifestation of the consequences of neoclassical economics taking hold of the economics profession, albeit one of the more illustrative ones: "The years of high theory" (Shackle 1967) generally marked the suppression of evolutionary approaches in economics. For the full story, the introduction of general equilibrium theory in the Anglo-Saxon community of economists following Hicks and Allen's work in consumer theory, the theory of market socialism etc., had to be taken into account. However, the preceding pages allow us to see that the suppression of evolutionary approaches in economics was more than merely a matter of increasing abstraction of theoretical concepts (e.g. the firm).

Briefly, the happenings in the nineteen thirties implied a change in *economic epistemics*: Whereas Marshall's agents had been ill-informed and fallible, the agents of neoclassical formalism were fully informed about all the relevant aspects of their problem-situations. The evolutionary framework embryonically present in Marshall's thought conceptually allowed the analyst to operate with a broad menu of behavioral assumptions, e.g. entrepreneurial creativity, rule-follwing etc. In neoclassical formalism, the only behavioral assumption left was maximizing. And since these maximizers were fully informed, it was possible to put forward propositions about aggregate outcomes from the analysis of single ("representative") agents; the explanatory procedure pioneered by Robinson (1933). In other words: The change in economic epistemics brought with it a change in the modes of explanations applied by economists. Replacing evolutionary modes of explanations (e.g. explicit invisible hand-explanations) were intentionalistic modes of explanation, where the notion of unintended outcomes became almost lost from the picture (as in modern rational expectations methodology).

All this was fundamentally a matter of the exclusion of *variety*: variety in terms of decision procedures followed by economic agents, knowledge held, internal organization, performance in the market place etc. It was only with Armen Alchian's (1950) famous and provocative paper, "Uncertainty, Evolution and Economic Theory", that the economic consequences of variety began to be systematically explored anew. Today, a new corpus of evolutionary economic theory (Nelson /Winter 1982 ; Dosi et al. 1988), strongly inspired by Alchian's paper, is rapidly expanding. The patron saint of this expanding corpus is Joseph Schumpeter. This paper suggests that Alfred Marshall is just as appropriate a patron saint for the new evolutionary economics-at least in the context of the theory of the firm.

References

Alchian, A.A. (1950) : "Uncertainty, Evolution and Economic Theory." In idem. (1979) : *Economic Forces at Work*. Indianapolis: Liberty Press.

Arthur, W.B. (1988): "Competing Technologies: An overview." In *Dosi et al.* (1988).

Chamberlin, E.H. (1933): *The Theory of Monopolistic Competition*. 8th ed. 1966. Cambridge, Mass.: Harvard University Press.

Clapham, J.H. (1922): "Of Empty Economic Boxes." *Economic Journal 32*: 305-314.

David, P.A. (1987): "Clio and the Economics of QWERTY." *American Economic Review 75*: 332-337.

Dennis, K.G. (1977): *"Competition" in the History of Economic Thought*. New York: Arno Press.

Dosi, G./C. Freeman/R.R. Nelson/G. Silverberg/L. Soete (eds.) (1988): *Technical Change and Economic Theory*. London: Pinter.

Downie, J. (1958): *The Competitive Process*. London: Macmillan.

Enke, S. (1951): "On Maximizing Profits: A Distinction Between Chamberlin and Robinson." *American Economic Review 51*: 566-578.

Friedman, M. (1953): "The Methodology of Positive Economics." In idem. (1953): *Essays in Positive Economics*. Chicago: University of Chicago Press.

Jaffe, W. (1976): "Jevons, Menger, and Walras De-Homogenized." *Economic Inquiry 14*: 511-524.

Jones , G. (1980) : *Social Darwinism and English Thought*. Brighton: Harvester Press.

Kamien, M.I/N.L. Schwartz (1982)K. : *Market Structure and Innovation*. Cambridge: Cambridge University Press.

Latsis, S. (1976a) : "A Research Program in Economics." In idem. (ed.) (1976) : *Method and Appraisal in Economics*. Cambridge: Cambridge University Press.

Latsis, S. (1976b) : "The Limitations of Single-Exit Models." *British Journal for the Philosophy of Science* 27: 51-60.

Levine, A.L. (1980): "Increasing Returns, the Competitive Model and the Enigma that was Alfred Marshall." *Scottish Journal of Political Economy* 27 : 260-275.

Loasby, B.J. (1989) : *The Minds and Methods of*

Economists.Cambridge: Cambridge University Press.
Marshall, A. (1925) : *Principles of Economics*. 8th ed. London: Macmillan.
Metcalfe, S. (1989) : "Evolution and Economic Change." In Silberston, A. (ed.) (1989) : *Technology and Economic Progress*. London: Macmillan.
Nelson, R.R./S.G. Winter (1982) : *An Evolutionary Theory of Economic Change*. Cambridge, Mass.: Bellknap Press.
Penrose, E.T. (1952) : "Biological Analogies in the Theory of the Firm." American Economic Review 52: 804-819.
Penrose, E.T. (1959) : *The Theory of the Growth of the Firm*. Oxford: Oxford University Press.
Pigou, A.C. (1928) : "An Analysis of Supply." *Economic Journal 38*: 238-257.
Robbins, L. (1928) : "The Representative Firm." *Economic Journal 38*: 387-404.
Robinson, J. (1932) : "Imperfect Competition and Falling Supply Price." *Economic Journal 42:* 544-554.
Robinson, J. (1933) : *The Economics of Imperfect Competiton*.2nd ed. 1969. London: Macmillan.
Schumpeter, J.A. (1934) : *The Theory of Economic Development*. Cambridge, Mass.: Harvard University Press.
Shackle, G.L.S. (1967) : *The Years of High Theory*. Cambridge: Cambridge University Press.
Shackle, G.L.S. (1972) : *Epistemics and Economics*. Cambridge: Cambridge University Press.
Shove, G. (1942) : "The Place of Marshall's Principles in the Development of Economic Theory." In Wood,J.C. (ed.) (1982) : *Alfred Marshall: Critical Assessments*. London: Croom Helm.
Sraffa, P. (1926) : "The Laws of Return under Competitive Conditions." In Stigler, G.J./K.E. Boulding (eds.) (1952) : *Readings in Price Theory*. Homewood: Irwin.
Stigler, G.J. (1957) : "Perfect Competiton Historically Contemplated." In idem. (1965) : *Essays in the History of Economics*. Chicago: University of Chicago Press.
Veblen, T. (1898) : "Why is Economics not an Evolutionary Science ?" *Quarterly Journal of Economics 12*: 373-397.
Weintraub, E.R. (1984) : *General Equilibrium Theory : Studies in Appraisal*. Cambridge: Cambridge University Press.
Winter, S.G. (1975) : " Optimization and Evolution in the Theory of the Firm." In Day, R.H./T. Groves (eds.) (1975) : *Adaptive Economic Models*. New York : Academic Press.

[18]

Solving Marshall's Problem with the Biological Analogy: Jack Downie's Competitive Process

John Nightingale*

Abstract:

The paper suggests that Marshall's text failed to explore the questions that naturally arose out of the 'biological analogy' that he was so strongly advocating. Instead, his mathematical background, and the already existing tradition of focussing on determination of market price and output, led him to the diagrams and mathematics of the footnotes and the Mathematical Appendix to make analytical sense of the story that he was telling. In essence, his theory of the firm, biological in nature, was left hanging in the air, without a solid analytical link to the market theory.

It was left to Andrews, following MacGregor, to elaborate a theory of price to go with Marshall's text, while it was Downie who took this framework of 'realistic' analysis (which for some reason he did not acknowledge as Andrews') to devise a theory of market process that relied on diversity and discontinuity for economic progress. It was Downie, in direct line from Marshall, who found the link between the theory of the firm and the market process that Marshall lacked, and that current authors now elaborate.

Marshall's *Principles of Economics* and Tension Between the Biological and the Mechanical Analogy.

Alfred Marshall was the first notable writer to give the firm a central place in theory, as Philip Williams (1978) so clearly demonstrated. He went beyond merely discussing the role of the entrepreneur, analysing the 'representative firm' in detail, its origin, its supply function, its growth and decline. Moreover, he popularised the tools of analysis that were to become the fundamentals of neoclassical theory. The internal consistency of his theory has long been a matter of controversy[1]. The very purpose of having an explicit theory of the firm also gives rise to question. Is his theory of the firm a necessary prerequisite for his theory of market and industry performance? Or is it really an irrelevancy, institutional padding to make the 'real' theory more palatable, easier to assimilate? Any thoroughgoing neoclassical economist would have to consider the latter very seriously indeed.

The fundamental shape of modern neoclassical partial equilibrium microeconomics was set by Marshall's work. Not only did he write at length of the analysis of all the problems of production and its distribution, he also presented diagrammatically the most important elements as footnotes to his text, and he set out their mathematical foundations in a concise appendix (pp.838-858 of the eighth edition and the Variorum).

The problem he created for later theorists was that his text espoused one theory while his graphical and mathematical notes required another. This inconsistency, seized upon by Paul Samuelson (Samuelson, 1967), and struggled with by scholars such as O'Brien and Loasby (eg. O'Brien, 1987, Loasby, 1989 & 1991), may have a resolution in the work of Jack Downie. Downie was educated at Oxford in the Marshallian tradition, imbibed the Cambridge economics of Joan Robinson, and rejected the latter to replace it with his own synthesis which, had it been taken more seriously as theory, could have led to a more progressive microeconomics of markets some 30 years earlier than is now emerging in the schools of evolutionary institutionalists and post-Schumpeterians. The central concept that gave Downie a key to the problem was that of diversity of firms, the driving force that leads markets' performance and structure in an ever changing pattern of, in Downie's view, progress.

The Darwinian World of the Firm in Marshall's Text.

Marshall explicitly built his theory on what he called "economic biology" (p.xiv). "...the central idea of economics, even when its Foundations alone are under discussion, must be that of living force and movement" (p.xv). The conclusion to Book IV, its chapter XIII, is the clearest statement of the economic biology of the firm. He gives a biographical history of the firm (pp.315-7), using the unincorporated firm as his norm. Central to his history is the ability of the undertaker or owner-manager and this person's goals in his (not her) business life. However, he does not neglect the joint-stock company. This he sees as being liable to stagnate rather than die. The reasons are what we would now call agency problems. The older and larger firm will have so lost "its elasticity and progressive force, that the advantages are no longer exclusively on its side in its competition with younger and smaller rivals" (p.316).

The biographical history of the firm:

> an able man gets a firm footing in the trade; he works hard, lives sparely, his own capital grows fast, etc; as the scale of his business increases, so do the advantages which he has over his competitors, this lowers the price at which he can afford to sell[2].
>
> This process may go on as long as his energy and enterprise, his inventive and organising power retain their full strength and freshness, and as long as the risks which are inseparable from business do not cause him exceptional losses; and if it could endure for a hundred years, he and one or two others like him would divide between them the whole of that branch of industry in which he in engaged.
>
> Here follows the parable of the trees of the forest as they struggle upwards through the benumbing shade of their older rivals (from pp.315-7).

Brian Loasby (1989) explores Marshall's methods and the context of his *Principles*. He sees Marshall as attempting something quite different from that which his orthodox successors imagined. He was not articulating a theory of value for the sake of determining the nature and conditions for equilibrium. He was setting out a theory of progress, in the tradition of Smith (Loasby, op cit, pp.48, 51-7). The terms he used were both those common to the then new neoclassical school of Walras, Jevons and so on, and innovative, in which case they were taken over by that school in the early part of this century. For this reason the story Marshall told was a mixture of real examples and theoretical analysis and of less rigour and elegance than the stories developed by the neoclassicals. In particular Loasby demonstrates Marshall's use of these concepts, showing that the modern usage is narrower, and often inconsistent (Internal and external economies, pp.57-60). Loasby does not labour Marshall's use of biological analogy, but he sees clearly the connection between Marshall's ideas and those of the modern evolutionary theorists (p.56). Moreover, Loasby argues that Marshall's industries were not the perfect competition constructs of the later theorists but were instead the competitive but oligopolistic industries whose analysis was later developed by both Andrews and Downie. The problems perceived by writers such as Samuelson, problems of failing to follow analysis to logical conclusions, asserting the importance of increasing returns in competitive industries, and so on (p.48), were then the product of errors of interpretation (pp.63-68). Their errors stemmed from the use which Marshall made of the mechanical analogy and of the equilibrium concept within that analogy.

Hodgson (1992, pp.6-8) argues that Marshall's biological analogy did not draw mainly from the influence of Darwin, but rather from Herbert Spencer. Spencer's version of biological thought, in Hodgson's view, is reductive and atomistic rather than 'organic', emphasising the typical or ideal and not the individual differences that Darwin's selection theory required. The representative firm concept, in Hodgson's view a Spencerian concept, avoids the central ideas of diversity of members of a population. Instead its focus is on the typical characteristics of the entity. Thus, on this argument, the use Marshall made of the biological analogy was crippled by the perspective from which he approached it. The small place accorded to diversity as a concept of theoretical importance is evidence of Marshall's leaning toward Spencer in his *Principles*[3]. Despite this, Marshall saw Darwin and his principle of gradual change as sufficiently important to make it his motto for the *Principles*.

The Mechanical Analogy of the Footnote Diagrams and Mathematical Appendix.

This is the theory with which we are familiar, the demand curve facing the industry, the supply curves, supply price, equilibrium price and output of the firm, internal and external economies of scale (the latter in post Pigovian writing is not quite what Marshall had in mind, but is something relentlessly logical instead[4]), all these and more were developed and presented as the means of expressing his ideas in precise form.

It is not the case that the mechanical analogy is confined to these places, there are many parts of the text where his exposition is essentially of the mechanical kind. He apologises for using mechanics rather than biology, excusing this as being due to his inability to use the latter. The Preface to the Eighth Edition makes this point plainly (p.xiv). An example is in his use of the idea of equilibrium which he singles out for attention as suggesting mechanics rather than biology: demand price = supply price. Marginal utility analysis and the aggregation of individual demands into market demand with no consideration of the possibility of interdependence of demands is another. Normal supply price is defined as a representation of the real cost of production, analysed into the efforts and sacrifices required to make the good being supplied (p.347). His discussion of the principle of substitution suggests the businessman carrying through mechanical calculations (Bk V, Ch IV).

On the other hand, he uses the biological analogy explicitly and implicitly when presenting historical analysis or the 'stylised facts' of some market or other institution of the economy. A good example is in Bk IV, Ch XII, § 5- § 12 where he discusses the development of business management in the alternative legal structures that have evolved to cope with differences in scale of operation. But this discussion ends with an analysis of the supply price of business ability which forces his analysis to focus on an equilibrating process in which this supply accommodates to the demand for it (p.313). It can be argued that Marshall's theoretical purpose is not clear. Is he intending to create a theory of market equilibrium or is he creating a theory of the firm in the market?

It is the former which captured the attention of his successors. The Pigovian synthesis took his market analysis and imposed a logic upon it, yielding neoclassical partial equilibrium theory as we know it today. It is the latter which the post Marshallian[5] writers attend to, emphasising the population dynamics of firms supplying a market. In this their links are to classical economics, of production and growth, rather than to the economics of exchange which neoclassical theory develops.

It is argued here that Marshall himself was consciously or unconsciously, attending to what are now two different research programmes. The one was what became the neoclassical programme, in which the focus of attention was on equilibrium price and output, on the market outcomes that can be observed, daily in the case of the produce markets. The other, what is the now burgeoning field of economic population dynamics, cried out for a focus on the evolution of market structures and performance outcomes. The biologists did not seek mainly to set down conditions for equilibrium population size, density etc, but instead tried to explain the emergence of differentiated species and their co-existence. In the same way the biological analogy used so enthusiastically by Marshall should have been the vehicle for the analysis of the rise and decline of firms within markets and industries, thereby explaining the progress of prices and outputs over time, and the obvious diversities within industries and how they lead to progress or decline. His inability to use biological analogy was not due to lack of logical and mathematical skills in analysis, it was due to attention being focussed on inappropriate theoretical goals, the goals of explaining equilibrium, its stability, and what became comparative statics. These goals are discussed in Clark & Juma (1988, pp.45-50), and also in Hammond (1991).

Marshall believed that both the mechanical and the biological analogies were useful and valid in their right place. What might be thought strange is that he found the notion of analogy so powerful in focussing theoretical development. Rather than inducing theory from the phenomena at hand he appeared to seek analogies with other scientific fields, and use their analyses. This was not an unusual feature of 19th century science (Clark & Juma, pp.203-6 for a discussion of the power of Cartesian/Newtonian mechanics in the thought of 19th century economists), nor of contemporary science, and perhaps reflects a faith in reductionism, and in the hierarchy of science, from physics at the top, to social sciences somewhere near the bottom.

Selection 14 of Pigou's *Memorials of Alfred Marshall* (1925) is "Mechanical and Biological Analogies in Economics". In this piece Marshall explores the limits of the mechanical analogy in coping with dynamics, concluding "Thus, then, dynamical solutions, in the physical sense, of economic problems are unattainable... It has been well said that analogies may help one into the saddle, but are encumbrances on a long journey... (I)s there...(a) serviceable analogy between the later stages of economic reasoning and the methods of physical dynamics? I think not. I think that in the later stages of economics better analogies are to be got from biology than from physics; and consequently... economic reasoning... should gradually become more biological in tone" (*Memorials*, pp.313-4). That being said, the substance of this little paper was directed at the use of the mechanical analogy, while noting both early in the paper (as quoted) and late in it, that the biological analogy would become necessary. The impression still remains, after taking this paper into account, that Marshall did not know how to employ that analogy beyond the exposition in Book IV of industrial organisation (see Book V, Ch 1, § 1). He wanted to journey to the Mecca of the biologist, but was unable to make that journey himself, hoping that those who followed would do so. The concept of equilibrium, whether in its mechanical or its Spencerian manifestation, held too strong a sway with him, and with those who followed[6].

Post-Marshallian Economists, and their Attempts to Keep Alive the Essence of Marshall's Text.

The post-Marshallians can be defined as those who held back from Pigou and Robinson in their logical extensions to Marshall's partial equilibrium analysis. Perhaps the most notable post-Marshallian was Philip Andrews, a man who saw himself as retrieving the real essence of Marshall from the depredations of the Pigovians. The clearest statement of Andrews' purpose is to be found in "Industrial Analysis in Economics" (1951). His task here was to show that the concept of industry as Marshall had used it was important to empirical work in industrial economics. Andrews had been educated in the modern Cambridge theories of monopolistic competition, in the 'microequilibrium' method, but had been forced to devise his own theory of the individual business and to then find that Marshall's theory of the competitive industry became of immediate and clear relevance to his own. "...(I)t was now possible to think consistently in terms of individual business, whereas Marshall did not push individual analysis beyond a few limited generalisations. The theory of the equilibrium of a competitive industry as presented by Marshall seemed meanwhile to take on the firmness which it must have had for him" (ibid, p141). Andrews defends Marshall's abstraction that suggested to the Pigovians that competition implied identical products by arguing that his long run price was the only requirement of the 'competitive market', that firms in such markets were never thought to be in a situation to sell any quantity at that price, and that reference to particular industries and his 'realistic asides' (p.143) was indication that industries consisted of firms selling non-identical products, and indeed, any firm would typically be selling many products (ibid). The subsequent neglect of this aspect stemmed from failure to appreciate Marshall's concepts of industry and market, one which Andrews saw as central. "The Marshallian industry will consist of businesses with a sufficiently common technical equipment, knowledge, experience, &s., for them to be able to turn over to making any 'range' of the given commodity or any of the particular commodities within the 'range'. Further, the business men can be assumed to be sufficiently 'in' the general market to be aware of the prices secured by producers of other types of commodities within the market" (pp.143-4).[7]

His *Manufacturing Business* (1949) takes themes familiar from Marshall and gives them an elaborate alternative price and market theory, based on the method of Marshall's text. In his later work, *On Competition in Economic Theory* (1964) he presented a detailed critique of the Pigovian system, and showed that his alternative was capable of dealing with all the orthodox questions, albeit without the formal elegance of the neoclassical models. Andrews did not, however, use biological analogies explicitly[8]. He did not mention them. Nor did he use any type of evolutionary dynamics to explain the time paths of industry structure or performance. The references for his theory were in the language of the world of manufacturing business as he knew it in England of the 1930s and 40s. Andrews integrated into economic theory the concepts of margin of profit, mark up over direct cost and full (more correctly, normal) cost pricing. He also gave the concept of cross entry, entry from adjacent industries, which were later developed in an explicitly neoclassical style by Baumol, Panzar and Willig, in their *Contestable Markets and Industrial Structure* (1982)[9]. The influence of these ideas was not as direct as he would have wished, but the use of the cost concepts in aggregative theories is now widespread, due to the simplicity and tractability of the mathematics of mark ups, and to their power to yield good predictions in macro models.

The major effort that Andrews made was directed against the notion of microequilibrium, the insistence that each and every firm be identical, and in equilibrium, before equilibrium of the industry could obtain. This effort took the larger part of *On Competition...* . His argument ran along the lines that Marshall had put forward 70 years previously, that firms were unique entities, possessing commonalities from common techniques of production, or, less importantly, common markets. The analysis upon which he embarked was essentially a refinement of Marshall's *Principles* and *Industry and Trade,* using the representative firm concept to bring back the determinate price and output. However, instead of supply curves dependent on marginal decisions, as in Marshall, he had normal costings and a vaguely defined competitive pressure (presumably on returns on funds invested) setting the costing margin that was able to be established within the industry. Andrews' theory accounted for observed changes from exogenous shocks, from cyclical or random fluctuations of demand, but in the static sense of setting the new equilibrium, for the industry, but not for the firm. Andrews' attack was on microequilibrium, not on the notion of equilibrium itself. Change and technical progress in particular remained outside Andrews' analysis. This was despite his own claim that differences in efficiency were the essence of competition "on any dynamic view" (p.145). While he laid open the processes of pricing and choice of product and market within the industrial culture of early to mid 20th century England, he did not go the further step to explore the dynamics of the processes. Instead, he saw innovation as "unsystematic" (ibid), relevant to the businesses doing the innovating, but not to the general picture of the industry. In other words, Andrews followed Marshall in failing to see the full significance of diversity within the population of firms in his industries, failed to see that diversity itself was the source of change in performance and structure of industries, the source of the secular fall of real costs and prices of especially manufactured goods.

It fell to Jack Downie to show that diversity was the engine driving the competitive system, and that population dynamics opened a new set of questions to explanation. In his one contribution to economic theory, a major but neglected one, Downie developed a model of industry (in the Andrews' sense of firms with a common technical capacity to produce) behaviour and performance. In this model it was precisely the differences between firms that drove the system through time. The industry then was seen to be following an evolutionary pathway, punctuated by revolutionary shocks of innovation whose origin was endogenous, though stochastic in timing and identity.

His model has many thoroughly contemporary insights. Examples to be explored include his notion that there needs to be 'grit in the system' to allow profit seekers to expect to enjoy benefits from a venture before they are competed away; the path dependence of his industries' history and 'destiny'; its non-ergodic nature in that a small change such as a firm's successful innovative effort can transform its industry, changing the time path of industry price, output and market structure[10].

Downie's book, *The Competitive Process* (1958) was written while he was at the Oxford Institute of Statistics, on leave from the Treasury where he spent almost the whole of his working life. His work was explicitly on the question of reform of monopoly and restrictive practices law, an exploration of the significance of the 'rules of the game' as he called them, for the efficacy of competition. This work was apparently quite different from his Treasury tasks, which in the latter part of his short career were monetary policy questions, and, from 1961, at the OECD where he was assistant secretary general in charge of the department of economics and statistics (*The Times*, Aug 13, 1963, p12)[11]. Apart from the book, his only other publication of relevance is his paper "How Should We Control Monopoly?" (1956), one of three bearing that title in a symposium in that issue.

Why did Downie Write *The Competitive Process* ?

When we put together the book and the *EJ* paper it can be seen that Downie saw monopoly policy as the reason for his research. Both the Preface and Introduction to the book make it clear that it is the effect of the regime of regulation on the working of competitive processes that is central. Is it the American anti-trust legislation that has allowed American industry to flourish (pp.11-2)? Is the common law and historic doctrines such as the restraint of trade doctrine efficacious, or is statute law required? But he saw the reason for asking the question in a quite different light to that of standard theory. Instead of the static efficiency arguments in the tradition of Harberger, his first and dominant concern was the effect of legislation on the diversity which he saw as the path to progress.

He saw his theory as a development of Marshall. "...in a sense I have done no more than try to rescue Marshall's notion (Downie specifically cites the trees in the forest analogy) from the damage it suffered when Mrs Robinson pointed out that pike in a pond might be a better analogy" (p.7). He went on immediately to note that "(i)n concentrating on growth and change rather than equilibrium I am swimming with the main stream of post-war economics and, of course, I have drawn much food for thought from Schumpeter. J. Steindl's book on *Maturity and Stagnation in American Capitalism* contains a model of the competitive process which is very like my own, although he places more emphasis on market imperfections..." (pp.7-8).

What is remarkable from the perspective of the 1990s, in the latter stages of the neoclassical hegemony, is that he thought he was in the mainstream. We now know that his work was largely ignored because it was far from the mainstream of either industrial economics, public economics or microeconomics in general. Mrs Robinson's *Imperfect Competition*, Professor Chamberlin, and American static micro-equilibrium theorists, were to dominate monopoly policy, going with the unimpressive productivity results which make the title of Steindl's book prophetic. He also apparently believed that his theory would be so unexceptionable (in the mainstream) that it did not require more than the relatively perfunctory exposition in the book. No journal articles of any kind appeared, let alone the heavily theoretical equivalent of Andrews' *On Competition...*, to draw the lines clearly around his theory, and exclude the neoclassical alternatives.

Further evidence of his beliefs can be found in his (*EJ*, 1956) paper. He defined the public interest (undefined in the legislation under discussion), quite unselfconsciously I would argue, as consisting in the two issues at the heart of his investigation. These were first, "the extent to which efficient and inefficient, low-cost and high-cost, firms co-exist in different industries. The second is the rate at which efficiency - now usually summarised as productivity - increases over time. ...(this) suggest(s), therefore, that we should take the public interest to be the securing of the minimum intra-industry dispersion of efficiency which is compatible with economic progress" (ibid, p.574). Note the complete absence of any concern for the traditionally acknowledged results of 'the monopoly problem', the efficiency criteria of orthodoxy.

It can be seen that Downie's public policy orientation created the demand for his theoretical work, and the theoretical work gave him the key to dealing with his public policy concerns.

The Significance of Downie's Theoretical Work.

There are many levels on which this question can be taken. At the least interesting, the extent to which it was directly seminal for further theoretical development can be measured by citation. The result, I suspect, would be to show it was not very influential. This paper is focussed on the place it has in the Marshallian tradition and its congruence with later Schumpeterian writing. Further papers will explore the extent to which Downie anticipated that later writing.

Downie and the Concepts Used by Orthodoxy

In his first theory chapter, Chapter II of the book, Downie reviews the orthodox theory and finds it wanting in relevance to the problems that he sees as central. Indeed the existence of his phenomena, i.e., differing efficiencies, persistence of those differences, and slowness to react to innovation, is denied by orthodoxy (pp.20-1). "The main preoccupation of the theory of the firm has been with aspects of economic performance where the quantitative effects of different rules of the game are likely to be small. The tolerance of the economic system for differences in efficiency and the rate of growth of efficiency over time... have received very much less attention" (p.24). The point he is making here is that relevant economic performance measures are not going to alter significantly with variation of variables seen as significant to orthodox theory.

He then disposes of the notion that the orthodox method of analysis might be worth saving (pp.24-9). Using argument reminiscent of that of Andrews' critique (Part I of *On Competition...*) Downie shows that the attempts to save the notion of the firm in equilibrium in the face of falling cost curves (Chamberlin) and horizontal long run demand curves (J.M. Clark) were in vain, or mutually incompatible. The static equilibrium criteria of orthodoxy have no meeting with the observable world.

Moreover, the efficiency criteria which fall out of the orthodox analysis are incompatible with the efficiency criteria of significance to firms, households and governments, namely, the progress of productivity over time.

Most significantly for our purposes, Downie recognises that the orthodox concept of equilibrium implies that "the path by which equilibrium is reached, and the speed with which firms move along it, have no influence on the nature of the equilibrium which is achieved or tended towards" (p.28), it is path independent and ergodic. To the contrary, inter-temporal efficiency depends on attempts to change what would have been the static conditions, on uncertainty about what objective conditions in the marketplace will be in the face of determined efforts to change them, on attempts to catch the market before opportunity has disappeared. Downie therefore set himself to the task that Marshall had failed to address. He concludes the chapter "we must start again, by abandoning the concept of equilbrium as defined in the theory of the firm. This is easy. Building a new set of concepts is not so easy. To this I now turn" (p.29).

Downie's Normative Concerns: the Problem of "efficiency"

Downie chose a difficult path in creating a single variable called "efficiency". He was attempting to quantify in a single measure his central normative concern with technical progress, an index of that progress which he wanted to relate to differing sets of 'rules of the game'. This is explicitly not a measure of the factors which affect a firm's relative market success, the success which sees firms growing rather than shrinking. Dozens of alternative measures are available in the productivity measurement literature. His choice may not be the best for this purpose, but alternatives will not alter the nature of the theory, merely its realisation.

With his background in practical statistics, evident in his early publication (1952), it is no surprise that his concern is with identifying an easily obtained statistic of firm performance. The measure is the ratio of costs to output for each firm. The costs measure is the sum of current costs (assuming that input prices are a good representation of relative scarcity) and the cost of capital (i.e., finance costs, defined as "the product of the value of the capital employed (as measured by the firm) and the average rate of profit in the industry" p.40). The output measure is, if anything, more problematical. His solution is to assume many firms produce any specific product, and all firms produce many products. Then to compare two firms' outputs (of different products), an index of quantity times all producers' average cost of each product is used for each firm. This works only where there are no common costs, and where no firm is "preponderant" (p.43). Because there are common costs, the next best solution is to use average price of each product, the worst to use the prices the firm charges, or obtains, in the market. The assumption here again, is that the market price, or the price charged by the firm, is a good representation of average total costs.

His efficiency measure, the ratio of cost to output, is influenced by both technical efficiency (current input cost and usage, funds employed), and by market performance (returns of funds, prices obtained). This he regards as a defect (p.44).

But it is not clear that it is, if the goal is a single measure on which to judge the socially important elements which do include both technical and market factors. A rise of prices, while input costs remain constant will be an increase of measured efficiency all round. So as well as falling input costs increasing efficiency, rising margins of prices over cost also increase efficiency. Perhaps this is why Downie was less than satisfied that a single index conflated technical and market efficiency, as the firm's market efficiency is indicated by a high margin, but it is technical efficiency that yields economic progress. But is this really so? Improved products gain market share at the expense of less desirable ones. The Transfer Mechanism (see below) deals with both in taking profit levels as the source of funds for investment in capacity. It can hardly be argued that economic progress is not furthered by improved product offerings. Nonetheless, rising prices are not a generally observed characteristic of technically progressive industries whether those industries are improving their products or simply lowering their costs.

His index allows inter-firm differences to be seen even where industry average prices are used in the index. Differences in firms' employment of funds will cause their efficiencies to differ. The reason is that the price change alters the average rate of profit, which in turn enters the efficiency index as the price of funds. So firms using more funds will be restricted in their rise in efficiency compared to firms using less funds (pp.46-7). This is indeed as it should be, given that *ceteris paribus* holds.

Our next question must be the advantage of defining a specific efficiency variable that is somewhat removed from the variable the capital market is supposed to rely upon in making judgements about whether to supply new funds to a firm, i.e., rate of profit on funds. First, as Downie says, "the latter (rate of profit) will...usually provide a fair guide" to the efficiency index ranking (p.46). In the absence of large changes of production processes over time, and in the absence of large differences between firms at any time, rate of profit may be enough for ordinal comparisons. But not always. Where the capital/output ratio differs very greatly between firms the efficiency ranking may differ from their profit rate ranking. Second, the efficiency index is one possible measure of total productivity, and so has the normative significance Downie required whereas rate of profit is without such significance, except in the most unusual conditions, that is of perfect competition in a world of no exogenous change.

It is not at all clear that the most efficient firms, in Downie's sense, are the most able firms in the relative growth sense of economic selection. Growth depends on both the ability to increase market share, or size of a market, and on the ability to command new funds. The latter is thought to be related to rate of profit for both internal and external funding. The former can depend on keen pricing relative to rivals, reducing the level of his efficiency index, while rate of profit may or may not be reduced by such behaviour.

The Transfer Mechanism

It is the Transfer Mechanism (TM) which marks Downie's contribution to economic theory, by which he lays claim to creating a link between Marshall and Schumpeter, or at least, the modern population dynamics school.

The verbal argument he uses to support his theory is very reminiscent of the words of the other Marshallians, Andrews in particular. Reasons for his failing to cite Andrews at all could be sought, and a detailed linguistic analysis may also reveal common threads. But neither of these is the present task. What is distinctive is his focus on market and industry growth, on the path of investment that maintains capacity usage constant (which he calls equilibrium).

He argues that prices, except for "new" industries (p.68fn), are of limited importance for growth of market or industry demand, because price elasticities are not great, nor is there scope for much variation of relative prices, while national income is of great importance for disposable income of buyers. Price is important as the supplier of cash flow to finance production and the level of investment to sustain capacity growth. Price and rate of growth are therefore determined (p.69). But for each firm, these differ with both cost efficiency and market success of each firm's range of products, so giving rise to the transfer of market share that is at the heart of the TM.

The rule that drives his system is the investment/disinvestment relation. Under this rule, all profits are invested in purchasing capacity, and negative profits are recovered by selling capacity. There is no external funding. Then differences in costs per unit of output determine the distribution of capacity among firms, while rate of growth of demand determines market size. His selection variable is thus profit (or costs equivalently) per unit of output.

The examples he uses at pp.70-2 indicate the power of the mechanism to change market structure. While this mechanism is crude and simplistic it does encapsulate some of the behaviour of firms. More importantly, it is useful as a simple example of the sort of forces that drive a system. One can imagine many more complex sets of forces, perhaps implying more complex selection variables, some weakening the force of the simple model, but all driven by diversity. Downie's view was that elaborations of the TM would only strengthen it. "So long as profits are the main determinant of potential growth the system will always show a strong intolerance of cost differences" (p.75)[12]. In other words, structure will change rapidly towards one of small cost difference.

Whether this also means that the most efficient firms prevail is a slightly different question. Downie's answer is that this will be the case except in most unusual circumstances. In his general model (pp.76-9) he presents a simple mathematical representation of a system in continuous equilibrium (as he defines it) under constraints specified earlier, and additionally, identical and constant capital output ratios and no entry or exit. His mathematics explores the behaviour of the variance of efficiency over time[13]. He uses a two period analysis to explain the current period's price and efficiency variance in terms of last period's values. He finds that both price and dispersion of efficiency will fall the more rapidly the greater the initial disperion. So we have an intimation of the analogue of the Fisher relation (the rate of change of population average on the selection variable is proportional to the variance of that selection variable) appearing. But note that it is the dispersion of efficiency, and not the dispersion of profit per unit of output that he analyses. In other words, it is because efficiency is so closely related to the selection variable, profit, that this result appears. The complexity of the result, containing a third moment term, is probably the outcome of this choice. A future task is to use profits, the selection variable, in the formula, and note the emergence of the Fisher relation.

Does the TM exhibit path dependence? Does Downie claim anything that might be interpreted as path dependence for the process of the TM? Path dependence means that the state of the system depends on the path that it has followed in its history. Where a system might find some kind of equilibrium, that equilibrium will differ depending on the path followed in reaching it. The second question can be answered in the negative. Downie saw that equilibrium as a steady state path of growth of capacity, detemined by the rate of growth of demand, almost completely exogenous to his system (pp.67-8). No matter what the initial state, he saw the path converging on that growth equilibrium. The first question is more difficult. The path at any point in time is dependent on its history, but that does not make the 'final' state path dependent. Whether that is the case is unclear from my understanding so far. Further formal analysis will be required to establish this property. What can, perhaps, be said is that the TM model is one for which history is clearly important, with a possible diminishing of that importance where conditions for steady state growth remain constant for many years. One difference between this and neoclassical growth models is that this model can run happily 'out of equilibrium' whereas the others are in some difficulty due to the nature of the production relations they require, i.e., the requirement of equilibrium for individual producers. The TM model assumes specifically that firms are not in any state which could be called 'equilibrium' by neoclassical theory.

What Downie has shown in his TM is that efficiency of the industry will increase if market share is able to be transferred to the more efficient and away from the less efficient. This is the main, and routine, means by which technical (and market) efficiency is translated into socially beneficial progress. Rules that impede this transfer are to be avoided, while arrangements that promote the success of the efficient firms relative to the inefficient are to be encouraged. What we see him to have achieved is an analysis of the dynamic change of market structure in response to selection pressures imposed by the market. Thus, Marshall's biological analogy has been completed, in a thoroughly gradualist Darwinian manner by Downie. However, what Downie proceeds to suggest goes well beyond the constraints of a Darwinian process. Nature is seen to jump.

The Innovation Mechanism

This mechanism is formally exogenous to his TM model. However, it is essentially part of the whole model, one which we can call 'punctuated equilibrium' following Mokyr (1990 and 1991). For a Darwinian model of population ecology, such as the

TM model, innovation represents purposive mutation that occurs randomly as far as the TM model is concerned. The innovation, when it is successful, transforms higher cost firms into lower cost firms. As an example, imagine a Poisson distribution of events that effect only one firm each event, only firms in the lowest x% of the distn of efficiency, e. The outcome is a new distn of e, and a new trajectory of relative growth for each firm, thus a new pathway to concentration and lower industry average cost.

Mokyr (1990) suggests that a taxonomy of technological change can be set up by analogy with genetic evolution. Phenotypical changes are equivalent to movements around known technologies; changes in gene dispersion are equivalent to Downie's TM, and to the many alternative formulations of this phenomena, that give rise to analogies of Fisher's Law; mutation is the equivalent of emergence of new ideas, but the Lamarkian aspect must be added in, as economic mutation is usually directed by goals and informed by learning[14]; speciation is equivalent to the rare event of an invention that transforms economic possibilities, Schumpeterian long cycles are set off by them, with the steam engine the most clearcut example. Mokyr calls these latter 'macroinventions' (ibid, p352). The Mokyr 'macroinventions' that lead to discontinuous change are of a much higher degree of discontinuity than Downie's innovations. That is, in the context of an industry, an innovation that transforms a firm's level of costs (or transforms a firm's market demand in a heterogeneous market) is not a Schumpeterian cataclysm for the economy as a whole. The industry's structure will be changed by a firm innovating as Downie suggests, but the industry's place in the economy may not be changed in any important respect. Downie's Innovation Mechanism (IM) fits into the Mokyr taxonomy as a mutation. Mokyr argues that this should be regarded as Darwinian, and continuous, rather than being a discontinuity. And from the macroeconomic viewpoint this may be appropriate. Nonetheless, we still have a discontinuity at market level, where the gradual process of concentration, and convergence upon best practice via the TM is disrupted. If, as Downie supposed, this disruption, though unusual, is quite certain in a statistical sense[15], then his analysis provides a means of understanding why concentration does not proceed toward the extreme, and why the leading firm does not maintain its position for more than a relatively few years (and why Robinson's 'pike in the pond' metaphor is rejected). But where an industry is constantly being upset by innovation, the TM process fails and another means of analysis must be sought. Downie himself notes (p.94) that these two sources of change, selection (TM) and mutation (IM) to follow Mokyr, may well operate "in a much more complex and continuous fashion than has been implied" (ibid). But his position remains at base one of separating the two clearly and of expecting the two to appear cyclically. As he concludes the analysis of the IM:

> "Nevertheless, the cyclical form in which I have found it most simple to expose the process may have more than merely pedagogic value. It is plausible to suppose that in reality also there will be periods of what may be called ingestion, during which the structure of efficiency-relatives is broadly undisturbed and the strong are engaged in consuming the weak, and that these will be followed by periods of revolution, when technique is in the

melting pot, old kings are being dethroned and new ones are coming to the fore. We should at least bear this in mind when confronting empirical material" (ibid).

A way of dealing with innovation that is quite consonant with Downie, but at odds with Mokyr at least on the surface, is that developed by Cyert and March using Simon's organisation theory (Cyert and March, 1963, but see also Cyert and March, 1956). Here the firm is stimulated only by failure to achieve targets. The firm attempts to reduce costs, eliminating organisational slack or pushing back the bounds of the firm's own knowledge, when it finds its profit goal underfulfilled, or its market share falling 'too much', 'too fast'. It is, of course, this set of ideas that Nelson & Winter (1982) took up in their model, a model which will be argued in another paper to have reinvented a number of Downie's ideas.

It is clear that the IM implies non-ergodicity. Success or failure of a particular innovation, the occurance of an innovation at all, can lead to change of the path taken by the industry in the future. Even if the innovation is small in impact on best practice costs, it will change that pathway, rather than being absorbed into an old pathway. Thus a departure even from one of his steady state growth paths will change the course of history. It also implies path dependence, which is a weaker condition than non-ergodicity[16]. The two mechanisms together thus demonstrate these two qualities that are characteristic of population dynamics models. The significance of history is assured.

One of his conclusions to the analysis of both mechanisms is not unlike that of Edith Penrose (1959), that there is nothing in the analysis of the competitive process that bears on the optimum size of the firm (p.95). His other conclusions are that progress consists in the tendency of cost dispersion to be eliminated, therefore no optimum dispersion can be determined; that there is no ideal rate of progress; that any relation between 'slow' progress and 'the rules of the game' must be explored by examination of the effect of these rules on such things as penalties for failure to innovate, rewards for efficiency, freedom to experiment, and the rate of diffusion of innovation.

Entry and Exit

It is here that Downie intersects with both Andrews and Penrose. Like Andrews, Downie sees entry as generally being by existing firms, moving into markets which their technical expertise can serve. Andrews called this 'cross entry'. Like Penrose, but unlike Andrews, Downie saw 'cross entry' as a phenomenon of large corporations seeking outlets for underused or inappropriately used resources. He saw it also as the dominant form of entry. But unlike both of them, his analysis of the effects of such entry is in terms of its effects on technical progress. The entrants are relatively efficient "largish" (p.101) and thus technically resourceful firms who believe their rate of growth can be improved by entering the new industry. This depends on the profitability which can be expected, on average, in the industry being entered, and on the relative advantage the firm expects in that industry (p.103). The latter he expected to be more important, as efficiency differences are greater than differences in average rates between industries. The industries from which entrants come will be those in which the dispersion of efficiency is no longer great, mature industries in other words, dominated by a few large firms. In such industries the innovations will be biased toward large scale methods, restricting the power of the mechanism to counter the concentrating effects of the TM (p.106). The capital export industry will not be as subject to the TM as without such export, as the efficient firms are moving capital elsewhere. This also weakens the IM as firms are under less pressure in that industry (p.107). But in the "colonised" (ibid) industries the effects will be the reverse, both mechanisms will be pushed harder by the inflow of capital of seemingly efficient firms. However countering the progressive effects of this capital inflow will be the market power of the new entrants, protected from the market's forces by the financial strength of the parents. Rates of profit may be no guide to selection (p.108). While Downie entitles this chapter (VIII) "On entry and exit", exit is not mentioned.

The contribution Downie makes in this chapter is the link between maturity, in terms of concentration and dispersion, and the relative rate of progress of the industries. His view of the success of entry by large existing firms is probably far too optimistic given the experience of merger in the past 40 years. His attempt to put the entry process in the context of diversification and link it to the selection and mutation processes of the market is still ahead of current model builders, probably because he was not confined by formality. This comment also applies to his final theoretical contribution, on the setting of prices and outputs through time, with emphasis on strategic behaviour by firms in an industry.

How Equilibrium is Achieved

His concept of equilibrium, the matched growth of demand and capacity, implies concern that firms' decisions to change their outputs will be consistent, not suffering the Richardson problem of over- or under-shooting due to the radical uncertainty of what competitors are choosing before their choices become obvious. He solves this, in a manner similar to that of Richardson (1953, 1960 & 1971), by positing "grit in the system" (Downie, 1956, p.575) as he called it in a slightly different context[17]. The argument is rather Andrewsian, normal price "provide(s) an anchor, which tends to confine price changes within not too wide a range" (p.110), and this normal price "approximates reasonably closely to the equilibrium price as I have defined it" (ibid). In other words, the short term fluctuations of demand that might create sudden price changes, and profit changes, thence capacity changes, which might be unjustified in the longer term, these are damped by the natural caution of businesspeople who have seen it all before. In other words, Downie is positing an adaptive expectations view of price and capacity setting.

It is in this chapter that exit is dealt with. The failing firm may wind slowly down, negative net profits preventing the firm from maintaining its asset base, but still able to produce and make a contribution toward interest costs and suchlike fixed charges. Or a more efficient firm may buy the failing firm, or its assets, and put it out of its misery quickly. This has the advantage that the more efficient will increase their profits and growth rate. This increases the efficacy of the TM, whereas the alternative slows the transfer of market share toward the more efficient (p.114).

The other constraint on rapid change in the market is the goodwill factor. Like Andrews, Downie regards customers as being, to greater or lesser extent, committed to their current supplier. To change supplier is a major policy initiative, not done lightly. Firms intent on increasing market share will attempt to "detach" customers of the most vulnerable firms, and "attach" them as firmly as possible (p.116). Where this process is facilitated by negotiation and commercial secrecy the TM operates more rapidly than where prices are posted and deals public (p.117). So goodwill is both a force for smoothing fluctuations and for slowing the transfer of market share from the inherently inefficient.

The declining industry provides a particular problem, as capacity is eroded only by time or innovation. And innovation is rare in such an industry, in Downie's view (p.119). While the notion of the normal price may restrict firms from indulging in marginal cost pricing, the longer the slump, the more likely discipline will break down. Under such conditions it is not always the efficient firms that stay solvent longest. The TM is thus suspended during such a slump, or in the death throes of the declining industry (ibid).

Downie's analysis of equilibrium of capacity to demand is less complete than his TM and IM models might wish to have as complements. But it must be said that the problem of strategy has not yet been dealt with happily by the post Schumpeterians either. Downie relies on behavioural traits that will differ from one economy to another, and from one time period to another. Nonetheless, the attempt was made. The critical insight, that immediate and complete reaction to any change, in the manner suggested by rational expectations models, is destructive of maintenance of equilbrium, was reached. The mechanisms which slowed reaction in Downie's case are those which Andrews developed in great detail in his *Manufacturing Business* (1949).

G.B. Richardson's doubts about the possibility of rational choice under competition or oligopoly were not published until 1960. Was it a coincidence that two minds in the same institution at about the same time developed the same ideas, in great detail in Richardson's case, and as an important subsidiary element in Downie's[18]. This result was only recently derived formally in a neoclassical context by Heiner (1989). Schumpeter's argument in *Capitalism, Socialism and Democracy* (Schumpeter, 1942), Ch VII, "Monopolistic Practices", is a possible source of Downie's idea, but Schumpeter takes the notion of beneficent restrictive practices much further toward the 'destructive competition' line of thinking which sees the nature of investment in sunk capital as requiring protection from the forces of competition.

Linking Marshall with Schumpeter

Downie's two mechanisms of competition can be seen as a formalisation of two sets of ideas, the Andrews post Marshallian ideas of the Oxford school that had its genesis in the Oxford studies in the price mechanism of the late 1930s; and Schumpeter's forces of creative destruction. While Schumpeter's focus was on the great movements of history that shaped modern industrial society, that of the post Marshallians was on the year by year passage of time and the evolution of markets and industries, their structure and performance. Where Andrews had failed to create a properly dynamic model, Downie used the Schumpeterian vision as a basis for his dynamics.

---

* Department of Economics, University of New England, Armidale, NSW 2351. The present work was carried out while on a year's study leave from the UNE. During that time I was fortunate to discuss this paper with Stan Metcalfe, Brian Loasby, Denis O'Brien, Alec Gee, Neil Kay, Dominique Foray, Geoff Hodgson, George Richardson, Martin Fransman and Norman Clark. Their encouragement and comments are gratefully acknowledged. The comments of the referees of this Journal have also been of great help in clarifying some issues.

Notes

1 Clark & Juma (1988) attempt to deal with Marshall's dilemma. However, they do not see that Marshall provided a substantial part of the basis for modern evolutionary thought, which is the burden of the present paper.

2 A theme important to Marshall, that of the long run tendency of real prices to fall with development of markets and techniques of production, can be suggested as the central idea with which the biological analogy is distinguished from the mechanical. This is to be explored in further work on Downie's contribution.

3 The relationship between the two analogies, and the full import of the biological analogy in Marshall can only be grasped by seeing *Industry and Trade* in the context of the *Principles*. The task of elaborating on this point is beyond the scope of this paper.

4 "Pigovian" is used to indicate work in which the full logical implications of the simple mechanical model is taken seriously. Whether Mr Pigou was the first, or whether Sraffa in his 1926 *EJ* paper (or his 1925 paper published in Italian) is really to blame is unclear to me. Loasby (1989), in his essay on the Cambridge economists' transformation from Marshall's economics to the timeless, ahistorical economics we accept as orthodoxy, "Joan Robinson's 'wrong turning'"(pp.71-85), notes that "with Pigou came an important shift of emphasis; historical development and the working of the competitive process faded into the background and formal analysis became more prominent" (p.75). See also pp.73-5 on increasing and decreasing returns, and Loasby, (ibid), Chapter 4, "Knowledge and organisation...".

5 Post Marshallians are writers such as MacGregor (see Lee, 1989) and Andrews, authors who resisted the Pigovian/Robinsonian synthesis, and maintained the need to see the business firm as a reality, and its behaviour as warranting explanation. As Andrews showed in his 1951 paper, the exit of many economists from the Cambridge orthodoxy in the first decades of the century was the beginning of the other business disciplines, at least in the UK.

6 The picture of Marshall leaning first to biology, then to mechanics, and so on, is drawn by Brinley Thomas in his recent paper (1991). The paper is unfortunately too brief to sustain the argument fully, but is highly suggestive of the conflict in directions taken in Marshall's development of his *Principles*.

7 The present author attempted to clarify these concepts in light of later writing of Andrews in his (1978).

8 He did, however, see the statictical nature of modern physics as analogous with his micro non-equilibrium views (Andrews and Brunner, 1951, p15).

9 There is some suggestion that Andrews' year at Harvard in the middle 1960s may have given some impetus to the work of Caves, whose seminal paper of 1977 was quoted by Baumol et al. It is still common for Americans to keep their citations local. The folklore of the transmission of ideas may be fascinating but no more than a footnote.

10 The reader unfamiliar with these concepts may find a convenient entry to them in W.B. Arthur's piece in *New Scientist*, 6 February, 1993, in a special supplement on complexity, all of which is worth reading.

11 It should be noted, however, that his Treasury position gave him privileged access to data. His empirical work for the book was based on raw data from the Census of Production, not the Standard Industrial Classification aggregations available to other researchers. This made his a difficult act to follow and may have contributed to his later neglect. My own view is that it was his unconventional framework that was more important to the neglect.

12 See Metcalfe (1989) for a modern account of profit as the selection variable.

13 There are also a couple of typographical errors in this section, the major one being carried through in the mathematics to a contradiction of his conclusion, viz, that " the rate at which prices fall will be the greater the smaller the capital intensity of the industry and the rate at which demand for its products is growing" (pp.78-9).

14 But for a contrary view, see Hannan and Freeman, (1989) pp.22-3, 76-7.

15 in the same way that cyclones are unusual for any specific location, but certain up to a probability distribution.

16 An economic process may be path dependent without being non-ergodic, but non-ergodicity implies path dependence.

17 Richardson's concerns with imperfect information and its relevance to economic efficiency was first flagged in his 1953 paper, but not developed in the form familiar from his 1960 and beyond. It has been suggested that 'grit' is similar to 'slack' as means of stabilising markets. In this context it may well be advisable to consider both Leibenstein's X-inefficiency concept and Hirschman's Exit/Voice dichotomy, to explore their relationship with Downie's adaptive expectations approach.

18 Richardson (1960). Downie's strong views on regulation of competition, coming from his Civil Servant's practical concern with the need for "grit in the system", to give the enterprising firm a reasonable run at profit making before being cut down by followers, did not introduce Richardson to the dilemma explored in his book. Richardson had little contact with Downie and does not remember ever discussing matters such as this with him, or coming into contact with Downie's ideas at all.

References

Andrews, P.W.S. 1951 "Industrial Analysis in Economics" in Wilson T. & Andrews, P.W.S. *Oxford Studies in the Price Mechanism*, Oxford, Clarendon, pp.139-172.

Andrews, P.W.S. & Brunner, E. 1951 *Capital Development in Steel*, Oxford, Basil Blackwell.

Barkley Rosser, J. 1992 "The dialogue between the economic and the ecologic theories of evolution" *Journal of Economic Behaviour and Organissation*, 17, pp.195-215.

Clark, N. & Juma, C. 1988 "Evolutionary theories in economic thought", in Dosi, G. et al, *Technical Change and Economic Theory*, London, Pinter, pp.197-228.

Cyert, R.M. & March, J.G. 1963 *Behavioural Theory of the Firm*, Englewood Cliffs, NJ, Prentice Hall.

___ 1956 "Organisational Factors in the Theory of Oligopoly" *QJE*, 70 pp.44-46.

Downie, J. 1952 "A note on the demand for food", *Economic Journal*, LXII, #248, pp.936-9

___ 1956 "How Should We Control Monopoly? II", *Economic Journal*, LXVI, #264, 573-7.

___ 1958 *The Competitive Process*, London, Duckworth.

Hammond, J.D. 1991 "Alfred Marshall's Methodology", *Methodus*, 3,1, pp.95-101.

Hannan, M.T. & Freeman, J. (1989) *Organisational Ecology*, Cambridge, Mass., Harvard University Press.

Heiner, R. 1989 "The Origin of Predictable Dynamic Behaviour", *Journal of Economic Behaviour and Organisation*, 12, pp.233-257.

Hodgson, G.M. 1992 "The Mecca of Alfred Marshall" unpublished manuscript, University of Northumbria.

Lee, F.S. 1989 "D.H. MacGregor and the Firm: a Neglected Chapter in the History of the Post Keynesian Theory of the Firm", *British Review of Economic Issues*, 11,24, pp.21-47.

Loasby, B. 1989 "Knowledge and organisation: Marshall's theory of economic progress and coordination" *The Mind and Method of the Economist*, Aldershot, Edward Elgar, pp.47-70.

___ "Joan Robinson's 'wrong turning'", pp.71-85 in *ibid*.

___ 1991 *Equilibrium and Evolution*, Manchester, MUP.

Metcalfe, J.S. 1989 "Evolution and Economic Change", in A. Silberston (ed) *Technology and Economic Progress*, Macmillan.

Mokyr, J. 1990 "Punctuated Equilibrium and Technological Progress" *AERPP*, May , pp.350-4.

___ 1991 *The Lever of Riches*, Oxford UP.

Nelson, R. & Winter, S. 1982 *An Evolutionary Theory of Economic Change*, Cambridge, Mass, Belknap Press

Nightingale, J. 1978 "On the Definition of Market and Industry", *Journal of Industrial Economics*, , pp.31-40.

O'Brien, D. 1990 "Marshall's Industrial Analysis", *Scottish Journal of Political Economy*, 37, 1, pp.61-84

Penrose, E.T. (1959) *The Theory of the Growth of the Firm*, Oxford, Basil Blackwell.

Pigou, A.C. 1925 *Memorials of Alfred Marshall*, London, Macmillan.

Richardson G.B. 1953 "Imperfect Knowledge and Economic Efficiency" *Oxford Economic Papers*, 1953, pp.136-56.

___ 1960 and 1990 *Information and Investment*, Oxford UP, Oxford.

___ 1971 "Planning versus Competition", *Soviet Studies*, 22, 3, pp.433-47, also in Richardson G.B., 1990.

Samuelson, P. 1967 "The Monopolistic Competition Revolution" in Kuenne, R.E. *Monopolistic Competition: Studies in Impact*, New York, Wiley.

Schumpeter, J. 1942 *Capitalism, Socialism and Democracy* New York, Harper & Brothers.

Thomas, Brinley 1991 "Alfred Marshall on Economic Biology", *Review of Political Economy*, 3.1 pp.1-14.

Williams, P.L. 1978 *The Emergence of the Theory of the Firm*, London, Macmillan.

Part V
Evolution, Optimization and Rationality

[19]

Economic Models in Ecology

The economics of resource allocation provide a framework for viewing ecological processes.

David J. Rapport and James E. Turner

Ecological processes have traditionally been studied from several vantage points. One approach focuses on energy flows through ecological communities from primary producers to consumers at higher trophic levels (*1*). Another approach considers species interactions in terms of population dynamics (*2*). A third explores the geographical distribution of species and the relationship between species diversity and area (*3*).

None of these approaches, however, explicitly address what some (*4, 5*) have regarded as one of the central problems of ecology—the ways in which scarce resources are allocated among alternative uses and users. This question is, of course, fundamental to economic thinking (more specifically to microeconomic theory) and it is for this reason that we have recently seen the introduction of essentially economic models and modes of thought in ecology (*6–21*). In some cases economic models and concepts have been transferred directly across disciplinary boundaries (*5, 7, 10–14, 16–18*), while in other instances ecologists have rediscovered economic principles in an ecological context (*6, 8, 9, 15, 19, 20, 21*).

These developments have occurred in a number of diverse areas of ecology, including models of optimal foraging (*6–8, 11, 12, 15, 16, 21*), reproduction strategies (*9, 12, 19, 20*), territoriality (*10*), altruism (*20*), and social caste systems (*17*). Viewed as a group these and other recent contributions may lay the foundations for an approach to ecology in terms of an economics of natural communities. In this article we review how economic analysis has contributed to our understanding of ecology and show how a comprehensive framework for economic analysis of ecological phenomena may emerge.

That economic principles are relevant to the study of ecology is by no means a new idea. H. G. Wells, Julian Huxley, and G. P. Wells (*22*) in their treatise *The Science of Life* defined ecology as biological economics or an extension of economics to the whole world of life. For these authors, economics is "the science of social subsistence, of needs and their satisfactions of work and wealth. It tries to elucidate the relations of producer, dealer, and consumer in the human community and show how the whole system carries on. Ecology broadens out this inquiry into a general study of the give and take, the effort, accumulation and consumption in every province of life" (*22*, p. 961).

In the history of science, biological-economic analogies have played a significant role. Malthus (*23*) borrowed from "the laws of natural increase in the animal and vegetable kingdom" in forecasting a dismal economic future for mankind. Darwin (*24*), as is well known, received a critical inspiration for formulating his theory of evolution by means of natural selection from a reading of Malthus's essay on population. It occurred to Darwin that not only man, but all other species too, are engaged in a struggle for existence owing to their requirement for limited resources, and that those species that evolved ways to use resources more efficiently would be favored in their struggle for survival.

Dissatisfied with the predominance of mechanical analogies in economic thinking, the economist Alfred Marshall (*25*), writing at the turn of this century, insisted that the Darwinian concept of natural selection is also the most important economic principle, and he frequently asserted that, as economics became a mature science, biological analogies would displace mechanical analogies. Some years later John Maynard Keynes (*26*) made the observation that the Darwinian "principle of survival of the fittest could be regarded as a vast generalization of Ricardian economics."

Several other examples of biological-economic analogies may be cited (*27*), but among the most colorful was Adam Smith's frustrated attempt to extend the invisible hand to the economy of nature

Dr. Rapport is environmentalist in the Office of the Senior Advisor on Integration, Statistics Canada, Ottawa, Ontario, Canada K1A 0T6; Dr. Turner is associate professor in the Department of Mathematics, McGill University, Montreal, Canada.

(28). In an early chapter of *The Wealth of Nations*, Smith concluded that while "a philosopher is not in genius and disposition half so different from a street porter, as a mastiff is from a greyhound, or a greyhound from a spaniel . . . those different tribes of animals, however, though all of the same species, are of scarce any use to one another. . . . The effects of those different geniuses and talents, for want of the power or disposition to barter and exchange, cannot be brought into a common stock, and do not in the least contribute to the better accommodation and conveniency of the species."

Numerous economic models have made their appearance in theoretical ecology within the past decade (6–21). If one adopts the classical definition of economic activity provided by Lionel Robbins (29), namely, that "any act has an economic aspect if time and the scarce means necessary to the achievement of one end involves the relinquishment of their use in the achievement of another," the applicability of economic concepts and models to resource allocation aspects of ecosystems can be shown to be rather pervasive. To place these diverse economic-ecological concepts and models into a coherent framework we group them into the three essential components of economic resource allocation systems—consumption, production, and consumer-producer interactions (30).

Consumer Behavior in Natural Communities

A plethora of theoretical models of the economics of consumer choice in natural communities now exists (6–8, 11, 15, 16, 21, 31, 32). Generally, these studies seek to determine the optimal feeding strategies of predators maximizing total energy intake, reproduction rates, or some other aspect of fitness.

It has been possible to use directly simple microeconomic models to describe important aspects of optimal foraging behavior (7, 11, 16, 31). The problem facing a consumer in terms of classical microeconomics is to choose the bundle of goods that maximizes utility within the budget constraints. Figure 1a illustrates a solution to this problem for the two goods case. Here the budget line is determined by the consumers' income constraints and the prices of goods A and B. The budget line forms the boundary between those bundles of goods obtainable and unobtainable by the consumer in a given time period. Benefits from consumption are represented by a family of indifference contours or isoclines,

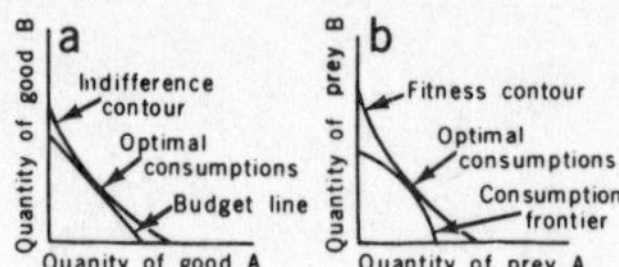

Fig. 1. (a) Optimal consumer. Tangency solution to maximize utility subject to budget constraint. (b) Optimal forager. Tangency solution to maximize fitness subject to consumption possibilities. Both (a) and (b) are in terms of rates of consumption per unit time.

each isocline indicating those bundles of goods A and B of equal satisfaction to the consumer. The solution to the dilemma of consumer choice is given by the tangency of the "highest" isocline with the budget line (33). The ecological model in Fig. 1b was derived directly from this economic model. Here the budget constraint (denoted as consumption frontier) is determined by a complex of ecological parameters (time and energy allocated to foraging, the ease of prey capture, prey abundance, competition among predators for prey). As in Fig. 1a, the budget constraint separates the alternative consumptions possible from those that are not and the family of fitness contours indicates the contributions of alternative prey combinations to the predators' welfare (34). The predators' best strategy is to consume that prey combination determined by the tangency of the highest fitness contour with the consumption frontier (35). The circumstances under which predators may shift from "generalist" to "specialist" strategies or from specialization on one prey type to another are readily determined within this context. In this regard a change in relative prey abundance acts as a change in relative prices for consumers. As Pulliam (31) points out, this economic model underscores the importance of relative prey abundance.

The concepts of substitute and complement resources, so basic to economic analysis, also play an important role in characterizing a predator's response to changes in prey abundance. If prey resources are "perfect" substitutes, slight changes in their relative abundance can cause a predator to switch from one prey type to another (7, 11, 36).

Laboratory experiments with predator-prey systems offer support for several of the assumptions and hypotheses derived from the economic foraging model. In experiments with protozoa, the ciliate *Stentor coeruleus* was fed on paired combinations of four prey species—two algal and two nonalgal species (37). Stentor food preferences were highly consistent (transitive), in that the stentor preferred nonalgal to algal prey and was indifferent in choosing among alternative algal species or alternative nonalgal species. In another set of experiments (38, 39), stentors' responsiveness to relative prey abundance (corresponding to relative prices in economics) was determined. Stentors increased their degree of preference for those prey types which became relatively more abundant (40). If greater abundance is interpreted in terms of reduced costs of capture or digestion, the stentor acts as a rational consumer, increasing its demand for relatively lower priced goods.

In order to determine the possible adaptive significance of food preference in stentor, glycogen accumulation, starvation times, and reproductive rates were measured in stentors maintained on alternative diets (38). In those cases in which stentor was indifferent to alternative prey combinations, it reproduced equally well on either prey type alone or on a combination of prey types fed sequentially. However, in the cases where stentor selected a particular combination of prey types in a nonrandom fashion, it reproduced better on a mixture of prey than on either prey type alone. These results suggest that stentor food preferences are highly adaptive, enabling this opportunistic species to increase its growth rate by exploiting complementary food resources in an economically efficient manner.

Holmberg (41) conducted similar experiments with the spider predator *Pardosa vancouveri* feeding on *Tenebrio* larvae, *Drosophila* adults, and young *Oncopeltus*. He found not only consistent (and nearly absolute) food preferences but also a correlation between food preferences and indicators of fitness. When spiders were fed preferred prey types their weight gain and size gain were significantly greater than achieved on alternative prey species. In those cases where spiders were indifferent to two prey types, there were no significant differences in any of the benefit criteria tested.

Simple microeconomic consumer behavior models have also been used to interpret field data on foraging. Tullock (16), in analyzing Gibbs' data on the predation by coal tits on insect larvae, concluded that the coal tit's behavior can be compared to that of a careful shopper. When the bird locates a region of high larval density it expends less energy in pine cone tapping per larva consumed. Therefore, a downward sloping demand function for larva in terms of coal tit energy expenditure can be inferred.

We now turn to examples of foraging models developed from within ecology which correspond to aspects of consumer economics. Among these is MacArthur's theory of the economics of consumer choice (*21*). MacArthur considered the economics of species behavior as an essential ingredient for understanding biogeographical patterns. He postulated that a forager will have "a fairly clear statistical expectation of the resources it will come upon" and that the expected yield to the predator in terms of grams of successfully captured prey per unit time will be maximized. From these postulates he derived the result that prudent predators should "pursue an item if and only if during the time the pursuit would take it would not expect to locate and catch a better item." This result as stated is an ecological equivalent of the opportunity cost concept familiar in many economic analyses.

In Schoener's development of the theory of foraging strategies (*15*), an explicit economic orientation is adopted at the outset. His optimal foraging framework consists of "choosing a currency—what is to be maximized or minimized, choosing the appropriate cost-benefit functions, and solving for the optimum." The parallel set of ideas in microeconomic theory is to specify measures of welfare (utility), budget constraints, and solve for the optimum (the tangency solution in the economic model). Schoener identifies two extreme strategists: energy maximizers and time minimizers. The energy maximizer allocates all its foraging time to prey capture, selecting prey in such a manner as to obtain the maximum net energy gain for the time expended on foraging. A time minimizer seeks a specified energy requirement, minimizing the time expended to obtain it.

In a review of optimality principles in ecology Cody (*6*) develops a model which focuses on generalist versus specialist strategies. A generalist consumes all prey species encountered (no preferences) while a specialist consumes only the prey type conferring maximum fitness. Using an economic cost-benefit analysis Cody finds that, as the proportion of preferred prey types available in a given habitat declines, a generalist strategy becomes more profitable to the organism. This is due to the increased costs (in terms of waiting time and energy expended for search) of being a selective (specialist) predator.

The foregoing examples serve to demonstrate that not only have some optimal foraging models in ecology been suggested by analogous models in consumer economics, but also that ecologically derived models can readily be reinterpreted in terms of the economics of consumer behavior. These models emphasize aspects of the problem of choice faced by many general predators, and yield insight into predator strategies such as those of energy maximizers, time minimizers, specialists, and generalists.

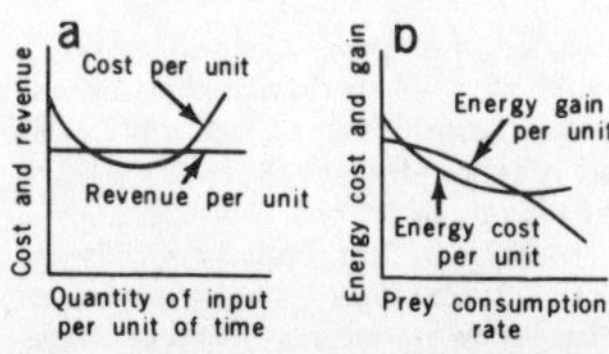

Fig. 2. (a) Economic cost and revenue per unit input as functions of input rate. The firm may profitably process inputs, for example, labor, land, capital, for some intermediate range of input rate where the average cost per unit of input is less than the average return on the input's contribution to the firm's output. (b) Energy cost and gain per unit of consumption as functions of consumption rate. Net reproduction can occur in the range where the cost of obtaining energy inputs is less than the assimilated energy derived from them.

Production in Natural Communities

The economics of production in natural communities covers a very broad spectrum of topics. Production to the ecologist is generally considered in terms of the manufacture of biomass either by growth or reproduction processes. From an economic perspective one desires to know the nature of the production function, that is, the relationship between factors of production (ecological equivalents to the economist's land, labor, and capital) and growth or reproductive output. Other questions concern the allocation of energy between growth and reproduction (*9*, *42*), the optimal division of labor in social caste systems (*17*), and strategies for territorial defense (*10*).

As in consumer choice theory, microeconomic models have been transferred rather directly to ecology in elucidating aspects of producer behavior. Consider for example the models shown in Fig. 2, a and b, in which the theory of the firm has been used in a description of the relationship between foraging activity and population growth (*12*). Both firms and organisms (viewed here as producers) are faced with the problem of determining the optimal quantities of inputs required for production per unit time.

A predator maximizing its net energy gain by consuming the quantity of prey that yields the largest difference between total energy gain and total energy cost is behaving in a similar fashion to a firm which seeks to employ the quantity of input that generates the largest difference between the total value of its product-added and its total costs. This economic perspective when applied to ecology enables one to relate the quantity and quality of available food resources to optimal consumption rates and population growth. For example, it has been shown with this approach that energy maximizing and time minimizing strategies converge as food becomes scarce (*12*). Further, this type of cost-benefit model permits one to explore the dependence of population growth on the quality and quantity of food resources and energy conversion efficiencies. Oster (*18*), in his development of the economics of the intricate relations between foraging and reproduction in bumblebee colonies, makes use of this structure of ideas. He describes the bee colony as analogous to the economy of a firm, relating the optimal population to the energy gains from harvesting activities (a complex function of flower density and nectar quality and quantity) and the energy costs of foraging activities and reproduction.

Schoener's optimal foraging models (*15*) should also be recalled here since they provide a striking example of the discovery in ecology of the economist's marginal cost—marginal revenue analysis of profitability. Schoener measures both costs and benefits in terms of offspring. As a predator feeds it incurs decreasing marginal benefits from ingesting lower quality foods and from less efficient conversion of food to offspring. At the same time the organism incurs increasing marginal costs, which here are measured in terms of offspring forgone by inadequate time for necessary reproductive activities such as courtship, nest building, and defense. The optimal time allocated to foraging is determined where marginal benefits equal marginal costs. Schoener's analysis is also similar to one economist's conceptualization of the household as a small factory which combines "capital goods, raw material and labor to clean, feed, procreate and otherwise produce useful commodities" (*43*).

Parental investment theory (*20*) furnishes another example of explicit economic analysis in describing aspects of production in natural communities. Viewing reproduction as an investment process, Trivers considers the contribution of each parent in terms of time and energy expenditures for all activities concerned with preparing for raising young. He suggests that monogamy, polygamy, and parental desertion can all be understood in terms of the relative parental investment made by each parent over time. For example, if the investment by females in offspring is large relative to males, a male may do better (in evolutionary terms) by deserting the female and engaging in polygamous behavior. In this case the expected return on a number of investments (in offspring of more than one female) exceeds the expected return of a single extensive investment (that is, including not only mating but also the care of offspring). Similar economic arguments are used to explain why male birds in most cases are more brightly colored and aggressive than females. Since females bear the brunt of the parental investment, they are the "scarce resource" in the production process and therefore there is a strong selective pressure for characteristics enabling males to compete for this limiting resource. It is interesting that in those species where male investment in a single brood of offspring is relatively large (Phalaropodidae and polyandrous species) the females are more brightly colored, aggressive, and exhibit polygamous behavior.

Life history strategies of species have also been viewed in terms of economic principles of investment behavior. Gadgil and Bossert (*9*) examined the returns (again in the currency of offspring) from allocations of energy to growth and reproduction. They pointed out that while a higher reproductive effort in a given year yields a higher expected number of surviving offspring, this is at the cost of lower adult survival probabilities and less adult growth. These costs reduce expected contributions to offspring in succeeding years. The exact forms of the cost and gain functions yield strategies ranging from repeated reproduction (iteroparous organisms) to "big-bang" reproduction in which a very large number of offspring are produced all at one time (semelparous organisms) (*44*). In all cases Gadgil and Bossert argue that natural selection "would tend to an adjustment of the reproductive effort at every age such that the overall fitness of the life history would be maximized" (*9*). In a similar manner, the investment decisions of individuals or firms take into account the opportunity costs of investment in terms of forgone consumption or reduced liquidity, and attempt to maximize benefits (profits, utility) over time.

In extending formal models of optimal life history strategies to more complex cases, Schaffer (*19*) has shown that "an optimal life history maximizes for each age class the expected fecundity at that age plus the sum of all future expected fecundities, each discounted by an appropriate power of e^{-m} where *m* is Fisher's Malthusian parameter." In this formulation the Malthusian parameter serves the function of an interest rate. Students of economics will recognize that the expected returns from a given investment are generally discounted to present value by the rate of interest.

Organisms, like firms, may change their "technology" in response to changes in resource availability. Heinrich (*45*) describes the foraging activities of the bumblebee in these terms. If nectar is abundant, the bee employs a high (energy) cost-gathering technique (flight), while the bee switches to a low-cost process (walking or crawling) when the flower density is low. Another example of the effect of resource availability on techniques of resource acquisition is provided by Cody's description of Mohave desert flocks (*6*). These flocks are more cohesive and better organized when food supplies dwindle than when food is abundant. Cody speculates that the change in behavior in response to resource scarcity serves to increase the success rate of gathering resources by regulating the return time of the group to the regeneration time of the resource.

Another aspect of the economics of production is the spacial relationships between the location of the producer and the location of resources gathered. This area of microeconomic theory has its origin in Losch's classic work on the economics of location (*46*). Using principles developed by Losch, Hamilton, and Watt (*10*) proposed a general theory of refuging systems which explores the relationships of the size of defended territory to the resources available, and spacing patterns of individuals or groups to the temporal and spacial pattern of the resource. Their approach enables one to account for the empirical finding that as the size of the group inhabiting a central location increases it becomes less probable that the foraging territory will be defended. In a recent review, Covich (*47*) discusses a wide range of similarities between economic and ecological location models, and demonstrates how economic concepts can be used to investigate the determinants of the shapes of foraging areas.

The division of labor in social insect societies is another area of ecological production amenable to economic analysis. In what he terms the "ergonomics" of insect societies, Wilson (*17*) has demonstrated how classic microeconomic techniques of linear programming are well suited to explain the division of labor among social insect castes. He considers the optimal number of castes and the proportion of workers in each caste required for the insect colony to function efficiently. This focus is the biological equivalent of the choice of types and proportions of land, labor, and capital by the firm. In social insect societies the objective function might be the production of queens at minimal energy cost (*18*). Wilson contends that in relatively constant environments the optimal number of castes should not exceed the number of separate tasks (defense and foraging, for example), and in general it is advantageous for the species to evolve so that in each mature colony there is one caste specialized to respond to each kind of contingency (*17*). A fluctuating environment can make a particular caste uneconomical and favors generalists over specialists even if the functions the caste performs remain as important as before.

Other aspects of the ergonomics of social insects have recently been explored by Oster (*18*) using the economics of contracts pioneered by the 19th-century economist Edgeworth (*48*). Within this explicit microeconomic framework, Oster shows how a reallocation of energy and population between castes in a given colony can increase the productivity of both castes. However, as in the standard economic models, after a certain degree of trading resources, a given caste (or contracting party in economics) can only improve its position at the expense of another.

Producer and Consumer Interactions as an Ecological Market

Writing several decades before Darwin, the geologist Lyell described population interactions in terms of a buffering effect, recently reinterpreted by Egerton (*49*) as "a biological example of the law of supply and demand." Today, reference to the role of supply and demand factors as elements in the balancing of predator-prey interactions is commonplace (*50–52*). Holling (*53*), for example, draws a specific analogy between predator-prey interactions and the supply and demand for land. Unsuccessful bidders for land are analogous to unsuccessful predators, and the behavior of both depends on the quality and availability of substitute resources. The supply of prey is regenerated by a reproduction process while land supply is governed by a resale process.

The economist Boulding has raised the question: "What, if anything, in the biosphere corresponds to the concept of a price system, and especially to an equilibrium price system, in economics?" (*51*). Energy has often been referred to as the currency of life, but as an answer to Boulding's query it is cumbersome because the energy cost of obtaining a particular prey type will differ for every species of predator (54, 55). A conceptually simpler approach considers prey density as equilibrating the availability of food supplies with the demands of predators (13, 52). In Fig. 3, the familiar supply-demand model from economics is compared with the harvest-yield model in ecology. For economic markets (Fig. 3a) "partial equilibrium" occurs at the price for which supply equals demand. In this classical economic model (30) [one which pertains to the agricultural sector of less-developed countries today as well as to foreign exchange and stock exchange markets (56)], if supply exceeds demand sellers lower prices to dispose of surplus goods. Conversely, if demand exceeds supply buyers bid up prices until the equilibrium price $\hat{p}$ is obtained. In ecological markets (Fig. 3b) the harvest function represents the total demand of all predators in a given habitat for a particular prey type as a function of prey density. The yield function indicates the number of prey available to predators at each prey density. If the prey harvest exceeds yield prey density declines, while if yield exceeds harvest prey density increases. The intersections of harvest and yield functions can generate stable, unstable, semistable, and multiple equilibriums as in the economic market models (52). From this representation of ecological producer-consumer interactions, the relation between prey density and predation rates of a single predator species (the functional response) (53) was extended to situations involving a community of predator and prey species interactions (13). The community is described in terms of moving attractor points, defined for each population and for the entire ecosystem. A change in abundance for a given prey species leads to adjustments in prey densities throughout the community through a series of interrelated harvest-yield function interactions. If the time constants of these interactions were specified it would be possible to explore stability and resilience properties of natural communities in these terms.

Just as theories of producer and consumer behavior have given rise to the theories of supply and demand, respectively, in economics, it can be shown that theories of biological production (in terms of energy gains and costs) and optimal foraging underlie the yield and harvest functions in ecology. The yield is governed by a delicate balance of energy gains and costs. As the density of the population increases, there may be both

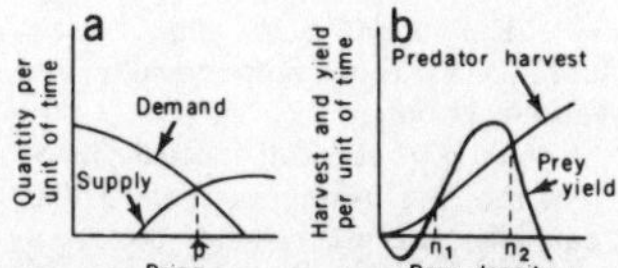

Fig. 3. (a) Supply and demand as functions of commodity price. In this case there is one intersection of the supply and demand curves. This intersection determines the market price ($\hat{p}$) and the quantity of goods purchased. (b) Prey yield and predator harvest as functions of prey density. There are two intersections of the harvest and yield functions in the above case. The first of these, n_1, is unstable. Should the prey population density decline below n_1 it would become extinct. Thus n_1 has been termed the extinction threshold. If the prey population exceeds n_1, it approaches the stable equilibrium n_2.

enhancement and competitive effects, these altering the profits to each of the individuals and, thus, their reproductive potential (12). The harvest is affected by changes in either the consumption opportunities or consumer preferences (11). Thus, models of ecological markets derived from theories of reproduction and optimal foraging have a parallel structure to models of economic markets derived from theories of producer and consumer behavior.

Economic models of consumer choice, reproductive strategies, and predator-prey interactions that fulfill the functions of the basic microeconomic processes of consumption, production, and exchange, respectively (57), have been described. We now turn briefly to a comparison of economic and ecological models of competition. Ecologists have placed primary emphasis on the partitioning of resources by competitors (21, 58) and the effects of competition on population numbers (2, 5). Economists have been more concerned with the efficiency of resource utilization (30). In both areas the stability of competitive interactions and the diversification of competitors to avoid the direct effects of competition have been of considerable interest.

Transfers of elements of competition theory from economics to ecology and from ecology to economics have occurred (5, 14, 59). Economic competition models have provided an energetic substructure for ecological population dynamics (5, 14), by relating classical Lotka-Volterra competitive outcomes to parameters such as the quality of the resource, and the efficiency with which the resource is exploited. Ecological models of competition (59) have served to introduce concepts of resource partitioning and ecological niche into the economic theory of the firm.

Uncertainty and Evolution

In the preceding sections, economic models of consumption, production, and exchange have been reinterpreted to describe corresponding ecological processes. Although these models embodied many simplifying assumptions about economic behavior (for example, perfect information, rationality) they served to provide a rudimentary framework for relating economic and ecological concepts and principles. In this section we consider how more realistic models of economic and ecological behavior take into consideration factors such as uncertainty and habitual behavior. Finally we consider evolutionary mechanisms in economic and ecological systems.

The assumption of optimal behavior on the part of economic agents has played a major role in the development of simple economic models (60). The validity of this assumption has subsequently been challenged in experimental studies of consumer behavior, in theories of decision-making and management, in economic anthropology, and in other areas (61). Consumers obviously do not have complete information concerning the consumption possibilities and the benefits of consumption. Producers equally face an uncertain and variable market for their products. Even when information is available, the consumer or producer may not have the computational ability to make optimal choices in the time available.

These objections to the assumption of optimal behavior in the narrow sense of making the best choice from all possibilities apply with equal force to other species of consumers and producers. Optimal behavior may be a limiting case to be expected only in those situations in which the consumer or producer does indeed have complete information or in which habits of consumption or techniques of production have evolved (by a trial and error procedure) over a considerable period of time in a predictable environment. While the consumption choices of predators are subject to natural selection, it should be noted that this does not imply that consumption choices in present environments are necessarily the most appropriate for survival and reproduction.

Johnson (62) has explored a number of ways in which introducing elements of uncertainty in economic analysis blurs the crisp precision of simple economic models. Johnson discusses the fact that, in the face of uncertainty, (i) households do not know the specific amounts of income they will receive in any given period in the future, nor do they know the time shape of their income stream, (ii) the household does not know its exact life-span, (iii) household tastes and preferences may change because of unforeseen and seemingly random events (for example, illness or changes in family size) as well as systematic factors such as aging, and (iv) the future course of prices, interest rates, and other parameters to the household are not known with perfect certainty. Analogous phenomena obviously pertain to consumers in natural communities. For example, foragers do not usually know their future foraging opportunities with certainty, or their exact life-span. Thus, for consumers in both natural (*21*) and human communities there may be statistical expectations of future conditions. These expectations are themselves subject to uncertainty and change.

An alternative assumption to optimal behavior of economic agents is satisficing behavior. A satisficer examines alternative courses of action and then chooses the first one that satisfies a set of minimal requirements (*61, 63*). The satisficing model is useful in explaining empirical data such as those collected by Wolpert (*64*) on farm productivity in one area of Sweden indicating that "less than half the area had performances more than 70 percent of the optimum" [see Haggett (*65*)]. This is attributed in part to "the simple fact that Swedish farmers were not aiming at optimum productivity but merely at a satisfactory (but suboptimal) level." Haggett points out the necessity of developing locational models on satisficer rather than optimizer principles. This approach may also prove useful for understanding the economics of populations in natural communities subject to variable conditions.

Another modification of traditional economic models would include a consideration of threshold behavior. Since the costs of acquiring information and determining the responses to changes in the environment may be considerable, organisms may be responsive only to stimuli which exceed thresholds rather than responsive to continuous variation in the environment. In economic models of consumer behavior, the central importance of threshold behavior has been examined by Devletoglou (*66*). In ecological models of predator-prey interactions, the importance of threshold behavior has long been recognized. For example, in the concept of search image "a predator does not learn and remember the worth of a food unless it reaches some threshold abundance (both relative and absolute). Thus foods below this density threshold are eaten proportionally less than when common . . ." (*53*).

Alchian (*67*) has reformulated the theory of the firm using an approach that "embodies the principles of biological evolution and natural selection by interpreting the economic system as an adaptive mechanism which chooses among exploratory actions generated by the adaptive pursuit of 'success' or 'profits.' " Alchian (*67*), and later Enke (*68*), Simon (*61*), Winters (*69*), and Lloyd *et al.* (*59*) argue that profit maximization is a poor single criterion for the behavior of the firm because of inadequate knowledge of opportunities and the uncertainty of the environment. Instead, they develop theories of reinforcement of successful (profitable) behavior and elimination of unsuccessful behavior.

A Transdisciplinary Focus

Economic models of ecological processes contribute a distinctive point of view to ecology. Optimal foraging, population growth, competition, life history strategies, and other ecological phenomena are brought into a common focus in terms of resource allocation processes. Natural communities are viewed in terms of the economics of consumption, production, and mechanisms for bringing into balance producer-consumer activities. This framework is suggestive of the Wells, Huxley, and Wells definition of ecology as biological economics (*22*). Microeconomic principles pertaining to the household, the firm, and markets have been related to their ecological theory counterparts.

Macroeconomic questions—the determinants of total economic activity (ecological productivity), its growth, and fluctuations—are also of obvious interest to ecologists. Hannon (*70*) has already described the energy and nutrient structure of total ecological activity in terms of the Leontieff input-output matrix.

Similarly, macroecological questions may prove of some interest to economists. For example, a study of how natural communities come to grips with resource limitations and achieve a no-growth economy (*55, 71*) may provide guidance for the management of human communities faced with the challenge of making the transition to a steady state economy.

What are the limitations of the comparative approach to economics and ecology? It is readily apparent that at a detailed level of analysis the fields are hardly isomorphic. Surely the organization of man's technology and society differs qualitatively from physiological, genetical, or behavioral rules governing the behavior and social organization of other species. At a finer level of detail the ecology of each species is unique as is the economics of each nation, industry, and firm.

It is at a more general level of description of ecological and economic systems that many similarities have been proposed. Holling (*50*) points to the limits to resources and limits to the responses of organisms to their resources as a fundamental similarity between ecological and economic systems. He further asserts that the diversity of interactions, historical components, spatial characteristics, and structural properties give social and ecological systems a similar degree of complexity which permits one to use the tools, approaches, and languages interchangeably among them. Although our exposition has stressed the manner in which ecology can be viewed in terms of economic principles, it is clear as we have noted in passing, that transfers have been made in both directions. It is, therefore, our belief that deep common principles underlie both fields enabling both economics and ecology to benefit from such transdisciplinary efforts.

A common framework for economic and ecological processes should make possible extensive transfers of concepts and theories between these fields. In this regard, the approach developed here contributes to the goals of general systems theory which attempts to unify areas of knowledge by searching for those "models, principles, and laws which apply to generalized systems irrespective of their particular kind, elements, and the forces involved" (*72*). The general systems viewpoint has been implicit in the work of many authors who have used economic or biological analogies in other disciplines. The 19th-century sociologist Emile Durkheim (*73*) wrote that the concept of the division of labor, for example, "applies to organisms as to societies . . . [and] is no longer considered only as a social institution that has its source in the intelligence and will of men, but is a phenomenon of general biology whose conditions must be sought in the properties of organized matter. The division of labor in society appears to be no more than a particular form of this general process, and societies, in conforming to that law, seem to be yielding to a movement that was born before them, and that similarly governs the entire world."

The existence of common ecological-economic models suggests that it is possible to unify methodologies, concepts, and theories which have independently developed in the two fields (*74*). This prospect should be of interest to strategic planners and managers of our resources. Communications between those whose concerns are with economic well-being and those who strive for ecological balance would be improved if common resource allocation principles were identified.

References and Notes

1. R. I. Lindemann, *Ecology* **23**, 399 (1942).
2. A. J. Lotka, *Elements of Physical Biology* (Williams & Wilkins, Baltimore, 1925); V. Volterra, *Mem. Accad. Naz. Lincei* **2**, 31 (1926); G. F. Gause, *The Struggle for Existence* (Williams & Wilkins, Baltimore, 1934).
3. R. H. MacArthur and E. O. Wilson, *The Theory of Island Biogeography* (Princeton Univ. Press, Princeton, N.J., 1967).
4. P. H. Klopfer, *Behavioral Aspects of Ecology* (Prentice-Hall, Englewood Cliffs, N.J., 1962). Klopfer suggests that the ecologist's fundamental questions concern the allocation of a finite amount of space and energy among species and the temporal dimension of this distribution. León and Tumpson (*5*) suggest that "The classical models of interspecific competition are phenomenological, that is, they purport to describe the trajectories followed by the abundances of both competitors, without specifying either mechanisms or the dynamics of what the competition is for, that is, resources. Yet the different outcomes of competition inferred from these models are most often interpreted in terms of resources."
5. J. A. León and D. B. Tumpson, *J. Theor. Biol.* **50**, 185 (1975).
6. M. L. Cody, *Science* **183**, 1156 (1974).
7. A. Covich, *Conn. Acad. Arts Sci.* **44**, 91 (1972).
8. J. M. Emlen, *Am. Nat.* **100**, 611 (1966); *ibid.* **102**, 385 (1968).
9. M. Gadgil and W. H. Bossert, *ibid.* **104**, 1 (1970).
10. W. J. Hamilton III and K. E. Watt, *Annu. Rev. Ecol. Syst.* **1**, 262 (1970).
11. D. J. Rapport, *Am. Nat.* **105**, 575 (1971).
12. ——— and J. E. Turner, *Ecology* **56**, 942 (1975).
13. ———, *J. Theor. Biol.* **51**, 169 (1975).
14. J. E. Turner and D. J. Rapport, in *Mathematical Problems in Biology*, P. Van den Driessche, Ed. (Springer-Verlag, New York, 1974), pp. 236–240.
15. T. W. Schoener, *Annu. Rev. Ecol. Syst.* **2**, 369 (1971).
16. G. Tullock, *Am. Nat.* **105**, 77 (1971).
17. E. O. Wilson, *Sociobiology* (Harvard Univ. Press, Cambridge, Mass., 1975).
18. G. Oster, *Am. Nat.* **110**, 215 (1976).
19. W. M. Schaffer, *Ecology* **55**, 291 (1974).
20. R. L. Trivers, in *Sexual Selection and the Descent of Man 1871–1971*, B. Campbell, Ed. (Aldine, Chicago, 1972), pp. 136–179.
21. R. H. MacArthur, *Geographical Ecology* (Harper & Row, New York, 1972).
22. H. G. Wells, J. Huxley, G. P. Wells, *The Science of Life* (Doubleday, Garden City, N.Y., 1933).
23. T. R. Malthus, *Population: The First Essay* (reprinted) (Univ. of Michigan Press, Ann Arbor, 1959).
24. C. Darwin, *The Origin of Species by Means of Natural Selection* (Murray, London, 1859).
25. A. Marshall, *Principles of Economics* (Macmillan, London, 1920).
26. J. M. Keynes, *The End of Laissez-Faire* (Hogarth, London, 1927).
27. See, for example, correspondence between Marx and Engels, in *Marx and Engels on Malthus* (Lawrence & Wishart, London, 1953).
28. A. Smith, *The Wealth of Nations* (Dent, London, 1910), p. 16.
29. L. Robbins, *An Essay on the Nature and Significance of Economic Science* (St. Martin's Press, New York, 1932).
30. C. Lloyd, *Microeconomic Analysis* (Irwin, Homewood, Ill., 1967).
31. H. R. Pulliam, *Am. Nat.* **108**, 59 (1974); *ibid.* **109**, 765 (1975).
32. J. M. Emlen and M. G. R. Emlen, *ibid.* **109**, 427 (1975); R. H. MacArthur and E. P. Pianka, *ibid.* **100**, 603 (1966); F. B. Gill and L. L. Wolf, *ibid.* **109**, 491 (1975).
33. In some cases a nontangency solution is obtained involving complete specialization in one type of good.
34. The fitness contours resemble Levins' concept of the adaptive function developed for a description of optimal phenotypes in changing environments [R. Levins, *Evolution in Changing Environments* (Princeton Univ. Press, Princeton, N.J., 1967)].
35. As in the economic model, nontangency solutions can also occur. If the consumption frontier is convex to the origin, the predator's optimal diet would be complete specialization on one prey type.
36. León and Tumpson (*5*) have shown the relevance of these concepts (substitute and complement resources) in models of ecological competition for resources. MacArthur (*21*) independently derived the notion of complementary resources in his competition model.
37. D. J. Rapport, J. Berger, D. B. Reid, *Biol. Bull. (Woods Hole, Mass.)* **142**, 103 (1972).
38. D. J. Rapport, in preparation.
39. Some of the data in (*38*) from these experiments have been given by W. Murdoch, S. Avery, M. E. B. Smyth, *Ecology* **56**, 1094 (1975).
40. Food preferences were not confounded with prey availability. Preference was determined by comparing food uptake in single and mixed cultures. Details of the method can be found in D. J. Rapport and J. E. Turner, *J. Theor. Biol.* **26**, 365 (1970).
41. R. G. Holmberg, in preparation.
42. W. M. Schaffer, *Ecology* **55**, 291 (1974).
43. G. S. Becker, *Econ. J.* **75**, 493 (1965).
44. Repeater producers allocate some energy to reproduction for many periods during their life cycle and comprise the majority of perennials, while "big-bang" reproducers "have a reproductive effort of zero for many ages followed by the suicidal reproductive effort of one. This category includes a few organisms such as the pacific salmon or the bamboo tree" (*9*).
45. B. Heinrich, *Sci. Am.* **228**, 96 (April 1973).
46. A. Losch, *The Economics of Location* (Yale Univ. Press, New Haven, Conn., 1963).
47. A. Covich, *Annu. Rev. Ecol. Syst.*, in press.
48. Edgeworth's theory of contracts [see Oster (*18*)] involves the famous Edgeworth box diagram within which trades among two parties possessing given proportions of two commodities can be analyzed. Edgeworth showed that trading resources could improve the welfare position of both parties up to the point that the "contract curve" was obtained. Further reallocations along the contract curve involve the improvement of one party's welfare at the expense of the other's.
49. F. N. Egerton, *Q. Rev. Biol.* **48**, 322 (1973).
50. C. S. Holling, *Brookhaven Symp. Biol.* **22**, 128 (1969); D. Pimentel, *Science* **159**, 1432 (1968); L. A. Real, *Theor. Pop. Biol.* **8**, 1 (1975).
51. K. E. Boulding, in *Challenging Biological Problems*, J. A. Behnke, Ed. (Oxford Univ. Press, London, 1972), p. 366.
52. D. J. Rapport and J. E. Turner, in *Mathematical Problems in Biology*, P. Van den Driessche, Ed. (Springer-Verlag, New York, 1974), pp. 206–209.
53. C. S. Holling, *Mem. Entomol. Soc. Can.* **45**, 5 (1965).
54. For a discussion of ecological markets in terms of energy price, see Hannon (*55*). Hannon develops the concepts of marginal product pricing in the ecosystem in terms of energetics. His underlying view of biological components as economic production units is strikingly similar to the theory of production in this article [see (*12*)].
55. B. Hannon, *J. Theor. Biol.* **56**, 253 (1976).
56. Hannon (*55*) points out that the economic conditions for perfect competition are probably better satisfied in natural communities than in economic systems.
57. It should be noted that while predator-prey interactions are hardly a mutually beneficial economic exchange, they contain the essential elements of economic market transactions, namely, an interaction of supply and demand factors. In this case supply is of course involuntary. A more exact economic analog in ecological systems is flowering plant–pollinator interactions.
58. T. W. Schoener, *Science* **185**, 27 (1974); in preparation; *Theor. Pop. Biol.* **6**, 265 (1974).
59. C. Lloyd, D. J. Rapport, J. E. Turner, in *Adaptive Economic Models*, R. H. Day and T. Groves, Eds. (Academic Press, New York, 1975), p. 119.
60. W. J. Baumol, *Economic Theory and Operations Analysis* (Prentice-Hall, Englewood Cliffs, N.J., 1961).
61. H. A. Simon, *Models of Man* (Wiley, New York, 1957).
62. M. B. Johnson, *Household Behavior: Consumption, Income and Wealth* (Penguin, Middlesex, England, 1971).
63. H. A. Simon, *Am. Econ. Rev.* **49**, 253 (1959); W. Isard, *General Theory: Social, Political, Economic and Regional* (MIT Press, Cambridge, Mass., 1969).
64. J. Wolpert, *Ann. Assoc. Am. Geog.* **52**, 176 (1964).
65. P. Haggett, *Locational Analysis in Human Geography* (St. Martins Press, New York, 1966).
66. N. E. Devletoglou, *Consumer Behavior* (Harper & Row, London, 1971).
67. A. A. Alchian, *J. Polit. Econ.* **58**, 211 (1950).
68. S. Enke, *Am. Econ. Rev.* **41**, 566 (1951).
69. S. Winters, in *Adaptive Economics Models*, R. H. Day and T. Groves, Eds. (Academic Press, New York, 1975), p. 73.
70. B. Hannon, *J. Theor. Biol.* **41**, 535 (1973).
71. E. P. Odum, *Science* **164**, 262 (1969).
72. L. V. Bertalanffy, *General Systems Theory* (Braziller, New York, 1968). See also M. D. Mesarovic, Ed., *Views on General Systems Theory* (Wiley, New York, 1964); I. Laszlo, *Relevance of General Systems Theory* (Braziller, New York, 1972); R. Rosen, *Optimality Principles in Biology* (Plenum, New York, 1967); in *Adaptive Economic Models*, R. H. Day and T. Groves, Eds. (Academic Press, New York, 1975), p. 39.
73. E. Durkheim, *The Rules of Sociological Method* (Collier-Macmillan, London, 1938).
74. H. A. Regier, P. L. Bishop, D. J. Rapport, *J. Fish. Res. Board Can.* **31**, 1683 (1974); H. A. Regier and D. J. Rapport, in *Proceedings of Symposium on Biological Evaluation of Environmental Impact* (Presidents Council on Environmental Quality, in press).

75. We thank D. Bloomberg, A. Covich, C. Lloyd, E. Rapport, T. Schoener, G. Tullock, A. Turnbull, P. Wollheim, and several anonymous reviewers for critical comments on the manuscript. We thank H. Regier for continuous encouragement and R. Holmberg for permission to use unpublished material. We acknowledge the support of the Canada Council through its I. W. Killam senior research fellowship program. This fellowship was held at Simon Fraser University, British Columbia, Canada.

Ann. Rev. Ecol. Syst. 1978. 9:31–56

OPTIMIZATION THEORY IN EVOLUTION

❖4134

J. Maynard Smith
School of Biological Sciences, University of Sussex, Brighton, Sussex, England

INTRODUCTION

In recent years there has been a growing attempt to use mathematical methods borrowed from engineering and economics in interpreting the diversity of life. It is assumed that evolution has occurred by natural selection, and hence that complex structures and behaviors are to be interpreted in terms of the contribution they make to the survival and reproduction of their possessors—that is, to Darwinian fitness. There is nothing particularly new in this logic, which is also the basis of functional anatomy, and indeed of much physiology and molecular biology. It was followed by Darwin himself in his studies of climbing and insectivorous plants, of fertilization mechanisms and devices to ensure cross-pollination.

What is new is the use of mathematical techniques such as control theory, dynamic programming, and the theory of games to generate a priori hypotheses, and the application of the method to behaviors and life history strategies. This change in method has led to the criticism (e.g. 54, 55) that the basic hypothesis of adaptation is untestable and therefore unscientific, and that the whole program of functional explanation through optimization has become a test of ingenuity rather than an enquiry into truth. Related to this is the criticism that there is no theoretical justification for any maximization principles in biology, and therefore that optimization is no substitute for an adequate genetic model.

My aim in this review is not to summarize the most important conclusions reached by optimization methods, but to discuss the methodology of the program and the criticisms that have been made of it. In doing so, I have taken as my starting point two articles by Lewontin (54, 55). I disagree with some of the views he expresses, but I believe that the development of evolution theory could benefit if workers in optimization paid serious attention to his criticisms.

I first outline the basic structure of optimization arguments, illustrating this with three examples, namely the sex ratio, the locomotion of mammals, and foraging behavior. I then discuss the possibility that some variation may be selectively neutral, and some structures maladaptive. I summarize and comment on criticisms made by Lewontin. The most damaging undoubtedly is the difficulty of testing the

0066-4162/78/1120-0031$01.00

hypotheses that are generated. The next section therefore discusses the methodology of testing; in this section I have relied heavily on the arguments of Curio (23). Finally I discuss mathematical methods. The intention here is not to give the details of the mathematics, but to identify the kinds of problems that have been attacked and the assumptions that have been made in doing so.

THE STRUCTURE OF OPTIMIZATION MODELS

In this section I illustrate the argument with three examples: (*a*) the sex ratio, based on Fisher's (28) treatment and later developments by Hamilton (34), Rosado & Robertson (85), Trivers & Willard (96), and Trivers & Hare (95); (*b*) the gaits of mammals—given a preliminary treatment by Maynard Smith & Savage (66), and further analyzed in several papers in Pedley (78); (*c*) foraging strategies. Theoretical work on the latter subject originated with the papers of Emlen (27) and MacArthur & Pianka (57). I have relied heavily on a recent review by Pyke et al (81). These authors suggest that models have in the main been concerned with four problems: choice by the animal of which types of food to eat (optimal diet); choice of which patch type to feed in; allocation of time to different patches; pattern and speed of movement. In what follows, I shall refer only to two of those—optimal diet and allocation of time to different patches.

All optimization models contain, implicitly or explicitly, an assumption about the "constraints" that are operating, an optimization criterion, and an assumption about heredity. I consider these in turn.

The Constraints: Phenotype Set and State Equations

The constraints are essentially of two kinds. In engineering applications, they concern the "strategy set," which specifies the range of control actions available, and the "state equations," which specify how the state of the system being controlled changes in time. In biological applications, the strategy set is replaced by an assumption about the set of possible phenotypes on which selection can operate.

It is clearly impossible to say what is the "best" phenotype unless one knows the range of possibilities. If there were no constraints on what is possible, the best phenotype would live for ever, would be impregnable to predators, would lay eggs at an infinite rate, and so on. It is therefore necessary to specify the set of possible phenotypes, or in some other way describe the limits on what can evolve. The "phenotype set" is an assumption about what can evolve and to what extent; the "state equations" describe features of the situation that are assumed not to change. This distinction will become clearer when particular examples are discussed. Let us consider the three problems in turn.

SEX RATIO For the sex ratio, the simplest assumption is that a parent can produce a fixed number N of offspring, and that the probability S that each birth will be a male can vary from parent to parent, over the complete range from 0 to 1; the phenotype set is then the set of values of S over this range. Fisher (28) extended this by supposing that males and females "cost" different amounts; i.e. he supposed that a parent could produce α males and β females, where α and β are constrained to lie on or below the line $\alpha + \beta\, k = N$, and k is the cost of a female relative to that of a male. He then concluded that the parent should equalize expenditure on males and females. MacArthur (56) further broadened the phenotype set by insisting only that α and β lie on or below a line of arbitrary shape, and concluded that a parent should maximize $\alpha\beta$. A similar assumption was used by Charnov et al (11) to analyze the evolution of hermaphroditism as opposed to dioecy. Finally, it is possible to ask (97) what is the optimal strategy if a parent can choose not merely a value of S, and hence of the expected sex ratio, but also the variance of the sex ratio.

The important point in the present context is that the optimal solution depends on the assumption made. For example, Crow & Kimura (21) conclude that the sex ratio should be unity, but they do so for a model that assumes that $N = \alpha + \beta$ is a constant.

GAITS In the analysis of gaits, it is assumed that the shapes of bones can vary, but the mechanical properties of bone, muscle and tendon cannot. It is also assumed that changes must be gradual; thus the gaits of ostrich, antelope and kangaroo are seen as different solutions to the same problem, not as solutions to different problems; i.e. they are different "adaptive peaks" (101).

FORAGING STRATEGY In models of foraging behavior, a common assumption is that the way in which an animal allocates its time among various activities (e.g. consuming one prey item rather than another, searching in one kind of patch rather than another, moving between patches rather than continuing to search in the same one) can vary, but the efficiency with which it performs each act cannot. Thus, for example, the length of time it takes to "handle" (capture and consume) a given item, the time and energy spent in moving from place to place, and the time taken to find a given prey item at a given prey density are taken as invariant. Thus the models of foraging so far developed treat the phenotype set as the set of possible behavioral strategies, and treat structure and locomotory or perceptual skills as constants contributing to the state equations (which determine how rapidly an animal adopting some strategy acquires food). In principle there is no reason why optimization models should not be applied to the evolution of structure or skill also; it is simply a question of how the phenotype set is defined.

The Optimization Criterion

Some assumption must then be made concerning what quantity is being maximized. The most satisfactory is the inclusive fitness (see the section on Games Between Relatives, below); in many contexts the individual fitness (expected number of offspring) is equally good. Often, as in the second and third of my examples, neither criterion is possible, and some other assumption is needed. Two points must be made. First, the assumption about what is maximized is an assumption about what selective forces have been responsible for the trait; second, this assumption is part of the hypothesis being tested.

In most theories of sex ratio the basic assumption is that the ratio is determined by a gene acting in a parent, and what is maximized is the number of copies of that gene in future generations. The maximization has therefore a sound basis. Other maximization criteria have been used. For example, Kalmus & Smith (41) propose that the sex ratio maximizes the probability that two individuals meeting will be of different sexes; it is hard to understand such an eccentric choice when the natural one is available.

An equally natural choice—the maximization of the expected number of offspring produced in a lifetime—is available in theories of the evolution of life history strategies. But often no such easy choice is available.

In the analysis of gaits, Maynard Smith & Savage (66) assumed that the energy expenditure at a given speed would be minimized (or, equivalently, that the speed for a given energy expenditure was maximized). This led to the prediction that the proportion of time spent with all four legs off the ground should increase with speed and decrease with size.

In foraging theory, the common assumption is that the animal is maximizing its energy intake per unit time spent foraging. Schoener (87) points out that this is an appropriate choice, whether the animal has a fixed energy requirement and aims to minimize the time spent feeding so as to leave more time for other activities ("time minimizers"), or has a fixed time in which to feed during which it aims to maximize its energy gain ("energy maximizers"). There will, however, be situations in which this is not an appropriate choice. For example, there may be a higher risk of predation for some types of foraging than others. For some animals, the problem may not be to maximize energy intake per unit time, but to take in a required amount of energy, protein, etc, without taking an excess of any one of a number of toxins (S. A. Altmann, personal communication).

Pyke et al (81) point out that the optimal strategy depends on the time scale over which optimization is carried out, for two reasons. First, an animal that has sole access to some resource (e.g. a territory-holder) can afford to manage that resource so as to maximize its yield over a whole season. Second, and more general, optimal behavior depends on a knowledge of the environment, which can be acquired only by experience; this means that, in order to acquire information of value in the long run, an animal may have to behave in a way that is inefficient in the short run.

Having considered the phenotype set and the optimization criterion, a word must be said about their relationship to Levins' (51) concept of a fitness set. Levins was explicitly concerned with defining fitness "in such a way that interpopulation selection would be expected to change a species towards the optimum (maximum fitness) structure." This essentially group-selectionist approach led him to conclusions (e.g. for the conditions for a stable polymorphism) different from those reached from the classic analysis of gene frequencies (93). Nevertheless, Levins' attempt to unite ecological and genetic approaches did lead him to recognize the need for the concept of a fitness set, i.e. the set of all possible phenotypes, each phenotype being characterized by its (individual) fitness in each of the environments in which it might find itself.

Levins' fitness set is thus a combination of what I have called the phenotype set and of a measure of the fitness of each phenotype in every possible environment. It did not allow for the fact that fitnesses may be frequency-dependent (see the section on Games, below). The valuable insight in Levins' approach is that it is only possible to discuss what course phenotypic evolution may take if one makes explicit assumptions about the constraints on what phenotypes are possible. It may be better to use the term "phenotype set" to define these constraints, both because a description of possible phenotypes is a process prior to and separable from an estimation of their fitnesses, and because of the group-selectionist associations of the term "fitness set."

An Assumption About Heredity

Because natural selection cannot produce adaptation unless there is heredity, some assumption, explicit or otherwise, is always present. The nature of this assumption can be important. Fisher (28) assumed that the sex ratio was determined by autosomal genes expressed in the parent, and that mating was random. Hamilton (34) showed that the predicted optima are greatly changed if these assumptions are altered. In particular, he considered the effects of inbreeding, and of genes for meiotic drive. Rosado & Robertson (85), Trivers & Willard (96), and Trivers & Hare (95) have analyzed the effects of genes acting in the children and (in Hymenoptera) in the sterile castes.

It is unusual for the way in which a trait is inherited to have such a crucial effect. Thus in models of mammalian gaits no explicit assumption is made; the implicit assumption is merely that like begets like. The same is true of models of foraging, although in this case "heredity" can be cultural as well as genetic [e.g. (72), for feeding behavior of oyster-catchers].

The question of how optimization models can be tested is the main topic of the next three sections. A few preliminary remarks are needed. Clearly, the first requirement of a model is that the conclusions should follow from the assumptions. This seems not to be the case, for example, for Zahavi's (102) theory of sexual selection (61). A more usual difficulty is that the conclusions depend on unstated assumptions. For example, Fisher does not state that his sex ratio argument assumes random mating, and this was not noticed until Hamilton's 1967 paper (34). Maynard Smith & Price (65) do not state that the idea of an ESS (evolutionarily stable strategy) assumes asexual inheritance. It is probably true that no model ever states all its assumptions explicitly. One reason for writing this review is to encourage authors to become more aware of their assumptions.

A particular model can be tested either by a direct test of its assumptions, or by comparing its predictions with observation. The essential point is that in testing a model we are *not* testing the general proposition that nature optimizes, but the specific hypotheses about constraints, optimization criteria, and heredity. Usually we test whether we have correctly identified the selective forces responsible for the trait in question. But we should not forget hypotheses about constraints or heredity. For example, the weakest feature of theories concerning the sex ratio is that there is little evidence for the existence of genetic variance of the kind assumed by Fisher [for references, see (63)]. It may be for this reason that the greatest successes of sex ratio theory (34, 95) have concerned Hymenoptera, in which it is easy to see how genes in the female parent can affect the sex of her children.

NEUTRALITY AND MALADAPTATION

I have said that when testing optimization models one is not testing the hypothesis that nature optimizes. But if it is not the case that the structure and behavior of organisms are nicely adapted to ensure their survival and reproduction, optimization models cannot be useful. What justification have we for assuming this?

The idea of adaptation is older than Darwinism. In the form of the argument from design it was a buttress of religious belief. For Darwin, the problem was not to prove that organisms were adapted but to explain how adaptation could arise without a creator. He was quite willing to accept that some characteristics are "selectively neutral." For example, he says (26) of the sterile dark red flower at the center of the umbel of the wild carrot: "That the modified central flower is of no functional importance to the plant is almost certain." Indeed, Darwin has been chided by Cain (8) for too readily accepting Owen's argument that the homology between bones of limbs of different vertebrates is nonadaptive. For Darwin the argument was welcome, because the resemblance could then be taken as evidence for genetic relationship (or, presumably, for a paucity of imagination on the part of the creator). But Cain points out that the homology would not have been preserved if it were not adaptive.

Biologists differ greatly in the extent to which they expect to find a detailed fit between structure and function. It may be symptomatic of the times that when, in conversation, I raised Darwin's example of the carrot, two different functional explanations were at once suggested. I suspect that these explanations were fanciful. But however much one may be in doubt about the function of the antlers of the Irish Elk or the tail of the peacock, one can hardly suppose them to be selectively neutral. In general, the structural and behavioral traits chosen for functional analysis are of a kind that rules out neutrality as a plausible explanation. Curio (23) makes the valid point that the ampullae of Lorenzini in elasmobranchs were studied for many years before their role in enabling a fish to locate prey buried in the mud was demonstrated (40), yet the one hypothesis that was never entertained was that the organ was functionless. The same could be said of Curio's own work (24) on the function of mobbing in birds; behavior so widespread, so constant, and so apparently dangerous calls for a functional explanation.

There are, however, exceptions to the rule that functional investigations are carried out with the aim of identifying particular selective forces, and not of demonstrating that traits are adaptive. The work initiated by Cain & Sheppard (9) on shell color and banding in *Cepaea* was in part aimed at refuting the claim that the variation was selectively neutral and explicable by genetic drift. To that extent, the work was aimed at demonstating adaptation as such; it is significant, however, that the work has been most successful when it has been possible to identify a particular selection pressure (e.g. predation by thrushes).

At present, of course, the major argument between neutral and selective theories concerns enzyme polymorphism. I cannot summarize the argument here, but a few points on methodology are relevant. The argument arose because of the formulation by Kimura (43) and King & Jukes (44) of the "neutral" hypothesis; one reason for proposing it was the difficulty of accounting for the extensive variation by selection. Hence the stimulus was quite different from that prompting most functional investigations; it was the existence of widespread variation in a trait of no obvious selective significance.

The neutral hypothesis is a good "Popperian" one; if it is false, it should be possible to show it. In contrast, the hypothesis of adaptation is virtually irrefutable. In practice, however, the statistical predictions of the neutral theory depend on so many unknowns (mutation rates, the past history of population number and structure, hitch-hiking from other loci) that it has proved hard to test (53). The difficulties have led some geneticists (e.g. 14) to propose that the only way in which the matter can be settled is by the classical methods of ecological genetics, i.e. by identifying the specific selection pressures associated with particular enzyme loci. The approach has had some success, but is always open to the objection that the loci for which the neutral hypothesis has been falsified are a small and biased sample.

In general, then, the problems raised by the neutral mutation theory and by optimization theory are wholly different. The latter is concerned with traits that differ between species and that can hardly be selectively neutral, but whose selective significance is not fully understood.

A more serious difficulty for optimization theory is the occurrence of maladaptive traits. Optimization is based on the assumption that the population is adapted to the contemporary environment, whereas evolution is a process of continuous change. Species lag behind a changing environment. This is particularly serious when studying species in an environment that has recently been drastically changed by man. For example, Lack (48) argued that the number of eggs laid by a bird maximizes the number of surviving young. Although there is much supporting evidence, there are some apparent exceptions. For example, the gannet *Sula bassana* lays a single egg. Studying gannets on the Bass Rock, Nelson (71) found that if a second egg is added the pair can successfully raise two young. The explanation can hardly be a lack of genetic variability, because species nesting in the Humboldt current off Peru lay and successfully raise two or even three eggs.

Lack (48) suggests that the environment for gannets may recently have improved, as evidenced by the recent increase in the population on the Bass Rock. Support for this interpretation comes from the work of Jarvis (39) on the closely related *S. capensis* in South Africa. This species typically lays one egg, but 1% of nests contain two. Using methods similar to Nelson's, Jarvis found that a pair can raise two chicks to fledgings, but that the average weight of twins was lower than singles, and in each nest one twin was always considerably lighter than its fellow. There is good evidence that birds fledging below the average weight are more likely to die soon after. Difficulties of a similar kind arise for the Glaucous Gull (see 45).

The undoubted existence of maladaptive traits, arising because evolutionary change is not instantaneous, is the most serious obstacle to the testing of optimization theories. The difficulty must arise; if species were perfectly adapted evolution would cease. There is no easy way out. Clearly a wholesale reliance on evolutionary lag to save hypotheses that would otherwise be falsified would be fatal to the whole research program. The best we can do is to invoke evolutionary lag sparingly, and only when there are independent grounds for believing that the environment has changed recently in a relevant way.

What then is the status of the concept of adaptation? In the strong form—that all organs are perfectly adapted—it is clearly false; the vermiform appendix is sufficient to refute it. For Darwin, adaptation was an obvious fact that required an explanation; this still seems a sensible point of view. Adaptation can also be seen as a necessary consequence of natural selection. The latter I regard as a refutable scientific theory (60); but it must be refuted, if at all, by genetic experiment and not by the observation of complex behavior.

CRITIQUES OF OPTIMIZATION THEORY

Lewontin (55) raises a number of criticisms, which I discuss in turn.

Do Organs Solve Problems?

Most organs have many functions. Therefore, if a hypothesis concerning function fails correctly to predict behavior, it can always be saved by proposing an additional function. Thus hypotheses become irrefutable and metaphysical, and the whole program merely a test of ingenuity in conceiving possible functions. Three examples follow; the first is one used by Lewontin.

Orians & Pearson (73) calculated the optimal food item size for a bird, on the assumption that food intake is to be maximized. They found that the items diverged from random in the expected direction, but did not fit the prediction quantitatively. They explained the discrepancy by saying that a bird must visit its nest frequently to discourage predators. Lewontin (54) comments:

> This is a paradigm for adaptive reconstruction. The problem is originally posed as efficiency for food-gathering. A deviation of behavior from random, in the direction predicted, is regarded as strong support for the adaptive explanation of the behavior and the discrepancy from the predicted optimum is accounted for by an ad hoc secondary problem which acts as a constraint on the solution to the first. . . . By allowing the theorist to postulate various combinations of "problems" to which manifest traits are optimal "solutions", the adaptationist programme makes of adaptation a metaphysical postulate, not only incapable of refutation, but necessarily confirmed by every observation. This is the caricature that was immanent in Darwin's insight that evolution is the product of natural selection.

It would be unfair to subject Orians alone to such criticism, so I offer two further examples from my own work.

First, as explained earlier, Maynard Smith & Savage (66) predicted qualitative features of mammalian gaits. However, their model failed to give a correct quantitative prediction. I suspect that if the model were modified to allow for wind resistance and the visco-elastic properties of muscle, the quantitative fit would be improved;

at present, however, this is pure speculation. In fact, it looks as if a model that gives quantitatively precise predictions will be hard to devise (1).

Second, Maynard Smith & Parker (64) predicted that populations will vary in persistence or aggressiveness in contest situations, but that individuals will not indicate their future behavior by varying levels of intensity of display. Rohwer (84) describes the expected variability in aggressivity in the Harris sparrow in winter flocks, but also finds a close correlation between aggressivity and a signal (amount of black in the plumage). I could point to the first observation as a confirmation of our theory, and explain how, by altering the model (by changing the phenotype set to permit the detection of cheating), one can explain the second.

What these examples, and many others, have in common is that a model gives predictions that are in part confirmed by observation but that are contradicted in some important respect. I agree with Lewontin that such discrepancies are inevitable if a simple model is used, particularly a model that assumes each organ or behavior to serve only one function. I also agree that if the investigator adds assumptions to his model to meet each discrepancy, there is no way in which the hypothesis of adaptation can be refuted. But the hypothesis of adaptation is not under test.

What is under test is the specific set of hypotheses in the particular model. Each of the three example models above has been falsified, at least as a complete explanation of these particular data. But since all have had some qualitative success, it seems quite appropriate to modify them (e.g. by allowing for predation, for wind resistance, for detection of cheating). What is not justified is to modify the model and at the same time to claim that the model is confirmed by observation. For example, Orians would have to show that his original model fits more closely in species less exposed to predation. I would have to show that Rohwer's data fit the "mixed ESS" model in other ways—in particular, that the fitness of the different morphs are approximately equal. If, as may well be the case, the latter prediction of the ESS model does not hold, it is hard to see how it could be saved.

If the ESS model proves irrelevant to the Harris sparrow, it does not follow, however, that it is never relevant. By analogy, the assertion is logically correct that there will be a stable polymorphism if the heterozygote at a locus with two alleles is fitter than either homozygote. The fact that there are polymorphisms not maintained by heterosis does not invalidate the logic. The (difficult) empirical question is whether polymorphisms are often maintained by heterosis. I claim a similar logical status for the prediction of a mixed ESS.

In population biology we need simple models that make predictions that hold qualitatively in a number of cases, even if they are contradicted in detail in all of them. One can say with some confidence, for example, that no model in May's *Stability and Complexity in Model Ecosystems* describes exactly any actual case, because no model could ever include all relevant features. Yet the models do make qualitative predictions that help to explain real ecosystems. In the analysis of complex systems, the best we can hope for are models that capture some essential feature.

To summarize my comments on this point, Lewontin is undoubtedly right to complain if an optimizer first explains the discrepancy between theory and observation by introducing a new hypothesis, and then claims that his modified theory has been confirmed. I think he is mistaken in supposing that the aim of optimization theories is to confirm a general concept of adaptation.

Is There Genetic Variance?

Natural selection can optimize only if there is appropriate genetic variance. What justification is there for assuming the existence of such variance? The main justification is that, with rare exceptions, artificial selection has always proved effective, whatever the organism or the selected character (53).

A particular difficulty arises because genes have pleiotropic effects, so that selection for trait A may alter trait B; in such cases, any attempt to explain the changes in B in functional terms is doomed to failure. There are good empirical grounds for doubting whether the difficulty is as serious as might be expected from the widespread nature of pleiotropy. The point can best be illustrated by a particular example. Lewontin (54) noted that in primates there is a constant allometric relationship between tooth size and body size. It would be a waste of time, therefore, to seek a functional explanation of the difference between the tooth size of the gorilla and of the rhesus monkey, since the difference is probably a simple consequence of the difference in body size.

It is quite true that for most teeth there is a constant allometric relationship between tooth and body size, but there is more to it than that (36). The canine teeth (and the teeth occluding with them) of male primates are often larger than those of females, even when allowance has been made for the difference in body size. This sex difference is greater in species in which males compete for females than in monogamous species, and greater in ground-living species (which are more exposed to predation) than in arboreal ones. Hence there is sex-limited genetic variance for canine tooth size, independent of body size, and the behavioral and ecological correlations suggest that this variance has been the basis of adaptation. It would be odd if there were tooth-specific, sex-limited variance, but no variance for the relative size of the teeth as a whole. However, there is some evidence for the latter. The size of the cheek teeth in females (relative to the size predicted from their body size) is significantly greater in those species with a higher proportion of leaves (as opposed to fruit, flowers, or animal matter) in their diets.

Thus, although at first sight the data on primate teeth suggest that there may be nothing to explain in functional terms, a more detailed analysis presents quite a different picture. More generally, changes in allometric relationships can and do occur during evolution (30).

I have quoted Lewontin as a critic of adaptive explanation, but it would misinterpret him to imply that he rejects all such explanations. He remarks (54) that "the serious methodological difficulties in the use of adaptive arguments should not blind us to the fact that many features of organisms are adaptations to obvious environmental 'problems.'" He goes on to argue that if natural selection is to produce adaptation, the mapping of character states into fitnesses must have two characteristics: "continuity" and "quasi-independence." By continuity is meant that small changes in a character result in small changes in the ecological relations of the organism; if this were not so it would be hard to improve a character for one role without ruining it for another. By quasi-independence is meant that the developmental paths are such that a variety of mutations may occur, all with the same effect on the primary character, but with different effects on other characters. It is hard to think of better evidence for quasi-independence than the evolution of primate canines.

To sum up this point, I accept the logic of Lewontin's argument. If I differ from him (and on this point he is his own strongest critic), it is in thinking that genetic variance of an appropriate kind will usually exist. But it may not always do so.

It has been an implicit assumption of optimization models that the optimal phenotype can breed true. There are two kinds of reasons why this might not be true. The first is that the optimal phenotype may be produced by a heterozygote. This would be a serious difficulty if one attempted to use optimization methods to analyze the genetic structure of populations, but I think that would be an inappropriate use of the method. Optimization models are useful for analyzing phenotypic evolution, but not the genetic structuring of populations. A second reason why the optimal phenotype may not breed true is more serious: the evolutionarily stable population may be phenotypically variable. This point is discussed further in the section on Games, below.

The assumption concerning the phenotype set is based on the range of variation observable within species, the phenotypes of related species, and on plausible guesses at what phenotypes might arise under selection. It is rare to have any information on the genetic basis of the phenotypic variability. Hence, although it is possible to introduce specific genetic assumptions into optimization models (e.g. 2, 89), this greatly complicates the analysis. In general, the assumption of "breeding true" is reasonable in particular applications; models in which genes appear explicitly need to be analyzed to decide in what situations the assumption may mislead us.

The Effects of History

If, as Wright (101) suggested, there are different "adaptive peaks" in the genetic landscape, then depending on initial conditions, different populations faced with identical "problems" may finish up in different stable states. Such divergence may be exaggerated if evolution takes the form of a "game" in which the optimal phenotype for one individual depends on what others are doing (see the section on Games, below). An example is Fisher's (28) theory of sexual selection, which can lead to an "auto-catalytic" exaggeration of initially small differences. Jaçob (38) has recently emphasized the importance of such historical accidents in evolution.

As an example of the difficulties that historical factors can raise for functional explanations, consider the evolution of parental care. A simple game-theory model (62) predicts that for a range of ecological parameters either of two patterns would be stable: male parental care only, or female care only. Many fish and amphibia show one or the other of these patterns. At first sight, the explanation of why some species show one pattern and others the other seems historical; the reasons seem lost in an unknown past. However, things may not be quite so bad. At a recent discussion of fish behavior at See-Wiesen the suggestion emerged that if uniparental care evolved from no parental care, it would be male care, whereas if it evolved from biparental care it would be female care. This prediction is plausible in the light of the original game-theory model, although not a necessary consequence of it. It is, however, testable by use of the comparative data; if it is true, male care should occur in families that also include species showing no care, and female care in families that include species showing biparental care. This may not prove to be the case; the example is given to show that even if there are alternative adaptive peaks, and in the absence of a relevant fossil record, it may still be possible to formulate testable hypotheses.

What Optimization Criterion Should One Use?

Suppose that, despite all difficulties, one has correctly identified the "problem." Suppose, for example, that in foraging it is indeed true that an animal should maximize *E*, its rate of energy intake. We must still decide in what circumstances to maximize *E*. If the animal is alone in a uniform environment, no difficulty arises. But if we allow for competition and for a changing environment, several choices of optimization procedure are possible. For example, three possibilities arise if we allow just for competition:

1. The "maximin" solution: Each animal maximizes *E* on the assumption that other individuals behave in the least favorable way for it.
2. The "Pareto" point: The members of the population behave so that no individual can improve its intake without harming others.
3. The ESS: The members of the population adopt feeding strategy *I* such that no mutant individual adopting a strategy other than *I* could do better than typical members.

These alternatives are discussed further in the section on Games, below. For the moment, it is sufficient to say that the choice among them is not arbitrary, but follows from assumptions about the mode of inheritance and the population structure. For individual selection and parthenogenetic inheritance, the ESS is the appropriate choice.

Lewontin's criticism would be valid if optimizers were in the habit of assuming the truth of what Haldane once called "Pangloss' theorem," which asserts that animals do those things that maximize the chance of survival of their species. If optimization rested on Pangloss' theorem it would be right to reject it. My reason for thinking that Lewontin regards optimization and Pangloss' theorem as equivalent is that he devotes the last section of his paper to showing that in *Drosophila* a characteristic may be established by individual selection and yet may reduce the competitive ability of the population relative to others. The point is correct and important, but in my view does not invalidate most recent applications of optimization.

THE METHODOLOGY OF TESTING

The crucial hypothesis under test is usually that the model correctly incorporates the selective forces responsible for the evolution of a trait. Optimization models sometimes make fairly precise quantitative predictions that can be tested. However, I shall discuss the question of how functional explanations can be tested more generally, including cases in which the predictions are only qualitative. It is convenient to distinguish comparative, quantitative, and individual-variation methods.

Comparative Tests

Given a functional hypothesis, there are usually testable predictions about the development of the trait in different species. For example, two main hypothesis have been proposed to account for the greater size of males in many mammalian species: It is a consequence of competition among males for females; or it arises because the two sexes use different resources. If the former hypothesis is true, dimorphism should be greater in harem-holding and group-living species, whereas if the latter is true it should be greater in monogamous ones, and in those with a relatively equal adult sex ratio.

Clutton-Brock et al (16) have tested these hypotheses by analyzing 42 species of primates (out of some 200 extant species) for which adequate breeding data are available. The data are consistent with the sexual selection hypothesis, and show no sign of the trend predicted by the resource differentiation hypothesis. The latter can therefore be rejected, at least as a major cause of sexual dimorphism in primates. It does not follow that inter-male competition is the only relevant selective factor (82). Nor do their observations say anything about the causes of sexual dimorphism in other groups. It is interesting (though not strictly relevant at this point) that the analysis also showed a strong correlation between female body size and degree of dimorphism. This trend, as was first noted by Rensch (83), occurs in a number of taxa, but has never received an entirely satisfactory explanation.

The comparative method requires some criterion for inclusion of species. This may be purely taxonomic (e.g. all primates, all passerine birds), or jointly taxonomic and geographic (e.g. all African ungulates, all passerines in a particular forest). Usually, some species must be omitted because data are not available. Studies on primates can include a substantial proportion of extant species (16, 68); in contrast, Schoener (86), in one of the earliest studies of this type, included all birds for which data were available and that also met certain criteria of territoriality, but he had to be content with a small fraction of extant species. It is therefore important to ask whether the sample of species is biased in ways likely to affect the hypothesis under test. Most important is that there be some criterion of inclusion, since otherwise species may be included simply because they confirm (or contradict) the hypothesis under test.

Most often, limitations of data will make it necessary to impose both taxonomic and geographic criteria. This need not prevent such data from being valuable, either in generating or in testing hypotheses; examples are analyses of flocking in birds (7, 31) and of breeding systems in forest plants (3, 4).

A second kind of difficulty concerns the design of significance tests. Different species cannot always be treated as statistically independent. For example, all gibbons are monogamous, and all are arboreal and frugivorous, but, since all may be descended from a single ancestor with these properties, they should be treated as a single case in any test of association (not that any is suspected). To take an actual example of this difficulty, Lack (49) criticized Verner & Willson's (98) conclusion that polygamy in passerines is associated with marsh and prairie habitats on the grounds that many of the species concerned belong to a single family, the Icteridae.

Statistical independence and other methodological problems in analyzing comparative data are discussed by Clutton-Brock & Harvey (17). In analyzing the primate data, they group together as a single observation all congeneric species belonging to the same ecological category. This is a conservative procedure, in that it is unlikely to find spurious cases of statistical significance. Their justification for treating genera, but not families, as units is that for their data there are significant differences between genera within families for seven of the eight ecological and behavioral variables, but significant additional variation between families for only two of them. It may be, however, that a more useful application of statistical methods is their use (17) of partial regression, which enables them to examine the effects of a particular variable when the effects of other variables have been removed, and to ask how much of the total variation in some trait is accounted for by particular variables.

Quantitative Tests

Quantitative tests can be illustrated by reference to some of the predictions of foraging theory. Consider first the problem of optimal diet. The following model situation has been widely assumed. There are a number of different kinds of food items. An animal can search simultaneously for all of them. Each item has a characteristic food value and "handling time" (the time taken to capture and consume it). For any given set of densities and hence frequencies of encounter, the animal must only decide which items it should consume and which ignore.

Pyke et al (81) remark that no fewer than eight authors have independently derived the following basic result. The animal should rank the items in order of $V =$ food value/handling time. Items should be added to the diet in rank order, provided that for each new item the value of V is greater than the rate of food intake for the diet without the addition. This basic result leads to three predictions:

1. Greater food abundance should lead to greater specialization. This qualitative prediction was first demonstrated by Ivlev (37) for various fish species in the laboratory, and data supporting it have been reviewed by Schoener (87). Curio (25) quotes a number of cases that do not fit.
2. For fixed densities, a food type should either be always taken, or never taken.
3. Whether a food item should be taken is independent of its density, and depends on the densities of food items of higher rank.

Werner & Hall (100) allowed bluegill sunfish to feed on *Daphnia* of three different size classes; the diets observed agreed well with the predictions of the model. Krebs et al (47) studied Great Tits foraging for parts of mealworms on a moving conveyor belt. They confirmed prediction 3 but not 2; that is, they found that whether small pieces were taken was independent of the density of small pieces, but, as food abundance rose, small pieces were dropped only gradually from the diet. Goss-

Custard (29) has provided field evidence confirming the model from a study of redshank feeding on marine worms of different sizes, and Pulliam (80) has confirmed it for Chipping Sparrows feeding on seeds.

Turning to the problem of how long an animal should stay in a patch before moving to another, there is again a simple prediction, which Charnov (10) has called the "Marginal Value Theorem" [the same theorem was derived independently by Parker & Stuart (77) in a different context]. It asserts that an animal should leave a patch when its rate of intake in the patch (its "marginal" rate) drops to the average rate of intake for the habitat as a whole. It is a corollary that the marginal rate should be the same for all patches in the habitat. Two laboratory experiments on tits (20, 46) agree well with the prediction.

A more general problem raised by these experiments is discussed by Pyke et al (81). How does an animal estimate the parameters it needs to know before it can perform the required optimization? How much time should it spend acquiring information? Sometimes these questions may receive a simple answer. Thus the results of Krebs et al (46) suggest that a bird leaves a patch if it has not found an item of food for some fixed period τ (which varied with the overall abundance of food). The bird seems to be using τ, or rather $1/\tau$, as an estimate of its marginal capture rate. But not all cases are so simple.

Individual Variation

The most direct way of testing a hypothesis about adaptation is to compare individuals with different phenotypes, to see whether their fitnesses vary in the way predicted by the hypothesis. This was the basis of Kettlewell's (42) classic demonstration of selection on industrial melanism in moths. In principle, the individual differences may be produced by experimental interference [Curio's (23) "method of altering a character"] or they may be genetic or of unknown origin (Curio's "method of variants"). Genetic differences are open to the objection that genes have pleiotropic effects, and occasionally are components of supergenes in which several closely linked loci affecting the same function are held in linkage disequilibrium, so that the phenotypic difference responsible for the change in fitness may not be the one on which attention is concentrated. This difficulty, however, is trivial compared to that which arises when two species are compared.

The real difficulty in applying this method to behavioral differences is that suitable individual differences are often absent and experimental interference is impractical. Although it is hard to alter behavior experimentally, it may be possible to alter its consequences. Tinbergen et al (94) tested the idea that gulls remove egg shells from the nest because the shells attract predators to their eggs and young; they placed egg shells close to eggs and recorded a higher predation rate.

However, the most obvious field of application of this method arises when a population is naturally variable. Natural variation in a phenotype may be maintained by frequency-dependent selection; in game-theoretical terms, the stable state may be a mixed strategy. If a particular case of phenotypic variability (genetic or not) is thought to be maintained in this way, it is important to measure the fitnesses of individuals with different phenotypes. At a mixed ESS (which assumes parthenogenetic inheritance) these fitnesses are equal; with sexual reproduction, exact equality is not guaranteed, but approximate equality is a reasonable expectation (91). If the differences are not genetic, we still expect a genotype to evolve that adopts the different strategies with frequencies that equalize their payoffs.

The only test of this kind known to me is Parker's (76) measurement of the mating success of male dungflies adopting different strategies. His results are consistent with a "mixed ESS" interpretation; it is not known whether the differences are genetic. The importance of tests of this kind lies in the fact that phenotypic variability can have other explanations; for example, it may arise from random environmental effects, or from genes with heterotic effects. In such cases, equality of fitness between phenotypes is not expected.

MATHEMATICAL APPROACHES TO OPTIMIZATION

During the past twenty years there has been a rapid development of mathematical techniques aimed at solving problems of optimization and control arising in economics and engineering. These stem from the concepts of "dynamic programming" (5) and of the "maximum principle" (79). The former is essentially a computer procedure to seek the best control policy in particular cases without the hopelessly time-consuming task of looking at every possibility. The latter is an extension of the classic methods of the calculus of variations that permits one to allow for "inequality" constraints on the state and control variables (e.g. in the resource allocation model discussed below, the proportion u of the available resources allocated to seeds must obey the constraint $u<1$).

This is not the place to describe these methods, even if I were competent to do so. Instead, I shall describe the kinds of problems that can be attacked. If a biologist has a problem of one of these kinds, he would do best to consult a mathematician. For anyone wishing to learn more of the mathematical background, Clark (12) provides an excellent introduction.

I discuss in turn "optimization," in which the problem is to choose an optimal policy in an environment without competitors; "games," in which the environment includes other "players" who are also attempting to optimize something; and "games of inclusive fitness," in which the "players" have genes in common. I shall use as an illustration the allocation of resources between growth and reproduction.

Optimization

CHOICE OF A SINGLE VALUE The simplest type of problem, which requires for its solution only the technique of differentiation, is the choice of a value for a single parameter. For example, in discussing the evolution of gaits, Maynard Smith & Savage (66) found an expression for P, the power output, as a function of the speed V, of size S, and of J, the fraction of time for which all four legs are off the ground. By solving the equation $\mathrm{d}P/\mathrm{d}J=0$, an equation $J=\mathrm{f}(V,S)$ was obtained, describing the optimum gait as a function of speed and size.

Few problems are as simple as this, but some more complex cases can be reduced to problems of this kind, as will appear below.

A SIMPLE PROBLEM IN SEQUENTIAL CONTROL Most optimization theory is concerned with how a series of sequential decisions should be taken. For example, consider the growth of an annual plant (19, 69). The rate at which the plant can accumulate resources depends on its size. The resources can be allocated either for further growth, or to seeds, or divided between them. For a fixed starting size and length of season, how should the plant allocate its resources so as to maximize the total number of seeds produced?

In this problem, the "state" of the system at any time is given simply by the plant's size, x; the "control variable" $u(t)$ is the fraction of the incoming resource allocated to seeds at time t; the "constraints" are the initial size, the length of the season, the fact that $u(t)$ must lie between 0 and 1, and the "state equation,"

$$dx/dt = F[x(t), u(t)], \qquad 1.$$

which describes how the system changes as a function of its state and of the control variable.

If equation 1 is linear in u, it can be shown that the optimal control is "bang-bang"—that is, $u(t) = 0$ up to some critical time t^*, and subsequently $u(t) = 1$. The problem is thus reduced to finding the single value, t^*. But if equation 1 is nonlinear, or has stochastic elements, the optimal control may be graded.

MORE COMPLEX CONTROL PROBLEMS Consider first the "state" of the system. This may require description by a vector rather than by a single variable. Thus suppose the plant could also allocate resources to the production of toxins that increased its chance of survival. Then its state would require measures of both size and toxicity. The state description must be sufficient for the production of a state equation analogous to equation 1. The state must also include any information used in determining the control function $u(t)$. This is particularly important when analyzing the behavior of an animal that can learn. Thus suppose that an animal is foraging, and that its decisions on whether to stay in a given patch or to move depend on information it has acquired about the distribution of food in patches; then this information is part of the state of the animal [for a discussion, see (20)].

Just as the state description may be multi-dimensional, so may the control function; for example, for the toxic plant the control function must specify the allocation both to seeds and to toxins.

The state equation may be stochastic. Thus the growth of a plant depends on whether it rains. A plant may be supposed to "know" the probability of rain (i.e. its genotype may be adapted to the frequency of rain in previous generations) but not whether it will actually rain. In this case, a stochastic state equation may require a graded control. This connection between stochasticity and a "compromise" response as opposed to an all-or-none one is a common feature of optimal control. A second example is the analysis by Oster & Wilson (75) of the optimal division into castes in social insects: A predictable environment is likely to call for a single type of worker, while an uncertain one probably calls for a division into several castes.

REVERSE OPTIMALITY McFarland (67) has suggested an alternative approach. The typical one is to ask how an organism should behave in order to maximize its fitness. Mathematically, this requires that one define an "objective function" that must be maximized ("objective" here means "aim" or "goal"); in the plant example, the objective function is the number of seeds produced, expressed as a function of x and $u(t)$. But a biologist may be faced with a different problem. Suppose that he knew, by experiment, how the plant actually allocates its resources. He could then ask what the plant is actually maximizing. If the plant is perfectly adapted, the objective function so obtained should correspond to what Sibly & McFarland (88) call the "cost function"—i.e. the function that should be maximized if the organism is maximizing its fitness. A discrepancy would indicate maladaptation.

There are difficulties in seeing how this process of reverse optimality can be used. Given that the organism's behavior is "consistent" (i.e. if it prefers A to B and B to C, it prefers A to C), it is certain that its behavior maximizes *some* objective function; in general there will be a set of functions maximized. Perfect adaptation then requires only that the cost function correspond to one member of this set. A more serious difficulty is that it is not clear what question is being asked. If a discrepancy is found, it would be hard to say whether this was because costs had been wrongly measured or because the organism was maladapted. This is a particular example of my general point that it is not sensible to test the hypothesis that animals optimize. But it may be that the reverse optimality approach will help to analyze how animals in fact take decisions.

Games

Optimization of the kind just discussed treats the environment as fixed, or as having fixed stochastic properties. It corresponds to that part of population genetics that assumes fitnesses to be independent of genotype frequencies. A number of selective processes have been proposed as frequency-dependent, including predation (13, 70) and disease (15, 32). The maintenance of polymorphism in a varied environment (50) is also best seen as a case of frequency-dependence (59). The concept can be applied directly to phenotypes.

The problem is best formulated in terms of the theory of games, first developed (99) to analyze human conflicts. The essence of a game is that the best strategy to adopt depends on what one's opponent will do; in the context of evolution, this means that the fitness of a phenotype depends on what others are present; i.e. fitnesses are frequency-dependent.

The essential concepts are those of a "strategy" and a "payoff matrix." A strategy is a specification of what a "player" will do in every situation in which it may find itself; in the plant example, a typical strategy would be to allocate all resources to growth for 20 days, and then divide resources equally between growth and seeds. A strategy may be "pure" (i.e. without chance elements) or "mixed" (i.e. of the form "do A with probability p and B with probability $1-p$," where A and B are pure strategies).

The "payoff" to an individual adopting strategy A in competition to one adopting B is written $E(A, B)$, which expresses the expected *change* in the fitness of the player adopting *A* if his opponent adopts *B.* The evolutionary model is then of a population of individuals adopting different strategies. They pair off at random, and their fitnesses change according to the payoff matrix. Each individual then produces offspring identical to itself, in numbers proportional to the payoff it has accumulated. Inheritance is thus parthenogenetic, and selection acts on the individual. It is also assumed that the population is infinite, so that the chance of meeting an opponent adopting a particular strategy is independent of one's own strategy.

The population will evolve to an evolutionarily stable strategy, or ESS, if one exists (64). An ESS is a strategy that, if almost all individuals adopt it, no rare mutant can invade. Thus let I be an ESS, and J a rare mutant strategy of frequency $p \ll 1$. Writing the fitnesses of I and J as $W(I)$ and $W(J)$,

$$W(I) = C + (1-p)\, E\,(I, I) + p\, E\,(I, J);$$

$$W(J) = C + (1-p)\, E\,(J, I) + p\, E\,(J, J).$$

In these equations C is the fitness of an individual before engaging in a contest. Since I is an ESS, $W(I) > W(J)$ for all $J \neq I$; that is, remembering that p is small, *either*

$$E\,(I, I) > E\,(J, I), \text{ or}$$
$$E\,(I, I) = E\,(J, I) \text{ and } E\,(I, J) > E\,(J, J). \qquad 2.$$

These conditions (expressions 2) are the definition of an ESS.

Consider the matrix in Table 1. For readers who prefer a biological interpretation, *A* is "Hawk" and *B* is "Dove"; thus *A* is a bad strategy to adopt against *A*, because of the risk of serious injury, but a good strategy to adopt against *B*, and so on.

The game has no pure ESS, because $E\,(A, A) < E\,(B, A)$ and $E\,(B, B) < E\,(A, B)$. It is easy to show that the mixed strategy—playing *A* and *B* with equal probability—is an ESS. It is useful to compare this with other "solutions," each of which has a possible biological interpretation:

THE MAXIMIN SOLUTION This is the pessimist's solution, playing the strategy that minimizes your losses if your opponent does what is worst for you. For our matrix, the maximin strategy is always to play *B.* Lewontin (52) suggested that this strategy is appropriate if the "player" is a species and its opponent nature: The species should minimize its chance of extinction when nature does its worst. This is the "existential game" of Slobodkin & Rapoport (92). It is hard to see how a

Table 1 Payoff matrix for a game; the values in the matrix give the payoff to Player 1

	Player 2	
	A	*B*
Player 1		
A	1	5
B	2	4

species could evolve this strategy, except by group selection. (Note that individual selection will not necessarily minimize the chance of death: A mutant that doubled the chance that an individual would die before maturity, but that quadrupled its fecundity if it did survive, would increase in frequency.)

THE NASH EQUILIBRIUM This is a pair of strategies, one for each player, such that neither would be tempted to change his strategy so long as the other continues with his. If in our matrix, player 1 plays *A* and 2 plays *B*, we have a Nash equilibrium; this is also the case if 1 plays *B* and 2 Plays *A*. A population can evolve to the Nash point if it is divided into two classes, and if members of one class compete only with members of the other. Hence it is the appropriate equilibrium in the "parental investment" game (62), in which all contests are between a male and a female. The ESS is subject to the added constraint that both players must adopt the same strategy.

THE GROUP SELECTION EQUILIBRIUM If the two players have the same genotype, genes in either will be favored that maximize the sum of their payoffs. For our matrix both must play strategy *B*. The problem of the stable strategy when the players are related but not identical is discussed in the section on Games Between Relatives, below.

It is possible to combine the game-theoretical and optimization approaches. Mirmirani & Oster (69) make this extension in their model of resource allocation in plants. They ask two questions. What is the ESS for a plant growing in competition with members of its own species? What is the ESS when two species compete with one another?

Thus consider two competing plants whose sizes at time t are P_1 and P_2. The effects of competition are allowed for by writing

$$dP_1/dt = (r_1 - e_1P_2)(1 - u_1)P_1,$$
$$dP_2/dt = (r_2 - e_2P_1)(1 - u_2)P_2, \qquad 3.$$

where u_1 and u_2 are the fractions of the available resources allocated to seeds. Let $J_1[u_1(t), u_2(t)]$ be the total seed production of plant 1 if it adopts the allocation strategy $u_1(t)$ and its competitor adopts $u_2(t)$. Mirmirani & Oster seek a stable pair of strategies $u_1^*(t)$, $u_2^*(t)$, such that

$$J_1[u_1(t), u_2^*(t)] \leq J_1[u_1^*(t), u_2^*(t)], \text{ and}$$
$$J_2[u_1^*(t), u_2(t)] \leq J_2[u_1^*(t), u_2^*(t)]. \qquad 4.$$

That is, they seek a Nash equilibrium, such that neither competitor could benefit by unilaterally altering its strategy. They find that the optimal strategies are again "bang-bang," but with earlier switching times than in the absence of competition. Strictly, the conditions indicated by expressions 4 are correct only when there is competition between species, and when individuals of one species compete only with individuals of the other; formally this would be so if the plants grew alternately in a linear array. The conditions indicated by expressions 4 are not appropriate for intra-specific competition, since they permit $u_1^*(t)$ and $u_2^*(t)$ to be different, which could not be the case unless individuals of one genotype competed only with individuals of the other. For intra-specific competition ($r_1 = r_2$, $e_1 = e_2$), the ESS is given by

$$J_1[u_1(t), u_1^*(t)] \leqslant J_1[u_1^*(t), u_1^*(t)]. \quad 5.$$

As it happens, for the plant growth example equations 4 and 5 give the same control function, but in general this need not be so.

The ESS model assumes parthenogenetic inheritance, whereas most interesting populations are sexual. If the ESS is a pure strategy, no difficulty arises; a genetically homgeneous sexual population adopting the strategy will also be stable. If the ESS is a mixed strategy that can be achieved by a single individual with a variable behavior, there is again no difficulty. If the ESS is a mixed one that can only be achieved by a population of pure strategists in the appropriate frequencies, two difficulties arise:

1. Even with the parthenogenetic model, the conditions expressed in expressions 2 do not guarantee stability. (This was first pointed out to me by Dr. C. Strobeck.) In such cases, therefore, it is best to check the stability of the equilibrium, if necessary by simulation; so far, experience suggests that stability, although not guaranteed, will usually be found.
2. The frequency distribution may be one that is incompatible with the genetic mechanism. This difficulty, first pointed out by Lewontin (52), has recently been investigated by Slatkin (89–91) and by Auslander et al (2). It is hard to say at present how serious it will prove to be; my hope is that a sexual population will usually evolve a frequency distribution as close to the ESS as its genetic mechanism will allow.

Games Between Relatives

The central concept is that of "inclusive fitness" (33). In classical population genetics we ascribe to a genotype I a "fitness" W_i, corresponding to the expected number of offspring produced by I. If, averaged over environments and genetic backgrounds, the effect of substituting allele A for a is to increase W, allele A will increase in frequency. Following Oster et al (74), but ignoring unequal sex ratios, Hamilton's proposal is that we should replace W_i by the inclusive fitness, Z_i, where

$$Z_i = \sum_{j=1}^{R} r_{ij} W_j, \quad 6.$$

where the summation is over all R relatives of I; r_{ij} is the fraction of J's genome that is identical by descent to alleles in I; and W_j is the expected number of offspring of the jth relative of I. (If $J = I$, then equation 6 refers to the component of inclusive fitness from an individual's own offspring.)

An allele *A* will increase in frequency if it increases *Z*, rather than just *W*. Three warnings are needed:

1. It is usual to calculate r_{ij} from the pedigree connecting *I* and *J* [as carried out, for example, by Malecot (58)]. However, if selection is occurring, r_{ij} so estimated is only approximate, as are predictions based on equation 6 (35).
2. Some difficulties arose in calculating appropriate values of r_{ij} for haplo-diploids; these were resolved by Crozier (22).
3. If the sex ratio is not unity, additional difficulties arise (74).

Mirmirani & Oster (69) have extended their plant-growth model along these lines to cover the case when the two competitors are genetically related. They show that as *r* increases, the switching time becomes earlier and the total yield higher.

CONCLUSION

The role of optimization theories in biology is not to demonstrate that organisms optimize. Rather, they are an attempt to understand the diversity of life.

Three sets of assumptions underlie an optimization model. First, there is an assumption about the kinds of phenotypes or strategies possible (i.e. a "phenotype set"). Second, there is an assumption about what is being maximized; ideally this should be the inclusive fitness of the individual, but often one must be satisfied with some component of fitness (e.g. rate of energy intake while foraging). Finally, there is an assumption, often tacit, about the mode of inheritance and the population structure; this will determine the type of equilibrium to which the population will move.

In testing an optimization model, one is testing the adequacy of these hypotheses to account for the evolution of the particular structures or patterns of behavior under study. In most cases the hypothesis that variation in the relevant phenotypes is selectively neutral is not a plausible alternative, because of the nature of the phenotypes chosen for study. However, it is often a plausible alternative that the phenotypes are not well adapted to current circumstances because the population is lagging behind a changing environment; this is a serious difficulty in testing optimization theories.

The most damaging criticism of optimization theories is that they are untestable. There is a real danger that the search for functional explanations in biology will degenerate into a test of ingenuity. An important task, therefore, is the development of an adequate methodology of testing. In many cases the comparative method is the most powerful; it is, however, essential to have clear criteria for inclusion or exclusion of species in comparative tests, and to use statistical methods with the same care as in the analysis of experimental results.

Tests of the quantitative predictions of optimization models in particular populations are beginning to be made. It is commonly found that a model correctly predicts qualitative features of the observations, but is contradicted in detail. In such cases, the Popperian view would be that the original model has been falsified. This is correct, but it does not follow that the model should be abandoned. In the analysis of complex systems it is most unlikely that any simple model, taking into account only a few factors, can give quantitatively exact predictions. Given that a simple model has been falsified by observations, the choice lies between abandoning it, and modifying it, usually by adding hypotheses. There can be no simple rule by which to make this choice; it will depend on how persuasive the qualitative predictions are, and on the availability of alternative models.

Mathematical methods of optimization have been developed with engineering and economic applications in mind. Two theoretical questions arise in applying these methods in biology. First, in those cases in which the fitnesses of phenotypes are frequency-dependent, the problem must be formulated in game-theoretical terms; some difficulties then arise in deciding to what type of equilibrium a population will tend. A second and related set of questions arise when specific genetic assumptions are incorporated in the model, because it may be that a population with the optimal phenotype cannot breed true. These questions need further study, but at present there is no reason to doubt the adequacy of the concepts of optimization and of evolutionary stability for studying phenotypic evolution.

ACKNOWLEDGMENTS

My thanks are due to Dr. R. C. Lewontin for sending me two manuscripts that formed the starting point of this review, and to Drs. G. Oster and R. Pulliam for their comments on an earlier draft. I was also greatly helped by preliminary discussions with Dr. E. Curio.

Literature Cited

1. Alexander, R. M. 1977. Mechanics and scaling of terrestrial locomotion. In *Scale Effects in Animal Locomotion,* ed. T. J. Pedley, pp. 93–110. London: Academic Press. 545 pp.
2. Auslander, D., Guckenheimer, J., Oster, G. 1978. Random evolutionarily stable strategies *Theor. Pop. Biol.* 13: In press
3. Baker, H. G. 1959. Reproductive methods as factors in speciation in flowering plants. *Cold Spring Harbor Symp. Quant. Biol.* 24:177–191
4. Bawa, K. S., Opler, P. A. 1975. Dioecism in tropical forest trees. *Evolution* 29:167–79
5. Bellman, R. 1957. *Dynamic Programming.* Princeton, NJ: Princeton Univ. Press. 342 pp.
6. Bishop, D. T., Cannings, C. 1978. A generalized war of attrition. *J. Theor. Biol.* 70:85–124
7. Buskirk, W. H. 1976. Social systems in tropical forest avifauna. *Am. Nat.* 110:293–310
8. Cain, A. J. 1964. The perfection of animals. In *Viewpoints in Biology,* ed. J. D. Carthy, C. L. Duddington, 3:36–63
9. Cain, A. J., Sheppard, P. H. 1954. Natural selection in *Cepaea. Genetics* 39: 89–116
10. Charnov, E. L. 1976. Optimal foraging, the marginal value theorem. *Theor. Pop. Biol.* 9:129–36
11. Charnov, E. L., Maynard Smith, J., Bull, J. J. 1976. Why be an hermaphrodite? *Nature* 263:125–26
12. Clark, C. W. 1976. *Mathematical Bioeconomics.* New York: Wiley. 351 pp.
13. Clarke, B. 1962. Balanced polymorphism and the diversity of sympatric species. In *Taxomony and Geography,* ed. D. Nichols, 4:47–70. London: Syst. Assoc. Publ.
14. Clarke, B. 1975. The contribution of ecological genetics to evolutionary theory: Detecting the direct effects of natural selection on particular polymorphic loci. *Genetics* 79:101–13
15. Clarke, B. 1976. The ecological genetics of host-parasite relationships. In *Genetic Aspects of Host-Parasite Relation-*

ships, ed. A. E. R. Taylor, R. Muller, pp. 87–103. Oxford: Blackwell
16. Clutton-Brock, T. H., Harvey, P. H. 1977. Primate ecology and social organisation. *J. Zool., London* 183:1–39
17. Clutton-Brock, T. H., Harvey, P. H. 1977. Species differences in feeding and ranging behaviour in primates. In *Primate Ecology*, ed. T. H. Clutton-Brock, pp. 557–84. London: Academic
18. Clutton-Brock, T. H., Harvey, P. H., Rudder, B. 1977. Sexual dimorphism, socionomic sex ratio and body weight in primates. *Nature* 269:797–800
19. Cohen, D. 1971. Maximising final yield when growth is limited by time or by limiting resources. *J. Theor. Biol.* 33: 299–307
20. Cowie, R. J. 1977. Optimal foraging in great tits (*Parus major*). *Nature* 268:137–39
21. Crow, J. F., Kimura, M. 1970. *An Introduction to Population Genetics Theory*. New York: Harper & Row. 589 pp.
22. Crozier, R. H. 1970. Coefficients of relationship and the identity of genes by descent in the Hymenoptera. *Am. Nat.* 104:216–17
23. Curio, E. 1973. Towards a methodology of teleonomy. *Experientia* 29:1045–58
24. Curio, E. 1975. The functional organisation of anti-predator behaviour in the pied flycatcher: a study of avian visual perception. *Anim. Behav.* 23:1–115
25. Curio, E. 1976. *The Ethology of Predation.* Berlin: Springer-Verlag. 250 pp.
26. Darwin, C. 1877. *The Different Forms of Flowers on Plants of the Same Species.* London: John Murray. 352 pp.
27. Emlen, J. M. 1966. The role of time and energy in food preference. *Am. Nat.* 100:611–17
28. Fisher, R. A. 1930. *The Genetical Theory of Natural Selection.* London: Oxford Univ. Press. 291 pp.
29. Goss-Custard, J. D. 1977. Optimal foraging and the size selection of worms by redshank, *Tringa totanus*, in the field. *Anim. Behav.* 25:10–29
30. Gould, S. J. 1971. Geometric scaling in allometric growth: a contribution to the problem of scaling in the evolution of size. *Am. Nat.* 105:113–36
31. Greig-Smith, P. W. 1978. The formation, structure and feeding of insectivorous bird flocks in West African savanna woodland. *Ibis.* In press
32. Haldane, J. B. S. 1949. Disease and evolution. *Ric. Sci.* Suppl. 19:68–76
33. Hamilton, W. D. 1964. The genetical theory of social behavior. I and II. *J. Theor. Biol.* 7:1–16; 17–32
34. Hamilton, W. D. 1967. Extraordinary sex ratios. *Science* 156:477–88
35. Hamilton, W. D. 1972. Altruism and related phenomena, mainly in social insects. *Ann. Rev. Ecol. Syst.* 3:193–232
36. Harvey, P. H., Kavanagh, M., Clutton-Brock, T. H. 1978. Sexual dimorphism in primate teeth. *J. Zool.* In press
37. Ivlev, V. S. 1961. *Experimental Ecology of the Feeding of Fishes.* New Haven: Yale Univ. Press
38. Jacob, F. 1977. Evolution and tinkering. *Science* 196:1161–66
39. Jarvis, M. J. F. 1974. The ecological significance of clutch size in the South African gannet [*Sula capensis.* (Lichtenstein)]. *J. Anim. Ecol.* 43:1–17
40. Kalmijn, A. J. 1971. The electric sense of sharks and rays. *J. Exp. Biol.* 55: 371–83
41. Kalmus, H., Smith, C. A. B. 1960. Evolutionary origin of sexual differentiation and the sex-ratio. *Nature* 186:1004–6
42. Kettlewell, H. B. D. 1956. Further selection experiments on industrial melanism in the Lepidoptera. *Heredity* 10:287–301
43. Kimura, M. 1968. Evolutionary rate at the molecular level. *Nature* 217:624–26
44. King, J. L., Jukes, T. H. 1969. Non-Darwinian Evolution: Random fixation of selectively neutral mutations. *Science* 164:788–98
45. Krebs, C. J. 1972. *Ecology.* New York: Harper & Row. p. 569
46. Krebs, J. R., Ryan, J. C., Charnov, E. L. 1974. Hunting by expectation or optimal foraging? A study of patch use by chickadees. *Anim. Behav.* 22:953–64
47. Krebs, J. R., Ericksen, J. T., Webber, M. I., Charnov, E. L. 1977. Optimal prey selection in the Great Tit (*Parus major*). *Anim. Behav.* 25:30–38
48. Lack, D. 1966. *Population Studies of Birds.* Oxford: Clarendon Press. 341 pp.
49. Lack, D. 1968. *Ecological Adaptations for Breeding in Birds.* London: Methuen. 409 pp.
50. Levene, H. 1953. Genetic equilibrium when more than one ecological niche is available. *Am. Nat.* 87:131–33
51. Levins, R. 1962. Theory of fitness in a heterogeneous environment. I. The fitness set and adaptive function. *Am. Nat.* 96:361–73
52. Lewontin, R. C. 1961. Evolution and the theory of games. *J. Theor. Biol.* 1: 382–403

53. Lewontin, R. C. 1974. *The Genetic Basis of Evolutionary Change.* New York: Columbia Univ. Press. 346 pp.
54. Lewontin, R. C. 1977. Adaptation. In *The Encyclopedia Einaudi.* Torino: Giulio Einaudi Edition.
55. Lewontin, R. C. 1978. Fitness, survival and optimality. In *Analysis of Ecological Systems,* ed. D. H. Horn, R. Mitchell, G. R. Stairs. Columbus, OH.: Ohio State Univ. Press
56. MacArthur, R. H. 1965. Ecological consequences of natural selection. In *Theoretical and Mathematical Biology,* ed. T. Waterman. H. Morowitz, pp. 388–97. New York: Blaisdell
57. MacArthur, R. H., Pianka, E. R. 1966. On optimal use of a patch environment. *Am. Nat.* 100:603–9
58. Malécot, G. 1969. *The Mathematics of Heredity,* transl. D. M. Yermanos. San Francisco: W. H. Freeman. 88 pp.
59. Maynard Smith, J. 1962. Disruptive selection, polymorphism and sympatric speciation. *Nature* 195:60–62
60. Maynard Smith, J. 1969. The status of neo-Darwinism. In *Towards a Theoretical Biology. 2: Sketches,* ed. C. H. Waddington, pp. 82–89. Edinburgh: Edinburgh Univ. Press
61. Maynard Smith, J. 1976. Sexual selection and the handicap principle. *J. Theor. Biol.* 57:239–42
62. Maynard Smith, J. 1977. Parental investment—a prospective analysis. *Anim. Behav.* 25:1–9
63. Maynard Smith, J. 1978. *The Evolution of Sex.* London: Cambridge Univ. Press. In press
64. Maynard Smith, J., Parker, G. A. 1976. The logic of asymmetric contests. *Anim. Behav.* 24:159–75
65. Maynard Smith, J., Price, G. R. 1973. The logic of animal conflict. *Nature* 246:15–18
66. Maynard Smith, J., Savage, R. J. G. 1956. Some locomotory adaptations in mammals. *Zool. J. Linn. Soc.* 42: 603–22
67. McFarland, D. J. 1977. Decision making in animals. *Nature* 269:15–21
68. Milton, K., May, M. L. 1976. Bodyweight, diet and home range area in primates. *Nature* 259:459–62
69. Mirmirani, M., Oster, G. 1978. Competition, kin selection and evolutionarily stable strategies. *Theor. Pop. Biol.* In press
70. Moment, G. 1962. Reflexive selection: a possible answer to an old puzzle. *Science* 136:262–63
71. Nelson, J. B. 1964. Factors influencing clutch size and chick growth in the North Atlantic Gannet, *Sula bassana. Ibis* 106:63–77
72. Norton-Griffiths, M. 1969. The organisation, control and development of parental feeding in the oystercatcher (*Haematopus ostralegus*). *Behavior* 34:55–114
73. Orians, G. H., Pearson, N. E. 1978. On the theory of central place foraging. In *Analysis of Ecological Systems,* ed. D. H. Horn, R. Mitchell, G. R. Stairs, Columbus: Ohio State Univ. Press
74. Oster, G., Eshel, I., Cohen, D. 1977. Worker-queen conflicts and the evolution of social insects. *Theor. Pop. Biol.* 12:49–85
75. Oster, G., Wilson, E. O. 1978. *Caste and Ecology in the Social Insects.* Princeton, NJ: Princeton Univ. Press. In press
76. Parker, G. A. 1974. The reproductive behaviour and the nature of sexual selection in *Scatophaga stercoraria* L. IX. Spatial distribution of fertilization rates and evolution of male search strategy within the reproductive area. *Evolution* 28:93–108
77. Parker, G. A., Stuart, R. A. 1976. Animal behaviour as a strategy optimizer: evolution of resource assessment strategies and optimal emigration thresholds. *Am. Nat.* 110:1055–76
78. Pedley, T. J. 1977. *Scale Effects in Animal Locomotion.* London: Academic Press. 545 pp.
79. Pontryagin, L. S., Boltyanskii, V. S., Gamkrelidze, R. V., Mishchenko, E. F. 1962. *The Mathematical Theory of Optimal Processes.* New York: Wiley
80. Pulliam, H. R. 1978. Do chipping sparrows forage optimally? A test of optimal foraging theory in nature. *Am. Nat.* In press
81. Pyke, G. H., Pulliam, H. R., Charnov, E. L. 1977. Optimal foraging: a selective review of theory and tests. *Q. Rev. Biol.* 52:137–54
82. Ralls, K. 1976. Mammals in which females are larger than males. *Q. Rev. Biol.* 51:245–76
83. Rensch, B. 1959. *Evolution above the Species Level.* New York: Columbia Univ. Press. 419 pp.
84. Rohwer, S. 1977. Status signaling in Harris sparrows: some experiments in deception. *Behaviour* 61:107–29
85. Rosado, J. M. C., Robertson, A. 1966. The genetic control of sex ratio. *J. Theor. Biol.* 13:324–29

86. Schoener, T. W. 1968. Sizes of feeding territories among birds. *Ecology* 49: 123–41
87. Schoener, T. W. 1971. Theory of feeding strategies. *Ann. Rev. Ecol. Syst.* 2:369–404
88. Sibly, R., McFarland, D. 1976. On the fitness of behaviour sequences. *Am. Nat.* 110:601–17
89. Slatkin, M. 1978. On the equilibration of fitnesses by natural selection. *Am. Nat.* In press
90. Slatkin, M. 1979. The evolutionary response to frequency and density dependence. I. A single species with distinct phenotypic classes. In press
91. Slatkin, M. 1979. The evolutionary response to frequency and density dependence. II. Interactions mediated by a quantitative character. In press
92. Slobodkin, L. B., Rapoport, A. 1974. An optimal strategy of evolution. *Q. Rev. Biol.* 49:181–200
93. Strobeck, C. 1975. Selection in a fine-grained environment. *Am. Nat.* 109: 419–25
94. Tinbergen, N., Broekhuysen, G. J., Feekes, F., Houghton, J. C. W., Kruuk, H., Szule, E. 1963. Egg shell removal by the Black-headed Gull, *Larus ridibundus* L.: a behaviour component of camouflage. *Behaviour* 19:74–117
95. Trivers, R. L., Hare, H. 1976. Haplodiploidy and the evolution of social insects. *Science* 191:249–63
96. Trivers, R. L., Willard, D. E. 1973. Natural selection of parental ability to vary the sex ratio of offspring. *Science* 179:90–92
97. Verner, J. 1965. Selection for sex ratio. *Am. Nat.* 19:419–21
98. Verner, J., Willson, M. F. 1966. The influence of habitats on mating systems of North American passerine birds. *Ecology* 47:143–47
99. Von Neumann, J., Morgenstern, O. 1953. *Theory of Games and Economic Behavior.* Princeton, NJ: Princeton Univ. Press. 641 pp.
100. Werner, E. E., Hall, D. J. 1974. Optimal foraging and size selection of prey by the bluegill sunfish (*Lepomis mochrochirus*). *Ecology* 55:1042–52
101. Wright, S. 1932. The roles of mutation, inbreeding, crossbreeding and selection in evolution. *Proc. Sixth. Int. Congr. Genet.* 1:356–66
102. Zahavi, A. 1975. Mate selection—a selection for a handicap. *J. Theor. Biol.* 53:205–14

Journal of Economic Behavior and Organization 12 (1989) 29–45. North-Holland

ARE PROFIT-MAXIMISERS THE BEST SURVIVORS?

A Darwinian Model of Economic Natural Selection

Mark E. SCHAFFER*

University of Sussex, Brighton BN1 9QN, UK

Received March 1988, final version received November 1988

This paper demonstrates that the Friedman conjecture that profit-maximisation 'summarises appropriately' the conditions for firm survival is not generally true. If firms have market power, profit-maximisers are not necessarily the best survivors because of the possibility of 'spiteful' behaviour of the following kind. Say a firm forgoes profit-maximisation and thus decreases its survival chances, but its deviation from maximisation harms its profit-maximising competitors more than itself. Though the firm will be less likely to survive than it would if it maximised its profits, it will still be more likely to survive than its competitors.

1. Introduction

'Economic natural selection' has sometimes been cited in support of the conventional neoclassical profit-maximisation model of the firm. In this view, the assumption of profit-maximisation by firms in formal economic models is plausible because in the real world, 'economic natural selection' drives non-maximisers out of the market. The most famous exposition of this position is in Friedman's 1953 methodological essay:

> The process of 'natural selection' helps to validate the hypothesis [of 'rational and informed maximization of returns'] – or, rather, given natural selection, acceptance of the hypothesis can be based largely on the judgment that it summarizes appropriately the conditions for survival.
>
> [Friedman (1953, p. 22)]

Though not without its critics [see, e.g., Nelson and Winter (1982)], this

*Revised version of a paper presented at the SSRC Summer Workshop, Georgetown University, July 1987, and written while the author was enrolled in the PhD programme at the London School of Economics and supported by fellowships from the National Science Foundation and the International Research and Exchanges Board. I would like to thank the editors and two anonymous referees, Stanislaw Gomulka, Herbert Levine, David de Meza, Ariel Rubenstein, Max Steuer, John Sutton, and a number of seminar audiences for helpful suggestions and discussions, and the NSF and IREX for their generous financial support. All remaining errors and omissions are mine.

argument seems intuitively convincing. Nevertheless, if it is to be accepted as valid, 'economic natural selection' would first need to be modelled explicitly. But when this is done, then, as I show in this paper, the Friedman conjecture is shown to be false in some important cases. Specifically, only in perfect competition, when firms lack market power, are profit-maximisers the best survivors.

The main result of the paper follows almost trivially from a Darwinian definition of 'economic natural selection', but nevertheless is at first surprising: absolute-profit maximisation does *not* 'summarise appropriately the conditions for survival'. The intuitive reason is that a firm maximising its own profit may help its non-maximising competitors to do even better. Put another way, a firm which does not maximise its profit may still earn profits which are larger than those of its profit-maximising competitors, if the costs to itself of its deviation from maximisation are smaller than the costs it imposes on the maximising competitors. The Friedman argument that economic natural selection will lead to the survival of profit-maximisers fails in the presence of this positive externality.[1] Only in the case of perfect competition, when firms have no market power and this externality disappears, is absolute-profit maximisation always an 'appropriate summary'. This result is a consequence of the Darwinian definition of economic natural selection, whereby it is the 'fittest' firms which survive.

The above result is essentially an application to economics of Hamilton's theory of 'spite' in evolutionary biology [Hamilton (1970, 1971)]. An act by an animal is 'spiteful' if the animal harms both itself and another. Hamilton demonstrated that such a trait could be selected for if the population was not very large. The condition for the selection of a spiteful trait is that the decrease in an animal's own Darwinian fitness is smaller than the decrease in the fitness of the average member of the rest of the population; since the holder of the spiteful trait thus has a higher fitness than that of his intra-species competitors, the trait will be selected for.

The relevance of Hamilton's theory to the Friedman conjecture is straightforward. When firms have market power, the potential for 'spiteful' behaviour exists. A firm which forgoes the opportunity to maximise its absolute profit may still enjoy a selective advantage over its competitors if its 'spiteful' deviation from profit-maximisation harms its competitors more than itself.

The simple formal model of economic natural selection which this paper presents is derived from the 'evolutionary game theory' (EGT) analysis used in evolutionary biology [see, e.g., Maynard Smith (1982)] and is Darwinian in spirit. The basic approach is directly analogous to that used in EGT to define an 'evolutionarily stable strategy' (ESS). In the paper which first

[1] Hansen and Samuelson (1988), in a paper which came to hand after this article was written, have also demonstrated this point.

introduced the concept, Maynard Smith and Price (1973, p. 73) give the intuition behind the ESS: 'Roughly, an ESS is a strategy such that, if most of the members of a population adopt it, there is no 'mutant' strategy that would give higher reproductive fitness.'

The standard EGT analysis assumes random pairwise contests between individuals drawn from an infinite population; two individuals are repeatedly chosen at random to play a given game. The intended application of the Friedman argument is firm behaviour in an industry, and so the model presented in this paper is instead based on the special case of the ESS defined for finite populations in which individuals 'play the field' [Schaffer (1988)].[2] 'Playing the field' means all the players in the game compete with each other simultaneously, which is the appropriate analogy for the standard model of competition between firms in an industry; the finite-population case is analogous to oligopoly.

In the model in the paper, the firms which are most likely to survive are not those which maximise the absolute level of their profits, but rather those which maximise their 'relative profits' (in a sense discussed below). This result is directly analogous to the 'spitefulness' of the evolutionary biology ESS in finite populations [Knowlton and Parker (1979); Schaffer (1988)]. It can also be interpreted as a formalisation of Alchian's statement in his 1950 paper on evolution and economic theory that 'success (survival) accompanies *relative* superiority' (p. 213, emphasis added). It must be stressed, however, that the model does *not* suggest maximisation of 'relative profits' as the best strategy for survival. In Hamilton's theory of spite, behaviour imposes costs on an animal, but larger costs on its competitors. Similarly, in the model which follows, 'relative-profit maximisation' can cause a firm to be less likely to survive; but it also means the firm is more likely to survive than its competitors.

2. An example

Before presenting the general model, we begin with a very simple example of quantity-setting duopoly to illustrate the main ideas. We have two identical firms which have no fixed costs and identical and constant marginal costs. Firm 1 sells quantity q_1 and earns profit π_1, and similarly for firm 2. The firms face a smooth, downward-sloping demand curve. When total supply equals Q^*, price is equal to marginal cost and both firms earn zero profits.

[2]That the definition of the standard infinite population ESS is inappropriate for finite populations was first shown by Riley (1979). The approach to evolutionary stability in finite populations drawn on here is not that suggested by Riley but rather that used in Schaffer (1988) [and independently proposed by Knowlton and Parker (1979) and Maynard Smith (1988)].

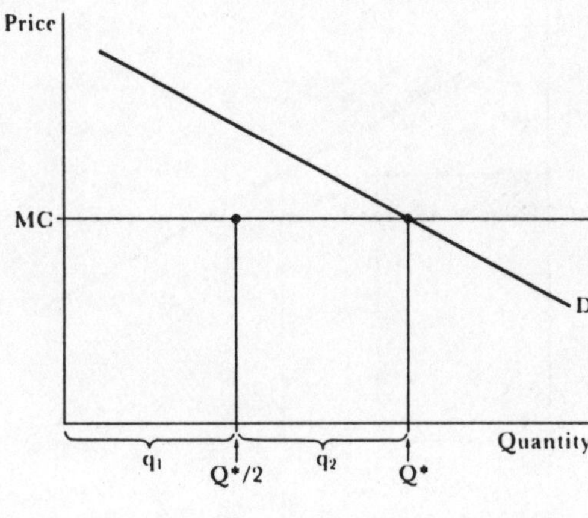

Fig. 1

Consider now a form of 'economic natural selection'. After the firms produce and sell their quantities of output, 'selection' takes place: with some probability p_i, firm i may or may not 'survive' to produce in the next period. We also require that $0<p_i<1$, so that neither firm can guarantee its 'survive'. The interpretation of a failure to 'survive' is left open for now. It could mean that the firm goes bankrupt; or the firm is forced to leave the market; or the firm stays in the market but the manager is fired; etc. This probability of survival must be related to profits in a way which captures the Darwinian notion of 'survival of the fittest'. We formalise this by a very natural requirement of 'monotonicity': $p_i>p_j$ if and only if $\pi_i>\pi_j$. This monotonicity requirement is fully in the spirit of biological models of natural selection: it means simply that if firm i has a larger profit than firm j, then firm i is more likely to survive than firm j.

Fig. 1 shows the case where both firms sell $Q^*/2$ units of output. The total quantity sold is Q^*, price is therefore equal to the marginal costs of both firms, and profits are zero. This is the symmetric competitive solution. It is also a 'symmetric evolutionary equilibrium' in the following sense: say firm 1 continues to sell $Q^*/2$ units of output, but firm 2 deviates and sells some other quantity. No matter what quantity the deviant firm 2 chooses to sell, firm 1 will always have a higher probability of survival than firm 2. In other words, the strategy of selling $Q^*/2$ units of output is analogous to the ESS of evolutionary biology in that a deviant ('mutant') firm which uses another strategy will always have a lower profit than a firm which sells $Q^*/2$ (compare the Maynard Smith and Price quote given earlier).

This is illustrated in figs. 2 and 3. In both figures, firm 1 sells $Q^*/2$. In fig. 2, firm 2 sells $q_2<Q^*/2$ and therefore earns itself positive profits π_2. But firm

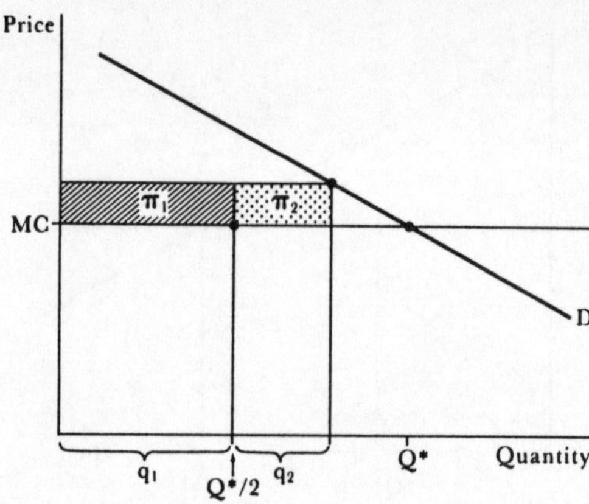

Fig. 2

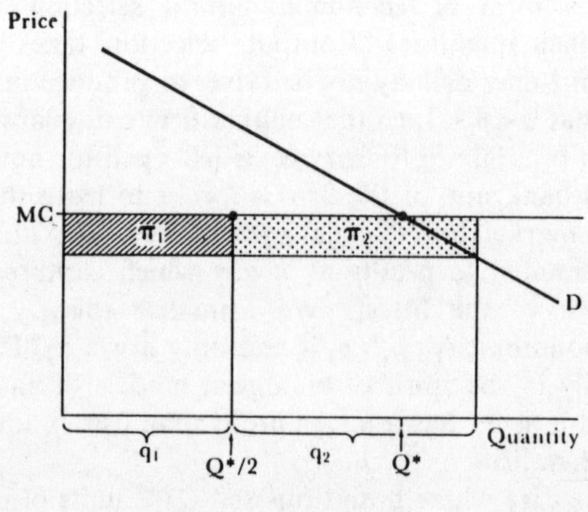

Fig. 3

1 is selling a larger quantity at the same price, and so its profits π_1 exceed the profits of firm 2. Similarly, in fig. 3, firm 2 sells $q_2 > Q^*/2$, driving price below marginal cost and thus suffering a loss. But firm 1 is selling a smaller quantity at the same price, and so its losses are smaller. In both cases firm 1 has a larger profit than that of the 'deviant' firm 2, and therefore a higher probability of survival.

It is important to emphasise that the above argument holds *even if survival is based on absolute profits.* Say that firm *i*'s probability of survival increases with its absolute level of profits: $p_i = f(\pi_i)$, $0 < f(\cdot) < 1$, $f' > 0$. But $f(\cdot)$ conforms to the monotonicity assumption above, and so we are still guaranteed that firm 1 will have a selective advantage should firm 2 sell some deviant quantity.

Indeed, note that in fig. 2 firm 2 is making positive profits. It is actually making larger profits than it would if it had continued to sell $Q^*/2$ units. In fact, taking firm 1's quantity as given, firm 2 may actually be maximising its profit. But firm 1 is making profits which are larger still. This is an important point: the non-profit-maximiser is here more likely to survive than the profit-maximiser. What is more, say that the probability of survival is an increasing function of the level of profits, as in the previous paragraph. Then maximising profits also maximises the probability of survival. So in fact the non-*survival*-maximiser firm 1 is more likely to survive than the *survival*-maximiser firm 2! Firm 2 has improved its survival chances by raising, indeed maximising, its profit; but by raising firm 1's profits even more, firm 2 now stands at a selective disadvantage.

I now move on to a demonstration of these points in a more general model.

3. The general model

There are N players. In period t, all engage in G_t, a play of the game G. The format of G_t is 'all versus all'; all the players engage each other simultaneously. N is constant for all t. Players are identical except possibly for their choice of strategy. Each player i has in each period t a strategy s_{it}, drawn from the set of pure strategies S, which it uses in G_t. I will consider only the case where $s_{it}=s_i$ for all t; the actual choices of strategy by individual players do not change as the game is played. Players are thus 'born' with strategies and cannot change them in response to changing circumstances. I am therefore assuming (non-rational) behaviour by players which is directly analogous to animal behaviour in the usual EGT approach. At the end of G_t, each player i receives a payoff π_{it} which is a function of his strategy and the strategies of the other players in that period; I will usually drop the t subscript. I will sometimes also write π_i as $\pi(s_i|s_{-i})$, where s_{-i} denotes the strategies of the other players.

We could think of players as corresponding to firms, as in the duopoly example above. Another interpretation which is perhaps more appealing (given that the industry size is assumed constant) is as follows. Players in the game represent the managers of firms in an industry of size N. Each firm is in the industry permanently, and its owners regularly hire and fire a manager. The manager's strategy determines the behaviour of the firm. Once hired the manager doesn't change his strategy, and the firm changes strategy by replacing the manager.

4. Entry, strategy choice, and survival

It is possible to divide 'economic natural selection' into three parts. First, there is the decision of whether or not to enter the game. In biology, this is the problem of whether to reproduce, and if so, how many offspring to produce. In economics, this is the 'entry' decision, for both firms and managers. In the model, N is assumed constant. This means the entry decision by players is assumed away: as soon as one player is selected out of the game ('dies', 'goes bankrupt', 'is fired'), a new player enters.

Second, there is the 'strategy choice rule', the rule which determines the choice of strategy by a new player. In biology, the strategy choice rule is given by genetic inheritance and chance mutation. In economics, it is a much more difficult problem to address. For now we assume the following role for 'mutation' in order to maintain the parallel between the model here and the standard evolutionary game theory model. Say we have a situation in which all N players share the same strategy. Now say one of the N players is selected out of the game and is replaced by a new player. This new player may with some positive probability choose any strategy in the strategy set S. I will return to the subject of the strategy choice rule later in the paper, when discussing evolutionary stability.

Third, there is the 'survival rule', the rule by which payoffs are associated with 'survival'. If players are interpreted as firms, the 'survival rule' summarises the market forces which drive poor performers out of the industry. In the managerial interpretation of the model, the 'survival rule' is the rule used by the owners of the firm to decide whether to fire the existing manager and hire a new one.

The survival rule in this model is applied to each player at the end of each period t; it determines p_{it}, the probability that player i survives to participate in G_{t+1}, the next play of the game. The main restriction on the survival rule is a form of monotonicity: $p_{it} > p_{jt}$ if and only if $\pi_{it} > \pi_{jt}$. This means, for example, firm i is more likely to survive market pressures than firm j, or the manager of firm i is more likely to keep his job than the manager of firm j, if and only if the profits of firm i exceed the profits of firm j. To ensure that some selection always takes place, we also assume that $0 < p_{it} < 1$, i.e. no player is ever guaranteed of survival or failure.[3]

The monotonicity assumption is compatible with a wide range of possibilities concerning survival. In particular, it is important to point out that monotonicity is compatible both with survival based on the absolute level of a player's payoff and with survival based on a player's performance compared to his competitors. For example, we could have $p_{it} = f(\pi_{it})$, $f' > 0$, so that survival of player i is based on the absolute level of his payoff. Or we

[3]This condition is rather stronger than is actually necessary, since monotonicity ensures that in a population with heterogeneous payoffs not everybody will be guaranteed of survival. It is stated this way mostly for clarity's sake.

could have $p_{it}=f(\pi_{it}/\Sigma\pi)$, $f'>0$, so that survival is based on player i's share of the total of payoffs earned by all players.

This wide range of possible survival rules mean we have a wide range of possible rationales for the model. Consider the managerial interpretation of the model. One possibility is in terms of principal–agent/imperfect information/moral hazard models. Unable to observe perfectly the actions of their manager, the owners choose an incentive scheme which determines whether or not the manager keeps his job. This incentive scheme may be based on the manager's absolute performance in generating profits for his firm; or it may reward the manager based on his performance relative to other managers [see, e.g., Lazear and Rosen (1981) and Holmstrom (1982)]; etc. Another possibility is that the owners of a firm are boundedly rational (as opposed to the managers, who are non-rational); unable to choose or control a manager perfectly, they use a rule of thumb in hiring and firing their manager. This rule of thumb may be based on the absolute level of the firm's profits; or it may be based on the firm's share of industry profits; etc. A similar range of rationales is possible if players are interpreted as firms.

Because players never change strategies, we can also think of the survival rule as operating on strategies. In other words, it is the fittest strategies which will best survive the process of economic natural selection. This is analogous to the EGT analysis in evolutionary biology, where genes determine strategies and the fittest genes survive.

Also analogous to the evolutionary biology analysis is the fact that because the model assumes that players do not change their strategies, the 'rationality' of any results of the model will come from the survival and strategy choice rules rather than directly from the 'rationality' of the players. The model is therefore, as already noted, Darwinian in spirit.

5. Definition of evolutionary equilibrium

The definition of the evolutionary biology finite-population ESS comes in two parts: an equilibrium condition, based on payoffs received when $N-1$ players have the ESS strategy and one mutant player has some other strategy; and a stability condition, based on payoffs when 2 or more mutants have some other strategy. (Note that in a sense the equilibrium condition therefore has a notion of stability built into it.) The model in this paper has been constructed so that the definition of a 'symmetric evolutionary equilibrium' (SEE) can proceed in the same fashion as the definition of the equilibrium condition for the finite-population ESS. Stability is discussed later in the paper.

We begin with a population in which $N-1$ players have the SEE strategy $s^{\mathrm{SEE}}\in S$, and so each receives payoff π^{SEE}. There is also one deviant player whose strategy $s^D \in S$ is one other than s^{SEE}, and whose payoff is π^D. For convenience, say this deviant player is player number d. So

$$\pi^{SEE} \equiv \pi(s^{SEE}|s^D, s^{SEE}, s^{SEE}, \ldots)$$

$$\equiv \pi_i \equiv \pi(s_i|s_{-i}) \quad \text{for} \quad i \neq d, \tag{1}$$

$$\pi^D \equiv \pi(s^D|s^{SEE}, s^{SEE}, s^{SEE}, \ldots)$$

$$\equiv \pi_d \equiv \pi(s_d|s_{-d}). \tag{2}$$

Definition. A strong (weak) SEE is given by a strategy $s^{SEE} \in S$ which has the property that, if $N-1$ players have this strategy and one deviant player has some other strategy s^D, then for any deviant strategy $s^D \in S$,

$$\pi^{SEE} > (\geqq) \pi^D, \tag{3}$$

where π^{SEE} and π^D are given in eqs. (1) and (2).

In other words, a strong (weak) SEE exists where, in a population of $N-1$ SEE players and one deviant player, the SEE players do strictly better than (at least as well as) the deviant player no matter what the deviant's strategy. The point is that, by monotonicity of the survival rule, the deviant thus has a lower probability of survival than his SEE strategist competitors. The intuition is identical to that behind the evolutionary biology ESS – see the Maynard Smith and Price quote at the beginning of the paper.

It is of interest to compare the SEE to the Nash equilibrium concept. We are considering the symmetric case, so we can define a strong (weak) symmetric Nash equilibrium (SNE) as a strategy $s^{SNE} \in S$ which, for any alternative strategy $s^D \in S$, satisfies

$$\pi(s^{SNE}|s^{SNE}, s^{SNE}, \ldots) > (\geqq) \pi(s^D|s^{SNE}, s^{SNE}, \ldots). \tag{4}$$

The difference between the SNE and the SEE is that the NE concept compares the payoffs for a single player under different strategies (with the strategies of the other players unchanging), whereas the SEE concept compares the payoffs of different players (with the strategies of all the players unchanging). The symmetric evolutionary *equilibrium concept* is thus based on *relative* payoffs, a result which reflects the Darwinian nature of selection among players. This is true in spite of the fact that in the model, *survival itself* for a player may well be based on the *absolute* level of his payoff, a point illustrated in the duopoly example above. The Nash *equilibrium concept*, by contrast, is based on *absolute* payoffs. In non-Darwinian 'evolutionary' economics models (e.g. satisficing models and learning models), Nash equilibria and 'absolute profit-maximisation' *will* be candidates for 'appropriate summaries' of the conditions for survival, or, perhaps, 'appropriate benchmarks'.[4]

It is useful to express the SEE as the Nash equilibrium of a different game. Say $N-1$ players are identical strong SEE strategists. Again the single deviant player is player number d with strategy s^D. The definition of a symmetric evolutionary equilibrium is equivalent to defining the SEE strategy as that s^D which solves

$$\max_{s^D \in S} \{\pi^D - \pi^{SEE}\}. \tag{5}$$

Since the SEE is symmetric by definition, we can write the payoff to an SEE player given by eq. (1) as the average of the payoffs of all the SEE players:

$$\pi^{SEE} \equiv \pi(s_i|s_{-i}) \quad \text{for} \quad i \neq d \qquad \equiv \frac{1}{N-1} \sum_{i \neq d}^{N} \pi(s_i|s_{-i}). \tag{6}$$

Substituting (6) and (2) into eq. (5), we have rewritten the definition of the symmetric evolutionary equilibrium strategy s^{SEE} as the symmetric solution to

$$\max_{s_d \in S} \{\pi(s_d|s_{-d}) - \frac{1}{N-1} \sum_{i \neq d}^{N} \pi(s_i|s_{-i})\}. \tag{7}$$

This is, in fact, the same definition as that for the symmetric non-cooperative Nash solution to Shubik's zero-sum 'beat-the-average' game [Shubik and Levitan (1980)]; it is easy to see how the game gets it name. The 'beat-the-average' (BTA) game is a zero-sum, *relative* maximisation game. Since the solution concepts for this evolutionary game and the 'beat-the-average' game coincide, we have here a demonstration that absolute-profit maximisation does not 'summarise appropriately the conditions for survival', and that relative-profit maximisation (in this model at least) is a more appropriate summary.

[4]Examples of non-Darwinian satisficing models and learning models are Nelson and Winter (1982) and Canning (1988), respectively. By contrast, Friedman and Rosenthal (1986) and Samuelson (1987) present game theoretic models which are essentially Darwinian in spirit. In these models selection takes place among strategies, and the change in the number of players using a particular strategy depends on the payoff to players using that strategy compared with the payoff to players using a different strategy. Selection in these models is therefore similar to selection in the model in this paper; as noted above, we can think of the selection rule in our model as operating on strategies, with the fittest strategies surviving.

More generally, there is a one-to-one correspondence between the SEE and the symmetric NE in the beat-the-average game. That any SNE in the BTA game is also an SEE can be demonstrated by assuming otherwise and showing this leads to a contradiction. Assume that there is an SNE in the BTA game which is not an SEE. Because it isn't an SEE, there exists a strategy s^{D} which, if all but one player adopts s^{BTA} and one adopts s^{D}, means that $\pi^{\mathrm{D}} > \pi^{\mathrm{BTA}}$. But then the player with strategy s^{D} must be beating the average. So s^{BTA} must not be a symmetric Nash solution to the BTA game, and we have a contradiction. Similarly, any SEE is also an SNE in the BTA game. Assume that there is an SEE which is not an SNE in the BTA game. Then there exists a strategy s^{D} such that, if player d adopts s^{D} and all the other players adopt s^{SEE}, then player d is beating the average,

$$\pi_d > \frac{1}{N-1} \sum_{i \neq d} \pi_i \qquad \text{i.e. } \pi^{\mathrm{D}} > \pi^{\mathrm{SEE}}.$$

But then s^{SEE} does not fit the definition of a symmetric evolutionary equilibrium strategy, and again we have a contradiction.

Now, what happens to the SEE in the case when players lack strategic power and are unable to influence directly each other's payoffs? In other words, what is the SEE in case of perfect competition, when players have no market power? Returning to eq. (7), say that player d cannot through his own actions change the payoffs of others; he lacks strategic power. Then the maximisation problem becomes simply

$$\max_{s_d \in S} \pi(s_d | s_{-d}),$$

i.e., maximise the *absolute* payoff. In the absence of strategic power, and only in this case, the problems of maximising relative and absolute payoffs will always coincide. That is, only under conditions of perfect competition is absolute-profit maximisation always an 'appropriate summary' of the conditions for survival.

Two points regarding this result should be noted. First, it applies only to choice variables which give players strategic power vis-à-vis each other. Whenever an agent's decision regarding a variable has no effect on his competitors' payoffs, relative- and absolute-maximisation coincide with respect to that variable. For example, a firm's choice of production technology may have no direct effects on its competitors, and so here absolute- and relative-profit maximisation (cost minimisation) coincide with respect to the choice of technology – even if the firm has market power via its choice of output. Similarly, local managers of a large firm with regional branches may be unable to influence each other's payoffs, and when comparing the survival probabilities of the regional managers, absolute-profit maximisation will be an 'appropriate summary' – even if a regional manager has market power vis-à-vis other firms within his region.

Second, the presence of strategic power is a necessary, but not a sufficient, condition for relative- and absolute-maximising behaviour to differ. Relative- and absolute-maximisation may coincide for some arrangements of payoffs, even when players have strategic power. For example, when the game is zero-sum to start with, the relative-maximisation SEE/BTA and the absolute-maximisation SNE coincide.[5]

It is worth noting that the SEE solution coincides not only with the symmetric solution to the 'beat-the-average' game but also with the symmetric solution to the 'maximise-profit-share' game [see Shubik and Levitan (1980)]. We can therefore also interpret the results of this section as providing an 'evolutionary' argument for studying these two relative-maximisation games.

6. Stability and dynamics

In this section we consider the question of 'evolutionary stability' – the behaviour of the model out of 'evolutionary equilibrium', with a mixture of SEE and non-SEE players.

The definition of the degree of stability used here is a natural extension of the definition of equilibrium, and is again borrowed from the analysis of the evolutionary biology finite-population ESS. We say that an SEE is Y-stable under a given strategy choice rule if, for a population with a total of anywhere from 2 to Y deviants with any deviant strategies, the payoff of an SEE player is strictly greater than the payoffs of all the deviants. An SEE is globally stable if this holds for any number of deviants up to $N-1$ (since we need at least one SEE player for the definition to make sense). Note that equilibrium is defined so that a single deviant will be at a selective disadvantage relative to his SEE competitors; stability is defined so that 2 or more deviants will be at a selective disadvantage.

A natural question to ask is the following: will an SEE strategy be the

[5]The proof is by contradiction. (1) Say we have a zero-sum game in which an SEE/BTA solution is not an absolute-maximisation SNE solution. Since it isn't an SNE, a player increases his payoff by deviating. Since it's a zero-sum game, the sum of the payoffs of the other players must then decrease. But then the deviant is now beating the average. Thus the original situation must not have been SEE/BTA solution, and we have a contradiction. (2) Say we have a zero-sum game in which an absolute-maximisation SNE is not an SEE/BTA. Then a player could beat the average by choosing a deviant strategy. Since the game is zero-sum to beat the average the deviant must have increased his payoff as well as lowered the sum of the payoffs of his competitors. But since he increased his payoff, the original situation must not have been an absolute-maximisation SNE, and we have a contradiction.

most frequently observed strategy in the long run? The answer is 'not necessarily', for four reasons. These reasons are particularly instructive because they apply both to the case of perfect competition (when the Friedman conjecture is valid) as well as to the case when players have market power.

6.1. The SEE may not be globally stable, or may not exist at all

For example, payoffs may be such that 'it pays to be different'. Say that if most firms in an industry sell product A and a minority sells the close substitute B, B has 'novelty value' and sells better; if most firms sell B and a minority sells A, A has 'novelty value'; and that product-specific fixed costs mean a firm cannot sell both A and B. An SEE does not exist for this example, because the deviants always do better. An 'evolutionary equilibrium' in such an industry would have a mixture of firms, some selling A, some B. The biological equivalent of this is a 'genetic polymorphism' [Maynard Smith (1982)].[6]

6.2. The stability of an SEE depends crucially on the strategy choice rule which determines the strategy a new player will use

This is why the strategy choice rule appears in the definition of stability above. Consider the following illustration. We first specify two possible strategy choice rules: (i) *imitation*, as suggested by Alchian in his 1950 paper. Specifically, we begin in a population using at most two different strategies; if only one strategy is being used by all players, a new player can choose either that strategy or some other strategy at random from the strategy set S; and if two strategies are in use, a new player chooses one of the two. This specification conforms to the 'mutation' assumption made earlier. The main feature of this strategy choice rule is that no more than two strategies will ever be in use in a population at any one time. (ii) *random choice*; new players choose their strategies at random from S, and their choice is not constrained. Under this strategy choice rule, any number of any of the strategies in S may be in use in a population at any moment.

The duopoly example at the beginning of the paper is easily extended to the N-firm case. The SEE strategy is for each firm to sell Q^*/N, which, as in the duopoly case, coincides with the symmetric zero-profit competitive solution. The proof that this is the SEE also proves that the SEE is globally stable under the imitation strategy choice rule. There are two cases. First, say that some firms are selling the SEE quantity Q^*/N, and the rest are selling some other deviant quantity $q^D < Q^*/N$. Price is now above marginal cost,

[6] Defining the stability conditions for a genetic polymorphism in a finite population is problematic, however; see Schaffer (1988).

and all firms are making profits. But the SEE firms are selling the larger quantity and thus are making the larger profits, and are therefore at a selective advantage relative to the deviant players. Similarly, say that some firms are selling the SEE quantity and the rest are selling $q^D > Q^*/N$. Price has been driven below marginal cost and all the firms are making losses; but the largest losses are being made by the deviants.

However, the SEE is not stable at all under the random strategy choice rule. Consider a population with $N-2$ SEE players, and two deviant players which sell quantities $q^{D1} > Q^*/N$ and $q^{D2} < Q^*/N$ such that $q^{D1} + q^{D2} \neq 2Q^*/N$. All the firms are now earning either positive or negative profits. But if positive profits are being earned, the largest belong to the deviant firm selling q^{D1}; and if the firms are making losses, the smallest losses are being made by the firm selling q^{D2}. The SEE players do not maintain their selective advantage when faced with such a 'simultaneous invasion'.[7]

The conclusions of evolutionary modelling can be very sensitive to behavioural assumptions; here, with respect to strategy choice. The model of this paper with random choice of strategy by new players is very much in the spirit of Friedman's argument. The quote from Friedman's methodological essay which begins this paper is preceded by the statement, 'Let the apparent immediate determinant of business behavior be anything at all – habitual reaction, random chance or what not'. The random choice of strategy corresponds to 'random chance', and the feature of the model that new players do not change their strategies corresponds to 'habitual reaction'. However, the preceding example demonstrates that the conclusions of the model can change drastically if choice of strategy is determined not by 'random chance' but by 'imitation' (or some other 'what not').

6.3. Bias in the strategy choice rule

The point here is straightforward. If new players predominantly choose some non-SEE strategy and avoid choosing the SEE strategy, then naturally the former will be frequently observed and the latter will not.

6.4. The 'absolute-payoff effect'

Say that the survival rule is a function of *absolute* profits, such that the probability of survival $p_{it} = f(\pi_{it})$, $f' > 0$. Say also that an SEE is globally stable under some strategy choice rule. An SEE player always has a selective advantage over a non-SEE competitor. But the payoff to an SEE player in a population of all or mostly SEE players may be very low on an absolute

[7]This 'simultaneous invasion' is similar to a simultaneous invasion in the standard EGT analysis [Maynard Smith (1982)], except that in the latter a successful simultaneous invasion requires *both* deviants to have a higher fitness than the ESS players.

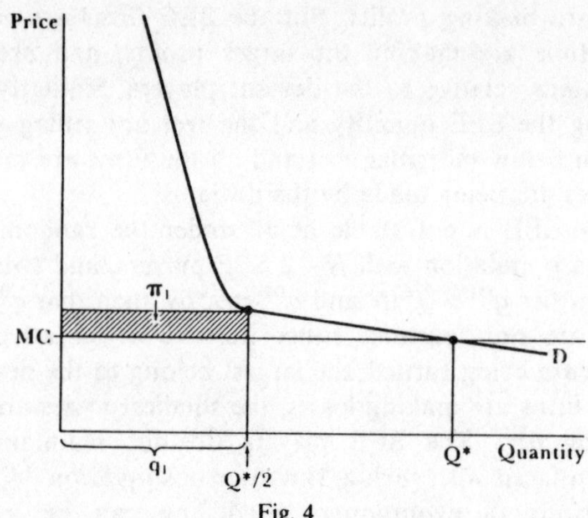

Fig. 4

scale, and the payoff to a non-SEE player in a population of all or mostly non-SEE players may be very high on an absolute scale (though if he has any SEE competitors, they will have even higher payoffs). With the above survival rule, populations with many SEE players will not persist long, and populations with few SEE players will persist longer. To take an extreme case, it may be possible that the largest possible payoffs are earned when *no* SEE players are present; such a state could persist a long time. (This 'absolute payoff effect' will not arise if the survival rule is a function of relative profits such as, say, $p_{it}=f(\pi_{it}/\Sigma\pi), f'>0$.)

Consider again the duopoly example. The shaded area in fig. 4 depicts the profit an SEE firm earns when his competitor sells nothing. This is the largest possible profit an SEE firm can earn. The two shaded areas in fig. 5 are the profits earned by two non-SEE firms which are selling very small quantities; say that they have formed a cartel and are splitting the monopoly profits. At these low quantities, demand is very inelastic and the profits earned by a cartel member are larger than the largest profit an SEE firm could earn. If the survival rule is base on absolute profits, the cartel could persist a long time.

Indeed, let us relax the restriction on the probability of survival and say that a firm is certain to survive selection at the end of the period if and only if its profits equal or exceed one-half the monopoly profits (i.e. the symmetric cartel profits).[8] Then an SEE firm will still always be at a selective

[8]It is not necessary in this example to relax the monotonicity assumption as well. This is because, by assumption, the monopoly profits are the largest industry profits which can be earned. If firm 1 is earning more than one-half the monopoly profits, firm 2 must be earning less than one-half the monopoly profits; thus $p_{1t}=1$ and $p_{2t}<1$. Only in the symmetric cartel will both firms be assured of survival.

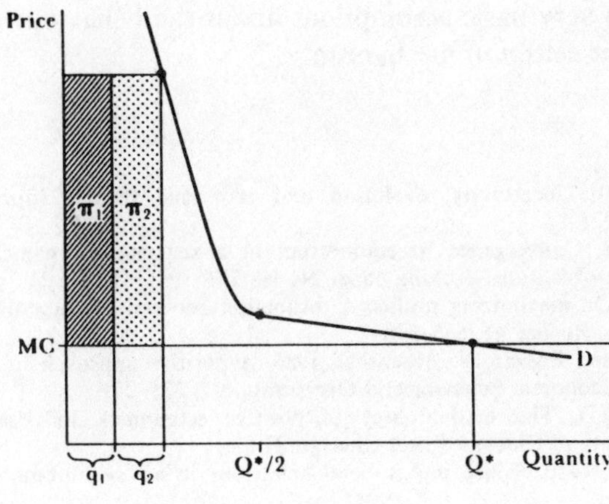

Fig. 5

advantage compared to a non-SEE competitor; but the cartel in fig. 5 would last forever. Note that a member of the cartel could raise his profits even more by expanding output. But if he did, he would drive the profits of the other firm down so that the other firm would *not* survive indefinitely; and when the other firm is replaced, it could well be with a firm which sells an even larger quantity, driving down the profits of the first firm so that now it too could not survive indefinitely.

The moral of this story is that a model of economic natural selection can have a Darwinian condition that the 'fittest survive' and yet feature the survival, the evolutionary success, of firms which maximise neither absolute profits nor relative profits.[9]

7. Conclusion

The basic argument of this paper is an application of Hamilton's evolutionary biology theory of 'spite' to the Friedman conjecture that profit-maximisation is an 'appropriate summary' of the conditions for survival. In a Darwinian 'survival of the fittest' regime, the Friedman conjecture is correct only in perfect competition. When firms have market power, the possibility of 'spiteful' behaviour exists: a firm may forgo profit-maximisation and lower its profits and even its survival chances, but if the profits of its competitors are lowered still further, the 'spiteful' firm will be the more likely survivor. This was formalised in a model using another theory borrowed from evolutionary biology, evolutionary game theory; other formalisations are also possible. The model also demonstrates the sensitivity of an economic natural

[9]A similar point is made in the context of a different model by Nelson and Winter (1982).

selection model to very basic assumptions about the behaviour of agents and the character of the selection mechanism.

References

Alchian, Armen, 1950, Uncertainty, evolution and economic theory, Journal of Political Economy 58, 211–221.

Canning, David, 1988, Convergence to equilibrium in a sequence of games with learning, European University Institute Working paper No. 88/331.

Enke, Stephen, 1951, On maximizing profits: A distinction between Chamberlin and Robinson, American Economic Review 41, 566–578.

Friedman, James W. and Robert W. Rosenthal, 1986, A positive approach to non-cooperative games, Journal of Economic Behavior and Organization 7, 235–251.

Friedman, Milton, 1953, The methodology of positive economics, in: Essays in positive economics (University of Chicago Press, Chicago, IL).

Hamilton, William D., 1970, Selfish and spiteful behaviour in an evolutionary model, Nature 228, 1218–1220.

Hamilton, William D., 1971, Selection of selfish and altruistic behavior in some extreme models, in: J.F. Eisenberg and Wilton S. Dillon, eds., Man and beast: Comparative social behavior (Smithsonian Institution, Washington, D.C.) 57–91.

Hansen, Robert G. and William F. Samuelson, 1988, Evolution in economic games, Journal of Economic Behavior and Organization 10, 315–338.

Holmstrom, Bengt, 1982, Moral hazard in teams, Bell Journal of Economics 13, 324–340.

Knowlton, N. and G.A. Parker, 1979, An evolutionarily stable strategy approach to indiscriminate spite, Nature 279, 419–421.

Lazear, Edward P. and Sherwin Rosen, 1981, Rank-order tournaments as optimum labor contracts, Journal of Political Economy 89, 841–864.

Matthews, R.O.C., 1984, Darwinism and economic change, Oxford Economic Papers (New Series) 36, 91–117.

Maynard Smith, John, 1982, Evolution and the theory of games (Cambridge University Press, Cambridge).

Maynard Smith, John, 1988, Can a mixed strategy be stable in a finite population?, Journal of Theoretical Biology 130, 247–251.

Maynard Smith, John and G.R. Price, 1973, The logic of animal conflict, Nature 246, 15–18.

Nelson, R.R. and S.G. Winter, 1982, An evolutionary theory of economic change (Belknap Press, Cambridge, MA and London).

Riley, John G., 1979, Evolutionary equilibrium strategies, Journal of Theoretical Biology 76, 109–123.

Samuelson, Larry, 1987, Evolutionary foundations of solution concepts for finite, two-player, normal-form games, Unpublished manuscript (Pennsylvania State University/University of Illinois).

Schaffer, Mark E., 1988, Evolutionarily stable strategies for a finite population and a variable contest size, Journal of Theoretical Biology 132, 469–478.

Shubik, Martin, 1954, Does the fittest necessarily survive?, in: Martin Shubik, ed., Readings in game theory and political behavior (Doubleday and Company, Inc., Garden City, NY) 43–46.

Shubik, Martin and Richard Levitan, 1980, Market structure and behavior (Harvard University Press, Cambridge, MA and London).

[22]

How Evolutionary Biology Challenges the Classical Theory of Rational Choice

W. S. COOPER

S.L.I.S.
University of California
Berkeley, CA 94720
U.S.A.

ABSTRACT: A fundamental philosophical question that arises in connection with evolutionary theory is whether the fittest patterns of behavior are always the most rational. Are fitness and rationality fully compatible? When behavioral rationality is characterized formally as in classical decision theory, the question becomes mathematically meaningful and can be explored systematically by investigating whether the optimally fit behavior predicted by evolutionary process models is decision-theoretically coherent. Upon investigation, it appears that in nontrivial evolutionary models the expected behavior is *not* always in accord with the norms of the standard theory of decision as ordinarily applied. Many classically irrational acts, e.g. betting on the occurrence of one event in the knowledge that the probabilities favor another, can under certain circumstances constitute adaptive behavior.

One interesting interpretation of this clash is that the criterion of rationality offered by classical decision theory is simply incorrect (or at least incomplete) as it stands, and that evolutionary theory should be called upon to provide a more generally applicable theory of rationality. Such a program, should it prove feasible, would amount to the logical reduction of the theory of rational choice to evolutionary theory.

KEY WORDS: Evolution, evolutionary biology, fitness, decision theory, theory of choice, rationality, rational behavior, reductionism.

The relationship of rationality to Darwinian fitness, though a subject of obvious importance and fascination, is not yet well understood. It is widely conceded that rational behavior could be a product of selective forces, but many questions remain unresolved. Perhaps the most fundamental is whether fitness and rationality are mutually compatible. Does optimal fitness entail perfect rationality, or could it sometimes give rise to irrationality?

In order to address this question systematically it is essential to start out with clear (if provisional) definitions of 'rationality' and 'fitness'. Rationality has been variously defined in disciplines ranging from economics (which treats of 'rational man') to deductive logic ('rational' inferences among propositions). However, so far as rational *behavior* is concerned, the characterization of rationality most widely accepted at the present time is the one presented in the standard theory of decision under risk and

Biology and Philosophy 4: 457–481, 1989.

uncertainty. This theory (actually a family of theories) will be referred to in this paper as *classical decision theory*, the phrase being intended here as a cover term for the formal systems of rational choice due to Ramsey (1926), von Neumann and Morgenstern (1953), Savage (1954/1972), and other more recent authors (surveyed e.g. by Fishburn (1981)). It is the system of decision analysis commonly taught in courses and presented in text books on decision theory (e.g. Raiffa 1968). Because of its logical persuasiveness and widespread acceptance as a source of normative rules for rational behavior, classical decision theory suggests itself as a plausible definition of rationality for an initial exploration of rationality vis-à-vis fitness.

The second concept, evolutionary fitness, has been defined by evolutionists in various ways, but the most commonly used mathematical measures of genotypic or populational fitness are, in essence, normalized versions of simple populational or genotypic growth rates (Wright 1931; Fisher 1930; Haldane 1949). These are the standard textbook measures of fitness. There is serious doubt whether they are absolute or universally appropriate characterizations of fitness (MacArthur & Wilson 1967; Stearns 1982; Cooper 1984; Endler 1986). However, most evolutionists would probably agree that under at least some conditions the growth measures do provide indicators of relative (i.e. ordinally valid) fitness. It would not seem unreasonable, therefore, to employ one of these growth formulae as a tentative characterization of fitness for exploratory purposes. For the present study one called the finite intrinsic rate of increase will be adopted; the precise definition will be given later.

Provisional definitions such as these make it possible to explore the relationship between rationality and fitness mathematically. Adopting the techniques of theoretical population biology, an evolutionary population process model may be used to predict the choice behavior of fitness-maximizing individuals in the population. These biologically predictable behavioral traits can in turn be compared against the classical decision-theoretic norms of rational behavior. This type of investigation makes it feasible to wrestle with such issues as: Is the evolutionary notion of fitness logically consistent with the kind of rationality described by classical decision theory? If so, might some logical relationship stronger than mere compatibility obtain, e.g. might success at fitness maximization logically *imply* that the resulting choice behavior is rational according to decision theory?

Pursuing this line of attack I have attempted elsewhere (Cooper 1987) to provide a mathematical proof that, for sufficiently simple population process models at least, the answer to the latter question would appear to be Yes. It seems the classical laws of rational choice theory (specifically, those of Savage *op. cit.*) are not only consistent with, but directly *derivable from*, the laws of adaptation and fitness maximization operative in sufficiently simplified evolutionary processes. One finds, in other words, that the forces of natural selection do more than merely abet or enforce independent rational criteria of external origin. Rather, these criteria are already included among the logical consequences of the evolutionary laws, so that in a sense the forces of selection *are* the rules of rationality. This means all truly adaptive behavior is inherently rational by classical standards, at least so far as one can tell from very simple evolutionary models.

Speculating on the significance of this implicative relationship between population biology and classical decision rules, it seems possible that it might provide the beginnings of an evolutionary foundation for all rational choice theory. Methodologically speaking, the evolutionary derivability of rational decision rules would seem to support a strong form of biological *reductionism*. In the reductionist view the entire theory of behavioral rationality could be considered, in principle, a branch of evolutionary theory. Evolutionary biology would supply the foundation, choice logic the superstructure. The philosophical ramifications of such a reduction, should it prove viable, could be far-reaching.

Qualifying these speculations, however, is an awkward fact. The mathematical demonstration of the biological reducibility of classical decision theory is based on highly simplified, indeed oversimplified, population process models. One naturally wonders: What about more elaborate population models, especially models that begin to approach a realistic description of the evolutionary forces shaping the behavior of organisms with complex cognitive processing capabilities? Is standard decision theory still implied by, or even compatible with, such models? If not, the simple reducibility relationship connecting evolutionary theory and classical decision theory might not be so straight-forward after all.

It is a justified worry. In what follows I shall try to show that classical decision theory, as ordinarily applied in typical textbook analyses at any rate, is probably *not* wholly consistent with the evolutionary notion of fitness maximization in more elaborate evolutionary models. It will be seen that generalized population models project their own rules of adaptive choice — rules the classical decision criteria capture only approximately. In the light of these more realistic models it will appear that even organisms that are fully fitness-maximizing could be expected to exhibit some classically unruly behavior. The behavioral anomalies could well seem illogical, inconsistent, incoherent, and contrary to common sense, at least until the evolutionary reasons for them are understood.

The upshot is that one is faced with a dilemma. Either rationality is not always the fittest policy, or else classical decision analysis is not as universally rational as is commonly claimed. If the latter horn of the dilemma is seized (and I shall argue that that is indeed the lesser of the evils), one is led to entertain the possibility of a new, nonclassical approach to decision theory founded on evolutionary theory rather than the unaided logical intuition.

BETTING AGAINST THE PROBABILITIES

As a way of fixing ideas and illustrating the aforementioned dilemma, I shall attempt to demonstrate the potential selective advantage of a specific pattern of choice behavior that apparently violates classical decision-theoretic norms as ordinarily interpreted. This problematic behavior will be referred to as 'betting against the probabilities'. As a simple illustration of a bet against the probabilities, suppose a coin is known on reliable grounds to be biased in favor of heads. Suppose too there is a fixed, known reward to an individual for guessing correctly, and a known penalty for guessing incorrectly, the outcome of the next flip. In these circumstances, could it ever be advantageous for the individual to bet on tails rather than heads?

Most of us would probably respond in the negative. To choose tails would be to ignore or misuse the crucial bit of information that heads is likelier than tails. The choice of tails seems clearly irrational; certainly it would run counter to garden-variety decision analysis. Nevertheless, as we shall try to show, under some circumstances this sort of bet against the known probabilities could well be an adaptive choice.

That such curious behavior could ever be adaptive is a consequence of a methodological fine point in population biology. In a temporally varying environment, in order to measure fitness a genotype's rate of increase has to be averaged over time. The averaging of multiplicative rates of increase is properly carried out using a geometric rather than an arithmetic mean (Crow & Kimura 1970). The implications of this technicality for the explanation of individual variation have been investigated by Gillespie (1974, 1977) and others. Kaplan and I have pointed out that one of its more interesting consequences is the prediction of a peculiar form of intra-genotypic strategy mixing which we call adaptive coin-flipping (Cooper & Kaplan 1982, Kaplan & Cooper 1984). The latter is an evolutionary mechanism in which it can be to the selective advantage of the genotype for its individual phenotypic expressions to make their choices randomly.

Adaptive coin-flipping can result in any of a number of strange behaviors (explored in our 1982 paper). Some of these appear to run contrary to the individuals' own best interests. The randomization that causes the anomalous behavior differs from the many other sources of individual variation that have been identified in the literature in that most of the latter either do not produce within-genotype variation at all or else do not lead to predictions of comparable behavioral oddities.

One of the nonclassical yet fit behaviors to which adaptive coin-flipping can give rise is betting against the probabilities. In order to understand the potential evolutionary advantage of sometimes placing bets against the probabilities (as well as other curious behavioral traits) it will be instructive to consider a series of examples illustrating the virtues of the coin-flipping that produces such bets. We shall start out with simple examples that make no overt reference to evolutionary processes and work up to the general evolutionary case of intra-genotypic strategy mixing. It is hoped that, in addition to introducing non-biologists to the subject, the examples may be of some service to evolutionists as a clarification of the difference between the kind of adaptive randomization that is relevant here and other more commonly discussed sources of individual variation and strategy mixing. Readers are asked to study the non-biological examples as closely as the biological, as all of the mathematics and most of the concepts will carry over to the evolutionary application.

EXAMPLE 1: *Hedging a Bet.* A blindfold draw is to be made from an urn containing sixty white balls and forty black balls. The balls have been thoroughly stirred and elaborate precautions have been taken to make the draw fair and truly random. You know all this and so are wholly convinced that the event that the drawn ball will be white has an objective probability of exactly 0.6. You may bet on an outcome of either a white or a black draw. The conditions of the bet are that if you predict the drawn color successfully you will double whatever sum of money you put up, but if you guess wrongly you will lose three quarters of it. You are allowed to place more than one bet.

Let Strategy A (the 'pure' strategy) be to bet all of one's money on white. Let Strategy B (the 'hedged' strategy) consist of putting 5/8 of one's money on white, with the remaining 3/8 placed in a separate bet on black. Which strategy do you prefer? Strategy A has the advantage of a higher expected monetary value. (The statistical expectation under Strategy A is that your initial capital will increase by a multiplicative factor of $0.6 \times 2 + 0.4 \times 0.25 \approx 1.30$, for an expected profit of 30%. Under Strategy B this factor is reduced to $0.6\,((5/8) \times 2 + (3/8) \times 0.25) + 0.4\,((5/8) \times 0.25 + (3/8) \times 2) \approx 1.17$, an expected profit of only 17%.) But there is something to be said for Strategy B too. In the unlucky event that black is drawn, under Strategy A you will lose 3/4 of your capital whereas under Strategy B you would lose only 3/32 of it. So if you are playing for large stakes and are risk-averse, you may well prefer Strategy B. Evidently it is not necessarily irrational to wager *part* of one's money against the probabilities, as a hedge.

EXAMPLE 2: *Hedging Successive Bets.* Suppose you are given the opportunity to repeat the foregoing gamble one thousand times in succession, with a new independent draw (with replacement) to be made from the (same) urn each time. All profits or losses are to be compounded; that is, after putting up your initial capital for the first gamble, no new capital may be introduced and in each gamble you must commit all of the proceeds from the previous gamble. Strategy A is to bet everything on white in each of the thousand gambles. Strategy B is to hedge each of the thousand bets by always putting 5/8 of one's current capital on white, 3/8 on black. Now which strategy do you prefer?

In a thousand independent trials with probability 0.6 of drawing white in each trial, it may be expected that around 600 of the draws will produce a white ball and around 400 black. Hence under Strategy A you might expect, after the thousandth gamble, to have multiplied your initial capital by a factor somewhere in the neighborhood of

$$2^{600}\,(0.25)^{400} \approx 6 \times 10^{-61}.$$

This is an almost unimaginably small number. In other words, your initial investment is very likely to have all but vanished. On the other hand, under Strategy B your initial capital will probably be multiplied by a factor of around

$$((5/8) \times 2 + (3/8) \times 0.25)^{600}\,((5/8) \times 0.25 + (3/8) \times 2)^{400} \approx 8 \times 10^{59}$$

by the thousandth draw, bringing you riches beyond the dreams of avarice.

Moreover, it can be calculated that the probability that a sequence of a thousand independent draws will contain enough white balls to make Strategy A more profitable than Strategy B is negligible (about 2×10^{-28}), so it is practically impossible to do better under A than B. True, the expected monetary value of Strategy A exceeds that of Strategy B, but that is academic. A person would have to have a pathological attitude indeed toward risk to prefer A to B. Once you have understood that Strategy B is virtually certain to make you fabulously wealthy, that Strategy A will almost certainly dissipate your initial capital, and that the chances of doing better under A than B are utterly remote, you will come around to Strategy B.

The example shows that consistently betting a portion of one's capital against the known probabilities can sometimes produce an enormously improved compound rate of return over time. It also illustrates that the commonly calculated expected monetary value of a gamble, which in this case favors the ruinous Strategy A over the brilliant Strategy B, serves poorly as an indicator of the best strategy when the gambles are to be repeated many times with returns compounded. The explanation commonly given of this kind of inadequacy is that the expected monetary value does not take into account the diminishing marginal utility of money. An alternative, and in this case more illuminating, explanation is that the expected monetary value of a strategy, as ordinarily calculated, is a probability-weighted *arithmetic* mean, whereas when successive change rates are to be multiplied together what is really wanted is a probability-weighted *geometric* mean of those rates.

To elaborate: Under Strategy A the geometrically expected rate of return on capital is

$$2^{0.6}\,(0.25)^{0.4} \approx 0.87$$

per gamble. This tells us that after many trials one's capital may be expected under the unhedged strategy to be depleted as though multiplied by a constant factor of about 0.87 with each trial. Under Strategy B the corresponding geometric mean change factor per trial is

$$((5/8) \times 2 + (3/8) \times 0.25)^{0.6}\,((5/8) \times 0.25 + (3/8) \times 2)^{0.4} \approx 1.15.$$

This indicates that in the long run the hedged bets should cause one's capital to grow at around that multiplicative rate per trial. Thus the geometric mean accurately identifies Strategy B as preferable to A, and it quantifies the extent of the advantage.

The superiority of the geometric over the arithmetic mean rate of return as a criterion measure of long range wealth-building potential is well known in investment portfolio theory. See for example Latane et al. (1975, pp. 564—573) for a detailed comparison and a demonstration that maximizing the geometric mean return gives "the largest compound rate of return over time" and "will result in a greater terminal wealth than other alternatives".

EXAMPLE 3: *Corporate Bet Hedging*. Next, let us imagine that our hypothetical urn problem is an accurate statistical model of a publicly available business investment. Some chance event in the world of commerce, corresponding to a 'draw' from the 'urn', is known by the investment community to have an objective probability of exactly 0.6 of coming out 'white' and 0.4 of turning out 'black'. There is just one 'urn' and its mixture doesn't change, but an independent random draw with replacement will be made from it once a week into the indefinite future. Each week, before the draw, shares or contracts for that week's draw are put on public sale. These contracts are of two types: (1) contracts in 'white', which will be worth double their former value immediately after the draw if the draw turns out to be a white ball, but will lose three quarters of their value if it turns out black; and (2) contracts in 'black' which will double their value in the event of a black draw and lose three quarters of it in the event of white. An inexhaustible supply of contracts is made available for purchase at the same fixed cost C per contract every week. Contract purchasers must sign up in person, and no individual is allowed to sign up for more than one contract for any given draw.

An investment company, recognizing that this opportunity could be immensely profitable if only there were a way to hedge, contrives the following scheme for getting around the one-contract-per-customer restriction. Each week before the draw the company quietly recruits enough private agents so that if each agent signs up for one contract, the firm's entire current fund of investment capital will be committed. Dividing its current assets up equally among the agents, the company instructs 5/8 of them to buy one 'white' contract each, and the remaining 3/8 to purchase one 'black' contract each. After the draw the agents are instructed to sell their contracts, return the proceeds to the firm, and the entire procedure is repeated the following week with another set of agents. The company's strategy is essentially Strategy B of the previous example. Clearly, such a firm could be expected to do fabulously well after a few years. If the agents are promised a share in the eventual profits, they will carry out their instructions with enthusiasm.

Notice that an onlooker, seeing intelligent individuals investing in black contracts, might be puzzled. Indeed such individuals would appear as first glance to be acting irrationally by betting on the wrong side of a known probability. However, the puzzle would be resolved when it was discovered they were secretly collaborating, investing not for their own immediate benefit but to enable their firm to hedge its corporate bets.

EXAMPLE 4: *Strategy Mixing*. Imagine now that for some reason the firm is unable to communicate with its agents before the draw in order to instruct them as to which of them should constitute the 5/8 buying into white and which the 3/8 choosing black. Suppose too that the agents cannot intercommunicate in order to organize this matter amongst themselves. A convenient way around the problem would be for each agent to decide privately which type of contract to buy through the use of an auxiliary chance device. For example, each week just before investing, each agent might make a private random draw from his own personal urn — an urn containing 5 white balls and 3 black — and buy a white or black contract accordingly. Provided there are enough agents, it is a fairly sure thing that under this 'strategy mixing' plan approximately 5/8 of the corporate funds will go into white and 3/8 into black in each trial, as desired under Strategy B. Because there would be no visible collusion or even communication among the agents, an onlooker might be even more mystified than in the previous example at the apparently rampant irrationality.

EXAMPLE 5: *Variable Payoffs*. Recall that C is the standard purchase cost of a contract. Suppose next that instead of only two possible selling prices $2C$ and $C/4$, any integral multiple of C (i.e. $0C$, $1C$, $2C$, $3C$, etc.) is possible as a selling price. Thus even when of the same color, different individual contracts can now sell at different prices, with the price received for any given contract depending upon various chance factors. The analysis of the firm's success will remain essentially unaffected by this minor elaboration provided it is assumed that the statistical distribution of all selling prices is such that the *average* (arithmetic mean) selling price of a contract in the drawn color is still $2C$, and the *average* selling price for a contract of the other type remains at $C/4$. The power of Strategy B remains intact.

In making the transition to the next example the reader may find it suggestive to imagine that following each draw each agent, after selling his contract for nC dollars, recruits and trains for the firm the n new agents who will be needed to reinvest these proceeds, dividing up the money equally among them in preparation for the next draw. One then has a fluctuating but automatically self-perpetuating population of agents, with lineages of descent comparable to those of an asexually breeding biological population.

EXAMPLE 6: *Intra-Genotypic Strategy Mixing.* Turning to biology, it is not hard to specify population processes that are exact mathematical analogs of the foregoing example. There is some conceptual analogy too. The firm corresponds to a genotype and its agents to the genotype's individual phenotypic expressions. The public urn becomes an unpredictable environmental event affecting all the population members. The private urns used by the agents to randomize their decisions become chance physiological or environmental factors, perhaps minor and seemingly irrelevant, to whose influence the phenotypic expressions are susceptible.

For the sake of a concrete example, consider a hypothetical population of organisms whose evolutionary fitness is highly dependent upon protective coloration. At a certain time each winter a certain species of predator passes through the region, decimating the numbers of those individuals within the population that can be spotted easily against the background terrain. If the black soil terrain happens to be covered with snow at the time, the best protective coloration is white; otherwise, black is best. The organisms' evolutionary dilemma is that in the autumn when the winter coloration is adopted, there is no way of telling whether or not there will be a snow cover at the crucial time during the ensuing winter.

Suppose that each year there is an objective probability of 0.6 of a snow cover at the crucial time, this probability being independent of whether or not there was snow the previous winter. Let us assume that protectively colored individuals can expect to survive the winter in enough numbers to leave an average of 2 surviving offspring each, while relative to their initial numbers the conspicuous ones leave on average only 0.25 offspring each. Thus if a census is taken every autumn, for the set of individuals adopting white coloration before a snowy winter or black before a snowless one the next-generation offspring will in the following autumn be about twice as numerous, while the conspicuous remainder of the population will shrink by a factor of about 4.

Let us assume a simplified evolutionary process model in which breeding is asexual, with the consequence that except for occasional mutations each individual is genetically identical with its (single) parent. Assume also that breeding is seasonal (i.e. offspring are produced only at a set time of year such as spring) and semelparous (each individual produces offspring only once per lifetime at the age of exactly one year). Adopting a broad definition of the term, we shall speak of all individuals whose genes affect winter coloration in the same way as being of the same *genotype* with respect to that characteristic. Assume there is no significant pleiotropy — no side effects of these genes for coloration on other characteristics which could prevent the selective forces on coloration from having their expected results.

The organisms will for simplicity be assumed to interact with the environment in a fashion called 'R-selecting' (Wilson 1975, MacArthur & Wilson *op. cit.*). R-selection implies that the intrinsic rate of increase R of the subpopulation of all individuals of a given genotype is a satisfactory measure of that genotype's Darwinian fitness. In case several genotypes coexist within the population, in an R-selecting process the genotype with the highest R is by definition likeliest to survive and become fixed in the population.

The genotypic growth rate R that is of interest is called an 'intrinsic' rate of increase because it is treated as mathematically separable from the effects of the regulatory forces that occasionally intervene under conditions of overpopulation to damp down population growth or cause the population size to drop. These regulatory pressures are assumed to be unbiased in their relative effects on the different genotypes, so that the intrinsic growth rate R is all that matters for comparative purposes. A genotype's intrinsic finite rate of increase R is defined mathematically as the multiplicative factor by which the size of the genotypic subpopulation is expected to increase in each season, in the absence of regulatory forces. Thus for instance a 5% increase per season would give a rate of $R = 1.05$. The finite rate of increase R is often denoted in the literature by λ or R_0 (Mertz 1970).

In models such as the present one in which a genotype's growth rate may change from season to season, a value of R must be used which has been averaged over time. Since the rates of change in population size are multiplicative, geometric averaging is called for. Although the two theories were developed independently, the grounds for using the geometric rather than arithmetic mean rate of population size change as an indicator of fitness in population biology are entirely parallel to the grounds for using the geometric mean rate of return as a criterion measure of long range wealth maximization potential in portfolio theory. Indeed the evolutionary process is the example *par excellence* of a situation in which compounding is multiplicative and in which what happens in the long run is what matters.

Now suppose two genotypes, call them A and B, are in competition within a large population. Assume individuals of Genotype A always have white winter coloration. In evolutionary terminology, A is a genotype with a uniquely determined phenotypic expression, namely the trait of whiteness in winter. Genotype B, on the other hand, gives rise each winter to some individuals with white coloration and some with black, the ratio staying constant at about 5/8 to 3/8 every winter. Thus Genotype B's phenotypic expression varies from individual to individual, with the result that although in winter each individual is either white all over or black all over, the set of all individuals of the type B genetic makeup is always mixed.

It is easy to show that Genotype B is fitter than Genotype A. Under the modelling assumptions that have been adopted, the two growth rates of interest are readily calculated using standard methods of population biology. These evolutionary computations are mathematically identical to the computations of the earlier example about investments. Thus the subpopulation consisting of all Genotype A individuals may be expected in the long run to be diminished by a multiplicative factor averaging about $R = 0.87$ per year, while those of Genotype B will increase at an annual multiplicative rate of about $R = 1.15$. Clearly, Genotype B is likely to win its evolutionary race handily and will eventually take over the population. Indeed the doomed Genotype A, with an intrinsic long run growth rate smaller than 1.0, could not be expected to maintain itself even in the absence of any competing genotypes. If one were to visit such a population one would therefore expect to find both white and dark individuals every winter in an approximate ratio of 5: 3.

How is it possible for one genotype to give rise to different phenotypic expressions in different individuals in a set ratio? There would appear to be no shortage of biological mechanisms that could serve as the proximate cause of such intra-genotypic variation. All that is required is that a chance mechanism with the desired probability characteristics be at work within each individual to determine its phenotype. The randomization could be accomplished, for example, through the conditioning of developmental events on unresolved developmental noise, through chance physiological phenomena, or even phenotypic responsiveness to random environmental events (Waddington 1957, Hutchinson 1981). As in the case of the agents' private urns in the earlier example, any chance mechanism will do so long as it has the desired statistical properties.

Note that when adaptive strategy mixing or randomization of this kind is present, the characteristic of interest (e.g. coloration) is still in a sense genetically controlled, but the control is only partial; it is only the statistical distribution of the characteristic that is genetically constrained. The genes determine the chance mechanism that will operate to produce the required distribution, and that chance mechanism in turn settles case by case the phenotypic character that will appear in each individual. For further biological particulars and examples the papers by Cooper and Kaplan (1982, 1984 *op. cit.*) and Walker (1986) may be consulted.

EXAMPLE 7: *Instinctive Behavioral Strategy Mixing.* "Regularities of behavior are as predictable and discernible as the color of plumage and the shape of eggs" (Tiger & Fox 1971, p. 17). Since adaptive behaviors can evolve as readily as adaptive morphological or physiological traits, the reasoning of the foregoing example extends immediately to the instinctive choices organisms make among available courses of action. Should a specific illustration be needed, the preceding example could be changed slightly to make it the color of the winter nest, rather than the winter color of the animal itself, that is critical. Given a free choice of white or black building materials, it will be less adaptive for all individuals to choose white materials than for all individuals to draw from private internal urns in such a way as to cause about 5/8 to choose white and about 3/8 black. Interestingly enough, those choosing black are in effect betting their very lives against the probabilities.

EXAMPLE 8: *Reasoned Strategy Mixing.* Next, suppose that something prevents the evolution of the appropriate behavior as a simple specialized instinct. It could be, for instance, that the specific numeric parameters of the decision problem — the relevant probabilities and conditional growth rates — keep changing from year to year in such rapid and unpredictable fashion that a fit behavior pattern has no time to arise as a fixed instinct. As a strong simplifying assumption, let us also postulate that the environment is *information-benign.* By this is meant that plenty of obvious environmental clues about the parameters relevant to the decision of interest are readily available to all individuals, and that these reliably indicate the exact values of the controlling probabilities and growth rates. Under such conditions it would be no surprise if in some organisms capacities were to evolve for internally processing these clues in a primitive kind of ratiocination. Selective pressures would favor a genotype whose individual members were, in each year, able to behave in such a manner as to mix the genotypic population optimally with respect to that year's environmental parameters.

Obviously, such ratiocination would not produce choices like that of classical decision theory, for it would not constitute optimally fit behavior for each individual to maximize its expected fitness separately using the classical expectation formula in the standard way. Instead, by an extension of the reasoning of the previous examples, genotypic strategy mixing using internalized randomizing devices would be more adaptive and hence likelier to evolve. This means that many individuals would be found taking such classically questionable courses of action as betting against the probabilities. Yet in spite of this classically anomalous behavior, genotypic fitness would be maximized.

INTERIM CONCLUSION

It appears that organisms can make evolutionarily correct (well-adapted) decisions that could look like blunders to a biologically unenlightened classical decision theorist. The seeming blunders could include betting against the probabilities and many other apparent irrationalities caused by adaptive choice randomization. This paradoxical choice behavior is brought about because, just as the agents in the earlier examples were secretly acting for the benefit of their firm, individual organisms tend to act as though for the benefit of their genotype. This pervasive phenomenon — a tendency toward maximization of genotypic fitness — is one of the most firmly established generalizations in all of evolutionary theory, and the consequent inclination of individuals to promote the welfare of their genes is a recurrent theme throughout the literature on ethology and sociobiology. What the examples show is that this evolutionary truism can have surprising consequences for decision logic — consequences that run counter to what a biologically uninformed statement of the classical theory of rational behavior might have led one to expect.

EXPLORING THE STRATEGY MIXING ADVANTAGE

Our analysis has suggested that even in an information-benign environment, it can be to a genotype's selective advantage for its members to randomize some of their decisions — to "flip coins" as it were. One has therefore a curiously regressive evolutionary tendency in which the effect of selective pressures will be to leave a bolt loose somewhere in the decision mechanism that develops. The loose bolt could be hard to spot, because it might hide under the appearance of various organismic design failures or inefficiencies attributable to developmental noise, incomplete adaptation, etc. (In humans, fuzzy-mindedness?) These apparent defects would nevertheless have an adaptive role. The real function of this superficially sloppy engineering would be to provide an internal 'urn' with beneficial statistical properties.

To the extent that this urn is well-adapted, its statistical properties should be susceptible to conventional optimization analysis. In the simple evolutionary model assumed for the examples, the optimal statistical mix is easily determined. Let a random environmental event have two possible outcomes, Outcome 1 with an objective probability of p and Outcome 2 with probability $1-p$. Assume (as in the examples) there are only two available acts, and the individuals of some genotype of interest have adopted a mixed strategy in which each individual has probability q of selecting Act 1 and probability $1-q$ of performing Act 2. Suppose a subpopulation of individuals performing the i'th act will, in a season in which the j'th outcome comes to pass, leave progeny which exceed them in number by a factor of $R_{i,j}$, the rate of increase for the group in a season of that type. The genotypic fitness (geometrically averaged finite rate of increase) resulting from such a mixed strategy is

$$r = (qr_{1,1} + (1-q)r_{2,1})^p (qr_{1,2} + (1-q)r_{2,2})^{1-p}. \quad (1)$$

The first derivative of this expression with respect to q has a root at

$$q = \frac{(1-p)r_{2,1}}{r_{2,1} - r_{1,1}} + \frac{pr_{2,2}}{r_{2,2} - r_{1,2}}. \quad (2)$$

It can be shown that there is a mixed (randomized) strategy superior to either pure strategy (pure means all individuals perform the same act) if and only if the value of q given by Equation (2) lies in the open interval between 0 and 1. When it does, q and $1-q$ specify the probabilities which a strategy mixing chance device would have to exhibit in order to maximize genotypic fitness. When it lies outside the unit interval, no randomization is called for and either Act 1 or Act 2 is best depending upon whether q is greater than 1 or less than 0.

Equation (2) may be thought of as encapsulating the correct (fit) logic of decision for all well adapted individuals in this particular population model. It is a comprehensive decision rule for binary choice making, telling whether an individual ought to opt outright for Act 1, opt outright for Act 2, or flip an internal coin to decide. If a coin-flip is indicated, it tells how the coin should be weighted. Selective pressures could be expected, other things being equal, to create an evolutionary tendency toward the use of this rule and these weights. To illustrate the application of Equations (1) and (2), in most of our examples $p = 0.6$, $r_{1,1} = r_{2,2} = 2$, and $r_{2,1} = r_{1,2} = 0.25$. Eq. (2) shows the optimal mixture to be at $q = 0.629$, or approximately 5/8 white. Substituting this value in Eq. (1) yields the Strategy B fitness of $r = 1.15$ as previously calculated.

From these formulae much can be learned about the character and robustness of the strategy mixing advantage. One finds for instance that the mixing probability q can be far from optimal and still yield at least some benefit. Thus for the probability value 0.6 and the growth rates of 2 and 0.25 assumed in the examples, one easily discovers that any value of q larger than 0.18 and smaller than 1.00 gives at least some advantage in fitness over the pure white strategy. Also, one finds the probability of the chance event need not necessarily be close to 0.5 to produce a strategy mixing advantage. For any value of p between 0.12 and 0.88 there is a mixed strategy that is fitter than the fittest pure strategy.

There can be a selective advantage not only to betting against the probabilities but also to betting against the payoffs. Suppose in the examples the value of p is lowered from 0.6 to a neutral 0.5, removing the probabilistic advantage of choosing white. To restore the advantage in another form, suppose that $R_{1,1}$ is raised to 2.25 and $R_{1,2}$ to 0.50, giving the choice of white both a larger potential reward and a more lenient penalty than that of black. There are no apparent compensating factors in black's favor, yet the formulas show that a mixed population will do much better than one in which all individuals choose white.

Some situations offer a choice between taking a risky gamble and not entering into the gamble at all. In our model this circumstance would obtain when, say, $p = 0.5$, $R_{1,1} = 2$, $R_{1,2} = 0.5$, and $R_{2,1} = R_{2,2} = 1$, where Act 1 is the risky gamble and Act 2 plays it safe. Upon substituting these values into the formulae one finds that any mixed strategy is fitter than either the pure Act 1 or the pure Act 2 strategy, a 50-50 mixture being optimal. Hence in a well adapted population one would expect to find both acts performed in about equal proportions. In decision and utility theory the traditional explanation of a situation in which some individuals accept a risky gamble and others decline it is that some individuals are more 'risk seeking' than others. As a scientific explanation this seems suspiciously circular — more like naming than explaining. The evolutionary analysis raises the possibility of a more substantive explanation: The genotype could be hedging its bets.

No strategy mixing advantage could exist were it not for the statistical dependencies allowed by the population model (e.g. snow for all or snow for none). The presence of such dependency is in fact the only thing that distinguishes the present model from the model of the earlier paper (Cooper 1987) in which the classical theory turned out to be biologically valid. The strongest dependencies produce the greatest strategy mixing advantage. The full benefit of strategy mixing will be realized only in the case of gambles in which all individuals of the same genotype experience identical chance event outcomes. If the chance event outcome is common only to those members of the genotype in a local population or deme, this benefit may be lessened. If the event is common to only part of the local population, the advantage could be weakened still further. In case the event of concern is not a single event affecting all individuals in the population alike, but rather a set of statistically correlated events of the same type, one for each individual, there will be a strategy mixing advantage whose significance will be dependent upon the strength of the correlation.

In the case of environments that are not entirely information-benign (and this surely includes most real environments), it can be shown that randomization can still be advantageous. That is to say, the fragmentary or subjective character of a decision maker's data about the relevant probabilities and payoffs does not eliminate the possibility that strategy mixing may be called for. To produce optimally fit behavior, some individuals might still have to bet contrary to the evidence provided by the available clues, or perform other classically incoherent acts. The extent of the need for strategy mixing will in general depend upon the amount and reliability of the fragmentary information available, the degree to which it is independent from individual to individual, and so on.

Strategy mixing is of the greatest benefit to a genotype when some of the differences between the possible payoffs (the $R_{i,j}$'s) are large. For decision situations in which these differences are all small, the intervals within which the mixing probabilities can confer a selective advantage are apt to be narrow and the magnitude of the conferred advantage slight. However, the present analysis has some severe limitations and it is not yet clear what would happen in more general models. Due to the magic of geometric compounding, even a minute advantage in the geometric mean growth rate, maintained over long stretches of evolutionary time, can give a genotype a dramatic competitive advantage. So while smaller stakes may in general give smaller mixing advantages, it has yet to be determined at what point the advantages of randomization become insignificant.

LIMITATIONS OF THE MODEL

The population model assumed for the sake of the examples is far too simple to offer an accurate representation of the evolutionary processes that produced the complex behaviors found in many animals including man. However, there is no reason to suppose that refining the model would somehow cancel out the benefit of choice randomization. The strategy mixing advantage is the product of a fundamental genotype-phenotype distinction implicit in all population genetics models.

Since most interesting species are not strictly R-selecting, more realistic population models would probably require a measure of evolutionary fitness of greater generality than the simple rate of increase R or its variants as presented in introductory textbooks on population biology. But the adoption of a more sophisticated measure of fitness is unlikely to weaken the case for a selective advantage to randomization. To the contrary, other known fitness measures, e.g. the so-called 'persistence' measures (Stearns 1982), would seem to support the case for a strategy mixing advantage to at least as great an extent. Examples of strategy mixing superiority have been constructed with fitness measured in terms of improbability of extinction (Cooper & Kaplan 1982 p. 146). Another important persistence measure with a broad range of applicability is 'expected time to extinction' (MacArthur & Wilson *op. cit.*, Cooper 1984). When this measure was used in a computer simulation of evolution in small populations, randomized choice-making was found to be fitter than the competing pure strategies (Kaplan *et al.* 1987). This evidence suggests that measuring fitness with R may, if anything, underestimate the importance of choice randomization.

CONTRASTS WITH CLASSICAL DECISION THEORY

As the standard decision logic is ordinarily interpreted and naively applied — that is to say, with the individual treated as an isolated locus of decision making and with the role of the genotype ignored — few of its laws are immune to evolutionary counterexamples. Consider for instance the underlying assumption that individual preferences are or should be stable. Traditionally it has been presumed that if a rational decision maker could be thrust repeatedly into the same decision situation with the same knowledge and tastes each time, the individual should continue to make the same choices. In our evolutionary analysis this comforting stability is not guaranteed, even for ideally adapted individuals reasoning perfectly in an information-benign environment, for in order to maximize genotypic fitness an individual might make choices by flipping internal coins at the time of the choice.

It might at first seem counterintuitive that random judgements could be a manifestation of fit thinking, but such a possibility is by no means in conflict with observation. There is by now considerable evidence that actual preferences among human subjects are in fact not very stable (e.g. Fischhoff *et al.* 1980). Perhaps some of the observed instability is due to adaptive strategy mixing. If so, instability would have to be reevaluated; when one is acting as an agent of one's genotype, it could sometimes be a sound strategy.

The specter of adaptive instability undermines many, perhaps most; classical postulates as customarily interpreted. Much of classical subjective probability theory (as ordinarily applied to individual reasoning at least) could be brought into question if the present analysis is correct. In many formalized systems of personal probability (e.g. Savage's), subjective probabilities are taken to be theoretical constructs defined wholly or partly in terms of preferences. But as we have seen, these preferences may themselves be unstable, undermining the very basis of the definition of personal probability. Our stock example, betting against the probabilities, illustrates this. We have seen that it is quite possible for an ideal reasoner found betting on an environmental event 'black' (for a predetermined reward and penalty) to be sure that the objective probability of a complementary event 'white' is exactly 0.6. Yet the classical criteria for deducing subjective probabilities from preferences would logically demand that such an individual have a personal probability for 'white' of no more than 0.5! This sort of contradiction raises doubts of the most fundamental kind about the currently received notion of coherence as an absolute law of reasonableness governing individual behavior.

Since contemporary theories of inductive logic frequently rely heavily upon a core of coherent subjective probability theory, much of inductive reasoning as we know it could be brought into question if the classical probability calculus does not hold for individual subjective reasoning. Even so sacrosanct a subject as deductive logic cannot escape all suspicion when applied as a supposedly adaptive system of individual reasoning, because it is inextricably interconnected with inductive logic (Carnap & Jeffrey 1971; de Finnetti 1974; Cooper 1978).

DISCUSSION

In defense of the standard logic of decision and probability, objections along some such lines as the following are apt to be raised by confirmed classical decision theorists:

DEFENSE # 1: The essential validity of the classical theory of choice has been firmly established and collectively endorsed by some of the most brilliant minds of the century. Your evolutionary analysis is interesting and possibly sound, but it does nothing to undermine the general thrust of the classical approach. To the contrary, your analysis is itself an application of that approach and an illustration of its versatility. The classical theory puts no restrictions on the objective function (criterion of desirability or utility) a rational agent might wish to adopt, this being a matter of personal aims which lies beyond the purview of logic. In particular, if individuals tend for biological reasons to behave in such a way as to optimize genotypic fitness (as may well be the case) then all one need conclude is that genotypic fitness is their objective function. That point once recognized, your proposed evolutionary analysis fits without difficulty into the general classical paradigm. No fundamental revision of decision theory is called for.

REPLY: The point is well taken but fails to face up to the seriousness of what it admits. Decision theory, if it is to be anything more than a sterile symbol system, has to be accompanied by rules of interpretation or application of some sort. These rules may be no more than implicit understandings, but they are nonetheless essential to the decision system as an applied whole. Now, one informal understanding implicit in virtually all conventional presentations of decision theory is this: In the absence of clear indications to the contrary, the individual can be treated as the sole locus of decision-making and has no motive for randomizing choices. It is only extraordinary situations — e.g. the secret corporate bet-hedging of our examples — that are supposed to require the theory to be applied in complex ways that would allow for oddities like betting against the probabilities. But if our evolutionary analysis has any merit, these situations are not extraordinary at all but pervasive; they don't require any secret collusion apart from membership in a genotype. Thus what traditional decision theory classifies as extraordinary, evolutionary theory reveals to be ordinary. While one might argue that decision theory as a pure abstraction remains undisturbed, the evolutionary analysis if taken seriously would greatly elaborate its rules of application. Only those who think that understandings about interpretation and application are unimportant to a paradigm could then maintain that the classical paradigm has been maintained unaltered.

DEFENSE # 2: Perhaps. But the larger classical framework includes game theory. It is well known that when cooperative or competitive considerations enter into decision making, the elementary theory of decision must be extended to accommodate game-theoretic elements, and in game theory randomized choices are commonplace. The members of the hypothetical biological populations of your examples are probably best classified as participants in some new type of quasi-cooperative game whose goal is to maximize the fitness of their shared genotype. It is hardly surprising, in that light, that randomization of their choice making should turn out to be rational and favored by natural selection.

REPLY: If it is hardly surprising, then decision and game theorists have been remiss in not allowing for it. Again it is a matter of the informal understandings that underlie decision and game analysis as traditionally practiced. In simple decision situations that do not clearly involve second-guessing other competing or cooperating decision makers, the custom has always been to assume that elementary decision theory is enough; there is supposed to be no need to invoke higher game theory. The circumstances of the kind analyzed in our biological examples are of this innocent-looking sort. Each individual appears, to the biologically untrained eye, to be facing only the personal consequences of some chance environmental event — an act of nature (like snow or no snow) whose occurrence is in no way controlled by the decisions of other individuals in the population. Under conventional decision-theoretic and game-theoretic understandings no game-theoretic treatment would be called for. The text books give no warning that every living creature is potentially entering a quasi-cooperative game every time it faces a choice involving a natural event that will also affect its fellow population members.

If our evolutionary analysis is accepted as biologically valid, and it is also agreed that the maximization of fitness is a ubiquitous goal, then the least that would seem to be called for is an honest admission that the classical understandings about interpretation and application are biologically naive and may have to be revised or elaborated. A more radical proposal would be to revise the classical theory itself at its mathematical core, letting biologically motivated decision rules (of which our Equation (2) is an example) replace or supplement the traditional ones as the basic decision rules. The classically conditioned mind may resist the latter proposal, arguing that biological detail should not be elevated to the status of pure logic. To the evolutionary reductionist, on the other hand, no such elevation would be involved because all adequate choice rules are seen as mere extensions of evolutionary principles anyway.

In the last analysis, whether it is the traditional rules of application or the classical theory proper that should be modified is a secondary issue. The essential point is that in either case the traditional package of theory-plus-interpretation known as classical decision analysis has to be rejected, as it stands, as a complete representation of fit organismic reasoning.

DEFENSE # 3. Your analysis seems motivated by an implicit assumption that utility is the same thing as fitness. All the analysis really shows is that that assumption is untenable.

REPLY: Our demonstration that nonclassical behavior can be fit was strictly biological. Though perhaps suggestive of some such relationship, it was in no way dependent upon a presupposition that evolutionary fitness can be identified with decision-theoretic utility. So, no matter what one thinks about the connection between fitness and utility, the fact remains that classically irrational behavior can be adaptive. This dilemma has somehow to be resolved, and denying the association between utility and fitness does nothing to resolve it.

DEFENSE # 4. Suppose however we assume explicitly that personal subjective utilities can be distinct from genotypic fitness, and that different individuals of the same genotype can have different subjective utility functions. This would provide for the strategy mixing needed to optimize fitness, yet each individual's private reasoning could still be in accord with classical norms.

REPLY: The reasoning could hardly be in accord with classical norms if it resulted in such behavior as, for instance, betting against known probabilities. In standard decision theory as it would ordinarily be used to exploit the known probabilities, there simply are no plausible utility functions consistent with such behavior. True, there could be pathological ones, such as (returning to the illustrations) functions that would assign a higher utility to being predated than to escaping predation. But these seem ruled out as candidates for fit utility assignments as they could get an individual into big trouble on other occasions such as a decision whether to flee a predator or run to its jaws.

DEFENSE # 5. Your attack on the validity of the classical theory is misguided, being based on an elementary confusion between descriptive and normative decision theory. Evolutionary biology may be capable of predicting what organisms probably will *do, and so may be able to contribute to* descriptive *decision theory. But biology has nothing to say about what decision makers* should *do to remain rational and coherent, this being the exclusive province of the* normative *(or prescriptive) logic of decision. It is of course the normative theory that the founders of decision and game theory had in mind.*

REPLY: The appeal to the normative/descriptive distinction fails to stand up under close scrutiny. When an observed behavior deviates from an accepted norm, a mistake is said to have occurred — an information processing error, perhaps. But the nonclassical organismic choices predicted by the evolutionary analysis can hardly be classified as mistakes. The evolutionary analysis is not an explanation of behavioral error. To the contrary, the entire thrust of our analysis has been that nonclassical behavior can constitute a *more* perfect adaptation to the environment than would naively applied classical decision rules. So, far from being merely descriptive, the analysis is primarily normative, and descriptive only to the extent that actual organisms tend to approach ideal fitness.

It should be remembered too that in decision theory, prescriptiveness has never implied deviation from the will of the decision maker. Thoughtful decision theorists freely admit that the classical theory is intended to be 'normative' only in the qualified sense of attempting to aid decision makers to arrive at choices that are in accord with their own ultimate goals. It is hard to see why a biologically founded decision system, based on the most accurate evolutionary inferences currently available about what an organism's goals are likely to be, should be regarded as any less normative than a classical analysis applied dogmatically in ignorance of those goals.

DEFENSE # 6: Still, betting against known probabilities and the other strange behaviors you describe are clearly irrational acts. They are obviously contrary to the individual's own personal welfare, however theoretically advantageous they might be for the genotype. Evolutionary theory may explain how such blundering instincts get imposed on hapless individuals by an impersonal process of genotypic selection, but that does not make the blunders any more individually rational. Indeed it would be a category error to suppose that biology or any other empirical science could ever offer counterevidence against a prescriptive system of logic such as decision theory, founded as it is upon enlightened logical intuition and pure reason and immune to empirical falsification. Can't you see that biology is simply irrelevant to the purposes for which the classical decision theory was created?

REPLY: This argument maintains it is obvious that nonclassical behaviors such as betting against the probabilities are detrimental to the reasoner's own welfare. But what if the individual identifies its own welfare with that of its genotype? Standard neo-Darwinist thought, fortified by recent theorizing in sociobiology, strongly suggests that individuals usually *do* tend to align their own desires with the evolutionary success of their genes. This entire body of thought is conveniently ignored by the above objection. Nor does the argument bother to refute the careful evolutionary reasoning to the effect that when individuals act for the perpetuation of their genes, nonclassical behaviors become perfectly reasonable and explainable.

On what authority, then, does this argument so confidently and vigorously oppose the modern evolutionary conception of what an individual's preference structure is likely to be like? The standard held up as the ultimate arbiter is the "enlightened logical intuition and pure reason" of classical decision theorists. But one wonders whether the founders of classical decision theory might not have presumed that their decision rules were in full accord with logical intuition largely because they could not at the time think of any significant counterexamples to them. Well, if they were not in a position to think of the counterexamples, perhaps contemporary evolutionists are.

DEFENSE # 7. The adaptive advantages of randomization predicted by the evolutionary model might well turn out to be too weak or too infrequent to be of practical significance for most real world decision situations.

REPLY: Granted. Without further investigation with the aid of more refined models, it is hard to say how often coin-flipping would be needed to optimize fitness in typical choice making situations. But the strategy-mixing advantage is robust enough to be of potential significance under a surprising variety of conditions (Cooper & Kaplan *op. cit.*), so it should not be discounted prematurely.

More significantly, the coin-flipping phenomenon establishes the important general principle that processes of fitness optimization do not always conform to classical preconceptions. This opens the door to the realization that there could be many other evolutionary phenomena, effects quite independent of those examined here, that further undermine the absolute rationality of the classical decision logic as ordinarily applied. A few such independent effects are already known. It can be shown, for instance, that the use of a different measure of Darwinian fitness can give rise to predictions of apparently nonclassical behavior, as can a relaxation of the simplifying assumption of semelparity (Cooper 1981; 1988).

It seems entirely possible, if not probable, that other classically disturbing effects await discovery as more refined evolutionary models are investigated. So while the particular nonclassical effect taken as a case study in this paper may or may not turn out to be of great practical significance, it has to be kept in mind that it is only one of a variety of potential evolutionary complications, any of which might upon examination turn out to upset classical expectations. The fact that most of the potential sources of nonclassical behavior remain to be investigated is no reason to assume that their combined influence on actual behavior will turn out to be insignificant.

SUMMARY AND CONCLUDING REMARKS

I have attempted to show that when 'rational' behavior is defined in terms of adherence to the principles of classical decision analysis as ordinarily understood and applied, and 'fitness' is defined using standard fitness measures in an evolutionary population model elaborate enough to allow for certain statistical dependencies, rationality and fitness are not always mutually compatible. Optimal fitness not only fails to imply behavior that is uniformly rational by classical standards, it logically entails the occurrence of behavior patterns that seem clearly irrational. Thus it is evolutionarily predictable that even perfectly adapted individuals may sometimes exhibit what could appear (classically) to be blatantly unreasonable behavior.

That much is biology. The philosophical question, of course, is how these behavioral peculiarities are to be regarded. Several possible positions could be taken:

> *Position* (*i*): The behavioral oddities in question seem at first to be irrational; however, on detailed examination they turn out to be rational and classically explainable within the larger framework of standard decision and game theory. Hence the classical theory of rationality remains valid as it stands.
>
> *Position* (*ii*): The predicted behaviors are clearly irrational. However, their biological predictability does nothing to undermine classical choice theory because that theory is intended to be normative rather than descriptive. Hence the classical theory of rationality remains valid as it stands.
>
> *Position* (*iii*): The nonclassical behaviors are admittedly troublesome in theory. However, in the real world these tendencies are so weak and infrequent that as a practical matter the classical theory of rationality remains valid as it stands.
>
> *Position* (*iv*): The predicted behavior patterns are irrational according to classical decision theory as traditionally applied. However, they are rational under a biologically enlightened redefinition of rationality based on fitness maximization. Hence the traditional theory of rationality is invalid as it stands, and in need of biological repair.

In the preceding section I indicated my reasons for thinking that Positions (i) and (ii) are flawed and (iii) is dubious. That leaves (iv), a stance not likely to be popular with confirmed classical decision theorists, but perhaps understandable to evolutionists, psychologists, philosophers, and others that have been impressed by the pervasive explanatory power of the modern evolutionary perspective.

According to Position (iv), the riginal provisional definition of rationality with which we started out (that is to say, the classical paradigm) is invalid or at least incomplete as ordinarily understood. In principle and perhaps in practice too, it needs to be significantly modified and elaborated, either at its mathematical core or in its informal guidelines for application. The particular modification examined in this paper as a case study is probably only a start. Further refinements might have to be added indefinitely as ever more elaborate process models and their accompanying measures of fitness are taken up. Thus to the extent (iv) is accepted, research into the foundations of decision theory becomes an ongoing process of successive approximation toward an accurate description of actual fit behavior and the evolutionary forces at work to produce it.

The strong reductionist view of decision theory mentioned earlier, according to which decision theory is seen as a branch of evolutionary biology, remains viable and is encouraged under policy (iv). It does, however, require a liberated notion of what decision theory is. Under the new approach decision theory would separate itself from the classical tradition of inventing 'rational' postulates *ab initio* – postulates that may be elegant and temporarily satisfying to the unaided logical intuition but are biologically naive. It would be allowed instead to progress through a process of drawing plausible consequences about choice behavior from evolutionary models, and of testing the hypotheses so formed against observational data about actual choice behavior.

This proposed bio-logical research program into the nature of rational choice as governed by natural selection, or 'Natural Decision Theory' as I have called it elsewhere (1981 *op. cit.*), would have as its ultimate aim a mature evolutionary science of the laws of rational behavior. The logic of decision would become a superstructure resting on biological foundations, with behavioral rationality interpreted in terms of fitness. It would be unrealistic to suppose that a rigorous system of natural decision theory could be quickly developed or easily validated. Indeed the very idea of pursuing such a course of research demands something of a paradigmatic shift away from traditional preconceptions about what decision logic is supposed to be and do. Still it does not seem unthinkable that a modest start in that direction might be made.

ACKNOWLEDGEMENTS

I am grateful to Yale Braunstein, Robert Kaplan, Baruch Fischhoff, Glenn Shafer, and Patrick Wilson for commenting on an early version of this paper, and to two anonymous referees who also helped improve it.

REFERENCES

Carnap, R. & R. Jeffrey: 1971, *Studies in Inductive Logic and Probability (1)*, University of California Press, Los Angeles, California.

Cooper, W. S.: 1978, *Foundations of Logico-linguistics: A Unified Theory of Information, Language, and Logic*, D. Reidel, Dordrecht, Holland.

Cooper, W. S.: 1981, 'Natural Decision Theory: A General Formalism for the Analysis of Evolved Characteristics,' *Journal of Theoretical Biology* **92**, 401–415.

Cooper, W. S.: 1984, 'Expected Time to Extinction and the Concept of Fundamental Fitness,' *Journal of Theoretical Biology* **107**, 603–629.

Cooper, W. S.: 1987, 'Decision Theory as a Branch of Evolutionary Theory: A Biological Derivation of the Savage Axioms,' *Psychological Review* **94** (4), 395–411.

Cooper, W. S.: 1988, *Is Classical Rationality Always Adaptive?* Xeroxed report, S.L.I.S., Univ. of California, Berkeley CA 94720.

Cooper, W. S. & R. H. Kaplan: 1982, 'Adaptive "Coin-flipping": A Decision-theoretic Examination of Natural Selection for Random Individual Variation', *Journal of Theoretical Biology* **94**, 135–151.

Crow, J. F. & M. Kimura: 1970, *An Introduction to Population Genetics Theory*, Harper and Row, New York.

de Finetti, B.: 1974, *Theory of Probability: A Critical Introductory Treatment*, John Wiley, New York.

Endler, J. A.: 1986, *Natural Selection In the Wild*, Princeton University Press, Princeton, N.J.

Fischhoff, B., Slovic, P. & Lichtenstein, S.: 1980, 'Knowing What You Want: Measuring Labile Values,' in T. S. Wallsten (ed.), *Cognitive Processes in Choice and Decision Behavior*, L. Erlbaum Associates, Hillsdale, N.J., pp. 117–141.

Fishburn, P. C.: 1981, 'Subjective Expected Utility: A Review of Normative Theories,' *Theory and Decision* **13**, 139–199.

Fisher, R. A.: 1930, *The Genetical Theory of Natural Selection*, Dover Publications, New York.

Gillespie, J. H.: 1974, 'Natural Selection for Within-generation Variance in Offspring Number,' *Genetics* **76**, 601–606.

Gillespie, J. H.: 1977, 'Natural Selection for Variances in Offspring Numbers: A New Evolutionary Principle,' *American Naturalist* **111**, 1010–1014.

Haldane, J. B. S.: 1949, 'Parental and Fraternal Correlations for Fitness,' *Ann. Eugen.* **14**, 288–292.

Hutchinson, G. E.: 1981, 'Random Adaptation and Imitation in Human Evolution', *American Scientist* **69**, 161–165.

Kaplan, R. H. & W. S. Cooper: 1984, 'The Evolution of Developmental Plasticity in Reproductive Characteristics: An Application of the 'Adaptive Coin-flipping' Principle,' *American Naturalist* **123**, 393–410.

Kaplan, R. H., P. C. Phillips, & W. S. Cooper: 1987, *Intra-genotypic Strategy Mixing in Small Populations: A Simulation Study*, xeroxed report, Dept. of Biology, Reed College, Portland, OR 97202.

Latane, H. A., D. L. Tuttle, & C. P. Jones: 1975, *Security Analysis and Portfolio Management* (2nd ed.), Ronald Press Co., New York.

MacArthur, R. H. & Wilson, E. O.: 1967, *The Theory of Island Biogeography*, Princeton University Press, Princeton, N.J.

Mertz, D. B.: 1970, 'Notes on the Methods Used in Life History Studies,' in J. H. Connell, D. B. Mertz & W. W. Murdoch (eds.), *Readings in Ecology and Ecological Genetics*, Harper and Row, New York, pp. 4–17.

Raiffa, H.: 1968, *Decision Analysis: Introductory Lectures on Choices Under Uncertainty*, Addison-Wesley, Reading, Mass.

Ramsey, F. P.: 1926, 'Truth and Probability,' in R. B. Brathwaite (Ed.), *The Foundations of Mathematics and Other Logical Essays*, The Humanities Press, New York (1950).

Savage, L.: 1954/1972, *The Foundations of Statistics* (2nd ed.), Dover, New York.

Stearns, S. C.: 1982, 'On Fitness,' in D. Mossakowski & G. Roth (eds.), *Environmental Adaptation and Evolution*, Gustav Fischer, New York, pp. 3–18.

Tiger, L. & Fox, R.: 1971, *The Imperial Animal*, Holt, Rinehart and Winston, New York.

von Neumann, J. & Morgenstern, O.: 1953, *Theory of Games and Economic Behavior* (3rd ed.), Princeton University Press, Princeton, N.J.

Waddington, C. H.: 1957, *The Strategy of the Genes*, George Allen and Unwin, London.

Walker, T. J.: 1986, 'Stochastic Polyphenism: Coping with Uncertainty,' *The Florida Entomologist* **62**, 46–62.

Wilson, E. O.: 1975, *Sociobiology: The New Synthesis*, Harvard University Press, Cambridge, Mass.

Wright, S.: 1931, 'Evolution in Mendellian Populations,' *Genetics* **16**, 97–159.

Part VI
Biology and Modern Economics

Holism, Individualism, and the Units of Selection[1]

Elliott Sober

University of Wisconsin, Madison

1. Holism and Individualism

The units of selection problem, as it is discussed within evolutionary theory, recapitulates some important elements in the dispute between methodological holism and methodological individualism. Holism and individualism have for a long time occupied favored positions in the stable of old warhorses owned and operated by philosophers of social science. These particular old warhorses are thought by many to be in retirement, although there is less than universal agreement about whether holism or individualism won the battle. Part of the point I will make about group versus individual selection is that biologists would do well _not_ to emulate certain aspects of the holism/individualism controversy. That they have done so already is a point that I will attempt to establish. And, conversely, the substantive empirical issues involved in the units of selection controversy suggest that the holism/individualism debate within the social sciences can be reformulated in a way that makes it nontrivial and also not decidable _a priori_. This offers some hope that the holism/individualism dispute need not remain a dismal philosophical problem of the "dismal sciences".

Holists and individualists disagree over whether social wholes are more than the sum of their parts (see Brodbeck [1968] for representative essays). Holists say they are and individualists say they are not. There is the _appearance_ of a disagreement here. But the appearance starts to appear illusory when one asks what each side means by "sum"; exactly what is meant when it is asserted, or denied, that the whole is more than the _sum_ of its parts?

Holists are concerned to avoid the sin of _atomism_. They do not think that social entities can be understood by taking individuals in isolation from each other. To understand social wholes, they insist, one must consider individuals in their relationship to each other and to the environment. When holists assert that the whole is more than

---

PSA 1980, Volume 2, pp. 93-121

the sum of its parts, they mean that properties of the whole are not determined by the unary, nonrelational, properties of the parts. To me, the point that holists are making is a truism. That relational properties must be taken into account seems obvious. It looks like this point is true, not just of *social* objects, but of *any* object which has parts. One might even suspect that the principle is *a priori*, or as *a priori* as anything can be.

Do individualists seriously propose to ignore relations? Are individualists really such benighted atomists? Not at all, say the individualists, who insist they not be confused with the straw man just discussed. Individualists concede that social facts cannot be understood by taking individuals in isolation from each other. But the crucial point is that the character of the whole is fixed by the properties and relations of its parts. The whole is nothing above and beyond those interactions among individuals. Individualists will deny being atomists. What accusation might they hurl back at the holists? Holists, they say, *hypostatize* (*reify*) social wholes. Holists, according to this indictment, think that properties of social wholes are not determined by the interactions that individuals have with each other and with the environment. Where, then, does this independent existence of social wholes come from? What is the secret added ingredient one must add to individuals, the environment, and their interactions to get social facts? Holism, thus construed, looks like old-fashioned vitalism; it isn't that some mysterious fluid must be added to matter to get life. Rather, holism is portrayed as holding that you must add some sort of occult social fluid to individuals and their interactions to get social groups.

This time it is the individualists who seem to be right. Reification is precisely what holists are up to, if they believe that the whole is not determined by its parts and their interactions with each other and the environment. Individualism does seem to be correct in claiming that properties of wholes are determined by properties of parts, in this sense.

So what has happened to this dismal dispute? One *could* embrace atomism on the one hand or hypostatis on the other, and doubtless there have been social scientists who have done so, in practice if not in theory. But if one rejects both of these alternatives, there seems to be no issue left. *Yes*, in one sense, the whole *is* more than the sum of its parts, but, in another sense, *no*, it is *not*. What else is there to talk about?

I will mention three problems which retain their interest in the face of these truisms. The first is epistemological. One can agree with the truisms and still wonder what the most fruitful research strategy might be in understanding a particular social phenomenon. Even if the truisms are true, it is still an open question what facts would be most interesting to look at in trying to understand the stock market crash of 1929; this social fact may be managable from a macroscopic perspective and completely intractable from a more individualist point of view (see Sober 1980 for the relevance of this distinction to the biological species concept). A second sort of question, also untouched by the truisms, concerns the amount of complexity and interaction among parts that needs to be taken into account to explain social facts. Historically the difference between self-styled holists and self-styled individualists has often concerned this question; the issue has not been whether the whole is reducible to the interaction of its parts, but in what ways the determination works (Wimsatt 1980 argues the centrality of this issue to the units of selection problem). A third question which is not addressed by the truisms can be grasped by distinguishing type from token.[2] What I have been discussing so far is the way in which single social events, like the stock market crash of 1929, are the upshot of interactions among individuals. That is, I have been talking about token social facts. A rather different question concerns the nature of various kinds of social facts. Here, one asks not for an explanation of a particular historical event, but of the nature of a social property. What is capitalism? What is a stock market crash? These questions about types may or may not be answerable in terms of individuals and their interactions. I raise these three questions only to set them to one side.

The truisms, then, do not concern how we might best attempt to understand a particular social fact, but concern that fact's causal connections with the world of individuals. The truisms do not concern the character of social properties, like the nature of crises or production in general, but the causality of single token events, like the stock market crash of 1929. Each whole is determined by interactions among its parts. This truism would be vouchsafed if causality were transitive. I'll assume that it is.[3] The stock market crash was caused, we might suppose, by interactions among various market conditions, which were themselves social facts. These social facts, in turn, obtained because various individuals did what they did in various physical environments. So the interactions among people caused the crash. If this is right, then it is an ill-conceived question which asks: "What caused the crash -- was it the market conditions or was it the way people acted?" One should respond to this question by asking: "What are you saying or for?" There is no asymmetry here. Causality, in virtue of its transitivity, gives aid and comfort neither to the holist nor to the individualist. The causal chain just keeps rolling along.

In what follows, it will be argued that the dispute about the units of selection resembles the holism/individualism dispute, but with the concept of natural selection replacing the more general idea of causality. This replacement makes all the difference in the world, however. Holists and individualists are, or should be, driven to disgruntled agreement by considerations that are not specifically sociological and appear to be almost a priori (like the fact that causality is transitive). In contrast, group selection and individual selection hypotheses admit of no such easy resolution; this dispute, properly construed, turns out to be an interesting empirical and specifically biological one. What is more, the lack of asymmetries just noted, when a question of social versus individual causation is broached, are replaced by asymmetries aplenty. It is a very real question to ask "Was a particular social characteristic caused by group or by individual selection?"

2. Historical and Conceptual Background

I just argued that holists and individualists interpret the cliché "the whole is more than the sum of its parts" in two different ways. The interpretations given *a priori* bias the case: holists interpret the slogan in such a way that it cannot fail to be true, whereas individualists tend to understand it in such a way that it cannot fail to be false. This same situation obtains, in much less virulent form, in the unit of selection controversy. I will address here the dispute between group and organismic selectionists, leaving to one side the issues raised concerning genic and molecular selection at one end of the spectrum, and interspecies and community selection at the other (although a brief comment will be made about this in section 6). Authors who believe that group selection has played a relatively minor role in evolution tend to use a definition of group selection that is extremely restrictive; authors who attribute greater potential importance to this selective force often use a more liberal, permissive, conception of group selection. What is more, each position has fairly cogent criticisms of some of the ideas on the other side.

The philosophical focus of this paper is on determining what group selection is; the hope is that we can then use this clarification to pinpoint what distinguishes group and individual processes generally. Yet, it is well to remember that biologists do not have this as their motivation for thinking about group selection, nor did they become interested in group selection as an idle conceptual exercise. The historical context for the recent incarnation of the group selection controversy is that group selection was hypothesized as an explanation of phenomena that allegedly could not be explained in any other way. In 1962, V. C. Wynne-Edwards published his book *Animal Dispersion in Relation to Social Behavior*. There, he argued that certain adaptations found in nature would be counterpredicted if individual selection were the only selective force at work. Wynne-Edwards talked about the ways in which prey populations react to the approach of predators. He discussed territoriality. He devoted a great deal of attention to the idea that organisms limit their own reproduction when the population approaches the environment's carrying capacity. Each of these categories involves traits which he thought were *altruistic*: organisms possessing such traits diminished their own reproductive chances while enhancing the fitness of the group. Altruism is always at a disadvantage when compared with selfishness, as far as individual selection is concerned. But groups of altruists may do better than groups of selfish individuals, and this, Wynne-Edwards argued, explains why altruism is such a common and stable phenomenon in nature.

Four years later, George C. Williams published his *Adaptation and Natural Selection*. Williams subjected group selection to two lines of attack. First, he looked at the alleged examples of altruism that

Wynne-Edwards had discussed and argued that they could be analyzed differently. Sentinel crows issue alarm cries when a predator approaches. Wynne-Edwards saw this as an example of altruism; the sentinel places itself in peril for the good of the group. But a number of alternative, individualist, construals can be offered: perhaps the sentinel's warnings benefit its own offspring more than they benefit unrelated individuals. If so, the issuing of warning cries is, like parental care, perfectly consistent with the selfish calculus of individual selection. Or perhaps, though the warning cries are heard by related and unrelated individuals alike, the accoustical properties of the cry do not expose the sentinel to increased risk; maybe predators can't localize them. Or, perhaps the cries have the effect of causing a flurry of activity in the flock, and thereby _conceal_ the sentinel from the approaching predator.

The occurrences of "perhaps" above deserve notice. The empirical details of sentinel crows, and of the other phenomena that Williams and Wynne-Edwards discuss, are incompletely understood. What Williams was doing was not providing known facts which, in every instance, _refuted_ Wynne-Edwards' suggestions. Rather, he was telling an alternative story which was capable of explaining the observations from the point of view of individual selection alone. So given our paucity of details about sentinel crows and the other examples that Wynne-Edwards and Williams discuss, we might say that there are _two_ possible explanations, at least, of the observations. One of them is provided by Wynne-Edwards' group selection hypothesis, the other by Williams' individual selection hypothesis. Do we have here a stand-off? According to Williams, we do not, since it is more _parsimonious_, he says, to invoke individual selection alone to account for these controversial cases.

Since I have discussed the principle of parsimony and its application to the group selection controversy elsewhere (1981b), I will not go into a great deal of detail in discussing the merits of such arguments in general or of Williams' argument in particular. However, a few comments are in order. One, not uncommon, reaction to Williams' parsimony argument is to dismiss it in such a way as to imply that considerations of parsimony never count for anything. As one biologist said to me: "The fact that Williams doesn't _need_ group selection has nothing to do with whether group selection _exists_." If the thought behind this remark were true, then Ockham's razor would be a purely aesthetic consideration, never offering us a reason for thinking that a given hypothesis is _true_.

I do not take this wholly negative view of Williams' parsimony argument, although there can be no doubt that parsimony alone does not place individual selection on a thoroughly satisfying theoretical basis. One of the limitations of parsimony arguments in general is that they do not offer us an explanation of _why_ the parsimonious hypothesis is true. Maybe we ought to believe that individual selection better accounts for the phenomena that Wynne-Edwards discussed. But this does not explain _why_ group selection has played so minor a role in the history of evolution. Sewall Wright (1978) discusses this point. He suggested to place the subject on a more secure foundation, we must create quantitative models of group selection, determine under what parameter values group selection would be efficacious, and then go to nature to see when, if ever, those parameter values are satisfied. Then we would have a more substantial reason for being parsimonious; we also would have an explanation of why group selection never, or rarely, occurs.

I believe that this limitation of parsimony arguments has the curious result of revealing why they can have a rational basis. Parsimony arguments are inductive arguments. Induction from a sample to a containing population does not provide one with an explanation of why the containing population is as it is. Williams wanted to explain the controversial phenomena over which he and Wynne-Edwards differed in a way in which everyone agreed the noncontroversial phenomena were to be explained. What was uncontroversial (at least to the participants in this dispute) was that individual selection was the mechanism behind numerous adaptations. Williams' parsimony argument was simply the assertion that we should use old mechanisms to explain new phenomena. Since the sampled, already understood, adaptations were due to individual selection, we infer that the new cases at issue are caused by the same thing.

Inductive arguments, I assume, can, if they are any good, provide us with reasons for believing their conclusions. So the issue of the quality of Williams' parsimony argument reduces to the issue of whether his inductive argument is strong. Are the known cases representative of the kinds of adaptations found in nature, or do they involve a biased sample? This and other questions are suggested by Wright's (1978) evaluation of the parsimony argument. What they show is that parsimony arguments can provide us with reasons, if they meet the standards of good induction. But even when they do this, they are always incomplete, from the point of view of a science which has explanation as a goal.

As I mentioned above, Williams offered a second line of argument which is supposed to count against the importance of group selection. This involved quantitative considerations based on Fisher's (1930) so-called Fundamental Theorem of Natural Selection. The upshot of these considerations (also discussed in Lewontin 1970) is that group selection will probably play a restricted, and relatively minor, role in the history of evolution, when compared with individual selection. These quantitative arguments do not show that group selection never exists, or that it couldn't exist. As we'll see, Williams believed that at least one real case of group selection has probably been found in nature, in any case. Although these quantitative considerations are separable from our goal of describing what group selection is, the definition we will arrive at has some ramifications for the quantitative question.

Wynne-Edwards' work and Williams' attack were followed by a series of theoretical papers (reviewed in Wade 1978) in which mathematical models were proposed and examined. The main result of these analyses has appeared to confirm Williams' orientation, in that the parameter values needed for group selection to have significant impact were generally found to be quite restrictive. This conclusion, however, has not gone unchallenged, in that it is arguable that the models contain several unrealistic assumptions that _a priori_ bias the case against group selection (Wade 1978). In my opinion, the quantitative question remains open.

As I have indicated, our interest here is not in the issue of how much of a difference group selection has made, but rather in the question of what group selection is. The various arguments and approaches that have fueled the biological controversy suggest that some rather different conceptions of group selection have been at work. Before we can identify these points of divergence, however, we ought to be clear on the common conceptual structure which is not in dispute.

For natural selection to act on a set of objects, there must be _variation_ -- the objects must be different. Moreover, the differences between the objects must include differences in their probabilities of reproductive success -- there must be _variation in fitness_. And lastly, it usually is assumed that the fitness of parents must be correlated with the fitness of offspring -- there must be _heritable variation in fitness_ (adapted from Lewontin 1970). This last requirement seems to me to be inessential for the existence of natural selection, although it is essential if cumulative genetic evolution by means of natural selection is to take place.

A word of clarification is in order concerning how the concept of fitness will be understood here. In any model of evolutionary processes which accords a role to random drift, fitness _cannot_ be defined as actual reproductive success (e.g., number of viable offspring). Since any realistic model must give drift its due, fitness is not identical with actual reproductive success. The so-called tautology of the survival of the fittest is no tautology at all; the fitter do _not_ always turn out to be more successful. The natural reaction to this fact is to think of fitness as an expectation, in the mathematical sense, of reproductive success (see, e.g., Crow and Kimura 1970, p. 178, Mills and Beatty 1979, and Sober 1981a for discussion). The fitness of an object is its propensity, or disposition, to be reproductively successful. Fitness differences, thus construed, may be the causes of reproductive differences.

The conditions set out above for natural selection to act on a set of objects -- namely that the objects should vary in fitness -- require supplementation to avoid the following problem. Consider a set of organisms which are causally isolated from each other; they may be at opposite ends of the universe and experience entirely different kinds of environmental stress. Suppose they are different in their fitness values. Still, it would be odd to conclude that there is a selection process in which they are all involved. One solution to this problem is to require that the objects be in _competition_ with each other. But, as Lewontin (1978) has argued, this is inessential; two bacterial strains may be subject to natural selection even when neither impinges on the other's access to resources. The strains, growing in an excess of nutrient broth, may have unlimited energy available, but selection may favor the strain with the faster division time. As Darwin remarked, "A plant at the edge of the desert is said to struggle for life against the drought." By implication, selection can favor the plant better suited to the desert conditions, even when the better and worse plants do not interfere with each other. To be sure, competition is a familiar way of thinking about natural selection; yet, curiously, the familiar cases of natural selection that serve as textbook examples do not involve competition. The evolution of industrial melanism and of immunity to DDT do not involve there being a common resource in short supply. Competition is a special case, not a defining characteristic, of natural selection.

A more general conception of what subsumes a set of objects under a single selection process is that there must be some common causal influence acting on the objects which affects their reproductive chances. This common influence I will call a force. Much latitude exists for determining whether two objects are subject to the same force. It may be appropriate to think of the organisms in geographically isolated local populations of the same species as all involved in a single selection process. If each experiences predation as its major environmental problem, this may suffice to say that they are exposed to the same force. If, however, some experience predation, others experience temperature fluctuation, and still others experience the disappearance of prey as the major environmental stress, it will be wrong to lump these organisms together and talk about a single selection process subsuming them all. The sameness of the forces impinging on different organisms will be determined not just by the physical characteristics of the environment, but also by the biology of the organisms involved. If a field is sprayed with one insecticide, and a second field is sprayed with a second insecticide, it may be perfectly correct to construe the two affected insect populations as part of the same selection process. This will be true if the physical differences in the insecticides make no difference in the way those chemicals impinge on the organisms. The idea of "sameness of force" needs to be read biologically.[4]

So far, I have talked about a set of objects satisfying certain conditions. What are these objects? How should the abstract structure of these conditions be interpreted? The classical, Darwinian, interpretation is that the objects are organisms that exist within the same population. Organismic, or individual, selection is generally understood as this sort of within group selection. Group selection, on the other hand, involves interpreting the structure so that the objects involved are groups. Groups differ in their capacity to contribute to the next generation. Group reproduction is here understood to require the founding of numerically distinct colonies; mere growth in size of the group isn't enough. So, to get started in considering what group selection is, imagine a set of groups which differ from each other in their expectations of reproductive success. Group selection will thereby involve selection between groups, whereas individual selection involves selection within groups.

3. The Artefact Argument

Can one define group selection in the way just suggested, as existing whenever there is heritable variation in the fitnesses of groups? I would say not, although some biologists have used this sort of permissive characterization. The defect of the definition is that differences in reproductive capacity that obtain between groups may merely be artefacts of the differences in fitness that obtain between organisms. Williams (1966) again and again deploys this idea in criticizing group selection hypotheses. The fact that natural selection has the effect that some groups are more reproductively successful than others is not enough to show that one has group selection. Selection at lower levels of organization can have this sort of "macroscopic" upshot.

Williams' artefact argument, as I will call it, asserts that the mere existence of differences in group productivity, or in group fitness, is not enough to demonstrate that there is group selection. The crucial question is where those differences came from: are they an artefact of selection processes occurring at other levels, or are they due to selection occurring at the level of groups? The distinction being made here must be spelled out in an adequate characterization of what group selection is.[5]

This line of thinking has its counterpart in the methodological holist versus methodological individualist controversy. Suppose holists argued that their position is confirmed by the fact that some social event, like the stock market crash of 1929, was caused by the occurrence of certain market conditions, which are themselves social events and states of affairs. Individualists might grant the causal claim, but argue that this by no means argues in favor of holism. After all, it still is possible, and indeed is to be expected, that individual interactions brought about those very market conditions. That social facts are causally efficacious does not show that their causal efficacy is irreducible. Individualists will often demand to be shown how social facts can exist without an individualist foundation. Williams, in his criticisms of group selection hypotheses, demands to be shown cases in which the causation of group properties is not reducible to individual selection.

Let's illustrate how the artefact argument works with a simple example. Imagine a system of populations, each of which is internally homogeneous with respect to height. All the individuals in population #1 are 1 foot tall, all those in population #2 are 2 feet tall, and so on, for six such populations. Now imagine that natural selection favors individuals which are taller over ones which are shorter. As a result, population #6 will be more reproductively successful than population #5, and so on. Is this a case of group selection? I doubt that many biologists would want to say that it is, and I am certain that Williams' artefact argument entails that it is not. What one has here is a case in which the differential reproductive success of groups is an artefact of differences in individual fitness. Group selection isn't to be equated with there being heritable variation in the fitnesses of groups.[6]

One of the assumptions underlying Williams' artefact argument is that group selection and individual selection are objectively distinct forces of evolution; in the above case, the group selection description is false while the individual selection description is true. Now it is conceivable that one might give up this assumption and view the concepts of group and individual selection as interchangable and equivalent, the way that some positivists have viewed the relationship between Euclidean and non-Euclidean geometry. In this vein, one might hold that whenever there is heritable variation in the fitness of groups, you can say that there is group selection or not, as you please. The choice would be one of convenience, in that both descriptions would be correct. According to this view, group selection and individual selection are not related to each other the way that mutation and migration are related to each other, namely, as two objectively distinct observer-independent forces of evolution.

Actually, this "conventionalist" attitude is not just conceivable, but is suggested by one of the oldest and most influential models of group selection, that of Sewall Wright (1931). Wright postulated a system of semi-isolated local populations. In virtue of their small size, random drift has more chance to operate, so that an allele might drift to a sufficiently high frequency for individual selection to take over and then drive the trait to fixation. The population would then send out migrants who would make over other local populations by the same process. Is this group selection? Well, it can be described as a case in which one has drift acting on *individuals* within a population, *individual* selection, and migration of *individuals*. One could, I suppose, define group selection as existing whenever these three individual-level processes occur. But then group selection is not a distinct evolutionary force, and Williams' artefact argument cannot be made.

4. Context Sensitivity of Fitness

How are we to strengthen our definition of group selection? What more is there to group selection beyond there being heritable variation in the fitness of groups? One natural suggestion is this: if the change in gene frequency one gets would not have happened if one had a single panmictic population, then one has group selection. That is, returning to our example of the populations distinguished by the heights of their inhabitants, we get this result: if the differential reproductive success that obtains in this situation differs from what would have happened if there had been a single interbreeding population made up of all the individuals, then we've got group selection. The idea here, which has obvious application to Wright's model, is that group selection exists whenever *population structure* affects reproductive success. A central point of Wright's model was to show how a system of small semi-isolated local populations could undergo evolutionary changes that would be extremely improbable in the kind of large panmictic population that R. A. Fisher (1930) considered.

Is this an adequate definition? Can one say that group selection exists whenever there is heritable variation in the fitness of groups, where those fitness values depend on population structure? I'll set to one side the problem of figuring out the character of the counterfactual situation we are supposed to consider; if the groups exist in different environments, what are we to imagine is the environment that the hypothetical single panmictic population occupies? This problem aside, it seems clear that the proposed definition is extremely liberal, in that it makes group selection a commonplace of evolution. It is a virtually universal fact about fitness that an organism's fitness depends on what the other organisms are like in the population. Thus, whenever one has a system of populations, one can expect individual fitnesses to depend in part on the way in which organisms are distributed into populations. In particular, one can expect the fitness values to differ from what they would be if there were a single panmictic population. Does this suffice for group selection? I would say not; group selection must involve more than the fact that fitness values are <u>context sensitive</u>.

Let me report a classic finding concerning this fact of context sensitivity. Levene, Pavlovsky, and Dobzhansky (1954) found that the so-called Arrowhead homozygote on the third chromosome of <u>Drosophila pseudoobscura</u> is fitter than the Chiricahua homozygote, under laboratory conditions in which just these two chromosome types competed. However, when a selection experiment was run in which Arrowhead and Chiricahua competed with the Standard chromosome type, Arrowhead turned out to be <u>less</u> fit than Chiricahua. This showed how relative fitness of a trait can depend, not just on the physical environment of the population, but on what other traits are present in the population itself. Now imagine two population cages, one containing Arrowhead and Standard, the other containing Chiricahua and Standard. Fitness values in the two pair-wise competitions would be different from what would obtain if Arrowhead, Chiricahua, and Standard were all present in a single population. But that there would be a difference in no way implies that the two pair-wise competitions involve group selection. Group selection must involve more than the idea that the fitness values of organisms is influenced by the kind of groups they are in.[7]

A parallel line of argument can be traced in the holism/individualism dispute. Holists sometimes argue for their position by citing cases in which the properties of individuals are influenced by the groups to which they belong. We will see later on that certain situations of this kind can be crucial for confirming holism; however, the mere fact that the properties of individuals are context sensitive does not win the day against individualism. For the individualist will simply point out that the group properties which shape the character of individuals are themselves the product of individuals and <u>their</u> interactions. Again, if one is unwilling to hypostatize groups, the individualist's assertion cannot be faulted. For the point being made is simply that the context sensitivity of individual properties -- the way in which they depend on group context -- is perfectly consistent with individuals being the material basis for all higher-level phenomena.

5. Altruism

So far, I have examined two rather permissive definitions of group selection and argued that they are inadequate. I argued for their inadequacy by taking seriously Williams' artefact argument. Group selection is not to be identified with there being heritable variation in the fitness of groups; nor should it be identified with there being heritable variation in the fitness of groups where organismic fitness is context sensitive. Neither of these conditions is sufficient for group selection.

In each of the two proposals, it was found that alleged cases of group selection could be analyzed in terms of individual-level processes alone. This is a standard ploy that individualists use to combat the arguments of holists. A natural response by holists to this line of argument is to try to find some social fact which would be counterpredicted by the assumptions of individualism. If this could be found, then the individualists' strategy of assimilating the phenomenon into their own framework would be blocked. Although phenomena which individualists can accommodate may not count as "real" group processes, ones that they cannot accommodate will qualify as paradigm cases of what holism is all about.

This thought may lead us back to the issue which fueled the fires of the group selection dispute initially. Altruism is counterpredicted by individual selection.[8] Group selection however, might be supposed to promote the existence of altruism, since groups which contain altruists may fare better than ones which do not. So, if one wants to argue for the efficacy of group selection, what better phenomenon to look for than cases in which altruism has emerged and remained prevalent owing to natural selection? Let us be careful here. There are two roles which the concept of altruism might be taken to play in the idea of group selection. One of them concerns how a biologist might try to discover cases of group selection: look for altruism. The other concerns what group selection is (not how we might find out about it); on this view, group selection must be selection for altruism. The difference here is that between an epistemological and an ontological consideration.

The ontological thesis, that group selection must work in a direction opposite to that of individual selection, has one virtue. It has the clear implication that group selection is objectively distinct from individual-level forces like individual selection. It thereby cannot be criticized by invoking Williams' artefact argument; the typical individualist ploy of reanalyzing alleged group-level phenomena as artefacts of individual-level processes has been forestalled.

So, does group selection have to involve selection for altruism? Before considering some biological examples which show that it need not, I want to note a rather abstract oddity of this idea. It implies that if there is group selection at work on a system of populations, individual selection must be acting as well. That is, we would have here a force of evolution which could not act alone. This, by itself, is not a conclusive reason for rejecting the idea, but it does show the proposed definition to conflict with a rather plausible requirement on evolutionary forces, and, perhaps, on all forces in general. It should be possible to describe the changes a force would bring about, if there were no other forces at work. That is, one might suppose that the use of the _ceteris paribus_ condition is not merely _permitted_ when it comes to describing a force, but that it is _necessary_ for the adequate description of a force that this be possible. This corresponds to the idea that a force should be isolatable in principle. I do not propose to defend this idea of isolatability, but merely note that it is rather standard fare in our conception of force. If group selection requires selection for altruism, this condition cannot be satisfied.

But the decisive reason for rejecting this view of group selection is more down to earth and biological. It is simply that some cases which seem clearly to be ones of group selection involve group and organismic selection acting in the same direction. A proper conception of group selection should be tailored to allow for this fact. Let me describe two examples, one of them being the sole case believed by Williams to be a real instance of group selection. Here I mean the investigation by Lewontin and Dunn (1960) of the segregator distorter _t_-allele in the house mouse _Mus musculus_.

Let me give an elementary description of how the process of segregation distortion, or meiotic drive, works (see Crow 1979 for details). Diploid organisms are ones whose chromosomes come in pairs. In the formation of sex cells, these pairs of chromosomes separate, so that sperms and eggs contain one chromosome each from each pair -- they are haploid. The normal pattern for this reduction is that 50% of the sex cells contain one chromosome and 50% the other, from each homologous pair. But when a segregator distorter allele is present on a chromosome, it "subverts" this equality of representation and secures for itself representation of greater than 50%.

This is what the _t_-allele does in the house mouse. Consider the males who are heterozygote for the _t_-allele. One might expect that 50% of the sperm pool of this group would be made of gametes containing the _t_-allele. In fact, the representation of the segregator distorter is 85%. So at this level there is strong selective pressure favoring chromosomes which contain the _t_-allele. Let us call this chromosomal selection. Chromosomes having the trait are at an advantage over ones lacking it.

If we go up a level or two, from chromosomes to organisms, the _t_-allele is _not_ favored by selection. Males who are homozygous for the _t_-allele are sterile. So there is strong organismic selection working against the _t_-allele.

Lewontin and Dunn combined this information about the chromosomal and organismic selection acting on the _t_-allele and derived a prediction of what the frequency of the _t_-allele should be in nature. It was wrong; the prediction erred by being too high. This suggested to them that some third force was acting against the t-allele. The third force was group selection. The population structure of the house mouse is one of small local demes. Whenever all the males in one of these small groups are homozygous for the t-allele, the entire deme goes extinct. Females living in a group all of whose males are homozygous will have no offspring. What is more, their fitnesses (or rather the component of fitness determined by this selection process) will be 0, owing to the fact that they belong to a group of a certain kind. Females within such a group may differ in phenotype and genotype as much as you like, but such differences make no difference; their reproductive chances have been destroyed by their belonging to the kind of group they're in. Since the frequency of t-alleles among females in such groups will, on average, be higher than the frequency of t-alleles among females in groups lacking this fatal flaw, the effect of group selection will be to reduce the frequency of the t-allele. Notice that in this case, organismic and group selection are in the same direction; both work against the t-allele. So one cannot require that group selection and individual selection always be opposing forces.

The other example I want to describe in which individual and group selection work in the same direction is a group selection experiment that Michael Wade (1976) carried out on the flour beetle, *Tribolium castaneum*. Wade's experiment involved setting up and monitoring four selection processes at once. In each of them, he started with 48 populations, each containing 16 beetles each. At the end of 37 days, he did his selecting. In one of the treatments, he selected for large populations; he located the population containing the largest number of adults and used it to found colonies of 16 individuals each until the population was exhausted. He then went to the next largest group and did the same, until 48 second generation populations were founded. He repeated this process for a number of generations. The average size of populations at the end of the selection process was higher than the average size of the populations in the first generation. Here we have group selection; groups were selected in virtue of their being large.

Another group selection procedure was carried out on a second set of 48 populations. Here, Wade selected for *small* populations. The regimen was as before, and at the end of the procedure the average size was much reduced from what it had been at the start.

A third selection treatment served as a control group. Again, there were 48 canisters. At the end of 37 days, one sample of 16 individuals was drawn *from each canister* and used to found a next generation population. The only selection process that took place here was within populations. Individuals within a canister competed with each other. But, roughly speaking, each group had the same chance of representation in the next generation as any other; each contributed one and only one colony of 16 individuals. This experimental treatment involved individual selection but no group selection. What happened in the process? Under individual selection alone, the average population size declined, owing to such factors as lengthened developmental time, reduced fecundity, and increased cannibalism.[9]

Now what happened in the control treatment also happened in the two group selection treatments just described. That is, within each canister in the group selection treatments, individual selection was going on as well. This force, we learn from the control treatment, promoted reduction in population size. In the group selection treatment, in which there was group selection for reduced population size, there were in fact two forces at work. Individual selection promoted reduction in population size, and group selection did the same thing. As one might expect, the magnitude of the reduction that took place in the group selection treatment was greater than that achieved by individual selection alone in the control treatment. Two forces are better than one. Here we have the same lesson as that obtained in the t-allele example. Group selection and individual selection can act in the same direction; group selection does not have to be selection for altruism.[10]

6. Group Selection Defined

My purpose in discussing these two examples has not merely been to argue that altruism is inessential. In addition, I wanted to add some data which may serve to constrain an adequate definition of group selection. Let me review the other requirements that a reasonable definition should fulfill. First, the definition should allow one to distinguish changes in group properties due to group selection from changes in group properties that are due to processes occurring at lower levels of organization. That is, an adequate definition should take seriously Williams' artefact argument. Secondly, the definition should not have the consequence that group selection exists whenever fitness values are context sensitive. Group selection does not exist simply in virtue of the fact that the fitness values of organisms depend on the character of the group they are in. And, thirdly, it should turn out that group selection can exist both in the presence or absence of organismic selection and can act in the same or opposite direction from it. This last consideration combines the rejection of altruism as a criterion of group selection with the earlier remarks to the effect that group selection should be an objectively distinct force of evolution.

With this elaborate preamble, the definition can be stated:

> Group selection acts on a set of groups if, and only if, there is a force impinging on those groups which makes it the case that for each group, there is some property of the group which determines one component of the fitness of every member of the group.

Let me try to state the intuitive idea in a less cumbersome way. When group selection occurs, all the organisms in the same group are bound together by a common fate. As far as this selective force is concerned, they are equally fit. What determines these identical fitness values (on the component of fitness at issue) is their membership in the same group. Individuals with radically different genotypes and phenotypes may have identical fitness values, owing to their belonging to the same group. And individuals with identical genotypes and phenotypes may have very different fitness values, owing to their belonging to different groups. Under group selection, what is causally efficacious in the production of reproductive differences among organisms is membership in groups of different kinds.

Let's apply this idea to the examples discussed so far, starting with the contrived example of populations in which everyone has the same height. Our definition explains why this is not a case of group selection. Although every individual in the same group has the same fitness value, the cause of this sameness is not common membership in a group of a certain kind. A simple explanation is also available of why our two pair-wise competitions between Arrowhead and Standard and between Chiricahua and Standard in adjacent population cages was not a case of group selection. Although the fitness of a fruit fly depended on the kind of group it was in, the members of the same group were not acted on as a unit. The members of the same group did not have the same fitness, on any component of fitness. Rather, group context served to determine the differential fitnesses of organisms with the group, in just the way that the environment can determine fitness differences in cases of ordinary individual selection. Group properties existed, but these failed to ramify back on the fitnesses of organisms in the appropriate way.

Our definition also explains why the two cases of group selection discussed before do really count as group selection. In the t-allele example, every mouse has fitness equal to 0, if it belongs to a group all of whose males are homozygous for the t-allele. What is crucial is that this common fitness value is caused by common membership in a group of a certain kind. The same is true of Wade's selection experiment. If there is group selection for groups of a certain size, then every individual in a group has an equal chance of finding its way into the next generation. The individuals within a population are bound together, their common fitness values determined by their common membership in a group of a certain size.

Before moving on to another example of group selection and to some further biological considerations, I want to point out a philosophically interesting feature of the definition proposed. The claim that a set of groups is subject to group selection will differ from the claim that a set of objects is subject to familiar physical forces like gravity or electromagnetism. Group selection may take endlessly many different physical forms; to say that some populations are undergoing a group selection process is not yet to say what physical properties are causally efficacious, but rather is just to say that some physical property or other is responsible for fitness values in a certain way. In contrast, claiming that a particular physical force is acting on a set of objects is a much more specific claim about the physical details; for example, to say that a physical object is in an electromagnetic field is to say that its charge and its distances from other objects play a specific kind of causal role. It is in this sense that claims about evolutionary forces can be more "abstract" than claims about physical forces. This greater degree of abstractness -- this formulation of generalizations which are true of objects which differ physically from each other -- is achieved in evolutionary theory by quantifying over properties. Besides the inevitable ontological commitment to numbers which any mathematical theory will involve, evolutionary theory is thereby Platonistic in an additional respect. This is one reason, among others (discussed at greater length in Sober 1981a) for thinking that a purely extensional ontology will be unsatisfactory for this science.

In order to give the reader some further grasp of the phenomenon that a definition of group selection is supposed to circumscribe, I want to describe another biological example which is often cited (e.g., by Lewontin 1970) as a probable case of group selection. The empirical details to be described have biological plausibility, but they may be revised or replaced by further information. Our interest, though, is not in whether they are true, but in what the assumption of their truth tells us about what group selection is.

Here I have in mind the coevolution in Australia of the disease virus myxoma and the rabbit Oryctolagus cuniculus. Myxoma was introduced into Australia to cut down on the rabbit population. Two familiar epidemiological events ensued. On the one hand, rabbits became more immune to the disease; on the other, the virus became less virulent. The explanation of the latter change is that the disease is spread from rabbit to rabbit by a mosquito which only bites live rabbits. Thus, an extremely virulent strain of myxoma, while it may become predominant within a single host, runs a good chance of never spreading through the rabbit population. Less virulent strains, on the other hand, while they succeed in expropriating a smaller number of the host's cells, nevertheless increase their chances of transmission.

Two, opposing, selection forces are at work here. Within each rabbit, strains of greater virulence will tend to consume a greater proportional share of the limiting resource -- namely the host's own cells. So there is individual (within group) selection for increased virulence. But a virus winning this race may thereby lose another -- that of spreading its genes to other rabbits. A virus population -- the assemblage of different strains within a single rabbit -- founds colonies, and roughly speaking, the lower the average virulence of a population, the better the chances are that a mosquito will transport a colonizing propagule from that population to another host. Assuming that these two selection forces are the main evolutionary forces at work, the fact that the virus declined in virulence shows that in this case the group selection force was stronger than the force of individual selection.

Less virulent strains of myxoma are "altruists". By being less virulent, they reduce their expectation of reproductive success within the population they are in, but thereby increase the group's chances of survival and reproduction by lowering the average virulence of the population. This example should correct the popular misconception that altruism must always be driven to extinction by a selection process.

Evolutionary theory entails no such theorem. Rather, what this example shows is that a crucial factor in determining the evolution of a system of this kind, in which group and individual selection oppose each other, is time. If mosquitoes bit rabbits much more rarely, or if myxoma expropriated host cells at a much faster rate, the decline in virulence of myxoma might never have occurred.

There is a theorem which represents this general idea, however. Fisher's fundamental theorem of natural selection (1930) states that the rate of evolution under natural selection is identical to the additive genetic variance in fitness. Since the fundamental theorem has to do with the rate of evolution, evolution will proceed faster, the shorter the generation time of the objects involved. But since groups almost always take longer to found new colonies than the individuals within the groups take to reproduce themselves, one again has the consequence that group selection will produce smaller changes than individual selection (Crow and Kimura 1970, Lewontin 1970). In the myxoma example, group selection was able to exert a powerful influence precisely because of the contingent facts concerning group and individual generation times.

Although I don't want to contest the correctness of applying Fisher's theorem in this case, it is important to identify a presupposition of using it in the general argument that group selection works more slowly than individual selection. It was pointed out earlier that the idea of group reproduction standardly used in discussing group selection is that of groups founding numerically distinct colonies. But there is no need to restrict our attention to this process, to the exclusion of considering the dynamics of population growth. Indeed, the definition of group selection we have arrived at is perfectly consistent with a system of groups undergoing a group selection process in which fitter groups increase in relative numbers. The total number of groups need not change at all. But if this kind of group selection process is considered, the argument based on Fisher's theorem cannot be made. Although individuals usually reproduce faster than their containing groups found colonies, it isn't quite so ubiquitous that individual reproduction takes place in the context of noncolonizing groups which are at their carrying capacity. This point leaves open the possibility, of course, that other broad differences between groups and organisms may be harnessed to Fisher's theorem in support of the claim that group selection is a weaker force of evolution than individual selection (see, for example, the argument of Lewontin 1970 concerning heritability).

Before drawing a few general lessons concerning what the definition of group selection implies about general features of the concepts of fitness and selection, I want to take up an objection to the proposed definition. According to the definition, the members of the same group must have precisely the same fitness values (on the component of fitness at issue) if group selection is at work. But this sounds too strong; for example, group selection might exist simply in virtue of the fact that membership in groups of different kinds had some percentage effect on some other fitness parameter. For example, each member of a particular group might have its overall fitness boosted by 5% by belonging to a group of a certain kind. What is crucial is *uniform effect*, in some sense; identical fitness values are not required, strictly speaking.

If a property of a group drives predators away, the individuals in the group need not benefit equally. Some might have been better than others in evading predators to begin with, and so the removal of danger may represent an unequal benefit. Still, this may be a genuine case of group selection. If some groups have properties which attract predators while others have properties which repel them, a group selection process may ensue. Though the numerical increments in fitness that members of the same group obtain from the shared group property may be unequal, the fundamental causal structure of a group selection process is still intact. The group's relation to the predator, in this case, is such that the predator reacts to the group *as a unit*. Although the numbers assigned to individuals may not transparently represent this, the biological relationship of the group to its predator subsumes each individual indifferently. Though fitness values within the group may differ, each individual encounters a predator to the degree that it does because of the property of the group it is in. Whether the biologist characterizes this aspect of the ecology in terms of a separate component of fitness or views it as a partial determinant of some more encompassing component is not what matters.

A number of consequences follow from our discussion concerning the concepts of fitness and selection. As soon as fitness is decoupled from actual reproductive success, it follows inevitably that one cannot read off fitness values from patterns of reproduction. The fact that some groups reproduce more than others does not mean that the more productive groups are fitter. Nor does the fact that some species speciate and persist more than others imply that species selection is occurring, or that some species are fitter than others (see Stanley 1975 and Gould 1980 for discussions of species selection). Fitness and selection are both causal concepts; they describe the causes of change and not the fact that there has been differential productivity.

Perhaps a more surprising consequence of our discussion is that fitness and selection are decoupled from each other. In spite of the fact that fitness values and selection coefficients are interdefinable in mathematical models (so that, typically, $s = 1 - w$), there is an important difference between these concepts. As we saw in our simple example of a series of populations which were each internally homogeneous for height, the fact that groups differ in fitness does not imply that there is group selection. The groups, in this example, differed in fitness in that they had different propensities to be reproductively successful. But the cause of these fitness differences was individual, not group, selection.

Selection is a richer concept than fitness. In fact, the relation of selection to fitness is somewhat like the relation of fitness to actual reproductive success. To say that group selection occurs is to say more than simply that groups differ in fitness; it is to say *why* those fitness differences obtain. Selection is the cause of fitness differences, just as fitness differences may be the cause of differences in actual reproductive success. It follows from this that just as one cannot read off the level of selection from facts about differential productivity, one cannot read off the level of selection from facts about differential fitness. The difference between individual and group selection is *not* the same as that between within-group and between-group variance in fitness. By the same token, even if some species could be shown to have a greater tendency to speciate, this would not suffice to establish the existence of species selection. The question that remains unanswered is the causal one of why these differences in the expectation of splitting obtain.

This difference between fitness and selection is not surprising, when one considers that fitness is a *disposition* while natural selection is a *force*. Although the forces at work determine certain dispositions in the objects present, the dispositions of those objects do not uniquely determine what forces are at work. Thus, to be told that two billiard balls are disposed to accelerate toward each other from their initial positions is not to say what force or forces endowed the objects with that disposition. On the other hand, to specify that the two objects generate an electromagnetic field determines one of their dispositions to move in certain ways.

Our analysis also reveals the inadequacy of two lines of argument that are sometimes offered in defense of lower-level -- either organismic or genic -- selectionism. It is sometimes pointed out that all of the alleged higher-level interactions which may obtain owing to population structure can be given mathematical representation in the fitness values of individual organisms or of individual genes. That is, the effects of processes at higher levels can be viewed as part of the environment of genes, and the whole selection story can be told in terms of the selection coefficients of individual genes. One criticism of this line of thinking is epistemological and, therefore, inconsequential: no one at present knows enough about any gene to define for it a selection coefficient which takes account of all this information. But this line of attack misses its mark since the proposal does not describe what *we* as theorists can successfully codify, but makes a claim about what *is* going on in nature.

The fundamental flaw in this kind of argument is that it confuses the task of formulating a predictively successful mathematical apparatus with the task of accurately describing the causal structure of selection processes. It is to be granted that all of the information about higher-level selection *can* be represented in the so-called selection coefficients of organisms or genes (Levins 1970, 1975; Wade 1979), but that simply does not imply that, in nature, it is individual or genic selection which is always occurring. Genes may be modelled as maximizing their fitnesses, but that leaves open the question of what causal processes propel changes in gene frequencies (Wilson 1980).

Earlier, I commented on the fact that the interdefinability of fitness values and selection coefficients should not mislead us into thinking that fitness and selection are essentially equivalent concepts. The same point applies here: it is essential not to confuse facts about the mathematics of our models with facts about the causal structure of the processes modelled. It is desirable, of course, that our models be realistic. But it is a naive realism which thinks that every biologically interesting distinction will be forced on us by the exigencies of mathematical modelling.

One last confusion which I hope this discussion lays to rest is that between the issue of the unit of selection and the issue of the unit of replication (see Hull 1980 and 1981 for discussion). Group selectionists do not deny that the gene is the mechanism by which biological objects pass on their characteristics; the issue of cultural evolution is not an issue here. But this shared assumption about the unit of replication simply cuts no ice. That genes are passed along leaves open the question of what causes their differential transmission (*pace* Dawkins 1976). This is not to say that facts about heritability are irrelevant to the question of how selection at different levels may produce cumulative evolution (see Lewontin 1970 for this kind of argument). But any such argument must do more than merely point out that genes are the devices by which characteristics are inherited.

7. Between Scylla and Charybdis

The stock market crash, which was a social fact, was caused by market conditions, which constitute other social facts. These market conditions, in turn, were caused by individual interactions. By transitivity of causality, the individual interactions caused the stock market crash. *If social facts cause something, so do individual facts.* Once we decide to avoid atomism on the one hand and hypostatis on the other, the sensible middle course appears to provide no asymmetry between the social and the individual; *both* are causally efficacious.

Yet, it is emphatically *not* the case that if group selection causes something, so does individual selection. Group selection and individual selection are objectively distinct forces. Individual selection does not require an atomistic view of the organism; it does not require one to ignore the fact that organismic fitness is context sensitive. Individual selection is a process that a sensible individualist can embrace. Similarly, group selection does not require a reification of the group; it does not force one to suppose that groups are something above and beyond the interactions of their member individuals and the environment. Group selection is a process that a sensible holist can embrace. And, best of all, it is a substantive empirical question what the role and importance of these two forms of selection has been in the history of evolution.

Holism and individualism in the social sciences should have such luck. To move beyond truisms to nontrivial empirical issues, holists and individualists need to formulate their dispute with reference to specific social forces. Although there is no real question involved in asking whether a certain evolutionary outcome was caused by properties of groups or by properties of individuals, there _is_ a substantive question involved in asking whether that outcome resulted from individual selection or from group selection. In just the same way, societies change because of the way their constituent groups interact, and these groups, ultimately, are caused to be the way they are by the individuals they contain. The debate between holism and individualism might become fruitful if specific mechanisms were considered and the question were then posed with respect to them: does their impact on individuals correspond to the causal structure we have identified in group selection processes, or does their activity represent a form of individual selection? Although it is probably a mistake to try to mimic the units of selection debate too closely, and there is no reason why the holism/individualism controversy _must_ be recast in its terms, let's explore, in conclusion, what individual and group selection would look like in the case of social processes mediated by cultural, rather than genetic, evolution.

Social institutions can be viewed as selection mechanisms. They discriminate among individuals in virtue of their having certain properties and differentially distribute effects on that basis. This description encompasses a great many, diverse, social processes and appears to be nontendentious, in that it is consistent with the outlook of neoclassical and Marxist social thought alike.

As an example, consider a college admissions test. The test discriminates among individuals, and, on the basis of that discrimination, the individual is either admitted or not to a particular college. Is this a case of individual or of group selection? The test tests _individuals_, of course, but that doesn't show that it embodies a kind of individual selection. And individuals are influenced in their ability to do well on the test by the groups to which they belong. But that doesn't show that the test is a form of group selection. As we have seen earlier, neither the fact that individuals are the material basis of groups nor the fact that individual properties are context sensitive suffices to decide the issue between individual and group selection.

The overall ability to do well on the test can presumably be broken down into a number of component abilities. Are there component abilities which an individual has, simply in virtue of its belonging to a group of some particular kind? Are the properties of the group which have this effect on individual ability the result of interaction among individuals? Could two individuals who are otherwise similar differ in ability simply in virtue of their belonging to different groups? Could two individuals who are otherwise quite different possess the same component ability simply in virtue of their belonging to the same group? If the answers to these questions are _yes_, then the admissions test would appear to have the earmarks of a mechanism of group selection.

Although each of us probably thinks that he or she can readily answer the above questions, a note of caution is in order. The mechanisms of selection processes are often difficult to discern, and it is a mistake to think that one can conclusively identify the character of a mechanism from the kinds of results it produces. Perhaps the admissions test gives greater than proportional representation to some particular group; it doesn't follow that the test involves group selection for membership in that group. In this case, a serious assessment of what the test is doing must be based on a serious understanding of the various abilities that affect the ability to do well on the test. Characterizing these components is a highly nontrivial task, one which we have barely begun to discharge. Although it is transparent that the admissions test is a form of selection, the character of this selection process is in many ways extremely opaque.

Another application to social processes that can be made of our distinction between group and individual selection involves the idea of the selection of selection processes. Besides wanting to answer the question of how the admissions test works, one would also like to know where it came from -- how it came to be used as the admissions test. Even if it were true that the admissions test embodied a form of individual selection, the possibility remains open that it evolved by a process of group selection. Perhaps part of the cause of its being used is that it has certain group level results; this may be true even if the test does not make its discriminations on the basis of group membership.

Marxist critiques of "bourgeois" social science often have two components (Keat and Urry 1977). First, bourgeois social science is allegedly too individualistic in its orientation, seeing the individual rather than the group as the correct unit of analysis. Secondly, it is claimed to be superficial in the kinds of questions it asks about society, typically focusing on issues concerning the regularities that social institutions obey, rather than on more structural questions having to do with why those institutions are as they are. These two lines of criticism are not unrelated, of course, since, for Marxists, an explanation of why particular social institutions have the form they do must crucially involve considerations of class conflict. From this point of view, the results of bourgeois social theory need not be false, but they must be incomplete. This means that if they are, mistakenly, taken to be complete, they will offer a distorted view of social life.

One might interpret this point of view as holding that social institutions, at least in bourgeois society, embody a form of individual selection, but that they evolved by a process of group selection. One of the differences between bourgeois and feudal society may consist in which properties of individuals determine how social institutions treat them. Whereas membership in particular social groups was used to decide all manner of social sortings out, these criteria are much less often the ones which are directly invoked in bourgeois society. Rather, the mechanisms have shifted toward the structure of individual selection. But this by no means implies that those social institutions do not themselves constitute a form of class interest, since they may have evolved by a process of group selection. From this point of view, holism and individualism may each be correct in a limited domain, if each is understood as claiming that certain sorts of selection processes are at work in a given society.

Although this articulation of the holism versus individualism debate is not the only one possible, it does have one virtue. It yields a conception of individualism which is untainted by atomism and a conception of holism which is unspoiled by hypostatis. In so doing, it turns the social science dispute into what it ought to be -- a question about the character of social causation which is not decidable by a priori argument but can only be addressed by the assessment of evidence and the development of theories which are specifically sociological. This reformulation makes the dispute harder than it was before; the road away from truisms and toward contentful hypotheses about causal mechanisms is never an easy one. But this presumably is a price that an explanatory science willingly pays.

Notes

[1] I am very grateful to James Crow, David Hull, Richard Lewontin, and William Wimsatt. Discussions with them have been invaluable to me in developing my ideas on evolutionary theory in general and on group selection in particular. The research discussed here was supported by the John Simon Guggenheim Foundation and by the Graduate School of the University of Wisconsin, Madison. I also wish to thank the Museum of Comparative Zoology, Harvard University, for its hospitality during 1980-81.

[2] The argument presented in Putnam (1975) and Fodor (1976) against identifying psychological and physical properties may be applicable to the relationship between social properties and the properties of individual psychology. Just as a given psychological property may be "multiply realizable" in indefinitely many physical forms, so a given social property may have indefinitely many realizations at the level of individual psychology. For an application of this line of thinking to the relationship of biological properties like fitness to physical properties, see Rosenberg (1978).

[3] The present discussion of holism and individualism and of causality assumes the truth of determinism, but this assumption is not essential to the points at issue. If quantum mechanical states at one time do not uniquely determine such states at a later time, then, on the assumption that macro-states are token/token identical with quantum mechanical states, it follows that macro-states at one time do not determine macro-states at a later time. Thus, from the point of view of causal determination, not only will facts about individuals fail to causally determine social facts; it will also be true that earlier social facts fail to causally determine later social facts. So, if both holism and individualism are construed as making claims which imply that social facts are causally determined (but disagree about what does

the determining), then both are mistaken. However, there still is scope for two other issues to be raised. First, if causality does not require causal determination (as in the theories of causality of Dretske and Snyder 1972 and of Mackie 1974), then it still is possible for social facts to be caused by individual facts, and for social facts to cause other social facts, as required above. Secondly, besides the question of the causal connections between and within levels, there is the possibility of identity relations obtaining between social and individual facts (and between macro- and micro-facts generally). This second possibility is enough to allow the holism and individualism issue to be addressed, even if the question of causality is set to one side.

[4]It is sometimes remarked that for selection to act on a set of objects, the objects must share a "common environment." I take it that this concept of a common environment is not definable in terms of spatio-temporal proximity, but will involve the idea that some causal influence affects the objects involved. (This includes, of course, the idea that they affect each other.) Even so, the requirement of a common environment still appears to represent too stringent a demand on the concept of natural selection. For consider again two prey populations which are geographically isolated from each other; suppose that they are preyed upon by two different populations of predators. If the two prey populations are conspecific, and the two predator populations are too, it may be appropriate to view the individuals in both prey populations as participating in a single selection process. The objects in a single selection process must be acted on by agents which are qualitatively similar, not necessarily numerically identical.

[5]In this paper, I will construe Williams' artefact argument as favoring individual selection hypotheses at the expense of group selection hypotheses. This does less than full justice to Williams' considered position, in which genic, rather than organismic, selection is the preferred level. However, a detailed discussion of genic selection must be postponed for another occasion.

[6]In the light of this argument, consider the common definition of group selection reported in Wade's (1978) review article: "Group selection is defined as that process of genetic change which is caused by differential extinction or proliferation of groups of organisms." Note that, besides failing to distinguish group from individual selection, this definition, taken at its word, fails to distinguish group selection from drift.

[7]I take it that this point undermines the definition of group selection presented in Wimsatt (1980, p. 236): "A unit of selection is any entity for which there is heritable context-independent variance in fitness among entities at that level which does not appear as heritable context-independent variance in fitness (and thus, for which the variance fitness is context-dependent) at any lower level of organization." As I understand it, this definition would imply that in our two pair-wise competitions between Arrowhead and Standard in one cage and between

118

Chiricahua and Standard in the other, we do not have a case of organismic, individual, selection. The reason is that the fitnesses of organisms in this situation are context-dependent.

[8] For more refined definitions of altruism, see Wilson (1980).

[9] Wade's fourth treatment he calls "random selection". Each canister is assigned a number and then a canister is chosen by picking a number at random. The chosen group is then used to found colonies of 16 until it is exhausted, at which point another canister is chosen at random. This is repeated until 48 next generation colonies are established. Although this process can be called "group selection", according to the definition of group selection used (see my footnote 6 above), it is not group selection, according to the definition to be presented in what follows. Moreover, if drift and selection are mutually distinct categories, it is hard to see how there could be such a thing as "random selection" at all.

[10] It is worth pointing out that if Wade's experiment provides genuine cases of group selection, then group selection need not involve groups with complex organizational properties or ones having especially intricate forms of sociality. Although interest in group selection sparked by the issue of altruism will naturally focus on such cases, this is not a consequence of the concept of group selection itself. Wade's group selection treatments selected for group properties which are absolutely universal when there are groups at all. Of course, even though it is no problem finding groups which vary in size, it is not quite so inevitable that this variation is heritable. This further requirement, as noted in Section 2, is needed if the selection process is to result in cumulative evolutionary change.

References

Brodbeck, M. (ed.). (1968). Readings in Philosophy of the Social Sciences. New York: MacMillan.

Crow, J. (1979). "Genes that Violate Mendel's Rules." Scientific American 240(2): 134-146.

-------- and Kimura, M. (1970). An Introduction to Population Genetics Theory. New York: Harper and Row.

Dawkins, R. (1976). The Selfish Gene. Oxford: Oxford University Press.

Dretske, F. and Snyder, A. (1972). "Causal Irregularity." Philosophy of Science 39: 69-71.

Fisher, R. (1930). The Genetical Theory of Natural Selection. New York: Dover.

Fodor, J. (1976). The Language of Thought. New York: Thomas Crowell.

Gould, S. (1980). "Is a New and General Theory of Evolution Emerging?" Paleobiology 6: 119-130.

Hull, D. (1980). "Individuality and Selection." Annual Review of Ecology and Systematics 11: 311-332.

-------. (1981). "The Herd as a Means." In PSA 1980, Volume 2. Edited by P.D. Asquith and R.N. Giere. East Lansing, Michigan: Philosophy of Science Associaton. Pages 73-92.

Keat, R. and Urry, J. (1977). Social Theory as Science. London: Routledge and Kegan Paul.

Leven, H., Pavlovsky, O., and Dobzhansky, T. (1954). "Interaction of the Adaptive Values in Polymorphic Experimental Populations of Drosophila pseudoobscura." Evolution 8: 335-349.

Levins, R. (1970). "Extinction." In Some Mathematical Questions in Biology, Volume 2. Edited by M. Gerstenhaber. Providence, Rhode Island: American Mathematical Society. Pages 75-108.

---------. (1975). "Evolution in Communities Near Equilibrium." In Ecology and Evolution of Communities. Edited by M. Cody and J. Diamond. Cambridge, Massachusetts: Harvard University Press. Pages 16-50.

Lewontin, R. (1970). "The Units of Selection." Annual Review of Ecology and Systematics 1: 1-18.

----------. (1978). "Adaptation." Scientific American 229(3): 156-169.

120

------------ and Dunn, R. (1960). "The Evolutionary Dynamics of a Polymorphism in the House Mouse." Genetics 45: 705-722.

Mackie, J. (1974). The Cement of the Universe. Oxford: Clarendon Press.

Mills, S. and Beatty, J. (1979). "The Propensity Interpretation of Fitness." Philosophy of Science 46: 263-286.

Putnam, H. (1967). "Psychological Predicates." In Art, Mind and Religion. Edited by W.H. Capitan and D.D. Merrill. Pittsburgh: University of Pittsburgh Press. Pages 37-48. (Reprinted as "The Nature of Mental States." In Mind, Language, and Reality. (Philosophical Papers, Volume 2.) Cambridge: Cambridge University Press, 1975. Pages 429-440.)

Rosenberg, A. (1978). "The Supervenience of Biological Concepts." Philosophy of Science 45: 368-386.

Sober, E. (1980). "Evolution, Population Thinking, and Essentialism." Philosophy of Science 47: 350-383.

--------. (1981a). "Evolutionary Theory and the Ontological Status of Properties." Philosophical Studies 40: 147-176.

--------. (1981b). "The Principle of Parsimony." British Journal for the Philosophy of Science 32: 145-156.

Stanley, S. (1975). "A Theory of Evolution Above the Species Level." Proceedings of the National Academy of Science, USA 72: 646-650.

Wade, M. (1976). "Group Selection Among Laboratory Populations of Tribolium." Proceedings of the National Academy of Sciences, USA 73: 4604-4607.

-------. (1978). "A Critical Review of the Models of Group Selection." Quarterly Review of Biology 53: 101-114.

-------. (1979). "The Evolution of Social Interactions by Family Selection." American Naturalist 113: 399-417.

Williams, G. (1966). Adaptation and Natural Selection. Princeton, New Jersey: Princeton University Press.

Wilson, D. (1980). The Natural Selection of Populations and Communities. Menlo Park, California: Benjamin/Cummings Publishing Co.

Wimsatt, W. (1980). "Reductionistic Research Strategies and Their Biases in the Units of Selection Controversy." In Scientific Discovery: Case Studies. Edited by T. Nickles. Dordrecht, North Holland: D. Reidel Publishing Co. Pages 213-259.

Wright, S. (1931). "Evolution in Mendelian Populations." Genetics 16: 97-159.

----------. (1978). Evolution and the Genetics of Populations. (Variability Within and Among Natural Populations, Volume IV.) Chicago: University of Chicago Press.

Wynne-Edwards, V. (1962). Animal Dispersion in Relation to Social Behavior. Edinburgh: Oliver and Boyd.

Economie appliquée, tome XXXIX - 1986 - N° 3, pp. 493-520

Technological variety and the process of competition*

*J.S. Metcalfe*** *and M. Gibbons****

** Department of Economics and PREST, University of Manchester
*** Department of Science and Technology Policy and PREST, University of Manchester

The purpose of this paper is to outline a framework for the analysis of innovation, in Schumpeter's classic sense of a process of creative destruction. It owes its origins both to a series of case studies of innovations in UK firms (Georghiou *et al.*) and a preliminary reading of some literature on evolutionary biology (Matthews, Sober). We shall argue that economic progress in capitalist economies is based upon two interdependent processes relating to, first, the mechanisms which generate a variety of technological and organizational forms, and, second, the mechanisms by which different forms acquire economic weight. For the economic impacts of a given technology depend directly upon the scale of application and we are not generally interested in technologies or organizational forms which do not acquire economic significance.

In developing our analysis, we find the biological metaphor useful. The biological concepts of selection, adaptation and mutation can be twinned with their economic counterparts, competition, imitation and innovation, and employed to generate useful insights into the competitive process. In this regard selection and adaptation are different mechanisms for reducing variety while mutation is a mechanism for generating variety. We argue below that the rate of progress in an industry is proportional to the degree of economic variety contained within it and so depends on the balance between the variety enhancing and variety diminishing aspects of technological competition. Of course, any metaphor must be translated with care across disciplines, the biological one no less so than its more

* We are grateful to participants at a seminar at the University of Rome for helpful comments on an early version of this paper. We are happy to record the financial support of the ESRC in preparing this paper.

familiar mechanical counterparts. The speed of operation of the variety generating process differs fundamentally between the natural and economic worlds, and there is nothing in the natural sphere to correspond to the directed, anticipatory behaviour which characterizes individuals and organizations in their economic behaviour. Nonetheless, we find the biological metaphor a useful basis for exploring technological change. In particular, the concept of isomorphism, that technologies, like species, are «adjusted» to fit their environmental circumstances, we believe to be of particular analytic value (Hannan and Freeman). How this adjustment takes place, be it by selection or by adaptative behaviour is at the heart of our discussion.

The paper is structured as follows. In Section I we discuss dimensions of firm behaviour relevant to the analysis of technological change. In Section II we discuss the competitive process focussing upon the contributions of Downie and Steindl. Section III is devoted to some analysis of selection processes in simple environments, where we focus upon the way in which technologies compete for economic weight.

I.

FIRM BEHAVIOUR AND INNOVATION

An understanding of the mechanism of technical change in modern capitalism requires analysis at two different levels: of the capacity of firms to generate a particular level and momentum of technological change; and of the interaction between firms within a «market» environment in which their technological differences are resolved into changes of economic weight. In the study of firm behaviour we have found it useful to divide the treatment of a technology into two components, namely, revealed technological performance and the knowledge base.

The revealed technological performance of a firm consists of its products and the processes employed to produce them, and these change over time as a consequence of innovation and imitative behaviour. Revealed performance is a basic unit of our analysis in that competition selects directly with respect to current products and processes not with respect to firms. Firms are only affected indirectly according to the superiority or otherwise of their revealed performance. Underpinning a firms's revealed performance is its knowledge base, that set of human skills and competences which define what can be achieved in practical terms. Within any technological area or paradigm (Dosi), a number of useful distinctions can be made with respect to the knowledge base. While major components are contained within firms, external knowledge held by other institutions, e.g. university departments and government laboratories is often important, as is any firm's ability to inwardly transfer knowledge from these external sources. A core of knowledge will often exist in a codified, publicly available form but for the competitive process it is the tacit, proprietary knowledge of individual firms which is of crucial importance. This knowledge exists in the minds of the firm's employees and its application is contingent upon how the organization pools their individual capacities. In understanding differences between firms in revealed technological performance, it is quite impossible to separate questions of strategy and organization from questions or technological knowledge proper. The routines and structures of organizations are critical to the process of technological differentiation. Typically, the knowledge base of a firm builds cumulatively, through experience, formal R. & D., and inward transfer of the knowledge contained in other organizations. It develops as it were as a technological landscape. Promising paths of development have a momentum of their own, and offer an agenda for change but equally they create inertia with respect to opportunities away from the chosen paths. Thus progress is predominantly incremental and localized. Organizations are not infinitely malleable, and they develop routinized responses to the opportunities they perceive. Given uncertainty and the role of human imagination, it is not surprising that we persistently observe firms exploring a common core of knowledge in quite different ways. Variety it appears is the basic norm of technological development. It is also the driving force behind technological competition.

While revealed technology is our primary unit of analysis, it is the behaviour of firms which links together knowledge bases with revealed performance. Thus we define the «firm» as an organization articulating a knowledge base in a profit seeking way. We assume that more profit is preferred to less profit but we do not imagine that any firm has the capacity to enumerate and evaluate all the opportunities open to it. Rationality is limited by the cognitive and intellectual capacities of the organization. Because information is scarce and costly to process, the idea of a uniform distribution of knowledge is simply incompatible with the idea of technological competition. We stress that in a majority of practical cases the relevant unit of organization is not the firm *simpliciter* but rather that sub-unit with the responsibility for articulating a particular product range and associated production methods. Often, relevant components of the knowledge base will lie in different parts of the umbrella organization, and the capacity to link these components together has often been observed to be an important element in innovative performance (Carter and Williams, Langrish *et al.*, Science Policy Research Unit).

In sum, in understanding levels and rates of changes of revealed technological performance, it is to the mechanisms by which firms acquire, store and articulate a knowledge base that investigators should look.

The Dimensions of Competitive Performance

To develop further the relation between technology and competition we assign to a «firm» three different dimensions of performance. The first dimension is the *efficiency* of the firm as measured by its revealed technological performance, the quality of its products and the productivity with which it produces them. The second dimension we term *fitness*, and define this as the ratio of the firm's growth rate of productive capacity to its profit margin per unit of output. In short, fitness summarizes the ability and willingness of the firm to transform profits into growth. The third dimension, by contrast, is more opaque. It is the *creativity* of the firm, as «measured» by its ability to enhance and improve its product range and its methods of production. The more creative firm is the one with the greater rate of improvement in revealed technological performance, whether this is achieved by directly augmenting its knowledge base of by articulating its existing knowledge base to greater effect. Creativity subsumes both innovation proper, and imitative behaviour.

Now the point to be emphasized is that firms differ in all three dimensions, and it is the differences which are the clue to the relation between competition and the environment. Within a given technological area, firms reveal products of differing quality and produce each product with different levels of unit cost. Indeed one of the enduring phenomena of industrial behaviour is the spread of efficiency, and the gap between best-practice and average practice that this implies (Salter, Iwai). Equally, firms differ in their fitness as we have defined it. Differences in the proportion of internal funds devoted to accumulation, differences in access to external funds, and different abilities to manage the process of capacity expansion (Penrose) determine the relation between growth rates and unit profit margins. Moreover, fitness may change systematically with the size or age of the organization, as Marshall's analogy of the trees in the forest was perhaps intended to suggest (Marshall). Finally, of course, firms differ in their creativity: because they have different perceptions of the agenda for improving revealed performance; because they have different financial and other resources to devote to R. & D.; because they have differential ability to manage the innovation process; because of differential degrees of organizational inertia; and, not least, because of the effects of serendipity.

It will be observed that the three dimensions are not independent. It is because firms differ in their creativity that they come to differ with respect to their efficiency. Similarly, differences in efficiency partially determine the resources to fund creativity. Moreover, the decision to allocate profits between, capacity expansion or R. & D., for example, is central to any firms long-term market performance. With respect to each of these dimensions of performance a rich literature exists, much of it outside the modern boundaries of industrial economics. Organizational and managerial literature helps provide a detailed understanding of differences between firms but it does not help to place such differences in their wider environmental and competitive context. Notice also that the dimensions of performance have significance quite independently of any postulate of maximizing behaviour. Efficiency, fitness and creativity are attributes of firms as they are, and how they might otherwise behave is quite irrelevant to the analysis of competitive performance or its relation to technological change. In short, the approach proposed by Nelson and Winter of decision making based upon satisfactory routines, forms a valuable starting point for understanding the origins of persistently diverse behaviour (Nelson and Winter).

II.

CONCEPTS OF COMPETITION

That a firm's command over product and process technology is crucual to its market performance needs only brief comment. The characteristics of a firm's products and processes relative to those of competing firms is a prime determinant of its profitability and thus its access to resources to enhance its market position. Profits determine the scope for expanding capacity, for influencing market perceptions of its products, via sales effort and advertising, and for improving its knowledge base. As a rule a firm will only enjoy above average profitability if its revealed technological performance is of above average practice levels. That is, if its costs of production are less than the average for the firms with which it competes, and if its product quality is such as to command a price premium relative to that commanded on average by its competitors. Of course, a firm may enjoy above average profitability even if it is below average in one dimension, providing there is a compensating excess above average in the other. The firm's technological performance, as revealed in its products and processes is the foundation for its competitive performance. Above average profitability provides the means to expand market share relative to rivals, either through a faster rate of capacity expansion, through a greater sales effort which attracts customers away from rivals, or, through a greater rate of improvement in the firm's products and process.

Thus, competition is driven by the differences between firms in technological performance, differences across which the market mechanism selects, differences which are continually changing over time with the evolution of technology. Competition is no dull equilibrium affair defined relative to firms with identical products and production methods. It is a vibrant affair driven by variety in performance, and in the long run no dimension of variety is more telling than that created by technological diversity.

The nature of the competitive struggle is placed in sharper focus when we recognize that a technology is rarely static. Rather when a technology first emerges it is imperfect and offers an agenda for future development limited by a state of technological maturity. Competitive success then depends not upon making a single innovation representing a stage in the evolution of the technology but in maintaining a momentum of technological advance - exploiting the agenda at least as effectively as do rival firms.

Given the significance of differences in firm behaviour it is surprising how little analysis there has been of the competitive consequences of diversity. However, two authors stand out as counterexamples, Joseph Steindl and Jack Downie. In a quite remarkable book published in 1952, Steindl developed a theory of profitability and changes in industrial concentration based upon empirically observed differences between firms in their costs of production. Where competition was defined as acute, the marginal producer earned zero net profits (i.e. a normal rate of return) and the remaining firms earned Ricardian rents in proportion to their differential efficiency. These rents provided the basis for internal accumulation, and the aggregate growth of the intra-marginal producers, in comparison with the growth rate of the market, determined the survival prospects of the marginal producers. In addition, Steindl sketched a theory of technical innovation in which cost reducing progress is related to the size of a firm. Not surprisingly, he found biological metaphors suggestive, illuminating the discussion of competition with appropriate allusions to the principle of natural selection and survival of the fittest.

Downie's analysis of the competition process, although developed quite independently, is remarkable in terms of its similarity. His purpose is to explain two aspects of competitive performance: the dispersion of efficiency between firms in the same line of business, and the «slow» diffusion of innovations. Diversity across firms in their cost structures is the basis for a competitive process called the *transfer mechanism*. Variety in efficiency leads to variety in profitability, such that the most efficient accumulate capacity more rapidly and squeeze the least efficient into bankruptcy. As with Steindl's theory, the account is rich with qualifications relating to the effects of profits taxation and of differences in capital: output ratios. However, the core, that competition is driven by variety, is the same in the two cases. In addition to the transfer mechanism, Downie also postulates an innovation mechanism. Unfortunately, the analysis is not well developed, and amounts to little more than the assertion that the probability of innovation is greatest for the least efficient firms which are under greatest competitive pressure.

The question which arises now, is which concepts of competition are best suited to the study of technological change? Clearly this is not an easy matter to resolve. A single word will never carry adequately a burden of different meanings and interpretations. However, it is apparent that the competitive concept employed by Steindl and Downie is quite different from that made familiar by Knight and subsequent neoclassical writers (Machlup). The source of the difference is not difficult to locate. While Downie and Steindl emphasize variety in cost conditions across firms, the traditional theory of industrial competition has found it convenient to treat firms as if they enjoy identical cost conditions. In the traditional theory, no firm has knowledge or organizational advantages which are in any sense proprietary. All fish with equal effectiveness in the common pool of knowledge. As a basis a theory of static resources allocation, the uniformity postulate is quite justifiable. Deviations from uniformity may be treated as of minor significance, or be anaesthetized by modifying the cost curves of the firm to include appropriate rents. By contrast, as a basis a theory of competition and innovation, of competition as a process rather than of competition as a state of equilibrium, it is simply not adequate (McNulty, Hayek). Differences between firms are at the heart of the problem, and the use to which differential rents are put is the key to how competition evolves. This Downie and Steindl make clear. At root their insights are an elaboration of Schumpeter's concept of creative destruction, a concept which cannot be made sense of within equilibrium conditions (Schumpeter).

In the following discussion, we will be concerned with competition as a process driven by variety, with market structure a consequence of competition not a test its existence. This process provides scope for entrepreneurship. For viewing competition as a race between unequals, in which prosperity and survival depend on a firm's position within a (multivariate) distribution of behaviour in the industry.

Typological vs. Population Thinking

A brief digression is in order, for the debate over uniformity and diversity in the theory of cost and competition is paralleled by a similar debate in evolutionary biology on the relative status of typological and population thinking. The issue in both cases is what sense can be made of variety (Sober, Mayr).

Typological, or essentialist, thinking is the doctrine of ideal types. Every phenomenon has a natural status, composed of its central characteristics, deviations from which are to be treated as aberrations containing nothing additional to the central core of properties. Variety is deviation generated by interfering forces. Now within the traditional theory of competition, the postulate of identical cost conditions is meant to capture the essence of behaviour, deviations are devoid of analytic significance and are caused by information imperfections. Pigou's equilibrium firm represents such an ideal type.

Unwittingly, or otherwise, Downie and Steindl reject essentialist thinking and replace it with what evolutionary biologists term population thinking. Each variation of form how has an independent, equivalent status. Variety is the natural state of affairs and ideal types are conceptual constructs. Uniformity is here the aberration, to be explained by the operation of interfering forces. Thus for Downie and Steindl, competition eliminates variety just as selection does for the evolutionary biologist. In other words, variety has a causal role in explaining the behaviour of a population aggregate. This population perspective has a number of important consequences. First, the behaviour of the population is a statistical construct, to be explained in terms of levels and changes in the mean, variance and higher moments of the population distribution. Secondly, the performance of any population member is only significant in terms of its position in the overall distribution of behaviour. Thirdly, the behaviour of the population aggregate need not be reducible to the behaviour of the corresponding population members. The whole is, of course, composed of the parts but changes in the whole do not necessarily entail changes in the corresponding characteristics of the parts. Reductionism is not always appropriate.

Each of the consequence we shall see at work in the following analysis.

III.

SELECTION PROCESSES AND TECHNOLOGICAL COMPETITION

We have suggested above that the behaviour of firms be interpreted in three dimensions — efficiency, fitness and creativity. We now turn to analyse how these dimensions of performance relate to the process of competitive selection. The core of the argument is that we must define both the degree of variety in behaviour and the selection environment, before the rate and direction of competitive change can be established.

a) Selection and Efficency

Consider first the relation between selection and efficiency. In making sense of the role of variety it is convenient to focus upon the following simple case. A number of process technologies are available for producing a single, homogeneous product. Each technology is articulated by one or more firms with a given technology base, and firms employing the same technology have identical unit costs of production. To incorporate differential «X-inefficiency» will be an important consideration but it is not essential to this argument. Each technology is of a constant returns kind and we let h_i denote the level of unit cost for the ith technology, and v_i denote the corresponding capital: output ratio, capacity increments being possible in infinitely variable amounts.

Starting from a given technology set, we now determine changes in the relative economic weight of the different technologies, the survival prospects of each, and whether a particular technology will emerge as the dominant design (Utterback and Abernathy). In short, we are to examine the working of a multi-technology diffusion process. For the purposes of this short paper we assume that the environment is of a particularly simple and stable kind. All firms face the same vector of input prices. This vector is independent of the aggregate scale of output of the commodity, and does not vary exogenously during the selection process. The price of the commodity does vary over time, according to the relation between supply potential and demand for the product, in a manner yet to be determined. Market demand is growing at the constant proportionate rate, g_D.

Following convention, each technology is exploited by profit seeking, organizations called firms, although each firm, or operating unit, is typically to be considered as a component part of a larger multi-product organization. At the common set of input prices, each technology will be associated with a different unit cost of production, and thus a different profit margin, since all firms receive the same price for their output. It is these differences in profit margins which are the basis for the selection process, and the changing economic weight of the different technologies.

We begin with the case of no technological change proper. There are neither changes to the technology set, nor variations within each technology in the set. In addition to its unit costs, each firm is characterized by its fitness. Fitness is determined by the ratio of the propensity to accumulate to the capital: output ratio. Letting each firm invest a fraction of its internal profits π_i, and supplement those with external funds in the proportion e_i, we define the ith firm's fitness as $f_i = \pi_i(1+e_i)/v_i$. Provided the firm is earning a rate of profits in excess of a normal rate, it invests in its own technology at the rate g_i, given by:

$$g_i = f_i(p - h_i);\ h_i < p \tag{1}$$

At a normal rate of profits, $p = h_i$, fitness drops to zero. Otherwise fitness is independent of the firm's rate of profits and is constant during the selection process. To allow firms to invest in other technologies besides their own is a straightforward extension of the argument (Turner and Soete).

Following Downie, we first analyse the relation between selection and efficiency under conditions of uniform fitness, $f_i = f$. Let s_i, the market share of the ith process technology, measure its economic weight. The aggregate growth rate of capacity, g, is then related to the average profit margin by:

$$g = \sum_i s_i g_i = f(p - \bar{h}) \qquad (2)$$

where $\bar{h}$ is average pratice unit cost, defined as

$$\sum_i s_i h_i,$$

with the summation in (2) applying only to those «dynamic» firms with above normal profitability.

The variation over time in the economic weight of the ith technology depends on the growth rate difference $g_i - g$, with:

$$\frac{ds_i}{dt} = s_i(g_i - g),$$

which from (1) and (2) becomes:

$$\frac{ds_i}{dt} = s_i f(\bar{h} - h_i);\ h_i < p \qquad (3)$$

The interpretation of (3) is straightforward. The economic weight of a given technology is expanding or contracting according to the position of that technology in the population distribution of efficiency, this distribution depending on the particular environmental vector of input prices. A technology which has units costs above average declines in economic weight, and conversely if units costs are below average. Provided unit costs are less than or equal to the product price, the technology survives.

In the case of two production inputs, the argument can be illustrated in terms of Figure 1 (Metcalfe). The solid convex area, t—t, denotes the technology set. It summarizes the extent of variety in terms of the two input:output coefficients a_1 and a_2. The given environment is represented by the relative price lines with slope

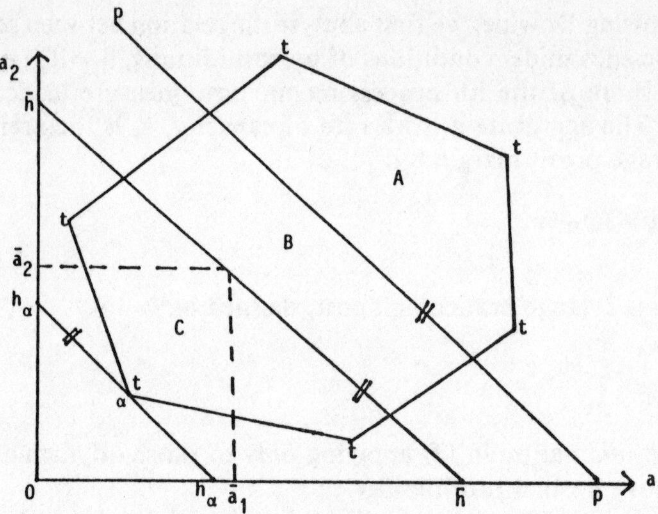

Fig. 1. The Technology Set.

(w_1/w_2). The number and distribution of technologies within the technology set need not be continuous and sections of the set may be empty. Note that only two technologies are required for the selection process to work. Given the environment, α is the best practice technology with unit costs h_α, and $\bar{h}$ is average practice unit cost with $\bar{a}_1$ and $\bar{a}_2$ the average practice input:output coefficients. The price of the product p, exceeds $\bar{h}$ by the amount required to finance the aggregate growth of the dynamic firms at rate g. On the basis of this information the technology set can be divided into three regions. Within region A. the technologies are redundant and the corresponding firms out of business, since $h_i > p$. Regions B and C contain dynamic firms and their technologies. Within B, any technology generates above normal profits so its capacity expands in absolute terms but, since $h_i > \bar{h}$, its market share and economic weight is declining. Within C are technologies with $h_i < \bar{h}$. Not only are these profitable and expanding in absolute terms their economic weight, market share, is increasing. At the boundaries between each region we have marginal (zero profit, technologies) distributed along p—p, and dynamically representative (constant market share) technologies distributed along $\bar{h}$-$\bar{h}$. Of course, with a different environment, the technology space will be divided differently and best practice may also be redefined. In short, given the environment, the competitive position of any one technology depends on its distance from average practive, $h_i - \bar{h}$, and this distance is related not to that technology's economic weight, s_i, but to the rate of change of its economic weight, ds_i/dt.

Figure 1 is, of course, a snapshot of a situation at a point in time, and it contains the seeds of its own destruction. The process of competition for economic weight continually redefines $\bar{h}$ and p and the relative subdivision of the technology set. From (3) and the definition of $\bar{h}$ we find that:

$$\frac{d\bar{h}}{dt} \sum_i \frac{ds_i}{dt} h_i = - fV_t(h_i), \; h_i < p \qquad (4)$$

where $V_t(h_t)$ is the variance in unit costs of dynamic firms in the technology set. Average practice unit cost is a population statistic, continually reduced by competitive selection and tending towards best practice unit cost as variety is eliminated. There is technical progress at the population level even though there is no technical progress proper. It is also clear that the technology which emerges as the dominant design is the best-practice technology. From (4) we see that the greater is the variety of efficiency, the greater is the rate of competitive selection. Furthermore, the rate of reduction in average practice cost depends on the fitness coefficient which varies directly with the flow of internal and external funds into investment and inversely with the capital: output ratio. Ultimately, $V_t(h_i)$ is driven to zero as $\bar{h}$ converges on h_α. Selection eliminates variety and with it the competition pressures which drive the changes in the population characteristic $\bar{h}$. We should note (4) has its parallel in evolutionary biology, *viz.*, R.A. Fisher's fundamental theorem of natural selection (Nelson and Winter).

Corresponding to the changes in $\bar{h}$ are changes in the average practice input:output coefficients $\bar{a}_1$ and $\bar{a}_2$. Since

$$\bar{a}_j = \sum_i s_i a_{ij}$$

it follows that the manner of variation of $\bar{a}_1$, say, is given by:

$$\frac{d\bar{a}_1}{dt} = -f[w_1 V_t(a_1) + w_2 C_t(a_1, a_2)] \quad (5)$$

where, w_1 and w_2 are the input prices, $V_t(a_1)$ is the variance in the use of a_1 and $C_t(a_1, a_2)$ is the co-variance of inoput use, again across the dynamic firms. A similar formula holds for $d\bar{a}_2/dt$ and combining these results we obtain:

$$V_t(h_i) = w_1^2 V_t(a_1) + w_2^2 V_t(a_2) + 2w_1 w_2 C_t(a_1 a_2) \quad (6)$$

the familiar decomposition of the variance of a sum. From (5) and (6) we can identify which dimensions of input use contribute most to selection pressure and how pressure is affected by different input price environments. Notice also that since $C_t(a_1 a_2)$ can be negative, it is possible for one (but not both) of the average practice coefficients to regress during the selection process. It is readily shown that the degree of input-saving bias generated during selection is given by

$$\frac{d}{dt}\log(\bar{a}_1/\bar{a}_2) = f[\frac{C_t(a_1, h_i)}{\bar{a}_1} - \frac{C_t(a_2, h_i)}{\bar{a}_2}] \quad (7)$$

In each of the expressions (4)-(7) we are relating movements in average population behaviour to higher order moments of the population distribution. Without variety in performance, such propositions would be impossible to derive. So far we have established the dynamics of selection and the principle of convergence upon best technology in a simple stable environment. We have not as yet determined either the aggregate growth rate of dynamic firms, g, or the price of the product and hence the range over which our population statistics are to be defined. To do this consider Figure 2, in which the price of the commodity is determined by the market demand curve $D_t(p)$ and the corresponding supply function $S_t(p)$ (Salter). Along this supply function, the length of each step denotes the amount of capacity invested in that particular technology at date t. At the ruling market equilibrium, the marginal technology is δ with unit cost $h_m = p$. Technology ε is redundant, while the remaining technologies are profitable and earn quasi-rents in proportion to their distance from h_m. It is these quasi-rents which, as with Steindl and Downie, drive the supply curve to the right over time. If we let

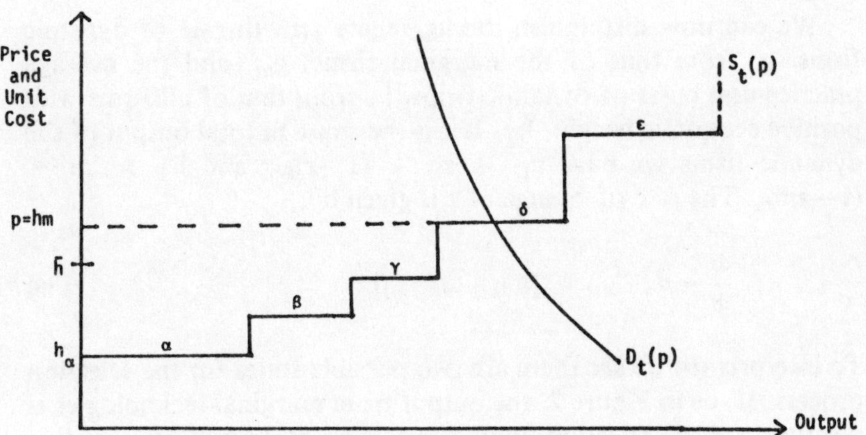

Fig. 2. Price, Costs and Rents.

ρ_i be the fraction of industry profits attributable to the ith technology, we find that:

$$\rho_i = \left(\frac{h_m - h_i}{h_m - \bar{h}}\right) s_i = \frac{f}{g}\,(h_m - h_i) s_i \qquad (8)$$

which relates the distribution of profits to market shares, to fitness, to the growth rate, and to distances from worst practice. In so far as creativity is linked to profits, this profit distribution plays an important part in developing an interaction between selection and technical change.

We now appear to have two explanations of the commodity price. A static demand and supply explanation, $p = h_m$, and a dynamic selection version, $p = g/f + \bar{h}$. The connection is provided by the distinction between marginal and dynamic firms. For a marginal firm, capacity accumulation has ceased and changes in its output correspond to changes in the utilization of existing capacity. By contrast, the dynamic firms produce at full capacity and expand capacity according to (1). In Marshallian terminology, the behaviour of the dynamic firms is interpretable by long-period methods of analysis, and of the marginal firms by short-period methods of analysis. Both methods are applied to the same point in the selection process.

We can now distinguish the aggregate growth rate of dynamic firms, g, from that of the marginal firms, g_m, and the average practice unit costs of dynamic firms, $\bar{h}$, from that of all firms with positive economic weight, $\bar{h}_T$. If z is the share in total output of the dynamic firms we have $g_D = zg + (1-z)g_m$ and $h_T = zh + (1-z)h_m$. The rate of change of z is given by:

$$\frac{dz}{dt} = z(g-g_D) = z\left[f(h_m-\bar{h}) - g_D\right] \qquad (9)$$

To interpret (9) we see there are two possible states for the selection process. If, as in Figure 2, the output from marginal technologies is positive, $z < 1$, selection equilibrium is characterized by $p = h_m$, $dp/dt = 0$ and $dg/dt = -f\,d\bar{h}/dt = = f^2V_t(h_i) > 0$. From (9) we have z rising or falling over time as $f(h_m-\bar{h} \gtrless g_D$ but either way the marginal technology is eventually eliminated. Either it is transferred into the redundant set if $dz/dt > 0$, or its capacity becomes fully utilized if $dz/dt < 0$, and p rises above h_m making the technology profitable. Thus we reach the second possible case in which all technologies generate positive profits and $z = 1$. We then have $g = g_D$ (Downie's case) and $dp/dt = dh/dt = -f\,V_t(h_i)$; price and average practice unit cost fall over time at the same rate.

That we have two possible states for the selection process implies that particular care is needed in defining average practice unit costs in an industry. Depending on z, the values of h_T and $\bar{h}$ may differ substantially and will vary at different rates with changes in z. Two other points are worth noting. First, the transfer of technologies from dynamism to redundancy has no effect on the evolution of $V_t(h_i)$, simply because when a technology becomes redundant, its economic weight has already reached zero. Selection in turbulent conditions could clearly affect this conclusion. Secondly, the value of $V_t(h_i)$ is independent of the growth rates g and g_D, *pace* Downie. This follows immediately, since the range of variety in unit costs, $p - h_\alpha$, is defined by D_t and S_t, i.e. by the levels of demand and supply potential, not by their rates of change.

We conclude this section with a number of exercises. Consider first the effect of innovations upon the selection process. An innovation is represented by an addition to the technology set simultaneously with the entry of new organizations and their respective knowledge basis. Notice that entry of new organizations is quite distinct from entry of capital into the industry, which is already taken care of by the role of external finance in the definition of fitness. Clearly entry has a shock effect on the existing pattern of market shares but from then on the entrant's fate is determined by its position within the overall distribution of units costs. Suppose, for example, that at entry, the new technology is superior to average practice but inferior to best practice. Then its diffusion curve, the path of market share over time, will behave as follows. Market share will rise at first, and continue to do so until average practice efficiency has fallen sufficiently to make the technology dynamically representative. From then on its market share falls progressively towards zero as it drops further behind average practice and moves closer to worst practice. Ultimately, the technology ceases to have economic weight. However, it may still survive in the sense of being intra-marginal and producing an increasing volume of output. In particular, the distinction between a technology having positive economic weight and its surviving is vital to an understanding of selection. With selection, the commodity price tends toward a value p_α, given by $p_\alpha = g_D/f + h_\alpha$. In this situation, all technologies satisfying $h_\alpha < h_i < p_\alpha$ will survive but each of them will have zero economic weight. Multi-technology diffusion processes are complex phenomena, and sigmoid diffusion curves are a limited reflection of their dynamics. Indeed, if economic weight is used to measure diffusion, only the dominant design will have a sigmoid diffusion curve with an upper asymptote of unity. All other technologies must ultimately experience declining diffusion levels. As in Gauss's famous principle, in this simple and stable environment all technologies but one are ultimately excluded in terms of their economic weight (Slobodkin). Notice that the survival of non-best-practice technologies is conditional upon g_D being positive, and that the survival range varies inversely with the degree of fitness. Again we see that the fitness coefficient is a measure of the degree of competitive pressure. Of course, if entrant technologies are superior to existing best-practice, this redefines the selection process rather more drastically. How this works out in terms of our selection principle is not difficult to see.

As our second brief exercise, we note that the selection process implies increasing concentration upon a declining number of technologies. Market structure in this sense is an endogenous consequence of the selection process not an independent test for the existence of competition. Of course, how market structure evolves in terms of firm concentration is more complex and depends ultimately on how many firms can acquire and articulate the best practice knowledge base.

To sum up. Technological variety, fitness and the selection environment define a competitive process in which the best-practice technology gradually acquires the status of the dominant design. How quickly this occurs depends on the characteristics of the technology set and the (uniform) fitness of the various firms. Although individual firms do not maximize it can be argued that the environment selects in a maximizing, i.e. cost-minimizing way. This does not imply in any sense that the dominant design firms maximize anything. Selection works with respect to firms as they are, not as they might otherwise be (Alchian). The environment «chooses» the best technology from the available set and the possibility that any technology could be articulated with greater efficiency is simply irrelevant (Winter). In a world of imperfect knowledge how could it be otherwise?

b) Selection and Non-Uniform Fitness

We now relax the assumption that all firms are of uniform fitness. This assumption has greatly simplified our discussion and the consequences of abandoning it are quite severe. We shall consider only two issues in this context: the possibility that the dominant design technology is not the best-practice technology; and the consequences of non-uniform fitness for the Fisher theorem (4). It is clearly important to take account of non-uniform fitness. In practice firms differ in their access to capital and in their capacity and willingness to grow. Such differences have significant effects on the diffusion of competing technologies.

The effect of non-uniform but time invariant fitness on the emergence of a dominant design may be introduced as follows. Imagine a technology set with a distribution of values h_i, and let all firms have zero fitness except the worst-practice technology. Investment takes place only in this worst-practice design and, while all technologies will remain viable, selection will bring this worst-practice technology to market dominance. Only it will acquire and sustain positive economic weight! To treat this problem more generally, consider Figure 3 which defines a selection set, analogous to the technology set of Figure 1, in terms of efficiency and inverse fitness values. Each firm is defined by a value of h_i and f_i^{-1} and the set of all points is bounded by the convex region t—t. Notice that this set depends on the environment via the dependence of h_i on the input price vector. Following the argument of the previous section, we can take a snapshot of the selection set at a point in time, dividing it into three segments. In A are the redundant technologies satisfying $p < h_i$. Notice that the redundant set is quite independent of the distribution of fitness. Divide the remaining region of dynamic firms in two, by locating the line q—p with a slope equal to the growth rate of market demand. All technologies in B and C are profitable but those in B are losing economic weight, $0 < g_i < g_D$ while those in C enjoy increasing economic weight, $g_i > g_D$. Along p—p technologies are marginal and along q—p they are dynamically representative. If we

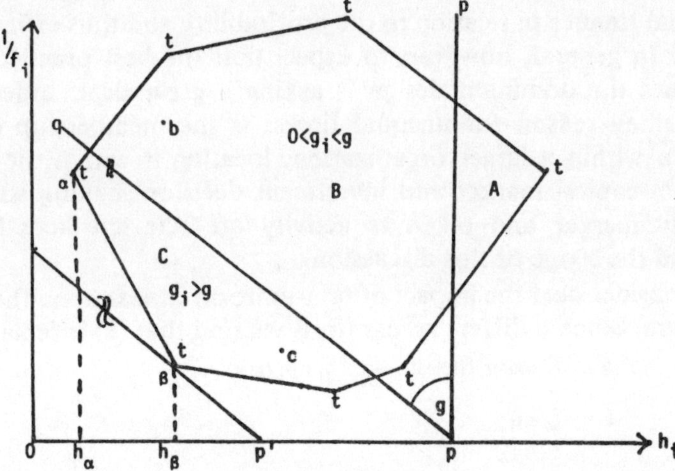

Fig. 3. The Selection Set.

compare the firms and their technologies represented by points b and c, we see why unequal fitness complicates the selection process. For b is a more efficient technology than c but nonetheless it is losing economic weight while c is gaining in importance. Why? Because firm b is so much more unfit than c that its superior profitability is transformed into an inferior growth rate of capacity, and relative loss of economic weight. We shall see below that this provides the rationale for $\bar{h}$ increasing at some stages during the selection process.

To determine the dominant design we note, as with Figure 1, that selection drives the industry to the boundary of its selection set. In this case, the process converges on point β, the dominant design technology, with the corresponding price of p'. All technologies with $h_i < p'$ survive but only β commands positive economic weight. However, β is not the best practice design, which is, in fact, technology α. With non-uniform fitness, it cannot be presumed that competitive selection converges on the economically best-practice technology. The conditions required to bring the best-practice design to market dominance are not difficult to establish. Either the growth rate of demand must be zero (so q—p coincides with p—p), or, given $g_D > 0$, the selection set must have the appropriate shape, necessarily entailing a negative correlation between fitness and efficiency values across the firms. One obvious way for this to be achieved is with an «efficient» capital market which allocates external finance in relation to the profitability and thus efficiency of firms. In general, however, to expect that the best practice design becomes the dominant design is asking a great deal. Indeed, one compelling reason for unequal fitness is the membership of each «firm» within a larger organization, locating it within the latter's internal capital market and investment decision making structure. Clearly merger and takeover activity are relevant here but are beyond the scope of this discussion.

Consider next the impact of non-uniform fitness upon the Fisher theorem. Since f_i differs across firms we find that (2) is replaced by:

$$g = \sum s_i g_i = \bar{f}(p - \bar{h}) - C_t(f_i, h_i); \; h_i < p \qquad (10)$$

with $\bar{f} = \sum_i s_i f_i$

being average fitness, and $C_t(f_i, h_i)$ being the covariance between fitness and efficiency across dynamic firms. Apart from the covariance term this is an obvious extension of (2). The rate of change of economic weight of a given technology is then determined according to:

$$\frac{ds_i}{dt} = s_i\,[(p-\bar{h})\,(f_i-\bar{f}) + f_i\,(\bar{h}-h_i) + C_t(f_i\,h_i)] \tag{11}$$

which reduces to (3) when $f_i = f$. Two conditions are favourable to a technology increasing its economic weight, above average efficiency and above average fitness. Notice that the effect of deviations from average fitness is proportional to the prevailing average profit margin. Again the presence of the covariance term indicates the significance of the distribution of population characteristics for the operation of the selection process. However, if we compare the relative performance of any pair of technologies i and j we find:

$$\frac{d}{dt}\log\left(\frac{s_i}{s_j}\right) = p(f_i-f_j) + f_if_j\left[\frac{h_j}{f_j}-\frac{h_i}{f_i}\right];\ h_i,\ h_j < p \tag{12}$$

which is independent of the covariance term, and varies only with p. To derive the analogue to the Fisher Law we focus on the population characteristic $\bar{h}$. Taking the rate of change of $\bar{h}$ in conjunction with (3) we have:

$$\frac{d\bar{h}}{dt} = \sum_i s_i(g_i-g)h_i = C_t(h_i,\ g_i) \tag{13}$$

so that average unit cost rises or diminishes over time according as there is a positive or negative correlation between efficiency and growth rates. With uniform fitness this correlation is necessarily negative, and indeed $C_t(h_ig_i) = -\,f\ V_t(h_i)$, the Fisher result. The general case is less clear cut, for with non-uniform fitness we cannot rule out phases of the selection process for which $C_t(h_i,\ g_i)$ is positive. Taking account of (11) we find that the formula for $d\bar{h}/dt$ reduces to:

$$\frac{d\bar{h}}{dt} = p\sum_i s_if_ih_i - \sum_i s_if_ih_i^2 - \bar{h}g$$

Now define $V^*_t(h_i)$ as the variance of h_i, constructed by using the contribution which each firm makes to average fitness as weights, $s_i f_i/\bar{f}$, rather than market shares. Substituting into the expression for $d\bar{h}/dt$ then yields:

$$\frac{d\bar{h}}{dt} = -\bar{f}\, V^*_t(h_i) + (p-\bar{h})\, C_t(f_i, h_i) \tag{14}$$

with $$V^*_t(h_i) = \sum_i \frac{s_i f_i}{\bar{f}} (h_i-\bar{h})^2,\ h_i < p$$

This is the closest we come to the Fisher Law with non-uniform fitness. If the correlation between fitness and efficiency is zero, then we have a direct analogue in terms of average and the fitness weighted variance in efficiency, $V^*_t(h_i)$. More generally, the Fisher Law does not hold, the rate of change of h depending on the covariance between fitness and efficiency in the manner indicated by (14).

Nonetheless, (14) and (4) conform to the same general proposition. The time evolution of average practice unit costs depends on the joint distribution of fitness and efficiency across the population of profitable firms and technologies. The Fisher Law is just a special case at one extreme of the possibilities.

c) Selection and Creativity

We turn finally and briefly to the most difficult of the three dimensions of performance, creativity, the capacity of the firm to improve its revealed technological performance through innovation or imitation. The significance of creativity is that it drives variations over time in the technology set, imitation operating to reduce variety and innovation having the opposite effect. We have already seen how the entry of new technologies affects the selection process; we now see how development within technologies interacts with selection. The general point is clear enough. By improving its technology, a firm may reduce its units relative to average practice and thus improve the prospects for increasing its economic weight and ultimately for survival. The key issue becomes the firm's momentum of change within a technology in relation to the average momentum of change for all the technologies competing in the environment (Georghiou *et al.*).

In this respect firms must be expected to differ substantially: in their perceptions of an agenda for improving technology; in their resources to devote to improving technology; in their perception of the profits from technical advances; and finally, in their ability to translate changes in their knowledge base into improvements of revealed performance. We cannot deal in any detail with these elements here, so we confine attention to two greatly simplified cases. In each case the rate of improvement within a technology is taken to be the same for all firms operating that technology. Returning to selection with uniform fitness, we investigate the relation between technical progress proper and the rate of improvement of average practice unit costs. From this we consider a simple example, in which the rate of progress at firm level depends on profitability and the perceived agenda for innovation.

Let λ_i be the rate of progress, rate of reduction in unit costs, in the ith technology, so that

$$\frac{dh_i}{dt} = \lambda_i h_i$$

Combining this with the definition of $\bar{h}$ we have:

$$\frac{d\bar{h}}{dt} = \sum_i \frac{ds_i}{dt} h_i + \sum_i s_i \frac{dh_i}{dt};\ h_i < p$$
$$= - [f\ V_t(h_i) + \sum_i s_i \lambda_i h_i] \tag{15}$$

Technical progress proper must accelerate the rate of reduction in average practice costs relative to that produced by selection alone. Simplifying further we note that:

$$\sum_i s_i \lambda_i h_i = C_t(\lambda_i, h_i) + \bar{\lambda}\bar{h},$$

where $C_t(h_i, \lambda_i)$ is the covariance between levels and rates of reduction in unit costs, and

$$\bar{\lambda} = \sum_i s_i \lambda_i$$

is the average rate of technical progress proper. However, $d\bar{\lambda}/dt = -f\, C_t(\lambda_i, h_i)$ so that the final expression for the average rate of cost reduction becomes:

$$\frac{d\bar{h}}{dt} = -\left\{f\, V_t(h_i) + \overline{\lambda h}\right\} + \frac{1}{f}\frac{d\bar{\lambda}}{dt} \tag{16}$$

Although $d\bar{h}/dt$ is necessarily negative, $d\bar{\lambda}/dt$ may be positive or negative. Indeed, if the more efficient firms tend to have lower values of λ_i, selection will work to diminish the average rate of technical progress proper. Again we see how the behaviour of population statistics depends on the joint distribution of firm performance.

Consider now a particular theoretical account of the rates of progress λ_i. Nothing is claimed for this example other than as an illustration of the method of analysis. Specifically, let λ_i be proportional to the product of two factors: the gap between a firm's current technology and its perception of the mature state of technology; and, the resources available to devote to improvements in technology. The latter we treat as proportional to the firm's ratio of profits to unit costs. Thus we can write:

$$\lambda_i = \alpha_i\left(\frac{p-h_i}{h_i}\right)(h_i - h_{Li}) \tag{17}$$

where α_i summarizes all other influence on the propensity to innovate and $h_i - h_{Li}$ is the firm's perception of the agenda for profitable technological advance. On substituting (17) into (15) and setting $\alpha_i = \alpha$ and $h_{Li} = h_L$ for all technologies we obtain:

$$\frac{d\bar{h}}{dt} = -\left\{(f-\alpha)\, V_t(h_i) + \alpha(p-\bar{h})(\bar{h}-h_L)\right\} \tag{18}$$

The second term in (18) is easy to interpret, it represents the product of the average profit margin with the average agenda for change. The interpretation of the first term is more complicated, for it indicates that a sufficiently high propensity to innovate, α, may reverse the efects of selection upon the rate of change of $\bar{h}$. Indeed, if $f < \alpha$, a greater variance of unit cost levels will slow down the rate of decline of $\bar{h}$, not accelerate it. Of course, this example is only proposed as an illustration of the complexity of selection processes. Other alternatives to (17) are worthy of closer attention, in particular, those which relate innovation to absolute profitability. Further important extension include the treatment of imitative behaviour, perhaps dependent on the distance of a firm from current best-practice, and the impact of different propensities to innovate. Indeed, the results obtained in these sample cases are suggestive of a rich menu of possibilities in which selection interacts with fitness, efficiency and creativity to shape the technology set and the evolution of population characteristics. In this process, the diffusion and survival prospects of competing technologies are simultaneously determined.

Conclusions: An Agenda for Research

We have sought in this paper to outline a framework for the analysis of innovation and the diffusion of innovation in multi-technology environments. The point to be emphasized is that patterns of technical progress depend on the variety of behaviour across firms and the characteristics of the environment in which those differences are resolved. Our simple sketches suggest fruitful avenues of research relating to: economies of scale, learning processes and product heterogeneity (Metcalfe) together with the study of more complex, locally differentiated and turbulent environments. At the empirical level this suggests the need to identify the forces which generate variety of behaviour in firms, and to specify the determinants of the agenda for change in a given technology. In following this enquiry, economists will find much to learn, and modify, from evolutionary biology.

ABSTRACT

This paper explores the relationship between the competitive process and technological variety, arguing that competition is driven by variety. Each technology and its associated firm is considered in relation to its market environment and the distribution of other technologies with which it competes. Firms are located in terms of three dimensions, efficiency, fitness and creativity. It is then shown how competitive selection operates with respect to each of these dimensions. Throughout the paper we draw upon the close conceptual relationship between the economics of technical change and the biological notions of selection, adaptation and mutation.

RÉSUMÉ

Cet article examine les relations entre le processus de concurrence et la variété des technologies, et développe l'idée que la concurrence est orientée par la variété. On considère chaque technologie et la firme qui lui est associée en relation avec son environnement de marché et avec la distribution des autres technologies avec lesquelles elle est en concurrence. On répartit les firmes par rapport à trois dimensions, l'efficience, lde degré d'adaptation et la créativité. On montre alors comment la sélection concurrentielle opère eu égard à chacune de ces dimensions. Nous insistons tout au long de l'article sur l'étroite relation conceptuelle entre l'économie du changement technique et les notions biologiques de sélection, d'adaptation et de mutation.

RÉFÉRENCES

Alchian, A.A. (1950). «Uncertainty, Evolution and Economic Theory», *Journal of Political Economy*, Vol. 58.

Carter, C.F. and Williams, B.R. (1957). *Industry and Technical Progress*, Oxford.

Dosi, G. (1982). «Technological Paradigms and Technological Trajectories», *Research Policy*.

Georghiou, L. *et al.* (1986). *Post Innovation Performance*, Macmillan, London.

Hannan, M.T. and Freeman, J. (1977). «The Population of Organizations», *American Journal of Sociology*, Vol. 82.

Hayek, F. (1946). «The Meaning of Competition», reprinted in 1948, *Individualism and Economic Order*, Chicago.

Iwai, K. (1984). «Schumpeterian Dynamics», *Journal of Economic Behaviour and Organization*, Vol. 4.

Knight, F. (1933). *The Economic Organization*, A.M. Kelly, New York, 1967.

Langrish, J. *et al.* (1972). *Wealth from Knowledge*, Macmillan, London.

Machlup, F. (1952). *The Economics of Seller's Competition*, John Hopkins.

Mathews, R.C.O. (1984). «Darvinism and Economic Change», in Collard, D.A. (eds.), *Economic Theory and Hicksian Themes*, Oxford.

Marshall, A. (1920). *Principles of Economics* (9th Ed.), Macmillan, London.

Mayr, E. (1982). *The Growth of Biological Thought*, Harvard.

McNulty, P. (1968). «Economic Theory and the Meaning of Competition», *Quarterly Journal of Economics*, Vol. 86.

Metcalfe, J.S. (1984). «Technological Innovation and the Competitive Process», *Greek Economic Review*, Vol. 6.

Nelson, R. and Winter, S. (1984). *An Evolutionary Theory of Economic Change*, Harvard.

Penrose, E. (1959). *The Theory of the Growth of the Firm*, Blackwell, Oxford.

Salter, W.E.G. (1966). *Productivity and Technical Change* (2nd Ed.), Cambridge.

Science Policy Research Unit (1972). *Success and Failure in Industrial Innovation*, Sussex University.

Schumpeter, J. (1943). *Capitalism, Socialism and Democracy*, Allen and Unwin, London.

Slobodkin, L.B. (1961). *Growth and Regulation in Animal Populations*, Dover, New York.

Sober, E. (1985). *The Nature of Selection*, MIT Press, Cambridge.

Steindl, J. (1952). *Maturity and Stagnation in American Capitalism*, Monthly Review Press, London.

Turner, R. and Soete, L. (1984). «Technology Diffusion and the Rate of Technological Change», *Economic Journal*, Vol. 94.

Utterback, J.M. and Abernathy, W.J. (1978). «A Dynamic Model of Product and Process Innovation», *Omega*, Vol. 3.

Winter, S. (1964). «Economic 'Natural Selection' and the Theory of the Firm», *Yale Economic Essays*, Vol. 4.

[25]

Information, variety and entropy in technoeconomic development *

P.P. SAVIOTTI

Department of Science and Technology Policy, University of Manchester, Manchester, M13 9PL, U.K.

Final version received June 1987

In this paper the trend towards an increasing variety of products and services offered to the consumer is considered as one of the most important in economic development. An approach to the analytical treatment of this problem is made by means of the concepts of variety and entropy. The increasing variety of products and services generated in the process of economic development increases the quantity of information required to produce and to use them. In order to reduce these information requirements both organisational and technological changes can be used. Two examples of organisational change, division of labour and hierarchical organisations, are discussed and it is shown that both of them can lead to a reduction in the information inputs used to generate a given output variety. Furthermore, the implications for variety and information of the emergence of new products, of product substitution, of specialisation, product diversification and of dominant designs, technological regimes, natural trajectories, technological paradigms and technological guideposts are examined. It is hoped that the approach contained in this paper can be useful in the development of evolutionary theories of technological change.

1. Introduction

One of the most striking characteristics of economic and technological development is the increasing variety of products and services which we use in our everyday life. Previously unknown products like computers, radio, television, motor cars, aircraft and telephones have come into existence within the last one hundred years. Naturally these are only a few examples, but the list of new products which have recently appeared and which continue to appear could be very long. Furthermore new products which have been available for a considerable time have undergone and are continually undergoing a process of diversification which increases the variety of services that they can perform for their users. Naturally the emergence of new products and services is accompanied by the disappearance of some pre-existing products and services. This happens when a pre-existing product is replaced by a new product. If this were the only process to occur then the total number of existing products and services would remain constant, or the net variety of existing products and services would not change. In this paper the net variety of existing products and services is assumed to grow although no empirical proof of it will be given. This implies that the process of substitution of an old product/service by a new one has not been the only process operating in technoeconomic development.

The increasing number of products and services available to the consumer has been accompanied by a number of related changes: the number of skills and of techniques required to produce this increased variety of final output has increased; the nature of competition has become less dependent on price and more based on products. The existence of non-price or imperfect forms of competition was first recognised in the early 1930s, when Joan Robinson [16] and Edwin Chamberlin [6] independently published their theories of imperfect competition. Later Schumpeter [19, p. 83] considered the new consumers' goods as one of the fundamental impulses that set and keep the capitalist engine in motion.

Clearly the availability of a wider variety of goods and services represents a benefit for the consumer but it is not necessarily an unmixed benefit. A system characterised by a greater variety of constituent elements is also a system which requires a greater amount of information to be

* The comments of Stan Metcalfe, Adrian Bowman and of two anonymous referees are gratefully acknowledged although the responsibility for any errors rests with the author.

Research Policy 17 (1988) 89–103
North-Holland

described. In other words a greater variety of goods and services also creates greater information requirements. These information requirements represent a cost. Therefore a type of economic development which creates both a greater variety of output and greater information requirements will proceed only if information costs do not grow as rapidly as the benefits produced by the increasing variety of services supplied to consumers.

Indeed, the trend towards an increasing variety of products and services is not the only trend in economic development. Other trends tend to limit the increasing information costs originated by the greater variety of products and services. New goods and services will in general tend to require new processes. Therefore a greater variety of goods and services will tend to be accompanied by a greater variety of the processes used to produce them. It is thus useful to distinguish between output variety (V_q) and process variety (V_p). While an increasing output variety can generally be interpreted as a benefit for users an increasing process variety will tend to increase the information required by producers to produce a given variety of output. In the normal course of economic development one would expect producers to attempt to decrease the information costs required to produce a given output variety, V_q. Information costs will depend not only on the quantity of information required to describe and understand the processes, but on the efficiency with which this information is processed and transmitted. Two types of approaches can be defined using the following symbols:

V_q = output variety;
V_p = process variety;
I_q = information required to describe products and services;
I_p = information required to describe processes;
$E(I_q)$ = product information efficiency;
$E(I_p)$ = process information efficiency

where $E(I_q)$ and $E(I_p)$ can be interpreted as the quantity of information that can be processed or transmitted per unit of labour employed in this particular task. For both cases V_q is assumed either to remain constant or to increase, since this represents a benefit for the users of services.

In the first approach I_p, the information required to produce a given variety of output is kept constant but information costs per unit of output caused to fall by increasing $E(I_p)$, the efficiency with which the required information is manipulated and transmitted. This can be achieved nowadays by the various applications of information technology. Computers, advanced software and telecommunications equipment greatly enhance the quantity of information that can be processed and transmitted per unit of labour employed.

In the second approach I_p, the information required to produce a given variety of output, is reduced without reducing V_q. Consequently information costs per unit of output variety fall even without any change in the efficiency with which information is processed. This can be achieved, for example, by redesigning a process (i.e. changing the number and type of operations performed by individual workers or institutional units) in such a way that the total information required to produce one unit of output variety falls.

Naturally neither of these two approaches is going to be followed exclusively by any real firm or organisation and a mixture of the two is going to be a more common type of behaviour. In other words, a firm is likely in general to attempt both to reduce the information (I_p) required to produce a given output variety V_q and to increase the efficiency $E(I_p)$ with which this information is processed.

The next two sections of this paper will be mainly concerned with the ways in which process information requirements can be reduced by changes in process organisation. In order to do this a number of other concepts will be introduced. Subsequently an attempt will be made to assess the contributions to variety and information of the process by which new products are introduced and adopted in the economic system.

In a complex economic system different trends can take place simultaneously, each of which is likely to make a different contribution to the variety, entropy and information of the system. In the final section an attempt will be made to approach the problem of how the changes in variety and information requirements of individual processes combine at the level of aggregation of the economic system.

Before proceeding, it has to be observed that in this paper an attempt is made to derive the information implications of production processes, be they processes that produce materials goods or services. No attempt is made to assess the information activities in an economy, for example by separating activities which produce predominantly information from activities which produce material goods, as is commonly done in many studies of the information economy (see for example [12,23]). On the contrary it is recognised that every process requires information and creates information requirements for the users of its output. An attempt is made to derive the information implications of some known trends in technoeconomic development.

2. Information, entropy and variety

In this paper the concept of variety has so far been used in a rather loose way. It is possibly to give a more rigorous definition of it [3, p. 124]. If an economic system is considered a set of elements then the variety of this set will increase when the number of distinguishable elements of the set increases. In information theory the variety of a set is defined as the logarithm in base 2 of the number of *distinguishable* elements in the set.

$$V = \log_2 n \tag{1}$$

where V = variety and n = number of distinguishable elements in the set. For the case of an economic system it would be the number of distinguishable products, services, operations, skills etc. of the system. An increase in the number of indistinguishable elements of the system will not lead to an increase in variety.

In the case of an economic system the usefulness of this definition of variety will depend on how easily distinguishable products, services, operations and skills are. Cases of product diversification which can be described as the same content with a new label or of partly overlapping skills could create difficulties. However, many new products which are continuously generated by the process of economic development are clearly distinguishable. For example, different models of aircraft (Piper, Tornado, Boeing 747), of microcomputers, of motor cars, of photocopiers, of machine tools etc., can be clearly distinguished even by means of quantitative techniques. Likewise, skills like welders, fitters, surgeons and software writers can be distinguished. The previous definition of variety will therefore be particularly useful in cases in which the elements of the system analysed are clearly distinguishable and less useful when the distinguishability of the elements is more problematic. The following treatment, based on the previous definition of variety, will be applicable to systems having elements which are distinguishable in principle. The number of such systems, as the previous examples imply, is sufficiently large to make this treatment worthwhile.

A concept related to that of variety but not identical to it is that of entropy. Entropy is a concept used to measure the randomness or uncertainty of a given set of elements [10, p. 28]. For example if we were to take a dictionary and to mix up all its letters in a completely disordered way we would obtain a state of the dictionary which could be described as random, disordered, disorganised, mixed, homogeneous. This state would have a higher entropy than the initial state of the dictionary, which by contrast could be described as a non-random, ordered, separated, inhomogeneous. Similarly if we had a very large billiard table with many billiard balls of different colours on it, the state with all the balls of the same colour grouped together would have a lower entropy than the state in which all the billiard balls are mixed at random. The state with the balls of the same colour grouped together will have the lowest possible entropy. However, many other dispositions of the billiard balls are possible. Each of these dispositions is called a microstate of the system. A real system, like a gas in a box, is a three-dimensional analogue of a billiard table with coloured balls. If we consider a mixture of gases the different types of atoms and molecules are the analogues of the billiard balls.

The gas itself will contain very large numbers of atoms or molecules in continual motion. Therefore there will be a very large number of microstates of the gas. Very few of these microstates will correspond to a disposition of the elements of the set (atoms, molecules) in which elements of each different type are all grouped together. There will be many more microstates in which the different types of atoms and molecules are mixed at random. Hence, the probability of finding the gas with the different types of atoms or molecules mixed at random is much higher than that of finding the gas with the molecules of each type grouped together. However, each microstate of the gas, whether it contains the atoms or molecules of different types in an ordered or disordered disposition is equally probable. As a consequence of these considerations most of the time we can expect to find the gas with a disposition of its constituent atoms or molecules as random as possible. Since entropy is supposed to measure the disorder of the system a higher entropy will be associated with a higher probability of finding the system in that state:

$$S = K \ln W \tag{2}$$

where S is entropy, K is a constant and W is the probability of finding the system in that state, which is given by the corresponding number of microstates.

All that was said previously is based on the assumption that all the individual microstates of the system (i.e., each individual disposition of its elements, in this case atoms and molecules) are equally probable. While this is a realistic assumption in the case of an ideal gas or of a billiard there are many cases in which the microstates of the system cannot be considered equiprobable. For example, not all the dispositions of letters obtained by mixing at random those contained in a dictionary are equiprobable. In particular, only one disposition of letters carries the full meaning of the dictionary. Hence, many systems are characterised by the non-equiprobability of their microstates. These considerations are particularly relevant in the case of social systems. For example, if one thinks about any organisation it is clear that not all the microstates obtained by mixing at random the members of the organisation are equivalent. In particular only one microstate allows the organisation to function at its best.

The non-equiprobability of the microstates of the system has important implications for what concerns its entropy. When the microstates of the system are independent (which again they cannot always be assumed to be) and equivalent then formula (2) becomes:

$$S = K \log(1/p_i) = -K \log p_i \tag{3}$$

where p_i is the probability of an individual microstate. If, however, the microstates of the system are not equiprobable formula (3) has to be modified, and it becomes:

$$S = -K p_i \log p_i. \tag{4}$$

This formula was introduced by Shannon and Weaver [20] in order to deal with the information content of messages. Clearly not all the microstates of a message composed of individual symbols (e.g., letters) are equiprobable. In general this formula is used to calculate changes in entropy between two different situations. The value of the constant K is not particularly important in many applications and in what follows it will always be considered equal to 1.

It is possible to demonstrate [10, p. 36] that a given set of elements will have its maximum entropy when all its microstates are independent and equiprobable. Both non-independence and non-equiprobability of microstates reduce the entropy of the system below its possible maximum value. An example of this could be given by an organisation in which all members had exactly the same skills, functions and power. It would then be possible to mix at random all the members of the organisation without changing its performance. Each microstate of the system (individual disposition of members) is equiprobable. If we then imagine that the members of the organisation are retrained and given completely different skills, and that consequently they perform different functions and occupy hierarchically different positions, it is clear that now a random mixing of the members of the organisation will not produce equiprobable microstates. It is also clear that in its initial state the system was far more random and potentially less structured than in its final state. The greater the degree of non-equiprobability and of non-independence of skills, functions and hierarchical positions the lower the entropy of the system.

Having introduced some general features of the concepts of entropy and variety it is now possible to begin the discussion of the concept of information. The word information in this paper will be used in a way which is very similar to that used in communications theory. In particular information in this sense must not be confused with meaning or knowledge [20, p. 8]. Information in the more specific and restricted sense in which it is used in communications theory refers to the freedom of choice when one selects a message. A situation in which there are only two messages a and b to choose from is characterised by one unit of information. This is true independently of the content of a and b and therefore of the quality of the messages to be chosen. In this sense information can be said to represent the *uncertainty* of the situation. The uncertainty would increase with the number of messages one had to choose from and the number of possible choices would correspondingly increase. It must be emphasised that these choices, and consequently the units of information, are equivalent.

The link between information and entropy can be made precisely by means of uncertainty. Since entropy measures the disorder or randomness of the system, a system with higher entropy will also be characterised by a greater uncertainty. Consequently, higher entropy will be associated with greater uncertainty and with greater information. More specifically, a greater amount of information will be required to choose one message out of a set of *n* messages the higher the entropy of the set of messages. This is true whatever is the nature of the individual messages. It is therefore understandable that entropy has been used as a measure of information in communications theory [10, pp. 47–52; 20, pp. 12–16].

Summarising the previous discussion one could say that the greater the uncertainty or randomness of a set of messages (and consequently the greater the entropy of the set) the greater the information required to choose one out of a series of messages. If one moves from the context of communications to that of organisations the analogue of the information required to choose one out of a set of messages becomes the information required by the top management of the organisation to choose one employee or a sub-unit out of the *n* employees/sub-units which constitute the organisation. In even simpler terms the information which is measured by entropy is the information which is required by top management (or by anyone else who needs it) to "know" the organisation.

The type of information which has been described above is not the only possible type of information. A communications engineer is interested in the capacity to transmit information. As Shannon and Weaver [20] put it "... this word 'information' in communications theory relates not so much to what you do say as to what you could say". This capacity is called by Gatlin [10, p. 48] *potential* information. Therefore potential information, which increases with messages variety and with freedom of choice, is measured by entropy.

It is not true, however, that as entropy increases information always increases. Let us take a simple example. A library contains information stored in the form of linear symbols ordered according to the constraints of a language. The sequences are contained in books and periodical which are classified and neatly catalogued in shelves. This is obviously a state of very high order. If we were to take each page of each book or periodical, cut them into single letter pieces and mix them at random the entropy of the system would increase but the information stored in the library would decrease to virtually zero. However, starting from this disordered state, many more meaningful combinations of letters could be formed than the one that was destroyed by cutting the books and periodicals into single letter pieces. Hence, while the actual information contained in the library decreased to virtually zero the information that it could contain increased. A difference has therefore to be made between *potential* information and *stored* information. In simpler terms a greater uncertainty or randomness of the system tends to increase its potential information while a greater order and constraint tend to increase its stored information.

These two types of information have analogues in the field of organisations. It has already been observed that potential information can be interpreted as the information required by top management to "know" the organisation. On the other hand, the purpose of an organisation is to transform some kinds of inputs, not necessarily material, into some kind of outputs. In so doing the organisation must have information about the types of inputs required, the processes to transform them into outputs and the external environment which is going to use these outputs. If one takes the view that the better informed an organisation is about these aspects the more likely it is to succeed, then the capacity to store information becomes crucial for its success. It has to be observed that the existence of these two types of information has already been discussed by organisation theorists. For example, according to Duncan and Weiss [9, p. 205]:

The objective of the kind of organisation structure that is implemented is twofold: (1) to generate information for decision making that reduces uncertainty, and (2) to generate information that will help to coordinate the diverse parts of the organisation.

Clearly there is a great similarity between (1) and stored information and between (2) and potential information.

If we now recall the previous discussion on the effect of the non-independence and non-equivalence of the microstates of the system on its entropy the following statements apply:

(a) the larger the number of non-distinguishable elements of the system, and consequently the greater its variety, the larger the amount of information required to *describe* the system.
(b) The greater the degree of non-independence and of non-equiprobability of the microstates of the system, the lower its entropy [10, p. 36] and consequently the lower the amount of information required to describe the system.
(c) A lower entropy of the system, due to non-independence and non-equiprobability of its microstates, is also associated with a greater capacity of the system to *store* information.

Before passing to the next section in which some examples will be discussed, three observations are in order. First, the concept of information as used in this paper does not describe all the types of information that an organisation uses in its decision-making processes. Types of information which would fall within the definition used in this paper are, for example, that required to choose a particular spare part from a store, to choose the employee who is knowledgeable about a particular topic or to calculate the wages of a group of workers. In other words, it is information of the type which is commonly described as factual. As already indicated, information is not meant to be equivalent to meaning or knowledge. However, the quantity of information of this type that has to be manipulated by organisations is so large that changes in organisational methods and technologies which decrease the costs of processing and transmitting this type of information are bound to have an important economic effect. Second, although from what was said before organisations of lower entropy should face lower information costs and be able to store more information, it is not always true that a lower entropy is an advantage. This can be understood by returning to the previous example of the dictionary. The state in which the dictionary is normally sold has obviously a lower entropy than the state obtained by mixing at random all its letters. Consequently, the information storage capacity of the dictionary in its normal state is much higher than that in its disordered state. However, starting from the disordered state it is possible to re-order the letters in many ways, the original state of the dictionary being only one of them. Many types of meanings can therefore be created starting from the disordered state. For this sense, the disordered state of a library has been described before as having a lower *stored* information but a higher *potential* information than the ordered state. The disordered state has a greater flexibility than any of the completely ordered states. In the case of reorganisations this implies that an organisation of lower entropy will be able to store a larger amount of specialised information which allows it to adapt well to a constant environment. On the other hand, an organisation of higher entropy will be more easily adaptable to changes in its external environment which required to store a different type of information. Normally we choose to store particular items of information in order to use them repeatedly. This is an effective strategy if the environment in which the information storing organisation operates is stable. Thus highly structured organisations are likely to be effective when a constant set of routines is appropriate. But if the environment changes quickly highly structured organisations are likely to experience difficulties. The information already stored in them blocks the channels through which new information might come: storing information reduces access to potential information. Third, the economic value of the same quantity of different types of information may be very different. Marschak [13] has argued that there is no relation between the number of bits conveyed and the gross value of the data producing service. Thus, for example, knowledge of the colour and style of a bride's dress (at least two bits of information) is unlikely to be twice as valuable as the knowledge of the future value of one's stocks (at least one bit of information). It is therefore impossible to compare the value of two qualitatively different pieces of information using the concepts of information theory.

Things are different if, however, one is comparing the quantity of information that two different organisational arrangements require to produce the same output. In this case the types of information will be the same for both organisational arrangements but the uncertainty of one arrangement will be greater and correspondingly its capacity to store information lower. Of course the comparison of the information requirements of two different organisational arrangements are valid only to the extent that no other changes take place simultaneously (e.g., changes in technology, strategy, skills etc.). Some examples of how the information requirements of a given process are influenced by changes in process organisation are now going to be discussed.

Some examples will now be given in order to discuss the previous concepts in a more specific context.

3. Examples

3.1. Example 1 – Division of labour

In this example two cases are going to be compared, one in which a given manufacturing process is carred out without division of labour and one in which the maximum division of labour is used. A process consists of a number of operations which are performed by different people. For simplicity in both cases the number n of operations will be considered equal to the number of people performing them.

Case 1

Each person carries out the n operations in a sequence, therefore producing the final product. Each person therefore works in parallel and independently of any other person involved in the process. In this system, therefore, there is no division of labour. In a formal sense this system does not constitute an organisation, rather each person carrying out the complete process constitutes a unit of production and organisation. This productive system constitutes a simplified model of a real system in which individual artisans produce finished products working independently of one another.

The total entropy of this process (formula 4) can be estimated by calculating the probabilities of the individual microstates of the system. We can imagine to derive each microstate of the system by drawing in sequence one person and one operation from two separate boxes and coupling them. A microstate of the system has been generated after n people and n operations have been drawn from separate boxes and coupled. A different microstate can be originated by putting back the people and operations in their separate boxes and drawing in a sequence n people and n operations and coupling them one to one. In this way all the possible microstates of the system can be originated. Each microstate of the system can be considered as a snapshot in which each person is "frozen" while performing one of the n operations. In a subsequent snapshot (microstate) each person will be found performing one operation different from the previous microstate.

In each microstate an operation is associated with each person. The following two are examples of microstates:

$$\text{(a)}\quad X_1O_1,\ X_2O_2,\ldots,\ X_nO_n \tag{5}$$

$$\text{(b)}\quad X_1O_3,\ X_2O_6,\ldots,\ X_nO_n \tag{6}$$

where $X_1,\ldots,X_n$ represent the people and $O_1,\ldots,O_n$ the operations. The probabilities of each of them are given by:

$$P_a = P[X_1O_1,\ X_2O_2,\ldots,\ X_nO_n] \tag{7}$$

$$P_b = P[X_1O_3,\ X_2O_6,\ldots,\ Z_nO_{22}]. \tag{8}$$

Given that each person works independently, P_a can be expressed as the product of the probabilities of each event X_1O_1, X_2O_2, ...

$$P_a = P[X_1O_1]\cdot P[X_2O_2]\ldots\cdot P[X_nO_n]. \tag{9}$$

Given that there is no specialisation and that consequently each person can perform equally well any of the n operations

$$\begin{aligned} P[X_1O_1] = P[X_1O_2] = \ldots &= P[X_1O_n] \\ = P[X_2O_1] = P[X_2O_2] = \ldots &= P[X_2O_n] \\ &= P[X_nO_n]. \end{aligned} \tag{10}$$

Consequently:

$$P_a = P_b = \text{probability of any other microstate } P_t. \tag{11}$$

All the microstates of the system are therefore equiprobable. Since the sum of the probabilities of the microstates must be equal to 1 then

$$P_1 = \frac{1}{n} \tag{12}$$

where n is the number of microstates of the system. Consequently, the entropy of the system will be

$$H = -\sum_{i=1}^{n} \frac{1}{n} \log \frac{1}{n} = +\sum_{i=1}^{n} \frac{1}{n} \log n = n \cdot \frac{1}{n} \log n$$

$$= \log n. \tag{13}$$

It can be noticed that here and in what follows formula (4) is used without the constant K because what is important is to estimate the change in entropy between two different situations and not its absolute value.

Given what was said before this will be the maximum possible entropy of the system of n workers and n operations.

Case 2

In this case the n operations which constitute the process remain constant but specialisation and division of labour are introduced in their most extreme form. Each person will then be able to perform only one of the n operations. The various microstates of the system can be originated by the same procedure used in Case 1. The same microstates will be originated except that now they will no longer be equiprobable. In particular, only one microstate, that in which each person is performing the operation that he/she has been trained to perform, has a non-zero probability and this probability is actually equal to 1. Shannon's expression for the entropy of the system is then reduced to a single term:

$$H = 1 \log 1 = 0. \tag{14}$$

In other words, passing from a system in which there was no division of labour and specialisation to one with the maximum possible specialisation and division of labour the entropy of the system has decreased from log n to zero. Since entropy can be considered a measure of the information which is required to describe the system, this example shows that the introduction of specialisation and division of labour decreases the information required to describe the process. Hence, the information that the organisation has to store to know itself and to coordinate its own internal processes, what was previously called potential information, decreases with increasing division of labour. Correspondingly, the information that the organisation can store about the environment in which it is operating and about the technologies it is using (stored information) increases. This is understandable if we think that information has to be stored or "embodied" in the human skills of an organisation. In absence of specialisation every person in the organisation would have to store the same types of information. On the other hand with division of labour every member of the organisation has to store only a very limited range of types of information and consequently can store a greater quantity of these types. Collectively the organisation can store more information.

In the context of organisations the difference between (a) potential and (b) stored information is analogous to the difference between (a) the information that the organisation requires to know itself and to coordinate its internal processes and, (b) the information that the organisation can store about its external environment, the technologies it is using etc. The roles of these two types of information can be better understood by comparing them to what happens in a computer. Particular types of information are stored in a computer at given locations. In order to retrieve this information the addresses of the location at which it is stored have to be known as well. The addresses are only part of the mechanism by which valuable information is stored. If the capacity of the computer is finite the more memory locations are used for addresses the less space there will be for the storage of valuable information. The uncertainty of the system in an organisation is the analogue of the number of addresses in a computer. In both cases the quantity of valuable information that can be stored increases with the uncertainty of the system or the number of addresses.

The two cases previously analysed are extreme cases. They are important, however, because any real process is likely to be included between these two. The entropy and the information requirements of any real process are therefore going to decrease as the process moves away from the extreme without any division of labour and toward that with the maximum division of labour.

The situation does not change substantially if the number of operations $n(O)$ is different from the number of people $n(x)$. Both for $n(O) < n(x)$ and $n(O) > n(x)$ the entropy of the system will be above its minimum that corresponds to the situation in which each person performs only one operation.

The representation of the division of labour

which was given in this section is clearly rather abstract. One feature of the process which has not been taken into account is the need to coordinate the tasks performed by different workers. Clearly this would require additional information and therefore cause additional costs. The presence of coordination costs actual information requirements would be determined by the balance between operation costs and coordination costs. The case previously illustrated is therefore an idealised one in which coordination costs can be considered negligible with respect to operation costs.

3.2. Example 2 – Hierarchical organisations

In this example two different structures of the same organisation will be compared, one with no departmental boundaries and one in which the organisation is constituted by a series of departments. Following Simon's terminology [21] the first case would be an example of a "flat" system with only one hierarchical level and with a "span" of control equal to the number of employees of the organisation. By introducing departments the number of hierarchical levels would have to increase to at least two, because now if all the departments but one were at the same hierarchical level the department in charge of overall coordination and planning would have to occupy a higher hierarchical level. Furthermore, the degree of non-equivalence would increase by introducing departments.

Case 1

The organisation is constituted by n people performing n operations which for the moment can be considered equivalent. In other words, it is as if every person in the organisation was performing the same operation. This assumption is made to distinguish the effect of the introduction of departmental boundaries from that of the division of labour. The organisation is then constituted by a set of n people and a set of n equivalent positions to which people can be assigned. All the microstates are equiprobable. Consequently the entropy of the system has its maximum possible value, given by the logarithm of the number of microstates of the system, which in this case is equal to the factorial of the number of people:

$$H = \log n! \tag{15}$$

It must be remembered that when the microstates are equiprobable the entropy of the system is given by Boltzmann's formula (2), which again turns out to be equal to its maximum possible value.

Case 2

The introduction of departmental boundaries implies that only microstates of the system obtained by moving people around within each department are now possible. A lower number of microstates can therefore be obtained with respect to the previous case. However, even in this case the microstates of the system are equiprobable. The change in entropy between Case 1 and Case 2 is given by:

$$\begin{aligned} \Delta S(1 \to 2) &= S(2) - S(1) \\ &= R \log p(2) - R \log p(1) \\ &= R \log \frac{p(2)}{p(1)} \end{aligned} \tag{16}$$

where $p(2)$ and $p(1)$ represent the numbers of microstates of the organisation in Case 2 and Case 1 respectively. If $n(1), n(2), \ldots, n(k)$ are the numbers of people employed in each department in Case 2 and n the number of people employed in the organisation as a whole then:

$$p(2) = N_1!N_2! \ldots N_k! \tag{17}$$

where $N_1!$, $N_2! \ldots N_k!$ are the factorials of $n(1), n(2), \ldots n(k)$.

Consequently:

$$\Delta S(1 \to 2) = R \log \frac{N_1!N_2! \ldots N_k}{N!}. \tag{18}$$

It can be proved that $\Delta S(1 \to 2)$ is less than zero. If we expand all the factorials:

$$\Delta S(1 \to 2) = \frac{1 \cdot 2 \cdot 3 \cdot 4 \cdot n(1) \cdot 1 \cdot 2 \cdot 3 \cdot n(2) \cdot 1 \cdot 2 \cdot 3 \cdot n(k)}{1 \cdot 2 \cdot 3 \cdot 4 \cdot \ldots \cdot n} \tag{19}$$

If we assume that factorials are ordered in the following way:

$$N_1! < N_2! < N_3! \ldots N_k! \tag{20}$$

and if we simplify the factors corresponding to the smallest factorial we find:

$$\Delta S(1 \to 2) = R \log \frac{1 \cdot 2 \cdot 3 \cdot n(2) \cdot 1 \cdot 2 \cdot 3 \cdot n(k)}{[n(1)+1] \cdot [n(1)+2] \cdot \ldots \cdot n(2) \cdot \ldots \cdot n}, \tag{21}$$

To each factor contributing to the second factorial in the numerator will correspond a larger factor in the denominator. Thus, for example, $n(1)+1$ will correspond to 1, $n(1)+2$ will correspond to 2 etc. The same will occur for each of the subsequent factorials. Consequently the denominator will always be greater than the numerator and $\Delta S(1 \rightarrow 2)$ will always be smaller than zero. This will occur provided only that departments are introduced into the organisation. The uncertainty of the system is limited by reducing the freedom of motion of employees within the organisation. From what was said before follows that increasing the number of departments leads to a fall in the entropy of the system. If in addition to introducing departments the various positions which can be occupied by the members of the organisation were made non-equivalent by introducing different operations and division of labour the entropy would undergo a further reduction. In other words the types of organisational change illustrated in example 1 and 2 can both lead to reductions in the entropy of a system and these reductions are cumulative.

According to Simon [21] hierarchical organisations tend to be more stable than unstructured organisations and therefore they have a higher probability of survival in an evolutionary process. On the other hand, if the process of creation of a hierarchical organisation leads to a reduction in entropy then the organisation itself must necessarily be an open system, since otherhwise a reduction in entropy would not lead to a stable state.

3.3. Examples – Trends in process technology

Studies of product and process technology have shown that there are some regularities in the evolution of technologies. For example, Abernathy and Utterback [1,2] found that a new technology is characterised in its early stages by a multiplicity of product designs and by very flexible, unstructured processes. When the technology matures the multiplicity of product designs is replaced by a dominant design and production processes become more structured and more rigid. Similarly, Nelson and Winter [14] have introduced the concepts of technological regimes and natural trajectories, Dosi [8] that of technological paradigms and Sahal [17] that of technological guideposts. All these concepts imply that in the process of selection which occurs during the evolution of a technology some constraints are imposed upon technology itself which limit the choices available to the producers. The imposition of a dominant design/ regime and trajectory/ paradigm/ guidepost on a technology would inhibit wide-ranging exploration of a rich field of potential information. By limiting the search in this way the dominant design/ regime and trajectory/ paradigm/ guidepost would create a relatively stable environment in which highly structured organisations, which store information efficiently, would perform particularly well. On the other hand, a complete change in the environment, such as a technological revolution, would invalidate much of the previous stored information and therefore put highly structured organisations at a disadvantage. Although no attempt is going to be made here to calculate the changes in entropy accompanying these changes in technology it seems that based on the previous considerations within a dominant design one could expect a decrease in entropy of both products and processes. As processes become more structured and more rigid their entropy decreases. Consequently both their information costs fall and the capacity of the organisations using them to store critical information increases. On the other hand, a Schumpeterian revolution would favour more flexible organisation characterised by lower stored information but higher potential information. From the previous discussion these organisations would also have a higher entropy. Consequently, even if the entropy of the system had decreased within a dominant design/ regime and trajectory/ paradigm/ guidepost it could increase during a revolution and then subsequently decrease within the new paradigm.

Furthermore, it must be observed that this model in its basic form apparently implies a decrease in output variety in passing from a multiplicity of product designs to a dominant design. However, this is not necessarily the case because the dominant design may only determine the fundamental features of the product and a very large degree of product differentiation can still be achieved by varying the extent and combination of the basic ingredients of the dominant design.

4. Information, variety and new products

The trends in process organisation described previously lead to a reduction in the quantity of information required to produce a given or increasing output variety. However, if an increasing variety of products and services is continuously introduced into the economic system this has implications for the processes by means of which these new goods are adopted by their users. These implications can be better understood by conceptualising products as two sets of characteristics, one describing the internal structure of the technology (technical characteristics) and one describing the services performed by the product (service characteristics). The two sets of characteristics are linked by a pattern of mapping, since the purpose of the internal structure of the technology is to supply the required services and changes in technical characteristics are going to be introduced only if they lead to improvements in services [18]. The following is a simplified representation of a product, based on the previous conceptual scheme:

$$(X_{ij}) \leftrightarrow (Y_{ip})$$

where (X_{ij}) and (Y_{ip}) represent the two vectors of technical and service characteristics of the ith product and the arrow represents the pattern of mapping.

On the basis of this conceptual framework a number of processes by means of which new products are adopted in the economic system and their implications for variety and entropy can be understood. Thus, for example, if a new product P_2 is introduced into an economic system in which another product P_1 already existed a number of situations can arise.

Situation 1: P_2 has a completely different internal structure with respect to P_1, and therefore needs qualitatively different technical characteristics to be represented, but supplies qualitatively identical services and therefore can be represented in the same service characteristics. This situation can be represented as follows:

$$P_2[(X_{2j}) \leftrightarrow (Y_{2l})]; \quad P_1[(X_{ij}) \leftrightarrow (Y_{2l})]$$

$$X_{2j} \neq X_{ij}; \quad Y_{2l} \equiv Y_{il}.$$

However, P_2 supplies the common services at a lower cost and is therefore going to be preferred by all users. From the moment in which P_2 appears in the economic system it will be preferred by all users and it will therefore replace completely P_1. This is an example of *pure substitution*. In such a situation output variety V_q does not change when P_2 substitutes P_1 and consequently neither new benefits nor new information requirements are created for the users of P_2, P_1. An example of this situation could be given by a mechanical watch (P_1) supplying only time and date and by a digital watch (P_2) which supplied only time and date but at a lower cost.

Situation 2: P_2 has a completely different internal structure with respect to P_1 and supplies a completely different set of services. Therefore P_2 will have to be represented by qualitatively different technical and service characteristics with respect to P_1. This situation is represented in the following formulae:

$$P_2[(X_{2j}) \leftrightarrow (Y_{2l})]; \quad P_1[(X_{ij}) \leftrightarrow (Y_{il})]$$

$$X_{2j} \neq X_{ij}; \quad Y_{2l} \neq Y_{il}.$$

In this case P_2 will diffuse in the economic system only if there is a demand for the new services which it supplies. This represents the emergence of a completely new product. If this new product is going to be produced alongside existing products it will obviously lead to an increase in output variety V_q and consequently in users' information requirements.

Situation 3: P_2 has a completely different internal structure with respect to P_1 and supplies services which are partly qualitatively different and partly qualitatively identical to those of P_1. This situation is represented as follows:

$$P_2[(X_{2j}) \leftrightarrow (Y_{2l})]; \quad P_1[(X_{1j}) \leftrightarrow (Y_{il})]$$

$$X_{2j} \neq X_{ij}; \quad Y_{21} = Y_{11}; \quad Y_{22} \neq Y_{12}; \quad Y_{23} = Y_{13}$$

$$\ldots \; Y_{2,l-1} = Y_{1,l-1}; \quad Y_{2,l} \neq Y_{1,l}.$$

In this case different users will prefer either P_2 or P_1 depending on the services in which they are most interested. If, for example,

$$Y_{22} \gg Y_{12}$$

users who have a particular interest in the second service characteristic will prefer P_2. If on the other hand:

$$Y_{2l} \ll Y_{1l}$$

users particularly interested in the lth characteristic will prefer P_1.

In this case, the most likely pattern of development is a situation in which P_2 and P_1 survive alongside, each occupying a subset of the market previously occupied by P_1. The output variety of the economic system is increased by the emergence of P_2, but not as much as it would have been increased by a completely new product, because some of the service characteristics of P_2 coincide with those of P_1. In this situation P_2 and and P_1 specialise in a particular subset of the original market of P_1. This case can therefore be called either *specialisation* or *market segmentation*. *Situation 4*: P_2 has an internal structure very similar to that of P_1 and supplies the same services as P_1, but in addition it supplies other new services:

$$P_2[(X_{2i}) \leftrightarrow (Y_{2m})]; \quad P_1[(X_{1j}) \leftrightarrow (Y_{1l})]$$

$$(i_{\max} > j_{\max}); \quad (m_{\max} > l_{\max})$$

$$X_{21} = X_{11},\ X_{22} = X_{12},\ \ldots\ X_{2j} = X_{1j},$$

$$\text{no } X_1 \text{ equal to } X_{2,j+1},\ \ldots\ X_{2,i}$$

$$Y_{21} = Y_{11},\ Y_{22} = Y_{12},\ \ldots\ Y_{2,m}.$$

In this case P_2 is an evolution of P_1, having a broadly similar internal structure to which some technical characteristics have been added which supply new services.

This case can be considered an example of either *product evolution* or *product diversification* and it bears some similarity to specialisation. Depending on how novel and important the new services are and on how large a niche can be found in the existing market for P_1, P_2 will either become a partial substitute for P_1 or it will specialize in a different niche.

Examples of this situation would be a digital watch to which a new function has been added, a car with four-wheel drive that allows it to go on roads on which a two-wheel drive car could not go, a microcomputer to which a new component has been added (e.g., a word processor chip) which allows it to perform a new function.

A comparison of these four situations shows that different processes by which new products are generated and diffuse in the economic system can make different contributions to the output variety of the system. Pure substitution and the emergence of a completely new product represent two extreme cases, the former leading to no change in variety and the second to the maximum possible change in variety. Other processes such as specialisation, lead to changes in output variety intermediate between those caused by substitution and new products respectively. This is due to the fact that in the case of specialisation or product diversification only some of the characteristics of the new products are distinguishable from those of the old products. This situation is schematically represented in Table 1.

An increase in output variety will generally lead to an increase in entropy and therefore in information requirements but not necessarily the same proportion. As in the case of process variety a change in entropy will be equal to a change in variety for a given system only when the microstates of the system are independent and equivalent. This is not always the case for the situations previously described.

For example, if the extra characteristics which have been added to a new product are not independent of the old characteristics, or in other words if there is constraint between different characteristics, the change in entropy will be lower than the change in variety. The change in variety for a given process of generation or diffusion of a new product represents the maximum value for the corresponding change in entropy and therefore in information requirements. However, one can still expect that in general the order of the changes in information requirements for the processes previously described will be the same as the order of the corresponding changes in variety.

The information requirements of a given product can be conceptualised in a different though related way. A stable multicharacteristics product, i.e., one which remains in the market for a sufficiently long time, is likely to emerge through a

Table 1
Contribution of different processes to output variety V_q. P_2 = new product, P_1 = existing product

Process	ΔV_q
P_2 completely substitutes P_1	0
P_2 almost identical to P_1 except for few new technical and service characteristics	> 0 small
P_2 new internal structure, some services similar to P_1, some new services	> 0 larger
P_2 new internal structure, new services	> 0 maximum

process of competition in which consumers by making choices will eliminate a series of products and leave only one dominant product [11]. These choices will decrease output uncertainty by means of information acquired by the consumers about products.

What changes in information requirements will be created by the process of generation and adoption of new products previously described? A greater output variety will in general be accompanied by a greater entropy and therefore by a greater uncertainty. This is the greater uncertainty which has to be faced by the users of the new products. A greater variety of goods and services will therefore lead to increased information requirements for the consumers of those goods and services. The analysis of the information implications of increasing output variety of users of goods and services would constitute the counterpart of the previous analysis, which was concerned with the information implications for producers of goods and services. Such a complete analysis will not be attempted in this paper. The following comments on users are therefore intended only to show that the principles of the analysis are very similar to those used for producers and not to provide a complete treatment for the problem.

It has so far been assumed that an increasing variety of goods and services is a benefit for consumers. However, together with those benefits due to increased variety there are also costs. For example, even in the case of homogeneous goods a variety of suppliers charging different prices can present the consumer with the problem of acquiring the information necessary to identify the cheapest supplier. The consumer has to undertake a search, and therefore to face search costs. (See, for example, [22].) Naturally, the search will be worthwhile only if its cost is lower than the potential saving to be made as a consequence of the search.

It is clear that this problem will become much more complicated for the consumer in passing from homogeneous to heterogeneous multicharacteristics goods. In the latter, not only the prices charged by different suppliers for the same goods will differ, but the relationship between price and quality and that between price and users' benefits will be much more problematic. In other words, the information required by consumers to make choices and consequently search costs can be considerably increased by the availability of a greater variety of goods and services. In this case, as well as in the case of manufacturing processes, ways had to be found to reduce the information requirements, and therefore the search costs, necessary to make a choice amongst the goods and services available. Better education, specialist publications and advertising supply consumers with an increased flow of information about the goods and services that they are supposed to choose. On the other hand, trade marks, brand names and even the reputation of particular chains of shops or supermarkets function as information savers because they replace the quantity of information that the consumer would need to evaluate the quality of the goods and services under consideration. Instead of scanning all the goods produced by different manufacturers a user can opt for the trade mark or brand name which in the past has been associated with good quality. In this way the user would not need to have a detailed knowledge (or a less detailed one) of the internal structure and even of the services performed by the product in order to make a choice. In other words, the trade mark or brand name would be equivalent to a source of expert choice for the user, thus reducing the quantity of information that he/she would need to acquire. Therefore, even on the consumer side, there are ways in which the information required to make the most rational choice amongst the goods and services available in order to enjoy an increasing variety of them can be reduced.

5. Trends in technoeconomic development

This paper began with the observation that the increasing variety of goods and services which is available to consumers is one of the most important trends in economic development. This increasing variety benefits consumers but it is also accompanied by increasing information requirements and therefore information costs. Some organisational changes which can lead to a reduction in the information required to produce one unit of output variety have been examined in the paper. Before summarising these considerations, it has to be observed that the trend towards an increasing variety of goods and services is historically relatively recent and it can be considered mainly a phenomenon of this century [4]. The beginning of the industrial revolution was characterised more by the greater efficiency with which cheap mass produced goods were manufactured than by the variety of goods that were offered to consumers. The tendency to product diversification and to the creation of new products became more important when the markets for basic goods had been saturated. In fact, both the multidivisional form [7] and the forms of competition based on new products and on product differentiation [6,16,19] are a phenomenon of this century.

As it has been previously argued this trend can in general be considered beneficial for consumers but it also creates increasing information requirements and therefore information costs for the suppliers of new goods and services. Ways to reduce these increasing information had to be found in order to allow the process of economic development to continue. This aim could be achieved either by means of organisational changes which reduced the uncertainty of the process and therefore the amount of information required to know it, or by increasing the efficiency with which a constant amount of information can be processed and transmitted. As it has been shown previously the division of labour, the emergence of hierarchical organisations (of which the U and M form are examples) and some trends in the evolution of productive processes, are types of organisational change which can reduce the amount of information required to produce a unit of output variety. Simultaneously with these organisational changes which reduced process information requirements new technologies were developed (e.g., telegraph, telephone, calculators, typing machines) which by being more efficient in the processing and transmission of information allowed to handle larger quantities of it. Both trends combined contributed to the possibility to provide consumers with an increasing variety of goods and services. Naturally, the combination of the two trends had to depend at least on the possibility to make progress within each of them. Thus, if advances in information processing were not very rapid this could be expected to create an inducement to reduce the amount of process information by organisational changes. Conversely, if new technologies which allowed to handle much larger quantities of information suddenly became available it would then be possible to use processes characterised by greater information requirements. This seems to have been what happened with the development first of very rigid mass manufacturing processes and with the more recent advances in information technology which seem to make possible much more flexible low scale processes.

According to the previous analysis together with processes which increase the variety of the economic system, there are other processes which tend to reduce the entropy, and consequently the information requirements of other parts of the economic system. The variety, entropy and information requirements of various parts and processes of the economic system have to be considered separately.

While output variety keeps increasing there are a number of organisational changes which can reduce process entropy and therefore process information costs. To the extent that this is a dominating feature in the process of technoeconomic development one can expect that organisations of lower entropy will be more efficient. As a consequence the entropy required to produce one unit of output variety in a given economic system can be expected to decrease with time.

A similar trend towards the reduction of the information requirements needed to produce a greater output variety can be found on the output side. Thus, trade marks, brand names and the reputation of some chains of shops can reduce the information required by consumers to make a choice amongst the variety of goods and services on offer. Likewise, technological advances can increase the amount of information which can be made available to consumers to help them in their decision-making processes. A good example of this could be given by advertising and by the importance that television and printing technology have for it.

Separate trends will then exist in the process of technoeconomic development, some leading to an increasing variety of the economic system and others tending to limit the entropy and information requirements of different parts of the system. In addition to the trends discussed in this paper, which are mainly due to the emergence of new goods, services or organisational forms, other trends, constituted by the diffusion of these innovations throughout the economic system, tend to reduce the variety of the economic system. The problem at the level of aggregation of the economic system as a whole then becomes some way to predict the outcome of the combination of the various trends which have been illustrated before. Based on these considerations alone, it would be very difficult to make any precise forecasts. A possible way in which the problem could be approached consists of considering a technoeconomic system as an open system. Such an open technoeconomic system may achieve a steady state in presence of exchanges of energy, materials and information with its environment. What is more important, such a system can evolve from a less ordered to a more ordered state, and therefore from a state of higher to a state of lower entropy [5]. It is therefore possible for an economic system as a whole to move to states of lower entropy. If this has to occur it means that even in presence of an increasing output variety entropy decreasing processes can predominate over entropy augmenting processes.

The work of Prigogine [15] acquires particular relevance in this context. The possibility that open systems moving away from equilibrium can move to different stationary states characterised simultaneously by order and heterogeneity is obviously of interest. In particular, according to Prigogine the properties of dissipative structures are not unique to physical systems and are common to biological and social systems as well. In each of these cases a balance of forces (innovations) and flows (diffusion of innovations) is responsible for the properties of dissipative structures and fluctuations can destabilise a particular stationary state leading to a different one. The problem for a technoeconomic system becomes to identify the relevant forces and flows, to determine the conditions for stability and the fluctuations which can induce transitions. This is a possible agenda for future research linked to the problems analysed in this paper.

References

[1] W.J. Abernathy and J.M. Utterback, A Dynamic Model of Process and Product Innovation, *Omega* 3 (6) (1975) 639–656.

[2] W.J. Abernathy and J.M. Utterback, Patterns of Industrial Innovation, *Technology Review* (1978) 41–47.

[3] W.R. Ashby, *An Introduction to Cybernetics* (Methuen, London, 1964).

[4] M.J. Baker, *Marketing Strategy and Management* (Macmillan, London, 1985).

[5] L. Von Bertalanffy, The Theory of Open Systems in Physics and Biology, in: F.E. Emery (ed.), *Systems Thinking*, 1 (Penguin Books, Harmondsworth, 1969).

[6] E.J. Chamberlin, *The Theory of Monopolistic Competition* (Harvard University Press, Cambridge, MA, 1933).

[7] A.D. Chandler, *Strategy and Structure* (MIT Press, Cambridge, MA, 1962).

[8] G. Dosi, Technological Paradigms and Technological Trajectories: a Suggested Interpretation of the Determinants and Directions of Technical Change, *Research Policy* 11 (1982).

[9] R. Duncan and A. Weiss, Organisational Learning: Implications for Organisational Design, *Research in Organisational Behaviour* 1 (1979) 75–123.

[10] L.L. Gatlin, *Information Theory and the Living System* (Columbia University Press, New York, 1972).

[11] R.A. Jenner, An Information Version of Pure Competition, *Economic Journal* 786–805, reprinted in D.M. Lamberton (ed.), *Economics of Information and Knowledge* (Penguin Books, Harmondsworth, 1971).

[12] C. Jonscher, The Economic Causes of Information Growth, *Intermedia* 10 (1982) 34–37.

[13] J. Marschak, Economics of Inquiring, Communicating, Deciding, *American Economic Review Papers and Proceedings* 58 (1958) 1–18.

[14] R. Nelson and S. Winter, In Search of Useful Theory of Innovation, *Research Policy* (1977) 36–76.

[15] I. Prigogine, Order through fluctuations in Self-Organisation and Social System, in: E. Jantsch and C.H. Waddington, *Evolution and Consciousness: Human Systems in Transition* (Addison Wesley, New York, 1976).

[16] J. Robinson, *The Economics of Imperfect Competition* (Macmillan, London, 1933).

[17] D. Sahal, Alternative Conceptions of Technology, *Research Policy* 10 (1981) 2–24.

[18] P.P. Saviotti and J.S. Metcalfe, A Theoretical Approach to the Construction of Technological Output Indicators, *Research Policy* 13 (1984) 141–151.

[19] J. Schumpeter, *Capitalism, Socialism and Democracy* (George Allen and Unwin, 1943, 5th Edition 1976).

[20] C.E. Shannon and W. Weaver, *The Mathematical Theory of Communication* (University of Illinois Press, Urbana, 1949).

[21] H.A. Simon, The Architecture of Complexity, *Proceedings of the American Philosophical Society* 106 (1962) 467–482, reprinted in: H.A. Simon, *The Sciences of the Artificial* (MIT Press, Cambridge, MA, 1981).

[22] G.J. Stigler, The Economics of Information, *Journal of Political Economy* 69 (1961) 213–25. Reprinted in: D.M. Lamberton (ed.), *Economics of Information and Knowledge* (Penguin Books, Harmondsworth, 1971).

[23] J.P. Voge, The Political Economics of Complexity, from the Information of the Economy to the Complexity Economy, *Information Economics and Policy* 1 (1983) 97–114.

[26]

Bulletin of Economic Research 43:2, 1991, 0307-3378 $2.00

EVOLUTIONARY BIOLOGY, TECHNOLOGICAL CHANGE AND ECONOMIC HISTORY*

Joel Mokyr

I

The idea that biology, and not physics, ought to inspire the science of economics has a long and venerable history, although not much seems to have been done about it, at least not until recently.[1] In particular, the application of the theory of Darwinian evolution to the economics of technology and the theory of the firm has been obviously appealing.[2] In a famous footnote, Karl Marx (1867, I, p. 372) drew an analogy between Darwinian selection and the emergence of the instruments of production. Alfred Marshall repeatedly drew examples from biology and called upon economists to use more biological analogies.[3] Ever since, vague ideas of 'selection', 'survival of the fittest', and even 'mutation' have been tossed about by economists. Although an increasing number of main-stream modern economists such as Kenneth Boulding (1981), Jack Hirschleifer (1985), Sidney Winter (1964, 1971) and Richard Nelson (1987, 1989) have pleaded for a greater use of evolutionary theory and biology in economics, standard microeconomics, even when it explicitly called itself 'evolutionary', has taken little notice. Until recently, the concepts of evolutionary biology were no match for the elegant if limited tools of comparative statics. Even those who tried their hand at the use of biological metaphors and who used words like 'evolution' and 'natural selection' left and right, have not always studied the literature of evolutionary biology carefully.[4] Had they done so, they would have realized that in fact the

*I am grateful to Louis Cain, Charles Calomiris, Roderick Floud, Geoffrey Hodgson, Jonathan Hughes and an anonymous referee for comments on an earlier version.

[1] For a recent history and criticism of the use of physics in economics, see Mirowski (1990).

[2] For a survey, see Clark and Juma (1988).

[3] Marshall ([1890], 1930), p. 777 warned that the analytical writings of Ricardo, which were devoid of biological analogies, were like 'sharp chisels with which it is easy to cut one's fingers because they have such awkward handles'. Cf. Brinley Thomas, 'Alfred Marshall on Economic Biology', unpublished manuscript, February 1990.

[4] The only essay in a recent collection on evolutionary economics (Hanusch (1988)) to make a short reference to the literature of biology is Klein (1988). Virtually no references to evolutionary biology can be found Batten, Casti and Johansson (1987). More recently, there has been a notable infusion of evolutionary theory into this literature. For some examples see Selten (1989), Metcalfe (1989), Silverberg (1988) and Hodgson (1990).

theory of evolution is at least as dispute-ridden as economics, which tends to make it interesting but also more hazardous to apply its insights to other fields. There are no easy theorems, and the mathematics is descriptive rather than analytical.

In recent years, microeconomics has come to realize the limitations of a theory based on the concept of a stable and unique equilibrium, and has become increasingly interested in describing dynamic processes. Evolutionary models, after all, are the best hope of economists trying to generate predictable or at least understandable outcomes without consciously optimizing agents or with bounded rationality (Alchian (1950); Day (1975); Sugden (1989)). Especially in game theory there has been strong interest in the work of John Maynard Smith, a biologist who has pioneered the work in evolutionary games. Yet despite the importance of that work to theoretical industrial organization, it is of limited interest to the economic historian. What economists have tried to learn from biologists here is how certain games generate what is known as ESS — evolutionary stable strategies. These strategies describe an evolutionary equilibrium, a situation in which the distribution of gene frequencies is constant. This is of interest to economists because most repeated games tend to generate a multiplicity of Nash equilibria, and evolutionary theory might help to reduce that number. But for my purposes, that is not the main insight yielded by evolutionary theory. Economic historians are interested in dynamic processes of historical change that cannot be described as equilibrium processes: how new techniques are created, how old techniques become extinct, and how the two interact and coexist in the meantime. The focus is more often on changes in the population as a whole, its diversity and the interaction of different techniques, than on the equilibrium properties of a representative agent or firm. Here, too, I submit, something can be learned from biologists. As Silverberg (1988, p. 532) has expressed it, in some deeper sense the laws applicable in biology have their counterparts in economics, not in a superficial one-to-one correspondence but in similar causal patterns and perhaps similar dynamic processes. Clearly, however, the most important lesson to be learned from the use of these models is that history matters, and that economics without history is an intellectual dead end. It is simply impossible to understand long-term economic growth without some kind of Schumpeterian theory of technological creativity and innovation. The neoclassical equilibrium paradigm seems singularly unsuited to that task.

Applying a paradigm from another science to one's own is a risky venture. Nevertheless, historians (Basalla (1988)) and economists (de Bresson (1987); Nelson (1987); Silverberg (1988); Metcalfe (1989); Selten (1989)) have suggested to adopt an evolutionary paradigm in the history of technological change. The idea behind the analogy is to look at technological change as a selective process imposed on random mutations occurring in an epistemological system. Genetics and technology are both informational systems determining the phenotypes (visible characteristics) of members of a group and are in some ways subject to comparable dynamic forces (Mokyr (1990c)).[5] Technology is an epistemological concept, it is something we *know*, consisting of information transmitted from generation to generation. Although DNA is not something that we 'know' *strictu sensu*, it, too, is information transmitted between generations.

These information systems are subject to change over time. Errors in the copying of DNA cause mutations which form the basis for evolution. Technological information is similarly subject to random errors and deviations from the norm, although they do not usually occur during intergenerational transmission. Most new technological ideas, like most mutants, are duds. However, every once in a while something novel and useful comes along, which might be termed a potential invention. If it is sufficiently viable, it could eventually join or supplant existing techniques. The outcomes of Darwinian processes, in biology as in history, are the consequence of neither fluke nor destiny but of a combination of highly stochastic disturbances and a deterministic selection mechanism.

The attractiveness of the idea of using the production technique as a unit of analysis is that techniques are picked out for survival by a single criterion, profitability.[6] Profitability bears a one-to-one relation with the concept of fitness used by evolutionary biologists (Nelson and Winter (1982), pp. 234–45). The selection mechanism operates, of course, in quite a different manner, but it is not absurd to think of all the techniques in use as a gene pool, and to compare the process of selecting the techniques to Darwinian selection. The diffusion of techniques is thus akin to changes in gene frequency, governed by natural selection. Inefficient techniques lose ground, sometimes rapidly, sometimes slowly. The way the technique is used (phenotype) is in part determined by technical knowledge (genotype) but in part by other factors, some individual to this technique, some a function of the local environment.

The role of the firm here is thus somewhat different from the Alchian model and those that it inspired, where it is the unit of selection.[7] Nelson and Winter (1982, pp. 18, 134–6), whose work has inspired much of what

[5] The same idea of applying Darwinian selection mechanisms imposed on blind variation has recently been applied to the history of science, in which scientific progress is explained by Darwinian processes (Campbell [1960], (1987)). For an excellent introduction, see Hull (1988).

[6] Strictly speaking the selection criterion is that techniques will be picked according to their marginal contribution to the objective function of the firm. In this, at least, the idea of evolution is applied more readily to the history of technology than to other cultural processes, including scientific progress, in which the selection criteria are more involved, and may itself be changing over time.

[7] The choice of the unit of selection depends largely on what kind of question we are asking and the time scale of the events in question. Exactly the same holds for evolutionary genetics. See Crow (1986), p. 3. It is crucial to choose a unit that has hereditable traits, which makes firms in that regard unattractive.

is to follow, view the 'routine' as the critical unit of the evolutionary process and compare it to genes. This leaves open the question what in their model the analogue is to the individual organism, how we distinguish between phenotypical and genotypical change (a fundamental distinction in all evolutionary models), and what the unit is on which selection occurs. Nelson and Winter's 'routines' are a general concept, and are behavioral and not just technical in nature. In much of their work evolution occurs because the successful firms expand and the unsuccessful ones contract.[8] In the analogy proposed here, the technique is the species, not the gene, and each occurrence of this technique within a firm is a specimen of the species.[9] Genes are analogous to ideas, and each technique, like a chromosome, contains many ideas that may have had different origins but are now located together in a combination that serves a specific purpose. The workers and equipment employing the technique are the analogue of individual living creatures, and biological reproduction is isomorphic to training, in which information is passed along between generations. A firm using just a single technique such as a handloom weaver would be like a lone tree, a single member of a species called handloom weaving technology. As noted, firms choose techniques on the basis of expected profitability (or possibly additional criteria) and it is in the sense of being selected in this way that a technique survives.[10] The marginal contribution of a technique to the objective function of the selecting agent (the firm) is analogous to the idea of fitness in biology. Note, however, that there is no equivalent in biology to the notion of a 'selecting agent'. In the present analogy, the firm is more like a forest, in which many species coexist, compete with, and complement each other.[11] Techniques compete among themselves to be chosen. Traditional competition between firms plays a less direct role here, but a hierarchy of competitive processes can easily be envisaged like the hierarchies of selective processes. Thus, if a firm is like a site within which various techniques interact and compete, more successful firms would be like habitable sites, though habitability here presupposes an accepted criterion for success.

[8] The confusion is illustrated by the fact that Selten (1989, p. 13) attributes to Nelson and Winter the view that the firm is the unit on which selection occurs and thus 'cannot see a close analogy to biological and cultural evolution'. The model employed in ch. 10 of Nelson and Winter (1982) is different from the first models and in it firms have no important role to play.

[9] For a similar approach, see Selten (1989), p. 14 and Vega-Redondo (1989).

[10] All that this selection criterion implies is that if there are two techniques, α and β, with profit levels π, the π's determine the chances that the technique will be employed next period. That is, $\pi(\alpha) > \pi(\beta) \rightarrow p(\alpha) > p(\beta)$. Like fitness, it is a purely statistical concept.

[11] The role of the firm in an evolutionary framework has been the subject of much thought, but remains problematical. The most coherent attempt is in Metcalfe and Gibbons (1989), yet their definition of the function of the firm is 'an operator, translating individual knowledge into collective, shared knowledge' (p. 167) has no obvious evolutionary interpretation.

Does evolution guarantee some kind of optimality in the 'survival of the fittest' tradition? As Gould and Lewontin have argued, evolution is not exclusively guided by selection mechanism, and selection does not guarantee optimality. The concept of optimality has been used quite differently by economists and evolutionary biologists. The Pareto concept of optimality is quite different from the panglossian view implied by global fitness maximization. One can envisage a world of allocative efficiency in which the marginal conditions for Pareto optimality are satisfied, but in which, due to historical contingencies, many opportunities were missed and the economy has a much lower living standard than could have been enjoyed in other circumstances. What I am arguing is, essentially, that if one believes that evolutionary models are useful, one is of necessity steered away from the Pareto concept of static efficiency toward a more Schumpeterian notion of historical progress or dynamic efficiency. Evolutionary biologists think in terms of fitness 'peaks' which are essentially local optima. In an evolutionary process, it is apt to ask not only whether the economy is at a peak at all and whether that peak is as high as the peak across the valley, but also whether the landscape is shifting so quickly that the peaks are of sandy dunes rather than hills.[12]

There are many pitfalls in the comparison, and I discuss these at length elsewhere (Mokyr (1990a, b)). One of them stands out: in cultural evolution (of which technological change is an example), the evolutionary process occurs through learning and imitation (Boyd and Richerson (1985); Cavalli-Sforza and Feldman (1981)). In biological evolution this does not occur: acquired traits are not transmitted to future generations. The theory of cultural evolution is Lamarck's ultimate revenge. Biased transmission, as these Lamarckian processes are known, is most pronounced when the firm is defined as the analogue of the specimen, because then functional units change their genotype through learning.[13] It should also be stressed that new ideas and mutations are inherently different in that mutations are copying errors, while ideas are deliberate attempts to make a change. Hence mutations are far more likely to be harmful than beneficial.[14] The intentionality behind technological change implies that the probabilities of a change to be deleterious, neutral, or harmful are very different than in nature. Yet because natural selection is inherently a statistical process, the likelihood of progress depends not only on the fitness distribution function but also on the frequency with which

[12] I discuss these issues at some length in Mokyr (1991).

[13] If the *technique* itself is likened to the species and every person using it is a specimen, the problem of biased transmission may appear less serious. The technological idea is the equivalent of the genotype so that the genetic information that determines the features of the technique is set for life. If someone changes the idea, a mutation has occurred and thus the genotype is altered and possibly a new species is born.

[14] It is sometimes speculated that mutations may be biased toward viable changes, though the evidence on this point is still much in dispute. See Nelson (1990), p. 194; 'How Blind is the Watchmaker', *The Economist*, 24 September 1988.

mutations occur, the degree of variability in the environment and its hospitality to change. Technological and biological change depend on similar parameters, although these parameters have very different values.

The mechanisms of change are, of course, totally different. Although scarcity and competition create selection forces that appear similar, the actual mode of intergenerational transmission of information is quite different. There are no neat Mendelian laws of inheritance in technological change, and simple rules like the Hardy–Weinberg principle which governs the binomial distribution of gene frequencies do not apply in a system in which the transmission of traits is not bi-parental. I have been unable to find an equivalent in economics to dominant and recessive alleles in genetics. The analogy cannot be and should not be stretched. Genetics may be to evolutionary biology what economic theory is to technological progress, a mechanism of change. But it would be futile to search for every important concept in one theory for its mirror image in the other.

Now, why is all this useful? Biological analogies do not have a good name in the social sciences, and for good reason. For one thing, the use of biological metaphors in the social sciences has resulted in such constructs as Eugenics and Sociobiology, which are highly unpopular in many circles. Moreover, evolutionary biology has little predictive power. Genetics, unlike evolutionary theory, makes clear and strong predictions: mix gene *a* with gene *b*, and you will get a predictable outcome. But we have no way of predicting the shape and looks of future animals and plants. Almost any outcome is possible, and a theory that predicts everything predicts nothing. Technically speaking, however, economic history does not predict either, it tries to explain the past in some way, just as paleontology and evolutionary biology try to make sense of an existing record. The shape of future technology is no more predictable than the shape of future life forms.

As Schumpeter has anticipated, evolutionary models have become indispensable in understanding why some areas choose certain techniques and others do not, and shed light on the problem of technological creativity.[15] They suggest that creative processes should be tracked by differential equations and Markov processes, rather than by linear simultaneous equations (Allen (1988)). They cast an entirely new light on concepts such as diversity and convergence, emphasizing something that historians have maintained all along: diversity and pluralism are the taproot of creativity and progress; convergence and conformity are not. Biologists, accustomed to concepts like the gene pool and Ronald Fisher's Fundamental Equation will find such notions obvious.[16] Yet neoclassical equilibrium models do not easily yield this conclusion.

[15] As evidence, see the many references to evolutionary models in various forms in the wide-ranging collection edited by Giovanni Dosi (1988).

[16] Fisher's equation states that the rate of change of the frequency of a specie is a function of the difference between its fitness and the average fitness of the reference population. Disequilibrium models in economics can reproduce this result. See Nelson and Winter (1982, p. 243, n. 2) and Metcalfe and Gibbons (1989, pp. 180–2).

Allen (1988) has argued that the essence of biological models is that they are non-mechanical and do not exhibit the timelessness and reversibility of equilibrium models. In fact, they may not exhibit equilibrium properties at all. As such, they confirm the importance of history in the understanding of technology. Initial conditions and seemingly unimportant choices on the way may become crucial in determining the observed historical outcomes. Below, I will venture into three different aspects of the economic history of technological change: the idea of path-dependency, the concept of progress itself, and the dynamic properties of technological change.

II

The importance of path dependency in technological change appears to be straightforward, and has been stressed recently by Basalla (1988) who argues that every technique has a parentage, and the new ideas are always and everywhere *local* improvements on existing ones. This accounts for the 'branched' feature of technology. Just as existing species can be traced through time to their ancestors, the technological structure of an economy is determined by history. This insight is neither very novel nor profound, but it does help drive home the message that once we specify a mechanism by which the past locks an economy into a specific technology, history matters. Strange phenomena become more readily explicable. Paul David's well-known example is the QWERTY keyboard which, once designed, proved resistant to what seemed obvious improvements. Another example is the cultivation of potatoes in Ireland. When they were first introduced, they were a radical innovation, a powerful new technique to produce food that eventually drove out most competing techniques. Because subsequent productivity gains in potato cultivation were modest, the potato was less conducive to productivity growth than cereals. Yet it turned out too difficult to abandon the potato altogether, because the potato was part of the Irish crop rotation and thus involved strong production externalities in an interrelated production system. Moreover, the infrastructure converting cereals into bread (bakeries and mills) was missing. In this fashion, history explains the slow growth in Irish agriculture.

As Brian Arthur (1989) has recently emphasized, in a world of path-dependency what seemed like a good choice at one point may eventually turn out to be costly or disastrous. This certainly is the case with the potato, but other examples come to mind. The adoption of camels as the primary source of motive power in North Africa and the Middle East after 100 BC led to a slow disappearance of wheeled transportation from the area, with incalculable effects on transportation technology, roadbuilding technology, and city layouts in these regions (Bulliet (1975)). There is no way to predict in advance how likely a technique is to give birth to further improvements. In other words, path dependence occurs when choices are *myopic*, taking into account only differences in fitness at a particular juncture. This means that, just as in biology, some new ideas and new species become successful and dominate, while others, *seemingly* just as adaptive and fit, come to a dead end.

Path dependency indicates the role of accident and chance in forming our environment. Such bifurcations are now widely believed to be of great importance in the evolution of some dynamic systems.[17] The evolution of technological history, just like our biological past, is not one of necessity; things could well have gone differently. Among *ex ante* roughly equivalent outcomes there is an element of chance and luck. One reason for this role of historical contingency is that there are what Arthur has called economies of adoption, including not only economies of scale but also network and other externalities, the diffusion of consumer information, learning effects and so on. Another mechanism, of substantial historical importance, is that cultural and political mechanisms are used to defend the technical *status quo* even when a superior alternative becomes available. The more important these externalities, the more likely it is that an economy will find itself 'locked' into an inferior technology. In biology, too, luck and contingency have played important roles. As Stephen J. Gould tirelessly points out, it is only by chance that *homo sapiens* evolved from more primitive mammals. Neutral mutations with phenotypic expression can become fixed or extinct through genetic drift or catastrophes, that is, entirely by chance.[18] Mildly deleterious mutations can become dominant and fitter species may become extinct this way. Gould and Woodruff (1990) have demonstrated how 'happenstance' can account for what is known as 'area effects', in which phenotypes happen to be constant in contiguous areas.

All the same, it is important not to overemphasize the concept of path dependency in technological history. The past imposes its constraints on technological options when there are scale effects, externalities, or complementarities in production that make it costly — but rarely impossible — to switch. Chance only operates within boundaries. If a mutation reduces fitness substantially, the chances of the gene to survive for many generations decline quickly. It surely is not due to chance that we have no insects

[17] Especially emphasized in the work of Richard Day (1975, 1987, 1989) and Brian Arthur (1988, 1989).

[18] An example of such accidents is the so-called 'founder effect' proposed by J. C. Willis to explain the spatial pattern of plants. Willis argued that a rare plant, confined to a small area, is not usually an adaptation to a specific ecotype. Instead the area occupied is a function of the age of the species. In other words, the success of one species compared to another can be explained by the accidental fact of who got there first (Willis (1922), pp. 1–9, 204–21). Brian Arthur (1988) points out that in the presence of economies of adoption, such founder effects will convey selectional advantages to a technique that happened to be first on the scene.

as large as cows or thousand-feet tall trees. Similarly, most techniques that have become 'extinct' were in some well-defined way inferior to the techniques that replaced them. The number of examples in technological history in which it made a genuine difference is not as large as one might think. In general, the most important path dependencies occurred in the presence of network externalities or complementarities between human and physical capital (such as the QWERTY keyboard). The past imposes costs, but if the payoff is high enough relative to those costs, the shackles of the past can be shed.

Where path dependency matters perhaps most is in the interaction between natural selection and changing environments. Consider an environment A which is such that mutation α has a high fitness and 'becomes fixed', that is, becomes homozygous throughout the population. Now suppose that for some reason (possibly but not necessarily a result of α) the environment changes to B. Assume that in B α is deleterious. If α has become fixed, the mutation is irreversible and the species cannot go back to its former genotype. *Ex post*, the mutation has turned out to reduce fitness. In technological change such absolute changes are less likely. Cases of complete technological oblivion are rare because technological information — unlike genetic information — can be stored in information banks (books) and fossil species (museum pieces). Unlike DNA, technological information can be cumulative, because it does not need to be embodied in living specimens (that is, currently employed in production).

A second set of issues in which biologists can teach economic historians something concerns the question of progress. Progress does not have to mean necessarily 'improvement' since the latter imposes an arbitrary welfare criterion. But in the deeper sense that there is an irreversibility, a unidirectionality in secular change, one can hardly miss the similarity between the two.[19] Unlike other forms of cultural evolution, it seems reasonable that technological progress, with few exceptions, moves into one direction and not another. The French ethnographer André Leroi-Gourhan (1945, Vol. 2, p. 322) wrote that societies might adopt less flexible languages or more primitive religions, but they never go back from the plough to the hoe. If there are any reversals, he argued, they are due to the temporary disruptions of war; the natural path leads clearly from less efficient to more efficient. This is not universally true, as the technological history of China demonstrates. It is, nevertheless, the norm.

Evolutionary biologists have had their difficulties with the term 'progress'. John Maynard Smith (1988, p. 219) summarizes the current consensus when he writes that 'the concept of progress has a bad name in

[19] In a different context, Marshall ([1890], 1930, p. 769) pointed out that 'biology itself teaches us that vertebrate organisms are the most highly developed. The modern economic organism is vertebrate.'

evolutionary biology'. Francisco Ayala (1988, p. 95) adds that 'if the term "progress" were completely obliterated from scientific discourse, I would be quite pleased'. This may come as a surprise to those who learned in their biology classes that Ronald Fisher's fundamental theorem of natural selection predicts that there will be an increase in mean fitness in any population. Unfortunately, the assumptions on which Fisher's theorem is based are so strong as to give predictions only for local and short-range processes. In any event, even mean fitness is only one criterion to judge progress by. Biologists seem to have been unable to settle on a clear answer to whether evolution is progressive. Of course, in the *very* long run life has progressed from simple to complex. Day (1989) submits that 'the emergence of successively more complex forms gives evolutionary dynamics its special character'. Similarly, Laszlo (1987, p. 82) argues that biological evolution converges toward higher and higher levels of development and complexity. Maynard Smith (1988), however, who lists a series of progressive stages of organism complexity, warns (p. 221) that there is little empirical support for this concept of progress except in the trivial sense that the complex creatures of today are more complex than the creatures at the beginning of life since the first living things were necessarily simple. George G. Simpson (1967) admits that the criterion that views humans at the top of the evolutionary ladder is anthropocentric, but nonetheless insists on its validity.

Is there a similar debate in economic history? Without any question there is, although the argument denying the unidirectional character of technological change is far weaker here. Just as nobody can deny that today's multicellular creatures are inherently more complex than the replicating molecules and prokaryotic cells that started life, it is obvious that technology today is more complex than it was millennia ago. Measured by our ability to control and manipulate nature for our needs, technology has steadily increased. An alternative measure, proposed by DeGregori (1985, p. 5) defines technological progress as the solution of problems and their replacement by simpler and easier ones. Movements were not entirely monotonic or irreversible, but the unidirectionality of the trend toward greater productivity was there.

Yet was it an improvement? Pessimists abound. Some economists, in the school of E. J. Mishan's, argue that increased income *per capita* does not improve welfare. Others argue with Basalla (1988, p. 218) that there is no evidence of a causal connection between technological progress and 'an overall betterment' of the human race. Technological progress is 'betterment' only on the mundane level of daily comforts. It affects not human happiness or satisfaction, but variables that make up Amartya Sen's (1987) concept of living standards in terms of 'functionings': physical health, life expectancy, nutritional status. At times technology is ineffective or even counterproductive in changing these, but the variables can be quantified and hypotheses regarding changes in infant mortality, nutritional status, and morbidity can be tested.

One reason why the concept of progress in economic history has remained problematical is the absence of much conclusive evidence that centuries of technological progress did much for the standard of living in most of Europe before the mid-nineteenth century.[20] It is fair to state that it is widely believed that by 1750, say, most signs indicate that *per capita* income and living standards in most of Europe — Britain and the Low Countries excepted — were not much higher than in 1250 or for perhaps in the time of Julius Caesar. Despite a long and distinguished record in technological progress, invention and innovation seem to have left European living standards largely unaffected. Does this diminish the role of technological change as the main progressive force in history?

The premise itself can be called into question. As far as *per capita* income is concerned, we should recall that the impact of technological change on living standards is always and everywhere understated by our national income accounting systems. This is because when product innovation occurs, new or superior products appear whose advantages by construction cannot be captured by aggregate measures. Consider two examples, 600 years apart. In about 1285, some anonymous Italian invented spectacles. Now the impact of spectacles on GNP of the time, even if we could measure it, was probably negligible. Yet the importance of spectacles in enhancing the welfare of those who needed it for reading or handicraft was quite extraordinary. Six centuries later, in 1899, Felix Hoffman, a chemist with Bayer's, discovered the wondrous properties of the acetyl compound of salicylic acid, later known as aspirin. The improvement in economic welfare in terms of *incremental consumer surplus* resulting from these inventions must have been considerable; the measurable aggregative effects were small. In process innovation, in principle, this bias should not happen, provided we can construct individual quantity and price indices for different commodities and provided process innovation is purely cost-reducing and not quality-improving. Purely cost-reducing inventions are rare, however. The cotton industry during the Industrial Revolution and electrical lighting a century later are examples of both occurring simultaneously, and thus their welfare effects are understated.

The other response to the concern about the impact of technological change on living standards is, of course, the standard Malthusian response that increases in living standards were preempted by rising population. Whether this is an accurate description of the European experience is not completely clear. The Malthusian model, according to which technological

[20] Some scholars would maintain that this is still true today. Lasch (1989, p. 231) writes that the trouble with statements relating progress to the improvements of the quality of life is not one of the definition of 'a better life' but that the evidence on the matter is ambiguous. Economists such as DeGregori (1985, esp. ch. 13) would whole-heartedly disagree.

progress initially raises living standards but is then followed by population increase erasing the progress, still seems accepted in many circles, despite mounting evidence that the factors regulating population were more complex. From a purely evolutionary point of view, however, population growth is the measure of success of a species, with the species here being the human species, and not a production technique. What matters in the evolutionary game is reproductive success and survival. In 1936, the eminent anthropologist V. Gordon Childe wrote that 'judged by the biological standard . . . the Industrial Revolution was a huge success. It has facilitated the survival and multiplication of the species' (Childe [1936], (1965), pp. 13–14). What we, as economists, are interested in — economic welfare — has no direct place here except insofar as it bears upon fecundity and longevity. Moreover, in some cases technological change was directly associated with non-adaptive features such as fertility control and delayed marriage.

In short, technological progress's impact on living standards depended on the extent to which it was translated into higher consumption of goods, increased numbers, or reduced work effort. In all cases there is some sense in which we can call the changes progress, although an exact assessment, as in evolutionary progress, depends on the criterion adopted by the observer.

III

Perhaps the most useful analogy between evolutionary biology and the economic history of technological change concerns the dynamics of change. There are two different kinds of change in nature, phenotypic and genotypic. Phenotypic change is achieved through what is known as error regulation in anatomical and physiological mechanisms. Animals, for example, need stable body temperature. To regulate it, they change other aspects of their phenotype such as their fur, their bodily functions, or change their habitat. These do not change the genetic make-up of the animal. They are comparable to what we see in economics in terms of technical responses to demand or supply shocks. The movement along an isoquant is of this nature: inputs are varied to cope with changing factor prices. By definition, however, there is no change in the information set.

Phenotypic change contrasts with genotypic change. Species are not concrete units themselves, they are embodied — literally — in living specimens. The informational material contained in the DNA is copied from generation to generation. As the amount of information is immense, copying errors are inevitable. Nature preserves the stability of the species by eliminating mutant specimens in which the DNA contains an error. In the history of technology the analogue to this process is the training of youngsters in the techniques of the elders. Although we rarely shoot our graduate students for failing their econometrics, the process of elimination of deviants in most cultural systems is just as ruthless.

Yet despite nature's built-in mechanisms for constancy, evolutionary history is not constant. The mechanisms preserving genotypic constancy have failed, and their failure is responsible for our existence. Every once in a while a minute fraction of the copying errors is able to survive the natural selection process and if its gene pool can beat the odds, to add to or supplant existing species. Successful mutations are uncommon, to say the least, and mutations that lead to speciation are even rarer. The fossil record shows, in fact, periods of drawn-out equilibrium, known as stasis, which are the rule rather than the exception.[21] These equilibria are punctuated by short bursts of rather rapid creation of new species and changes in existing ones, a feature I shall return to momentarily. There is thus a tenuous equilibrium between the forces of stability and the forces for change.

The history of technology is similar in that it too reveals strong forces preserving the existing order, periodically interrupted by waves of new inventions. Most societies have been rather strict in their dealings with innovations and thus experienced technological stasis. There seems no obvious, one-line explanation why such periods occur in some economies whereas others become technologically creative. Evolutionary biology can suggest how to ask the right questions. The frequency of successful mutations depends on the intensity of mutagens in the environment, which determines the number of copying errors made, and on the friendliness of the environment to deviants, that is, the strength of the mechanisms trying to eliminate them. Similarly, the success of new techniques depends both on the level of inventive activity and the receptivity of the surrounding economy to new ideas. Any study of technological creativity and why and how it occurs has to start with that distinction.

A related issue on which the debates between biologists could be instructive to economic historians is the feedback between changes in a species and its environment. The environment for any given species tends to deteriorate, in part because competing species improve through natural selection, and in part because success eventually causes overcrowding. The changing environment, in this view, becomes a crucial factor in evolution, as previously neutral alleles may turn suddenly favorable. Stenseth (1985, p. 65) shows formally that depending on the value of certain parameters, a physically constant environment may continue to experience evolution forever or converge to stasis. Like the Red Queen in Alice in Wonderland, evolution at times has to run in order to stay at the same place. In economics, it might seem at first glance that technological evolu-

[21] There still is some question about whether such periods of stasis are in fact a correct inference of the fossil record. It is clear that the issue cannot be decided on *a priori* grounds (Maynard Smith (1988), p. 132).

tion could occur just as well in a stable environment because inter- and intra-firm competition of techniques favors the survival chances of the fitter (that is, more profitable) techniques.[22] The Red Queen hypothesis postulates that changes in one technique are treated by all others as parametric changes in the environment, and that such changes are regarded as positive stimuli toward further innovation. Without competition between techniques, indeed, Darwinian selection mechanisms in technical choice cannot work.

The Red Queen hypothesis has a deeper significance for technological history, because it explicitly refers to *inter*species interaction. A successful mutation in one species is generally regarded as a negative change in the environment for all other species who compete with it for resources. It is, however, a positive change for species that prey on it or live in symbiosis with it. In technological history it is just as likely that successful inventions in one technique turn out to be favorable environmental changes for another. This is not only because techniques can be complements (an invention increasing the productivity in spinning will benefit weavers) but also because useful new knowledge can travel across techniques — a mechanism that, of course, is absent in evolutionary biology. Moreover, it is possible that successful inventions in one industry could turn previously unsuccessful inventions in another industry into beneficial changes.[23]

Nevertheless, any dynamic theory based on Darwinian selection will have to explain the many long periods of technological stasis and observed sharp variations in the rate of successful mutations. Not all stable environments are equally conducive to technological change and many may have led to the technological equivalent of ESS, so that a 'ruling' technique could not be invaded, that is, replaced by a new technology.

An interesting insight from the analogy between biological evolution and technological progress can be attained from the arguments among biologists whether evolution proceeds smoothly or whether it can occur in leaps and bounds. Although the time scale of evolution naturally is very different from that of technological history, the question how 'evolutionary' evolution is has been heatedly debated by evolutionary biologists.[24] The same question keeps cropping up in economic history. Economic historians have long been arguing over whether technological change was sudden or gradual. Little did the gradualists, from Alfred Marshall ([1890], 1930) to S. C. Gilfillan (1935) to E. L. Jones (1988),

[22] Klein (1988) compares evolutionary progress, defined by him as 'the adaptation of species to new circumstances' to Schumpeter's idea of creative destruction. Yet there appears nothing in Schumpeter's views that demands changing circumstances. Instead, the *primum movens* is technological change itself.

[23] An example is the invention of the pneumatic tire by R. W. Thomson in 1845. These 'aerial' tires were invented, experimented with, patented, and then forgotten. In 1888 they were reinvented by Dunlop. In the intervening years the economic and technological environment had changed sufficiently to change the 'fitness' of this invention.

[24] See Dawkins (1987) and Stanley (1982) for a summary of the debate.

who all relied on biological metaphors to underline their gradualist position, realize that biologists could not agree whether evolution itself was necessarily gradual.[25]

To be sure, the neo-Darwinist synthesis which emerged after 1945 was firmly rooted in gradualism, as was, of course, Darwin himself. Population genetics was deeply influenced by Ronald Fisher's classic *The Genetical Theory of Natural Selection* which argued strictly that evolution proceeds typically by a succession of small incremental steps. Saltationists, those who believed that *natura facit saltum*, were regarded at best as eccentrics, at worst as crypto Creationists. But in the late 1970s, an attack on the conventional wisdom was launched that could not be ignored, because it came from people who had the evidence: the paleontologists. The role of paleontologists in evolutionary biology until then had been somewhat similar to that of economic historians in economics. As Maynard Smith recounts it, the paleontologist rash enough to offer an opinion on evolutionary theory was told by population geneticists to go away and find another fossil, and not bother the grownups. But Gould, Eldredge and Stanley, among others, piled up evidence showing that the gradual and continuous path of evolution was not consistent with the record.[26] This rude behavior caused great confusion in the placid camp of evolutionary biologists. To be sure, the concept of punctuated equilibrium is by no means a consensus opinion among evolutionary biologists.[27] By now, however, there is growing agreement that even if the new view of evolution may have overstated its claims, there may be something to it.

What, then, are the claims of Gould and his colleagues, and how could these possibly be relevant to economic history? The fossil evidence suggests that evolutionary progress occurred in a discontinuous fashion, with periods of long stagnation or 'stasis' punctuated by sudden bursts of rather abrupt change. Hence the concept of 'punctuated equilibria'. The image of long periods of stasis punctuated by bursts of fundamental change, as I noted above, is congenial to the pattern of technological change in the past two millennia. The hard truth is that most societies that ever were, were not technologically creative, and those that were, were so for relatively brief periods, a phenomenon I have called Cardwell's Law (Mokyr (1990b)). In the economic history of technological change, stasis has been the rule, not the exception. Nonetheless, despite what may or may

[25] The idea that evolutionary biology suggests that all inventions have close parentage and that there is nothing new under the sun, as argued emphatically by Basalla, seems to me either a tautology or incorrect. If what he is saying is that at any time $X_t = X_{t-1} + \varepsilon$, where X is some representation of the technology in use, he is stating the obvious. If the argument is, however, that historically ε has always been small so that technological progress is slow and gradual, his version of technological evolution is open to criticism.

[26] Introductions to the ideas and evidence associated with the punctuationist view of evolution can be found in Stanley (1981), Gould (1982a, b) and Eldredge (1985).

[27] The concept is also known as 'quantum evolution' or 'quantum speciation'. For a summary, see Stanley (1981) and a critique Stenseth (1985) or Dawkins (1986, ch. 9).

not have happened to GNP, from time to time a wave of radical inventions and discoveries stirred the usually placid water of production technology.

To buttress their views, the new punctuationists turned back to a geneticist active in the first half of the century by the name of Richard Goldschmidt. In a controversial and later neglected book (1940), Goldschmidt made a strong argument for a special view of evolution. He distinguished between macromutations and micromutations, a terminology which economists will find perhaps infelicitous. Successful macromutations in his view are rare and unusual, but when they do occur, they create a new species altogether which in some cases may survive. In Goldschmidt's words, macromutations created 'hopeful monsters', radical mutations with profound phenotypic consequences which under certain circumstances would indeed mean a new evolutionary departure. In order to make it in the brutal world of Darwinian selection, however, such a new species will have to undergo secondary alterations and fine tuning, allowing the descendants of the new species to fully adapt to their environment. Goldschmidt termed these further changes micromutations. The two processes should be thought of as complementary. Macromutations created new viable species, and micromutations perfected them.

The distinctions that Goldschmidt drew and the dynamics that he envisaged may be of use in the history of technology despite the distance in subject matter. What I am proposing is to distinguish between macroinventions creating a new technique and microinventions that refine and improve it. Macroinventions tend to be abrupt and discontinuous, microinventions usually satisfy the *natura non facit saltum* rule. Following a typical macroinvention, a large number of microinventions (some of them, of course, far from trivial) improved upon the new idea and made it workable. Indeed, the term 'hopeful monstrosity' seems an apt description of Gutenberg's first printing press or Newcomen's 1712 Dudley Castle machine.

One lesson that this foray into biology may suggest is that the debate whether radical and large inventions or small cumulative improvements are responsible for most gains in productivity is not enlightening. Without subsequent improvements, most if not all major inventions would have remained in the domain of curiosa. But without radical breakthroughs, with only gradual and local improvements and learning-by-doing effects, we would be riding today in perfectly designed horse-and-buggies, and lighting our houses with marvelously efficient oil lamps. The process of further refinement and improvement of existing techniques runs eventually into diminishing returns. A macroinvention increases the marginal productivity of the search for secondary improvements and debuggings.

A number of qualifications to anticipate some inevitable objections. First, macroinventions are abrupt, but they do not necessarily come in one blow. The steam engine, for instance, a macroinvention by any account, was not invented by any single person. In some cases, however, the crucial insight appeared instantaneously in more or less complete fashion. This must have been the case with the verge-and-foliot escapement mechanism, the hot air balloon, and the alternating-current induction motor. In other cases, the distinction is blurred because what appears to be a secondary invention could equally be classified as a major breakthrough itself: adding a pendulum to a mechanical clock or a separate condenser to an atmospheric engine is more than a marginal refinement.

This raises the next issue whether all new techniques require macro-inventions or whether they can also emerge by cumulative small inventions. The analogous question in evolutionary biology is whether new species can emerge by an accumulation of micromutations. Richard Goldschmidt argued that the answer was negative, whereas orthodox neo-Darwinism held that this is the *only* way in which new species emerge. A modern punctuationist would take an intermediate position that speciation can and did occur in both ways, though the relative importance of the two is still in dispute. In technological progress too, totally new techniques can arise by small, cumulative increments, although such gradual processes appear to be the exception, not the rule. The classic example is perhaps the sailing ship which was picked by Gilfillan as a case of slow and incremental change. Agriculture and mining, too, are characterized by relatively smooth and continuous processes of invention. Nonetheless, genuinely discontinuous changes did occur even here: it is hard to imagine a smooth transition from steering-oar to sternpost rudder, and no sequence of microinventions could ever have turned oats into potatoes.

Finally, if we define the technique itself as the unit of selection, and if a macroinvention is defined as the emergence of a new technique, it may be objected that there is no clear way to measure 'radicalness' and that therefore we have no clear-cut criterion to judge where an old technique ends and new one begins. In the absence of such a metric, the best approach is to use examples. Few will object to the statement that a self-actor is indeed different from a spinning wheel, that a Bessemer converter is a different 'species' from a Huntsman crucible, and that a Diesel engine is different from an Otto-type four stroke engine. When we make such distinctions, gray areas are inevitable, and perhaps here they are quite large. We should recall, however, Edmund Burke's statement that he could not draw an exact line between night and day but he sure could tell one from the other. It is of some consolation, perhaps, that a similar problem exists in biology. Although reproductive isolation is supposed to distinguish one species from another, different species often produce fertile hybrids, and matings of seemingly identical species prove to produce sterile or inviable hybrids (Maynard Smith (1988), p. 127).

It is a mistake to assume that *all* technological change is of one type or another.[28] The extreme positions of the old 'heroic' school of inventions,

[28] A recent example of such a view is Persson (1988).

and the reactions to it by scholars who claimed that all was gradual and smooth and that individual acts and insights never mattered, seem to me equally flawed. Complementarity between the two types of invention is fundamental to the paradigm I am proposing. All the same, the evidence suggests that in most cases, macroinventions were the *primum movens* that got the ball rolling.

The economic and social factors that affect the activities leading to macro- and microinventions are quite different. The history of micro-inventions is described by the standard literature of the economics of technological change whch relates inputs such as research and development to output such as patents or cost-reductions. Microinventions respond to incentives in a predictable if stochastic way, and are sensitive to factor prices, geographical constraints, labor relations and what not. This kind of technological change moves mostly by small incremental steps, but stays within the same technological paradigm. Bursts of macroinventions are attributable, however, to a totally different mechanism that is poorly understood.

This biological analogy is thus of some help in interpreting the Industrial Revolution and to respond to those who would like to abolish the term altogether. The Industrial Revolution can and should be interpreted as a 'burst of inventions', a 'wave of gadgets' if you wish, punctuating periods of stasis. Between 1760 and 1820 more radical inventions occurred in Western Europe than ever before in so short a period. Nothing like it had occurred before 1700. Indeed, one is hard-pressed to find many successful macroinventions at all in the sixteenth and seventeenth centuries. Nonetheless, the period between 1500 and 1700 was not really one of complete stasis. Microinventions kept increasing the efficiency of techniques that had evolved through earlier radical improvements such as the spinning wheel and the blast furnace. But by the beginning of the eighteenth century, these improvements were reaching a point close to exhaustion. What was needed were some hopeful monsters.[29]

The chances of generating such a monster whose hopes are fulfilled, in both evolutionary biology and the economic history of technology, depend on three factors. The first is the actual rate of mutation. Just as we know that certain environmental factors such as radiation and chemicals speed up the rate of mutation in a population, we can identify certain factors that will stimulate the emergence of original ideas. Second, bold ideas are never enough: Renaissance and Baroque Europe witnessed dozens of brilliant men of the Leonardo mold, whose 'monsters' saw their hopes dashed by hostile and reactionary environments or the inability of the workmanship and materials of the time to carry out their ideas. In evolutionary biology,

[29] For a more detailed analysis of the Industrial Revolution from this point of view, see Mokyr (1990a).

too, we can identify features of an environment that enhance the survival chances of hopeful monsters to create a new and successful species (Mayr (1970)).[30] Third, the success of a new technique is determined by the complementarity between macro- and microprocesses I mentioned above. Consider again the steam engine: after Guericke and Torricelli had demonstrated the existence of the atmosphere, the idea of using atmospheric pressure against a vacuum to convert thermal energy into kinetic energy seemed obvious enough. Christiaan Huygens, the great Dutch mathematician, proposed an internal combustion engine using gunpowder. His assistant, the Frenchman Denis Papin, in fact built a steam-engine prototype, and has as much claim to the title of inventor of the steam engine as anyone. But to actually build a machine that would work and work well, good engineers were needed in addition to genius, and these were to be found preponderantly in Britain. Mechanical aptitude and dexterity were as important in developing the Newcomen engine as the brilliant insight into the principle itself. A constant stream of microinventions associated with people such as Josiah Hornblower and John Smeaton improved the early steam engine and increased its efficiency. In the British environment after 1700, the correct combination of macro- and microinventions could emerge. In fact, Britain owed its success to a comparative advantage in *micro*inventions. Many of its macroinventions were imported from elsewhere, but as a Swiss observer remarked in 1766 with some exaggeration, for something to work it has to be invented in France and perfected in Britain (Wadsworth and Mann (1931), p. 413). In short, much as it sounds somehow far-fetched, the Industrial Revolution conforms to the dynamic models suggested by the punctuationists and their conceptual tools can contribute to its explanation.

The theory I have outlined is far from complete. I have said little about the causes of clustering in technological change, nor have I dealt in detail with the mechanisms that suppress inventions and lead to stasis. The theory does, however, what economic theory should do for economic historians, namely suggest what kind of facts may be worthwhile investigating and what kind of questions might be asked from the evidence. The odd thing is that there is an enormous amount of evidence: the five massive volumes of the Singer *A History of Technology* are no more than an appetizer. Yet with the exception of a few brilliant writers such as Lynn White and Paul David, little theoretical work exists to assist us in picking the raisins in that huge cake. Perhaps an analogy with evolutionary biology may be helpful in writing the economic history of technological change in

[30] Genetics suggests an analogy to inventions that cannot be built because they are 'premature'. Some mutations are recessive without any visible effects on the phenotype until the appropriate complementarity is encountered or until the environment changes. Dominant or recessive genes are not fixed in that status forever but can be changed by future mutations.

the context it deserves as the most fundamental force shaping the current economic world.

Department of Economics and History,
Northwestern University,
Evanston, IL 60201, USA

Invited paper,
final version received
December 1990

REFERENCES

Alchian, A. (1950). 'Uncertainty, Evolution, and Economic Theory', *Journal of Political Economy*, Vol. 58, pp. 211–21.

Allen, P. M. (1988). 'Evolution, Innovation and Economics', in Dosi, G. *et al.* (eds.), *Technical Change and Economic Theory*, pp. 95–119, London and New York, Pinter Publishers.

Arthur, W. B. (1988). 'Competing Technologies: An Overview', in Dosi, G. *et al.* (eds.), *Technical Change and Economic Theory*, pp. 590–607, London and New York, Pinter Publishers.

Arthur, W. B. (1989). 'Competing Technologies, Increasing Returns, and Lock-in by Historical Events', *Economic Journal*, Vol. 99 (March), pp. 116–31.

Ayala, F. J. (1988). 'Can "Progress" be Defined as a Biological Concept?', in Nitecki, M. (ed.), *Evolutionary Progress*, pp. 75–96, Chicago, University of Chicago Press.

Basalla, G. (1988). *The Evolution of Technology*, Cambridge, Cambridge University Press.

Batten, D., Casti, J. L. and Johansson, B. (1987). *Economic Evolution and Structural Adjustment*, Berlin, Springer Verlag.

Boulding, K. (1981). *Evolutionary Economics*, Beverly Hills, Sage Publications.

Boyd, R. and Richerson, P. J. (1985). *Culture and the Evolutionary Process*, Chicago, University of Chicago Press.

Bulliet, R. W. (1975). *The Camel and the Wheel*, Cambridge, Harvard University Press.

Campbell, D. T. [1960] (1987). 'Blind Variation and Selective Retention in Creative Thought as in Other Knowledge Processes', in Radnitzky, G. and Bartley, W. W. (eds.), *Evolutionary Epistemology, Rationality, and the Sociology of Knowledge*, Vol. III, pp. 91–114, La Salle, Ill., Open Court.

Cavalli-Sforza, C. C. and Feldman, M. W. (1981). *Cultural Transmission and Evolution: A Quantitative Approach*, Princeton, Princeton University Press.

Childe, V. G. [1936] (1965). *Man Makes Himself*, Fourth edition, London,Watts & Co.

Clark, N. and Juma, C. (1988). 'Evolutionary Theories in Economic Thought', in Dosi, G. *et al.* (eds.), *Technical Change and Economic Theory*, pp. 197–218, London and New York, Pinter Publishers.

Crow, J. F. (1986). *Basic Concepts in Population, Quantitative, and Evolutionary Genetics*, New York, W. H. Freeman.

David, P. A. (1985). 'Clio and the Economics of QWERTY', *American Economic Review*, Vol. 75 (May), pp. 332–7.

David, P. A. (1986). 'Understanding the Economics of QWERTY: The Necessity of History', in Parker, W. N. (ed.), *Economic History and the Modern Economist*, pp. 30–49, Oxford, Basil Blackwell.

David, P. A. (1988). 'Path Dependence: Putting the Past into the Future of Economics', Unpublished paper, Stanford University.

Dawkins, R. (1987). *The Blind Watchmaker*, New York, W. W. Norton.

Day, R. H. (1975). 'Adaptive Processes and Economic Theory', in Day, R. H. and Groves, T. (eds.), *Adaptive Economic Systems*, New York, Academic Press.

Day, R. H. (1987). 'The General Theory of Disequilibrium Economics and Economic Evolution', in Batten, D., Casti, J. L. and Johansson, B. (eds.), *Economic Evolution and Structural Adjustment*, Berlin, Springer Verlag.

Day, R. H. (1989). 'Dynamical Systems, Adaptation, and Economic Evolution', Unpublished manuscript, USC.

De Bresson, C. (1987). 'The Evolutionary Paradigm and the Economics of Technological Change', *Journal of Economic Issues*, Vol. 21 (June), pp. 751–61.

DeGregori, T. R. (1985). *A Theory of Technology*, Ames, Iowa, Iowa State University Press.

Eldredge, N. (1985). *Time Frames: The Rethinking of Darwinian Evolution and the Theory of Punctuated Equilibria*, New York, Simon and Schuster.

Gilfillan, S. C. (1935). *The Sociology of Invention*, Cambridge, MA, MIT Press.

Goldschmidt, R. (1940). *The Material Basis of Evolution*, New Haven, Yale University Press.

Gould, S. J. (1980a). 'Is a New and General Theory of Evolution Emerging?', *Paleobiology*, Vol. 6, No. 1, pp. 119–30.

Gould, S. J. (1980b). *Ever Since Darwin*, New York, Norton.

Gould, S. J. (1981). *The Mismeasurement of Man*, New York, Norton.

Gould, S. J. (1982a). 'Darwinism and the Expansion of Evolutionary Theory', *Science*, Vol. 216 (April), pp. 380–7.

Gould, S. J. (1982b). 'The Meaning of Punctuated Equilibrium and its Role in Validating a Hierarchical Approach to Macroevolution', in Milkman, R. (ed.), *Perspectives on Evolution*, pp. 83–104, Sunderland, MA, Sinauer Publishing Co.

Gould, S. J. and Lewontin, R. C. (1979). 'The Spandrels of San Marco and the Panglossian Paradigm: A Critique of the Adaptationist Programme', *Proceedings of the Royal Society of London*, Vol. 205, pp. 581–98.

Gould, S. J. and Woodruff, D. S. (1990). 'History as a Cause of Area Effects', *Biological Journal of the Linnean Society*, Vol. 40, pp. 67–98.

Hanusch, H. (ed.) (1988). *Evolutionary Economics*, Cambridge, Cambridge University Press.

Harris, M. (1977). *Cannibals and Kings: The Origins of our Cultures*, New York, Vintage Books.

Hirschleifer, J. (1985). 'The Expanding Domain of Economics', *American Economic Review*, Vol. 75, pp. 53–68.

Hodgson, G. M. (1990). 'Optimization and Evolution: Winter's Critique of Friedman Revisited', Unpublished Manuscript, Newcastle upon Tyne Polytechnic.

Hull, D. L. (1988a). 'A Mechanism and its Metaphysics: An Evolutionary Account of the Social and Conceptual Development of Science', *Biology and Philosophy*, Vol. 3, pp. 123–55.

Hull, D. L. (1988b). *Science as a Progress*, Chicago, University of Chicago Press.

Hull, D. L. (1988c). 'Progress in Ideas of Progress', in Nitecki, M. (ed.), *Evolutionary Progress*, pp. 27–48, Chicago, University of Chicago Press.

Jones, E. L. (1988). *Growth Recurring: Economic Change in World History*, Oxford, The Clarendon Press.

Klein, B. H. (1988). 'Luck, Necessity, and Dynamic Flexibility', in Hanusch, H. (ed.), pp. 95–127.

Lasch, C. (1989). 'The Idea of Progress in our Time', in Goldman, S. (ed.), *Science, Technology, and Social Progress*, Bethlehem, PA, Lehigh University Press.

Laszlo, E. (1987). *Evolution: The Grand Synthesis*, Boston, New Science Library.

Leroi-Gourhan, A. (1945). *Milieu et Techniques*, Paris, Albin Michel.

Lewontin, R. C. (1974). *The Genetic Basis of Evolutionary Change*, New York, Columbia University Press.

Marshall, A. [1890] (1930). *Principles of Economics*, London, Macmillan.

Marx, K. [1867] (1967). *Capital*, New York, International Publishers.

Maynard Smith, J. (1972). *On Evolution*, Edinburgh, Edinburgh University Press.

Maynard Smith, J. (1982). *Evolution and the Theory of Games*, Cambridge, Cambridge University Press.

Maynard Smith, J. (1988). *Did Darwin get it Right?*, New York, Chapman and Hall.

Mayr, E. (1970). *Population, Species, and Evolution*, Cambridge, MA, the Belknap Press.

Metcalfe, J. S. (1989). 'Evolution and Economic Change', in Silberstein, A. (ed.), *Technology and Economic Progress*, pp. 54–85, London, Macmillan.

Metcalfe, J. S. and Gibbons, M. (1989). 'Technology, Variety, and Organization', *Research on Technological Innovation, Management and Policy*, Vol. 4, pp. 153–93.

Mirowski, P. (1990). *More Heat than Light*, New York, Cambridge University Press.

Mokyr, J. (1990a). 'Was There a British Industrial Evolution?', in Mokyr J. (ed.), *The Vital One: Essays Presented to Jonathan R. T. Hughes*, Greenwich, CT, JAI Press.

Mokyr, J. (1990b). *The Lever of Riches: Technological Creativity and Economic Progress*, New York, Oxford University Press.

Mokyr, J. (1990c). 'Punctuated Equilibria and Technological Progress', *American Economic Review*, Vol. 80, No. 2 (May), pp. 350–4.

Mokyr, J. (1991). 'Is Economic Change Optimal?', *Australian Economic History Review*, forthcoming.

Nelson, R. R. (1987). *Understanding Technical Change as an Evolutionary Process*, Amsterdam, North Holland.

Nelson, R. R. (1990). 'Capitalism as an Engine of Progress', *Research Policy*, Vol. 19, pp. 193–214.

Nelson, R. R. and Winter, S. (1982). *An Evolutionary Theory of Economic Change*, Cambridge, The Belknap Press.

Persson, K. G. (1988). *Pre-Industrial Growth: Social Organization and Technological Progress in Europe*, Oxford, Basil Blackwell.

Ruse, M. (1986). *Taking Darwin Seriously*, Oxford, Basil Blackwell.

Ruse, M. (1988). 'Molecules to Men: Evolutionary Biology and Thoughts of Progress', in Nitecki, M. (ed.), *Evolutionary Progress*, pp. 97–126, Chicago, University of Chicago Press.

Selten, R. (1989). 'Evolution, Learning, and Economic Behavior', Nancy L. Schwartz Memorial Lecture, Northwestern University, J. L. Kellogg Graduate School of Management.

Sen, A. (1987). *The Standard of Living*, Cambridge, Cambridge University Press.

Silverberg, G. (1988). 'Modelling Economic Dynamics and Technical Change: Mathematical Approaches to Self-Organization and Evolution', in Dosi, G. *et al.* (eds.), *Technical Change and Economic Theory*, pp. 531–59, London and New York, Pinter Publishers.

Simpson, G. G. (1967). *The Meaning of Evolution*, 2nd revised edition, New Haven, Yale University Press.

Stanley, S. M. (1979). *Macroevolution: Pattern and Process*, San Francisco, W. H. Freeman.

Stanley, S. M. (1981). *The New Evolutionary Timetable*, New York, Basic Books.

Stenseth, N. C. (1985). 'Darwinian Evolution in Ecosystems: The Red Queen View', in Greenwood, P. J., Harvey, P. H. and Slatkin, M. (eds.), *Evolution: Essays in honour of John Maynard Smith*, Cambridge, Cambridge University Press.

Sugden, R. (1989). 'Spontaneous Order', *Journal of Economic Perspectives*, Vol. 3, No. 4 (Fall), pp. 85–97.

Vega-Redondo, F. (1989). 'An Evolutionary Model of Technological Progress', Unpublished Paper, Barcelona.

Wadsworth, A. P. and Mann, J. De L. (1931). *The Cotton Trade and Industrial Lancashire*, Manchester, Manchester University Press.

Willis, J. C. (1922). *Age and Area: A Study in Geographical Distribution and Origin of the Species*, Cambridge, Cambridge University Press.

Winter, S. G. (1964). 'Economic Natural Selection and the Theory of the Firm', *Yale Economic Essays*, Vol. 4, pp. 225–72.

Winter, S. G. (1971). 'Satisficing, Selection and the Innovating Remnant', *Quarterly Journal of Economics*, Vol. 85, pp. 237–61.

[27]

Ecological Modelling, 38 (1987) 107–121
Elsevier Science Publishers B.V., Amsterdam – Printed in The Netherlands

ECONOMICS AS MECHANICS AND THE DEMISE OF BIOLOGICAL DIVERSITY

RICHARD B. NORGAARD

Department of Agricultural and Resource Economics, 207 Giannini Hall, University of California, Berkeley, CA 94720 (U.S.A.)

ABSTRACT

Norgaard, R.B., 1987. Economics as mechanics and the demise of biological diversity. *Ecol. Modelling*, 38: 107–121.

Macro explanations of the loss of biological diversity have emphasized how higher population levels have forced the transformation of relatively undisturbed areas and how industrial pollutants and energy-intensive agriculture have put new, and relatively uniform, selective pressures on species. This paper explores how a third macro phenomena, social organization based on specialization and exchange, has contributed to the demise of biological diversity.

The world was a patchwork quilt of nearly independent regions until a century ago. Knowledge, technologies and supporting social structures evolved relatively independently within each of the patches of the quilt. With only regional exchange, a wide variety of crops were grown within each patch for subsistence. Hence, people applied diverse selective pressure on the biological system within and across the patches. This pattern, combined with low population levels such that people only applied selective pressure to a portion of each patch, meant that people had relatively little detrimental impact on biological diversity overall and in some cases even enhanced biological diversity.

During this past century the patchwork quilt has transformed into a global exchange economy supporting a fourfold increase in population. The global order is organized around a monolithic vision based on comparative advantage, specialization, and exchange. This understanding, common to both capitalist and socialist countries, has resulted in a reduction in the number of crops grown over broad regions. Yet since each region responds to the market signals generated by changes in all of the other regions, there has been more variation within each region with respect to which crops are grown in any given year. Specialization has reduced the diversity of selective pressure of agricultural practices on species, while increased annual variation within each region has selected against species with narrow niches.

The dominant vision of social organization stems from the Newtonian model of systems consisting of mechanically related atomistic parts. This view contrasts with our model of ecological systems consisting of tightly coevolved parts and relations. The maintenance of biological diversity will require moderation of the dominant vision and social organization more often designed around a coevolutionary world view.

Giannini Foundation No. 834.

0304-3800/87/$03.50

INTRODUCTION

The loss of biological diversity is generally attributed to two macro phenomena. Human population growth has increased the stress on biological systems overall and forced relatively undisturbed areas into the ranks of agricultural land. Resource extraction, industrial pollution, and agricultural technologies since the rise of Western science have increasingly disrupted natural systems. Population growth and technological change have worked together, each complementing the other. A third macro phenomena, the transformation of social organization, is frequently included in other descriptions of the process of modernization but is rarely mentioned in explanations of the loss of biological diversity. This essay explores how the rise of social organization based on specialization and exchange works with population growth and Western technology to reduce biological diversity.

This exploration is conceptual rather than specific. How we think we understand complex systems influences how we organize socially. Or, from a more cynical perspective, our models of systems help us rationalize the existing order and prevents us from making but marginal adjustments. Our current social order is rationalized by the Newtonian paradigm with its emphasis on static systems of mechanically related atomistic parts. This atomistic-mechanical view of a system, especially as it is reflected in our economic thinking (Georgescu-Roegen, 1971; Blaug, 1980), is inconsistent with the evolutionary view of a system which explains how species evolve and become extinct. And thus the demise of biological diversity is partly rooted in the conceptual incongruities between the Newtonian and Darwinian paradigms. The essay, as it pursues the implications of alternative sciences of systems, should be read as a "thought experiment" rather than as a scientific consensus backed by an accumulation of evidence.

DEVELOPMENT AND DIVERSITY BEFORE THE GLOBAL EXCHANGE ECONOMY

People have coexisted with other species for some three million years. While there is considerable evidence that people extinguished species in the past, earlier rates of extinction were far lower than current or projected rates. We have a pretty good idea of how the modern world works, but we tend to think of the past as simply less of what we have today. The world was traditional rather than modern, pre-industrial rather than industrial, and simply earlier on the road of progress. Surprisingly, neither neoclassical nor Marxist economic theory explains how the human population doubled eight times between the agricultural and industrial revolutions (Norgaard,

1984b). The following coevolutionary model of our past explains how we coexisted with other species more successfully in the past.

The world before the rise of the global exchange economy can be viewed as a mosaic of coevolving social and ecological systems. Within each area of the mosaic, species were selected for characteristics according to how well they fit the evolving values, knowledge, social organization, and technologies of the local peoples. At the same time, each of these components of the social system was also evolving under the selective pressure of how well it fit the evolving ecological system and the other social components. Local knowledge, embedded in myths and traditions, was correct for it had proven fit and become consistent with, through selective evolutionary pressure, the components of the social and ecological systems it explained (Norgaard, 1984a).

Within the coevolving world-mosaic the boundaries of each area were not distinct or fixed. Myths, values, social organization, technologies, species, and their genetic characteristics spilled over the boundaries of the areas of the mosaic within which they initially coevolved to become exotics in other areas. Some of these exotics proved fit as they arrived and thrived; some adapted; and some died out. But to some extent they all influenced the further coevolution of system characteristics in their new areas, resetting the dynamics of the system's change in area, composition, and structure. Spillovers were immensely important as a force of change. The possible combinations of spillovers and rooting of exotics into different parts was infinite. The plethora of combinations meant the pattern of coevolving species, myths, organization, and technology remained patchy, albeit a constantly changing patchy. This coevolutionary vision of our past combines the evolution of belief systems with biological systems and suggests how each has contributed to the diversity of the other.

A few tattered remnants of coevolutionary agricultural developments remain to give us clues to the past. Several agricultural scientists during the past decade have followed the path of anthropologists and discovered a wide array of traditional agroecosystems (Gliessman, et al., 1981; Altieri and Letourneau, 1982; Chacon and Gliessman, 1982). In nearly all of these, farmers deliberately intermix many crop and noncrop, and occasionally animal, species. These agroecosystems coevolved with the values, beliefs about nature, technologies, and social organization of indigenous peoples over centuries or millennia. Farmers selected for adequate and stable rates of food production through as much of the growing season as possible. A dependable food supply was achieved in part by planting many different crops in different places at different times and relying on the law of large numbers (Richards, 1985). Peasants evolved a portfolio theory well before modern professors of finance. But to a large extent the dependability of food supply resulted from the ecological stability achieved through high species diversity within each system [1].

The increased interest in agroecology coincides with an increased recognition of people as biological participants (Ellenberg, 1979). Whereas natural historians, on the basis of Western experience, have consistently portrayed man's influence to be destructive of natural systems, we are now beginning to learn how traditional peoples contributed to the growth and maintenance of genetic diversity (Brush, 1982; Alcorn, 1984; Altieri and Merrick, 1987). Traditional peoples created agroecosystems within which plants and microorganisms coevolved under different selective pressures than in environments which were only marginally disturbed by people. Technological uniformity was not imposed; farmers developed different approaches for different microenvironments, adding to variation in selective pressure (Richards, 1985).

A significant reservoir of biological diversity remains within existing traditional agricultural systems. But these systems and their diversity are disappearing fast. Agroecologists argue that conservation of genetic diversity is possible through the maintenance of traditional cultures and the transfer of some of their practices to modern agriculture (Alcorn, 1984; Altieri and Merrick, 1987). They also argue for the adoption of practices which favored diversity over millennia. Diversity, biological as well as cultural, is intimately linked to coevolutionary agricultural development. Diversity in coevolving agricultural systems is greater than in global exchange economies because coevolution is a local process, specific to local cultural knowledge, technology, and social organization. Biological diversity assures a broad genetic base for subsequent coevolution. Ayala and Valentine (1979, p. 94) argue: "the amount of genetic variation present in a population is about 5000 times greater than that acquired each generation by mutation." Systems without inherent diversity have little potential for continued coevolution for new traits evolve slowly.

Recent development has been distinctly different from the coevolving mosaic of the past. The mechanistic grid of universal truths developed by Western science has boldly overlayed and destroyed most of the coevolutionary mosaic. The global adoption of Western knowledge and technologies

[1] Mindful of the treacherous definitional currents of the diversity-stability debate in ecology (May, 1973; Goodman, 1975; Murdoch, 1975; Westman, 1978), I here use the term 'stability' to mean little variation in food output under varying environmental conditions as MacArthur (1955) used the term early on. Agroecologists (Risch et al., 1983) used the same definition in a summary of 150 studies covering 198 herbivore species and concluded that pest populations are less abundant, and hence a stable food supply more likely, in polycultures compared to monocultures in 62% of the cases and more abundant in only 11%.

has set disparate cultures on convergent paths. And the environment has not been immune to this globally unifying process. Environments are merging through common land management practices while biological diversity is narrowing because of the common selective pressure from the cropping, fertilization and pest control practices of modern agriculture. Global markets, global values, global social organization, and global technologies have resulted in global criteria for environmental fitness. Diversity of all kinds has been lost. The bold grid of Western science has simplified the elaborate coevolutionary mosaic.

GLOBAL EXCHANGE ECONOMY

The global exchange economy evolved over several centuries and began to characterize the global order during the past century. While exchange was underway well before economists began to theorize about the global system, economic understanding has since complemented and rationalized the development of the global exchange economy. The economic model now affects the design of policies which affect individual decisions which affect biological diversity. Development policies are heavily influenced by institutions such as the World Bank where there are 692 economists occupying positions with economics in the title and numerous other economists in other positions (World Bank, 1986) and only one biologist on the staff. How economists conceptualize social systems affects the maintainance of existing features and design of new components of the global order.

The concepts of comparative advantage, specialization, and the gains from exchange are central to the Western economic model. Comparative advantage stems from differences in the productivities of people, tools, and land in various economic activities. It immediately follows that total output can be increased through specialization of people, tools, and land in those activities for which they have a comparative advantage. Producers then exchange with each other until they have a mix of goods which makes each as happy as possible given the willingness of others to exchange. Comparative advantage, the efficiency of specialization, and the gains through exchange are basic to our understanding of economic systems and to our understanding of the development process. Capitalists and socialists disagree as to whether specialization and exchange should be optimized through the invisible hand of free markets or through the central direction of government planners. Nearly every country picks a mix of the two. But in whatever form or mix, we now think of economies as consisting of interconnected people rather than a mere collection of individuals because exchange is central to our understanding of economic systems.

This framing of social order has affected diversity in two ways. First, the encouragement of development through capturing the gains of exchange has encouraged specialization and a reduction in crop and supporting species in every region. Second, when exogenous factors change, comparative advantage and the pattern of specialization and exchange changes. Variation in aggregate economic welfare is reduced through increased variation in the activities of individual actors. This increased variation imposes stress on biological species that leads to extinction.

The gains from trade argument underlies many development policies and justifies many specific projects. Road construction, much of it financed by international lending agencies, has encouraged traditional farmers to switch to cash crop agriculture, specializing in only a few crops according to market prices rather than to criteria of sustainable environmental management. The gains from trade argument has also supported road and port development and free-trade policies which have encouraged third world farmers to respond to international agricultural markets.

Farmers, who once planted diverse crops for subsistence, connected into the global exchange system and began to specialize. Other subsistence farmers were simply bought out or moved out by larger commercial or centrally planned agricultural ventures. Since labor with specific skills as well as special tools can be purchased in the market and managerial skills can be learned, comparative advantage is effectively dictated by the physical environment. For this reason, physically homogeneous regions now specialize in but a few crops.

The reduction in the number of crop species grown results in an even larger reduction in the number of supporting species. The locally specific nitrogen-fixing bacteria, mycorrhizae that facilitate nutrient intake, predators of pests, pollinators and seed dispersers, and other species which coevolved over centuries to provide environmental services to traditional agroecosystems have gone extinct or had their genetic base dramatically narrowed. Deprived of the flora with which they coevolved, soil microbes disappear. Environmental services take time to coevolve with an agroecosystem. The best fitting nitrogen fixing bacteria, most effective predators of crop pests, and most complementary host plants for each of these are particular to the farmer's field and cannot be purchased with the seed of the cash crop. Specialization, exchange, and the consequent regional homogeneity of crop species has dramatically reduced biological diversity.

Participating in the global exchange, economy also transforms local agroecosystems because it forces farmers to produce as much as possible at low cost to stay competitive with other farmers who have been put in the same bind. This encourages the use of fertilizers, pesticides, and high-yielding seed varieties, which are productive in the short run. The use of common inputs in commercial agriculture eliminates much of the remaining regional differences. Soil is reduced to a medium for fertilizer. Pesticides reduce both good and bad weeds and insects. Not only are many species and genetic traits being lost which could prove important to the future of agriculture, but numerous relations affecting the productivity and control of ecosystems will never be known (Myers, 1979).

Global exchange induces areal constancy, thereby reducing biological diversity. Species go extinct in the global exchange economy for a second reason. The global exchange economy induces temporal variation for which species have not evolved coping strategies.

Crops fail due to bad weather, new technologies are developed, and tastes change. Perhaps more importantly, institutions change. Interest rates, lending and repayment policies, the strength of cartels, and trade barriers vary, sometimes dramatically. These changes redefine which people, as well as which tools and land, have a comparative advantage in particular productive activities. This redefinition is accommodated, at least in theory,through people, tools, and land shifting their specialization to different lines of production and redefining the pattern of exchange. Economists assume that factors of production are mobile, that labor, capital, and land can shift between lines of production, that labor and capital can move to new locations, and that each adjusts in a way that optimizes for the good of all.

Economists envision economies as mechanical systems that can freely shift along a continuum of stable equilibria. When rice production is down in Brazil because of poor rains, the price of rice rises inducing farmers around the world to bring more land into rice production and to farm existing land more intensively. Workers, tools, and land shift from the production of other crops to the production of rice. Higher wages and land rents for rice production induce the shift. When Brazilian rice production returns to normal, the rest of the world returns to its old equilibrium.

These adjustments to exogenous change, other things being equal, maximize economic well-being as economists define it. With all producers adjusting to best compensate for the failure in the rice crop in Brazil, the impact of the failure is minimized. The adjustments keep aggregate well-being as close to the undisturbed maximum as possible and hence more stable than it would be if the adjustments did not take place. But this stabilizing process for the whole increases the amount of change at the individual level in terms of who does what and with which tools and land. Variation in aggregate economic welfare is reduced through increased variability at the level of the activities of the individual components in the economic system.

The economic model is used for purposes of designing exchange policies with the implicit assumption that land can move between uses much like people and tools. Land, however, is a little more complex than a tractor.

Economists have given little thought to the environmental services which help give land its value and have implicitly assumed they are mobile. The problem, put simply, is that environmental services cannot freely shift from the support of rice, to the support of cotton, to suburban lawns, to concrete, to alfalfa, to marsh habitat for waterfowl, and back to rice the same as a reasonably adaptive person might shift from being a farmer, to a urban gardener, to a game warden, and back to being a farmer.

There are many similarities between economic and ecological models (Rapport and Turner, 1977). Economic models have people with different capabilities filling different niches much like different species fill different niches. But the two models differ dramatically with respect to how the systems are presumed to, and do, adjust to exogenous change. The differences help explain why the use of the neoclassical economic model has led to extinction.

Biological species evolve to fill their niches, outcompeting other species for various aspects of the niche. During the last few decades biologists have put more emphasis on how ecological relations between species affect evolution, how species coevolve (Ehrlich and Raven, 1964; Baker and Hurd, 1968). The shift from thinking of each species evolving in response to a changing physical environment to thinking of species coevolving together has led to a new understanding of evolutionary dynamics (Lewin, 1986). The new emphasis also stresses how the coevolutionary process defines the niches themselves. Ecologists do not assume that predefined species sort themselves into predefined niches according to their comparative advantages, optimizing for what is 'best for all', given the exogenous influences at the time.

Under different circumstances biological species do alter their behavior. Predators of multiple prey will shift to whichever happens to be the most available at the time, disproportionately predating the most available. When food is scarce, less vocal chicks are left to starve. Although a fit coping strategy must assure the survival of the species' prey, ecologists do not explain the shift in the behavior of individual species in terms of a simultaneous optimization of what is 'best for all'. These strategies for coping with change evolved. Fit strategies assured survival; unfit strategies led to extinction (Ricklefs, 1976).

May's (1973) mathematical models of ecological systems led him to an evolutionary explanation of the correlation between complexity and stability [2]. Biological diversity is greater in the tropics than in the arctic because

[2] Natural historians, conservationists, and practitioners of public land management have long presumed that more diverse ecological systems are more stable. During the 1950s and early 1960s, ecologists assembled empirical evidence and conceptual arguments in support of

the climatic constancy facilitated the evolution of greater niche specialization. This conjecture matches theory with evidence very nicely and has considerable appeal. Climates with little variation lead to the evolution of highly specialized species dependent on particular conditions. Conversely, increased variation in an ecosystem with many tightly interconnected species which had evolved under environmental constancy would lead to extinction. A small change from the conditions around which species coevolved in a tropical rainforest ecosystem is more likely to lead to extinction than a change of comparable magnitude in an arctic tundra system, but in both cases increased variation favors fewer, less tightly connected species. This explains why the tropical rainforests with their immense diversity of species and complex relations between them have proven so vulnerable to changes wrought by modern technologies.

No doubt, some species are evolving strategies to cope with the changing agricultural conditions dictated by the exchange economy. Some of the loss in diversity, however, is attributable to the increase in environmental variation with the transition from the slowly changing practices based on traditional subsistence needs to the rapidly changing practices dictated by the global exchange economy.

There would not be a problem if the species that supply the environmental services appropriate to particular crops could coevolve to fill their supporting niches as fast as the global exchange economy leads farmers to shift crops. In this sense, the mismatch between economic and ecological models can be reduced to differences in the speed of their adjustment. Within economics, concern over the factor mobility assumption is frequently stated in terms of rates of adjustment. Doctors can switch from treating a flu epidemic in March to advising on hay fever in April. The auto industry, however, cannot shift from the production of low-fuel to high-fuel efficiency cars and back again as fast as the Organization of Petroleum Exporting Countries coalesced and raised the price of oil and collapsed and let it fall. The oil price perturbation and difference in adjustment rates have resulted in the extinction of many small firms that supported the auto industry. Dramatic fluctuations in farm prices have had the same impact on agricult-

---

this conventional wisdom (Odum, 1953; MacArthur, 1955; Elton, 1958; Hutchinson, 1959; and Pimentel, 1961). Robert May (1973) explored many of these explanations using mathematical models of ecosystems and found the explanations unlikely to be true. Relatively simple mathematics induced a flurry of rethinking about ecological systems (Goodman, 1975; Murdoch, 1975; Westman, 1978) that continues still (Pimm, 1984). Subsequent ecology texts and traning have hedged on the matter of diversity and stability, uneasily balancing myth, mathematical models, specific ecological feedbacks, and empirical evidence.

ural firms. In a sense, this paper simply extends the argument to supporting biological species.

The difference between how economic and ecological models are presumed to respond to change stems from different degrees of mechanical and evolutionary thinking in the two disciplines. The economy is modeled as if it had predefined atomistic parts which mechanically adjust through market signals or central planning to optimize the performance of the system as a whole. There is not a comparable formal model in ecology. Species and their interrelations in ecological systems coevolve in response to the particular conditions of the place and time. For this reason, ecologists are more hesitant to generalize than economists.

Nevertheless, ecologists have not been blind to the beauty of calculus. Optimization models have been constructed to explore various hypotheses (Smith, 1978; Pielou, 1981). Do species forage in patterns which minimize risk or maximize net energy gained? Do species reproduce to maximize offspring over their lifetime? But ecologists use mathematics to explore ideas, to better understand how things might work in nature. They have given up on the idea that nature is in fact optimizing. And ecologists are forever warning themselves against the dangers of mathematics (Smith, 1978; Oster and Wilson, 1978). The bottom line is always that evolution is a tinkerer, not an engineer (Jacob, 1977).

Nor have economists been immune to the seductiveness of evolutionary thinking. They recognize that the skills of workers, the knowledge that leads to technology, and the tools themselves evolve over time in complex ways. Evolution is implicit in their written explanations of development. Several economists have tried to explicitly reframe economic issues around evolutionary principles Haavelmo, 1954; Boulding, 1978, 1981; Nelson and Winter, 1982). But the formal models of economics remain mechanical even while some of the most effective economic rhetoric is evolutionary (McCloskey, 1985).

In economics there is a consensus on a clearly defined model which, being basically mechanical, is mathematically tractable. Economists modify the basic mode, when feeling creative or pushed, with evolutionary thinking, losing tractability and predictive and prescriptive power in the process. In ecology there is a consensus that the characteristics and behavior of species and relationships between them evolved, but there is not a clearly defined, let alone tractable, model of the resulting system. Ecologists use mechanical models as a tactical tool for exploring the implications of possible sets of relations, but eschew the idea that these experimental aids can be used for prediction or prescription in policy arenas.

The emphasis on exchange and tractability in economics is underscored by the paucity of explanations for non-market forms of economic organization. Unions, industry associations, professional licensing, and government services in general are explained with respect to whether they facilitate or restrain exchange. The firm, let alone the modern multinational corporation, is a black box wherein profit maximizing exchange decisions are made.

The tractable, formal models of economics, however poor the predictions and prescriptions in retrospect, dominate development policy and generate the arguments for exchange. But linking into global exchange forces all participants in the economy to respond to each other. The difficulties of adjusting imposed upon capitalists, entrepreneurs, and laborers are not a part of the tractable model. But the hardships are very well acknowledged informally and in practice. Every reasonably developed economy has additional mechanisms such as unemployment insurance, the expensing of moving costs, and capital loss write offs to cushion and reduce the hardships of adjustment.

Our informal acknowledgement of the hardship, however, has not been extended to biological species. By basing the design of development institutions only on the insights gleaned from the economic model and the obvious difficulties this creates for people, we have ignored the links with our understanding of ecology characterized by our ecological models. As a minimal remedial measure, we should protect biological species from the hardships of adjustment to the exchange economy much like we protect people.

CONCLUSIONS

Species extinction is occurring at the most rapid rate since the hypothesized meeting with the asteroid that raised the dust that terminated the dinosaurs (Alvarez et al., 1980; Ehrlich and Ehrlich, 1981; Lewin, 1983). We also seem to have reached a turning point after an intense century during which our technology, economic system, and political organization have been molded around the Newtonian paradigm (Capra, 1982; Merchant, 1983; Berman, 1981). The coincidence of the rise of the atomistic-mechanistic model and the rapid decline in species diversity is not mere chance. All agree that to some extent the technology, economic decisions, and social organization stemming from this model will have to change to sustain species diversity.

The coincidence, however, has not encouraged a creative response from a broader base of understanding. Economists have simply argued that species die out because no one can own and manage species over the long run without others enjoying the gains, hence all exploit them for immediate profit. Species are driven to extinction because both economically rational entrepreneurs and responsible public officials divest the species and invest where earnings are higher. Lastly, extinction is forever, but economic decisions are necessarily made over specific time horizons with incomplete knowledge of the future. The 'trouble' with extinction is that it is irreversible (Miller, 1978; Simon and Wildavsky, 1984; Brown, 1985; Norgaard, 1985, 1987; Fisher and Hanemann, 1986).

Nor has the coincidence between the rise of Western science and extinction led biologists to question their stance. While biologists increasingly acknowledge the role of people in the evolutionary process, their policy prescriptions reflect only the negative influence on a 'natural' world apart from people. Biologists stress how people reduce species diversity and advocate the preservation of diversity in undisturbed areas, zoos, seed banks, and liquified nitrogen. Their alarms and prescriptions may ring hollow because their epistomological stance still does not fully acknowledge the role of people in the evolutionary process.

People and the economic decisions they make are an integral part of the ecological system. To think of them separately is one of the unfortunate consequences of the idea of objective knowledge, the idea that knowledge of nature can be independent of the use of knowledge and nature by people as individuals and members of cultures. The diversity of the ecological system is intimately linked to the diversity of economic decisions people make. There was considerable economic diversity in the past due to cultural diversity. How people interact with ecological systems today is heavily influenced by the monotonous signals of the global exchange system built around the economic model. Biological diversity has declined with economic diversity.

The economic model has imposed additional species loss through increased intertemporal instability. More biological speciation and niche specialization is possible in a stable system. But comparative advantage, specialization, and trade lead all to adjust to each other so that an economic event in Japan induces a temporary response in Kenya. Thus further extinction occurs through temporal instability.

Regions cannot develop through coevolutionary processes if they are, on the one hand, planting vast monocultures, on the other, adjusting cropping yearly to accommodate the fluctuations of international prices. Local biological and social systems, the culture of agriculture, are destroyed when international markets dictate that corn should be planted throughout the region one year, wheat the next, and soybeans the third. Species conservation and the continued coevolution of cultural knowledge, local technologies, and unique forms of social organization need more areal diversity and temporal stability than the global exchange economy provides.

The process of species extinction is seen in the incongruencies between our economic and ecological models of reality. A comparison of the two models from a coevolutionary vantage indicates that the economic argument of specialization, comparative advantage, and the gains from trade has been oversold. Our ecological model is nebulous, but it posits numerous and complex relations between species. Our economic model is well specified and barren, positing only exchange relations.

Species loss occurs because of a mismatch between technologies and environmental systems. This mismatch is typically attributed to the stupidity of planners, the greed of capitalists, the desperation of peasants, and the disciplinary blinders of the scientists who developed the technologies and described our environments for us in the first place. Not denying any of these, this paper shows how the mismatch and the roles of each of the major actors can be traced to discrepancies in how we think about systems, to the fact that we emphasize atomistic–mechanical relations in the design of social order while more fully acknowledging the evolutionary basis of ecological systems.

ACKNOWLEDGEMENTS

Craig Allen, Stephen Brush, Andrew Cohen, George Ledec, Philippe Martin, Robert May, Laurel Prevetti, Michael Soule and two anonymous reviewers caught the drift of the original draft and helped me channel the arguments into a steady flow. Conflicts in their suggestions have made it impossible to respond fully to all of their comments.

REFERENCES

Alcorn, J.B., 1984. Development policy, forests, and peasant farms: reflections on Huastec-managed forests' contributions to commercial production and resource conservation. Econ. Bot., 38: 389–406.

Altieri, M.A. and Letourneau, D.K., 1982. Vegetation management and biological control in agroecosystems. Crop Prot., 1: 405–430.

Altieri, M.A. and Merrick, L.C., 1987. In situ conservation of crop genetic resources through maintenance of traditional farming systems. Econ. Bot., 41: 86–96.

Alvarez, L., Alvarez, W.W., Asaro, F. and Michel, H.V., 1980. Extraterrestrial cause for the cretacious-tertiary extinction. Science, 208: 1095–1108.

Ayala, F.J. and Valentine, J.W., 1979. Evolving: The Theory and Processes of Organic Evolution. Benjamin/Cummings, Menlo Park, CA, 452 pp.

Baker, H.G. and Hurd, P.D., 1968. Intrafloral ecology. Annu. Rev. Entomol., 13: 385–414.

Berman, M., 1981. The Reenchantment of the World. Cornell University Press, Ithaca, NY. Republished by Bantam, New York, 1984, 366 pp.

Blaug, M., 1980. The methodology of economics: or how economists explain. Cambridge University Press, Cambridge, 296 pp.

Boulding, K.E., 1978. Ecodynamics: A New Theory of Societal Evolution. Sage, Beverly Hills, CA, 367 pp.

Boulding, K.E., 1981. Evolutionary Economics. Sage, Beverly Hills, CA, 200 pp.

Brown, G., Jr., 1985. Valuation of genetic resources. Paper prepared for the Workshop on Conservation of Genetic Resources, 12–16 June, Lake Wilderness, Washington.

Brush, S.B., 1982. The natural and human environment of the Central Andes. Mt. Res. Dev., 2: 14–38.

Capra, F., 1982. The Turning Point: Science, Society, and the Rising Culture. Simon and Schuster, New York, 464 pp.

Chacon, J.C. and Gliessman, S.R., 1982. Use of the 'non-weed' concept in traditional agroecosystems of south-eastern Mexico. Agroecosystems, 8: 1–11.

Ehrlich, P.R. and Ehrlich, A.H., 1981. Extinction: The Causes and Consequences of the Disappearance of Species. Random House, New York.

Ehrlich, P.R. and Raven, P.H., 1964. Butterflies and plants, a study of coevolution. Evolution, 18: 586–608.

Ellenberg, H., 1979. Man's influence on tropical mountain ecosystems in South America. J. Ecol., 67: 401–416.

Elton, C.S., 1958. The Ecology of Invasions by Animals and Plants. Methuen, London.

Fisher, A.C. and Hanemann, W.M., 1986. Option value and the extinction of species. In: K. Smith (Editor), Advances in Applied Microeconomics. JAI Press, Greenwich, CT.

Georgescu-Roegen, N., 1971. The Entropy Law and the Economic Process. Harvard University Press, Cambridge, MA, 457 pp.

Gliessman, S.R., Garcia, E.R. and Amador, A.M., 1981. The ecological basis for the application of traditional agricultural technology in the management of tropical agroecosystems. Agroecosystems, 7: 173–185.

Goodman, D., 1975. The theory of diversity–stability relationships in ecology. Q. Rev. Biol., 50: 237–266.

Haavelmo, T., 1954. A Study in the Theory of Economic Evolution. North-Holland, Amsterdam.

Hutchinson, G.E., 1959. Homage to Santa Rosalia, or why are there so many kinds of animals? Am. Nat., 93: 145–159.

Jacob, F., 1977. Evolution and tinkering. Science, 196: 1161–166.

Lewin, R., 1983. Extinctions and the history of life. Science, 221: 935–937.

Lewin, R., 1986. Punctuated equilibrium is now old hat. Science, 231: 672–673.

MacArthur, R.H., 1955. Fluctuations of animal populations, and a measure of community stability. Ecology, 36: 533–536.

May, R.M., 1973. Stability and Complexity of Model Ecosystems. Princeton University Press, Princeton, NJ, 235 pp.

McCloskey, D.M., 1985. The rhetoric of economics. University of Wisconsin, Madison, WI, 209 pp.

Merchant, C., 1983. The Death of Nature: Women, Ecolocy, and the Scientific Revolution. Harper and Row, San Francisco, CA, 348 pp.

Miller, J., 1978. A simple economic model of endangered species protection in the United States. J. Environ. Econ. Manage., 8: 292–300.

Murdoch, W.W., 1975. Diversity, complexity, stability, and pest control. J. Appl. Ecol., 12: 795–807.

Myers, N., 1979. The Sinking Ark. Pergamon Press, Oxford.

Myers, N., 1984. The Primary Source: Tropical Forests and Our Future. Norton, New York, 399 pp.

Nelson, R.R. and Winter, S.G., 1982. An Evolutionary Theory of Economic Change. Harvard University Press, Cambridge, MA, 437 pp.

Norgaard, R.B., 1984a. Coevolutionary agricultural development. Econ. Dev. Cult. Change, 32: 525–546.

Norgaard, R.B., 1984b. Coevolutionary development potential. Land Econ., 60: 160–173.

Norgaard, R.B., 1985. Environmental economics: an evolutionary critique and a plea for pluralism. J. Environ. Econ. Manage., 12: 382–393.

Norgaard, R.B., 1987. The economics of biological diversity: apologetics or theory. In: D.R. Southgate and J. Disinger (Editors), Sustainable Development of Natural Resources in the Third World, 3. Westview Press, Boulder, CO.

Odum, E.P., 1953. Fundamentals of Ecology. Saunders, Philadelphia, PA, 574 pp.

Oster, G. and Wilson, E.O. (Editors), 1978. A critique of optimization theory. In: Caste and Ecology in the Social Insects, 8. Princeton University Press, Princeton, NJ. Reprinted as Chapter 16 in: E. Sober (Editor), Conceptual Issues in Evolutionary Biology: An Anthology. Massachusetts Institute of Technology, Cambridge, MA, 1984, pp. 271–288.

Pielou, E.C., 1981. The usefulness of ecological models: a stock-taking. Q. Rev. Biol., 56: 17–31.

Pimentel, D., 1961. Species diversity and insect population outbreaks. Ann. Entomol. Soc. Am., 54: 76–86.

Pimm, S.L., 1984. The complexity and stability of ecosystems. Nature, 307: 321–326.

Rapport, D.J. and Turner, J.E., 1977. Economic models and ecology. Science, 195: 367–373.

Richards, P., 1985. Indigenous Agricultural Revolution: Ecology and Food Production in West Africa. Hutchinson, London/Westview Press, Boulder, CO, 192 pp.

Ricklefs, R.E., 1976. The Economy of Nature. Chiron, Portland, OR, 455 pp.

Risch, S.J., Andow, D. and Altieri, M.A., 1983. Agroecosystem diversity and pest control: data, tentative conclusions, and new research directions. Environ. Entomol., 12: 625–629.

Simon, J.L. and Wildavsky, A., 1984. On species loss, the absence of data, and risks to humanity. In: J.L. Simon and H. Kahn (Editors), The Resourceful Earth: A Response to Global 2000. Blackwell, Oxford, pp. 171–183.

Smith, J.M., 1978. Optimization theory in evolution. Annu. Rev. Ecol. Syst., 9: 31–56. Reprinted as Chapter 17 in: E. Sober (Editor), Conceptual Issues in Evolutionary Biology: An Anthology. Massachusetts Institute of Technology, Cambridge, MA, 1984, pp. 289–315.

Westman, W.E., 1978. Measuring the inertia and resilience of ecosystems. Bioscience, 28: 705–710.

World Bank, 1986. Thomas A. Blinkhorn, Chief, Public Affairs Division, personal communication, 30 April 1986.

[28]

Methodus December 1992

Economics and Biology: Eight Areas of Research

*Elias L. Khalil**
Ohio State University, Mansfield

I try to organize the contemporary economic literature which relates in one form or another to biology. While I do not attempt to cover all of the literature, I do try to delineate all the possible areas of research. I identify eight separate problem areas: First, does the appeal to a universal scientific methodology necessarily involve reductionist reasoning? Second, can biology shed light on the limitations of the model of rational self-interested man? Third, can biology teach us about the origin of principles and rules which underpin ordered economic organizations? Fourth, can ecology provide tools for the analysis of self-feeding mechanisms which engender spontaneously ordered structures? Five, is there a similarity between human and non-human production activities? Sixth, does economic organization age like lower-level, biological organization? Seventh, is the mechanism *and* unit of human socio-cultural-technological evolution similar to non-human evolution? Eighth, can we map the theory of biological evolution onto scientific evolution?

Once biology is mentioned among economists, it is customary — at least in Anglo-Saxon circles — to pay homage to Alfred Marshall:

> "The main concern of economics is ... with human beings who are impelled, for good and evil, to change and progress. Fragmentary statistical hypotheses are used as temporary auxiliaries to dynamical — or rather biological — conceptions: but the central idea of economics, even when its Foundations alone are under discussion, must be that of living force and movement" [Alfred Marshall, 1920, p. xiii].

However, a whole string of German economists — stretching from Friedrich List to Adam Müller — have employed the biological metaphor more extensively than Marshall. As recent scholarship indicates [Moss, 1982], Marshall referred to evolutionary biology only to buttress his victorian, anti-revolutionary belief that change occurs mostly gradually — as opposed to radically. Furthermore, Marshall made little use of biology [Thomas, 1991; cf. Niman, 1991]. This is probably the case because, as he admits, "biological conceptions are more complex than those of mechanics" [Marshall, 1920, p. xii; cf. Marshall, 1966].

Economists started earnestly in the 1950's to appeal to biological conceptions [e.g., Alchian, 1950; Friedman, 1953, pp. 16-23; Houthakher, 1956].[1] Although the different appeals were insightful, they were soon shown to involve great difficulties [see Penrose, 1952]. One lesson could be drawn from the experience: In order for the progeny of the intercourse between the two disciplines to be fruitful, one has to carefully specify which biological conceptions are pertinent to what economic questions. Otherwise, the intercourse would be a fleetingly exciting summer encounter.

The task ahead is to identify the diverse economic questions and delineate the separate possible links between the two disciplines. Such a task would be worthless if one believes that the invocation of biology should be restricted to superficial metaphors. There is no room in this survey for superficial metaphors.

To clarify, there are four general types of metaphors separated by fuzzy boundaries. Given such boundaries, one can devise more types in order to attain greater rigor and detail. However, one would lose simplicity. Given such diversity, some critical thinkers — like Michel Foucault, Mary Douglas, and lately Philip Mirowski — went as far as disparaging, in general, the attempt to classify metaphors. They considered it another culturally instigated impulse to bring order, which is supposedly non-consciously imaged after social order, to what is objectively orderless nature. That is, they regarded the attempt of classification a quixotic reconstruction of nature after socially negotiated categories. Nonetheless, the mind cannot rest without clarity. Even the minds of such deconstructionists assume, at a higher type of reasoning, an understanding of what is nature — as many of their critics have pointed out.

The four types of metaphor are the superficial, homologous, heterologous (analogous), and unificational. Each expresses a different kind of similarity which the observer conjectures among apparently unrelated phenomena.

The superficial metaphor includes statements like "the coconut is shaped after the cat's head," "the car speeded like the wind," "the fertile stretches of land form a crescent," or "her face is rounded like the moon." The observed similarities of shape or movement are not meant to indicate any functional likeness, common origin, or the outcome of the same law.

To use the biological distinction between heterologous and homologous (or analogous) traits, we have two other kinds of metaphors. When a metaphor highlights a feature in one phenomenon by alluring to a functionally similar but unrelated — in terms of context, underpinning framework, or what biologists call "structure" — it highlights heterology. For example, the wings of a fly and the wings of a bat are heterologous. Likewise, the driving of an automobile to work and the driving of the automobile for the pleasure of it expresses an heterologous similarity.

In contrast, when a metaphor points out a characteristic in one phenomenon by referring to a corresponding phenomenon of the same type, it usually shows homology. Biologists describe two organs in different species as homologous, as opposed to heterologous, when they occupy the same type of organization and emanate from a common origin. In this light, the forelegs of a mouse and the wings of a bat are homologous. This is what was intended when Marshall likened division of labor within the firm to the specialization of organs within the organism. Likewise, the driving of an automobile to work and then driving a truck to deliver goods highlights a homologous similarity.

Although it is not that easy to distinguish, there is a difference, although a penumbral one, between homologous metaphors and heterologous metaphors. Whether a similarity is homologous or heterologous is probably a major point of contention in many scientific controversies. Nonetheless, their distinction is crucial if one seeks greater conceptual clarity.

Still, homologous metaphor is different from the fourth type, the unificational metaphor which expresses sameness. Newton's law of gravitation established a unity between celestial motion and terrestrial acceleration of bodies as they fall downward. Both disparate events are regulated by the *same* law of gravity. Of course, no sameness is intended when the firm is likened to an organism.

There is an "identificational slip" when a superficial metaphor is considered heterologous, a heterologous metaphor is treated as homologous, or when a homologous metaphor is taken as unity. Of course, it is a double or triple identificational slip to jump a wider gap. For example, as alluded to below, Nicholas Georgescu-Roegen [1971; cf. Khalil, 1991] committed a triple slip: While the heat death and the economic process exhibit a superficial similarity, he conceived them not only heterologously and homologously related, but also considered the two non-reversible phenomena as the manifestation of the *same* law, viz., the entropy law.[2]

With an interest only in homologous metaphors, I discern in the literature, which has emerged in the past four decades, eight possible links between the two disciplines. In the next eight sections, I discuss, respectively the problems of reductionism, rationality, economic organization, economic structure, production, aging, evolution, and evolutionary epistemology.

In order to make the reference section manageable, I include only the burgeoning literature in economics.[3] Given the constraint of space, there is the all-too familiar tradeoff between depth of analysis and comprehensiveness of coverage. Given the aims set here, the essay tilts towards the latter.

1. The Problem of Individualism and Biological Reductionism

Does the advocacy of a unified scientific methodology à la Karl Popper necessarily involve biological reductionism? In other words, does the appeal to modes of explanation in biology translate into the thesis that, e.g., income differentials could be, to a great extent, explained by genetic variation? The question, in fact, encompasses two distinct ones: First, is the naturalist argument, i.e., the continuity of all the sciences, intrinsically connected with ontological individualism? Second, does ontological individualism in the social sciences entail reduction to biological factors?

To start with, ontological individualism should be differentiated from what is commonly known in the literature as "methodological individualism." The distinction is not usually made clearly in many debates. Put simply, ontological individualism or reductionism stipulates that, e.g., we need only to know the tastes and endowments of the input owners in order to determine the course of action of the household or the firm. At the scale of the state, ontological individualist reasoning considers constitutional authority as the result of an explicit and complete contractual arrangement among rational, calculating agents. In contrast, methodological individualist reasoning does not offer a *substantive* theory about the organization of the household, firm, or state. Rather, it is about the *method* of analyzing a phenomenon, i.e., about how to proceed. It recommends simply that the best way to understand a complex organization is to start at the micro level. This need not assume that the agent's traits are determined prior to entering social interaction or that the context is almost fully determined by the traits of the constitutive parts. It could be very well that the micro-level starting point encompasses as well the socio-cultural milieu.[4] Although the issue of method is important, I focus here on the substantive thesis, viz., the implications of ontological individualism with regard to naturalism and biological reductionism.

With regard to the first question, one needs to distinguish between the quest for a unified, naturalist discourse and the specific mode of conception one adopts. For example, H. Thoben [1982] shows that one could advocate a naturalist discourse and equally subscribe to either mechanistic (reductionist) as opposed to organismic (holistic) models for economic discourse.[5] This is possible because there is a difference between the naturalist postulate and the reductionist postulate. The naturalist postulate entails the thesis that the same method of explanation should apply to all the sciences or, which is not the same thing, similar features, dynamics, and processes are observed at diverse domains of reality. In contrast, the reductionist postulate involves the thesis that features of the whole could be explained almost totally by the pre-determined features of the components.

Practitioners and critics alike usually conflate, to the detriment of social theory, the naturalist postulate with the reductionist postulate. Consequently, as Martin O'Connor [1988, p. 33] observes: "the exploratory, experimental, indeed enigmatic character of social life is denied by the dominant naturalistic discourses of our day." The denial of the enigmatic character of social life has been blamed on naturalism, rather than on the reductionist practice in specific. As a result, a naturalist outlook has been assumed to involve trans-historical reasoning, where novelty is reduced to supposed immutable nature. Such confusion would vanish once naturalism is separated from the reductionist agenda. In fact, nature should not be opposed to society which is supposedly ever-changing. That is, the natural realm of inanimate and animate matter could also be conceived as exploratory, experimental, and enigmatic.

The conflation between the reductionist and naturalist postulates might have risen from the fact that they have been explicitly combined in the practices of some social theorists, notably neoclassical economists and behaviorists. The fruit of such a combination has been the conception of human action as empty of intentionality, free will, imagination, virtue, deep psychological motivations, and so on.

In light of the neglect of intentionality, and armed with the distinction drawn by Kant and a host of German romanticists between human and non-human entities, some researchers have understandably resisted making economics into a branch of natural science. Similar to the thesis of vitalism — i.e., the discontinuity between animate and inanimate matter — such researchers would like to draw a radical break between nature and the human sphere, which came to be called the natural/social dichotomy.

The question of the relation between social and natural sciences winds in dark alleys of metaphysical character. The metaphysical question, which is different from epistemological and other concerns, asks whether the world is made of one *kind* of entities: Do we need to appeal to non-natural beings like gods, angels, ancestral spirits, and souls in order to explain natural events? More specifically, does the study of human choice requires *deus ex machina* concepts, i.e., extra-natural concepts which are different from, or in addition to, the perceived concepts used in the investigation of atoms, cells, rocks, planets, and non-human organisms?

Supposed extra-natural concepts have been advocated by Austrian (entrepreneurship), institutional (idle curiosity), and classical/Marxist (the drive of capital) economists. This does not necessarily indicate that such economists advocate the nature/human dichotomy or what is also known as the autonomy-of-social-sciences thesis.[6] This is so because the thesis rests on a subtle assumption, viz., non-human entities lack will, risk-taking, and purposeful drive to survive. There are enormous data, however, which show that everything which Kant and Dilthey thought to be uniquely human are present in non-human animals.[7]

Thus, the naturalist postulate does not have to rob human action from will, trust, sociality, and intentionality. The natural realm, after all, might not be as divisible as Nineteenth Century Newtonian scientists believed. Thus, whether the thesis about the nature/human continuity implies ontological individualism depends greatly on our implicit assumption of what is natural. That is, the naturalist, continuity postulate could accommodate diverse modes of conception. In fact, this is supposed to be the case because the former is about metaphysical concerns, while the latter is about ontological matters. In short, there is no necessary link between the naturalist postulate and ontological individualism.

With regard to the second question, there is also no necessary link between ontological individualism and biological reductionism. A good example is how tastes of individuals are modelled in the neoclassical theory of choice or Austrian economics. They are usually taken as data which need not be explained, as George Stigler and Gary Becker [1977] argue, or could be explained by appeal to free will, as Ludwig von Mises maintains. That is, if individual traits are not seen as the product of higher-level determinants (socio-cultural context), they are not necessarily as the product of lower-level determinants (the genome). As I show below, even when Becker [1976] borrows the inclusive fitness hypothesis from sociobiology, he reserves the make up of the mathematical argument, not genetic reductionism.

In addition, experimental economists who use laboratory animals [e.g., Battalio, et al., 1981] in order to prove the maximization axiom of neoclassical economics are not usually involved in biological reductionism. They simply try to show the universality of the neoclassical hypothesis that behavior is a solution to the constrained optimization problem. Along these lines one may interpret the work of some neoclassical theorists, like Gordon Tullock [1971, 1978; see also Boulier & Goldfarb, 1991], who attempt to make positive contributions to evolutionary biology. In fact, Jack Hirshleifer [1978] argues — and seconded by biologists like Edward Wilson [1978] and Michael Ghiselin [1978] — that biology, or "natural economy," and economics, or "political economy," should be regarded as two branches of knowledge called general economics.

The fusion of neoclassical economics and neo-Darwinian biology should not be surprising [Khalil, 1992a]. To recall, the choice of the most efficient route, as stipulated by the neoclassical theory, does not require conscious deliberation. Thus, experiments with animals and the generalization of the maximization axiom do not explain human action by referring to genes, but rather attempt to show how all organisms, including humans, follow the same rules of efficiency.

Thus, the extension of neoclassical economics to biology amounts to the epitome of naturalist practice. Such naturalism does not commit biological reductionism, but rather ontological individualism. The distinction between the two is apt irrespective of how one assesses the value of the neoclassical axioms or to what extent the animal experiments give them support.

In this light, the traditional resistance of social scientists to biological metaphors and insights is more based on the confusion of naturalism with reductionism, on one hand, and reductionism with biological reductionism, on the other. The disassociation of the naturalist postulate from reductionism in general is expected to encourage more open-mindedness towards biology on the part of social scientists who have witnessed only the neo-classical/neo-Darwinian marriage.

2. Theory of Rationality

Can biology provide insights on how to deal with the anomalies which confront the theory of rational self-interested man? As is well known, the phenomena of kindness, beneficence, commitment to sub-optimal principles, and cooperation present a problem to the traditional *Homo economicus* view.[8]

One solution of the problem of cooperation is game theory, which instigated a huge literature in the past two decades. Given the focus here, one relevant line of research, and most favored by neoclassical economists, is Robert Axelrod's [1984] model of the evolution of cooperation among egoists. In his model, the suboptimal outcome of the familiar prisoners' dilemma fails to arise because the game is repeatable. In an iterated game characterized by tit-for-tat, egoistic players choose cooperative strategy. This resembles John Maynard Smith's game theoretic account of the rise of mutual aid among organisms.

Another solution is the appeal to sociobiology. Gary Becker [1976; cf. Hirshleifer, 1977b; Tullock, 1977] borrows the inclusive fitness hypothesis of sociobiology as championed by Edward Wilson and Richard Dawkins. The hypothesis postulates that genes do not act, via the organism, to maximize only their own fitness. Rather, they also act to maximize the fitness of duplicate genes which happen to be carried by kin-related organisms. That is, mutual aid stems from the strategy of genes to increase the probability of their survival. In this fashion, the concept of self-interest has been expanded.[9]

Likewise, neoclassical theory à la Becker posits

the pursuit of beneficence and the adherence to sub-optimal principles as an expanded set of tastes. For example, the agent enjoys directly the eating of a banana or indirectly by giving it to a dear person. This is the case because, for Becker, the utility function of the agent *includes* as well the utility function of the dear person. In this light, beneficence, loyalty, and trust are not really far-sighted strategies of self-interest à la Axelrod. Rather, they are tastes in themselves.[10]

Jack Hirshleifer [1977a, 1982] also regards cooperation and loyalty as tastes, i.e., not merely contingent outcomes of educated self-interested calculations. However, he regards such tastes as genetically guided because, in order for social contracts to counter the free-riding problem, the taste for cooperation must be hardy or "inbuilt":

> "[E]conomic man's behavior is constrained by inbuilt emotions and tastes. While these no doubt contain accidental elements, they are not completely arbitrary. What tastes sweet to us is mainly what serves our own interest, and our 'irrational' or 'unselfish' drives have largely met the evolutionary test of enabling us the better to compete via group membership" [Hirshleifer, 1987, p. 263].[11]

Robert Frank [1987, 1988], whose work is surprisingly celebrated by heterodox economists, seems also to regard "unselfish" tastes to be genetically programmed.[12] Frank blends neoclassical analytical tools with Darwinian selection mechanism in order to explain the prominence of "irrational" sentiments. He treats the tastes for conscience, revenge, and food as analytically part of a continuous utility function. For example, Frank considers revenge as a taste favored by natural selection because it serves, most of the time nonconsciously, as an *ex ante* deterrence against hostile actions by others.

In short, I enumerated three strategies, which are not exhaustive, on how to solve the problem of "unselfish" taste without dispensing of the *Homo economicus* model: First, such taste is far-sighted self-interest à la Axelrod. Second, the taste is chosen for its sake à la Becker. Third, it is genetically built à la Hirshleifer and Frank.

3. Economic Organization

Can biology enlighten us about how does economic organization — ranging from the household and the firm to the national economy — coordinate its divided functions? Stated differently, can metaphors from biology shed light on spontaneous as well as designed coordination of divided labor which characterize organizations at all levels of hierarchy?

In order to answer the question, it needs to be separated from the theory of evolution. The theory of organization asks about the organizing principles, which could be universal, behind the division of labor. Put differently, it asks about the way an economic organization works irrespective of the process of change. In contrast, the theory of evolution deals with *what* level of organization and *how* does it mutate during the process of change. With respect to the *what*, the debate is about the unit of evolution or the role of underpinning frameworks (institutions) of organization. With respect to the *how*, the question is about the role of blind forces versus purposefulness. These two issues are dealt with in the section on evolution below.

To make the discussion of economic organization transparent, I divide the pertinent literature into two subsections. The first one deals with the literature on the theory of the firm. The second subsection examines the literature on the theory of organization at large, like the social division of labor at the national level. At both levels of hierarchy, the same conceptual issues arise. In order to avoid redundancy, I divide the issues in this manner: At the level of the firm, I restrict the discussion to ontological individualism or reductionism. At the level of the national economy, I focus on the related issue of command versus the spontaneous working of the invisible hand which touches on the work of Friedrich Hayek.

3.1 The Theory of the Firm

Do agents form, at first level of approximation, their tastes, expectations, and strategies independently of their particular organization and the socio-cultural context at large? If so, the firm could be understood as a contingent contractual entity, i.e., a black box that facilitates the pursuits of such agents. In fact, such an image of the firm emerges from the orthodox approach of Ronald Coase and Oliver Williamson, where the firm is ultimately portrayed as an efficient mechanism which reduces transaction cost [Khalil, 1992c, 1993b]. To what extent such an image conflicts with Alfred Marshall's metaphor of the firm as an organism with differentiated functions?

To start with, how do biologists conceive the organism? As it turns out, orthodox neo-Darwinists also view the organism as a black box which facilitates the survival of pre-constituted, selfish genes. Thus, the simple appeal to biology is no life saver for the critics who would like to see the firm as an individual and not merely a nexus of contracts.

To elaborate, the organism is not seen as an individual by orthodox neo-Darwinists like Richard Dawkins and sociobiologists like Edward Wilson, George Williams, and Richard Alexander. They basically view the organism as a vehicle or an epiphenomenon devised by genes to reproduce themselves. This parallels the reductionist view of the firm in neoclassical theory of production. The firm is not seen as an individual in its own right. Rather, it is the mean by which agents pursue pre-given goals. This entails that each agent receives an income equals to her marginal productivity. As behavioral economists like Harvey Leibenstein have highlighted, the productivity of workers depend on organizational factors, the corporate cultural, and the willing of managers to deliver what they promise [Khalil, 1992a].

Once one admits in the context of biology or economics that the agent's effort intensity depends on the organizational context, it becomes hard to argue that the market or nature rewards individual agents or genes. This has given rise in biology to the notion of group selection, as promoted by anti-reductionists as Richard Lewontin, David Wilson, Elliott Sober, Steven Stanley, Niles Eldredge, and Stephen Jay Gould [Hodgson, 1991].

In economics, the most prominent thinker to adopt from biology the idea of group selection is, surprisingly, Hayek [1967, 1988; see also Witt, 1985; Sugden, 1989]. This is surprising, as Geoffrey Hodgson [1991] and Viktor Vanberg [1986] point out, because Hayek has been identified with a strong version of reductionism à la ontological individualism. Hayek argues that the rules followed by agents — which somewhat differ from the consequent, unintended order — become viable if they afford the group, in this case the firm, a greater survival chance. As Vanberg emphasizes, the argument is functionalist and, hence, is riddled with the free-rider problem: Why rules, which are beneficial for the group, would be obeyed by self-seeking agents?[13]

3.2 The Theory of Economic Organization at Large

This raises the related question of organization theory, viz., the role of command, which I will discuss here at the level of the national economy. Is organization basically ordered through spontaneous interaction of elements and, hence, any commanding or designing elements must be intrusive and external as Hayek vehemently maintains?[14]

Hayek's zeal to deny any role for state planning underlies his well-known dichotomy between design, which is supposedly artificial, and evolutionary rules which are natural. Hayek's vision is premised on the treatment of organization as the spontaneous order which arises unintentionally from purposefully acting agents. Such a view presents the economic society as a self-organized entity, i.e., a society which does not ultimately need a reflective or commanding center. While unintended consequences explain the rise of spontaneous cooperation, they cannot account for the commanding elements found in modern organizations. The mistaken identification of economic organizations as only self-organizations is responsible for treating "design" as an external element imposed by fatally conceited planners.

Hayek and others have appealed to similar notions of self-organization in biology, especially "autopoiesis" (literally: self-production) which is spearheaded by Francisco Varela [Khalil, 1992b]. Vilmos Csanyi uses a different term, "autogenesis," for basically the same notion [see Pantzar & Csanyi, 1991]. The autopoiesis and autogenesis research programs highlight that the components of cells or organisms have functions which are adjusted to each other. The output of each component enters as inputs for the other functional activities. Such input/output production is conceived, at first approximation, abstractly from the commanding function of genetic information. Thus, the organization of the cell or organism is seen as arising spontaneously, with no regard to the natural history and genetic endowment of the organism.[15]

Janos Kornai offers an alternative vision of economic organization with regard to the issue of command. For Kornai [1971, p. 176-187], one should distinguish between automatic functions, on one hand, and higher functions, on the other. He borrows the distinction from physiology. Some activities like the pumping of the heart and auto-immune system are automatic. In contrast, other activities like breathing are more controlled at a higher level of the neurological system. And certainly activities like mobility are fully commanded. Spontaneous and designed activities of the body are indispensable to each other. For Kornai, economic organization is also characterized simultaneously by automatic functions and commanded regulations and intervention. Both should be seen as integral to the organization of economic affairs. The controlling functions should not be viewed as an appendage to the automatic ones, as much as the brain is not an external organ in relation to other organs.

Kenneth Boulding [1989b] calls the commanding aspect of economic organization the "integrative system," one of the three faces of power. The integrative system employs ideology, general interest, principles, and common roots. As for Kornai, Boulding finds that the organization is also characterized by the "exchange system" of spontaneous relations, which Hayek highlighted exclusively. These two facets of power are preferable to the use of brute force — the "threat system"[16]

In short, the roles of the genome in cells, the brain in the body, and the pack leader in the society of wolves might be worth investigating as homologous metaphors of the designing state in human economy. But one could state with more certainty that the manner in which cells and organisms function cannot buttress Hayek's vision of self-organization, i.e., organization abstracted from the element of command.

4. Economic Structure

Can ecology provide tools for the analysis of self-feeding mechanisms which engender spontaneously ordered structures? In order to answer this, I need to explain positive feedbacks which make the consequent economic structure radically distinct from economic organization just discussed.

Although it might be the most unfamiliar and controversial, I cannot fully substantiate here my distinction between the economic organization and economic structure.[17] However, put tersely, the organizational and structural phenomena are two aspects of everyday exchanges. While they are different, they are not exclusive of each other. As an organization, the economy is a more-or-less stable division of labor ordered by trust, property rights, purposeful initiatives, and the commanding state taking the role of entrepreneurial leadership. As a structure, the economy is the collection of chaotic markets ordered by autocatalytic mechanisms which give rise, *inter alios*, to business cycles and geographical core/periphery bifurcations. Such cycles and bifurcations are ultimately ruled by equilibrating forces. In contrast, evolutionary processes are the property of the economy as an organization.

If we see economic structure and economic organization as complementary, as much as the business cycle and the secular trend, there would be no need to conceive of "equilibrium" and "evolution" as exclusive concepts as many do [e.g., Loasby, 1991; Hodgson, 1993].

To clarify further, the way I use the term "structure" here is related neither to the technological/organizational regime of division of labor and property rights nor to the relative size of economic sectors and firms (which are really matters about economic organization). I rather use the term "structure" to indicate a spontaneous ordering pattern which pushes, within limits, the market away from equilibrium as a result of positive feedbacks.

Of course, the organizational and structural moments of the economy influence each other. But their ordering mechanisms and ordering principles are not the same. The difference is also noted in biology. The distinction is illustrated by the boundary between the study of the organization of organisms and the structure of ecosystems. To be clear, the organism — like human society — also contains structural aspects which resemble the ordering mechanism of ecosystems. But this does not mean that the organism is a miniature ecosystem.[18]

Since the focus here is on economic structure, it is good to start with the work of the Nobel laureate Ilya Prigogine. He investigated the autocatalytic mechanisms which push thermodynamic systems far away from equilibrium by amplifying initial, hard to detect conditions. The consequent pattern, which he called, "dissipative structures," could be sustained as long as the system is open to a high influx of energy/matter.

Prigogine's notion of spontaneous dissipative structures gained recognition from many workers in different disciplines. Prigogine, however, committed a major identificational slip: He elucidated economic and biological organizations with the same concepts suitable for economic and biological structures. Such an identificational slip has been followed by economists [e.g., Buchanan & Vanberg, 1991] who attempt to hang the ideas about economic organization and its creative development on Prigogine's spontaneous dissipative structures. Such a slip should not prevent us from examining the ramifications of spontaneous arrangements with respect to a narrower field, viz., the study of structures in general and economic structures in particular [Khalil, 1993a].

Prigogine employs the entropy law in a way which radically differs from Georgescu-Roegen's [1971]. Rather than worrying about the effect of production on resources and levels of pollution, Prigogine wants to illuminate spontaneous arrangements or patterns. Prigogine does not identify useful resources with negative entropy as Georgescu-Roegen does, but rather identifies self-ordering structures with negative entropy.

For Prigogine, a structure, like a spontaneous hurricane or Benard cells, is basically the outcome of the effort to minimize entropy at the expense of increasing entropy in the environment. Stated differently, structures are autocatalytic systems spun into existence without command because they are caught in a potential energy/matter. This means the system's boundaries are not closed, but are open to the influx of energy/matter.

Prigogine's concept of dissipative structure is useful for the study of economic structure like the business cycle because it also arises without command. In fact, as the work of Peter Allen shows, there is no need to use the notion of minimum entropy production or thermodynamics in general in order to explain spontaneous structures. One could describe such structures with the aid of chaos theory, which was pioneered by the meteorologist Edward H. Lorenz in the 1960's. What really matters is the modeling of nonergodic dynamics and how it unleashes self-reinforcing mechanisms which gives rise to spontaneous structures or self-structure phenomena.

Allen [in Dosi, 1988] presents an ecological model where positive feedbacks make the optimization hypothesis inapplicable. He studies how fishing boats process information and react to uncertainty. The consequent geographical diffusion of boats forms a far-from-equilibrium, spontaneous structure. In this context one could also place Kenneth Boulding's [1978, 1981] dynamics models of disequilibrium markets.

The contribution of post Keynesian theory with respect to the business cycle is pertinent here [e.g., Goodwin, 199o; see also Khalil, 1987]. It elucidates the self-feeding temporal dynamics of economic growth [Day, 1982]. The consequent models are very similar to Robert May's biological population dynamics. The structure of business cycle is based on the inherent asymmetry of demand. While the investment decision by firm X secures the demand for the products of other firms, it does not directly translate into the demand for its own products. However, once a firm's investment is confirmed by the market, it ensures a self-feeding investment activity. This means that investments, following expectations, are temporally bunched in the upturn and downturn of the business cycle. Such dynamics provide the seeds for the possibility of chaotic phenomena which have been gaining attention lately [e.g., Baumol & Quandt, 1985; Baumol & Benhabib, 1989; Boldrin, Brock in Anderson, et al., 1988; Barnett, et al., 1989; Radzicki, 1990; cf. Mirowski, 1990].

With regard to space, C. Dyke [1988] uses the tools of Prigogine's analysis of self-feeding mechanisms to show how cities, in relation to their environs, emerge as attracting centers of economic activity. The location of cities could be acts of historical accident — like the founding of early settlements in North America. Once established, cities and their environs grow as far-from-equilibrium structures as a result of nonergodic bifurcation over space. At larger scales, the same bifurcation structure explains the core/periphery polarization highlighted by dependency theorists like Andre Gunder Frank and Immanuel Wallerstein.

The core/periphery structure is taken up by Paul Krugman [1991] and explained as the result of increasing returns to scale, which Allyn Young and Nicholas Kaldor have emphasized. Krugman advances further the analytic of such autocatalytic feedbacks by borrowing from Brian Arthur [1988, 1990]. But Arthur's specific study of technological trajectories is related, as shown below, to developmental/evolutionary processes, not the spontaneous rise of structural patterns. In any case, Krugman shows how high fixed costs and costs of transportation induce firms to concentrate their investment in few plants and in regions close to the population center. The move towards such a center makes it, in turn, more attractive to other firms — which prompts nonergodic, uneven regional development.

In short, puzzles like the business cycle and geographical uneven development defy the equilibrium outlook of negative feedbacks. In contrast, with the help of ecological and population models of positive feedbacks, it would be possible to render such far-from-equilibrium structures as subject to endogenous variables. Expectedly, the study of economic structures would become a more respected pursuit in economics.

5. Production

Is there a similarity between human and non-human production activities? Already economic anthropologists have borrowed most of their tools of analyzing production from theories developed initially to describe optimum foraging behavior of animals.

The optimal diet theory, first developed by the ecologists Robert MacArthur and E.R. Pianka, has been put to describe the strategy of foragers in hunting and gathering bands. Such foragers are usually aware of horticultural societies which live near by. They choose foraging instead of agriculture not simply because of the force of tradition. As one !Kung man told an economic anthropologist, Richard Lee: "Why should we plant when there are so many mongongo nuts in the world?" [quoted in Cashdan, 1989, p. 26].In fact, there is an increasing empirical evidence supporting, with some qualifications, optimum foraging theories. Such theories attempt to explain the composition of food type demanded by hunters and gatherers. It is found that more-or-less human foragers opt for the food types which afford the highest calories per unit of effort [Cashdan, 1989, pp. 28-33].[19] Thus, human foragers substitute among food sources in the attempt to economize.

Thus, the common denominator among human and non-human foragers is that the harnessing of nature's gifts involves inescapable effort-expenditure. From the viewpoint of the actor, such effort is wasteful. This implies that production is inefficient: The agent cannot appropriate 100% of nature's gifts. Put in modern terminology, consumer surplus could never equal the gross utility of products because there is no free lunch. Or in the lexicon of classical/Marxian economics, surplus value is always less than the value of output because of the positive value of means of production.

The best that humans and non-humans can do is to minimize the inevitable waste through the search for the least costly means. Alfred J. Lotka called it the "energy principle." For Lotka, Darwin's natural selection is deficient without the energy principle: Nature selects the most efficient users of energy.

More recently, the ecologist Howard Odum employed the energy principle under the name "maximum power principle." He defined it as the rate of useful transformation of available energy. This insight has been developed further by ecological Darwinists like Bruce Weber, David Depew, Stanley Salthe, Eric Schneider, Robert Ulanowicz, and Jeffrey S. Wicken. They have used the maximum power principle to supplement the neo-Darwinian mechanism. In this manner, they have attempted to emphasize the flows of matter/energy in nature. Lotka's principle and the ideas of matter/energy flows have also impressed a number of ecological economists like Herman Daly [1968].

Georgescu-Roegen [1971; see also Faber, et al., 1987] has drawn the attention to the similarity between the inevitable inefficiency of production and the inevitable inefficiency of the Carnot cycle. As well known, the Carnot cycle, or any attempt of generating energy from a chaotic source, necessitates the waste of some of the inputs into a sink. The inefficiency of the Carnot originates from the *second* law of thermodynamics (entropy law). This has prompted Georgescu-Roegen, in a sophisticated argument, also to ground the inefficiency of production on the entropy law. However, the inefficiency of production, highlighted by the ecologists, emanates from the *first* law of thermodynamics (conservation law). The fact that the Carnot cycle and production are ineluctably inefficient does not mean they arise from the same law, viz., the entropy law. In this light, Georgescu-Roegen should have written a somewhat different book, titled *The Conservation Law and the Economic Process*, rather than *The Entropy Law and the Economic Process* [Khalil, 1991].

In summary, economists could learn from the entropy law (as well as the chaos theory) about positive feedbacks in open systems and the possible rise of far-from-equilibrium economic structures. However, economists should turn to the conservation law in order to decipher the wasteful nature of production and its impact on the cycling ability of the ecosystem.

6. Aging

Does an economic organization age like a lower-level, biological organization? Alfred Marshall likened the fortunes of a firm to the living process of an organism, i.e., prospering for three generations before starting to lose vigor. The question is worth investigating, especially if, as discussed above, the division of social labor and the differentiation of biological functions are *homologous*.

Given the inevitability of biological aging, economists have been surprisingly slow, if not mute, with regard to drawing insights from it. Even heterodox economists and theorists of decline like Mancur Olson [1982] do not derive their critical insights from biology. One reason might reside in the difficulty of conceptualizing how a firm or a nation might die. After all, the members of such organizations go on living. However, what is at hand is the death of the organization, not its members. In fact, the same conceptual difficulty is encountered with regard to the death of cells and organisms: Their fundamental members, the genes, continue on living from one generation to the next. Thus, the loss of vigor of a firm and its rebirth under new management or branching through subsidiaries are similar to the aging of the organism and its rejuvenation through the cultivation of the germ afresh, i.e., outside the aging organization. The difficulty of seeing the parallel between the two phenomena might be the result of our epistemological viewpoint. That is, as individuals we could easily witness the death of other individuals, but not so easily witness the death of the group of which they are part.

A second reason for why social scientists have not drawn lessons from biological aging is that, to start with, biological aging has been the most perplexing phenomenon for biologists. It is the weakest link in theoretical biology because there are no apparent reasons why organisms should age and die. The phenomenon proves to be independent of the question of depletion of nutrients. As the experiment of Leonard Hayflick [1965] has shown, replication of cells *in vitro* (test tube) comes to a halt after few generations, even though there are plenty of nutrients available.

There are as many theories of senescence as there are researchers working on it [Hall, 1984, ch. 2]. It is becoming more apparent that the diversity of theories does not express incompatibility as much as the fact that aging is a multi-faceted problem. Aging takes place concurrently at different levels of hierarchy (from organelles, cells to organs, and organisms). This makes it harder to isolate the initial cause, if there is any.

Nonetheless, one could divide quasi-speculative theories of aging into two major approaches: Different researchers have called them by different names. Raymond Tice [in Schneider, 1978, pp. 53] calls them "genetic programming" vs. "error accumulation." The genetic programming approach postulates that senescence is a continuation of growth and differentiation, and, furthermore, is determined according the neo-Darwinian criterion of fitness, like body size. According to David Wilson [in Rockstein, 1974, p. 11], "there are direct or indirect selective advantages to limiting life span through senescence."

In contrast, the error accumulation approach argues that the main aging event is stochastic, governed by chance, and expresses itself by accumulation of errors in DNA, RNA, protein, or in a combination of the three. Others have called the error accumulation approach "epiphenomenalist," since it locates the factors behind aging as lying outside the cell [Behnke, et al., 1978, pp. 7-14]. In general, the epiphenomenalist approach has been identified by the work of Alex Comfort [1979]. In specific, Johan Bjorksten's [in Rockstein, 1974] theory of crosslinkages is the best example of this approach. According to him, floating agents, typified by small molecules, accidentally cross-link macromolecules such as protein and DNA. In fact, Bjorksten uses the metaphor of factory production and how it would slow down if workers in an assembly line are chained together. The crosslinking of molecules makes them dysfunctional — the basis of the aging process. Defense mechanism and excision are not fast enough to break these chains.

There are other theories of aging that defy simple classification. Examples include the wear and tear theory and, inspired by radiation-stimulated cancer, somatic mutation theory (as opposed to mutation of germ cells like sperms). It would become easier to classify those theories if we use the terminology of Behnke, et al., [1978], Strehler [1977], and Hall [1984]. Namely, it would be better to employ "intrinsic" in place of "genetic programming" and "extrinsic" instead of "error accumulation." In this fashion, a wear and tear theory could be intrinsic or extrinsic, depending on where it locates the cause of degradation. Likewise, somatic cell mutation theory is intrinsic if looked upon from the standpoint of organ or organism, but extrinsic if observed from the level of genome.

The extrinsic and intrinsic approaches to senescence are not necessarily exclusive. According to Hall [1984, p. 47], intrinsic approaches deal with the theoretical path of an organism as determined by internal factors, while the actual path is modified in light of external factors. He uses the metaphor, which should be taken in a superficial manner, of the flight path of a projectile. Theoretically speaking, the parabola is determined by the intrinsic factors of mass, force, and angle. But, actually speaking, the parabola is modified by extrinsic factors like friction of air and its variation at different atmospheric levels. In this manner, the extrinsic factors which affect aging are superimposed on the intrinsic path which is defined by the constitution of the organism.

Is there anything for economists to learn from extrinsic and intrinsic theories of aging? In fact, most economists already practice, without knowing, extrinsic theories of aging. For example, the slowdown of productivity in Western economies in the past two decades has been blamed on external causes like the rise of energy costs, union power, the Japanese challenge, the increased ratio of women and other low-skilled groups in the labor force, high taxes, low saving rates, excessive regulations, myopic management concerned with immediate profits, and so on. Such factors resemble the explanation of aging as a result of bad diet, accidents, lack of exercise, lack of sleep, and so on.

It would be interesting and challenging to examine if there are intrinsic variables, as discussed by the literature on the logic of collective action and the free-riding problem, which set the economic organization on a quasi-determined path of aging. However, such a challenge should be undertaken with great caution. While the effort might lead to a dead end, it is worth the risk.

Methodus December 1992

7. Evolution

Is human socio-cultural-technological evolution similar to non-human evolution? The question, in fact, involves two separate ones. The first concerns the theory of evolution which specifies the *mechanism* or how evolution comes about: Does evolution emerge because of the blind forces of natural selection à la neo-Darwinism; or does it arise as a result of the purposeful action of the agents à la neo-Lamarckianism? The second involves the theory of evolution which specifies the *level* or unit of evolution: Does evolution mostly occur at the surface level and, hence, is gradual; or does it happen as well at deeper hierarchical levels of frameworks/regimes and, hence, is punctuated?

I cannot do justice here to the enormous theoretical difficulties concerning the nature of biological as opposed to non-biological evolution. But it is helpful to reformulate Lotka's distinction between the two [see Georgescu-Roegen, 1971, p. 307]: Biological evolution is endosomatic since the emerging tools like long wings, sharp claws, wide teeth, and tough skins, and organizations like organs are part of the body. In contrast, human evolution is exosomatic since the emerging tools like sticks, wheels,, arrows, and trucks, and organizations like nations, firms, and households are separate from the body.

With regard to the first question, mechanism of evolution, Milton Friedman saw a homologous correspondence between biological and non-biological mechanisms. In his widely commented essay on methodology, Friedman resorts to the mindless, non-conscious theory of natural selection to buttress his thesis that a scientific hypothesis need not be consciously followed in order to be used:

> "Confidence in the maximization-of-returns hypothesis is justified by evidence of a very different character. This evidence is in part similar to that adduced on behalf of the billiard-player hypothesis — unless the behavior of businessmen in some way or other approximated behavior consistent with the maximization of return, it seems unlikely that they would remain in business for long. Let the apparent immediate determinant of business behavior be anything at all — habitual reaction, random chance, or whatnot. Whenever this determinant happens to lead to behavior consistent with rational and informed maximization of returns, the business will prosper and acquire resources with which to expand; whenever it does not, the business will tend to lose resources and can be kept in existence only by the addition of resources from outside. The process of "natural selection" thus helps to validate the hypothesis — or, rather, given natural selection, acceptance of the hypothesis can be based largely on the judgment that it summarizes appropriately the conditions for survival" [Friedman, 1953, p. 22].[20]

In a classic essay, Armen Alchian [1950] dispenses with the maximization hypothesis in light of uncertainty. He anticipates the concept of "satisficing," which later figures prominently in the works of behavioral (Leibenstein and Simon), evolutionary (Nelson & Winter), and institutional economists (Veblen). Alchian presents the economic system as an adoptive pursuit of success or profit, which rewards results rather than motivations of the agent. As a result of "realized positive profits," rather than "maximized profits," rules which succeeded through trial-and-error are replicated.

E. Penrose [1952] was quick to point out that Alchian's appeal to natural selection is misguided because Alchian's theory of "environmental adoption" resembles, in fact, the discredited Lamarckian theory of the inheritance of acquired characteristics. The most important feature of neo-Darwinism is that the mutation of genes ("rules") do not appear in anticipation of their fitness ("results"). In response, Alchian [1952] dispenses of the biological metaphor, but maintains the economic model.

Richard Nelson and Sidney Winter carry Alchian's environmental adoption further. However, they insist on the relevance of the biological metaphor. But their biological benchmark is not mainly the neo-Darwinian mechanism, but rather the Lamarckian one. They take issue with what they call the "orthodox" emphasis on maximization, which their evolutionary economics repudiates:

> "[W]e reject the notion of maximizing behavior as an explanation of why decision rules are what they are; indeed, we dispense with all three components of the maximization model — the global objective function, the well-defined choice set, and the maximization choice rationalization of firms' actions. ..."
>
> "Our general term for all regular and predictable behavioral patterns of firms is "routine." ...In our evolutionary theory, these routines play the role that genes play in biological evolutionary theory. They are a persistent feature of the organism and

determine its possible behavior" [Nelson & Winter, 1982, p. 14].

While Nelson and Winter recognize the role of "blind" natural selection in augmenting routines, they put more emphasis on Lamarckian "deliberate" goal-seeking:

It is neither difficult nor implausible to develop models of firm behavior that interweave "blind" and "deliberate" processes. Indeed, in human problem solving itself, both elements are involved and difficult to disentangle. Relatedly, our theory is unabashedly Lamarckian: it contemplates both the "inheritance" of acquired characteristics and the timely appearance of variation under the stimulus of adversity [Nelson & Winter, 1982, p. 11].

Nelson and Winter's Lamarckian approach and the emphasis on routines were already anticipated by Thorstein Veblen's [1898] evolutionary economics. However, he was given little credit for them [Winter, 1987, p. 616].[21]

Aside from the Darwinian vs. Lamarckian mechanism, what about the second question, viz., the unit of evolution in the sense of levels of hierarchy? That is, aside from the apparent level like the firm, does the more fundamental levels of the hierarchy of organizations evolve? How does the evolution of the firm's routines affect or affected by the evolution of its underpinning technological/organizational regime, or what is known in the biological literature as higher-level (deeper-level) framework which underlines species within the same order or class?

Kenneth Boulding [1989a] takes up the question of the unit of evolution with reference to Niles Eldredge and Stephen Jay Gould's theory of punctuated equilibria. It is also addressed by many of the papers in the collection edited by Giovanni Dosi, et al., [1988]. The collection marshes on the familiar tracks laid out by Joseph Schumpeter's [1949; see Kleinknecht, 1987] vision of technological trajectories and capitalist gales of creative destruction. The collection also leans on the literature on long waves and the French regulation school [see Boyer in Dosi, et al., 1988].

G. Dosi and L. Orsenigo [in Dosi, et al., 1988] blend Schumpetarian insights about technological pathways of development and diffusion with stabilizing institutions in the face of uncertainty. As a result, according to them, it is possible to have "evolutionary equilibria," i.e., well-defined and stable trajectories which engender a number of small innovations.

Like its biological counterpart, Schumpetarian processes involve two interrelated theses: First, everyday market activity is underlined by a deep organization/technological regime. The regime involves the web of the primary technology, physical infrastructure, and the property rights arrangement. This is similar to the idea that traits of organisms are underlined by enduring schemes shared by many species who are members of higher taxa (i.e., genus, family, order, class, and phylum). Second, the evolution of such regimes, or what Christopher Freeman and Carlota Perez [in Dosi, et al., 1988] call "techno-economic paradigm," do not occur gradually. Rather, they stay stable for a long time before they peter out in a relatively short period. This is similar to the fossil record which shows great stability for tens of millions of years to be followed by drastic extinctions and the rise of new frameworks (higher taxa) within the span of a few million years.

In this context, one should place Paul David's [1985] and Brian Arthur's [1988, 1990] works on the path-dependency of technological diffusion. They show how a technology which was superior at the time of adoption becomes entrenched and inflexible as a result of learning-by-doing. That is, it becomes difficult over time to switch to a superior, but unimproved, technology. Thus, the choice of technology over the life span of a regime of production is usually limited as a result of irreversible processes of development.

In a similar vein, Paul David [1985] discusses the typewriter's keyboard. The QWERTY set-up, which slows down typing, was adopted because it minimizes the serious problem of jamming. However, the relatively inefficient QWERTY set up persists despite the fact that new technology took care of the jamming problem. The transaction costs, especially in human training, of switching to a more efficient lay out must be very high relative to the benefits.

Douglass North [1990, ch. 11] refers to Arthur's and David's works when he discusses the persistence of inefficient institutions in economic history. North argues that besides high transaction costs of setting new institutions, inefficient frameworks of property rights and rules persist because of their nonergodic character. Once institutions are set up, they engender increasing returns because of learning-by-doing and the adaptive, self-reinforcing character of expectations. That is, expectations formed by the institutions become self-fulfilling because they are "historically derived subjective modeling." Thus, inefficient institutions are expected to last longer than what the transaction cost approach predicts.

However, underpinning regimes change when enough stress builds up. This amounts to the evolution of the underpinning framework, which is different from the evolution of the firm's routines. Thus, we need to distinguish two levels of processes. At the gradual one, everyday activity elaborates on and takes for granted the technological/organizational regime. Thus, everyday activity helps the regime to become more entrenched or inflexible as North has argued. At the punctuated level, the regime itself becomes subject to a critical crisis which might stimulate, but not usually successfully, its replacement with a more efficient, updated one.[22] A fresh regime could easily strike new major technological trajectory which could liberate everyday life from previous rigidities. This involves discontinuous or punctuated change.[23]

Once gradual/punctuated processes are delineated, it would be possible to improve evolutionary economics. I would not be surprised if aging is related to the gradual process of development. If the incorporation of the two is accomplished successfully, the theory of evolution could focus exclusively on the punctuated process.

Process philosophy, as best formulated by Alfred Whitehead and Henri Bergson, could be helpful in describing the irreversible, punctuated process of evolution. Georgescu-Roegen [1971, pp. 41-47, 69-72] embraces its organismic viewpoint.[24] He makes a useful distinction between arithmomorphic concepts (i.e., nominal or fictional concepts which help us control the world) and dialectic concepts (i.e., concepts which express real forms which have penumbra-kind boundaries). Contrary to his argument however, the entropy law should not be the entry point to the study of dialectical entities and evolutionary processes.

I do not attempt here to provide an evolutionary theory of the economy. I merely call attention to the possibility of guidance from Lamarckian theory and the theory of punctuated equilibria. Lamarckian theory emphasizes non-Darwinian mechanisms like the role of purposeful deliberation, learning-by-doing, and the adoption of techniques in light of their usefulness. Punctuated equilibria theory shows that the unit of evolution is not only the individual, but also could be the group of individuals when the underpinning regime runs out of steam. While these heterodox biological ideas are worth studying insofar as they shed light on economics, they have been gaining ground lately in biology as the anomalies facing neo-Darwinism have become harder to manage [see Khalil, 1992a].

8. Evolutionary Epistemology

Can we map the theory of biological evolution onto scientific evolution? As soon as Charles Darwin published *The Origin of Species* in 1859, some philosophers took the opportunity to ground the evolution of science according to the theory of natural selection. Most recently, David Hull [1992] provides the most eloquent statement of Darwinian evolutionary epistemology. As summed up by Bruce Caldwell, (Darwinian) evolutionary epistemology,

> "provides the epistemological foundations for critical rationalism. This doctrine emphasizes the similarities between the growth of animal (including human) knowledge and the evolution of species. Bold conjectures are analogous to blind variations (mutations) in nature; the process of criticism is analogous to theprocess of natural selection. Evolutionary epistemology provides an empirical basis for epistemology (in processes found in nature) as well as an argument for realism (the survival of both ideas and organisms depends on their fit within their environment, and the assumption of an existing environment is consistent with realism). The goal of the evolutionary epistemologist is to create an "ecology of rationality" in which the optimal amount of critical discourse is able to flourish" [Caldwell, 1991, pp. 23-24].

Karl Popper is a strong proponent of the "ecology of rationality." Such ecology, like Darwin's natural selection, assures the survival of fittest ideas. According to Popper [1981, p. 95], "the objectivity and the rationality of progress in science is not due to the personal objectivity and rationality of the scientist." W.W. Bartley goes one step further and argues that epistemology should be treated as a branch of economics [Bartley, 1990, p. 89]: Evolutionary epistemology is about the market of ideas. Like all markets, its outcome is non-intentional, but rather is guided by the invisible hand. Such hand ensures that only optimum ideas — even when they are the outcome of self-interested scientists — are the winners [see also, Hands, 1991].

However, is the Darwinian story an adequate representation of the evolution of economic thought? One needs only to take a closer look at Darwin's theory to find some troubling questions. For Darwin and neo-Darwinians, evolutionary novelty arises out of blind forces selecting traits which originate from random mutation. This raises a few questions: First, do economic ideas emerge without the anticipation of the critical selecting forces or without regard to the concrete policy questions of the day? Second, is the market of ideas efficient in the sense that what survives must be the optimum theory of all available theories? Third, are paradigms unimportant as units of evolution like groups and higher taxa in neo-Darwinian theory? Fourth, since the neo-Darwinian theory denies the phenomenon of progress and emphasizes instead fitness relative to the particular environment, is it impossible to adjudicate — as Imre Lakatos argues — among different paradigms and not treat them as equally suited to their particular environments and ideologies?

Given these deep problems, should one discard altogether the appropriateness of evolutionary epistemology? Before doing this, one should realize that there are alternative evolutionary epistemologies being developed after non-Darwinian theories of biological evolution. Some philosophers of science have resorted to C.H. Waddington's theory of embryonic development, which is somewhat related to Lamarck's theory, as a better metaphor of how knowledge evolves [Hahlweg & Hooker, 1989].

In short, evolutionary epistemology is not going to be an easy exit out of the impasse in which economic methodologists find themselves. They are destined to echo the same disagreements, but adorned instead with biological metaphors.

9. Conclusion

It is fruitless to attempt a summary of the survey. Maybe a single lesson could be extracted from the intercourse between economics and biology: Economists who venture across the hall to the biology department must be careful in order not to fall into one of many identificational slips.

To summarize some identificational slips, it is misleading to study biological population dynamics in order to model the evolutionary trend of an economy. It is also important to distinguish a theory of organization, which Hayek strips it from the element of design, from the theory of evolution. In addition, the spontaneous order of ecological and thermodynamic systems, as theorized by Prigogine, is the wrong area to rummage in order to shed light on the organization of division of labor in the economic society as a whole. Also, one should not commit Georgescu-Roegen's identification of the non-reversibility of the expansion of entropy, on one hand, with the non-reversibility of aging, biological evolution, and human economic processes, on the other. Furthermore, the problem of aging which accompanies development is not the same as long-term evolutionary processes.

One must be careful in order to avoid such identificational slips. But once caution and critical interrogation are continuously applied, economics and biology could enter a stimulating and lasting partnership.

Notes

* I appreciate the extensive comments of Ulrich Witt. I would like to thank also Carole Brown and Patricia Markley for their technical help. None, however, should be held responsible for any remaining shortcoming.

1. For reviews of the history of, and perspectives on, evolutionary theßories in economics, see N. Clark and C. Juma [in Dosi, et al., 1988] and Ulrich Witt [1992a, 1992b].
2. Claude Menard [1988] reviews several cases of how metaphors from mechanics and biology have been misused in economics.
3. With respect to the question of aging, however, I refer to texts in biology since there has been little work done by economists stimulated by the biological theories of aging.
4. In this light, it would be interesting to rethink whether Popper, Schumpeter, Hayek, or the Chicago economists subscribe to ontological or methodological individualism.
5. To caution, Thoben identifies the holisticapproach with cybernetics. The latter is merely an engineering device best seen as mechanics turned upside down.
6. The same debate rages in biology, i.e., whether it needs to appeal to extra-natural forces beyond what chemistry and physics employ. An affirmative answer has been called the autonomy-of-biological-sciences thesis.
7. For example, consult the work of Donald Griffin on the minds and thinking processes of animals.
8. I avoid using the term "altruism" to denote beneficence for the same reason that I shun using the term "selfishness" interchangeably with self-interest. A convincing argument could be made, although I cannot develop here, that from a cognitive standpoint, altruism involves denial of legitimate self-interest which could arise, in fact, from weakness, guilt, obsession, transmuted selfishness, neurosis, and other pathologies.
9. Gordon Tullock [e.g., 1978] offers an insightful critique of the inclusive fitness hypothesis by pointing out that cooperation is noticed among animals who are not related. In fact, new findings report that cooperation exists more than has been suspected among organisms who belong to different species.
10. To be clear, the importation of the inclusive fitness hypothesis does not amount to biological reductionism. This is the case because, as discussed earlier, ontological individualism does not lead necessarily to biological reductionism. Becker imports only the superficial make up of the inclusive fitness hypothesis, not its biological content. Becker explains the allocation of endowments between self-interest and other-interest on the basis of maximizing the agent's utility function—not his/her genetic fitness.
11. The competition via group membership advanced by Hirshleifer amounts to the advocacy of evolution via group-selection, as opposed to via individual-selection. Group-selection is vehemently opposed by ultra-Darwinists like Dawkins and, I may add, is also opposed by orthodox neoclassical economists.
12. One may conjecture that Robert Frank's work is celebrated by heterodox, anti-neoclassical economists because they only examined its conclusions, not its neoclassical foundation. This goes to support the thesis that neoclassical tools are almost neutral and could be used to support diverse policy actions.

13. Maybe the reason behind Hayek's inconsistency is that he lacks a theory of underpinning institutions or frameworks which presuppose market activity. To be precise, Hayek's rules appear in the same spontaneous manner in which spontaneous markets appear. He resorted to the anti-reductionist idea of cultural-level selection in order to deny that there are pre-market rules which could be designed by the state.
14. Without being able to defend my choice here, I am implicitly arguing that Hayek's theory of spontaneous order is more a theory of organization, as far as it adheres to ontological individualism, than a theory of evolution. Insofar it is a theory of the evolution of rules, it is inconsistent as Vanberg and Hodgson have shown.
15. While the autopoiesis and autogenesis research programs fall within the concerns of organizational theory, this is not the case with Ilya Prigogine's work. As argued in the section on economic structure, Prigogine's work is about self-structure, rather than self-organization. The distinction, which is lost to many [e.g., Buchanan & Vanberg, 1991], is explained below.
16. Unlike Kornai, Boulding seems to believe that the integrative system is uniquely human, arising from the linguistic ability:
Because of the capacity for language and therefore for images that extend far beyond immediate personal experience, the human race has developed a group of genetic organizers for which there is practically no parallel in biology... In the human race, communication by means of language, other symbols, behavioral signs, and so on becomes a process of complex mutuality and feedback among numbers of individuals that leads to the development of organizations, institutions, and other social structures which affect behavior and material and personal products. There seem to be three major groups of these organizers which I have identified as the Threat system, the Integrative system, and the Exchange system [Boulding, 1978, pp. 15-16].
17. The distinction between economic organization and economic structure reflects, respectively, the much wide-ranging dichotomy between "natural complex" and "natural system" detailed elsewhere [Khalil, 1990a].
18. Alfred Lotka's followers, who I describe below as ecological Darwinists, assert that the organism is essentially a miniature ecosystem. It is interesting to contrast such a view with James Lovelock's Gaia hypothesis which treats the ecosystem as a superorganism.
19. Effort is composed of search time and, once the prey is collected, processing or handling time.
20. See Mark Schaffer [1989; cf. Matthews, 1984] for a more rigorous version of Friedman's argument.
21. To note however, it was lost to Veblen that the Darwinian model does not support his vision of the evolution of institutions, routines, and habits [see Jones, 1986]. This is still not recognized by traditional institutionalists — except for a few [e.g., Hodgson, 1993].
22. A series of regimes could still be underlined by a greater scheme which would be subject to a grander, punctuated process of evolution.
23 The theory of punctuated evolution could benefit from, as well as shed light upon, the phenomenon of political revolutions.
24 Organismic philosophy should not be confused with vitalism. While vitalism believes that only animate matter possesses vitae, organismic philosophy contends that all matter (including atoms and particles) possesses a living substance.

References

Alchian, Armen A. "Uncertainty, Evolution, and Economic Theory." Journal of Political Economy, June 1950, 58:3, pp. 211-221.

___. "Biological Analogies in the Theory of the Firm: Comment." American Economic Review, 1952, 42, pp. 820-823.

Anderson, Philip W., K. J. Arrow, and David Pines (eds.). The Economy as an Evolving Complex System. Redwood City, CA: Addison-Wesley, 1988.

Arthur, W. Brian. "Self-Reinforcing Mechanisms in Economics." In Anderson, Philip W., K. J. Arrow, and David Pines (eds.) The Economy as an Evolving Complex System. Redwood City, CA: Addison-Wesley, 1988, pp. 9-31.

___. "Positive Feedbacks in the Economy." Scientific American, February 1990, 262:2, pp. 92-99.

Axelrod, Robert. The Evolution of Cooperation. New York: Basic Books, 1984.

Barnett, William A., John Geweke, and Karl Shell (eds.). Economic Complexity: Chaos, Sunspots, Bubbles and Nonlinearity. Cambridge: Cambridge University Press, 1989.

Bartley, W.W. III. Unfathomed Knowledge, Unmeasured Wealth. La Salle, IL: Open Court, 1990.

Battalio, Raymond C., et al. "Income-Leisure Tradeoffs of Animal Workers." American Economic Review, September 1981, 71:4, pp. 621-32.

Baumol, William J. and R. Quandt. "Chaos Models and Their Implications for Forecasting." Eastern Economic Journal, January-March 1985, 11:1, pp. 3-15.

Baumol, William J. and Jess Benhabib. "Chaos: Significance, Mechanism, and Economic Applications." Journal of Economic Perspectives, Winter 1989, 3:1, pp. 77-105.

Becker, Gary S. "Altruism, Egoism, and Genetic Fitness: Economics and Sociobiology." Journal of Economic Literature, Sept. 1976, 4:3, pp. 817-26.

Behnke, John A., Caleb E. Finch, and Gairdner B. Moment (eds.). The Biology of Aging. New York: Plenum Press, 1978.

Boulding, Kenneth E. Ecodynamics. Beverly Hills: Sage, 1978.

___. Evolutionary Economics. Beverly Hills: Sage, 1981.

___. "Punctuationalism in Societal Evolution." Journal of Social and Biological Structures, April/July 1989a, 12:2/3, pp. 213-223.

___. Three Faces of Power. Newbury Park, CA: Sage, 1989b.

Boulier, Bryan L. and Robert S. Goldfarb. "Pisces Economicus: The Fish as Economic Man." Economics and Philosophy, April 1991, 7:1, pp. 83-86.

Buchanan, James M. and Viktor J. Vanberg. "The Market as a Creative Process." Economics and Philosophy, October 1991, 7:2, pp. 167-186.

Caldwell, Bruce J. "Clarifying Popper." Journal of Economic Literature, 1991, 29, pp. 1-33.

Cashdan, Elizabeth. "Hunters and Gatherers: Economic Behavior in Bands." In Stuart Plattner (ed.) Economic Anthropology. Stanford, CA: Stanford University Press, 1989, pp. 21-48.

Comfort, Alex. The Biology of Senescence. New York: Elsevier, 1979.

Daly, Herman E. "On Economics as a Life Science." Journal of Political Economy, May/June 1968, 76:3, pp. 392-406.

David, Paul. "Clio and the Economics of QWERTY." American Economic Review, May 1985, 75:2, pp. 332-337.

Day, Richard H. "Irregular Growth Cycles." American Economic Review, June 1982, 72:3, pp. 406-414.

Dosi, Giovanni, Christopher Freeman, Richard Nelson, Gerald Silverberg, and Luc Soete (eds.). Technical Change and Economic Theory. London & New York: Pinter, 1988.

Dyke, C. "Cities as Dissipative Structures." In Bruce H. Weber, David J. Depew, and James D. Smith (eds.) Entropy, Information, and Evolution: New Perspectives on Physical and Biological Evolution. Cambridge, MA: MIT, 1988, pp. 355-367.

Faber, Malte, Horst Niemes, and Gunter Stephan, with the cooperation of L. Freytag. Entropy, Environment and Resources: An Essay in Physico-Economics, trans. from the German by I. Pellengahr. New York: Springer, 1987.

Frank, Robert W. "If Homo Economicus Could Choose His Own Utility Function, Would He Want One With a Conscience?" The American Economic Review, September 1987, 77:4, pp. 593-604.

___. Passions Within Reason: The Strategic Role of the Emotions. New York: W.W. Norton, 1988.

Friedman, Milton. "The Methodology of Positive Economics." In M. Friedman Essays in Positive Economics. Chicago: The University of Chicago Press, 1953, pp. 3-43.

Georgescu-Roegen, Nicholas. The Entropy Law and the Economic Process. Cambridge, MA: Harvard University Press, 1971.

Ghiselin, Michael T. "The Economy of the Body." American Economic Review, Papers and Proceedings, May 1978, 68:2, pp. 133-137.

Goodwin, Richard M. Chaotic Economic Dynamics. Oxford: Clarendon Press, 1990.

Hahlweg, Kai and C.A. Hooker. "Evolutionary Epistemology and Philosophy of Science." In Kai Hahlweg and C.A. Hooker (eds.) Issues in Evolutionary Epistemology. Albany, NY: State University of New York Press, 1989.

Hall, David A. The Biomedical Basis of Gerontology. Bristol: John Wright, 1984.

Hands, D. Wade. "Virtue and Vice in the Popperian Approach to Economic Methodology." Cahiers d'épistémologie (Université du Québec à Montréal), 1991, n. 9121.

Hayek, Friedrich A. "Notes on the Evolution of Systems of Rules of Conduct: The Interplay between Rules of Individual Conduct and the Social Order of Actions." In Studies in Philosophy, Politics, and Economics. Chicago: The University of Chicago Press, 1967, ch. 4, pp. 66-81.

___. The Fatal Conceit: The Errors of Socialism. London: Routledge, 1988.

Hayflick, Leonard. "The Limited in vitro Lifetime of Human Diploid Strains." Experimental Cell Research, 1965, 37.

Hirshleifer, Jack. "Economics from a Biological Viewpoint." Journal of Law and Economics, April 1977a, 20:1, pp. 1-52. (In file).

___. "Shakespeare vs. Becker on Altruism: The Importance of Having the Last Word." Journal of Economic Literature, 1977b, 15, pp. 500-502.

___. "Natural Economy versus Political Economy." Journal of Social and Biological Structures, October 1978, 1:4, pp. 319-337.

___. "Evolutionary Models in Economics and Law: Cooperation versus Conflict Strategies." In J. Hirshleifer Economic Behaviour in Adversity. Brighton, Sussex: Wheatsheaf, 1987, pp. 211-272. (Originally published in Research in Law and Economics, 1982, 4, pp. 1-60.)

Hodgson, Geoffrey M. "Hayek's Theory of Cultural Evolution: An Evaluation in Light of Vanberg's Critique." Economics and Philosophy, April 1991, 7:1, pp. 67-82.

___. Economics and Evolution: Bringing Back Life into Economics. Oxford: Polity Press, 1993.

Houthakher, H.S. "Economics and Biology." Office of Naval Research Technical Report no. 30, January 1956.

Hull, David. "An Evolutionary Account of Science: A Response to Rosenberg's Critical Notice." Biology and Philosophy, April 1992, 7:2, pp. 229-236.

Jones, Lamar B. "The Institutionalists and On the Origin of Species: A Case of Mistaken Identity." Southern Economic Journal, April 1986, 52:4, pp. 1043-1055.

Khalil, Elias L. "The Process of Capitalist Accumulation: A Review Essay of David Levine's Contribution." Review of Radical Political Economics, Winter 1987, 19:4, pp. 76-85.

___. "Natural Complex vs. Natural System." Journal of Social and Biological Structures, February 1990, 13:1, pp. 11-31. (Reprinted in General Systems Yearbook, 32.)

___. "Entropy Law and Nicholas Georgescu-Roegen's Paradigm: A Reply." Ecological Economics, July 1991, 3:2, pp. 161-163.

___. "Neoclassical Economics and Neo-Darwinism: Clearing the Way for Historical Thinking." In Edward Nell, Jaspal Chatha, and Ronald Blackwell (eds.) Economics as Worldly Philosophy: Essays on Political and Historical Economics in Honour of Robert Heilbroner. London: Macmillan, 1992a, pp. 22-72.

___. "Hayek's Spontaneous Order and Varela's Autopoiesis: A Comment." Human Systems Management, 1992b, 11:2, pp. 101-105.

___. "Between Culture and Efficient Rationality: A Review of Douglass C. North's Institutions, Institutional Change and Economic Performance." Journal of Evolutionary Economics, December 1992c, 2:4, in press

___. "Entropy and Economics." In Geoffrey M. Hodgson, Marc

Tool, and Warren J. Samuels (eds.) Handbook on Institutional and Evolutionary Economics, vol. 1. Cheltenham, UK: Edward Elgar, 1993a, in press.

___. "Rules." In Geoffrey M. Hodgson, Marc Tool, and Warren J. Samuels (eds.) Handbook on Institutional and Evolutionary Economics, vol. 2.Cheltenham, UK: Edward Elgar, 1993b, in press.

Kleinknecht, A. Innovation Patterns in Crisis and Prosperity: Schumpeter's Long Cycle Reconsidered, foreword by Jan Tinbergen. London: Macmillan, 1987.

Kornai J. Anti-Equilibrium: On Economic Systems Theory and the Tasks of Research. Amsterdam: North-Holland, 1972.

Krugman, Paul. Geography and Trade. Leuven, Belgium: Leuven University Press jointly with Cambridge, MA: The MIT Press, 1991.

Loasby, Brian. Equilibrium and Evolution. Manchester: Manchester University Press, 1991.

Marshall, Alfred. Principles of Economics. London: Macmillan, 1920.

___. "Mechanical and Biological Analogies in Economics" (1898). In A.C. Pigou Memorials of Alfred Marshall, New York: Kelly, 1966.

Matthews, R.C.O. "Darwinism and Economic Change." Oxford Economic Papers, November 1984, New Series, 36:supplement, pp. 91-117.

Menard, Claude. "The Machine and the Heart: An Essay on Analogies in Economic Reasoning." Social Concept, December 1988, 5:1, pp. 81-95.

Mirowski, Philip. "From Mandelbrot to Chaos in Economic Theory." Southern Economic Journal, October 1990, 57:2, pp. 289-307.

Moss, Laurence. "Biological Theory and Technological Entrepreneurship in Marshall's Writings." Eastern Economic Journal, January 1982, 8:1, pp. 3-13.

Nelson, Richard R. and Sidney G. Winter. An Evolutionary Theory of Economic Change. Cambridge, MA: Harvard University Press, 1982.

Niman, Neil B. "Biological Analogies in Marshall's Work." Journal of the History of Economic Thought, Spring 1991, 13:1, pp. 19-36.

North, Douglass C. Institutions, Institutional Change and Economic Performance. Cambridge: Cambridge University Press, 1990.

O'Connor, Martin. "Convolution and Involution: The Career of the Biological Organism." Social Concept, December 1988, 5:1, pp. 3-40.

Olson, Mancur. The Rise and Decline of Nations. New Haven, CT: Yale University Press, 1982.

Pantzar, Mika and Vilmos Csanyi. "The Replicative Model of the Evolution of the Business Organization." Journal of Social and Biological Structures, May 1991, 14:2, pp. 149-163.

Penrose, E.T. "Biological Analogies in the Theory of the Firm." American Economic Review, December 1952, 42:5, pp. 804-819.

Popper, Karl. "The Rationality of Scientific Revolutions." In Ian Hacking (ed.) Scientific Revolutions. Oxford: Oxford University Press, 1981, pp. 80-106.

Radzicki, Michael J. "Institutional Dynamics, Deterministic Chaos, and Self-Organizing Systems." Journal of Economic Issues, March 1990, 24:1, pp. 57-102.

Rockstein, Morris, with Marvin L. Sussman and Jeffrey Chesky (eds.). Theoretical Aspects of Aging. New York: Academic Press, 1974.

Schaffer, Mark E. "Are Profit-Maximizers the Best Survivors? A Darwinian Model of Economic Natural Selection." Journal of Economic Behavior and Organization, 1989, 12, pp. 29-45.

Schneider, Edward L. (ed.) The Genetics of Aging. New York: Plenum Press, 1978.

Schumpeter, Joseph A. The Theory of Economic Development. Cambridge, MA: Harvard University Press, (1912) 1949.

Stigler, George J. and Gary S. Becker. "DE Gustibus Non Est Disputandum." The American Economic Review, March 1977, 67:1, pp. 76-90.

Strehler, B.L. Time, Cell and Aging. New York: Academic Press, 1977.

Sugden, Robert. "Spontaneous Order." Journal of Economic Perspectives, Fall 1989, 3:4, pp. 85-97.

Thoben, H. "Mechanistic and Organistic Analogies in Economics Reconsidered." Kyklos, 1982, 35:2, pp. 292-306

Thomas, Brinley. "Alfred Marshall on Economic Biology." Review of Political Economy, January 1991, 3:1, pp. 1-14.

Tullock, Gordon. "The Coal Tit as a Careful Shopper." American Naturalist, 1971, 105, pp. 77-80.

___. "Economics and Sociobiology: A Comment." Journal of Economic Literature, 1977, 15, pp. 502-506.

___. "Altruism, Malice and Public Goods." Journal of Social and Biological Structures, January 1978, 1:1, pp. 3-9.

Vanberg, Viktor. "Spontaneous Market Order and Social Rules: A Critical Examination of F.A. Hayek's Theory of Cultural Evolution." Economics and Philosophy, April 1986, 2:1, pp. 75-100.

Veblen, Thorstein. "Why is Economics not an Evolutionary Science?" Quarterly Journal of Economics, July 1898, 12:3, pp. 373-397.

Wilson, Edward O. "The Ergonomics of Caste in the Social Insects." American Economic Review, 1978, 68, pp. 13-35.

Winter, Sidney G. "Natural Selection and Evolution." In John Eatwell, Murray Milgate, and Peter Newman (eds.) The New Palgrave: A Dictionary of Economics, volume three. London: Macmillan Press, 1987, pp. 614-617.

Witt, Ulrich. "Coordination of Individual Economic Activities as an Evolving Process of Self-Organization." Economie Appliquée, 1985, 37, pp. 569-595.

___. Evolutionary Economics. Cheltenham, U.K.: Edward Elgar, 1992a.

___. (ed.). Explaining Process and Change: Approaches to Evolutionary Economics. Ann Arbor, MI: University of Michigan Press, 1992b.

[29]

Why the Problem of Reductionism in Biology Has Implications for Economics

GEOFFREY M. HODGSON

The Judge Institute of Management Studies, University of Cambridge, Cambridge CB2 1RX, UK

ABSTRACT: For several decades, economists have been preoccupied with an attempt to place their entire subject on the 'sound microfoundations' of general equilibrium theory, with its individualistic premises. However, this project has run into seemingly intractable problems. This essay examines underlying questions such as the appropriate building block of analysis and the structure of explanation in economics. The examination of biology is found to be instructive, due to debates concerning the limitations of reductionism within that discipline. The final part of the paper argues for the autonomy of a non-reductionist macroeconomics, based on the institution as the unit of analysis.

KEYWORDS: atomism, biology, economics, hierarchy, individualism, reductionism

Economics today is in confusion and disorder. The comfortable consensus of the postwar years is long gone. There is a plethora of rival approaches and schools. 'Hard core' notions such as rationality and equilibrium are being questioned, even by mainstream theorists. Textbook attempts to make neoclassical theory operational, with aggregated functions, the 'law of demand' and so on, have been found to lack generality and to depend upon a seemingly increasing number of *ad hoc* presuppositions. The precise resolution of this crisis in this subject is not, of course, an easy matter. But nevertheless an examination of some of the fundamental ontological and methodological issues suggests a route of advance that may well repay further intellectual investment.

Part I of this essay addresses some of the ontological and methodological issues involved in the atomistic world view, and in the individualistic version of atomism found in economics. In Part II there is a brief review of some developments in biology which lead away from atomistic and reductionist philosophies. Finally, in Part III, some tentative ideas concerning the future development of economics are proposed, influenced in particular by developments in biology, and involving a discussion of the appropriate levels of reduction in economic science.

World Futures Vol. 37. pp. 69–90
Reprints available directly from the publisher
Photocopying permitted by license only

I. ATOMISM AND REDUCTIONISM IN SCIENCE AND ECONOMICS

Atomism in Science

In an atomist ontology, entities possess qualities independently of their relations with other entities. In the world of atoms 'all qualitative diversity is reduced to differences in configuration and motion of the homogeneous and permanent elements' (Capek, 1961:5). The origins of atomism in the West can be traced back Greek civilisation, and to Leucippus and Democritus in particular. Embracing a deterministic outlook, they believed that everything is composed of atoms which are physically indivisible.

In contrast, Aristotle rejected atomism, and his ideas were prominent in medieval Europe. The move back to atomism, led by Galileo, Descartes, Newton and others, helped to establish the foundations of modern science. In particular, Newtonian physics was built on the analysis of particles and their motions in accord with the assumed fundamental laws. The analytical success of atomism related to the development of methods by which complex phenomena could be broken down and understood in terms of their fundamental components and the interactions between them, involving an impressive analytical reduction of wholes to parts. The new scientific method was thereby characterized by its fusion of an atomist ontology with a reductionist approach to analysis.

The post-medieval rebirth of atomism coincided—not accidentally—with the development of liberal and individualistic doctrines in political science, in the writings of Hobbes and Locke, for example. There is a familiar yet resilient argument that the growth of these ideas was related in some degree to the social and economic changes associated with the development of commodity trade.

In the social sphere the human individual was seen as the fundamental unit of analysis: the indivisible particle in motion. Of course, it is accepted that individuals, like particles, are affected by their circumstances in the manner of the forces and constraints that impinge upon them. But in such an atomist social ontology the essential aspects of human personality and motivation are conceived as independent of the social relations with others. We have a picture of the 'abstract individual . . . pictured abstractly as given, with given interests, wants, purposes, needs, etc.', as Steven Lukes (1973:73) puts it. As a key part of this outlook, individual tastes and preferences are taken as given.

Many examples of atomism and reductionism can be found in both the natural and the social sciences to the present day. For instance, the physicist and Nobel Laureate Steven Weinberg (1974:56) has written: 'One of man's enduring hopes has been to find a few simple laws that would explain why nature with all its seeming complexity and variety is the way it is. . . . At the present moment the closest we can come to a unified view of nature is a description in terms of elementary particles and their mutual interactions.'

Atomism, Individualism and Reductionism in Economics

With a few notable exceptions, the ideas of atomism and its special expression as a form of individualism have dominated economics since its emergence as a science.[1] Since Adam Smith, mainstream economists has taken for granted the analytical primacy either of the individual or of the household. Topics such as growth and distribution have been frequently addressed, but it has been a general belief that such aggregate or social phenomena should, where possible, be explained via an understanding of the behavior of the individuals involved.

The rise of neoclassical economics after 1870 further consolidated this reductionism by providing an analytical framework in which to place the choosing individual, adjusting his or her endowments according to given individual functions of utility or preference and with due heed to prices and constraints.

Thus the dilemmas of choice under constraint increasingly became the dominant theme, reinforcing the maximizing and utility-driven individual as the elemental component of the science. This development has been further consolidated in recent years with attempts to break down the analysis of previously undivided units, such as the government or the family or the firm, into the individual behavioral elements composing them.[2]

At the core of general equilibrium theory the individual atom still remains. Like others, general equilibrium theorist Kenneth Arrow (1968:641) reflects the view that explanations of economic phenomena should be reduced to the behavior of individuals, seeing this as a salutary 'rejection of the organism approach to social problems'. In a mood of disenchantment with aggregative macroeconomic theory, there has been a strong movement since the 1970s to place that arm of the subject on secure microeconomic foundations derived from Walrasian general equilibrium theory (Weintraub, 1979).

The atomistic and reductionist outlook is also endorsed by non-neoclassical authors, such as the Austrian School of Ludwig von Mises and Friedrich Hayek. It is even ratified by the new type of 'rational choice' or 'analytical' Marxism which proudly employs 'standard tools of microeconomic analysis' (Roemer, 1988:172) including versions of general equilibrium and game theory.

John Elster, a leading member of the latter school, expresses well the individualistic presumptions which he shares with orthodoxy: 'The basic building block in the social sciences, the elementary unit of explanation, is the individual action guided by some intention. . . . Generally speaking, the scientific practice is to seek an explanation at a lower level than the explandum. . . . The *search for micro-foundations*, to use a fashionable term from recent controversies in economics, is in reality a pervasive and omnipresent feature of science' (Elster, 1983:20–24).

Methodological Individualism

Clearly, the individualistic version of atomism, as found in the social sciences, has both ontological and methodological aspects. Methodological individualism, in particular, amounts to the view that explanations of social and economic phenomena should be made in individual terms. In other words, social phenomena should be reduced to their individual constituents and the relations between them. A long controversy surrounds the term 'methodological individualism' and it is not possible to go into all the details here.[3]

Faced with the assertion that individual tastes and preferences may be moulded by social circumstances, the methodological individualist responds that these circumstances can and should be themselves explained in individual terms. However, this response involves a problem of infinite regress and cannot establish the analytical supremacy of the individual alone. Just as social phenomena can often be explained in terms of individuals, individuals may also be explained in terms of their social circumstances. Neither has *a priori* theoretical primacy.

A further difficulty for the methodological individualist is why the individual should be chosen as the unit of analysis. After all if 'the scientific practice is to seek an explanation at a lower level than the explandum', as Elster puts it, then why stop with the individual? Why not delve into the psyche, and further, observe the firing of the neurons and the electrochemistry of the brain? As Barry Hindess (1989:91) suggests, just as there may be conflicts of objectives within organizations, thereby ruling out a unitary conception of their operation, there may be diverse and sometimes conflicting objectives within the minds of single individuals. A paradox of methodological individualism is that by its own reductionist canons it is not reductionist enough.

However, several stratagems have been employed to prevent the degenerative rigours of further reductionism, beneath the level of the individual. Hayek (1948:67) seems to speak for neoclassical economists as well as the Austrian school when he asserts that the task of explaining the formation and moulding of individual tastes and preferences is a matter for 'psychology but not for economics . . . or any other social science'. Leaving aside the questionable reduction of such explanations to psychology alone, Hayek is here reinforcing the idea that economics must be a blinkered science. Deeper analysis of the individual by economists is prevented, because if they dare to enter this underworld it is so decreed that thereby they cease to be economists.

Another stratagem involves a Cartesian and dualistic separation of the world. Thus Von Mises (1949:8) writes: 'Reason and experience show us two separate realms, the external world of the physical, chemical and psychological phenomena and the internal world of thought, feeling, valuation and purposeful action'. With such a 'methodological dualism', the individual, now virtually a ghost in the machine, can be rendered safe from further dissection.

Extending this idea, Mises (1960:11) surmises that 'the same situation has a different effect on different men' giving scope for notions of 'free will, of the irrationality of what is human, spiritual, or historical, of individuality in history'. We are thus led to Ludwig Lachmann's (1969:63) notion of individual plans not being a response 'to anything pre-existent' and to George Shackle's (1989:51) premise that 'economics is about choice as a *first cause*.'

In arguing that the forces moulding expectation and decision cannot be explained at all, the position of Shackle and Lachmann is different from that of

Hayek, who suggests that they could possibly be explained by psychology but it would not be legitimate to do so, and from that of neoclassical theorists, who 'explain' behavior by reference to all-determining and exogenous preference functions. The implication of the tenet of Lachmann and Shackle is that reductionism is obliged to stop at the level of the individual precisely because of the indeterminate or uncaused nature of individual decision and action.

The possibility of some indeterminacy of action and decision may be accepted (Hodgson, 1988). Indeed, such an assumption may be necessary to affirm the existence of free will and the reality of choice.[4] A problem, however, is that the existence of either caused or uncaused causes can neither be proved or disproved. And if they exist, why should their location be confined to the human mind? If such indeterminacy is possible, why shouldn't it be located in other living things, or even elsewhere in the universe? With the development of quantum theory, Pandora's box has been opened. As Sir Karl Popper has declared: 'The "natural" view of the universe seems to be indeterministic' (Popper and Eccles, 1977:32; see also Popper, 1982). Hence the trouble with the Lachmann-Shackle defence of reductionism is that it cannot ultimately control the demon of indeterminacy that it has chosen to release.

The general idea of a reduction to parts is not being overturned here. Some degree of reduction to elemental units is inevitable. Science cannot proceed without some dissection and some analysis of parts. However, the process of analysis cannot be extended to the most elementary sub-atomic particles presently known to science. Complete reductionism would be hopeless and interminable. As Sir Karl Popper has declared: 'I do not think that there are any examples of a successful reduction' to elemental units in science (Popper and Eccles, 1977:18). Reduction is necessary to some extent, but it can never be complete. What is contentious, is not reductionism *per se*, but its chosen scope and extent, and the ultimate reliance placed upon it in comparison with other general methodological procedures.

The Failure of the Microfoundations Project

Mainstream theory has been engaged in a longlasting attempt to place economics on secure and individualistic microfoundations. However, it was realized at the outset that the potential diversity amongst individuals threatened the feasibility of the project. Many types of interaction between the individuals have to be ignored. Even with the psychological and epistemological limitations of the standard assumptions of rational behavior, severe difficulties are faced. As Arrow (1986:S388) has been led to declare: 'In the aggregate, the hypothesis of rational behavior has in general no implications.' Consequently, it is widely assumed that all individuals have the same utility function. Amongst other things this denies the possibility of 'gains from trade arising from individual differences' (Arrow, 1986:S390).

Today, it is no exaggeration to say that the microfoundations enterprise has effectively collapsed, and for reasons well known to and understood by the leading theorists of the genre. The gravity of the present crisis for mainstream economics can be illustrated by considering a number of central theoretical topics.[5]

First, theoretical work in game theory and elsewhere has raised questions about the very meaning of 'hard core' notions such as rationality. Yanis Varoufakis (1990) surveys some of the recent results concerning the problems of rational decision making in the circumstances where a limited number of other actors are believed to be capable of 'irrational' acts. Such 'irrationality' need not stem from stupidity; it is sufficient to consider the possibilities that rational actors may have incomplete information, limited computational capacities, slight misperceptions of reality, or doubts concerning the attributes of their adversaries. Agents do not have to be substantially irrational for irrationality to matter. Irrational behavior may emerge simply where some people are uncertain that everybody else is rational. For similar reasons, Robert Sugden (1990:89) observes that 'game theory may rest on a concept of rationality that is ultimately little more than a convention'. These are indeed striking conclusions.

Second, after the door being bolted for decades, mainstream theorists now, albeit in a limited fashion, admit discussion of problems of imperfect or asymmetric information and even 'bounded rationality'. Whilst these are welcome developments they have created havoc with orthodox presuppositions. For instance, as Joseph Stiglitz (1987) has elaborated, where prices signal quality to the consumer, standard demand analysis and the so-called 'law of demand' become overturned.

Third, the intrusion of chaos theory into economics has put paid to the general idea that economics can proceed simply on the criterion of 'correct predictions'. With non-linear models, outcomes are over-sensitive to initial conditions and thereby reliable predictions are impossible to make in regard to any extended time period. In particular, chaos theory has confounded the rational expectations theorists by showing that even if most agents knew the basic structure of the economic model, in general they cannot derive reliable predictions of outcomes and thereby form any meaningful 'rational expectations' of the future (Grandmont, 1987). We shall discuss some further implications of chaos theory below.

Fourth, recent research into the problems of the uniqueness and stability of general equilibria has shown that they may be indeterminate and unstable unless very strong assumptions are made, such as the supposition that society as a whole behaves as if it was a single individual (Coricelli and Dosi, 1988). This disrupts the entire microfoundations project. Facing such profound problems, Alan Kirman (1989:138) concludes: 'If we are to progress further we may well be forced to theorize in terms of groups who have collectively coherent behavior. . . . The idea that we should start at the level of the isolated individual is one which we may well have to abandon.'

The theoretical implications of these uniqueness and stability results for general equilibrium theory are devastating and dramatic. A fundamental consequence is the breakdown of the types of analysis based on individualistic or atomistic ontologies. The indeterminacy and instability results produced by contemporary theory lead to the conclusion that an economy made up of atomistic agents has not structure enough to survive, as its equilibria may be evanescent states from which the system tends to depart (Ingrao and Israel, 1985, 1990; Kirman, 1989). Furthermore, as Donald Katzner (1991) has argued, it is not possible to aggregate from individual supply and demand functions to such aggregated functions at the level of the market if considerations of ignorance and historical time are taken into account.

Typically, the textbook macroeconomics that is spun out of neoclassical theory goes well beyond the rigours of general equilibrium theory, to make bold and general claims concerning the relationship between wages and unemployment, and inflation and the money supply. Only the more honest and careful neoclassical theorists have questioned such macroeconomic derivations from microeconomic assumptions. For instance, Arrow (1986:S386) states that he knows 'of no serious derivation of the demand for money from a rational optimization.' In an extensive examination of orthodox, textbook, macroeconomic theories, John Weeks (1989:236) shows that they 'suffer from serious flaws of internal logic. Accepting these models and proceeding as if they were analytically sound is essentially an act of politically-motivated faith.'

There are many other problems in modern economics, from capital theory to monetary analysis, from the theory of the firm to the economics of welfare. For the moment we have confined ourselves to some special cases only. These conspire to undermine the very ontological and methodological foundations of orthodoxy.

II. BEYOND ATOMISM AND REDUCTIONISM

Analytical Intractability in Biology and Elsewhere

As in other sciences, there is a strong reductionist tradition in biology. One of the best known cases is the work of Richard Dawkins (1976) where he takes the views that the behaviors of organisms, groups and whole species, can and should be explained in terms of their genes. Similarly, sociobiologists such as Edward Wilson (1975) attempt to explain the social behavior of animals and humans entirely in terms of the constituent genes, without adequate recognition of the explanatory autonomy of social culture.

However, biological reductionism likewise encounters unmanageable computational problems. Consider the prediction of evolution at a single locus with multiple alleles: 'even the simplest multi-locus case of two alleles at each of two loci is analytically intractable. This should not be surprising: 'the problem of dimensionality nine (there are nine possible genotypes, with independently specifiable fitness parameters) is already more complicated than the three-body problem of classical mechanics' (Wimsatt, 1980:223). Like the three-body problem, this biological computation has been solved for a variety of special cases (Roughgarden, 1979:111–33) but has not been solved in general.

To assess the dimensions of analytical difficulty, consider the 'less complex' case of the three-body problem in mechanics. Whilst this problem has been solved for two bodies, the differential equations that result from applying these laws to three bodies are so complicated that a general solution has not been found. Instead, partial solutions have been achieved by resorting to approximations or constraints of various kinds, such the assumption that one body has negligible mass (Young, 1968:258; Stewart, 1989:66–72).

Hence mathematical solutions cannot be found to configurations of this very first level of complexity, involving just three bodies. This gives little hope to the biological or economic reductionist who aims to break down all complex phenomena to the interactive behavior of atomistic or individual parts.

Chaos theorists have shown that in non-linear systems, tiny changes in crucial parameters can lead to dramatic consequences (Gleick, 1988; Stewart, 1989). The result is not simply to make prediction difficult or impossible; there are serious implications for the notion of reductive explanation in science. We cannot in complete confidence associate a given outcome with a given set of initial conditions, because we can never be sure that the computations traced out from those initial conditions are precise enough, and that the initial conditions themselves have been defined with sufficient precision. Hence in chaos theory the very notion of explanation of a phenomenon by reference to a system and its initial conditions is challenged.

As leading mathematicians of chaos have themselves proclaimed, chaos theory 'brings a new challenge to the reductionist view that a system can be understood by breaking it down and studying each piece' (Crutchfield et al, 1986:48). The impact of chaos theory for science as a whole is likely to be profound. Not only is the common obsession with precise prediction confounded; the whole atomistic tradition in science of attempting to reduce each phenomenon to its component parts is placed into question.

However, this does not mean that such non-linear equations relating to a lower level of analysis are worthless. Although they may be of limited computational or predictive use, they retain some explanatory power. Furthermore, as noted later below, chaotic systems do exhibit some kind of order from which deductions may be drawn.

The Limitations and Biases of the Counter-Strategies

Strategies have been devised to deal with such complex systems, in biology and elsewhere. For instance, Herbert Simon (1968) has examined 'the hypothesis of near decomposability' through which it is assumed that a complex system can be decomposed into a set of subsystems. For this to be feasible, all strong interactions must be contained within the boundaries of subsystems, and interactions between variables or entities in different subsystems must be appreciably weaker than those relating variables or entities in the same subsystem. If this is the case then a short run approximation to the behavior of the system can be made by ignoring the interactions between subsystems, and analysing each one as if it were isolated.

However, the general applicability of this principle is in doubt. Apart from the remaining problem of long-term interactions, biologists have shown that under feasible conditions there can be permanent and substantial linkage disequilibrium between subsystems (Lewontin, 1974; Maynard Smith, 1978, ch. 5; Roughgarden, 1979). This means that, in general, systems cannot be treated as being nearly decomposable.

In a seminal work of genetic reductionism, George C. Williams (1966) claims that reductive problems can be solved one locus at a time and then extended to a global solution by 'iterating over all loci'. This is now recognised by critics as invalid. Williams wrongly presumes that gene frequency alone is an adequate basis for a deterministic theory of evolutionary change, and ignores context dependence. This refers to a situation where the fitness or behavior of an organism may be significantly dependent on its environmental context, often leading to two-way interactions between a unit and its environment. As William Wimsatt (1980:240) argues: 'Illegitimate assumptions of context-independence are a frequent error in reductionist analyses.'

In the course of his argument, Wimsatt (1980:241) highlights 'the practical impossibility of generating an exhaustive, quasi-algorithmic, or exact analysis of the behavior of the system and its environment'. In response to this complexity 'the reductionist must start simplifying. In general, simplifying assumptions will have to be made everywhere, but given his interest in studying relations *internal* to the system, he will tend to order his list of economic priorities so as to simplify, first and more extremely, in his description, observation, control, and analysis of the environment than in the system he is studying. After all, simplifications internal to the system face the danger of simplifying out of existence the very phenomena and mechanisms he wishes to study.' However, there are clear pitfalls in ignoring the complexities of the environment and some of its interactions with the system in question. Therefore the reductionist research strategy, Wimsatt rightly concludes, has an inbuilt bias towards the inclusion of certain types of relations and the exclusion of others.

The Revival of Organicism in Biology

The dispute between reductionists and non-reductionists in biology has flared up periodically. Partly because of the ongoing prestige enjoyed by the basic physical sciences, ever since Darwin published his *Origin of Species* biologists have been faced with the claim that biological phenomena could be reduced to and explained in terms of classical physics and chemistry. It has been upheld that every living organism must obey the same laws as those that apply to inert matter and that there are no other laws. In the past, some biologists adopted this physicalist viewpoint, and ventured to explain biological phenomena mechanistically and deterministically in terms of particles, movements and forces. Max Hartmann, Hermann Helmholtz, Jacques Loeb, Carl Ludwig, Julius Sachs and August Weismann took this physicalist view. Although it has since declined in adherents, it has persisted as late as the postwar period. Note the words of Nobel Laureate Francis Crick (1966:10): 'the ultimate aim of the modern movement in biology is in fact to explain *all* biology in terms of physics and chemistry.'[6]

For a long time the opposition to physicalism from within biology came from those who followed Aristotle and proposed that a living organism had some kind of constituent that clearly distinguished it from inert matter. This 'vital force' was deemed not to obey the laws of physics and chemistry. 'For a vitalist, at least an extreme vitalist, there are two entirely separate worlds, that of the physical sciences and that of the world of life' (Mayr, 1985:45). Leading biologists such as Hans Driesch and J. B. S. Haldane adopted vitalism. Mayr (1985:46) evaluates this group as follows: 'There is little doubt that some of the much-maligned vitalists had a far more profound understanding of the living organism than their mechanistic opponents.' Since the 1940s, however, vitalism has had no significant following.

With conceptual developments in postwar biology, physicalism also went into decline. Instead, the refined synthesis between Darwinism and Mendelian genetics focussed the attention of many on the gene as the unit of analysis. However, a thoroughgoing reductionist should not be content with explanations based on the gene alone. This unit should in turn be reduced to its constituent elements. Accordingly, there is a controversy over the possibility of the reduction of Mendelian genetics to molecular biology.[7]

In addition, there is a related quarrel over the unit of evolutionary selection. On this central issue there is as yet no consensus amongst biologists, and views range from the idea of the gene as the exclusive unit of selection as in the work of Dawkins, through the possibility of group or species selection, up to the selection of ecosystems.[8]

Even with such a diversity of views, biology fosters an intuition about the wholeness of living systems. As Mayr (1985:44) retorts: 'every biologist would insist that to dissect complex biological systems into elementary particles would be by all odds the worst way to study nature'. Mayr's (1985:57–58) own argument goes further: 'Nowhere in the inanimate world can one find a system, even a complex system, that has the ordered internal cohesion and coadaptation of even the simplest of biological systems. And this requires an entirely different approach from that of the classical philosophy of science.'

An earlier postwar challenge to atomism and reductionism came from the set of biologists, including Ludwig von Bertalanffy (1971) and Paul Weiss (1973), who had become the pioneers of general systems theory. Although the reductionist tradition remains strong, there have been further moves against genetic reductionism in biology in recent years. These are found in the work of Niles Eldredge, Stephen Jay Gould, Richard Lewontin and Ernst Mayr, amongst others.[9]

The Principles of Hierarchy and Emergence

Along with some philosophers of biology, the view is proposed here that the key to this alternative approach is through an exploration of the organising principles of complex, hierarchical, open systems. We proceed by noting, first, that systems or sub-systems at each level of the hierarchy have a dual character, acting both as wholes themselves and as parts of other wholes (Miller, 1978). Arthur Koestler (1967:383) has attempted to capture this dual quality of each system with the term 'holon': 'Biological holons are self-regulating open systems which display both the autonomous properties of wholes and the dependent properties of parts.' According to Koestler (1978:57), each holon combines two opposite but complementary tendencies: an integrative tendency to function as a part of the larger whole, and a self-assertive tendency to preserve its individual autonomy.

Further, Donald Campbell (1974:182) has drawn attention to the way in which wholes, through what he calls downward causation, can affect the properties of components at lower levels. Thus in addition to the notion of the whole being greater than the sum of the parts, to some extent the whole determines the properties of the parts.

In a related vein, Mayr (1985:58) argues: 'Systems at each hierarchical level have two characteristics. They act as wholes (as if they were a homogeneous entity), and their characteristics cannot (not even in theory) be deduced from the most complete knowledge of the components, taken separately or in other partial combinations. In other words, when such systems are assembled from their components, new characteristics of the new whole emerge that could not have been predicted from a knowledge of the components.'

This principle of emergence is a fundamental characteristic of complex, hierarchical systems. Reductionism is thwarted by the existence of such emergent properties at each level of the hierarchy. As Mayr (1985:58) contends: 'Recognition of the importance of emergence demonstrates, of course, the invalidity of extreme reductionism. By the time we have dissected an organism down to atoms and elementary particles we have lost everything that is characteristic of a living system.' Furthermore: 'Such emergence is quite universal, occurring also, of course, in inanimate systems, but nowhere else plays the important role that it does in living organisms.'

This hierarchic ontology also counters strict determinism, for the existence of emergent properties suggests that some phenomena are uncaused, at least in the traditional sense in terms of the dissectable combination of forces acting upon them. As Popper (1974:281) has remarked: 'We live in a universe of emergent novelty.'

Chaos Theory and Novelty

Chaos theory suggests that apparent novelty may arise from a deterministic system. Nevertheless, this does not give outright victory to determinism in its old battle against indeterminacy. On the contrary, chaos theory suggests that the rules of engagement have changed. Even if the world is deterministic, the theory suggests that we should have to treat it as if it were indeterministic and unpredictable. Even if novelty is caused, it may appear as entirely spontaneous and free.

Thus the very distinction between determinacy and indeterminacy is undermined. We can never know for sure if any event is caused or uncaused, but chaos theory suggests that we have to treat complex systems as if they were indeterministic. As Philip Mirowski (1990:305) writes: 'The chaos literature instead reveals the curious symbiosis of randomness and determinism, the blurring of the boundaries between order and chaos.'

Correspondingly, chaos theory combines the notions of order and novelty. Significantly, James Crutchfield et al (1986:49) relate this to the concept of evolution:

> Chaos is often seen in terms of the limitations it implies, such as lack of predictability. Nature may, however, employ chaos constructively. Through amplification of small fluctuations it can provide natural systems with access to novelty. . . . Biological evolution demands genetic variability; chaos provides a means of structuring random

changes, thereby providing the possibility of putting variability under evolutionary control.

A dynamic system that exhibits chaotic behavior may in fact be performing complex oscillations around an attractor. Chaotic attractors are complex configurations within which the behavior of seemingly random and unpredictable systems is constrained. As Ervin Laszlo (1987:41–42) puts it, chaos theory 'studies processes that appear chaotic on the surface but on detailed analysis prove to manifest subtle strands of order'. Thus the chaos generated out of orderly mathematical functions generates a kind of order at a higher level.[10]

The Unity of Science

Mayr (1985:52) observes that 'evolutionary biology, with its interest in historical processes, is in some respects as closely allied to the humanities as it is to the exact sciences' (p. 52). Thus greater direct inspiration for economics may be derived from modern biology. This is partly because of the way in which biology addresses diversity, complexity and change, but also to do with the claim that biology may encompass a wider set of principles than physics. In short, biology embraces life.

Following such a trail, a number of writers have developed schemata for the unity of science as a whole, including both its natural and its social branches. In general terms, of course, this is an old idea. But what marks out the new attempts at unity is the incorporation of the principles of hierarchy and emergence, as described above.[11]

The unity is not achieved in a reductionist manner, by breaking phenomena down into atomistic units and observing the interactions between them in a complete model. The formulation of a complete mechanistic system of this kind was the dream of Laplace. Such a mechanical reduction is not only unobtainable in practice; attempts to work extensively in and exclusively in such a manner destroy the very life, spontaneity and complexity of nature, and of systems containing living things.

The principles of hierarchy and emergence combine to prevent the reduction of all this complexity to common, simple units, whether they be ontological particles or theoretical laws. Each level in the hierarchy has its own autonomy, and thereby its own principles of explanation and its own units of analysis. However, this autonomy is not absolute. Phenomena at one level are underlain by phenomena at the level below and affected by those at the level above. Explanations at each level are in some respects compatible with those at different tiers.

Paul Oppenheim and Hilary Putnam (1968) have put forward a sketch of a future, unified science, discussing six 'reductive levels': social groups, multicellular living things, cells, molecules, atoms, and elementary particles. More recently, addressing some additional methodological questions and taking heed of some of the developments in the philosophy of biology discussed above, Nancy Maull contrasts two approaches to the unity of science. On the one hand, there is the limited and traditional approach of 'derivational reduction'. On the other, there is an 'interlevel theory' which 'by establishing, explaining, and warranting the connections between different levels' (Maull, 1977:158) bridges different tiers in the hierarchy.

In an equally ambitious work, Laszlo (1987) portends the unification of science within an evolutionary framework. He addresses ideas about dissipative structures and 'self-organization' in complex systems (Nicolis and Prigogine, 1977; Prigogine and Stengers, 1984) and concerning autopoietic systems (Varela *et al*, 1974; Maturana, 1975; Benseler *et al*, 1980; Zeleny, 1980, 1981, 1987) which 'can maintain themselves in time only if they evolve the capacity to replicate or reproduce their structure' (Laszlo, 1987:38). Laszlo's work offers some useful suggestions for economic theory, some of which are discussed in the next section below.

An important feature of the hierarchically ordered view of reality is that different levels are both divided and interconnected. It is important to neglect neither the interconnectness nor the division of the hierarchy. Marshall Sahlins's (1977) spirited critique of sociobiology is an example of an error of the former kind. He goes too far by sealing off the social and cultural, on the one hand, from natural phenomena, on the other. His anti-reductionism thus builds Chinese Walls, completely detaching the realm of the social from the realm of the natural upon which in reality it depends. In contrast, an anti-reductionism of a hierarchically-structured kind may be able to accommodate some notions of genetic causation at the social level, without reducing social explanations wholly or largely to lower-level, biological causes. The ontology of the structured hierarchy thus promotes the connectedness of methods, without denying the methodologies of the social and the life sciences some respective autonomy.

The converse error is to ignore the divided character of the hierarchy, and the autonomy of its different levels. This error is committed by Dawkins (1976) and Wilson (1975). Generally, atomistic reductionism is mistaken in this regard. However, some presentations of holism are likewise reductionist, by suggesting that we can somehow study wholes directly without considering the workings of their constituent parts. Such a version of holism is another kind of reductionism, and simply the obverse of the mistaken, atomistic view that systems can be completely understood simply by addressing the interactions between their constituent parts. The term 'holism' can only be acceptable if it is defined in a non-reductionist way, accepting the relative autonomy of the parts as well as the wholes.

IV. BRINGING LIFE BACK INTO ECONOMICS

The Autonomy of Macroeconomics

One thing that is remarkable about modern, complex economic systems is their enduring stability and resilience over long periods of time, despite the multitude of decisions and actions, and the plethora of variety at the microeconomic level. We may conjecture that for years or sometimes even decades, socio-economic systems become locked-in to a fixed overall patterns of dynamic development. Whilst there will be *parametric* change in economic variables such as output and employment, there may be years or decades of overall and relative *structural* stability. Such structural stability, based on a set of dominant socio-economic relations, creates the possibility of macroeconomic analysis and modelling.

Support for such a notion can be found in the modern theory of nonlinear systems. As Jay Forrester (1987:108) argues:

> A rich representation of nonlinearities leads to a model that is relatively insensitive to parameter values. Being insensitive to parameter values is also a characteristic of most social systems. . . . In fact, the operating point of a system tends to move along the changing slopes of its nonlinearities until it finds an operating region that is determined more by the structure of the system than be plausible differences in parameter values. In a high-order nonlinear system, one can move many parameters within a plausible range with little effect on essential behavior.

The modern theory of complex systems has led to the idea of autopoiesis. An autopoietic system is not in a state of equilibrium, at least in the normal senses of that term. Precisely because it is far from a thermodynamic or mechanical equilibrium such an open system must absorb energy from its environment. Autopoietic systems 'can maintain themselves in time only if they evolve the capacity to replicate or reproduce their structure' (Laszlo, 1987:38). Like living animals and plants, such systems maintain an autonomy and continuity of pattern 'despite the endless turnover of their constituents' (Zeleny, 1987:393). Clearly, economic systems may well exhibit autopoietic self-replication and growth.

It is important to note that, just as the features of a plant may change during its growth, autopoietic development in economic systems does not, within limits, exclude changes in technology and tastes. The structural stability implied is not rigid; it is simply sufficient to provide coherence and a consistent mode of self-organization. A socio-economic system in an autopoietic phase will be one that is exhibiting particular patterns of growth and development. The growth rate and economic fluctuations will be within a broad range. Socioeconomic structures and institutions will be subject to piecemeal rather than fundamental change.

In contrast, there may be apparent randomness at the micro-level, with substantial variety in the structure and behavior of individual units. However, the interactions between these elements help to generate a degree of (impermanent) stability and coherence at the macro-level. Such an argument is reminiscent of the 'principle of *stratified determinism*' adduced by Paul Weiss (1969), i.e. the 'principle of *determinacy in the gross despite demonstrable indeterminacy in the small*'. Today, however, with the insights of chaos theory it has to be accepted that even apparent indeterminacy may have deterministic roots. Thus, paraphrasing Weiss, an autopoietic system exhibits a high degree of order at the macro level, in contrast to variety and chaos at the micro level. At the higher and more complex level, spanning many territories and units, the behavior of institutions is more stable, and more determined or weighed down by cumulative interactions in the system and the constraints of its past. Variations are buffered out and rendered inconsequential.

Through this feature of 'self-organization', as the work of Ilya Prigogine and his collaborators shows order can result from chaos. Indeed, although individual variations are rendered inconsequential in systems in this state, the degree of homoeostatic self-regulation vitally *depends upon* extensive diversity and chaos at the micro level. Without the latter, the system as a whole would be more vulnerable to aggregative and cumulative feedback effects and prone to instability itself.

Elements of these modern arguments for self-organization and periods of relative stability can be found in the work of Thorstein Veblen. He observed that routines have a stable and inert quality, and tend to sustain and thus 'pass on' their important characteristics through time: 'The situation of today shapes the institutions of tomorrow through a selective, coercive process, by acting upon men's habitual view of things, and so altering or fortifying a point of view or a mental attitude handed down from the past' (Veblen, 1899:190–1).

According to Veblen (1919:239), institutions are 'settled habits of thought common to the generality of men'. They are seen as both outgrowths and reinforcers of the routinized thought processes that are shared by a number of persons in a given society. As Walton Hamilton (1963:84) elaborates, the term 'institution . . . connotes a way of thought or action of some prevalence and permanence, which is embedded in the habits of a group or the customs of a people. . . . Institutions fix the confines of and impose form upon the activities of human beings.'

On this basis Veblen (1899, 1919) argued that economic development is best regarded as an evolutionary process. He suggested that organizational structures, habits and routines play a similar evolutionary role to that of the gene in the natural world. Whilst these are more malleable and do not mutate in the same way as their analogue in biology, structures and routines do have a sufficient degree of durability to regard them as having quasi-genetic qualities.

The power and durability of institutions and routines are manifest in a number of ways. With the benefit of modern developments in modern anthropology and psychology it can be seen that institutions play an essential role in providing a cognitive framework for interpreting sense data and in providing intellectual habits or routines for transforming information into useful knowledge (Hodgson, 1988). These cultural and cognitive functions have been investigated by anthropologists such as Mary Douglas (1973, 1987) and Barbara Lloyd (1972). Reference to the cognitive functions of institutions and routines is important in understanding their relative stability and capacity to replicate. Indeed, the strong, reinforcing interaction between social institutions and individual cognition provides some significant stability in socio-economic systems in their autopoeitic phase, partly by buffering the diverse and variable actions of many agents.

On the basis of these typically self-reinforcing norms of perception and behavior, the economy can exhibit some structural stability for periods of time. However, these are punctuated by occasions where such conventions may 'change violently as the result of sudden fluctuations of opinion' (Keynes, 1936:154). As Nicholas Georgescu-Roegen (1971:127) has argued in general terms, the history 'of an individual or of a society, seems to be the result of two factors: a hysteresis process and the emergence of novelty'.

The periods of structural stability make macroeconomic modelling and estimation feasible; the periods of crisis undermine firm predictions, particularly regarding the more volatile variables. However, as John Maynard Keynes made clear, it is not only impossible to make reliable predictions during a period of high turbulence in the economy, but the timing of such disruptive episodes cannot be forecast with any assurance.[12]

Nevertheless, the macroeconomist must make do. Empirical work should involve the search for regularities and tendencies as part of the process of establishing plausible causal linkages. As Tony Lawson (1989:65) asserts, 'to the extent that any manifest phenomenon appears to reveal some degree of uniformity, generality, or persistency, albeit by no means complete in such respects, it would seem to provide a *prima facie* case for supposing that some enduring generative mechanisms are at work'. Lawson argues that such an approach is both compatible with philosophical realism and the methodological essentials of the macroeconomic work of Post Keynesians such as Nicholas Kaldor. It is also notable that it is consistent with the autonomous and non-reductionist status of macroeconomic theory proposed in this essay.

In Defence of the Ad Hoc

The old charge against the type of macroeconomics associated with the Post Keynesians is that it is 'ad hoc'. Such is the rallying cry of the reductionist, dismissing all theoretical formulations based on aggregated terms, and condemning all such constructions because of the absence of secure microfoundations. Such a charge, however, is dubious and misconceived.

In fact, all attempts to find secure microfoundations must inevitably involve gross simplifications and ad hoc assumptions of another kind. As Lawson (1989) points out, neoclassical general equilibrium theory involves a number of arbitrary assumptions or 'axioms'. Some of these axioms, like 'people have preferences', are 'relatively contentless'. Others are added to make the mathematics tractable, such as the assumption of a production function in a Cobb-Douglas form.

However, both types of assumption are restrictive and ad hoc. The 'people have preferences' assumption, for instance, is interpreted in such a way that it is inconsistent with lexicographic choice (Earl, 1983). As noted above, most existing general equilibrium theory goes even further by assuming that all individuals are identical. Hence another ad hoc, restrictive and unrealistic assumption is made. Again, heroic assumptions about the well-behaved and stable character of a 'production function' show adhocness in a most fanciful and confident mood.

There is also the problem of explaining why reduction should stop short at the level of the individual. For the thoroughgoing reductionist to stop short of reduction at any level other than the most elemental subatomic particle currently known to science requires some explanation. Furthermore, because the most elemental level is never actually reached, a degree of adhocness is inevitable, thus committing the very same crime with which Keynesians and others have been charged.

In general, as Larry Laudan (1977:114–8) has argued, adhocness in scientific theories cannot be entirely avoided. Most major and prestigious theories, including Newton's and Darwin's, are ad hoc. Furthermore, he insists, adhocness with theories is generally a cognitive virtue rather than a vice, because it becomes a pragmatic lever in the process of problem solving.

The ontological ideas discussed above, particularly the view that reality is hierarchically ordered, sustain a methodology which endorses a kind of adhocness in relation to each level in the system. Because each level has a degree of autonomy, assumptions cannot be justified in reductionist terms, that is by basing them entirely upon the characteristics of entities discerned at a lower level. However, because the levels are connected, assumptions made in regard to a particular level cannot be arbitrary, and attempts must be made to render them consistent with other assumptions or results, at lower, higher, or equivalent levels. A principle upon which legitimate but conditional theoretical aggregations may be based is discussed in the concluding section.

In Conclusion: Institutions as Units of Analysis

Among the primary tasks of scientific analysis are taxonomy and classification: the assignment of sameness and difference. Classification, by bringing together entities in discrete groups, must refer to common qualities.[13] For classification to work, it must be assumed that the common qualities themselves must be invariant. However, as Mirowski (1989:397) puts it: 'No posited invariance holds without exceptions and qualifications. We live in a world of broken symmetries and partial invariances.' As Georgescu-Roegen (1971) has insisted, operational concepts have a contradictory or dialectical quality; they uneasily encompass their opposites.

The structured hierarchy of theories and concepts incorporates a web of partial invariances at each level. The problem, then, is to develop meaningful and operational principles of invariance upon which analysis can be founded. In social science, the institutionalist tradition has a tentative answer to this problem, locating invariances in the (imperfect) self-reinforcing mechanisms of (partially) stable social institutions: 'such as the institutions of accounting conventions (say, Werner Sombart or David Ellerman) or in the legal definition of property rights (John R. Commons), or else in money itself (Knapp and the German Historicist School)' (Mirowski, 1989:400).

Institutions, in short, are taken as the units and entities of analysis. This should apply to both microeconomics and macroeconomics. Theories based on aggregates become plausible when based on corresponding social institutions. Money is a legitimate unit of account because money itself is an institutionally-sanctioned medium. Aggregate consumption functions should relate to a set of persons with strong institutional and cultural links, and so on. This contrasts with of the approach based on reasoning from bare axioms based on the supposed universals of individual behavior. This approach based on institutional specifics rather than ahistorical universals is characteristic of institutional, Marxian and Keynesian economics.

American institutionalists such as Veblen and Commons, saw the relationship between the relatively invariant qualities of social institutions and the 'genetic' elements of biological evolution. They thus implied that biology and economics were on different ontological levels but united by some broad and common evolutionary themes. The grand synthesis proposed in recent years was thus foreshadowed.

Despite these insights, the American institutionalists were never able to develop a comprehensive theoretical system. But the fortification of their general theoretical approach by recent developments in the biological and even physical sciences gives the institutionalist school a renewed impetus. Nevertheless, the approach sketched out here is tentative and provisional, and the ideas in this essay require much development and clarification.

One point that has been established is that recent developments in biology and the philosophy of biology are of great relevance for economics and indeed the other social sciences. In particular they may rescue economics from its implicit atomist ontology and reductionist obsessions. Long ago Alfred Marshall (1949:xii) wrote that 'the Mecca of the economist lies in economic biology rather than in economic dynamics'.[14] Indeed, the interaction of biology with economics goes back even earlier than the inspiration that Charles Darwin drew from the writings of Thomas Robert Malthus (Schweber, 1977; Jones, 1989; Hodgson, 1993). The suggestion here is that there is much to be gained from a renewed exchange of ideas.

It is a sign of the times that an orthodox theorist of the stature of Frank Hahn (1991:48–50) has predicted that in the next hundred years 'the subject will return to its Marshallian affinities to biology,' noting that evolutionary theories are already beginning to flourish. His successors, he concludes, will not be so preoccupied with 'grand unifying theory' or so immersed in 'the pleasures of theorems and proof.' What will take their place? Hahn candidly writes: 'the uncertain embrace of history and sociology and biology.' Such would be a victory for a kind of economics that is able once again to draw inspiration from the sciences of life.

Acknowledgments

The author wishes to acknowledge gratefully the supportive facilities of a fellowship at the Swedish Collegium for Advanced Study in the Social Sciences in writing this paper, and to thank several colleagues, particularly Uskali Mäki and Allan Pred, for discussions. Thanks are also due to Mika Pantzar for editorial advice.

Notes

1. Arguably, notable exceptions are Karl Marx, John Maynard Keynes, John Hobson, and the American institutionalists. For a relevant debate on Keynes see, for example, Winslow (1986, 1989), O'Donnell (1989:127–36, 177–8) and Davis (1989, 1989–90). On Hobson see Freeden (1990). On Keynes and the institutionalists see Gruchy (1948).
2. Note, for example, the neoclassical analyses of the family by Gary Becker (1976); of the firm by Alchian and Demsetz (1972) and Oliver Williamson (1975, 1985); and of government by Anthony Downs (1957) and James Buchanan and Gordon Tullock (1962).
3. For a more extensive discussion, with references to the literature, see Hodgson (1988, ch. 3).
4. Thorp (1980) argues that the defence of free will has precisely to be located in the neurophysiological indeterminacy of the nervous system, and, following a suggestion of Sir John Eccles, that such indeterminacy is both real and indeterminate in the deeper sense that it is not governed by a probability function. However, Thorp's argument does not entertain the possibility that the firing of the neurons may not be a case of indeterminacy but deterministic chaos. Indeed, chaos theory might put a new perspective on these controversies.

5. The crisis in economic theory afflicts heterodox as well as orthodox traditions but for reasons of brevity the other schools of thought are not discussed in detail here.
6. As a result of the dominance of the physicalist view 'there was an almost total neglect of specific biological phenomena in the literature of the philosophy of science' Mayr (1985:45).
7. See, for example, Hull (1976), Maull (1977), Nagel (1961:428–46), Ruse (1976), Schaffner (1976), Wimsatt (1976).
8. After attack from Dawkins, the notion of group selection has been refined and defended by a number of authors, particularly Sober (1984a). See Brandon and Burian (1984) and Hodgson (1991a, 1992) for discussions and references.
9. See, in particular, Eldredge (1985), Gould (1982).
10. Conversely, Prigogine and Stengers (1984) start from chaotic interactions and show that self-organisation and order can arise in complex systems. This insight complements chaos theory; order can emerge from chaos just as chaos can be spun from order.
11. See, for example, Laszlo (1987), Jantsch (1980).
12. For further discussion, with econometric tests, of a related idea of punctuated autopoietic growth see Hodgson (1991b). This, of course, relates to the idea of punctuated equilibrium in biology (Eldredge and Gould, 1972, 1977; Gould, 1982).
13. Classification must transcend the old dilemma of nominalism versus essentialism. Mary Douglas (1987:397) rightly remarks that 'it is naive to think that the quality of sameness, which characterizes members of a class, as if it were a quality inherent in things or as a power of recognition inherent in the mind.' The latter subjectivism implies that the human mind can be treated as unitary and self-contained, the former essentialism an atomism of things in themselves.
14. For discussions of Marshall's use of biology see Thomas (1991) and Hodgson (1993).

References

Alchian, A. A. and Demsetz, H. 1972. 'Production, Information Costs, and Economic Organization', *American Economic Review*, 62:777–95.

Arrow, K. J. 1968. 'Mathematical Models in the Social Sciences', in M. Brodbeck (ed.) 1968. *Readings in the Philosophy of the Social Sciences*. New York: Macmillan.

Arrow, K. J. 1986. 'Rationality of Self and Others in an Economic System', *Journal of Business*, 59:S385–S399. Reprinted in R. M. Hogarth and M. W. Reder (eds.) 1987: *Rational Choice: The Contrast Between Economics and Psychology*. Chicago: University of Chicago Press.

Ayala, F. J. and Dobzhansky, T. (eds.) 1974. *Studies in the Philosophy of Biology*. Berkeley and Los Angeles: University of California Press.

Becker, G. S. 1976. *The Economic Approach to Human Behavior*. Chicago: University of Chicago Press.

Benseler, F., Hejl, P. M. and Koeck, W. K. (eds.) 1980. *Autopoiesis, Communication and Society*. Frankfurt: Campus.

Bertalanffy, L. von 1971. *General System Theory: Foundation Development Applications*. London: Allen Lane.

Brandon, R. N. and Burian, R. M. (eds.) 1984. *Genes, Organisms, Populations: Controversies Over the Units of Selection*. Cambridge: MIT Press.

Buchanan, J. M. and Tullock, G. 1962. *The Calculus of Consent*. Ann Arbor: University of Michigan Press.

Campbell, D. T. 1974. '"Downward Causation" in Hierarchically Organized Biological Systems'. In Ayala and Dobzhansky (1974).

Capek, M. 1961. *The Philosophical Impact of Contemporary Physics*. Princeton: Van Nostrand.

Cohen, R. S. *et al* (eds.) 1976: *Philosophy of Science Association 1974*. Dordrecht: Reidel.

Coricelli, F. and Dosi, G. 1988. 'Coordination and Order in Economic Change and the Interpretative Power of Economic Theory'. In Dosi, G., Freeman, C., Nelson, R. R., Silverberg, G., and Soete, L. (eds.): *Technical Change and Economic Theory*. London: Pinter.

Crick, F. 1966. *Of Molecules and Men*. Seattle: University of Washington Press.

Crutchfield, J. P., Farmer, J. D., Packard, N. H., Shaw, R. S. 1986. 'Chaos', *Scientific American*, 255:38–49.

Davis, J. B. 1989. 'Keynes on Atomism and Organicism'. *The Economic Journal*, 99:1159–72.

Davis, J. B. 1989–90. 'Keynes and Organicism'. *Journal of Post Keynesian Economics*, 12:308–15.

Dawkins, R. 1976. *The Selfish Gene*. Oxford: Oxford University Press.

Douglas, M. (ed.) 1973. *Rules and Meanings*. Harmondsworth: Penguin.

Douglas, M. 1987. *How Institutions Think*. London: Routledge and Kegan Paul.

Downs, A. 1957. *An Economic Theory of Democracy*. New York: Harper.

Earl, P. E. 1983. *The Economic Imagination: Towards a Behavioual Analysis of Choice*. Brighton: Wheatsheaf.

Eldredge, N. 1985. *Unfinished Synthesis: Biological Hierarchies and Modern Evolutionary Thought*. Oxford: Oxford University Press.

Eldredge, N. and Gould, S. J. 1972. 'Punctuated Equilibria: An Alternative to Phyletic Gradualism'. In Schopf, T. J. M. (ed.) *Models in Paleobiology*. San Francisco: Freeman, Cooper and Co.

Eldredge, N. and Gould, S. J. 1977. 'Punctuated Equilibria: The Tempo and Mode of Evolution Reconsidered'. *Paleobiology*, 3:115–51.

Elster, J. 1983. *Explaining Technical Change*. Cambridge: Cambridge University Press.

Forrester, J. W. 1987. 'Nonlinearity in High-Order Models of Social Systems'. *European Journal of Operational Research*, 30:104–9.

Freeden, M. (ed.) 1990. *Reappraising J. A. Hobson: Humanism and Welfare*. London: Unwin Hyman.

Georgescu-Roegen, N. 1971. *The Entropy Law and the Economic Process*. Cambridge: Harvard University Press.

Gleick, J. 1988. *Chaos: Making a New Science*. London: Heinemann.

Gould, S. J. 1982. 'The Meaning of Punctuated Equilibrium and its Role in Validating a Hierarchical Approach to Macroevolution'. In Milkman, R. (ed.) *Perspectives on Evolution*. Sunderland: Sinauer Associates.

Grandmont, J.-M. (ed.) 1987. *Nonlinear Economic Dynamics*. New York: Academic Press.

Gruchy, A. G. 1948. 'The Philosophical Basis of the New Keynesian Economics'. *Ethics*, 58:235–44.

Hahn, F. H. 1991. 'The Next Hundred Years'. *The Economic Journal*, 101:47–50.

Hamilton, W. H. 1963. 'Institution'. In Seligman, E. R. A. and Johnson, A. (eds.): *Encyclopaedia of the Social Sciences*, 7:84–89.

Hayek, F. A. 1948. *Individualism and Economic Order*. Chicago: University of Chicago Press.

Hindess, B. 1989. *Political Choice and Social Structure*. Aldershot: Edward Elgar.

Hodgson, G. M. 1988. *Economics and Institutions: A Manifesto for a Modern Institutional Economics*. Cambridge: Polity Press.

Hodgson, G. M. 1991a. 'Hayek's Theory of Cultural Evolution: An Evaluation in the Light of Vanberg's Critique'. *Economics and Philosophy*, 7:67–82.

Hodgson, G. M. 1991b. 'Socio-Political Disruption and Economic Development'. In Hodgson, G. M. and Screpanti, E. (eds.): *Rethinking Economics: Markets, Technology and Economic Evolution*. Aldershot: Edward Elgar.

Hodgson, G. M. 1993. *Economics and Evolution*. Cambridge: Polity Press (forthcoming).

Hull, D. L. 1976. 'Informal Aspects of Theory Reduction'. In Cohen *et al*, 1976:653–70. Reprinted in Sober (1984b).

Ingrao, B. and Israel, G. 1985. 'General Economic Equilibrium: A History of Ineffectual Paradigmatic Shift'. *Fundamenta Scientiae*, 6:1–45, 89–125.

Ingrao, B. and Israel, G. 1990. *The Invisible Hand: Economic Equilibrium in the History of Science*. Cambridge: MIT Press.

Jantsch, E. 1980. *The Self-Organizing Universe: Scientific and Human Implications of the Emerging Paradigm of Evolution*. Oxford and New York: Pergamon Press.

Jones, L. B. 1989. 'Schumpeter versus Darwin: In re Malthus'. *Southern Economic Journal*, 56:410–22.

Katzner, D. W. 1991. 'Aggregation and the Analysis of Markets'. *Review of Political Economy*, 3:220–31.

Keynes, J. M. 1936. *The General Theory of Employment, Interest and Money*. London: Macmillan.

Kirman, A. 1989. 'The Intrinsic Limits of Modern Economic Theory: The Emperor Has No Clothes'. *The Economic Journal (Conference Papers)*, 99:126–139.

Koestler, A. 1967. *The Ghost in the Machine*. London: Hutchinson.

Koestler, A. 1978. *Janus—A Summing Up*. London: Hutchinson.

Lachmann, L. M. 1969. 'Methodological Individualism and the Market Economy'. In Streissler, E. (ed.): *Roads to Freedom: Essays in Honour of Friedrich A. von Hayek*. London: Routledge and Kegan Paul. Reprinted in Lachman, L. M. 1977. *Capital, Expectations and the Market Process*. Kansas City: Sheed Andrews and McMeel.

Laszlo, E. 1987. *Evolution: The Grand Synthesis*. Boston: New Science Library—Shambhala.

Laudan, L. 1977. *Progress and its Problems: Towards a Theory of Scientific Growth*. London: Routledge and Kegan Paul.

Lawson, A. 1989. 'Abstraction, Tendencies and Stylised Facts: A Realist Approach to Economic Analysis'. *Cambridge Journal of Economics*, 13:59–78. Reprinted in Lawson, A., Palma, J. G., and Sender, J. (eds.) 1989: *Kaldor's Political Economy*. London: Academic Press.

Lewontin, R. C. 1970. 'The Units of Selection'. *Annual Review of Ecology and Systematics*, 1:1–18.

Lewontin, R. C. 1974. *The Genetic Basis of Evolutionary Change*. New York: Columbia University Press.

Lloyd, B. B. 1972. *Perception and Cognition: A Cross-Cultural Perspective*. Harmondsworth: Penguin.

Lukes, S. 1973. *Individualism*. Oxford: Basil Blackwell.

Marshall, A. 1949. *The Principles of Economics*. 8th reset edn. London: Macmillan.

Maturana, H. R. 1975. 'The Organisation of the Living: A Theory of the Living Organisation'. *International Journal of Man-Machine Studies*, 7:313–32.

Maull, N. 1977. 'Unifying Science Without Reduction'. *Studies in the History and Philosophy of Science*, 9:143–62. Reprinted in Sober (1984b).

Maynard Smith, J. 1978. *The Evolution of Sex*. London: Cambridge University Press.

Mayr, E. 1985. 'How Biology Differs from the Physical Sciences'. In Depew, D. J. and Weber, B. H. (eds.): *Evolution at the Crossroads: The New Biology and the New Philosophy of Science*. Cambridge: MIT Press.

Miller, J. G. 1978. *Living Systems*. New York: McGraw-Hill.

Mirowski, P. 1989. *More Heat Than Light: Economics as Social Physics, Physics as Nature's Economics*. Cambridge: Cambridge University Press.

Mirowski, P. 1990. 'From Mandelbrot to Chaos in Economic Theory'. *Southern Economic Journal*, 57:289–307.

Mises, L. von 1949. *Human Action: A Treatise on Economics*. London: William Hodge.

Mises, L. von 1960. *Epistemological Problems of Economics*. New York: Van Nostrand.

Nagel, E. 1961. *The Structure of Science*. Indianapolis: Hackett Publishing.

Nicolis, G. and Prigogine, I. 1977. *Self-Organization in Non-Equilibrium Systems: From Dissipative Structures to Order Through Fluctuations*. New York: Wiley.

O'Donnell, R. M. 1989. *Keynes: Philosophy, Economics and Politics*. London: Macmillan.

Oppenheim, P. and Putnam, H. 1968. 'Unity of Science as a Working Hypothesis'. In Feigl, H., Scriven, M., and Maxwell, M. and G. (eds.): *Concepts, Theories, and the Mind-Body Problem, Minnesota Studies in the Philosophy of Science, Vol. 2*. Minneapolis: University of Minnesota Press.

Popper, K. R. 1974. 'Scientific Reduction and the Essential Incompleteness of All Science'. In Ayala and Dobzhansky (1974).

Popper, K. R. 1982. *The Open Universe: An Argument for Indeterminism*. In Barley, W. W., III (ed.): *Postscript to the Logic of Scientific Discovery*. London: Hutchinson.

Popper, K. R. and Eccles, J. C. 1977. *The Self and Its Brain*. Berlin: Springer International.

Prigogine, I. and Stengers, I. 1984. *Order Out of Chaos: Man's New Dialogue With Nature*. London: Heinemann.

Roemer, J. E. 1988. *Free to Lose: An Introduction to Marxist Economic Philosophy*. Cambridge: Harvard University Press.

Roughgarden, J. 1979. *Theory of Population Genetics and Evolutionary Ecology: An Introduction*. New York: Macmillan.

Ruse, M. 1976. 'Reduction in Genetics'. In Cohen *et al* (1976:653–670). Reprinted in Sober (1984b).

Sahlins, M. D. 1977. *The Use and Abuse of Biology: An Anthropological Critique of Sociobiology*. London: Tavistock.

Schaffner, K. F. 1976. 'Reduction in Biology: Prospects and Problems'. In Cohen *et al* (1976:613–32). Reprinted in Sober (1984b).

Schweber, S. S. 1977. 'The Origin of the *Origin* Revisited'. *Journal of the History of Biology*, 10:229–316.

Shackle, G. L. S. 1989. 'What Did the "General Theory" Do?'. In Pheby, J. (ed.): *New Directions in Post-Keynesian Economics*. Aldershot: Edward Elgar.

Simon, H. A. 1968. *The Sciences of the Artificial*. Cambridge: MIT Press.

Sober, E. 1984a. *The Nature of Selection: Evolutionary Theory in Philosophical Focus*. Cambridge: MIT Press.

Sober, E. (ed.) 1984b. *Conceptual Issues in Evolutionary Biology: An Anthology*. Cambridge: MIT Press.

Stewart, I. 1989. *Does God Play Dice? The Mathematics of Chaos*. Oxford: Basil Blackwell.

Stiglitz, J. E. 1987. 'The Causes and Consequences of the Dependence of Quality on Price'. *Journal of Economic Literature*, 25:1–48.

Sugden, R. 1990. 'Convention, Creativity and Conflict'. In Varoufakis and Young (1990).

Thomas, B. 1991. 'Alfred Marshall on Economic Biology'. *Review of Political Economy*, 3:1–14.

Thorp, J. 1980. *Free Will: A Defence Against Neurophysiological Determinism*. London: Routledge and Kegan Paul.

Varela, F. Maturana, H. R. and Uribe, R. 1974. 'Autopoiesis: The Organization of Living Systems, Its Characterization and a Model'. *Bio-Systems*, 5.

Varoufakis, Y. 1990. 'Conflict in Equilibrium'. In Varoufakis and Young (1990).

Varoufakis, Y. and Young, D. (eds.) 1990. *Conflict in Economics*. Hemel Hempstead: Harvester Wheatsheaf.

Veblen, T. B. 1899. *The Theory of the Leisure Class: An Economic Study of Institutions*. New York: Macmillan.

Veblen, T. B. 1919. *The Place of Science in Modern Civilisation and Other Essays*. New York: Huebsch. Reprinted 1990 with a new introduction by Samuels, W. J. New Brunswick: Transaction Publishers.

Weeks, J. 1989. *A Critique of Neoclassical Macroeconomics*. Basingstoke: Macmillan.

Weinberg, S. 1974. 'Unified Theories of Elementary-Particle Interaction'. *Scientific American*, no. 231.

Weintraub, E. R. 1979. *Microfoundations*. Cambridge: Cambridge University Press.

Weiss, P. A. 1969. 'The Living System: Determinism Stratified'. In Koestler, A. and Smythies, J. R. (eds.): *Beyond Reductionism: New Perspectives in the Life Sciences*. London: Hutchinson.

Weiss, P. A. 1973. *The Science of Life*. Mt. Kisco: Futura.

Williams, G. C. 1966. *Adaptation and Natural Selection*. Princeton: Princeton University Press.

Williamson, O. E. 1975. *Markets and Hierarchies: Analysis and Anti-Trust Implications: A Study in the Economics of Internal Organization*. New York: Free Press.

Williamson, O. E. 1985. *The Economic Institutions of Capitalism: Firms, Markets, Relational Contracting*. London: Macmillan.

Wilson, E. O. 1975. *Sociobiology*. Cambridge: Harvard University Press.

Wimsatt, W. C. 1976. 'Reductive Explanation: A Functional Account'. In Cohen et al (1976:671–710). Reprinted in Sober (1984b).

Wimsatt, W. C. 1980. 'Reductionist Research Strategies and Their Biases in the Units of Selection Controversy'. In Nickles, T. (ed.): *Scientific Discovery, Volume II, Historical and Scientific Case Studies*. Dordrecht: Reidel. Extracted in Brandon and Burian (1984) and reprinted in Sober (1984b).

Winslow, E. A. 1986. '"Human Logic" and Keynes's Economics'. *Eastern Economic Journal*, 12:413–30.

Winslow, E. A. 1989. 'Organic Interdependence, Uncertainty and Economic Analysis'. *The Economic Journal*, 99:1173–82.

Young, H. D. 1968. *Fundamentals of Optics and Modern physics*. New York.

Zeleny, M. (ed.) 1980. *Autopoiesis, Dissipative Structures, and Spontaneous Social Orders*. Boulder: Westview Press.

Zeleny, M. (ed.) 1981. *Autopoiesis: A Theory of Living Systems*. New York: North-Holland.

Zeleny, M. 1987. 'Autopoiesis'. In Singh, M. G. (ed.): *Systems and Control Encyclopedia. Theory, Technology, Applications*. Oxford: Pergamon Press.

[30]

Neo-classical Economics and Neo-Darwinism: Clearing the Way for Historical Thinking

Elias L. Khalil*

> [E]conomics has never interested me primarily as a 'kit of tools' for the examination or repair of the existing social mechanism. Perhaps because my first serious work plunged me into the worlds of Adam Smith, David Ricardo, John Stuart Mill, and Karl Marx, I have always found the greatest attraction of economics to lie elsewhere, in the astonishing capabilities of the discipline to elucidate the problem of large-scale historical . . . change. (Heilbroner, 1970, p. xii)

3.1 INTRODUCTION

In his contributions to different fields of economics, Professor Robert L. Heilbroner has advanced many arguments, but the one which made the most lasting impression on me is his call to exploit the capabilities of economics for the study of large-scale historical change. His advice as a teacher was unambiguous: one should not seek guidance from neo-classical economics, since it is ahistorical. The great worldly philosophers of the not too distant past are the proper guides to follow. This calls for a return to an older tradition of grand visions of historical evolution.

Putting my central argument succinctly, the neo-classical (hereafter: NC) paradigm[1], in its textbook version at least, is ahistorical because it is the progeny of reductionist and efficient modes of conception. Although these two complement each other, they are distinct. Reductionist economics ignores organization of production on the ground of having no bearing on the analysis of the constitutive economic agents. Agents are assumed independent and defined prior to the constitution of the organization. Albeit, the disavowal of reductionism by itself, as in the cases of behavioural economics of Herbert Simon and Harvey Leibenstein,

* This chapter was presented as a paper at the meeting of the International Society for the History, Philosophy and Social Studies of Biology, University of Western Ontario, London, Ontario, Canada, 22 June 1989. I appreciate the response of the audience at that meeting. I thank also Stanley Sâlthe, Jeffrey Wicken, David Depew for safeguarding my ventures into biology, and also Edward Nell, Roger D. Masters, and Jack Hirshleifer. I thank Kamel Merarda and Carole Brown for some technical help. The usual disclaimer applies.

is insufficient for historical thinking. One still has to address the question whether the organization or agent behaves according to purpose or efficient cause.

Economics emphasizes efficient causality (in the Aristotelian sense) at the expense of final causality (purposeful behaviour). Agents are assumed passive and unimaginative within the model. That is, initiative and creativity are viewed as exogenous. However, the repudiation of efficient reasoning by itself, as in the case of Austrian economics, is insufficient for historical thinking. One still has to answer the question as to whether organization is a congeries of sub-agents or an integral, organic unit.

Put tersely, historical thinking calls for the replacement of reductionism with an organic view, and efficient thinking with teleological reasoning. One should note that historical thinking involves more than theorizing about the business cycle and market dynamics. It deals with large-scale economic change – a topic which has enthralled Heilbroner. The mark of large-scale change is irreversibility. Otherwise, it is a form of business cycle. Examples of processes which usually do not proceed backwards include the development or evolution of consumer needs, major technological innovations, and the exhaustion of the carrying capacity of an environmental niche. They are as much irreversible as the processes of aging and the evolution of species.

In order to qualify as history, a process's reversibility should be pronounced impossible on theoretical rather than statistical grounds. To illustrate, heat always moves from hot to cold masses, not because the opposite motion is theoretically impossible, but because it is highly improbable. Thus, the motion of heat is *not* historically irreversible – which Boltzmann's version of the entropy law acknowledges (Khalil, 1990c).

Thus, to submit that a certain type of economic change is historical means that it is, like aging, irreversible at the theoretical, not the statistical level. A great part of the core conception of NC theory needs to be repudiated since it conceives economic phenomena exclusively according to efficient causality. That is, it fails to treat economic phenomena differently from the motion of heat. In order to disavow efficient reasoning, one has to recognize that households, firms and governments pursue goals like accumulation of wealth and growth, and act to maintain their integrity for the sake of it. This entails the adoption of – to use a much disdained term – teleological reasoning.

I need not repeat the familiar story of how modern science in general had originated as a revolution against the teleological thought of the scholastic and Aristotelian traditions. While that thought has been justly criticized, the anti-teleological zeal has gone to excess. The observation that economic agents pursue reproduction and the accumulation of capital for its own sake, need not be grounded on an extravagant teleological cosmology or theology. Teleological reasoning can be much humbler, enough to recognize phenomena like the striving of economists to publish in order to achieve respect, and that firms grow in order to attain power. Purposeful behaviour is copious; it arises from duty, ambition, self-respect, and less lofty values like status, wealth, and even includes negative drives like envy and self-aggrandizement.

Englis (1986) was not afraid to call economics a teleological inquiry since one has to specify the values which economic means are supposed to meet. Adam Smith (1976a) considered human conduct to be prompted by – beside the sentiments – the desire to do what is praiseworthy. Praiseworthiness cannot be explained by the want for public applause *à la* the stimulus–response framework (see Khalil, 1990a). Duty and responsibility prompt humans to do what is right. This principle is reminiscent of John Locke's much neglected concept of *fides*, 'the duty to observe mutual undertakings and the virtue of consistently discharging this duty' (quoted by Dunn in Gambetta, 1988, p. 81).

One way to attain satisfaction is to act according to duty and praiseworthiness. This goes beyond the NC modelling of human behaviour as a series of responses to stimuli, governed by the utility function. To Adam Smith, satisfaction is not a function of the absolute, but relative size of goods in regard to expectations (Khalil, n.d.; cf. Frank, 1989). When a student, for example in an exam attains the expected C grade, it is more satisfying than achieving a B grade when an A grade was expected. The fact that a person with limited means is more likely to be satisfied than a rich person, a favourite theme of Smith (1976a, pp. 149–53), indicates that satisfaction is not the product of a mechanistic utility, but of the proximity of actual achievement to specified goals.

Thus, the pursuit of satisfaction, at a basic level, should not be conceived as a response to a stimulus *à la* B.F. Skinner's behaviourism. The stimulus–response framework may explain some categories of behaviour, but not all. Satisfaction is, for the greater part, the fulfilling of self-made, multilayered final goals, which are not rigidly defined. Final goals are normally the result of an on-going fusion of individual and communal values of what is the proper ends to pursue during the irreversible process of growth.

Such innocuous observations go, for the most part, unremarked in the mainstream enterprise, in order for it to attain its dubious scientific precision. This enterprise amounts to producing pen-and-paper models about utility maximization, which resemble Byzantine theology and pre-Copernican astronomy. But 'precision' is not the fish I want to fry.[2] Rather, I am concerned with the truth content of NC economics.

When under fire, NC theorists seek other sciences. Darwinism, and neo-Darwinism (hereafter ND) have been a favourite haven. Yet, the Darwinian shelter, in the textbook version at least, suffers from deep faults, not different from the ones that permeate the NC edifice. The parallel is astounding – given that both have evolved independently.

It is true that Darwin was influenced by Malthus's principles of population, but NC economics was still to be born at the time of the publication of *The Origins of Species* in 1859. Moreover, the progenitors of NC economics – Menger, Walras, and Jevons – were oblivious to Darwinism and more interested in utilitarianism and engineering. This has prompted Veblen (1898) to admonish economics for not being evolutionary. Furthermore, it is true that NC and ND paradigms have been involved in cross-fertilization in the past decade, but the love has struck too late to conceive new core concepts.

Thus, the similarity of the core of both orthodoxies must be attributed to the circumambient scientific milieu within which both disciplines were incubated. The milieu has been dominated by the Newtonian framework, which, as Appendix 3.1 argues, is underpinned by efficient and reductionist conceptions. These two conceptions underlie the Darwinian approach. It is no surprise that NC economics finds Darwinism a haven.

Despite its metamorphosis over the past century (Depew and Weber, 1989), Darwinism is still a reductionist and efficient scheme, which postulates an ahistorical view of events.[3] Darwinism is praised for that reason (Ghiselin, 1969). The modern version, neo-Darwinism, has perfected that irony:

> 'new Darwinism' has been able to displace the historical perspective from the center stage of evolutionary science . . . It [evolution] is but the tailings of the instantaneous selective process much as the pile of sawdust is the accumulated residue of the cutting action of a saw blade upon logs in a saw mill. (Campbell, in Weber *et al.*, 1988, p. 275)

Similar judgements have been articulated by increasing numbers of scholars. Depew and Weber (in Weber *et al.*, 1988) view the ND approach as a progeny of the Newtonian framework; Wicken (1986, 1987) calls for the injection of ND with thermodynamics to attain historical directionality (see Matsuno and Ho, in Ho and Saunders, 1984). These indictments do not stem from the mystical cosmologies of Bergson (1913) and Teilhard de Chardin (1959).[4]

The anomalies, which have been budding and chipping at the edges of NC and ND paradigms, have emboldened heterodox approaches recently. The platform which the critics of both orthodoxies share is the advocacy of a historical paradigm.[5] It is no surprise that heterodox biology parallels heterodox economics. Each heterodoxy may fortify the other.

Given the similarity of their core theoretical approaches, it was natural for the two orthodoxies to exchange support once they met. An increasing number of articles have appeared in the past decade that apply the tools of NC economics – concepts like maximization of utility, work/leisure trade-off, and transaction–cost analysis – to study how rats, pigeons, and honeybees supposedly supply labour, reveal preferences for goods, and enter cooperative behaviour (*inter alia*, Battalio *et al.*, 1979, 1981a, 1981b; Kagel *et al.*, 1975, 1980a, 1980b; Landa and Wallis, 1988; cf. Rapport and Turner, 1977). Likewise, NC economists (Alchian, 1950; Becker, 1976; Hirshleifer, 1977, 1978a, 1978b, 1982; Ursprung, 1988) borrow heavily from ND concepts like natural selection and survival of the fittest.

No one can object *per se* to cross-fertilization between the disciplines. There are insights, beyond metaphors, to be learned from each other. For instance, Marshall's theory of the aging of firms and industries is conceived after biological senescence. But I have reservations about the cross-fertilization between the NC and ND orthodoxies. If each is defective at the core, the progeny are likely to be freakish!

This chapter has two main parts. The first part, in four sections, explains the conceptual cores of NC and ND paradigms. The second part recounts, in the same order, the heterodox challenges in both disciplines. At the end I reflect on how the challenges of different schools of heterodox economics can be synthesized.

3.2 THE CONCEPTUAL CORES

3.2.1 Overview

In his classic work, Robbins (1932, p. 38) views economics as concerned with efficient means and given ends. Means have to be selected efficiently since they are scarce. For the NC scheme, if there were no scarcity, there would be no economic problem. The NC approach expresses the economic problem in a four-word tenet, *maximization subject to constraints*. The maximized variable is the utility derived from goods; the constraints are resources. The NC tenet assumes that the scarcity constraints are fungible: there is more than one way to skin a cat. The economic problem is about the best way to rearrange the fungibles, so that output maximizes the given utility function (Walsh and Gram, 1980).[6]

The fundamental problem facing organisms, according to ND, is scarcity – similar to the contention of neo-classical economics. The amount of nutrients/prey is supposed to be given; otherwise, natural selection would not work.[7] Nature has to select (disregarding the animistic connotation) efficient traits which make the best use of given nutrients/prey. That is, nature encourages the maximization of a fitness function which is indicated in the reproductive success. This may also be expressed by the four-word tenet, *maximization subject to constraints*. The maximized variable is fitness of traits;[8] the constraints are nutrients/prey. The ND tenet assumes that nutrients/prey and gene frequency are fungible, i.e. can produce a variety of traits. In this manner, evolution is about producing the best composition of traits which, given the niche, maximizes the fitness function.

Sociobiologists (e.g. Wilson, 1975) have expanded the meaning of trait to include behaviour, ranging from selfishness to altruism.[9] Behaviour is subject to fitness pressure which causes 'evolutionary stable strategy' (ESS). The term 'strategy' denotes preprogrammed behaviour not consciously worked out. The word 'stable' means equilibrium. That is, fitness pressure engenders behaviour which, *ceteris paribus*, cannot be improved: no gene which alters the genetic ratios can successfully invade a population at ESS – reminiscent of Nash equilibrium in economics.

The parallelism between NC and ND paradigms is unmistakable. Both postulate the maximization of a variable, utility or fitness, via selection. For NC, the selected set of products determines the set of efficient firms. For ND, the selected set of traits ascertains the set of fit organisms. Albeit, selection would not occur if there were no constraints and exogenous variables. The variables which are specified as exogenous by both orthodoxies are remarkably analogous. Similarly, the endogenous variables, firms and organisms, are highly parallel. Causality runs in one direction: a change in the equilibrium product compositions or trait frequency is the result of a change of exogenous variables. Both orthodoxies give an *ad hoc* account of why exogenous variables change; they usually explain the change away as fortuitous in origin.

Before going into detail, let me sketch the conceptual cores. The given 'resources' in NC theory include primordial labour, materials, and land. Similarly, the exogenous 'nutrients' in ND theory include prey (in the broad sense) and territory. In Table 3.1, I place these constraints in the first column under the general heading 'factors'. Recalling Aristotle's categories of causation, factors can be identified with material cause. The second constraint in NC scheme is 'technology', and in ND paradigm is 'genotype' (as opposed to phenotype).[10] I locate these constraints in the second column under the general heading 'information', which can be identified with formal cause. Factors and information are put together in NC theory to generate product and through it to maintain the firm, or in short 'product/firm'. Equivalently, factors and information are put together in the ND approach to generate trait and through it to sustain the organism, or in short 'trait/organism'. I set these outputs in the third column under the general heading 'yield/thing', which can be identified with material cause since it is a mere rearrangement of factors. Moreover, there would be no maximization of utility or fitness without selectors. The screening device in the NC scheme is 'preferences' of consumer and in ND theory is 'nature'. I situate them in the fourth column under the general heading 'selector', which can be identified with efficient cause.

Instructive though such parallelism is, we need to go further. In one case, resources are ordered by technology to produce a product/firm which is subjected to selection by preferences. In another case, nutrients are ordered by genotype to produce a trait/organism which is subjected to selection by nature. Put in general terms, factors are ordered by information to produce a yield/entity which is screened by the selector. In both cases, the yield is under direct selection pressure, while the entity is selected indirectly as a result. The firm or organism is treated as a passive object; its existence is contingent on external causes. Moreover, the

Table 3.1 Parallelism of NC and ND conceptual cores

Factors (Material cause)	+	*Information (Formal cause)*	→	*Yield/Thing (Material cause)*	←	*Selector (Efficient cause)*
Given NC resources	+	Given technology	→	Passive product/firm	←	Given preferences
Given ND nutrients	+	Given genotype	→	Passive trait/organism	←	Given nature

firm or organism amounts to a patch of well-defined, independent products or traits. Thus, from the perspective of historical thinking NC and ND paradigms have two conceptual flaws: they deny that the firm or organism acts according to purpose; they deny that the firm or organism is an integral, organic whole.

There are some differences between the two orthodoxies. However, they stem from the dissimilarity of the subject of study, rather than the mode of conception. One difference is related to the constitution of the selector. The selector in the NC approach, preferences, is carried by agents who also make up the producer, the firm. In contrast, the selector in ND theory, nature, is segregated from the producer, the organism. This difference is superficial, however. The preferences are assumed by NC theory to be independent of producers. This difference calls for a qualification which neutralizes it. In the economy, according to NC theory, the rules of justice (property rights) are observed. There are no such observances in the jungle.

The second difference is related to awareness. Nature obviously does not select traits consciously, while agents calculate what products to consume. This difference is also more apparent than real. Agents in the economy, with respect to NC theory, are dormant rather than vigorous, passive rather than active, and inert rather than entrepreneurial. That is, agents act 'as if' they are conscious, but in fact it does not matter; they are the dummies and the pre-determined preferences are the ventriloquists. NC economics expunges creativity, initiative, and purposeful behaviour from its tool kit. This resembles the crux of the ND paradigm, where no room is allowed for teleological explanations of evolution. As Table 3.1 shows, the fact that economic agents are aware has not prompted NC orthodoxy to recognize final cause.

The third difference is related to the unit of evolution. According to ND, the organism does not evolve but the population does. It occurs as a result of the failure of the relatively unfit organisms to leave proportionate scion behind. In contrast, NC theory recognizes that inefficient firms need not perish if they adjust. This difference, though, is non-substantive.

Given these differences, one can assert that the parallelism of the two mainstreams is striking. It is the outcome of disregarding teleological and organic conceptions. Certainly, many phenomena should not be explained through such conceptions, for example the gyration of stocks or ecological change. But other phenomena, like the firm or the organism, require teleological and organic views.[11] The orthodox rejection of these views has made economic or biological organization look no different from chaotic forms. In fact, the theoretical core of both orthodoxies resembles the mechanical gas law and entropy law. The gas law, as expressed by J.D. van der Waals, states:

$$\{p + a(n/V)^2\}\ (V - nb) = nRT$$

Where p, V, T are the state variables of pressure, volume, absolute temperature, R the universal gas constant, and n the number of molecules (moles) (Fenn, 1982,

p. 43–7). A good illustration is the balloon. As temperature and/or pressure increase, the volume of the balloon expands. This equation depicts real gases since the parameters *a* and *b* specify its identity.

Rosen (1987) argues that the equation, on one hand, masquerades as the difference between parameters and state variables and, on the other, camouflages the functional relationship between exogenous (pressure and temperature) and endogenous (volume) variables. Thus, he rewrites it as:

$$\Phi_{abR}, n \mid (T, p) \rightarrow (V)$$

Where the parameters *a*, *b*, *R* act as coordinates in the functional space Φ, given *n*. They specify the function of a particular gas from a range of functions. The variable *V* is rewritten to show clearly that it is a function of *T* and *p*. In Table 3.2, I show the mechanical core of the gas law, using Aristotle's categories of causation. The gas law turns out to be no different from the cores of NC and ND paradigms. The number of molecules (the factors which make up the system) can be identified with material cause, parameters (the informational identity of the system) with formal cause, volume (the entity under focus) with material cause since it is the form which molecules take, and temperature and pressure (the conditioning selector) with efficient causes. Final cause is fittingly absent since volume changes for an efficient, not purposeful reason.

Moreover, as shown in Table 3.2, the mechanical entropy law repeats the cores of NC and ND theories. The law observes that a closed system tends towards equilibrium like an ice cube in a glass of water where the ice melts. The variable that measures the degree of melting is dubbed entropy. Each system has its individuality specified by the parameters. In Table 3.2, I demonstrate the entropy law in thermodynamic terms (not statistical ones). The number of molecules can be identified with material cause, parameters with formal cause, entropy with

Table 3.2 Parallelism of gas law, entropy law, NC, and ND conceptual cores

	Factors (Material cause)	+	*Information (Formal cause)*	→	*Yield/Thing (Material cause)*	←	*Selector (Efficient cause)*
Gas law:	Molecules	+	Parameters	→	Volume	←	Temp./Pres.
Entropy law:	Molecules	+	Parameters	→	Entropy	←	Temp./Heat
NC:	Resources	+	Technology	→	Product/firm	←	Preferences
ND:	Nutrients	+	Genotype	→	Trait/organism	←	Nature

material cause since it is the form which molecules take, and temperature and heat with efficient causes. For the same fitting reason, final cause is absent.[12]

Table 3.2 shows that the core of NC and ND theories is no different from the law which describes chaotic gases. This is not accidental but the outcome of conscious attempt to purge teleology from scientific reasoning. Teleological conception need not be alarming, however. It does not have to be derived from vitalist conceptions. That is, final cause need not be the character of some strange force in living matter. With aid of quantum mechanics, physicists like David Bohm trace teleology to the behaviour of subatomic matter.

Quantum mechanics has raised troubling questions about the classical view of nature. David Bohm views matter as an organic, integral unit (Khalil, 1989g). Matter is a potential with penumbral boundaries. The 1982 experiment by Alain Aspect and his colleagues at the University of Paris-South confirmed that matter does not occupy the ordinary space we are familiar with. To Bohm, matter constantly moves from the realm of abstract space to the concrete.[13] This movement implies purpose. Rosen (1987; see also 1985a, 1985b) finds this idea relevant to living matter. Thus, one need not whimsically introduce *vita* to living matter to explain purpose.[14] Hence one need not apologize for teleology. Teleological reasoning is materialist, after all.

Before presenting the critique, I discuss the three variables which ND considers as given. The treatment of factors, information, and selector as given underpins the 'efficient' conception of NC and ND. I seldom take notice of auxiliary qualifications. I present orthodoxy in its virgin or textbook form in order to sharpen the image of the core. That is, I take public choice and new household economics as the purest forms of the NC paradigm (Khalil, 1987b). Similarly, I find socio-biology and Dawkins's approach the quintessence of ND. In this manner, I can focus on the meta-theoretical questions.

3.2.2 Factors: Given

The NC paradigm

Factors of production are called 'resources'. NC models usually stipulate that resources are scarce endowments, like manna fallen from heaven. Robinson Crusoe or a nation faces given resources, consisting of an X amount of labour, Y quantity of raw materials, and Z measure of land. They are the material cause which could be formed into alternative products at the production possibility frontier. The economic question is limited to determining the position on the frontier, not the quantity of resources. A change of the quantity of resources is considered an external shock, not an endogenous event.

The view of resources does not change when we move to the level of one producer among others, the firm. The firm is faced with the challenge of choosing the correct combination of resources in such a manner that, given their relative prices, its budget constraint generates maximum output. This is the idea behind the tangency of the firm's output isoquants with the budget constraint: the tangency point is the equality of the resources' relative marginal product with their relative prices. In this way, the firm is maximizing its output given its total budget constraint and the scarcity prices of the resources.

The concept of scarcity in the NC scheme is not the niggardliness of nature which purposeful agents face in production, but rather it is a mathematical constraint. In this manner, the model is concerned with how the exogenously given constraint is allocated in order to maximize satisfaction. In this sense, the NC term 'scarcity' has no relation to the common meaning. In day-to-day usage, a commodity is scarce if quantity demanded is greater than quantity supplied at a certain price, while in NC theory the price is restricted to zero. This appears an innocuous linguistic innovation. It implies, though, that a commodity is essentially free; if its price is not zero, it is in order to attenuate quantity demanded and bring it to equal given quantity supplied. Thus, the cost of purposeful production does not enter the picture at first approximation, as if resources are handed on a silver platter.

This abstract mode of conceptualization is not without practical consequences. The national income accounts treat resources as if, indeed, they were handed on a silver platter. While it has a provision for depreciation, it is restricted for man-made assets, such as tools and buildings. The provision does not cover rivers and soil which are polluted and exhausted as a result of production. The depreciated natural capital is not written off against the *gross* national products. As a result, the rate of growth of *net* national product is inflated. More seriously, growth and prosperity would suffer greatly if resources were actually replaced at the same rate of replenishment.

The ND paradigm

Organisms obviously do not possess resources like raw materials and land. They have, though, something equivalent dubbed 'nutrients', like prey and territory. In this manner, prey is equivalent to raw materials. Besides hunted rabbits and deer, prey includes plants and what they depend on like solar energy, minerals in the ground, and compounds in the air, without which no organism can survive (Ricklefs, 1979, pp. 780 ff.). Likewise, territory is equivalent to land, which most organisms need and defend to secure prey and sexual partners. Nutrients are the material cause in Aristotle's categories.

Similar to the treatment of resources by NC theory, nutrients are figured by ND to be given, not altered by the organism. Otherwise, the selection by nature is nullified. The given nutrients correspond to the concept of budget constraint in economics (Rapport and Turner, 1977, p. 368). The organism's 'budget constraint' is determined by a variety of ecological parameters. In comparison to orthodox economics, the time and energy allocated to foraging corresponds to the total budget, and the relative ease of capturing fungible nutrients/prey to relative prices. The relative ease is determined by the relative scarcity of nutrients/prey, accentuated by the intensity of competition among predators for prey.

According to orthodox biology (e.g. MacArthur, 1972), the given nutrients determine the organism's foraging strategy, since it attempts to maximize the captured nutrients/prey. Put differently, the organism chooses the correct combination of preys in a way which maximizes its fitness function. In such manner, a unit of captured prey is produced with minimal energy expenditure. For insect societies, the fitness function is the production of queens. Wilson (1975) explains division of labour in insect colonies using neo-classical linear programming. The number of castes and their relative size in a colony is similar to the number of factors of production and their relative size in a firm. If the environment does not change, castes and their relative sizes stay stable. That is, there is a substitution among factors of production of queens, depending on their relative availability.

In such manner, scarce nutrients are used efficiently to maximize output and fitness. This means maximum net energy gain. The gain could either be translated into current growth of bio-mass or investment in reproduction – future growth of one's descendants – or a combination of both. This is similar to maximum output in economics, which is the surrogate of maximum profit. The profit could either be translated into current consumption or investment, or a combination of both (Rapport and Turner, 1977).

R. Levins (1967) calls the fitness function 'adaptive function', since the selector of nature determines which organism, and hence genotype, is relatively more fit in transforming scarce nutrients into phenotypes. Stated differently, natural selection determines which organisms score best in the employment of given nutrients. If organisms could create new nutrients, Darwinian selection would not work, and the mathematical exercise of fitness maximization would be void.

3.2.3 Information: Given

The NC paradigm

Information is called 'technology'. It is the formal cause behind the production of tools, upgrading of labour skills, and improvement of land. NC economics sees technology as information, i.e. given, distinct rules about how to attain definite products. They are precisely grafted in human capital, the capital stock, and improved land. This view consists of two relatively independent theses: technology as exogenous; technology as definite.

Technology as exogenous. Instructions on how to assemble a product from resources run in one way: from the given technology to the product. Feedback is not allowed. The thesis that information is exogenous rules out improvement of know-how as a result of practice. Production does not entail the generation of new technology, but the execution of what is given.

NC economists recognize technological innovations. They are, however, treated as external shocks to the system. The theory fails to incorporate technological change as an endogenous feature. Of course, when NC-trained economists roll up their sleeves to do empirical work, some of these assumptions are revised, and sometimes played with to generate more sophisticated models. This should not blind us to the fact that technological improvements are essentially viewed as exogenous. Discovery is considered idiosyncratic or serendipitous, and hence cannot be subjected to theoretical inquiry. Technological change is not considered the result of feedbacks from experience. Hence there is no surprise that NC theorists resist the idea that change is usually an irreversible process.

Technology as definite. Once technology is considered given and not influenced by the purposeful process of production, it is deemed rigid and self-defined. Technology is assumed to be analyzable into self-contained parts, whose contributions could be calculated precisely. This is the origin of the concept of marginal productivity and the production function.

The production function is a mathematical formula whose variables could vary independently of each other. Technology is represented as another feature of production, independent of labour and raw materials. Technology is deemed to be an exact commodity, like traffic signals and computational codes. In this capacity, technology is capable of specifying each step of production, insulated from the process itself. Instances through time are seen as reversible since technology is assumed to be self-defined, unaffected by past experience.

The ND paradigm

Information is called 'genotype'. It is the formal cause behind organs and their function. Similar to the NC view, ND sees genotype as information, i.e. given, distinct rules on how to attain definite traits. Rules are exactly grafted on organs and behaviour. This view consists of two relatively separate theses: genotype as exogenous; genotype as definite.

Genotype as exogenous. According to ND, the mutation of genotype rules arises from random causes. Jacques Monod (1972) has established himself as biologist-turned-philosopher in his forceful defence of the view that chance lies behind mutation. According to him, mutations give rise to more or less complex organisms. If there is a rise of complexity during evolution, it is the result of natural selection, which indicates that greater complexity confers greater fitness.

The doctrine of random mutation is concomitant with the belief that genotype is a set of passive rules like traffic regulation, not a set of self-seeking, self-defining principles. As rules, they are inert; they do not determine their own mutation. Rules are the starting point which determine the phenotype: genotype $\rightarrow$ phenotype. The claim that the phenotype does not react and affect the genotype in a loop-fashion is the basic citadel of the ND programme. Any physical alteration which arises from experience, will, or accident does not affect the genotype, and most certainly cannot be passed on to progeny. That is, the germ (sex) cells are supposedly insulated from somatic (body) cells.

This came to be called Weismann's barrier, after August Weismann. It postulates that acquired characteristics cannot penetrate germ (sex) cells. That is, germ cells, while giving rise to a variety of organisms, are passed on to progeny intact. The Weismann barrier is at the core of the ND programme. This makes Lamarck (1984), who postulated the inheritance of acquired characteristics, the archpriest of heresy in the temples of orthodoxy.[15]

With regard to ND, the genetic code spells out the differentiation of cells into different positions and functions during development. The synthesis of proteins proceeds according to instructions sent by the DNA. There is no feedback which alters the DNA of cells. It is recognized that enzymes suppress and activate certain genes. Albeit, the activity of enzymes is dictated by the genetic code and it does not alter, after all, the DNA.

If Weismann's barrier is made of steel, what gives rise to new proteins and traits? Darwin struggled with an explanation. In later editions of *Origin* (1959), particularly the last (sixth) edition, he conceded to the Lamarckian notion of the inheritance of acquired characteristics. Modern genetics, as first introduced by Dobzhansky (1982), Mayr (1982), and Simpson (1984), came to the rescue by proposing random mutation of germ cells as the basis of new traits.[16] This addition came to be called the modern synthesis or ND.

Parallel to the NC view of technological innovation, the idea of random mutation presents the genotype as insulated from the process of maintaining the organism. Any change which occurs is fortuitous in origin, not the result of feedbacks from experience. Not surprisingly, ND theorists resist the idea that evolution is usually an irreversible process.

Genotype as definite. The view of genotype as exogenous implies that it is self-defined and explicit. That is, the genotype sends unambiguous messages, not subject to interpretation. Otherwise, the environment might influence the genotype, and make it endogenous.

The assumed explicitness of the DNA makes it available for slicing into tidbits. Each tidbit is supposed to be a precise instruction for the 'machinery' of the cell and the organism. Genes are seen as bits of information which transmit unclouded messages, like a computer programme. In fact, a huge cottage industry has sprung up around likening the genetic code to C. Shannon's information theory, designed initially to transmit intelligence signals. These signals, measured by bits of information, became more than a metaphor. Genes became conceived as self-contained bits of information. The organism became a mere vehicle for genetic rules (see Dawkins, 1976). A genetic message, like the NC view of technology, is capable of specifying each step of production, insulated from the process itself. Instances through time are seen as reversible since genes are presumably unaffected by experience.

3.2.4 Selector: Given

The NC paradigm

The pertinent selector is called 'preferences'. It is the efficient cause which solves the economic problem, the position along the production frontier. Thus, preferences of consumers are designated as the sovereign of the economy. Given the distribution of endowments, the composition of GNP, as selected by consumers, represents maximum allocative efficiency.

Once consumers determine the product composition, allocation of resources is determined indirectly. Consumers' tastes are not determined endogenously, especially not by firms. Otherwise, the maximum efficiency criterion would be undermined. Stigler and Becker (1977) offer the classic defence of this posture. To them, economists need not be concerned with preferences since they originate from eccentric sources. They call them 'tastes' in order to underline their whimsical nature. It is possible that consumers, for no economic reason, start favouring horse-pulled carriages over cars and ice-boxes over electric refrigerators. To wit, there is no *a priori* reason why needs should be considered irreversible. As a corollary, technological change is also viewed as reversible since products are subject to consumers' tastes. Put differently, technological change is not necessarily unidirectional since the sovereign, preferences, could reverse itself.

This highlights the arbitrary link between goods and the consumer as portrayed by the NC approach. This is expressed by the NC utility function, where goods are represented as fungible: there is no endurable connection between particular goods and the consumer; all goods serve equally a homogeneous utility function. In this fashion, consumers have no particular attachments arising from habit or consistency of personality. Consumers are ready to switch among fungible goods in order to maximize the utility function. This presumes that consumers act optimally; i.e. they choose among goods in such a way which equalizes the relative prices with the subjective marginal rate of substitution. Furthermore, this presumes that they have perfect knowledge, even in the form of statistical expectation, of all opportunities and prices in the present and future markets.

Given these perfectly prudent consumers, inefficient producers are not spared. The assumption that goods are fungible is essential to the view that preferences is an efficient selector.

The ND paradigm

The relevant selector is called 'nature'. Nature, as an efficient selector, allows the relatively fit organisms to increase their share; the propitious organisms validate their genotype via differential copulation. Given external conditions, the frequency of traits of organisms adjust accordingly; i.e. nature makes population fit.

Selectors include abiotic and biotic nature. In relation to the biotic nature, predators, MacArthur (1972) argues that they are efficient selectors in two senses

– resembling the NC assumptions about consumer behaviour. First, they act optimally; that is, no predator expends more energy on capturing a prey than opportunity cost. Although MacArthur does not use the term 'opportunity cost', he postulates that predators maximize the returns in terms of grams of captured prey per unit of time. Second, predators have perfect knowledge; that is, they have a clear statistical expectations of the location of prey. With these assumptions at hand, a predator is made into a prudent selector.

The selector is not influenced by the fitness process. In other words, the selector is not manipulated by the organism, since the organism is seen as a helpless entity. Otherwise, nature would be incapable of acting as an arbitrator; it would be unable to maximize the fitness function. That does not imply that the environment does not change, but the change is exogenous in origin. The change might be reversed, which allows, with random mutations, for the return of old gene frequencies. Although the statistical likelihood of reversals is nil, as stated by Dollo's Law, reversals are not ruled out at the theoretical level. Thus, according to ND, genetic change is not theoretically irreversible, since the sovereign, nature, could reverse itself.

3.3 A CRITIQUE OF THE CONCEPTUAL CORES

3.3.1 Overview

I have attempted to show that NC economics is ahistorical. An appeal to ND provides no consolation, since it is also ahistorical. Both treat time as a backdrop for events rather than a thread in the fabric of events. Non-conventional approaches in economics may be emboldened by their counterparts in biology.

The ahistorical conception is the outcome of treating factors of production, information, and selector as given. The handling of these key variables as exogenous should not come as a surprise. It is expected after treating the organism or the firm as exclusively governed by efficient causes. Such an explanation strips the agent of purposefulness since it accents efficient cause, at the expense of final cause. It should not come as a revelation that the critiques levelled at them have great affinities.

Within each discipline, the critics are not monolithic. Each critic may question one or another key orthodox concept. Once purposeful behaviour is admitted, it might be feasible to reach a synthesis among the critics. Factors, information, and selector would be seen as determined by purposeful behaviour. Heterodoxies within each discipline would appear to match like mortise and tenon.

Put together, heterodoxies treat factors of production, information and selector as partially endogenously determined. Table 3.3 sums up such findings. In comparison to Table 3.2, there are two major related departures: final cause is recognized and the other categories of causes are not taken as exogenous, but partially (as shown by the arrows) determined by the final cause. In Table 3.3, resources and nutrients in the first column are called 'inputs' to signify their continuous flux. Inputs are still identified with material cause. In the second column, technology and genotype are dubbed 'knowledge' to denote their penumbral organizational quality. Knowledge is still identified with formal cause. In the third column, the firm and organism are named 'organization', which is no longer subsumed to the product or the trait. This signifies that it is a purposeful agent and hence identified with final cause. Consumers' preferences and nature are flexible and labelled 'environment'. The environment is still identified with efficient cause.

The critical exposition below is divided into three parts. The axioms about factors, information and selector are examined in turn.

3.3.2 Inputs: Not Given Factors

Heterodox economics

People make choices. This phenomenon is taken by NC theory as the only behavioural imperative, since the economic problem is exclusively identified with scarcity, i.e. given factors. This makes the economy a closed system, and the only price is scarcity price or opportunity cost. Those who use real cost instead are usually taunted as accountants.

The opportunity cost concept is counter-intuitive; first, it implies that the cost of production is zero – as if goods are given by a cornucopia; second, profit is not considered a return above the cost of production, but rather a specific kind of opportunity cost. A major assumption underlies the opportunity cost concept: all goods are fungible, i.e. could be substituted for each other. As a corollary, orthodoxy ignores limits to growth posed by natural resources, since depleted resources could easily be substituted. This is one of the greatest ironies in the history of ideas: the NC idea of scarcity leads to the postulate that there is no ecological limits to growth.[17]

The opportunity cost concept is alien to classical economists. From Adam Smith to Karl Marx, they recognize real cost – the effort it takes to procure

Table 3.3 Parallelism of the critiques of NC and ND conceptual cores

	Inputs (Material cause)	+	*Knowledge (Formal cause)*	↔	*Organization (Final cause)*	↔	*Environment (Efficient cause)*
Heterodox economics	Resource influx	+	Organizational technology	↔	Purposeful firm	↔	Flexible preferences
Heterodox biology	Nutrient influx	+	Organizational genotype	↔	Purposeful organism	↔	Flexible nature

resources. According to them, the economic problem is the securing of returns which at least offset effort and, if possible, secure a surplus for reproduction on a greater scale. This surplus is not seen as part of cost, as NC economists postulate, the 'cost of capital'.

Thus, there is a behavioural imperative beside making choices, since at a more fundamental level humans do not deal with scarce, given resources. To the contrary, they deal with a multilayered, underdetermined amount of resources, which become available only upon the expenditure of effort. Thus, the economic problem is not scarce resources, but securing the appropriation of resources at steady and even extended scales.

This calls for a distinction which is usually overlooked by conventional analyses. The actor and the tools of labour must be distinguished from what is acted upon. As an actor, the agency of production expends effort to procure inputs, both exhaustible and renewable, from the biophysical environment. The agency of production is the potential and the drive behind the processing of raw inputs. The drive to work is a purposeful action, and the inputs are ingredients to be worked on.

Thus, the agency of labour should not be part of resource input, the first column in Table 3.3. But rather, the agency of labour is constitutive of the organization of production, since it is a final cause. After all, the organization of labour and its tools determines the continuous influx of resources.

This amounts to stating that the economic problem is not about scarce inputs. I may add that it is not about the scarce agency of labour either. Labour, though, is not scarce for a different reason. While inputs are not scarce because they are sought out by the agency of production, labour is not scarce because of procreation. This means that the purposeful agency of production has a longer life than the lifespan of the individual. That may explain why humans do not see their effort is wasted in vain. Future generations are counted to enjoy the fruits of the effort – as if the time horizon is infinite and mortality is irrelevant.

A person would consider the agency of production scarce if work is seen, in a fundamental sense, as an alien tool to attain higher indifference curves. The view of labour as scarce is epitomized by new household economics, spearheaded by Gary Becker (1981). At first examination, it is true that work is drudgery, but at a higher level, work is part of an endless chain of projects. Thus, work is not a mere tool but the life process itself.

The non-scarcity view of inputs and labour has been articulated lately by a new heterodox school called ecological economics (Christensen, 1989; Daly, 1977; Jansson, 1984; Perrings, 1987; Proops, 1989). The heterodox view has come of age with the initiation in 1989 of a new journal, *Ecological Economics*. It acknowledges the role of the ecosystem in renewing inputs by absorbing pollution and waste (Faber *et al.*, 1987). It repudiates the NC representation of the GNP as the circular flow of goods and services, insulated from the biophysical sphere. The NC model implies that the ecosystem either does not exist or its capacity is large enough to be of no concern to economics. The non-scarcity view argues that the capacity of the ecosystem is fragile beyond a critical point. Thus, it rectifies the ironic orthodox position, which, on one hand, asserts scarcity as the perennial problem and, on the other, ignores the capacity of the ecosystem.

Ecological economists can seek inspiration from classical theorists, since they, beside rejecting the scarcity theory of price, have recognized input limits to growth. Malthus, Ricardo and Mill have realized the niggardliness of land fertility and the constraint it places on accumulation. They did not portray a rosy picture of the prospects of commercial society. Technological innovations cannot, in the final analysis, reverse the downhill slide. This is the origin of the cliché about economics as the 'the dismal science'.

In Georgescu-Roegen's (1971) work, the dismal science reaches its acme; he predicts doomsday since the dowry of earth's resources are on an irreversible course of dispersion. His premonition of doldrums is based on the concept of resources as self-defined in the abstract, independent of the particular agency of production. Inputs, though, cannot be defined in the abstract. For example, oil companies find different resources in Alaska from what the Eskimo tribes did. Minerals on Mars are not inputs for human society since the organizational capacity and technology is not yet created. The rub is that the ecosystem capacity is not given, but demarcated by the complexity of the purposeful agency of production. I show elsewhere (Khalil, 1990c) that Georgescu-Roegen's misuse of the entropy law has contributed to his erroneous view of ecosystem capacity as an absolutely defined dowry.[18]

Another erroneous extension of the entropy law follows the work of the chemist Ilya Prigogine (1980). Prigogine uses the entropy law to explain spontaneously emerging patterns, 'dissipative structures', in far-from-equilibrium systems. He and others (e.g. Schneider, Dyke, Wiley, Brooks in Weber *et al.*, 1988; Allen, in Dosi *et al.*, 1988; Artigiani, 1987) extend dissipative structures to analyze biological and social organization. The project amounts to explaining the constitution of organization, its irreversible development and evolution after the explanation of the structure of storm systems or ocean currents. This is an erroneous explanation since dissipative structures are chaotic systems, while organizations are purposeful complexes (Khalil, 1990b, 1989f).

To explain irreversibility of biological and social processes, there is no need to seek help from Prigogine's notions of entropy.[19] The observation made above about the limitations posed by ecosystem capacity is adequate to explain – in conjunction with other variables discussed below – irreversibility of historical change. Wicken (1986) weaves a scenario of socio-economic evolution as the result of the drive to reverse the degradation of the capacity of the ecological niche. With each fresh regime of institutional and technological infrastructure, a new gate is opened to a more vigorous carrying capacity. Thus, change is driven by the exhaustion of ecological niches. Since exhausted niches cannot be reused, evolution cannot be reversed.

Heterodox biology

Parallel to the view of ecological economists, heterodox biologists (e.g. Harrison, Johnson, Depew and Weber, Schneider, Wicken, in Weber *et al.*, 1988) introduce input influx to evolutionary theory. Although they retain Darwin's idea of natural selection, they introduce a major theoretical consideration: the ability to process input influx is more important than passive traits in determining fitness.

Inputs are not given nutrients which the organism is obliged to endure while selection activity is taking place. Rather, the organism actively manipulates the influx of inputs. This challenges the ND axiom of given nutrients. According to Wicken (1986, 1987), inputs are not given in nature in a ready form. Except for parasites, all others have to work. Expenditure of effort is essential for, on the one hand, obtaining nutrients and, on the other hand, altering them by the body's digestive system into goods ready for consumption.

Lotka (1925) and Odum (1971) propose the concept 'maximum power principle' to complete Darwin's natural selection. Organisms attempt to maximize the rate of transformation of given input into useful output by minimizing waste. Waste cannot be eliminated totally – analogous to the case of heat engines – but there is a pressure to minimize it.

Beside the drive for greater efficiency, organisms attempt to muster materials and energy as much as they can by penetrating larger portions of the environment, which Ulanowicz (1986) calls 'ascendancy'. That is, beside minimizing waste, there is a need to increase the influx of inputs. In order to increase the input influx, the organism has to prolong the search or hunting period. There are strong grounds for the thesis that ascendancy is more pertinent for survival and evolution than efficiency. In either case, organisms are under pressure to attain greater efficiency and ascendancy. Otherwise, they will be swept away, since they are afflicted with the Red Queen Paradox (although the metaphor was first expressed by Van Valen, 1973, it is put to better use by Campbell, in Depew and Weber, 1985). The Queen, in Alice's Wonderland, has to to keep running in order to stay in the same place.

Put differently, nature selects the more *efficient* in transforming given input, and the more *productive* in harnessing inputs from the environment.[20] The fact that organisms work to transform and harness nutrients from a territory highlights the isomorphism of the economic problem. Organisms have to expend effort since they, like humans, cannot find what is needed immediately available, placed on a silver platter. The effort to produce are aided with tools, not too dissimilar from human tools. Spiders, for example, build webs, beavers construct dams, and higher primates use twigs. Most organisms, though, do not employ tools in the strict sense; rather they use tools like eyes, legs, skin, claws, teeth, wings, etc. They are part of the agency of purposefully directed effort, and hence are capital tools in the broader sense. Lotka (1945) calls them 'endosomatic instruments', to separate them from 'exosomatic instruments' like webs, nets, wheels, arrows, etc.

Endosomatic instruments should not be lumped together with inputs. It amounts to the confusion of the actor with what is acted upon – reminiscent of the confusion committed by conventional economics. For example, the claws of a vulture belong to the vulture and should not be lumped with the prey. The size of inputs is contingent on the capability of the actor, its degree of experience, and its territory. Any improvements of those variables assist the organism to process greater amounts of input, attaining greater ascendancy. With ascendancy, ecological connections (nodes) become more stable. Stability cannot endure, since the carrying capacity of the environment is finite to some extent. Pertinent nutrients in the ecological niche eventually deplete by the sheer fact of production activity, even though it is conducted at the same scale. Ironically, when the carrying capacity is expanded as a result of the employment of more sophisticated instruments, i.e. evolution, the deterioration of the environment is accelerated.

Wicken (1986, 1987) views the rise of more complex instruments a remedy to the on-going deterioration of the input influx. Greater complexity allows the organism to appropriate more food than others and makes some nutrients useful when they were not before; i.e. the carrying capacity of the environment is expanded. Wicken (in Ho and Saunders, 1984) calls this phenomenon anagenesis to indicate that evolution favours the more complex. That is, evolution is the irreversible process of the rise of complexity. The depletion of input influx necessitates evolutionary change to favour the more complex. Otherwise, a population becomes unable to explore deeper resources in the environment. This goes against the ethos of ND which cannot assert that evolution is irreversible theoretically.[21]

3.3.3 Knowledge: Not Given Information

Heterodox economics

Economists, throughout the history of the discipline, have levelled criticisms at the axiom of given technological information. To recapitulate, the orthodox view involves two fairly distinguishable statements: technology as exogenous; technology as definite.

Technology as non-exogenous. Heterodox economists assert that technological innovation, and so productivity, is normally endogenous. They appeal to Smith's postulate that innovation is a function of learning-by-doing and the growth of demand, i.e. production and the market at large.

Smith (1976b, chapter 1) argues that division of labour heightens productivity gains. It engenders greater labour dexterity, time saving, and replacement of monotonous tasks with tools. The productivity gain allows external economies; unit cost drops as output rises. This rebuts the NC law of supply (Young, 1928; Kaldor, 1972; Kurdas, 1988).[22]

While productivity is a function of division of labour, the latter is a function of the extent of the market facing a firm. Smith (1976b, chapter 3) argues that the greater the demand for a certain good, the more the firm can afford further division of labour – which enhances its innovation and productivity. Thus, the growth of demand facing a firm indirectly induces innovation.

The growth of demand facing a firm need not be exogenously induced. As innovative activity of a firm rises, it expands further. As a result of vertical linkages, this has unintended spill-over effects – the expansion of one firm spurs demand facing other firms (Levine, 1981). I call this macroexternality 'asymmetry of demand' (Khalil, 1987c). As other firms expand, demand facing the original firm may rise, and hence *ex post* confirm the initial expansion. Thus, growth of demand is endogenously induced (Nell, 1992).

To sum up the story of one firm, growth of demand which indirectly encourages innovation is itself induced initially by innovation. Figure 3.1 depicts the virtuous circle: growth of specific demand induces division of labour, which in turn invite innovation, productivity, and expansion of the firm. Expansion of one firm enhances growth of aggregate demand. The latter may spill over and stir specific demand facing the firm. This envelops the circle and shows that innovation is endogenous.[23]

Likewise, Karl Marx conceived innovative activity to be endogenous in the sense of being the product of the purposeful activity of capital to accumulate. In *Capital*, Marx presented technical innovation in volume 1 as part of accumulation, prior to the presentation of circulation of capital in volume 2, and competition in volume 3. This indicates that, for Marx, innovation is not primarily the outcome of market structure as NC theory claims, but which empirical findings by and large fail to corroborate (Coombs, in Dosi *et al.*, 1988b). For Marx, innovation is sought after even by monopolistic firms, since it generates absolute surplus value (increased productivity independent of intensified effort).

Despite the unbridgeable ideological divide, Marx was admired by Joseph Schumpeter (1949), who also elevated accumulation and innovation to the centre of theory. In his work, technological innovation and product innovation are not desultory, competition-driven, or serendipitous activities. Innovative activities are rather purposeful endeavours, pursued earnestly by the entrepreneur. Schumpeter postulated that the ebbs and flows of accumulation are punctuated by the introduction of major technological innovations. Without innovations and the entrepreneurial spirit behind them, capitalism would perish.

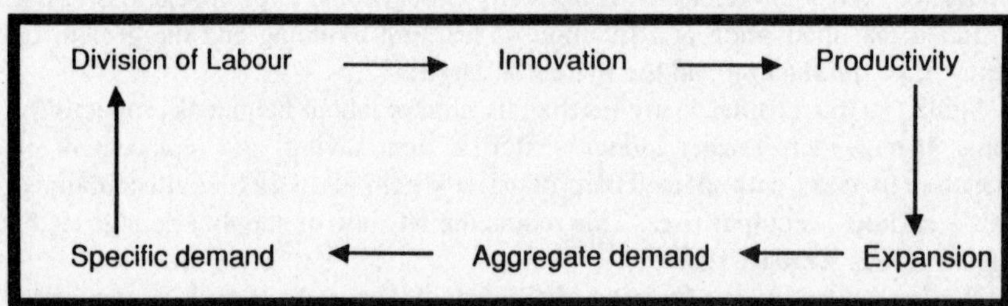

Figure 3.1 Endogenously determined innovations

Schumpeter is a good representative of Austrian economics. Austrian economics, at least the strand which emphasizes subjective human behaviour, views the economy as a process of creation and discovery (O'Driscoll and Rizzo, 1985). It emphasizes purposeful human action (von Mises, 1966). It faults NC theory for ignoring entrepreneurship. The idea of entrepreneurship is also advanced by evolutionary economists like Nelson and Winter (1982). They propose a theory of the firm which includes purposeful innovative activity, which are embodied in R & D departments (Nelson, in Dosi *et al.*, 1988b).

Dosi (1988a, and in Dosi *et al.*, 1988b, p. 221 ff.) argues likewise that innovations are pursued by the firm independently of market structure. To him, technological improvements proceed according to a well-recognized trajectory, which is discerned from antecedent historical events. The general outline is specified by what he calls the 'technological paradigm', which defines the range of innovations. Improvements are not pulled out of a hat, but rather out of solving puzzles generated and outlined by the paradigm (Nell, 1992, esp. Ch. 16).

Rosenberg (1976b) calls the paradigm a set of 'focusing devices', which identify the problems and their solution. Similarly, the French regulation school (Boyer, in Dosi *et al.*, 1988b) calls it an 'accumulation regime', which stabilizes and provides impetus to accumulation. The accumulation regime does not change continuously, but is transformed in the face of punctuated economic doldrums. Radical institutionalists (Gordon *et al.*, in Cherry *et al.*, 1987) give a similar version and call it the 'social structure of accumulation'. Nell (1988 and 1992) explains the same phenomenon under the name 'transformational growth'. Freeman and Perez (in Dosi *et al.*, 1988b) call it 'techno-economic paradigm', and distinguish it from innovations sponsored by it. These accumulation paradigms are probably behind Kondratieff's finding about long waves (van Duijn, 1983).

Most of these ideas fail in one regard – they lack coherent theoretical account. This failing, though, pales next to the disregard from which these findings suffer at the hand of NC economists. Given the NC tool kit, long waves and regime change stand as stubborn thorns – reminiscent of the difficulty hard-core neo-Darwinian theorists have with punctuated evolutionary change. In contrast, such large-scale changes are the bread and butter for approaches which embrace innovative activity as endogenous.

Technology as non-definite. NC economists view technology as discrete bits of information, like signals in communication theory. Heterodox economists challenge such reductionism. While some techniques are discrete rules, the rest are integral organizations who function in light of to the environment. As a corollary, the firm should not be viewed as a black box.

At the bottom of this reductionism is the conflation between knowledge and information. While knowledge is fuzzy and made of contingent principles, information is precise and composed of self-defined rules (Khalil, 1989d). There are certain canons which are bits of information, like engineering rules and codes of computer programmes. Others should be considered as knowledge, like the technological know-how to make an axe or bread.

According to Jean Piaget (see Russell, 1978), the acquisition of knowledge is a biological process. The person has to maintain a harmonious field to make sense of new acquisitions. The nervous system is not a bag of potatoes which can be stuffed with information, but a coherent organizer. For accumulated knowledge to function, the components have to blend well together. Similarly, Gestalt psychology describes perception and thoughts as attempts to build holistic forms of the sensory fields (Kohler, 1969). In the essay on the history of astronomy, Smith (1980) argues that knowledge amounts to making links between the familiar and unfamiliar to ease the tension of the imagination (Khalil, 1989e).

As the mind reaches a new harmony among acquired experiences, the components of knowledge coexist in a flexible balance. While each component complements the other, insightful reorganization may lead to improvements, since the meaning of each part is not self- but topologically-defined. This makes knowledge a versatile potential, taking different forms depending on the context. By contrast, information is context free, not open for interpretation, since its units are self-defined. If the bits are reassembled, the message is destroyed since each bit is rigid, cannot be defined by other bits.

Given this distinction, most technical know-how is not composed of self-defined bits of information, but formed of fuzzy principles of abstract potential which are organically connected. This makes technology susceptible to the environment of consumers' needs. Homologous to how Waddington's epigenetic landscape explains environmental shaping of the organism, discussed below, consumers' needs shape the development of technology in unique ways. Technology takes shape through unique producer–consumer interaction, which Lundvall (in Dosi *et al.*, 1988b) calls 'organized market'. Unique surroundings shape the way technology grows. The actual product is contingent upon the particular and personal way an agent applies the technology.

Dosi (ibid., pp. 221 ff.) expounds a similar thesis. He views technical know-how as personal knowledge – reminiscent of Michael Polanyi's (1958) central proposition. It cannot be made fully explicit through the transmission of self-defined information. In fact, knowledge loses effectiveness when it is broken down for transmission.

That explains, according to Fagerberg (in Dosi *et al.*, 1988b), the failure of the developing countries to import technology. He shows that growth rate differentials among nations are a function of nationally induced technological activity, which cannot be transplanted. He argues that the key to unlock the vicious cycle of underdevelopment is a national policy that encourages innovative activity at the local level. Local experiences need to develop in an authentic fashion with the help of the government. Modern Japan is a case in point, according to Freeman (ibid.).

Thus, for technology to work it has to be at least partly home-grown. Technology is the outcome of historically accumulated, particular experiences. Thus, it is part of the 'personality' of a firm. To treat technology as mere transferable information amounts to viewing the firm as a black box with no character (Rosenberg, 1982). In the NC approach the firm is treated as an entity that simply transforms, according to a production function, given resources with the help of given information into a precise output.

Within the NC view, it is anomalous to observe two firms with identical information but different productivities. This is not anomalous according to Leibenstein (1987; see Khalil, 1989a). He rejects the view of the firm as an informational blueprint. While two firms may have identical production functions, it does not establish that effort expended on the part of labour is identical. The extraction of effort, which Marx calls relative surplus value, can be impeded by workers disgruntled by unfulfilled expectations promised by the firm.[24]

Cultural heritage also explains divergent productivities. Maurice *et al.* (1986) have shown amply how the difference in industrial relations between France and Germany untangles the conspicuous difference in the productivity performance, although there is no difference in the quantity and quality of investment. Performance by a nation or a firm depends on its historical record; each producing agency has a personality developed through unique conventions. The firm is the embodiment of its particular experiences and specific technological tradition. This, to some extent, insulates, in an unrestricted market, inefficient firms or nations from competition; their unique personality may have developed committed consumers. According to Metcalfe (in Dosi *et al.*, 1988b), diffusion of innovations, even under competitive pressure, is not as homogeneous and rapid as NC theory make us expect. It is rather erratic, since each nation or firm has its own personal conditions which cause it to ignore new technologies.

This suggests that technology is not an extraneous shirt. What is at stake is the identity of the firm. Technology is not only capital goods, but also the organization of the division of labour, the break-up of tasks, the accumulated technical experience by the labour force, and even includes the marketing apparatus (Levine, 1981). Technology permeates the producing agency and makes it into an organic whole. Thus, according to heterodox theorists (see Robinson, 1953, 1970; Pasinetti, 1966), it is ludicrous to suggest *à la* NC theory of capital that, within a certain technological organization, the relative composition of labour, capital and land is fungible. That is, they cannot be rearranged according to changes in relative prices. This is the origin of the reswitching of technique debate between Cambridge, USA and Cambridge, UK (see Moss, in Nell, 1980). Most critics of orthodoxy have focused on the logical and mathematical inadequacies of NC capital theory. Meanwhile, the conceptual failing was almost lost in the tussle. Factors, within certain limits, are not substitutable, since technological know-how permeates and unites the firm as an organic whole (Nell, 1992).

The basis of the view of factors of production as fungible is the conception of the firm as a mere contractual entity, a black box. This reductionist conception sees the firm as contingently premised on the independent will of owners of factors (Coase, 1937; Alchian and Demsetz, 1972). Owners of factors are assumed to form firms to avoid relatively higher transaction costs (Williamson, 1985). While this question is legitimate, it should not be the whole story – particularly when the concern is with the nature of organization. In this regard, vertically dependent firms should be considered as a single organization since their technologies are locked in, even when subcontracting is not explicitly evident. Although vertical transactions are conducted via the market, firms form an organic organization. They produce products according to the specification of others (see Lorenz, in Gambetta, 1988).

This signifies that a firm is more than the negation of the market. The firm is part of the vertical division of labour which expresses technological know-how. The firm, in a profound sense, cannot be severed into factors. These factors are not preconstituted, and hence cannot replace each other according to relative prices. They are organically joined by knowledge.

One cannot simply rearrange technology. It is not a congeries of self-defined bits of information. A mechanical reorganization of the components of technology may well generate undesired outcomes. Technology should be handled carefully if one intends to create an improved product or process of production. Components of technology are fuzzy know-how that engender products only through historical interaction between producer and environments.

Heterodox biology

Darwin's theory was rescued from decline by injecting it with modern genetics in the 1940s. The synthesis, ND, postulates that the genotype is given. To recapitulate, this axiom consists of two relatively separate statements: the genotype as exogenous; the genotype as definite.

Genotype as non-exogenous. The tenet that genotype is exogenous entails that genes are insulated from experience and purposeful will. If a gene mutates, it presumably occurs for random and extraneous reasons. The heterodox idea that gene mutation is directed (non-random), epitomized by the work of Lamarck, became something of a pariah in the hallways of ND orthodoxy.

One implication of the random mutation idea is that species evolve gradually. It is, however, unsupported by the fossil record unearthed by paleontologists. The record shows that species remain largely stable for long periods of time. Periods of prolonged stasis are interrupted by sudden appearances of new species in relatively short periods. The new species are usually more elaborate and complex forms of their lineage – reminiscent of technological regime change in economics. The rhythmic character of change suggests that the genotype does not mutate randomly or exogenously.[25]

A second implication of the random mutation idea is that the outcome of genetic mutation is open: anything goes. The soft-core version of ND, however, recognizes that genes operate within families, which confine the range of outcomes (Bateson, in Gambetta, 1988). In this light, Gould (in Milkman, 1982) has redefined the meaning of randomness: it does not mean that outcomes are equally probable but that they occur in disregard to expected benefit.

This redefinition of randomness, to Grasse (1977, p. 245), does not save ND. It does not matter how long the genome is shuffled, the DNA of bacteria does not have enough components to engender the DNA of mice. Random mutations are simply rearrangements of what already exists. Complex organisms require complex gene families which cannot be constructed from simpler ones by random mutations. Furthermore, random mutations are rare; there is a chemical 'proof-reader' which ensures that newborn cells carry the same genes as parent cells. Moreover, if a random mutation occurs, it would most likely be fatal. If it is not fatal, it would more probably be neutral, since there is no one–to–one correlation between genetic change and phenotypic change. The probability of a propitious mutation dwindles even further in light of the fact that most traits require the cooperation of multitudes of genes. That is, the chance of apropos genes randomly mutating in complementary fashion is astronomically low (Noda, 1982; Schoffeniels, 1976, *passim*; Moorhead and Kaplan, 1987).[26]

Furthermore, random mutation, as the origin of substantial and evolutionary change, is highly unlikely. The work of Cairns *et al.* (1988) suggests an alternative. He and his collaborators cultured a strain of bacteria that cannot digest lactose, in a dish with only lactose in it. Most cells starved to death; a few managed to develop the proper enzyme to digest lactose. The likelihood of this mutation occurring randomly is reckoned to be ludicrously small. More surprisingly, the mutation was passed on to daughter cells. They concluded that not only did the bacteria seem to have directed their mutation, but they also managed to pass the acquired character to progeny.[27] This challenges the orthodox idea of mutation as exogenous – similar to the case nurtured by heterodox economics in respect to innovations.

Other workers (e.g. Cullis, Steele *et al.*, Temin and Engels, in Pollard, 1984) extend the directed mutation and Lamarckian inheritance ideas to multicellular organisms. In multicellular organisms, cells may direct their genetic mutation through the enzymatic machinery. The idea of directed mutation should not sound radical, since it is the normal way of life for sexually reproducing species. Sexual organisms usually exercise power over the progeny through sexual selection. Humans assist such sexual selection through breeding and domestication of animals (Campbell, in Depew and Weber, 1985, p. 150).

Matsuno (in Ho and Saunders, 1984) shows that studies on the origin of life suggests an 'active agent' behind the assembly of non-living into living matter. To Campbell (in Milkman, 1982, pp. 200–1), the active agent is present at the lowest levels of hierarchy, the gene. Genes are crafty agents which modify their own structure according to circumstances. They team together and form families which shield members, even when they are defective. Families also help transport members anywhere, even to other species (Pollard, in Ho and Saunders, 1984). This 'colonialism' could change gene expression drastically if high ranking genes are involved (Hunkapillar *et al.* in Milkman, 1982).

A problem still needs to be confronted: how directed mutations are transferred from somatic (body) cells to germ (sex) cells, so that they can be passed on to progeny. This is discussed in Appendix 3.2. Meanwhile, I have shown that heterodox biologists, like their counterpart in economics, argue that change of know-how is at least partially directed by agents to promote their survival.

Genotype as non-definite. As explained above, orthodox biologists conceive genes as definite bits of information, similar to signals in communication theory. Heterodox biologists challenge such reductionism; while some genes are definite, the rest are organizations with somewhat flexible functions. As a corollary, heterodoxy does not conceive the organism as a black box. These ideas are reminiscent of heterodox views on technology and the firm.

Surroundings which influence genes include other genes, the cytoplasm (the protoplasm encircling the cell's nucleus), and, to a lesser extent, the organism, population, and natural habitat at large. Here, I am dealing with a different type of influence from the one I discussed in the previous subsection, where I argued that genes in many cases undergo directed rather than random mutations, as ND claims. The source of these mutations is learning feedbacks and the purposeful determination to survive. In this subsection, I am not dealing with genetic mutation but with genetic ambiguity, which allows the surroundings to interpret genetic messages in a liberal fashion.

As all interpretative activity has proven, the product depends, to some extent, on the interpreter. That is, interpreters with different contexts interpret the same genetic message differently; the circumstance of the interpreter matters to an extent. This is similar to what hermeneutics claims with respect to classic texts: there is no definite, precise meaning in biblical or Aristotelian texts (Gadamer, 1975). Likewise, genes are not definitive in themselves; they do not have precise messages. In order for a genetic message actually to become precise, it needs an interpreter to make sense of it.

Ptashne (1989) shows how the surroundings shape the messages of genes. This signifies that the DNA, for the most part, is not a self-defined entity, but, according to Wright (1988), is an organizational knowledge that possesses 'meaning'. The idea of DNA as possessing 'meaning' is iconoclastic, supposing that genes have, within reason, many ways of manifesting themselves. This may explain to baffled scientists how the immune system is capable of producing a large variety of antigens whose number could well surpass the number of genes. This versatility shows that the DNA is a supple organization capable of diverse behavioural strategies.[28] The RNA has been found to exhibit such diversity as well.[29]

The behaviour strategy of an organism is also versatile. It involves flexible actions ranging from self-promotion to mutual aid. It suggests that at least some genes do not emit self-defined rules, but fuzzy principles. The inclusive fitness hypothesis of sociobiology may be the last bulwark against such a suggestion; it insists that behaviour, following genes, is rigid. It expounds that mutual aid is disguised selfishness. An organism aids only relatives, in order to promote its own genes. Some empirical findings are not supportive of such an explanation. Queller *et al.* (1988), for example, have shown that members of a species of wasps undertake altruistic behaviour with no regard to kin.

Such flexibility of behaviour suggests that genes are not a blueprint. The fuzziness of some genes invites the participation of environments to shape the development of the organism. Wolterick (Ho and Saunders, 1984, p. 269) calls the confrontation a 'norm of reaction', since the organism is not defined until it confronts the environment. Waddington's (1957) metaphor of epigenetic landscape highlights the role of milieu in embryogenesis. He uses the metaphor to depict the development of a trait as a ball rolling down a genetically fixed path. Given gradient heights, the ball skirts the path when external factors exceed certain thresholds. In this manner, external, environmental factors participate in shaping the organism, which indicates that the genotype is fuzzy.[30]

Likewise, Lovtrup (in Ho and Saunders, 1984) views ontogeny (the development of organism to adult form) as the historical unfolding of abstract body plan into particular organisms. In this sense, according to von Baer's Law, phylogeny (the evolution of a lineage), like ontogeny, is the unfolding of the general into the particular. That is, ontogeny, broadly speaking, does not recapitulate phylogeny as asserted by Ernst Haeckel's biogenetic law (Gould, 1977). The earliest embryonic stages of related species are identical since they share the same abstract body plan before distinguishing features emerge during development. This suggests, as elaborated in Appendix 3.3, that evolution is highly related to development (ibid.).

Thus, ontogeny and phylogeny, from the heterodox view, show that the organism is not exclusively the product of a genetic blueprint. Besides the genotype, the organism is shaped by pressures from a multitude of environments. The consequent acquired characteristics are different from the ones prompted by the Lamarckian will. Regardless, traits changed by milieu also amount to nothing without evidence of their inheritance, as discussed in Appendix 3.2.

In light of this, the organism and its traits are not epiphenomena of some well-defined genotype. Contrary to Dawkins's (1976) view, the organism is not a black box for the genome to make another genome, a medium between genes and environment (Ho and Fox, 1988, *passim*). Some soft neo-Darwinists have conceded as much; they point out that genotype and phenotype may not correspond one to one (e.g. Eldredge, in Khalil and Boulding, 1993). They have failed, though, to draw the conclusion that activity of genes is to some extent a function of the organization of which they are members.

Campbell (in Milkman, 1982; in Depew and Weber, 1985; in Weber *et al.*, 1988; cf. Khalil, 1989f) emphasizes the integrity of organization running from multigene families to the organism (see also Hunkapillar *et al.*, in Milkman, 1982). Likewise, Varela (1979; cf. Kauffman, in Depew and Weber, 1985) views the organism as an 'autopoiesis', a self-reproducing, integral organization. Similarly, Edelman's (1988, 1989) idea of topobiology attempts to recover the organism from reductionism. According to him, current interactions of any cell depend on its current and past positions. Past history is important in the life of a cell since the kind of neighbours a cell used to have affects its current individuality and uniqueness. Such place-dependent interactions are most crucial in embryonic development, and continue throughout the organism's life.[31]

An earlier attempt to save the organism from the black-box conception is the work of D'Arcy Thompson (1961), an inspiration for many modern cladists (Janvier, in Pollard, 1984). Thompson charges that Darwin explained away the remarkable persistence of organizational form throughout evolution as a result of common origin (Kauffman, in Depew and Weber, 1985; Goodwin, in Pollard, 1984). Thompson's work is given a respectful, albeit lukewarm, attention in the history of biological thought. In most cases, it is misunderstood as highlighting physical forces in shaping the plan of the body (e.g. O'Grady and Brooks, in Weber *et al.*, 1988). Thus, it is assumed to complement ND. It is, however, an alternative to ND and suggests that evolution is the variation of the same body plan – which still needs to be explained.

A similar non-reductionist view of the organism and evolution is expressed by Webster and Goodwin (1982; in Ho and Saunders, 1984; in Pollard, 1984). Although their approach may have problems, they advance the unique conception of the organism as a field that cannot be reduced to insulated bits of information. Like Thompson, they do not attempt to explain diversity, but homological invariance. Universal homology suggests a generative field underlying all processes (cf. Ho, Saunders, in Ho and Saunders, 1984).[32] The field idea was first proposed by the arch-vitalist Hans Driesch in response to the remarkable ability of sea-urchin embryos to recover parts after being severed (see Sheldrake, 1988, pp. 79–80). Webster and Goodwin call their approach 'structuralism' since it rejects the genetic reductionism of ND and emphasizes the role of the cytoplasm.

The notion of the organism as a generative field which unfolds from the abstract to the concrete indicates that the genotype is not completely self-defined. Instead, the genotype is a form of organizational knowledge, defined partially through the assimilation of historical experience.

3.3.4 Environment: Not Given Selector

Heterodox economics

Alchian (1950) employed the neo-Darwinian notion of natural selection to expound the view that extant firms, by virtue of survival, signify efficiency.[33] The selector, made up of preferences, must be assumed to be given in order for the efficiency thesis to work. If agents manipulate the selector, less than optimal efficiency would persist. The axiom of a given selector has two untenable parts – similar to the neo-Darwinian view of nature: first, selectors are perfectly efficient because of perfect knowledge and hyper-rationality. Second, selectors are unyielding to the manipulations of firms because their preferences are well-defined before entering the market.

Under attack, NC theorists opted for the notion that agents have statistical rather than perfect knowledge of the prices of goods in all markets, spatially and temporally spread. The statistical qualification (even the subjective variety) is no response to critics like Frank Knight (1971; see O'Driscoll and Rizzo, 1985) and G.L.S. Shackle (1970) who insist that subjective or objective uncertainty cannot be reduced to probabilistic risk. No one denies that agents actually do not know all the opportunities and prices of goods in current markets, not to mention future markets. When this thesis is incorporated theoretically, the clout of agents as efficient selectors is clipped.

Furthermore, the hyper-rationality tenet comes under heavy fire from Simon (1978). He calls it 'substantive' rationality, in distinction to his view of rationality as 'procedural'. Regarding the NC substantive view, information is processed to generate an unambiguous, single-exit solution (Latsis, in Latsis, 1976). It presumes that agents are hyper-rational, capable of superseding their habits, historical uniqueness, and pragmatic rules of thumb. According to Simon's procedural view, information is knowledge which carries meaning and subject to interpretation. Agents are not automata but carry tacit, personal knowledge.

Thus, agents make decisions according to past knowledge; they are not exempt from the recency effect or inertia. According to Simon, their behaviour over time is more or less consistent; it is not erratically determined by an extraneous utility function. Decisions are part of a chain of events, from which agents cannot extricate themselves at the whim of price gyrations. Agents do not stand on suprahistorical grounds. They are defined by biological, cultural, and individual habits, which it is possible to overthrow, but not instantaneously.

Classical institutional thinkers, like Veblen (see Coats, in Latsis, 1976), have likewise emphasized the role of habits and tradition in moulding agents. Despite the new avenues they have opened, by neo-institutionalists (Langlois, 1986), arrive at conclusions reached by classical institutionalists, but through NC axioms. The neo-institutionalists postulate the ineluctability of rules from the perspective of hyper-rationality. Heiner (in Dosi *et al.*, 1988), for instance, reasons that rules arise because agents lack the competence to make prudent decisions.

Classical institutional economics and Simon's behaviouralism stand for the thesis that agents exhibit satisficing behaviour. That is, agents choose the first opportunity or course of action which satisfies their minimum requirement, rather than optimize an imagined utility function. Agents act according to inertia and habit, and are not ready to change behaviour in response to marginal stimuli. Habits emerge because agents' satisfaction arises from the act of consumption.

Thus, goods are not perfectly fungible. Consumers develop attachments to particular goods which express their personality (see Levine, 1988, chapter 1) as it develops biological and socially. That is, consumers relate to goods in a non-arbitrary manner. The array of goods exhibits some coherence which reflects the integrity of consumers. Consequently, consumers, within reason, do not substitute goods as relative prices change. Thus, preferences of consumers cannot act as the efficient selector as envisaged by NC theory. Preferences do not put the underachiever out of business. This explains the anomalous coexistence of firms with diverse rates of profit. The environment is multilayered, and hence inefficient firms can survive in the long run.

The fact that preferences are hypoefficient permits producers to mould and manipulate them. Preferences, after all, are not rigid enough; they yield to the manipulation of firms and are not absolutely sovereign as claimed. The environment is not an ironclad selector. Consumers are usually not precisely aware of their preferences, which are ductile enough to be moulded by advertisement and socialization forces.

Moreover, because preferences are hyporational and flexible explains the ability of most firms to develop special connections with their clients. Each firm carves a niche in the economy. This permits firms producing the same good to coexist, despite long-term profit rate gradients – reminiscent of the wide intra-population genetic frequency. As Galbraith argues (1958), firms have power to shape preferences (and even politics), rather than the other way around. Firms cultivate specific tastes that can be almost exclusively met by them.

Consequently, preferences are not the guardian angels that screen out the inefficient. The term 'efficiency' is non-operational and hazy in a world of hyporationality and flexible consumers' preferences. The fact that preferences are not given undermines the thesis that the satisfaction of consumers is the gauge of economic efficiency. There cannot be such a neutral criterion, since the environment can never be exogenously given. The environment is like an intaglio impressed upon by the cameo of purposefully acting producers.

Heterodox biology

The axiom that nature is given underlies the ND term 'adaptation', which denotes the act of fitting organisms to given habitats. The axiom involves two parts: first, nature is a hyperefficient selector (similar to the idea of hyper-rationality in economics); second, nature is unyielding (coinciding with the idea of well-defined preferences in economics). If nature is less than hyperefficient, and yields to agents' manoeuvres, it could not make an organism adapt to its habitat. Heterodoxy challenges the idea of adaptation and its underlying axiom that nature is given.

Heterodox biologists highlight the fact that intra-population frequency of a gene allele is wider than ND leads us to expect. This would not be the case if nature were a hyperefficient selector. The excessive intra-population variability is explained away by ND as the result of meiotic division and sexual recombination. This did not, however, stop some workers from questioning the efficiency of nature. Large differences among organisms of the same population were taken as serious anomalies, implying that nature is not a rigid selector. Organisms of various abilities could coexist for long periods of time – similar to the coexistence of firms with different rates of profit. This indicates that nature is a multilayered habitat, which allows diverse abilities to live side by side.

Specifically in relation to predators, studies have shown that these animals do not have perfect knowledge, even in the statistical form. They look for prey in a trial and error or iterative process. Furthermore, they do not forage in an optimal fashion, but rather pursue a course which seems to satisfy their minimum requirement. Thus, the selector, after all, is not hyperefficient.

This allows the organism to mould and manipulate native to an extent. The agent, within limits, may carve certain habitats after its own image rather than adapt to what is given. The common example, and sometimes mistaken to be the exclusive one, is the transfiguring of nature by humans. In fact, almost all living forms carve their own niche and exercise some power over the environment (Lewontin, 1984). The most primordial form of such power is the motion of animals and the roots of plants, which allow the organism to seek nutrients. More obvious examples of the manipulation of habitat include nests, dens, burrows, and colonies.

Thus, the environment yields to 'persuasion'; it is flexible in the face of the potency of organisms. This repudiates the orthodox thesis that nature is given. Nature is not the absolute arbiter of the fate of organisms, since nature is, to some extent; manipulated by organisms.

3.4 REFLECTIONS

When economists appeal to the core of ND in order to buttress the axioms of orthodoxy, they open a can of worms. ND is hard pressed to offer any help since it is under attack for the same reasons that the axioms of NC economics are under attack. The umbrella tenet which unites these attacks in both disciplines is the principle of purposeful behaviour. The principle puts non-conventional ideas in context and provides a deeper rationale for them.

The rejection of the precept of given material cause implies that the agent partially determines input influx. The repudiation of the tenet of given formal cause signifies that initiative and need to some extent determine technological and genetic innovations. The renunciation of the axiom of given efficient cause suggests that producers are somewhat able to redefine the environment. Put succinctly, the different challenges to NC and ND axioms are underpinned by the principle of purposeful action.

Orthodox theorists recognize purposeful behaviour, of course. But they do not really include it at the theoretical level in the textbook version of their approaches. The outcome is a theory which relies exclusively on efficient causality: phenomena like institutional arrangements are presented as contingent on exogenous causes, not a function of purposeful action. To NC theory, such arrangements are theoretically reversible since they depend on capriciously given variables. Orthodoxy, at the first level of approximation, is not equipped to discern temporal continuity.

To clear the way for historical theorizing, variables like resources, technology, and preferences must be treated as partially endogenous, determined to some extent by purposeful action. This makes theoretical endeavours more difficult. The gain, though, is worth the effort. Then, one can conceive historical trends theoretically: availability of resources, the evolution of technology, and development of preferences are the outcomes (some unintended) of irreversible purposeful action. These three moments contribute differently to the irreversible historical process. The detailed blend of these variables can be expressed in diverse scenarios. This chapter is not the place to develop them. But for a scenario to be historical, it must conceive one kind of action as self-seeking, purposeful behaviour.

Conventional theory finds teleology unpalatable. It does not need to be. Teleology is not necessarily the brainchild of wild metaphysics. Purposeful behaviour simply *completes* the organizational framework of humans:

> Humans are self-organizing and self-constructing. Committing oneself to goals not yet accomplished creates incomplete organization. Incomplete organization or disorganization elicits efforts to transform it into some coherent organizational form. When progress towards, or accomplishment of, a set of current concerns is not occurring, an incomplete behavior episode (i.e. incomplete organization) exists. A person will try to create organizational coherence, either by increased striving to accomplish current goals or abandonment of them (at least temporarily). (Ford, 1987, p. 408)

Organization, like household, firm, or government agency, is essentially incoherent. In order to eradicate incoherence, the agent has to pursue goals: 'The drama of real life reveal (sic) the importance of human purpose in ways sterile laboratory conditions cannot' (ibid., p. 394). If there are no goals to pursue, the organization would degenerate and perish. The absence of purpose is the most frequent cause of suicide and, to some extent, sickness. Purpose does not need to be fully attained. What matters is its presence:

> Without the direction which purposes give to life, there can be no coherent organization and no reference against which to evaluate one's activities and experiences. Without direction, life is meaningless. Like a ship on a stormy sea without someone steering it, one gets pushed around by the winds and waves of life until one capsizes and sinks to oblivion. Given the fundamental importance of the directive function in human life, it is sad that science has for so long treated it as an epiphenomenon. (ibid., p. 395)

The function of purpose in life is to end incoherence and incompleteness of organization – which really cannot be willed (Elster, 1983). This suggests that organization is not a self-constituted, well-defined agency – similar to technological knowledge discussed above. That is, the worth of an agent of production cannot be determined independently of the actual pursuit of production. The agent acquires different attributes depending on the greater organizational context. Thus, when incomplete, fuzzy organizations of production join hands to form a greater organiza-tion, the productivity of labour, for example, is *not* the sum of independent productivities. The productivity of each agent cannot be determined in isolation from the organic context. An agent's productivity is a potential with diverse actualities, depending on how the agent relates to others. Thus, the firm's productivity is not the sum of the productivity of its agents'.

Therefore, the whole organization has to be specified in order to know the actual productivity of the constitutive agents. This sheds doubt on the other conceptual pillar of NC economics, reductionism. For that matter, it is also the pillar of ND. The firm is not a black box, an entity. It is not a congeries of agents; the way agents are connected is a crucial matter. Heterodox biologists have registered similar ideas in regard to the organism.

The upshot is that NC theory, at the first theoretical approximation, not equipped to handle organization. The way agents are connected, in the NC world, is capricious, the function of relative prices. The fungibility of inputs, as stipulated by the NC production function, indicates that the firm lacks an organizational integrity. The idea of fungibility makes job differentiation or the rise of complexity contingent on relative prices, and hence reversible.[34]

Williamson (1985) tries to remedy the situation. However, the picture does not improve much, since his concern is still the NC emphasis on the size of the firm. He adds a twist to the NC explanation. The size is a function of transaction cost. While market structure is a sound inquiry, it is insufficient.

One needs to combine the organic idea of organization with the earlier assertion, the teleological idea of action, in order to clear the way for historical thinking. Each idea complements the other. Purposeful action means the agent is incomplete, and incomplete organization drives the agent to act purposefully. Unfortunately, most heterodox views have incorporated one idea at the expense of the other. Some have recognized the organic idea, but retained the efficient view; others have accepted teleology, but kept reductionism. Consequently, these traditions have only produced partial historical thinking.

The first type includes Leibenstein's (1987; see Khalil, 1989a) theory of the firm. He holds organic views, but does not entertain teleology. To him, the agent is not a purposeful actor that defines the influx of resources, technology, and preferences. It is not surprising that Leibenstein's study of the inefficiency of US firms relative to Japanese firms lacks a historical perspective. He blames hierarchy and the individualist ethos (which generates prisoner dilemma outcomes) for inefficiency in US industry, rather than seeing the expenditive of effort as the subject of historical development.[35]

The second type of heterodox traditions includes Austrian economics. It advocates teleology, but fails to subscribe to organic views.[36] In fact, the Austrian school is a forceful proponent of reductionism. Schumpeter's work is a good representative. His analysis of purposeful entrepreneurship is not complemented with an organic view of organization. There could be only one type of correct organization, namely, the small, independent entrepreneur. History for him hence is not an on-going process of evolution of organization, but a motion which terminates with the society of small entrepreneurs. His prognostication of the appearance of large firms and socialism leads him to pessimism, which further substantiates my point: Schumpeter's view of history is ahistorical (cf. Heilbroner, 1986, chapter 10).

In another paper (Khalil, 1992; cf. Khalil 1990d), I show in detail that Marx's view of the agent is similar to the Austrian programme: Marx's conception of action is teleological, but falls short of organic views. He is not, though, a reductionist. His vision is non-organic in another sense: he advocates a functionalist view of organization which amounts to portraying it as a mere entity. This is clearest in Marx's writings on abstract labour and the dominance of capital.

The concept of abstract labour means that labour-power is fungible; there is no irreversible technical division of labour. Dominance of capital for Marx is a moment which subsumes all others. Organization of production is totally subsumed under the yoke of capital. The firm is portrayed as a unidimensional agent which is only interested in the valorization of capital. There are, though, other dimensions to the firm. The firm is interested in its reputation, satisfying different sectors – like consumers and owners – and maintaining its constitutive suborganizations. This multi-faceted complexity is ignored by Marx at the first level of approximation. For him, there could be only one type of correct organization, namely, the association of producers who are free from the yoke of capital. Similar to Schumpeter, Marx sees history not as an endless process of development of organization, but as a motion which terminates with the society of free producers. Thus, Marx's view of history is ahistorical as well.

Thus, for clear historical thinking, organic conception should be combined with teleology. If the organic view is infused into Schumpeter's and Marx's analyses, history would be seen as an endless process of evaluation, not as an ideal telos to reach. If teleological reasoning is infused into Leibenstein's analysis, X-efficiency would be seen in a historical context.

While teleological conception has been repudiated for its mystical connotations, the organic conception has been rebuked for its imprecision. I may add that there might be a common rationale for the castigation of teleological and organic conceptions. Namely, it is the commitment to crude, pre-quantum materialism, which seems to be the ethos of mainstream scientific milieu. It is crude since it portrays itself as committed mainly to tangible objects, which excludes 'ghostly' things like final cause and organic interaction. In the light of quantum mechanics, matter after all is neither located in space in a point-like way nor bounded by sharp edges.

Such crude materialism is supposed to save us from teleology, which is usually identified with mystical speculations. The teleological conception has been castigated as non-scientific since it opens a Pandora's box of theology, metaphysics, and mysticism. With reference to the above discussion, I hope that I have demonstrated that teleological thinking need not be extravagant speculation. Furthermore, teleology should not be identified with an enigmatic, predestined telos which presumably guides development and evolution from an Olympian height.

Another promise made by the crude materialist ethos is the delivery of precise prediction. Precise prediction, however, has not been the silver lining of orthodoxy. So, why champion precision, and pay the high expense of relevance? If one champions relevance instead, its price – imprecision – is not too high, given the need of the intellect to understand and for public policy to be sagacious.

Action and organization should not, respectively, be reasoned in exclusively efficient and reductionist frameworks. As things stand now, those who try to shake the scales off their eyes and explain large-scale historical change are seen by the majority of on-lookers as peculiar. The audience, however, changes in the larger theatre of human ideas.

58

Appendix 3.1 The Newtonian Framework

The Newtonian framework is reductionist and efficient. The Newtonian law of gravity is the epitome of reductionism. The law is underpinned by the apparently innocuous assumptions that matter is independent of space, and both are analytically conceived apart from time and force. Thus, the movement of terrestrial and celestial masses is explained, when there is no contiguous force, as an action at-a-distance between objects, while the spatial/temporal matrix serves as a mere background. This allows the break-up of a phenomenon into its constitutive parts, as if the parts are independent and self-constituted. In this manner, the Newtonian framework has no room for the concept of organization as an integral, organic unit.

Newton's three laws of motion – inertia, acceleration, and action/reaction – are the quintessence of efficient conception. They relate mobility to contiguous forces, like pushing. Aristotle's efficient causality is emphasized at the expense of final causality. Classical, pre-twentieth-century physics perceives the world as a colossal machine or a huge billiard table which is mechanically determined. Along these lines, the behaviour of organization is conceived exclusively as a response to stimulus, similar to the response to contiguous force in the Newtonian world. In this manner, the Newtonian framework has no room for the concept of action as self-seeking, purposeful behaviour.

The Cartesian strategy is also reductionist and efficient. It reduces phenomena to kinematic and geometrical quantities, like mobility, impenetrability, and extension. It views the organism as a machine, and hence cannot be the basis of purposeful action. Any intentional action must have a separate ground that can be appended to the machine.

59

Appendix 3.2 The Inheritance of Acquired Characteristics

Characteristics may be acquired through purposeful will or the moulding of experience. They would amount to nothing, as far as evolutionary theory is concerned, if they cannot be inherited. That is, it has to be shown that Weismann's barrier is permeable.

To recapitulate, the barrier postulates that, in multicellular organisms, germ (sex) cells are totally insulated from somatic cells. In this fashion, an occurrence at the somatic level cannot be passed on to progeny. A number of workers are questioning the thesis that the germline is inviolate from the soma. Particles contained in somatic cells, called pangenes, can be influenced by environment and the organs containing them. Pangenes can move via blood to germ cells and influence the course of heredity. Steele (1979) proposes another mechanism inspired by Temin's protovirus hypothesis. He suggests that endogenous retroviruses targeted at the germline may act as vectors for the mutant somatic information by capturing RNAs from somatic cells and transducing them to germ cells. This scenario runs into problems in cases where cells do not divide as often or do not move. Steele offers solutions which need not concern us here.

It has been shown empirically that acquired traits by adults can be inherited in organisms as diverse as the ciliate protozoa and drosophila (Ho and Saunders, 1984, p. 225 ff.). Steele and Pollard (1987) have explained this through the process of reverse transcription. It is similar to Reidl's postulate of the feedback loop from the phenome to genome: 'This feedback information causes to develop, by trial and error, those gene interactions which improve their own adaptive speed or success' (Reidl, 1978, pp. xv–xvi).

The feedback loop for Ho (in Ho and Saunders, 1984, p. 275) is between the cytoplasm (the protoplasm outside the cell's nucleus) and the phenome; the genome only plays a secondary role. She places great emphasis on the cytoplasm since it is actually the whole organism at the zygote stage (Ho, in Ho and Saunders, 1984, p. 280). She conceives the cytoplasm of the ovum as crucial for the instigation and suppression of gene expression and cell differentiation. The cytoplasm registers the experience of the organism, while the genome records the experiences of the species. The experiences of the organism are assimilated and transmitted through the cytoplasm, and indirectly through the genome, to progeny:

> Organisms develop in accordance partly with the assimilated experiences of their forebears and partly with their own experiences. Development evolves through the internalization of new environments. The material link between organism and environment, and development and evolution alike is the hereditary apparatus which realistically includes both cytoplasm and nuclear genes. The cytoplasm registers the somatic imprint of experienced environments which can be transmitted to the next generation independently of the nuclear genes. At the same time, it acts as a true communication channel between the environment and the nuclear genome in the coordination of developmental and evolutionary processes. (Ho, in Ho and Saunders, 1984, p. 284; cf. Pollard, in Ho and Saunders, 1984; Campbell, in Milkman, 1982)

The role she accords to the cytoplasm and non-genetic inheritance complements Webster and Goodwin's structuralist alternative to ND. They provide ways to explain the inheritance of acquired characteristics.

More evidence is being discovered each day that acquired characteristics could be inherited under certain circumstances. This heterodox thesis is no longer on the defensive. It undermines the basic tenet of orthodoxy – Weismann's barrier – and makes it look like a wall with holes. That is, the genetic change of somatic cells can influence the germ cells.

Appendix 3.3 Development and Evolution

Von Baer's Law, after Karl Ernst von Baer, a nineteenth-century embryologist, fosters a developmental view of evolution – which more biologists are recognizing (e.g. Gould, 1977; Marx, 1988). Von Baer's Law stipulates that evolution, like development, is largely a process of differentiation from the general to the more particular. Such a process entails the rise of complexity of biological functions, which were tacitly implied in ancestral forms. That is, evolution is not about adding something totally new, but is rather the elaboration of what already exists – although in a relatively undifferentiated form.

In sympathy with von Baer's Law, Stephen Jay Gould (1977) argues that evolutionary change arises *during* the development of an organism through the change of the rate of reaching adulthood. The rate of unfolding from the general to the particular could be speeded up or retarded, which provides an opportunity for other rates to proceed into new territories. The opportunity to experiment is most crucial in the cases where the environment becomes hostile. According to Gould, the change of rate of development might engender successful species – even a higher taxon.

Gould's view supersedes the biogenetic law, also propagated by a nineteenth-century embryologist, Ernst Haeckel. The biogenetic law relates development to evolution in an opposite fashion to von Baer's Law. Haeckel's biogenetic law stipulates that the development of an organism recapitulates the features of ancestral *adult* forms before adding its own novelty on top (Gould, 1977, pp. 39–45). Advocates of recapitulation usually use the gill slits in a human embryo (see pictures in Sheldrake, 1988, p. 16) as an example of the recapitulation of a feature of adult fish. Such a feature is supposedly pushed back by others added on top of it during evolution. In respect of this example, Gould puts the difference between Haeckel's biogenetic law and von Baer's Law at the outset of his magisterial account:

> Haeckel interpreted the gill slits of human embryos as features of ancestral *adult* fishes, pushed back into the early stages of human ontogeny by a universal acceleration of developmental rates in evolving lineages. Von Baer argued that human gill slits do not reflect a change in developmental timing. They are not adult stages of ancestors pushed back into the embryos of descendants; they merely represent a stage common to the early ontogeny of all vertebrates (embryonic fish also have gill slits, after all). (Gould, 1977, pp. 2–3)

Stated differently, von Baer argues that the human embryo resembles embryos of other vertebrates because they are the most general foundations which give rise to the different lineages. This entails that, according to von Baer's Law, evolution is not a process of adding on totally unrelated features on top of others exhibited by ancestral adults. Rather, evolution is the reworking in new and more complex directions of the *same* general outline which humans, fish, and other schemes share.

Thus, the processes of evolution and development are intricately connected. Both entail the unfolding of the general into the particular. This should weaken the neo-Darwinian theses that mutations are random, and that evolutionary regularities are the outcome of the blind forces of natural selection.

Notes

1. Some prefer to expunge the term 'paradigm' from the English language for its widespread abuse (see Khalil, 1987a). In order to avoid tiresome and lengthy periphrases, however, I use it loosely to mean, what Schumpeter calls, the pre-analytical vision. That is, it should not denote relativistic epistemology.
2. Hollis and Nell (1975) have argued that NC concepts are bogus since positivism, which NC theorists adhere to, stands on shaky grounds. However, first, it has been observed (e.g. Blaug, 1980; Hirsch and de Marchi, 1986) that NC economists in practice are not positivists. Second, NC axioms do not stand or fall with the proclaimed epistemology.
3. It might come as a surprise that mainstream evolutionary theory is ahistorical. Part of the bewilderment stems from the failure to delineate between the *general* theory of evolution, which advocates the reality of the historical change of species, and the *specific* theory of evolution, which proposes an explanation of the general theory. Darwin's mechanism, natural selection, is a specific theory of evolution. The identification of the general theory with Darwinism was not helped by Darwin's popularized writings.
4. The vitalist doctrine submits that life in living organisms is caused and sustained by a vital force. This force is assumed to be distinct from and in addition to all primodial physical and chemical forces. Put differently, the doctrine draws a thick boundary between living and non-living matter.
5. The critics share another platform, the animosity towards the bourgeois ideological underpinning of both orthodoxies, like self-interest, survival of the fittest, *laissez-faire*, and competition. I do not develop this here. It has been attempted by others (Nell, 1972; Kitcher, 1985).
6. Equilibrium, no surplus, and complete market axioms are central to the NC enterprise. Albeit, they are ignored, since the concern of this chapter is with purposeful behaviour and large-scale historical change, while the idea of equilibrium is concerned only with the character of market dynamics. Hence one should deal with the two concerns separately (Khalil, 1990b).

   Some heterodox economists (e.g. Robinson, 1979) have helped convolute the two concerns. She considered the notion of equilibrium to contravene historical thinking. The notion of equilibrium, though, can be defended as an underlying force which need *not* be inconsistent with historical analysis. After all, historical–classical economics upheld the idea of natural price as the centre of gravity of market fluctuation (Eatwell, 1983).
7. Natural selection is the principle agency of evolution according to Darwin. Its modern version espouses the tenet that the genetic frequency of a population changes through time, and so evolves. Evolution occurs for two reasons: first, organisms are heterogenous in regard to hereditary materials. Second, those endowed with traits best fit for survival and reproduction will be overrepresented in the progeny. It is different from genetic drift and random statistical fluctuations.

   Hard-core Darwinians emphasize lower levels of the hierarchy like organisms and genes as the units of selection. Soft-core Darwinians stress that the units of natural selection are higher levels of the hierarchy like species and genus.

   Another related concept is the survival of the fittest, an expression coined by Herbert Spencer to refer to natural selection. Survival of the fittest, though, is no substitute for natural selection since it measures survival *prior* to selection, while natural selection measures fitness *after* the ousting of unfit organisms. Both principles are tautological. This is not necessarily a flaw. Some philosophers argue that theory by definition is a tautology. Thus, I do not entertain this line of criticism.
8. The quantity or property which nature maximizes is more accurately called 'net

reproductive advantage'. The word 'net' indicates that the measurement of fertility, the basis of fitness, makes allowance for mortality.

9. Wilson employs the concept 'inclusive fitness' to explain altruism. An organism supposedly strives for its fitness plus all its influence on the fitness of its relatives other than direct descendants. It is related to kin selection theory. Kin includes brothers, sisters, parents, and cousins. The theory argues that one or more organisms favour the survival and reproduction of relatives who are likely to possess the same genes by common descent.
10. Genotype is the totality of the genetic material of cells; genome is the sum total of genetic material in a fertilized egg. It is supposedly antecedent of phenotype, the external appearance.
11. In another paper (Khalil, 1990b), I show the difference between the phenomena (natural complex) which are organized and require final cause and the phenomena (natural system) which are chaotic and does not require it. The distinction does not run along the traditional separation between living and non-living matter. For example, agents interact in the market chaotically and non-living matter, as quantum mechanics postulates, interact organically (see Khalil, 1989g).
12. The fact that a closed system tends spontaneously towards maximum entropy (maximum melting) has misled many thinkers, notably N. Georgescu-Roegen (1971), to postulate that the entropy law is teleological. Therefore, they have concluded erroneously that the entropy law is the exemplar of, and the impetus behind, social and biological development (Khalil, 1990c, 1991).
13. Bohm conceives matter as a never-ending process of becoming. He postulates an order, called implicate, which gives rise to tangible order, called explicate. While the former is hidden, the latter is accessible to measurements. The philosopher Bhaskar (1978) made a similar distinction between the level of reality (plan of generative structures) and the level of actuality (the place of manifested events).
14. This implies that purposefulness does not necessitate consciousness. The quest to survive is not specifically human. Anyhow, the fact that humans are conscious, not to mention self-conscious, did not stop behaviourist psychologists and NC economists from ignoring purpose and will.
15. Lamarck is also castigated, mostly in Anglo-American circles, for another reason. He is admonished for advocating purposeful behaviour, which he unfortunately equated with 'vital force'. Since classical Greece, philosophers have been divided over whether organs were created for purpose or simply found their purpose after they had been created. Lamarck supported the former position and Darwin the latter one. Lamarck (1984, pp. 355–61) postulated that a trait develops for a purpose as a result of the organism's response to its needs by an appropriate self-modification. This explicitly recognizes the role of will, especially in vertebrate organisms which possess higher nervous systems. Thus, Lamarckianism entails two independent doctrines: the inheritance of acquired characteristics (which may happen for a multitude of reasons) and the more radical notion of will (a particular way of acquiring a characteristic). It is possible to embrace the former and reject the latter radical doctrine – as Darwin did in later editions of *Origin*.
16. A mutation is any physical or functional heritable variation. Two types of mutations are distinguished: *gene mutations* due to changes in the genetic code, and *chromosomal mutations* resulting from modification of the order of the genes (e.g. inversion of a segment).
17. This ecological insensitivity is epitomized by the celebrated Hotelling's (1931) model. Hotelling finds that an exhaustible resource should be used when its present value exceeds its current price. This ignores the needs of future generations.
18. The dwindle of resources is defined by the agency of labour. While the dispersion of heat (greater entropy) is objective, independent of human agency. Thus, the waste

generated by economic organization is conceptually different from the 'waste' generated by the entropy law. The fact that both tendencies are irreversible does not mean they are identical. Otherwise, it would be analogous to the claim that aeroplanes are subject to Newton's law of action and reaction since they rise in the air like rockets (Khalil, 1989b). At the bottom of the confusion of the two kinds of wastes is the failure to view the entropy law as devoid of purposeful agency – as Table 3.2 above shows – and its irreversibility is statistical, not theoretical in nature.

19. Prigogine's notion of dissipative structure, along with the new science of chaos, is more suited to explain feedbacks, which give rise to the chaotic business cycle and regional polarization (Khalil, 1989c). Albeit, they are outside my concern here, since I investigate purposeful organization.
20. This distinction between efficiency and productivity also applies to economics: the change of technique is about efficiency, since it involves the production of a greater amount of products with the same inputs; while innovation is about productivity, since it means ability to process a greater amount of inputs (Khalil, 1990c).
21. The irreversibility of evolution has been widely and erroneously identified with the entropy law – reminiscent of Georgescu-Roegen's fumble. This is taken to extremes by Brooks and Wiley (e.g. in Weber *et al.*, 1988), whose position has come under fire, even from other devotees of the relevance of non-scarcity view of input influx (Weber *et al.*, 1988; Khalil, 1989f).
22. Thus, Kaldor and other Post-Keynesians conclude that general equilibrium theory is untenable. Arrow (1962), though, shows that learning-by-doing, and its implications, can be accommodated in the general equilibrium framework. This is done, though, with highly contrived assumptions.
23. This circle would accelerate and the economy would grow faster if innovative activity or productivity gain is mostly occurring in the main sector of the economy, since it has disproportionate weight. This has been empirically established by Verdoon and popularized by Kaldor (1975). It came to be called the Verdoon or Kaldor law (Thirlwall, 1983). It postulates that the rate of growth of GNP would be faster than productivity growth, if the latter is occurring in manufacturing – taken to be the main sector.
24. This is the story of breakdown of trust (see Khalil, 1993), which is a more plausible explanation of the attenuation of effort expenditure on the part of workers than the explanation that workers simply resent the domination of capitalist bosses (e.g. Gordon *et al.*, in Cherry *et al.*, 1987). One may ask the latter approach, why workers did not question capitalist domination prior to the decline of productivity? Meanwhile, there are many explanations for the abrupt breakdown of trust. One of them is the process of senescence which relations within institutions go through. Marshall (Whitaker, in Black, 1986; cf. Penrose, 1952) and Boulding (1950, p. 34) have supported such a view.
25. Another suggestion, the 'punctuated equilibria' hypothesis (Gould, in Milkman 1982; Eldredge, 1985a, 1986b; Stanley, 1979), attempts to explain this anomaly without challenging the orthodox dogma that genotype is exogenous. The hypothesis proposes that the unit of selection is mainly the species and higher taxa, rather than the organism. This hierarchical, non-reductionist view jibes with ND, as Buss (1987) shows. Buss views the history of life as a history of changing units of selection from molecules, cells, multicellular organisms, to higher taxa. Although Sâlthe (1985) has given systemic theoretical exposition of the hierarchical perspective, he (1987) admits that it, along with ND, fails to give an account of purposeful behaviour.
26. Hall (1988) has shown that for bacteria to adapt to a new environment, two independent mutations are required. The chance of both occurring consecutively makes it almost an impossible event.

27. In response, others have tried to explain it away as random mutation (Partridge and Morgan, 1988; Charlesworth *et al.*, 1988; Lenski *et al.*, 1989).
28. This is explained by Grasse (1977, p. 224n) as the result of the holographic nature of 'information': 'The information in an organized being is not at all localized as in a computer. Each cell, i.e. each executant, contains the whole of it. There are as many memories as there are cells.'
29. It has been shown in the past two years that the RNA could be manipulated by variables other than the DNA. Bass and Weintraub (1988) in a serendipitous way found that a double-stranded RNA has been covalently modified by an unwinding activity, without the intervention of the DNA.
30. Waddington departs from ND in this fashion: while he upholds natural selection as the rule which weeds out unfit variations, variations do not originate only from randomness as ND postulates, but are also encouraged by environmental factors.
31. Edelman's work on cell interaction in embryos led to the discovery of cell-adhesion molecule (CAM). CAM and other molecules are complex proteins that regulate interactions among cell surfaces. Such surface interactions influence gene expression, cell shape, movement, and function.
32. The idea of a generative field is reminiscent of Noam Chomsky's (1965) linguistic theory that all languages share a deep structure.
33. In this way, NC theorists can defend marginalism and hyper-rationality without pretending realism. What matters, to Friedman's (1953) brand of positivism, is the predictiveness of assumptions, not their realism.
34. Karl Marx's concept of abstract labour is equivalent to the NC idea of fungibility of technique. For Marx, labour-time is comparable and the basis of exchange value since it has the abstract potential to undertake *any* job. That is, labour-power is a fungible commodity. Thus, job differentiation could be reversed and hence the firm lacks organizational integrity (see Khalil, 1992).
35. The same could be said in respect to advocates of punctuated equilibria, like Gould and Eldredge. They recognize the organism as an integral, imprecise unit, and even view population and higher taxation as individuals, but still cling to the Darwinian apprehension about teleology.
36. The work of Reidl (1978) also advocates teleology and fails to subscribe to organic views of organism. (I owe this note to Stanley Sâlthe.)

References

Alchian, Armen A. (1950) 'Uncertainty, Evolution, and Economic Theory', *Journal of Political Economy*, June, vol. 58, no. 3, pp. 211–21.

Alchian, Armen A. and Harold Demsetz (1972) 'Production, Information Costs, and Economic Organization', *American Economic Review*, December, vol. 62, no. 5, pp. 777–95.

Arrow, Kenneth J. (1962) 'The Economic Implications of Learning by Doing', *Review of Economic Studies*, vol. 29, pp. 155–73.

Artigiani, Robert (1987) 'Revolution and Evolution: Applying Prigogine's Dissipative Structures Model', *Journal of Social and Biological Structures*, July, vol. 10, no. 3, pp. 249–64.

Bass, Brenda L. and Harold Weintraub (1988) 'An Unwinding Activity that Covalently Modifies Its Double-stranded RNA Substrate', *Cell*, 23 December, vol. 55, no. 6, pp. 1089–98.

Battalio, Raymond C. *et al.* (1979) 'Labor Supply of Animal Workers: Towards an Experimental Analysis', *Research in Experimental Economics*, 1, pp. 231–53.

Battalio, Raymond C. *et al.* (1981a) 'Commodity-choice Behavior with Pigeons as Subjects', *Journal of Political Economy*, February, vol. 89, no. 1, pp. 67–91.

Battalio, Raymond C. *et al.* (1981b) 'Income–Leisure Tradeoffs of Animal Workers', *American Economic Review*, September, vol. 71, no. 4, pp. 621–32.

Becker, Gary S. (1976) 'Altruism, Egoism, and Genetic Fitness: Economics and Sociobiology', *Journal of Economic Literature*, September, vol. 4, no. 3, pp. 817–26.

Becker, Gary S. (1981) *A Treatise on the Family* (Cambridge, Mass.: Harvard University Press).

Bergson, Henri (1913) *Creative Evolution* (New York: Holt).

Berry, R. J. (1982) *Neo-Darwinism* (London: Edward Arnold).

Bhaskar, Roy (1978) *A Realist Theory of Science* (Hassocks, Sussex: Harvester Press Atlantic Highlands, NJ: Humanities Press).

Black, R. D. Collison (ed.) (1986) *Ideas in Economics* (Totowa, NJ: Barnes & Noble).

Blaug, Mark (1980) *The Methodology of Economics: Or How Economists Explain* (Cambridge: Cambridge University Press).

Boulding, Kenneth E. (1950) *A Reconstruction of Economics* (New York: John Wiley).

Buss, Leo W. (1987) *The Evolution of Individuality* (Princeton, NJ: Princeton University Press).

Cairns, John, Julie Overbaugh and Stephen Miller (1988) 'The Origin of Mutants', *Nature*, September, vol. 335, no. 6186, pp. 142–5.

Charlesworth, D., *et al.* (1988) 'Origin of Mutants Disputed', *Nature*, 8 December, vol. 336, no. 6199, pp. 525–8.

Cherry, Robert, *et al.* (eds) (1987) *The Imperiled Economy: Book 1* (New York: Union for Radical Political Economics).

Chomsky, Noam (1965) *Aspects of the Theory of Syntax* (Cambridge, Mass.: MIT Press).

Christensen, Paul P. (1989) 'Historical Roots for Ecological Economics – Biophysical Versus Allocative Approaches', *Ecological Economics*, February, vol. 1, no. 1, pp. 17–36.

Coase, R. H. (1937) 'The Nature of the Firm', *Economica*, November, vol. 4, pp. 386–405. (Reprinted in G. J. Stigler and K. E. Boulding (eds) *Readings in Price Theory* (Homewood, Ill.: Irwin, 1952, pp. 331–51).

Daly, Herman E. (1977) *Steady State Economics* (San Francisco: Freeman).

Darwin, Charles (1959) *The Origins of Species*, A Variorum Text, ed. by Morse Peckham (Philadelphia: University of Pennsylvania Press (1859–72).

Dawkins, Richard (1976) *The Selfish Gene* (New York: Oxford University Press).

Depew, David and Bruce Weber (eds) (1985) *Evolution at a Crossroads: The New Biology and the New Philosophy of Science* (Cambridge, Mass.: MIT Press).

Depew, David and Bruce Weber (1989) 'The Evolution of the Darwinian Research Tradition', *Systems Research*, vol. 6.

Dobzhansky, Theodosius (1982) *Genetics and the Origin of Species* (New York: Columbia University Press).

Dosi, Giovanni (1988a) 'Sources, Procedures, and Microeconomic Effects of Innovation', *Journal of Economic Literature*, September, vol. 26, no. 3, pp. 1120–71

Dosi, Giovanni, Christopher Freeman, Richard Nelson, Gerald Silverberg and Luc Soete (eds) (1988b) *Technical Change and Economic Theory* (London and New York: Pinter).

Duijn, J. J. van (1983) *The Long Wave in Economic Life* (London: Unwin Hyman).

Eatwell, John (1983) 'Theories of Value, Output and Employment', in John Eatwell and Murray Milgate (eds), *Keynes's Economics and the Theory of Value and Distribution* (London: Duckworth).

Edelman, Gerald M. (1988) *Topobiology: An Introduction to Molecular Embryology* (New York: Basic Books).

Edelman, Gerald M. (1989) 'Topobiology', *Scientific American*, May, vol. 260, no. 5, pp. 76–88.

Eldredge, Niles (1986a) *Unfinished Synthesis: Biological Hierarchies and Modern Evolutionary Thought* (New York: Oxford University Press).

Eldredge, Niles (1986b) *Time Frames: The Rethinking of Darwinian Evolution and the Theory of Punctuated Equilibria* (New York: Simon & Schuster).

Elster, Jon (1983) *Sour Grapes: Studies in the Subversion of Rationality* (Cambridge: Cambridge University Press)

Englis, Karel (1986) *An Essay on Economic Systems: A Teleological Approach*, trans. by Ivo Moravcik (Boulder, Col.: East European Monographs).

Faber, Malte, Horst Niemes and Gunter Stephen, with the cooperation of L. Freytag (1987) *Entropy, Environment and Resources: An Essay in Physico-Economics*, trans. from the German by I. Pellengahr (New York: Springer).

Fenn, John B. (1982) *Engines, Energy, and Entropy* (San Francisco: Freeman).

Ford, Donald H. (1987) *Humans as Self-Constructing Living Systems: A Developmental Perspective on Behavior and Personality* (Hillsdale, NJ: Lawrence Erlbaum).

Frank, Robert (1989) 'Frames of Reference and the Quality of Life', *American Economic Review*, May, vol. 79, no. 2, pp. 80–5.

Friedman, Milton (1953) *Essays in Positive Economics* (Chicago: University of Chicago Press).

Gadamer H. (1975) *Truth and Method* (New York: Seabury).

Galbraith, J. K. (1958) *The Affluent Society* (Boston: Houghton-Mifflin).

Gambetta, Diego (ed.) (1988) *Trust: Making and Breaking Cooperative Relations* (New York and Oxford: Blackwell).

Georgescu-Roegen, Nicholas (1971) *The Entropy Law and the Economic Process* (Cambridge, Mass.: Harvard University Press).

Ghiselin, Michael T. (1969) *The Triumph of the Darwinian Method* (Berkeley: University of California Press).

Gould, Stephen Jay (1977) *Ontogeny and Phylogeny* (Cambridge, Mass.: Harvard University Press).

Grasse, Pierre-P. (1977) *Evolution of Living Organisms: Evidence for a New Theory of Transformation* (New York: Academic Press).

Hall, Barry G. (1988) 'Adaptive Evolution that Requires Multiple Spontaneous Mutations. I: Mutations Involving an Insertion Sequence', *Genetics*, December, vol. 120, no. 4, pp. 887–97.

Heilbroner, Robert L. (1970) *Between Capitalism and Socialism: Essays in Political Economics* (New York: Vintage Books).

Heilbroner, Robert L. (1986) *The Worldly Philosophers: The Lives, Times, and Ideas of the Great Economic Thinkers* (New York: Simon & Schuster).

Hirsch, Abraham and Neil de Marchi (1986) 'Making a Case When Theory Is Unfalsifiable: Friedman's Monetary History', *Economics and Philosophy*, April, vol. 2, no. 1, pp. 1–21.

Hirshleifer, Jack (1977) 'Economics from a Biological Viewpoint', *Journal of Law and Economics*, April, vol. 20, no. 1, pp. 1–52.

Hirshleifer, Jack (1978a) 'Competition, Cooperation, and Conflict in Economics and Biology', *American Economic Review*, May, vol. 68, no. 2, pp. 238–43.

Hirshleifer, Jack (1978b) 'Natural Economy versus Political Economy', *Journal of Social and Biological Structures*, October, vol. 1, no. 4, pp. 319–37.

Hirshleifer, Jack (1982) 'Evolutionary Models in Economics and Law: Cooperation versus Conflict Strategies', *Research in Law and Economics*, vol. 4, pp. 1–60.

Ho, Mae-Wan and Peter T. Saunders (eds) (1984) *Beyond Neo-Darwinism: An Introduction to the New Evolutionary Paradigm* (London: Academic Press).

Ho, Mae-Wan and Sidney W. Fox (eds) (1988) *Evolutionary Processes and Metaphors* (New York: John Wiley).

Hollis, Martin and Edward J. Nell (1975) *Rational Economic Man: A Philosophical Critique of Neo-classical Economics* (London: Cambridge University Press).

Hotelling, Harold (1931) 'The Economics of Exhaustible Resources', *Journal of Political Economy*, April, vol. 39, no. 2.

Jansson, Ann-Mari (ed.) (1984) *Integration of Economy and Ecology: An Outlook for the Eighties*, Proceedings from the Wallenberg Symposia, Asko Laboratory (Stockholm: University of Stockholm).

Kagel, John H. *et al.* (1975) 'Experimental Studies of Consumer Demand Behavior Using Laboratory Animals', *Economic Inquiry*, March, vol. 13, no. 1, pp. 22–38.

Kagel, John H. *et al.* (1980a) 'Token Economy and Animal Models for the Experimental Analysis of Economic Behavior', in Jan Kmenta and James B. Ramsey (eds), *Evaluation of Econometric Models* (New York: Academic Press).

Kagel, John H. and *et al.* (1980b) 'Consumer Demand Theory Applied to Choice Behavior of Rats', in John E. R. Staddon (ed.), *Limits to Action: The Allocation of Individual Behavior* (New York: Academic Press).

Kaldor, Nicholas (1972) 'The Irrelevance of Equilibrium Economics', *Economic Journal*, December, vol. 82, no. 328, pp. 1237–55.

Kaldor, Nicholas (1975) 'Economic Growth and the Verdoon Law – A Comment on Mr Rowthorn's Article', *Economic Journal*, December, vol. 85, no. 4, pp. 891–6.

Khalil, Elias L. (1987a) 'Kuhn, Lakatos, and the History of Economic Thought', *International Journal of Social Economics*, vol. 14, nos. 3–5, pp. 118–31.

Khalil, Elias L. (1987b) 'Sir James Steuart vs. Professor James Buchanan: Critical Notes on Modern Public Choice', *Review of Social Economy*, October, vol. 45, no. 2, pp. 113–32.

Khalil, Elias L. (1987c) 'The Process of Capitalist Accumulation: A Review Essay of David Levine's Contribution', *Review of Radical Political Economics*, Winter, vol. 19, no. 4, pp. 76–85.

Khalil, Elias L. (1989a) 'A Review of Harvey Leibenstein's *Inside the Firm: The Inefficiencies of Hierarchy*', *Journal of Economic Issues*, March, vol. 23, no. 1, pp. 297–300.

Khalil, Elias L. (1989b) 'A Review of M. Faber, H. Niemes and G. Stephan's *Entropy, Environment and Resources: An Essay in Physico-Economics*', *Journal of Economic Literature*, June, vol. 27, no. 2, pp. 647–9.

Khalil, Elias L. (1989c) 'A Review of P. W. Anderson, K. J. Arrow and D. Pines's (eds) *The Economy as an Evolving Complex System*', *Southern Economic Journal*, July, vol. 56, no. 1, pp. 266–8.

Khalil, Elias L. (1989d) 'Principles, Rules, and Ideology', *Forum for Social Economics*, Spring/Fall, vols. 18/19, nos. 2/1, pp. 41–54.

Khalil, Elias L. (1989e) 'Adam Smith and Albert Einstein: The Aesthetic Principle of Truth', *History of Economics Society Bulletin*, Fall, vol. 11, no. 2, pp. 222–37.

Khalil, Elias L. (1989f) 'A Review of Bruce H. Weber, David J. Depew and James D. Smith's (eds) *Entropy, Information, and Evolution: New Perspectives on Physical and Biological Evolution*', *Journal of Social and Biological Structures*, October, vol. 12, no. 4, pp. 389–91.

Khalil, Elias L. (1989g) 'A Review of B. J. Hiley and F. David Peat's (eds) *Quantum Implications: Essays in Honour of David Bohm*', *Journal of Social and Biological Structures*, October, vol. 12, no. 4, pp. 391–5.

Khalil, Elias L. (1990a) 'Beyond Self-interest and Altruism: A Reconstruction of Adam Smith's Theory of Human Conduct', *Economics and Philosophy*, October, vol. 6, no. 2, pp. 255–73.

Khalil, Elias L. (1990b) 'Natural Complex vs. Natural System', *Journal of Social and Biological Structures*, February, vol. 13, no. 1, pp. 11–31. Reprinted in *General Systems Yearbook* (cap R, vol. 32).

Khalil, Elias L. (1990c) 'Entropy Law and the Exhaustion of Natural Resources: Is Nicholas Georgescu-Roegen's Paradigm Defensible?' *Ecological Economics*, May, vol. 2, no. 2, pp. 163–78.

Khalil, Elias L. (1990d) 'Rationality and Social Labor in Marx', *Critical Review*, Winter/Spring, vol. 4, nos. 1 & 2, pp. 239–65.

Khalil, Elias L. (1991) 'Entropy Law and Nicholas Georgescu-Roegen's Paradigm: A Reply', *Ecological Economics*, July, vol. 3, no. 2, pp. 161–3.

Khalil, Elias L. (1992) 'Nature and Abstract Labor in Marx', *Social Concept*, vol. 6, no. 2.

Khalil, Elias L. (1993) 'Trust', in Geoff Hodgson, Marc Tool and Warren J. Samuels's (eds) *Handbook on Institutional and Evolutionary Economics*, vol. 2 (Cheltenham, UK: Edward Elgar), in press.

Khalil, Elias L. (n.d.) 'Admiration vs. Respect: A Reformulation of Adam Smith's Theory of Social Rank and Satisfaction', unpublished paper.

Khalil, Elias L. and Kenneth E. Boulding (eds) (1993). *Social and Natural Complexity* (to appear).

Kitcher, Philip (1985) *Vaulting Ambition: Sociobiology and the Quest for Human Nature* (Cambridge, Mass.: MIT Press).

Knight, Frank H. (1971) *Risk, Uncertainty and Profit*, intr. by George J. Stigler (Chicago: University of Chicago Press).

Kohler, Wolfgang (1969) *The Task of Gestalt Psychology* (Princeton, NJ: Princeton University Press).

Kurdas, Cigdem (1988) 'The "Whig Historian" on Adam Smith: Paul Samuelson's Canonical Classical Model", *History of Economic Society Bulletin*, Spring, vol. 10, no. 1, pp. 13–23.

Lamarck, J. B. (1984) *Zoological Philosophy: An Exposition with Regard to the Natural History of Animals*, trans. by Hugh Elliot (Chicago: University of Chicago Press).

Landa, Janet T. and Anthony Wallis (1988) 'Socio-economic Organization of Honeybee Colonies: A Transaction–Cost Approach', *Journal of Social and Biological Structures*, July, vol. 11, no. 3, pp. 353–63.

Langlois, Richard N. (ed.) (1986) *Economics as a Process: Essays in The New Institutional Economics* (Cambridge: Cambridge University Press).

Latsis, S. J. (ed.) (1976) *Method and Appraisal in Economics* (Cambridge: Cambridge University Press).

Leibenstein, Harvey J. (1987) *Inside the Firm: The Inefficiencies of Hierarchy* (Cambridge, Mass.: Harvard University Press).

Lenski, Richard *et al.* (1989) 'Another Alternative to Directed Mutation', *Nature*, 12 January, vol. 337, no. 6203, pp. 123–4.

Levine, David P. (1981) *Economic Theory*, vol. 2: *The System of Economic Relations as a Whole* (London: Routledge & Kegan Paul).

Levine, David P. (1988) *Needs, Rights and the Market* (Boulder and London: Lynne Rienner).

Levins, Richard (1967) *Evolution in Changing Environments* (Princeton, NJ: Princeton University Press).

Lewontin, Richard C. (1984) 'Adaptation', in Elliot Sober (ed.), *Conceptual Issues in Evolutionary Biology: An Anthology* (Cambridge, Mass.: MIT Press), pp. 235–51.

Lotka, Alfred J. (1925) *Elements of Physical Biology* (Baltimore: Williams & Wilkins).

Lotka, Alfred J. (1945) 'The Law of Evolution as a Maximal Principle', *Human Biology*, p. 17.

MacArthur, Robert H. (1972) *Geographical Ecology* (New York: Harper & Row).

Marx, Jean L. (1988) 'Evolution Link to Development Explored', *Science*, 13 May, 1988, vol. 240, no. 4854, pp. 880–2.

Masters, Roger D. (1983) 'The Biological Nature of the State', *World Politics*, vol. 25, pp. 161–93.

Masters, Roger D. (1989) *The Nature of Politics* (New Haven, Conn.: Yale University Press).

Maurice, Marc Francois Sellier and Jean-Jacques Silvestre (1986) *The Social Foundations of Industrial Power: A Comparison of France and Germany*, trans. by Arthur Goldhammer (Cambridge, Mass.: MIT Press).

Mayr, Ernst (1982) *Systematics and the Origin of Species* (New York: Columbia University Press).

Milkman, R. (ed.) (1982) *Perspectives of Evolution* (Sunderland, Mass.: Sinaver Associations).

Mises, Ludwig von (1966) *Human Action: A Treatise on Economics* (Chicago: Contemporary Books).

Monod, Jacques (1972) *Chance and Necessity* (New York: Knopf).

Moorhead, P. S. and M. M. Kaplan (eds) (1987) *Mathematical Challenges of Neo-Darwinian Interpretation of Evolution* (Philadelphia: Wistar Institute Press).

Nell, Edward (1972) 'Economics: The Revival of Political Economy', Robin Blackburn (ed.), *Ideology in Social Science: Readings in Critical Social Theory* (Isle of Man, UK: Fontana), pp. 76–95.

Nell, Edward (1980) (ed.) *Growth, Profits, and Property* (Cambridge: Cambridge University Press).

Nell, Edward (1988) *Prosperity and Public Spending: Transformational Growth and the Role of Government* (London: Unwin Hyman).

Nell, Edward (1992) *Transformational Growth and Effective Demand: Economics After the Capital Critique* (London: Macmillan, and New York: New York University Press).

Nelson, Richard R. and Sidney G. Winter (1982) *An Evolutionary Theory of Economic Change* (Cambridge, Mass.: Harvard University Press).

Noda, H. (1982) 'Probability of Life, Rareness of Realization in Evolution', *Journal of Theoretical Biology*, vol. 95, pp. 145–50.

O'Driscoll, Gerald P. and Mario J. Rizzo (1985) *The Economics of Time and Ignorance* (Oxford: Blackwell).

Odum, Howard T. (1971) *Environment, Power, and Society* (New York: Wiley-Interscience).

Partridge, Linda and Michael J. Morgan (1988) 'Is Bacterial Evolution Random or Selective?' *Nature*, 3 November, vol. 336, no. 6194, p. 22.

Pasinetti, Luigi L. (1966) 'Changes in the Rate of Profit and Switches of Techniques', *Quarterly Journal of Economics*, November, vol. 80, no. 4, pp. 503–17.

Penrose, E. T. (1952) 'Biological Analogies in the Theory of the Firm', *American Economic Review*, December, vol. 42, no. 5, pp. 804–19.

Perrings, Charles (1987) *Economy and Environment: A Theoretical Essay on the Interdependence of Economic and Environmental Systems* (Cambridge: Cambridge University Press).

Polanyi, Michael (1958) *Personal Knowledge: Towards a Post-Critical Philosophy* (New York: Harper & Row).

Pollard, Jeffrey W. (ed.) (1984) *Evolutionary Theory: Paths into the Future* (New York: John Wiley).

Prigogine, Ilya (1980) *From Being into Becoming* (San Francisco: Freeman).

Proops, John L. R. (1989) 'Ecological Economics: Rationale and Problem Areas', *Ecological Economics*, February, vol. 1, no. 1, pp. 59–76.

Ptashne, Mark (1989) 'How Gene Activators Work', *Scientific American*, January, vol. 260, no. 1, pp. 40–7.

Queller, David C., *et al.* (1988) 'Genetic Relatedness in Colonies of Tropical Wasps with Multiple Queens', *Science*, 25 November, vol. 242, no. 4882, pp. 1155–7.

Rapport, David J. and James E. Turner (1977) 'Economic Models in Ecology', *Science*, 28 January, vol. 195, no. 4276, pp. 367–73.

Reidl, Ruppert (1978) *Order in Living Organisms: A System Analysis of Evolution* (New York: John Wiley).

Ricklefs, Robert E. (1979) *Ecology* (New York: Chiron Press).

Robbins, Lionel (1932) *An Essay on the Nature and Significance of Economic Science* (London: Macmillan).

Robinson, Joan (1953) 'The Production Function and the Theory of Capital', *Review of Economic Studies*, vol. 21, pp. 81–106.

Robinson, Joan (1970) 'Capital Theory Up to Date', *Canadian Journal of Economics*, vol. 3, pp. 309–17. (Reprinted in Jesse G. Schwartz and E. K. Hunt (eds), *A Critique of Economic Theory: Selected Readings* (Harmondsworth, Middlesex: Penguin, 1972) pp. 233–44).

Robinson, Joan (1979) 'History Versus Equilibrium', in *Collected Economic Papers*, vol. 5 (Oxford: Oxford University Press).

Rosen, Robert (1985a) 'Organisms as Causal Systems which are not Mechanisms: An Essay into the Nature of Complexity', in Robert Rosen (ed.) *Theoretical Biology and Complexity: Three Essays on the Natural Philosophy of Complex Systems* (Orlando, Flor.: Academic Press).

Rosen, Robert (1985b) *Anticipatory Systems* (Oxford: Pergamon Press).

Rosen, Robert (1987) 'Some Epistemological Issues in Physics and Biology', in Hiley, B. J. and F. David Peat (eds) *Quantum Implications: Essays in Honour of David Bohm* (London and New York: Routledge & Kegan Paul), pp. 314–27.

Rosenberg, Nathan (1976) *Perspectives in Technology* (Cambridge: Cambridge University Press).

Rosenberg, Nathan (1982) *Inside the Black Box* (Cambridge: Cambridge University Press).

Russell, James (1978) *The Acquisition of Knowledge* (New York: St Martin's Press).

Sâlthe, Stanley N. (1985) *Evolving Hierarchical Systems* (New York: Columbia University Press).

Sâlthe, Stanley N. (1987) 'On the Trail of the Unknown in Biology', *The Journal of Heredity*, May/June, vol. 78, no. 3, pp. 213–14. (A book review of Gustafson, Perry J., et al. (eds) *Genetics, Development, and Evolution* (New York: Plenum Press, 1986).

Schoffeniels, E. (1976) *Anti-Chance* (New York: Pergamon).

Schubert, Glendon (1989) *Evolutionary Politics* (Carbondale: Southern Illinois University Press).

Schumpeter, Joseph (1949) *The Theory of Economic Development* (Cambridge, Mass.: Harvard University Press).

Schwartz, Barry (1986) *The Battle for Human Nature* (New York: W.W. Norton).

Shackle, G. L. S. (1970) *Expectations, Enterprise and Profit* (London: Allen & Unwin).

Sheldrake, Rupert (1988) *The Presence of the Past: Morphic Resonance and Habits of Nature* (New York: Times Books (Random House)).

Simon, Herbert A. (1978) 'Rationality as Process and as Product of Thought', *American Economic Review*, May, vol. 68, no. 2, pp. 1–16.

Simpson, George Gaylord (1984) *Tempo and Mode in Evolution* (New York: Columbia University Press).

Smith, Adam (1976a) *The Theory of Moral Sentiments*, ed. by D. D. Raphael and A. L. Macfie (Oxford: Clarendon Press).

Smith, Adam (1976b) *An Inquiry into the Nature and Causes of the Wealth of Nations*, in 2 volumes, general eds R. H. Campbell and A. S. Skinner, text ed. W. B. Todd (Oxford: Clarendon Press).

Smith, Adam (1980) *Essays on Philosophical Subjects*, gen. eds D. D. Raphael and A. S. Skinner, eds W. P. D. Wightman, J. C. Bryce, and I. S. Ross (Oxford: Clarendon Press).

Stanley, Steven M. (1979) *Macroevolution: Pattern and Process* (San Francisco: Freeman).

Steele, E. J. (1979) *Somatic Selection and Adaptive Evolution: On the Inheritance of Acquired Characters* (Chicago: University of Chicago Press).

Steele, E. J. and J. W. Pollard (1987) 'Hypothesis: Somatic Hypermutation by Gene Conversion via the Error Prone DNA → RNA → DNA Information Loop", *Molecular Immunology*, June, vol. 24, no. 6, pp. 667–73.

Stigler, George J. and Gary S. Becker (1977) '*De Gustibus Non Est Disputandum*', *American Economic Review*, March, vol. no. 67, no. 1, pp. 76–90.

Teilhard de Chardin, Pierre (1959) *The Phenomenon of Man*, trans. by B. Wall (New York: Harper & Row).

Thirlwall, A. P. (1983) 'A Plain Man's Guide to Kaldor's Growth Laws', *Journal of Post Keynesian Economics*, Spring, vol. 5, no. 3, pp. 345–59.

Thompson, D'Arcy Wentworth (1961) *On Growth and Form*, ed. by J. T. Bonner. (Cambridge: Cambridge University Press).

Ulanowicz, Robert E. (1986) *Growth and Development: A Phenomenological Perspective* (New York: Springer Verlag).

Ursprung, Heinrich W. (1988) 'Evolution and the Economic Approach to Human Behavior', *Journal of Social and Biological Structures*, April, vol. 11, no. 2, pp. 257–79.

Van Valen, L. (1973) 'A New Evolutionary Law', *Evolutionary Theory*, vol. 1, pp. 1–30.

Varela, F. (1979) *Principles of Biological Autonomy* (New York: Kluwer).

Veblen, Thorstein (1898) 'Why is Economics not an Evolutionary Science?', *Quarterly Journal of Economics*, July, vol. 12, no. 3, pp. 373–97.

Waddington, C. H. (1957) *The Strategy of the Genes* (London: Unwin Hyman).

Walsh, Vivian and Harvey Gram (1980) *Classical and Neoclassical Theories of General Equilibrium: Historical Origins and Mathematical Structure* (New York: Oxford University Press).

Weber, Bruce H., David J. Depew, and James D. Smith (eds) (1988) *Entropy, Information, and Evolution: New Perspectives on Physical and Biological Evolution* (Cambridge, Mass.: MIT Press).

Webster, G. C. and B. C. Goodwin (1982) 'The Origin of Species: A Structuralist Approach', *Journal of Social and Biological Structures*, January, vol. 5, no. 1, pp. 15–47.

Wicken, Jeffrey S. (1986) 'Evolutionary Self-Organization and Entropic Dissipation in Biological and Socioeconomic Systems', *Journal of Social and Biological Structures*, July, vol. 9, no. 3, pp. 261–73.

Wicken, Jeffrey S. (1987) *Evolution, Thermodynamics, and Information: Extending the Darwinian Program* (New York: Oxford University Press).

Williamson, Oliver E. (1985) *The Economic Institutions of Capitalism: Firms, Markets, Relational Contracting* (New York: Free Press).

Wilson, Edward O. (1975) *Sociobiology: The New Synthesis* (Cambridge, Mass.: Harvard University Press).

Wright, Robert (1988) *Three Scientists and their Gods: Looking for Meaning in an Age of Information* (New York: Times Books).

Young, Allyn A. (1928) 'Increasing Returns and Economic Progress', *Economic Journal*, December, vol. 38, no. 152, pp. 527–42.

Name Index

The International Library of Critical Writings in Economics

1. Multinational Corporations
   Mark Casson

2. The Economics of Innovation
   Christopher Freeman

3. Entrepreneurship
   Mark Casson

4. International Investment
   Peter J. Buckley

5. Game Theory in Economics
   Ariel Rubinstein

6. The History of Economic Thought
   Mark Blaug

7. Monetary Theory
   Thomas Mayer

8. Joint Production of Commodities
   Neri Salvadori and Ian Steedman

9. Industrial Organization
   Oliver E. Williamson

10. Growth Theory (Volumes I, II and III)
    R. Becker and E. Burmeister

11. Microeconomics: Theoretical and Applied (Volumes I, II and III)
    Robert E. Kuenne

12. The Economics of Health (Volumes I and II)
    A.J. Culyer

13. Recent Developments in Macroeconomics (Volumes I, II and III)
    Edmund S. Phelps

14. Urban and Regional Economics
    Paul C. Cheshire and Alan W. Evans

15. Modern Public Finance (Volumes I and II)
    A.B. Atkinson

16. Exchange Rate Economics (Volumes I and II)
    Ronald MacDonald and Mark P. Taylor

17. The Economic Value of Education: Studies in the Economics of Education
Mark Blaug

18. Development Economics (Volumes I, II, III and IV)
Deepak Lal

19. The New Classical Macroeconomics (Volumes I, II and III)
Kevin D. Hoover

20. The Economics of the Environment
Wallace E. Oates

21. Post Keynesian Theory of Growth and Distribution
Carlo Panico and Neri Salvadori

22. Dynamic Labor Demand and Adjustment Costs
Giorgio Galeazzi and Daniel S. Hamermesh

23. The Philosophy and Methodology of Economics (Volumes I, II and III)
Bruce J. Caldwell

24. Public Choice Theory (Volumes I, II and III)
Charles K. Rowley

25. Evolutionary Economics
Ulrich Witt

26. Economics and Psychology
Shlomo Maital and Sharone L. Maital

27. Social Choice Theory (Volumes I, II and III)
Charles K. Rowley

28. Non-Linear Dynamics in Economic Theory
Marc Jarsulic

29. Recent Developments in Experimental Economics (Volumes I and II)
John D. Hey and Graham Loomes

30. Monopoly and Competition Policy (Volumes I and II)
F.M. Scherer

31. The Economics of Technical Change
Edwin Mansfield and Elizabeth Mansfield

32. The Economics of Exhaustible Resources
Geoffrey Heal

33. The Economics of Institutions
Geoffrey M. Hodgson

34. The Economics of Transport (Volumes I and II)
Herbert Mohring

35. Implicit Contract Theory
Sherwin Rosen

36. Foundations of Analytical Marxism (Volumes I and II)
John E. Roemer

37. The Economics of Product Differentiation (Volumes I and II)
Jacques-François Thisse and George Norman

38. Economic Growth in Theory and Practice: A Kaldorian Perspective
John E. King

39. Markets and Socialism
Alec Nove and Ian D. Thatcher

40. Recent Developments in the Economics of Education
Elchanan Cohn and Geraint Johnes

41. The Theory of Inflation
Michael Parkin

42. The Economics of Location (Volumes I, II and III)
Melvin L. Greenhut and George Norman

43. Financial Intermediaries
Mervyn K. Lewis

44. The Political Economy of Privatization and Deregulation
Elizabeth E. Bailey and Janet Rothenberg Pack

45. Gender and Economics
Jane Humphries

46. Macroeconomics and Imperfect Competition
Jean-Pascal Bénassy

47. Labor Economics (Volumes I, II, III and IV)
Orley C. Ashenfelter and Kevin F. Hallock

48. The Economics of Altruism
Stefano Zamagni

49. The Economic Analysis of Rent Seeking
Robert D. Tollison and Roger D. Congleton

50. Economics and Biology
Geoffrey M. Hodgson

Future titles will include:

Economics and Discrimination
William A. Darity, Jr

The Economics of Information
David K. Levine and Steven A. Lippman

Fiscal and Monetary Policy
Thomas Mayer and Stephen Sheffrin

Transaction Cost Economics
Oliver Williamson and Scott Masten

The Economics of Ageing
John Creedy

Long Wave Theory
Christopher Freeman

International Trade
J. Peter Neary

Agricultural Economics
G.H. Peters

International Debt
Graham Bird and P.N. Snowdon

Small Firms and Economic Growth
Zoltan Acs

Business Cycle Theory
Finn E. Kydland

General Equilibrium Theory
Gerard Debreu

The Money Supply in the Economic Process
Marco Musella and Carlo Panico

Producer Cooperatives and Labor-Managed Systems
David L. Prychitko and Jaroslav Vanek

The Foundations of Public Finance
Peter Jackson

International Finance
Robert Z. Aliber

Welfare Economics
William J. Baumol and Janusz A. Ordover

The Theory of the Firm
Mark Casson

The Economics of Inequality and Poverty
A.B. Atkinson

The Economics of Housing
John M. Quigley

Population Economics
Julian L. Simon

The Economics of Crime
Isaac Ehrlich

The Economics of Integration
Willem Molle

The Rhetoric of Economics
Donald McCloskey

Ethics and Economics
Alan Hamlin

Migration
Oded Stark

Economic Forecasting
Paul Ormerod

The Economics of Training
Robert J. LaLonde and Orley Ashenfelter

The Economics of Defence
Keith Hartley and Nicholas Hooper

Consumer Theory
Kelvin Lancaster

Law and Economics
Judge Richard A. Posner

The Economics of Business Policy
John Kay

Microeconomic Theories of Imperfect Competition
Jacques Thisse and Jean Gabszewicz

The Economics of Increasing Returns
Geoffrey Heal

The Balance of Payments
Michael J. Artis

The Economics of the Family
Nancy Folbre

Cost-Benefit Analysis
Arnold Harberger and Glenn P. Jenkins

The New Growth Theory
Gene M. Grossman

Economic Theory and Chaos Theory
W. Davis Dechert

The Economics of Unemployment
P.N. Junankar

Mathematical Economics
Graciela Chichilnisky

Economic Growth in the Long Run
Bart van Ark

Gender in Economic and Social History
K.J. Humphries and J. Lewis

The Economics of Communication and Innovation
Donald M. Lamberton

The Economics of Uncertainty
John D. Hey